TREATISE
ON THE
LOVE OF GOD

ST. FRANCIS DE SALES
1567-1622
Bishop, Founder of the Visitation
and Doctor of the Church

TREATISE
ON THE
LOVE OF GOD

By

St. Francis de Sales
DOCTOR OF THE CHURCH

Translated by

Rev. Henry Benedict Mackey, O.S.B.

Under the Direction and Patronage of His Lordship the
Right Rev. John Cuthbert Hedley, O.S.B.
BISHOP OF NEWPORT

*"A truly admirable book, which has as many admirers of the sweetness
of its author as it has readers. I have carefully arranged that it shall be
read throughout our Society, as the universal remedy for all feeble ones,
the goad of slothful ones, the stimulus of love, and the ladder of those who
are tending to perfection. Oh! that all would study it as it deserves! There
should be no one to escape its heat."*

—St. Vincent de Paul

TAN BOOKS AND PUBLISHERS, INC.
Rockford, Illinois 61105

Originally published in approximately 1884 by Burns & Oates, Limited, London and Benziger Brothers, New York as Volume II of the series "Library of St. Francis de Sales." This edition photographically reproduced from the Third Edition by arrangement with Burns & Oates.

Library of Congress Catalog Card No.: 95-60646

ISBN 0-89555-526-3

Cover illustration: Portrait of St. Francis de Sales by J. J. Owens (early 20th century), based on the Turin portrait. Courtesy of De Sales Resource Center, Niagara Falls, New York.

Printed and bound in the United States of America.

TAN BOOKS AND PUBLISHERS, INC.
P.O. Box 424
Rockford, Illinois 61105
1997

DEDICATION

I have dedicated this work to the Mother of dilection and to the Father of cordial love, as I dedicated the *Introduction* to the Divine child who is the Saviour of lovers and the love of the saved. And as women, while they are strong and able to bring forth their children with ease, choose commonly their worldly friends to be godfathers, but when their feebleness and indisposition make their delivery hard and dangerous invoke the Saints of heaven, and vow to have their children stood to by some poor body or by some devout soul in the name of S. Joseph, S. Francis of Assisi, S. Francis of Paula, S. Nicholas, or some other of the blessed, who may obtain of God their safe delivery and that the child may be born alive: so I, while I was not yet bishop, having more leisure and less fears for my writings, dedicated my little works to princes of the earth, but now being weighed down with my charge, and having a thousand difficulties in writing, I consecrate all to the princes of heaven, that they may obtain for me the light requisite, and that if such be the Divine will, these my writings may be fruitful and profitable to many.

Annecy, the day of the most loving Apostles
S. Peter and S. Paul, 1616.
BLESSED BE GOD.

—St. Francis de Sales
From The Preface (*Pages 15-16*)

TRANSLATOR'S INTRODUCTION.

THE following Treatise presents, at first sight, considerable difficulties. They do not arise from any defect in the Saint's mode of expression, but are inherent in his subject and manner of treatment, " going deep down into the roots" of the Love of God. Thus he speaks in his Preface, and continues : " The first four books, and some chapters of the others might doubtless have been omitted without disadvantage to such souls as seek only the practice of holy love. . . . I have been forced to say many things which will appear more obscure than they are. The depths of science are always somewhat hard to sound." But he tells us that the state of the minds of his age required this deeper treatment ; and whatever may be thought as to the best way of presenting modern religious teaching to an age so ignorant, so shallow and so unthinking as is our own with regard to spiritual truths, there can be no question that this masterpiece of the chief doctor of ascetic theology must not be brought down to our level, but that we must raise ourselves towards it. The necessity of giving some explanation of the sequence of its doctrine, and of the difficulties which occur, must be our chief excuse for daring to place words of ours by the side of this finished work of S. Francis de Sales.

A second reason lies in the fact that the "Treatise on the Love of God " was, with others of his writings, the chief subject of the celebrated controversy between Fénélon and Bossuet. There can be little doubt that this lowered the authority of the work. Not because the mere fact of a discussion seemed to throw over it an air of unsafeness or

suspicion. Descriptions of the sublime and mysterious operations
of the soul under the influence of grace are always capable of
being misunderstood, and "wrested" from their proper sense,
and no Christian mystic, from S. Paul downwards, has escaped
this danger. The shameless abuse of the Saint's authority by
the Jansenists left it eventually quite unimpaired. Hence
the mistakes of Molinos, Père Lacombe, Madame Guyon, and
even of Fénélon himself would have thrown no permanent
discredit on this treatise, if Bossuet had defended it in a proper
spirit and with full knowledge and discretion. Incredible as
the fact may seem, it is nevertheless true that neither Fénélon
nor Bossuet had properly studied the works in dispute. The
former went to them prepossessed. His opinions were already
formed, and he merely sought a confirmation of them. He
read in a most superficial manner. He precipitately chose
out what seemed to suit his purpose, and neglected important
statements and obvious interpretations which were inconsistent
with it. He even went so far in what must be called a sincere
dishonesty of misapprehension, as to insist on clinging to mistakes he had fallen into through using Bailly's Lyons edition
of the "Conferences" (1628), which Bossuet had proved to be
spurious. Bossuet, on his side, admits that he had not
previously read it properly, he only studied what seemed
necessary to answer his opponent, and lacked that high complete knowledge of S. Francis's teaching as a whole which
was necessary for taking a proper view of details and parts.
Indeed he only then (1695) began those profounder studies of
mystic theology which enabled him later to write his treatises
on matters which to S. Francis, by the experience of sanctity
more even than by the studies of a lifetime, were as familiar
as the sights and sounds of home. Hence it came about that
while he easily justified the teaching of the Saint, he not only
failed to give the full influence of his genius and authority to
unassailably establish its triumphant reputation, but on the
contrary he incidentally disparaged it. He says, for instance:
" S. Francis is a great saint, and I have always maintained

that his doctrine which is objected against us is entirely for us
as to the matters in question : but we must not therefore make
him infallible, and it cannot be forgotten that he has shown
more good intention than knowledge on some points." For-
tunately Bossuet mentions these points, and the reader shall
see directly Bossuet's entire misapprehension of the Saint's
meaning, and meanwhile "it cannot be forgotten" that while
Bossuet refused the title " infallible" to S. Francis, for whom
no one claims it, he refused it to the successor of S. Peter to
whose office it really belongs. Bossuet says further : " According to the spirit of his time he had perhaps less read the
Fathers than the modern Scholastics." Did Bossuet remember
that he was speaking of the age of Sirmond, of Bellarmine,
of Venerable Canisius, and, we may say, of Petavius ? Francis
was a master and a leader of his age, and, as is clear from this
Treatise alone, was excellently versed both in the Fathers and
the Scholastics, if any distinction is to be made between them.
In conclusion, Bossuet presumes to say : " In these places
and in some others his theology might be more exact and his
principles more sure . . . . one would not follow him in
certain condescensions which I will not particularize." In
this also it will be shown that Bossuet is most unjust, but for
the present we may consider that he neutralizes his own
objection, when in the same sentence he says : " As director of
souls he is truly sublime." In answer to these attacks, Fénélon
gladly changed places with Bossuet, but his hasty defence
was not so complete as the charges were unwarranted and
presumptuous.*

We shall briefly touch upon these controverted points as
they occur among the difficulties of the Treatise. Of these
difficulties Book I. contains by far the largest proportion, and
we will give an abstract of this Book sufficiently complete to

---

* For our authorities and full information on this important controversy
we refer our readers to the admirable "Dissertation," by Baudry, in the
supplementary volume (ix.) of Migne's edition of the "Works of S. Francis
and S. Jane Frances." There is an anonymous dissertation in vol. vi. which
bears on the same subject.

prevent the necessity, not indeed of studying it, but, of a too
laborious study.*

In this first Book the Saint treats in general of the will and
its affections, in particular of its chief affection, love, and
of the will's natural inclination towards a sovereign love of
God.

The first chapter is to show that the unity required for the
beauty of that assemblage of perfections called man, lies in this,
that all his powers are grouped round the will and subordinated
to it.   Then (c. 2) it is shown that the will exercises its authority in different ways, according to the different nature of
human powers.   It governs: (*a*) exterior movements, at its
pleasure, like slaves; (*b*) the senses and corporal functions, by
a certain management, like horses or hawks; (*c*) the fancy,
memory, understanding, by direction and command, like wife
and children, who are able to disobey if they choose; (*d*) the
sensual appetite (c. 3), in the same manner as the last-named;
it is still less under the will's control, but there is no moral guilt
so long as the will refuses to consent to or adopt its wrong
desires.   Then are described the twelve movements of this
sensual appetite,—viz., desire, hatred, hope, &c., which are called
perturbations or passions.   They are all forms of the chief, and,
in a sense, the only passion, love.   These passions are left in
man on purpose to exercise his will.   A universal experience,
testified to in effect even by those who pretend to deny it, such
as the Stoics, proves that these movements are necessary
qualities of human nature.   Love being (c. 4) the root of the
others their action is good or bad according as the love is rightly
or wrongly placed.   Nay the very will is bad or good according
to its love; and its supremacy does not lie in this that it can
reject all love, but in this that it can choose amongst the loves
presented to it, by directing the understanding to consider one
more favourably or more attentively than another.   In the

---

* The following part of our Introduction—viz., the analysis of Books i.,
ii., will probably be found more intelligible and useful after reading the
Saint's text.

will, now defined (c. 5) as "the reasonable appetite," there are affections, that is, movements or forms of love, similar to the passions of the sensual appetite. Having different and higher objects they often run counter to the passions, and the reasonable will often forces a soul to remain in circumstances most repugnant to its sensual inclinations. These affections or tendencies of the will are divided into four classes according to their dignity, that is, the dignity of their objects: 1°. Natural affections, where the word natural is not used in opposition to supernatural (as in this sense the next class would also be natural), but to signify those first and spontaneous affections which by the very natural constitution of our reason arise from the perception of sensible goods. Indeed the word sensible exactly explains his use of the word natural, provided that we carefully remember that he is speaking not of the movements of the merely sensual appetite or concupiscence which are anterior to reason, but of our reasonable and lawful affections for sensible goods. Such are the affections we have for health, food, agreeable society. 2°. Reasonable affections, where it will now easily be understood that the word, which could be applied also to the preceding class, is restricted to those which are *par excellence* reasonable, that is, the affections which arise in the spiritual part of reason, from the light of nature indeed, but from the higher light of nature—such as the affections for the moral virtues. 3°. Christian affections, which spring from the consideration of truths of the Christian revelation, such as affections for poverty, chastity, heavenly glory. 4°. Divine, or (entirely) supernatural affections which God effects in us, and which tend to him as known by a light entirely above that of nature. These supernatural affections are primarily three: love for the beautiful in the mysteries of faith, love for the useful in the promises of hope, and love for the sovereign good which is the Divinity.

The essential supremacy of divine love is proved (c. 6), and there follows a wondrous description in four chapters of the nature and qualities of love in general. Divine love or

charity is not defined till chapter 13, and is not specifically
described till the last chapter of Book II.

There are (c. 7) five points in the process of love: 1.
Natural affinity of the will with good. 2. Delectation or
complacency in it. 3. A movement, following this complacency,
towards union. 4. Taking the means required for union.
5. Union itself.* It is in 2 and 3, complacency and movement,
that love more properly consists, and most precisely in 3, the
movement or outflowing of heart. Complacency has appeared
to some to be the really essential point of love, but it is not
so, because love is a true passion or affection, that is, a movement. Complacency spreads the wings, love actually flies.
When the object loved is present and the lover has but to
grasp it, the love is called a love of complacency, because
complacency has no sooner produced the movement of love
than it ends in a second complacency. When the object is
absent, or, like God, not as present as it may become, the
tending, advancing, aspiring movement is called a love of
desire, that is, the cupidity of what we have not but hope to
have. After certain exquisite distinctions between various
kinds of desires, he returns (c. 8) to the correspondence or
affinity with good which is the root of love, and which consists
not exclusively in resemblance, but in a certain relation
between things which makes them apt to union for their
mutual perfection. Finally, coming to union and the means
thereto, it is exquisitely proved (c. 9) that love tends to union
but (c. 10) to a spiritual union, and that carnal union, instead
of being an expression of true love or a help to it, is positively
a hindrance, a deviation, a degradation.

The next two chapters (11, 12) treat the important distinction between the two parts of the soul, the inferior and
the superior. It will clear matters to notice that the Saint

* This division is the connecting chain of the whole Treatise, and it will
be found that each Book treats of one or more of its parts. Thus the three
following Books are on point 3, Book v. on point 2, Books vi.–ix. on points
4 and 5 (viz., union by affective and by effective love), x.–xii. on point 3.

means the two parts of the reasonable soul, and that in
the first two paragraphs of chapter 11 he simply says that
his distinction does not refer to the soul as a mere animating
principle, or, again, as the principle of that life which man
shares with plants and animals. He speaks of the human
soul as such, that is, as having the gift of reason.

Even the inferior part of the soul truly reasons and wills (so
that his distinction of inferior and superior is not the distinction
between concupiscence and reason), but it is inferior because it
only reasons and wills according to data furnished by the senses :
the superior part reasons and wills on intellectual and spiritual
considerations. But it must be noticed that these considerations
are not necessarily supernatural. The distinction between the
inferior and the superior part of the reasonable soul is quite
independent of revelation : it rests on the distinction between
what we have called the lower light of nature and that higher
light which, for instance, heathen philosophers used, when, for
love of country or moral virtue, they chose to submit to
sensible pain or even to death which their lower reason would
direct them to avoid. The existence of this lower reason is
clearly shown in Our Blessed Saviour's prayer in the garden.
Willing and praying are acts of reason, yet in this case they
were acts of a lower reason which Christ permitted to
manifest itself, but which had to give way to higher considerations.

Now the inferior part of reason forms by itself one degree
of the reason, but the superior part has three degrees; in
the lowest of which we reason according to higher natural
light, or as the Saint calls it, " human sciences," in the next
according to faith, and in the highest we do not properly
reason, but, " by a simple view of the understanding, and
simple acquiescence," or assent, " of the will" we correspond
with God's action, when he spreads faith, hope and charity in
this supreme point of our reasonable soul. The distinction
corresponds exactly with that made in chapter 5, into natural,
reasonable, Christian and divine. The Saint there spoke of

affections or tendencies, he here speaks of reasonings and willings which are the fulfilment of those tendencies. We may remark here, as an instance of the superficial way in which Fénélon and Bossuet studied this Treatise, that they take a totally different ground of distinction in separating the soul into superior and inferior (viz., sensible perception and intellectual cognition), and yet do not perceive that they are differing from the Saint.* To sum up (cc. 11, 12): in man there are some powers altogether below reason; and reason, which is of course one and simple in itself, has four degrees, according to the rank of the objects presented for its consideration and love,— sensible things, spiritual things known by the light of nature, spiritual things known by the revelation of Christ, and spiritual knowledge communicated by the immediate communication of God's light. Between the last and the last but one there is not exactly a difference of rank in the objects, but a difference in clearness of perception and strength of acceptance.

Having finished this subject, which is to some extent a digression, the Saint returns to the consideration of love, and gives (c. 13) its two main divisions,—viz., love of cupidity when we love good for our own sake, and love of benevolence when we love good for its sake—*i.e.* love of self-interest and disinterested love. He has already, in chapter 7, sub-divided the love of cupidity into love of benevolence and love of desire, according as the loved good is present or absent, and now he applies the same division and the same ground of division to the love of benevolence. This also is either a love of complacency or a love of desire according as the good is present to or absent from the person we love : we rejoice in the good he

* Certain expressions on p. 50 require explanation. It is there said that in the superior part of the soul there are *two* degrees of reason—the answer is that the Saint for the moment puts out of consideration the lowest degree of the higher reason, and concerns himself with the two supernatural degrees. And a little lower down he speaks of the action of faith "in the inferior part of the soul," but he really means in the lower one of the two highest degrees.

already has, we desire him the good he has not. This double form of the love of benevolence, besides occurring frequently throughout, enters particularly into the structure of Book V., and is importantly needed for the full understanding of Book VIII. It is necessary here to point out that whereas he has just placed the names complacency and desire under the generic head, benevolence, he afterwards uses the word benevolence, specifically, instead of desire, as if dividing benevolence into complacency, and benevolence proper. This use of the word in the sense of desire agrees with its etymology,—*bene-volentia, bien-veuillance,* well-wishing.

Cupidity alone is exercised in the inferior reason, but in the superior reason both find place. The love of God for his own sake which is necessary for eternal life belongs exclusively to the supreme degree of the superior reason, but the Saint teaches (as Bossuet has clearly shown against Fénélon) that there is a reasonable, high love of cupidity, that is, a love of God as good to us, even in the highest degree and supreme point of the spirit. This indeed is the precise motive of Christian hope, which must be kept subordinate to disinterested love, but can only be separated from it by abstraction and by a non-permanent act.

The love of benevolence is called friendship when it is mutual. This friendship has degrees. When it is beyond all comparison with other friendships, supereminent, sovereign, it is called charity—the friendship or mutual love of God and man.

The Saint shows (c. 14) that to employ the word love instead of charity is not against the use of Scripture, and he mentions one reason for his preferring the word love which gives us an important help to the understanding of the Treatise. It is, he says, because he is speaking for the most part not of the *habitual* charity, or state of friendship between God and the soul in grace, but of *actual* charity, that is, of the acts of love which at once express and increase the state of charity. Even in the three following books, in which he is speaking of the formation, or progress, or loss, of habitual charity, he is still chiefly concerned with the acts by which this is done.

In the remaining four chapters preparation is made for the account of the communication of grace and charity to the soul. He shows (c. 15) that there is a natural affinity of the soul with its God which is the root of love; that thus, by a glorious paradox, God and man need one another for their mutual perfection; that we have (c. 16) a natural inclination to love God above all things; that (c. 17) we cannot fulfil this inclination by natural powers; but (c. 18) that still the inclination is not left in our hearts for nothing, as it makes possible the communication of grace, and is the handle by which grace takes hold of us.

It is chiefly against these three chapters that Bossuet's animadversions are directed. He accuses the Saint of two errors: 1°. in saying (p. 61) that God would give grace to one who did his best by the forces of nature as certainly as he would give a further grace to one who corresponded with a first grace; 2°. of saying (p. 57) that in the state of original justice our love of God would not be supernatural.

Fénélon misapprehends the Saint's meaning, and gives a very confused, imperfect answer to the two objections. The real answer to the first is that Bossuet is quite outside the question. S. Francis is not speaking of the step by which a man passes from the natural to the supernatural order, but of the process by which his natural inclination to love God above all things ripens into that actual love of him above all things which belongs still to the natural order.*

Bossuet falls into a somewhat similar error in his second objection. S. Francis is considering, separately, the natural

---

* It is true that elsewhere (Book iv. c. v.) S. Francis says, after S. Thomas and S. Francis Xavier, that God is sure to give grace to those who fulfil the natural law, but, since in the state of fallen nature the natural law itself cannot be fully observed without grace, there is already supposed in the hearts of such persons the existence of grace which draws the further grace. This the Saint expressly states (xi. 1).

love of God which those would have who might be in the state
of original justice, who would, of course, by the very terms,
have supernatural love. Not only is Bossuet's criticism
ridiculously irrelevant, but his language, to ears which have
heard the Saint declared " Doctor of the Church," sounds
almost like impertinence. " What," he says, " would this humble
servant of God have done if it had been represented to him
that in the state of original justice we should have loved God
supernaturally ? Would he not have confessed that he was
forgetting the most essential condition of that state ?" And it
is after these mistakes that Bossuet complacently observes :
" These opinions rectify themselves in practice when the intention is good ;" and " In some points his theology might be more
exact and his principles more sure."

Book II. describes the generation of charity, which, being
supernatural, must be created in the soul as a new quality. And
after two introductory chapters, the remaining twenty are
evenly divided between the history of the action of God in
bestowing, and the action of man in appropriating this gift.
The two introductory chapters, which seem at first sight somewhat foreign to the subject of the book, are directed to put
steadily and unmistakeably before us the truth that when theologians speak of many perfections, many acts, a most various
order of decrees and execution, this is only according to the
human method of viewing, and that our God is really but one
perfection and one act, which is himself. This truth is de-
veloped partly also to introduce a description of the perfections
of the God of whose love the Saint is speaking. At the end
of the Treatise he refers to these chapters as his chief treatment of the chief motive of love—the infinite goodness of God
in himself.

After this caution and preface, he begins (c. 3) his account
of the action of God in the production of charity. He speaks,
first, of God's providence in general, including under this title
his actual providing or foreseeing, his creating, and his
governance. Then (c. 4) he comes to the divine decree to

The Love of God.

create Christ's Humanity, angels and men for him, inferior
creatures for men—following here the Scotist teaching that
Christ would have become man (though of course he would
not have died) even if Adam had not sinned. God decreed to
create angels and man in the supernatural state of charity, and,
foreseeing that some angels and the whole nature or race of
man would fall from this state, God decreed to condemn the
former, but to redeem the latter by his Son's death, making
the state of redemption a hundred times better than the state
of innocence. God decreed (c. 6) special favours, such as the
Immaculate Conception of Mary, for certain rare creatures who
were to come nearest to his Son, and then for men in general
an immense abundance and universal showers of grace, an all-
illuminating light. He gives a whole exquisite chapter (c. 8) to
show the sincerity and strength of the desire God thus manifests
that we should love him, and then comes (c. 9) to the effecting
this desire by preventing our hearts with his grace, taking hold
of our natural inclination to love him. We can (c. 10) repulse
his grace, not because (c. 11) there is anything wanting in
God's offer, but (c. 12) as an inevitable consequence of our
having free-will; in case we accept it, we begin to mingle our
action with God's. Here we must remark that the Saint is
not concerned with the sacramental action of God which creates
or re-creates charity in the soul by baptism or penance, still
less does he treat the semi-miraculous production of charity
by Baptism in souls which have not yet the use of reason,
but he speaks of the intellectual and moral process or set of acts
by which a soul gifted with the use of reason is conducted from
infidelity to faith and charity, he treats of the justification
which is made by love even before the actual reception of a
Sacrament.

Our first act under divine inspiration is (c. 13) the consenting to those first stirrings of love which God causes in the soul
even before it has faith. Then (c. 14) comes the production
of faith. This may follow after argument and the acceptance
of the fact of miracles, but it is not precisely an effect of these.

Such things make truths of faith extremely credible, but God alone makes them actually believed. And the effect is from God not only in this sense that the extremest effort of natural intelligence could not attain to faith, but also because a moving of the *will* is required and is contained in the intellectual act of faith itself, what the Saint calls an affectionate sentiment of complacency in the beauty and sweetness of the truth accepted, so that faith is an acquiescence, an assent, an assurance. The Jews saw the force of the argument from Christ's miracles, but they did not assent to the conclusion because they loved it not. Hence faith includes a certain commencement of love in the will, but a love not as yet enough for eternal life.

Then (cc. 15, 16, 17) comes the production of hope, which brings yet closer to charity. As soon as faith shows the divine object of man's affections, there arises a movement of complacency and desiring love. This desire would be a torment to us unless we had an assurance that we might obtain its object. God gives this assurance by his promise, and this promise, while it makes desire stronger, causes at the same time a sense of calm which the Saint calls the "root" of hope. From it spring two movements or acts of the soul, the one by which she expects from God the promised happiness, and this is really the chief element of hope—*esperer*, the other by which she excites herself to do all that is required on her part—*aspirer*. This aspiration is the condition but not the positive ground of our esperation (to coin a word). That is to say, we may not expect the fruition of God except in so far as we have a courageous design to do all we can; then, we may infalliby expect it, yet still ever from the pure mercy of God. Hope, then, is defined "an expecting and aspiring love," or "the loving complacency we take in the expecting and seeking our soverign good." It is then a distinct advance in love. Faith includes a beginning of love in the movement of the will though its real seat is the intelligence; hope is all love, and its seat is the will. However hope as such is still insufficient, because, however noble, it is a love of cupidity, and not that love of God for his own sake which is necessary for eternal life. By it we love God sovereignly, because we desire him above all other goods, yet our love is not sovereign, because it is not the highest kind of love. The Saint is of course speaking of the action of hope before charity. Hope remains also after charity, existing, as we have said, in the very heights of perfect love, and after charity its acts merit before those of every other virtue.

Then comes the production of penitence or repentance. He distinguishes (c. 18) first, a merely human repentance; secondly, a religious repentance belonging to the merely natural order; thirdly, a supernatural inferior repentance, which (c. 19) is good but insufficient; and fourthly (c. 20), perfect repentance, that is, sorrow for sin arising from the loving consideration of the sovereignly amiable goodness which has been offended thereby. This is not precisely charity, because charity is, precisely, a movement towards union, whereas repentance is, precisely, a movement of separation (from sin); but though it is not precisely charity and therefore has not the sweetness of charity, it has the virtue and uniting property of charity, because the object of its movement of separation from sin is union with God. In practice there is no means, or need, to distinguish, because perfect repentance is always immediately followed or preceded by charity, or else the one is born within the other.

The Saint then reminds us (c. 21) that all this has been done by the loving action of God's grace, which, after awakening our souls and inspiring them to pray has brought them through faith and hope to penitence and perfect love. In conclusion (c. 22) he describes charity.

Book III. treats of the progress and perseverance of the soul in charity on earth, and of the perfection of triumphant charity in heaven. We have only one remark to make on this book. The Abbé Baudry expresses surprise that the Saint when speaking (c. 2) of the increase of charity by good works does not mention its increase by the Sacraments. But he includes them under the name good-works, and in Book IV., c. 4, where he sums up this part of Book III. mentions them explicitly. He does not dwell on them because his object in chapter 2 is to show how easy God has made the increase of charity. He takes therefore as his examples the smallest works, such as the giving a cup of cold water, and he leaves us to draw the conclusion that the faithful and loving reception of God's Sacraments would *à fortiori* increase love. Still it is true that neither here nor elsewhere does he treat the Sacraments except quite incidentally, and the explanation of this fact gives us a further insight into the true character and object of the Treatise. He is concerned with the action of grace in general, not with its action by particular means; he is more concerned with the interior movements of man under grace than with the effects worked on him, as it were from outside; and, as he is treating of actual charity, he is more concerned with the good acts for which God gives (whether by Sacraments or in any other way) an increase of grace, than he is concerned with the actual reception of the grace. We mention this to show that one must not be surprised at not finding a fuller treatment of, for instance, the Blessed Eucharist. We must also remember that this Treatise supposes the "Introduction to a Devout Life" as a foundation. And though he only introduces the Sacraments incidentally, he does not fail to speak of them frequently, and with such magnificent praises as we should expect from the Saint of love. As when he says (ii. 22) that the communication of Christ's body and blood is the very consummation of the charity he is writing of, and the crown of God's love-dealings with us; or as when he says, speaking of the return of the penitent soul to reunite herself, immediately, with her God: "Go and cry God's mercy in the very ear of your confessor" (ix. 7).

Book IV. describes the relations of love and sin. The following five Books treat of the exercise of benevolence in its generic sense—the sovereign love of God for his own sake.

Book V. treats in general of the double action or manifestation of this love,—in complacency, and in benevolence in its specific sense, that is, desire.

Books VI. and VII. treat of union with God by affection, that is, by prayer; the former treating of meditation, and of contemplation as far as union, the latter of union itself. The various degrees of the prayer of quiet are treated in these books, and Quietists bring forward passages from them, as from other parts of the Saint's works, in support of their extravagant system of annihilation of the powers and of purely passive prayer. We have said elsewhere* as much as we think it necessary to say to overthrow these allegations. But it is important to show that Fénélon was utterly wrong in appealing to the Saint's authority in support of his erroneous doctrine on this point in his " Maximes des Saints." Bossuet has exposed these errors and given a full explanation of the passages cited from S. Francis; particularly in the 8th and 9th Books of his " *Instruction pastorale sur les états d'oraison.*" The Saint expresses in this as in all things the very teaching of the Church. He rightly teaches that there is, even short of suspension and ecstasy, a kind of prayer in which God takes into his own hands the powers of the soul, and produces in it acts far above the ordinary operations of faith, hope and charity. When God lifts a soul to this prayer, and also to some extent in preparation and expectancy of this elevation, the will acts, by a placing of itself (*remise*) in the hands of God, and even continues to act, though insensibly: hence the soul is not purely passive, but the action of God is so mighty, and so far beyond all proportion to that of the will, that S. Francis says this is " as it were passive." And as the soul must offer itself to be lifted, and must co-operate with God, therefore also must it help to acquire and preserve that " quiet" which is the condition of God's operation : it must abstain from intrusive acts of reasoning and from other acts of the will, especially from violent ones.

* " Four Essays on the Life and Writings of S. Francis de Sales," Essay III. p. 88.

But this prayer, however frequent, long, uninterrupted, absorbing, it may become, is of itself a non-permanent state, and not of the nature of a habit, but is always an act of charity. And far from saying that for perfection it is necessary to be raised to and to keep oneself in this state, the Saint teaches in a hundred places that the soul, however perfect, must exercise itself in all ordinary acts of prayer, faith, hope, petition, which are only put on one side for the time in which God has raised it. The practice of S. Jane Frances, whose authority was invoked even more speciously than that of her saintly director by the advocates of passive prayer, bears on this. We are told that : " She wrote out and signed with her blood a long prayer which she had composed of petitions, praises, thanksgivings, for general and particular favours, for relations and friends, for the living and the dead, in fine for all intentions to which she considered herself obliged, with the Credo of the Missal, also signed with her blood. She carried this in a little bag night and day round her neck, and she had made a loving covenant with Our Lord that whenever she pressed this to her heart she should be taken to have made all the acts of faith, the thanks and the petitions she had written."* And, at last, prayer is not a character of perfection, but a means to it, and the two following statements of S. Francis in his second Conference absolutely settle the whole question as to his teaching. " It happens often enough that Our Lord gives these quietudes and tranquillities to souls that are far from perfection." . . . . and on the other hand : " There are persons who are very perfect to whom Our Lord has never given such sweetnesses nor such quietudes ; who do all with the superior part of the soul, and make their will die in the will of God by main force, and with the supreme point of the reason ; and this death is the death of the cross, much more excellent than that other, which should rather be called a slumber than a death."

* From her life by Maupas, quoted by Bossuet in the "Instr. Past. sur les états d'oraison," viii.

As in treating affective love Book VII. completes Book VI.,
so in treating effective love Book VIII., which treats of
obedience to the already signified will of God, is completed by
Book IX., which treats of indifference, or the state of perfect
readiness to accept all that God's good-pleasure may choose to
send us.

On the doctrine of indifference we venture again to refer
the reader to our Essay* just quoted. We add a few words to
show how completely Fénélon erred in appealing to this
Treatise to support his extravagant and condemned propositions that indifference extends to eternal salvation as *our*
salvation, and to virtuousness as such. The Saint expressly
teaches that while God's glory must be our principal end, we
may, indeed we must—our nature so requires—desire salvation
and virtue as good also in themselves. Much less can we
acquiesce in a supposed decree of damnation, with that species
of absolute act which Fénélon requires as the last test of the
disinterestedness of love.† With regard to eternal salvation,
we have only to study the sentiments the Saint places in the
hearts and mouths of those whose love is refined to its highest
point at the moment of death (v. 10, vii. 11, 12). He has a
chapter to prove that the preceding desire of heaven increases
the enjoyment of it (iii. 10) ; and he teaches that not only
mercenary hope but also servile fear remain in the soul as part
of its habit of charity so long as it is in this life (xi. 17).
With regard to virtues he says (xi. 13) : " Let us love the particular virtues, but principally because they are agreeable to
God ;" and : " We must make this heavenly good-pleasure the
soul of our actions, loving the goodness and beauty of virtue
principally because it is agreeable to God." Here the word
" principally " is the key of the whole question.

Bossuet triumphantly vindicates‡ the Saint's *doctrine* on

* Pp. 82-4.
† The Saint is careful to qualify any ambiguous statement (as in ix. 4)
by declaring that he speaks " *par imagination de chose impossible.*"
‡ In the same " Instruction, &c."

indifference, but has a very ill-judged criticism on his use of the word. He is quite right in saying that indifference is only a degree of resignation, but he forgets how far ordinary resignation is below indifference. Bossuet gives a full explanation of all the passages alleged by Fénélon from S. Francis, but he was hampered, as Fénélon was totally misled, by Maupas's erroneous account of S. Francis's famous temptation to despair.

Of the remaining three books, Book X. is dedicated entirely to the commandment of loving God above all things; Books XI. and XII. are on the theory and practice of the particular virtues. Indeed it must be remembered that the object of the Treatise, even in its speculative parts, is exclusively practical. And as we have shown that in its theory it is free from error, so we may now be allowed to indicate some of its glorious truths, particularly with regard to the practice of holy living.

It is not a book, like other spiritual books, treating only a section or a single element of the devout life, but it is one by which and on which the whole spiritual life can be formed; it is, with the " Introduction to a Devout Life," a perfect book, a " complete food," containing all the ingredients necessary for spiritual sustenance.

It contains in the first place an immense mass of instruction, dogmatic and moral, on the science of the love of God. It treats not only in broad outline but also in subtle detail of God and the soul, this world and the world to come, grace and free-will, holiness and sin, commandments and counsels, ordinary virtue and perfection, all questions of prayer; it treats the virtues in detail, not only the virtue of charity in all its parts, but also faith, hope and fear, zeal, obedience, resignation. The direct course of the Treatise takes us through all these, and they are not only treated fully in themselves, but so treated as to bring out in illustrating them a hundred related truths. A whole theology of Mary might be gathered as we pass along; her Immaculate Conception (ii. 3), her graces and privileges (iii. 8.; ix. 14.; vii. 13, 14), her praise of God (v. 11), her heavenly death (vii. 13, 14). A new light is thrown on the sense of Holy Scripture, and on the principles and actions of the Saints.

But, in the second place, we more particularly wish to point out some of his practical principles and rules, the manner of loving and serving God. The most important of these is what may be called the Saint's general idea or philosophy of life. It begins thus: " We know by faith that the divinity is an incomprehensible abyss of all perfection. . . . . And this truth which faith teaches we consider attentively by meditation, regarding this immensity of goods which are in God. . . . . Now when we have made our understanding very attentive to the greatness of the goods which are in this divine object, it is impossible that our will should not be touched with complacency in this good . . . . and especially when we see amidst his perfections that of his infinite love excellently shining" (v. 1, 2.) The loving soul does not stay in complacency but goes on to benevolence, wishing her God all possible goods ; but as she is at the very same time exulting in the thought that nothing is wanting to him, she can at first but spend herself in desiring him what he already has, in desiring to be able to give him something, and in praises, ever rising higher and higher until at last she finds a sort of rest in the sense that her utter inability to desire him anything which he has not, or to praise him fully, is the best proof of the infinity of the goods he has. This delight in God and these loving desires are an important part of her service, but they would be barren if she did not go further. She turns, then, to her own powers, and finds that exercising them in herself by internal acts of prayer (affective love), and outside herself, amid creatures, by external acts of the virtues (effective love), she can increase the glory of her beloved, not in itself, but in and by herself. Thus the various interior and exterior acts are brought into one, and the soul's life consists, on the one hand, in " a continual progress in the sweet searching out of motives which may continually urge her" (v. 7), and, on the other hand, in acts of prayer, in obedience, and in submission. She " employs every occasion," " does everything most perfectly," and, by the practice of Intention, Offering, and Ejaculatory Prayer (according to methods minutely described in Book XI. 13, 14, 20, and throughout Book XII.), subordinates and ranges every interior movement and every exterior action to the service of divine love.

This " view" of life, this continual gazing at the beloved Master for whom we work, this regarding the acts of life as a mere series of acts or offerings of love, is the very central point of the ascetic teaching of S. Francis. It not only gives the nobleness, the intensity, the meritoriousness of charity to every act, but it gives also at the same time a great simplicity and largeness, preserving the soul from formality and from getting lost or wearied in the multitudinous details and minute practices of the spiritual life ; it creates a loving detachment and liberty of spirit, with a readiness to follow every slightest indication of God's will. Finally, it gives order to our various duties. For instance, it puts in their proper place, in serene majesty above the cavils of worldlings, the works of religion and " piety." These are the immediate services of the beloved, the first effects of charity, and therefore charity itself teaches that : "Amongst all virtuous actions we should carefully practise those of religion and reverence to divine things, those of faith, hope and the most holy fear of God ;—often talking of heavenly things, thinking of and aspiring after eternity, frequenting churches and holy services, reading spiritual books, observing the ceremonies of the Christian religion ; for holy love feeds at will amid these exercises, and spreads its graces and properties more abundantly over them than over the simply human virtues" (xi. 3). Yet there is no fanaticism. The human virtues find their proper place at the proper time, and, inferior in themselves, are raised by love, that is, by the fact that for the time they are the will of God, to the highest rank in the eyes of the loving soul,—" For in little and low exercises, charity is practised not only more frequently, but also as a rule more humbly, and therefore more profitably and more holily" (xii. 6). He has two glorious chapters on the truth that legitimate occupations, be they even in court or camp, hinder not the practice of divine love. "Curiosity, ambition, disquiet, together with inadvertence to, or not considering, the end for which we are in this world, are the causes why we have a hundred times more hindrances than affairs ; and it is these embarrassments, that is, the silly, vain, superfluous undertakings with which we charge ourselves that turn us from the love of God, and not the true and lawful exercise of our vocations" (xii. 4). In the one great principle of doing all for love we have signalized two conditions or negative aspects of the same. 1°. The intellect must be kept "very attentive." As the Saint says in the "Introduction to a Devout Life" (v. 17), so here, consideration "is supposed throughout the entire work," the whole edifice is built on it, and therefore the want of it, "*inconsidération*," is the ruin of the whole spiritual life (xi. 7.) This "consideration" need not be called by the alarming name of mental prayer, but whatever it is called it consists in a most serious attention to spiritual truths according to the capacity of the individual : there must be one great esteem, and therefore the energy of the intellect cannot be given primarily to anything else. So (2°) in the will, there must be but one great affection, one aim, one desire—"One to one." " The desire of exalting God separates from inferior pleasures" (v. 7) ; and : " to have the desire of sacred love we must cut off other desires" (xii. 3). " Those souls who ever abound in desires, designs and projects never desire holy celestial love as they ought :" " He who aspires to heavenly love must carefully reserve for it his leisure, his spirit, and his affections :"—words which should be written in letters of flame for the guidance of such as seek the right way to perfection.

We will not stay to give examples of his more particular principles with regard to prayer, but we select a few with regard to the virtues. The truly loving heart not only observes the commandments, but loves the observance, of them (viii. 5). "Inclination is neither vice nor virtue. . . . . How many by natural disposition are sober, simple, silent, even chaste ? All this seems to be virtue, but it is not, until on such natural humours we have grafted free and voluntary consent." The whole chapter "On the imperfection of the virtues of the pagans" (xi. 7.) is of the most practical importance at the present day. The general, but surely most constraining, principle of mortification,—that other pleasures and other desires must be put down for the sake of divine love,—is applied to the *interior* in such more particular methods as this :—irregular affections can be put down either on the principle of curing contraries by contraries, or on the principle of curing likes by likes : the inclination to trust in earthly things may be overcome either by thinking of the vanity of earthly hopes or of the solidity of heavenly hopes ; desire of riches or of sensual pleasure may be kept down either by the contempt of them or by the esteem of heavenly goods, "as fire is extinguished either by water or by lightning"(xi. 20). It is applied to the *exterior* thus : "It is useless to give orders of abstinence to the palate, but the hands must be ordered to furnish the mouth with meat and drink only in such and such a measure. . . . . If we desire our eyes not to see we must turn them away, or (he has just compared our sensual appetite to a hawk) cover them with their natural hood . . . . it would be folly to command a horse not to wax fat, not to grow, not to kick,—to effect all this, stop his corn" (i. 2). In this connection, and to show how beautiful, how consistent, and how feasible his teaching is, it should be studied with his life, as his life should be explained by his teaching. That his extraordinary and almost unreasonable meekness sprang from no weakness or ignorance, but was founded on the deepest wisdom and sincere humility, we realize when we study his teaching (x.) on zeal and anger. His extremely affectionate expressions towards his friends find their justification in the truth that "the union to which love aspires is spiritual" (i. 10). The ground of his missionary spirit and life is found in v. 9, and the whole work is the explanation of his absolute devotion of himself to the loving service of God and his neighbour.

In the third place, the Treatise contains a full exposition of

the motives for serving God, the *why* of a spiritual life. This
is all reduced to the one great motive of the infinite perfections—especially the amiableness, the love, the goodness of
God—brought before us in a hundred ways. His mere descriptions are enough to bring home this motive to the heart
that reads them with attention, but the Saint himself puts
them together (xii., 11, 12) with the exact method of
applying them. But besides the direct treatment of the
motives, the Treatise is pervaded by a heavenly persuasive
unction, which ever urges them. This is why S. Vincent calls
it " the goad of the slothful and the stimulus of love." While
S. Francis seems only to be making us clearly understand what
virtue is, he at the same time makes us esteem and love it; his
reasons for loving God and practising virtue are not cold, dry
logic, but reach the heart, and command assent; and while he
is apparently only fixing our attention on the way to practise
virtue he is at the same time gently but effectively touching
the springs of the will to make us love and prepare to effect it.
But besides this continual stimulation he has direct exhortations; he stops, as it were, in his course to preach. One chapter
is headed : " An exhortation to the amorous submission which
we owe to the decrees of divine Providence" (iv. 8). Another
is his exposition of S. Paul's,—" The charity of Christ presseth
us." Another—" An exhortation to the sacrifice we ought
to make to God of our free-will" (xii. 10). And other chapters,
though not precisely in the form of exhortations, contain the
virtue of them. Such are the chapters " On condolence and
complacency in the Passion of Our Lord" (v. 5); on the
" Marvellous history of a gentleman who died of love on Mount
Olivet" (vii. 12) ; and the last chapter of all : " That Mount
Calvary is the true academy of love."

But, in the fourth place, this Treatise is not only a manual
and a guide to perfection, but it is also a meditation-book, and
a prayer-book. In such chapters as those just mentioned the
devout soul will find all the materials of most excellent meditations;—not only deep pregnant thoughts, but also a **very**

fountain of affections and ejaculations, most pressing movements of the will, and most effective resolutions. The sum-
ming up of motives, and method of using them is already in
the very form of meditation. But almost every chapter could
be used as such. For instance, if one wished to strengthen
the groundwork of love—the realization of the perfections of
God—after thinking out Book v. cc. 1. 2., he could add Book i.
cc. 15, 18, Book ii. cc. 1, 2, 8, 15, 22, and Book iii. cc. 11, 12,
13. This Book III. furnishes grand meditations on heaven,
and every Book is full of the excellences of charity, than which
no consideration could be more touching or more practical.

Then, the Treatise is a prayer-book. Very frequently the
Saint ends his chapter with an exquisite prayer, himself giving the expression of the ardours with which he has filled
our hearts. All Book V. is a prayer;—for instance, c. 5
on the Passion, c. 6 on Desires. Profound dogma, having
permeated the intellect, exhales itself, as it were, to God
on the apex of the spirit in such burning words as
his—"Ah! then I am not made for this world, &c." (i. 15),
or—"Ah! Jesus, who will give me grace to be one single
spirit with thee, &c!" (vii. 3.)

We have now to speak of our text and rendering. We
have followed the text of Vivès's edition of the "Œuvres
Complètes," which, with a little improvement from subse-
quent editions, is a reproduction of the original work, published at Lyons by Rigaud in 1616. We therefore follow in
our quotations the spelling and accentuation of the old French.
We have of course used the ordinary Catholic translation of
the Bible, except where the Saint leaves the Vulgate for the
Septuagint or the Hebrew, which he occasionally does, not, as
he says, to get the true sense, but "to explain and confirm the
true sense." We have consulted the originals for the citations
from the Fathers, but the Saint himself quotes them with a
certain freedom, and we have not thought it necessary to give
the exact references, as the student can easily find them in
Vivès or Migne. It has been decided to omit or modify in

this popular edition a few sentences in which the Saint refers
to certain delicate matters—in particular to certain Bible
narratives which to his original readers were matters of
familiar knowledge—with the happy simplicity of his day. As
he says in his Preface, " it is of extreme importance to remember the age in which one writes," and there can be no doubt
that if he had been writing for this age he would have
consulted its requirements, and would have conformed to the
universal practice of modern spiritual writers by forbearing
reference to these subjects. He only introduces them incidentally and merely for the purpose of illustrating his main
argument. The omissions or alterations taken altogether
would not amount to more than two pages.*

We are acquainted with only two English versions of the
Treatise. The first was made by Father Car, from the eighteenth
French edition,† and we had at first intended to take this as
the basis of ours; but when we came to actually test it
by the original, we determined to make our translation completely independent of it, and in many parts we did not refer
to it at all. As to the substance of the work it is satisfactory;
though there are many slight omissions, and a few somewhat
serious mistakes. As to style, taken by itself, it is a good and
a very interesting specimen of the racy, vigorous English of
that day; but taken as a translation, the rendering is un-
warrantably free, and Father Car's manner is far too rugged
to represent that of the Saint, which is always graceful and
flowing, even when the thought is closest and the passion
strongest. Father Car gives the structure correctly, but his
manipulation of conjunctions and adverbs, particularly in the
more argumentative parts, is painfully cumbrous. We should
expect his diction to be archaic, but some of his words are

* They occur in i. 5, 10; iv. 10; v. 1; vi. 15; vii. 1; viii. 1; ix. 10;
x. 7, 9; xi. 4, 10, 11, 14.

† " A Treatise of the Love of God." Written in French by B. Francis de
Sales, Bishope and Prince of Geneva. Translated into English by Miles
Car, priest of the English Colledge of Doway. The eighteenth edition.
Printed at Doway by Gerard Pinchon, at the sign of Coleyn, 1630.

quite obsolete.* He is occasionally mistaken in his use of words, as when he translates *bonté*, "bounty," instead of "goodness;" he makes curious mistakes in words which are spelt nearly alike.† We have laboured to preserve his delightful air of antiqueness, which is singularly appropriate to the Saint's work.

The modern English translation, which was made, we believe, early in the present century by an Irish lady, and which has been reprinted by various publishers, is not worth criticizing. It is not so much a translation as a very bad adaptation. A good deal of the substance of the book is left out, and the translator, who was not properly acquainted either with the Saint's language or her own, substitutes her style for his. We have no hesitation in saying that there is not a page without important errors on commission or omission.

We may add a few words on our own work. It is sometimes said that a translation should read as if it were composed in the language in which it appears, and, again, that a translator must not attend immediately to the words of his text, but must, in the first place, aim at producing the same impression on the minds of his readers as the author would produce on the minds of those for whom he originally wrote. We cannot but consider both these rules or principles to be fallacious. A Frenchman, for instance, is different from an Englishman, and there are many words which necessarily make a very different impression, according as they fall on a French or on an English mind. So, again, the French tongue has national peculiarities and differences which an English translator may not ignore, but which he cannot represent in strict accordance with the genius of his own tongue. S. Francis's work would have been totally different, both in itself and in its effect, if he had been an Englishman writing for his countrymen in their

---

* We would gladly have reintroduced such a fine old word as "yert," which represents the now untranslateable *eslan* or *eslancement*.

† For instance *nuisance* as if it were *naissance; jeusnes et veilles*, as if they were *jeunes et vieilles*.

native language. The most that a translator can do is to put
the foreign reader in as good a position as he would be in if he
had a familiar knowledge of the original. When an Englishman having a familiar knowledge of French reads a book
written in that language, he does not indeed usually advert to
the expression therein of the national characteristics—vivacity,
use of gesture, frequent expression of emotion, strong sense of
personality—because he has for the time put on his French
form of mind, but there is certainly a latent sense of foreign-
ness, of which he becomes conscious when these peculiarities
are exaggerated, as in such a writer as Victor Hugo.

We say this in explanation of the general structure of the
work, which could not be altered without being revolution-
ized, but as regards particular words and phrases, we have
tried our best to spare our readers the disagreeable jar which
is caused by the introduction of a foreign idiom. In this
matter the Treatise presents less difficulty than is found in the
more colloquial writings, because its argument is very substantial, and its text largely consists of quotations from the
Holy Scriptures, the Fathers, and philosophers. The difficulty
lies deeper, and one must be extremely careful, in obliterating
Gallicisms, not to injure or destroy what belongs to the very
texture of the style. S. Francis's work cannot be made to read
as easily as do the empty, superficial writings of the day, or to
appear in a spick-and-span modern English dress. He is a
classic, he is a master of thought, having his individual
characteristics, who wrote scientifically on profoundest religious truths three ages back.

His style is old-world, antique. Words with him have more
of their fresh native simplicity than they now retain after
having done service for three hundred years. Some of them
he was the first to bring out of their classic use into modern
circulation. Hence, we make no difficulty in using such words
as "contemplation," "sensible," "civil," in their original and
more proper sense, as English religious writers of his age—
Hooker, Taylor or Milton—used them.

Again, he is scientific—theological and philosophical. He writes a Treatise. The world, which is only interested in its own matters, will not admit the rights of the scientific writer on religion. Catholics of the English-speaking race are placed at a double disadvantage, on account of the small proportion their numbers bear to the mass of their countrymen. But surely we are not to acquiesce in allowing terms to be prohibited which are necessary or useful for properly and safely expressing the distinctive truths of our religion: there is an interest at stake not merely literary, but religious, and also patriotic. We claim, therefore, the right to use, for instance, the words " religion," "religious," " professed," in our technical Catholic sense, for the state and the persons of those who have bound themselves to the service of God by vow.

S. Francis also had his special characteristics, which, therefore, are not French but Salesian. He was slightly old-fashioned, even in his own time. He was a patriarch of French literature, and devoted, in language as in other things, to the old times, though so glorious a pioneer of the new. He is simple in expression amongst the simple. But each word is charged with thought and reflection, and sometimes an exclamation which one might at first be tempted to suppress as a French superfluity, turns out to be a "word," and welded into the substance of the phrase. He was a Saint, also, and what would be an exclamation in others is an ejaculation in him.

But, after all, our object is devotional and not literary; we are far from wishing to indulge any literary fancies or crotchets and have no intention of straining our principles of translation. Our one aim is to make the true teachings of S. Francis de Sales accessible, profitable, and attractive to English readers, and so to contribute our poor efforts to advance the divine Art of Holy Loving.

WEOBLEY,

Feast of our most holy Father S. Benedict, 1884.

TABLE OF CONTENTS.

BOOK I.

CONTAINING A PREPARATION FOR THE WHOLE TREATISE.

Contents.

BOOK II.

THE HISTORY OF THE GENERATION AND HEAVENLY BIRTH OF DIVINE LOVE.

BOOK III.

OF THE PROGRESS AND PERFECTION OF LOVE.

BOOK IV.

OF THE DECAY AND RUIN OF CHARITY.

BOOK V.

OF THE TWO PRINCIPAL EXERCISES OF HOLY LOVE WHICH CONSIST IN COMPLACENCY AND BENEVOLENCE.

BOOK VI.

OF THE EXERCISES OF HOLY LOVE IN PRAYER.

BOOK VII.

OF THE UNION OF THE SOUL WITH HER GOD, WHICH IS PERFECTED IN PRAYER.

BOOK VIII.

OF THE LOVE OF CONFORMITY, BY WHICH WE UNITE OUR WILL TO THE WILL OF GOD, SIGNIFIED UNTO US BY HIS COMMANDMENTS, COUNSELS AND INSPIRATIONS.

Contents.

xliii

BOOK IX.

OF THE LOVE OF SUBMISSION, WHEREBY OUR WILL IS UNITED TO GOD'S GOOD-PLEASURE.

BOOK X.

OF THE COMMANDMENT OF LOVING GOD ABOVE ALL THINGS.

BOOK XI.

OF THE SOVEREIGN AUTHORITY WHICH SACRED LOVE HOLDS OVER ALL THE VIRTUES, ACTIONS AND PERFECTIONS OF THE SOUL.

BOOK XII.

CONTAINING CERTAIN COUNSELS FOR THE PROGRESS OF THE SOUL IN HOLY LOVE.

TREATISE
ON THE
LOVE OF GOD

Dedicatory Prayer

Most holy Mother of God, vessel of incomparable election, Queen of sovereign dilection, thou art the most lovely, the most loving and most beloved of all creatures! The love of the heavenly Father found its good pleasure in thee from all eternity, destining thy chaste heart to the perfection of holy love, to the end that one day thou mightest love his only Son with unique motherly love as he had done from all eternity with unique fatherly love. O Saviour Jesus, to whom could I better dedicate words on thy love, than to the most amiable heart of the well-beloved of thy soul?

But O all triumphant Mother! Who can cast his eyes upon thy majesty without seeing at thy right hand him whom for the love of thee thy Son deigned so often to honour with the title of father, having united him unto thee by the celestial bond of a most virginal marriage, that he might be thy coadjutor and helper in the charge of the direction and education of his divine infancy? O great S. Joseph! Most beloved spouse of the well-beloved Mother, ah! how often hast thou borne in thy arms the love of heaven and earth, while, inflamed with the sweet embraces and kisses of this Divine child, thy soul melted away with joy while he tenderly whispered in thy ears (O God what sweetness!) that thou wast his great friend and his well-beloved father?

Of old the lamps of the ancient temple were placed upon golden lilies. O Mary and Joseph, Pair without peer! Sacred lilies of incomparable beauty, amongst which the well-beloved

feeds himself and feeds all his lovers—ah ! if I may give myself
any hope that this love-writing may enlighten and inflame the
children of light, where can I better lay it than amongst your
lilies, wherein the Sun of Justice, the splendour and brightness
of the eternal light, did so sovereignly recreate himself that he
there fulfilled the delights of the ineffable love of his heart
towards us ?　　O well-beloved mother of the well-beloved Son, O
well-beloved spouse of the well-beloved mother ! Prostrate
before the feet of you who bore my Saviour, I dedicate and
consecrate this little work of love to the immense greatness of
your love.　Ah! I conjure you by the heart of your sweet
Jesus, King of hearts, whom your hearts adore—animate my
heart, and all hearts that shall read this writing, by your all-
powerful favour with the Holy Ghost, that henceforth we may
offer up in holocaust all our affections to his divine goodness, to
live, die, and live again for ever, amid the flames of this heavenly
fire, which Our Lord your son has so much desired to kindle in
our hearts, that he never ceased to labour and sigh for this until
death, even the death of the cross.

VIVE JÉSUS.

———•◦•———

PREFACE.

The Holy Ghost teaches that the lips of the heavenly Spouse, that is The Church, resemble *scarlet* and the *dropping honey-comb*,* to let every one know that all the doctrine which she announces consists in sacred love; of a more resplendent red than scarlet on account of the blood of the spouse whose love inflames her, sweeter than honey on account of the sweetness of the beloved who crowns her with delights. So this heavenly spouse when he thought good to begin the promulgation of his law, cast down upon the assembly of those disciples whom he had deputed for this work a shower of fiery tongues, sufficiently intimating thereby that the preaching of the gospel was wholly designed for the inflaming of hearts.

Represent to yourself beautiful doves amidst the rays of the sun; you will see their plumage break into as many different colours as you change your point of viewing them; because their feathers are so fitted to display the light, that when the sun comes to spread his splendour on them, a multitude of reflections are made, producing a great variety of tints and glancing colours, colours so agreeable to the eye that they surpass all other colours, even the enamel of richest jewels; colours so resplendent and so delicately gilded that the gilding makes their own colours more bright than ever; for it was this sight which made the royal prophet say *If you sleep among the midst of lots; you shall be as the wings of a dove covered with silver, and the hinder parts of her back with the paleness of gold.*† The Church is indeed adorned with an excellent variety of teachings,

* Cant. iv. † Ps. lxvii. 14.

3

sermons, treatises and spiritual books, all very beautiful and pleasant to the sight by reason of the admirable mingling which the Sun of Justice makes of his divine wisdom with the tongues of his pastors, which are their feathers, and with their pens, which sometimes hold the place of tongues, and form the rich plumage of this mystic dove. But amongst all the divers colours of the doctrine which she displays, the fine gold of holy Charity is everywhere spread, and makes itself excellently visible, gilding all the science of the saints with its incomparable lustre, and raising it above every other science. All is love's, and in love, for love, and of love, in the holy Church.

But as we are not ignorant that all the light of the day proceeds from the sun and yet we ordinarily say that the sun does not shine, except only when it openly sends out its beams here or there ; in like manner, though all Christian doctrine be about sacred love, yet we do not honour all theology indifferently with the title of this divine love, but only those parts of it which regard the birth, nature, properties and operations thereof in particular.

Now it is true that divers writers have already handled this subject ; above all those ancient Fathers, who as they did lovingly serve God so did they speak divinely of his love. O how good it is to hear S. Paul speak of heavenly things, who learned them even in heaven itself, and how good to see those souls who were nursed in the bosom of love write of its holy sweetness ! For this reason those amongst the schoolmen that discoursed the most and the best of it, did also most excel in piety. S. Thomas has made a treatise on it worthy of S. Thomas ; S. Bonaventure and B. Denis the Carthusian have made divers most excellent ones on it under various titles, and as for John Gerson, Chancellor of the University of Paris, Sixtus Senensis speaks of him thus : " He has so worthily discoursed of the fifty properties of divine love which are described in the course of the Canticle of Canticles, that he alone would seem to have taken proper account of the affections of the love of God." Truly this man was extremely learned, judicious and devout.

And that we may know this kind of writings to be made more successfully by the devotion of lovers than by the learning of the wise, it has pleased the Holy Ghost that many women should work wonders in it. Who has ever better expressed the heavenly passions of sacred love, than S. Catharine of Genoa, S. Angela of Foligno, S. Catharine of Siena, S. Mechtilde?

In our age also many have written upon this subject, whose works I have not had leisure to read distinctly but only here and there so far forth as was requisite to discover whether this book might yet find place. Father Louis of Granada, that great doctor of piety, has placed a treatise of the love of God in his Memorial, which is sufficiently commended in saying it is his. Diego Stella, of the Order of S. Francis, made another, which is very effective and profitable for prayer. Christopher Fonseca, an Augustinian, brought out one still larger, wherein he has many excellent things. Father Louis Richeome of the Society has also published a book under the title of *The Art of Loving God by his Creatures*, and this author is so amiable in his person and in his beautiful writings that doubtless he is even more so when writing of love itself. Father John of Jesus Maria, a discalced Carmelite, has composed a little book which is also called *The Art of Loving God*, and which is much esteemed. That great and celebrated Cardinal Bellarmine has also lately issued a little book entitled: *The Ladder for Ascending unto God by his Creatures*, which cannot be but admirable coming from that most learned hand and most devout soul, who has written so much and so wisely in the Church's behalf. I will say nothing of the *Parenetic* of that river of eloquence* who flows at present through all France in the multitude and variety of his sermons and noble writings. The close spiritual consanguinity which my soul has contracted with his, when by the imposition of my hands he received the sacred character of the episcopal order, to the great happiness of the diocese of Belley and to the honour of the Church, besides a thousand ties of a sincere friendship which fasten us together, permits me not to speak with praise of his works, amongst which this *Parenetic of divine love* was one of the first sallies of the matchless wealth of intellect which every one admires in him.

* M. Camus.

We see further a goodly and magnificent palace which the R. Father Laurence of Paris, a Capuchin preacher, erected in honour of heavenly love, which being finished will be a complete course of the Art of loving well. And lastly the B. Mother (S.) Teresa of Jesus, has written so accurately of the sacred movements of love in all the books she has left us, that one is amazed to see so much eloquence masked under such profound humility, such great solidity of wit in such great simplicity : and her most learned ignorance makes the knowledge of many learned men appear ignorant, who after long and laborious study have to blush at not understanding what she so happily puts down touching the practice of holy love. Thus does God raise the throne of his power upon the ground of our infirmity, *making use of weak things to confound the strong.**

And although, my dear reader, this Treatise which I now present you, comes far short of those excellent works, without hope of ever running even with them, yet have I such confidence in the favour of the two heavenly lovers to whom I dedicate it, that still it may be in some way serviceable to you, and that in it you will meet with many wholesome considerations which you would not elsewhere so easily find, as again you may elsewhere find many beautiful things which are not here. Indeed, it even seems to me that my design is not the same as that of others except in general, inasmuch as we all look towards the glory of holy love. But this you will see by reading it.

Truly my intention is only to represent simply and naïvely, without art, still more without false colours, the history of the birth, progress, decay, operations, properties, advantages and excellences of divine love. And if besides this you find other things, these are but excrescences which it is almost impossible for such as me who write amidst many distractions to avoid. But still I think that there will be nothing without some utility. Nature herself, who is so skilful a workwoman, intending to produce grapes, produces at the same time, as by a prudent inadvertence, such an abundance of leaves and branches, that there are very few vines which have not in their season to be pruned of leaves and shoots.

* 1 Cor. i. 27.

Writers are often treated too harshly : the censures that are passed on them are given hastily, and very often with more incorrectness than they committed imprudence in hastening to publish their writings. Precipitation of judgment greatly puts in danger the conscience of the judge, and the innocence of the accused. Many write amiss and many censure foolishly. The kindness of the reader makes his reading sweet and profitable. And, my dear reader, to have you more favourable, I will here give you an explanation of some points which might peradventure otherwise put you out of humour.

Some perhaps will think that I have said too much, and that it was not requisite to go so deep down into the roots of the subject, but I am of opinion that heavenly love is a plant like to that which we call Angelica, whose root is no less odoriferous and wholesome than the stalk and the branches. The four first books and some chapters of the rest might without doubt have been omitted, without disadvantage to such souls as only seek the practice of holy love, yet all of it will be profitable unto them if they behold it with a devout eye : while others also might have been disappointed not to have had the whole of what belongs to the treatise of divine love. I have taken into consideration as I should do, the state of the minds of this age : it much imports to remember in what age we are writing.

I cite Scripture sometimes in other terms than those of the ordinary edition (the Vulgate). For God's sake, my dear reader do me not therefore the wrong to think that I wish to depart from that edition. Ah no ! For I know the Holy Ghost has authorized it by the sacred Council of Trent, and that therefore all of us ought to keep to it : on the contrary I only use the other versions for the service of this, when they explain and confirm its true sense. For example what the heavenly spouse says to his spouse : *Thou hast wounded my heart :** is greatly illustrated by the other version : *Thou hast taken away my heart*, or, *Thou hast snatched away and ravished my heart.* That which our Saviour said : *Blessed are the poor in spirit :* is much amplified and cleared by the Greek : *Blessed are the beggars in spirit :* and so with others.

* Cant. iv. 9.

I have often cited the sacred Psalmist in verse, and this to
recreate your mind and on account of the ease with which I
could do it, by the beautiful translation of Phillip des Portes,
Abbot of Tiron. This however I have sometimes departed
from ; not of course thinking I could improve the verses of this
famous poet (for I should be too impertinent if never having
so much as thought of this kind of writing, I should pretend to
be happy in it in an age and condition of life which would
oblige me to retire from it in case I had ever been engaged
therein), but in some places where the sense might be variously
taken, I have not followed his verse, because I would not follow
his sense, as in Psalm cxxxii., where he has taken a certain
Latin word for the fringe of the garment which I thought
ought to be taken for the collar, wherefore I have translated it
to my own mind.

I have said nothing which I have not learned of others, yet it
is impossible for me to remember whence I had everything in
particular ; but believe me, if I had taken any lengthy and
remarkable passages out of any author, I would make it a
matter of conscience not to let him have the deserved honour
of it, and to remove a suspicion which you may conceive against
my sincerity in this matter, I warn you that the 13th chapter
of Book VII. is extracted from a sermon which I delivered at
Paris at S. John's *en Grève* upon the feast of the Assumption
of our Blessed Lady, 1602.

I have not always expressed the sequence of the chapters, but
if you notice you will easily find the links of their connection.
In that and several other things I had a care to spare my own
leisure and your patience. After I had caused the *Introduction
to a Devout Life* to be printed, my Lord Archbishop of Vienne,
Peter de Villars, did me the favour of writing his opinion of it
in terms so advantageous to that little book and to me, that I
should never dare to rehearse them : and exhorting me to apply
the most of my leisure to the like works, amongst many rare
counsels he favoured me with, one was that as far as the matter
would permit I should always be short in the chapters. For as,
said he, travellers knowing that there is a fair garden some
twenty or twenty-five paces out of their way, readily turn aside

so short a distance to go see it, which they would not do if it were further distant; even so those who know that there is but little distance between the beginning and end of a chapter do willingly undertake to read it, which they would not do though the subject were never so delightful, if a long time were required for the reading of it. And therefore I had good reason to follow my own inclination in this respect since it was agreeable to this great personage who was one of the most saintly prelates and learned doctors that the Church has had in our age, and who at the time that he honoured me with his letter was the most ancient of all the doctors of the faculty of Paris.

A great servant of God informed me not long ago that by addressing my speech to Philothea in the *Introduction to a Devout Life*, I hindered many men from profiting by it: because they did not esteem advice given to a woman, to be worthy of a man. I marvelled that there were men who, to be thought men, showed themselves in effect so little men, for I leave it to your consideration, my dear reader, whether devotion be not as well for men as for women, and whether we are not to read with as great attention and reverence the second Epistle of S. John which was addressed to the holy lady Electa, as the third which he directs to Caius, and whether a thousand thousand Epistles and excellent Treatises of the ancient fathers of the Church ought to be held unprofitable to men, because they are addressed to holy women of those times. But, besides, it is the soul which aspires to devotion that I call Philothea, and men have souls as well as women.

Nevertheless, to imitate the great Apostle in this occasion, who esteemed himself *a debtor to every one*, I have changed my address in this treatise and speak to Theotimus, but if perchance there should be any woman (and such an unreasonableness would be more tolerable in them) who would not read the instructions which are given to men, I beg them to know that Theotimus to whom I speak is the human spirit desirous of making progress in holy love, which spirit is equally in women as in men.

This Treatise then is made for a soul already devout that she may be able to advance in her design, and hence I have been forced to say many things somewhat unknown to the generality, and which will therefore appear more obscure than they are. The depths of science are always somewhat hard to sound, and there are few divers who care and are able to descend and gather the pearls and other precious stones which are in the womb of the ocean. But if you have the courage fairly to penetrate these words which I have written, it will truly be with you as with the divers, who, says Pliny, see clearly in the deepest caves of the sea the light of the sun: for you will find in the hardest parts of this discourse a good and fair light. Moreover, as I do not follow them that despise books treating of a certain supereminently perfect life, so for my part, I do not speak of such a supereminence ; for I can neither censure the authors, nor authorize the censors of a doctrine which I do not understand.

I have touched on a number of theological questions, proposing simply, not so much what I anciently learnt in disputations, as what attention to the service of souls, and my twenty-four years spent in holy preaching have made me think most conducive to the glory of the Gospel and of the Church.

For the rest some men of note in various places have signified to me that certain little books have been published simply under the first letters of their author's name which are the same as mine. This made some believe that they were my works, not without some little scandal to such as supposed thereby that I had bidden adieu to my simplicity, to puff up my style with pompous words, my argument with worldly conceit, and my conceptions with a lofty and plumed eloquence. For this cause my dear reader, I will tell you, that as those who engrave or cut precious stones, having their sight tired by keeping it continually fixed upon the small lines of their work, are glad to keep before them some fair emerald that by beholding it from time to time they may be recreated with its greenness and restore their weakened sight to its natural condition,—so in this press of business which my office daily draws upon me I have ever little projects of some treatise of piety, which I look at when I can, to revive and unweary my mind.

However, I do not profess myself a writer; for the dulness of my spirit and the condition of my life, subject to the service and requirements of many, would not permit me so to be. Wherefore I have written very little and have published much less, and following the counsel and will of my friends I will tell you what I have written that you may not attribute the praises of another's labours to him who deserves none for his own.

It is now nineteen years since that, being at Thonon, a small town situated upon the Lake of Geneva, which was then being little by little converted to the Catholic faith, the minister, an adversary of the Church, was proclaiming everywhere that the Catholic article of the real presence of our Saviour's body in the Eucharist destroyed the symbol and the analogy of faith (for he was glad to mouth this word analogy not understood by his auditors, in order to appear very learned); and upon this the rest of the Catholic preachers with whom I was pressed me to write something in refutation of this vanity. I did what seemed suitable, framing a brief meditation upon the Creed to confirm the truth : all the copies were distributed in this diocese where now I find not one of them.

Soon afterwards his Highness came over the mountains, and finding the bailiwicks of Chablais, Gaillard and Ternier, which are in the environs of Geneva, well disposed to receive the Catholic faith which had been banished thence by force of wars and re-volts about seventy years before, he resolved to re-establish the exercise thereof in all the parishes, and to abolish that of heresy, and whereas on the one side there were many obstacles to this great blessing from those considerations which are called reasons of State, and on the other side some persons as yet not well instructed in the truth made resistance against this so much-desired establishment, his Highness surmounted the first diffi-culty by the invincible constancy of his zeal for the Catholic religion, and the second by an extraordinary gentleness and prudence. For he had the chief and most obstinate called together, and made a speech unto them with so lovingly per-suasive an eloquence that almost all, vanquished by the sweet violence of his fatherly love towards them, cast the weapons of their obstinacy at his feet, and their souls into the hands of Holy Church.

And allow me, my dear reader, I pray you, to say this word

in passing. One may praise many rich actions of this great
Prince, in which I see the proof of his valour and military
knowledge, which with just cause is admired through all Europe.
But for my part I cannot sufficiently extol the re-establishment
of the Catholic religion in these three bailiwicks which I have
just mentioned, having seen in it so many marks of piety, united
with so many and various acts of prudence, constancy, magnanimity, justice and mildness, that I seemed to see in this one little
trait, as in a miniature, all that is praised in princes who have
in times past with most fervour striven to advance the glory of
God and the Church. The stage was small, but the action great.
And as that ancient craftsman was never so much esteemed for
his great pieces as he was admired for making a ship of ivory
fitted with all its gear, in so tiny a volume that the wings
of a bee covered all, so I esteem more that which this great
Prince did at that time in this small corner of his dominions,
than many more brilliant actions which others extol to the
heavens.

Now on this occasion the victorious ensigns of the cross were
replanted in all the ways and public places of those quarters, and
whereas a little before there had been one erected very solemnly
at Annemasse close to Geneva, a certain minister made a little
treatise against the honour thereof, which was a burning and
venomous invective, and to which therefore it was deemed fit to
make answer. My Lord Claude de Granier, my predecessor,
whose memory is in benediction, imposed the burden upon me
according to the power which he had over me, who beheld him
not only as my Bishop but also as a holy servant of God. I
made therefore this answer, under the title : *Defence of the
Standard of the Cross,* and dedicated it to his Highness, partly
to testify unto him my most humble submission, and partly to
render him some small thanksgiving for the care which he took
of the Church in those parts.

Now lately this *Defence* has been reprinted under the prodigious title of *Panthalogy,* or *Treasure of the Cross:* a title whereof
I never dreamed, as in truth I am not a man of that study and
leisure, nor of that memory, to be able to put together so many
pieces of worth in one book as to let it deserve the name of

Treasure or Panthalogy, besides I have a horror of such insolent frontispieces :

> A sot, or senseless creature we him call,
> Who makes his portal greater than his hall.

In the year 1602, were celebrated at Paris, where I was, the obsequies of that magnanimous prince Philip Emanuel of Lorraine, Duke of Mercœur, who had performed so many brave exploits against the Turks in Hungary that all Christianity was bound to conspire to honour his memory. But especially Madam Mary of Luxembourg, his widow, did for her part all that her heart and the love of the deceased could suggest to her to make his funeral solemn. And because my father, grandfather, and great grandfather had been brought up pages to the most illustrious princes of Martigues her father and his predecessors, she regarded me as an hereditary servant of her house; and made choice of me to preach the funeral sermon in that great celebration, where there were not only several Cardinals and Prelates but a number of princes also, princesses, marshals of France, knights of the Order,* and even the Court of Parliament in a body. I made then this funeral oration and pronounced it in this great assembly in the great Church of Paris, and as it contained a true abridgment of the heroic feats of the deceased prince, I willingly had it printed, at the request of the widow-princess, whose request was to me a law. I dedicated this piece to Madam the Duchess of Vendôme, as yet a girl, and a very young princess, yet one in whom were very clearly to be recognized the signs of that excellent virtue and piety which now adorn her, and which show her to be worthy of the bringing forth and educating by so devout and pious a mother.

While this sermon was in the press, I heard that I had been made Bishop, so that I came here to be consecrated and to begin residence. And at first there was pointed out to me the necessity of instructing Confessors on some important points. For this reason I wrote twenty-five instructions, which I had printed to get them more easily spread amongst those to whom I directed them; since then they have been reprinted in various places.

* Of the Holy Spirit. (Tr.)

Three or four years afterwards I published the *Introduction to a Devout Life*, upon the occasion and in the manner which I have put down in the preface thereof: regarding which I have nothing to say to you, my dear reader, save only that though this little book has generally had a gracious and kind acceptance, yes even amongst the most grave prelates and doctors of the Church, yet it did not escape the rude censure of some who did not merely blame me but bitterly attacked me in public because I tell Philothea that dancing is an action indifferent in itself, and that for recreation's sake one may make *quodlibets;* and I, knowing the quality of these censors, praise their intention which I think was good. I should have desired them however to please to consider that the first proposition is drawn from the common and true doctrine of the most holy and learned divines, that I was writing for such as live in the world and in courts; that withal I carefully inculcate the extreme dangers which are found in dancing;—and that as to the second proposition it is not mine, but S. Louis's, that admirable king, a doctor worthy to be followed in the art of rightly conducting courtiers to a devout life. For, I believe if they had weighed this, their charity and discretion would never have permitted their zeal, how vigorous and austere soever, to arm their indignation against me.

And therefore, my dear reader, I conjure you to be gracious and good to me in reading this Treatise. And if you find the style a little (though I am sure it will be but a very little) different from that which I used in the *Defence of the Cross,* know that in nineteen years one learns and unlearns many things, that the language of war differs from that of peace, and that a man uses one manner of speech to young apprentices and another to old fellow-craftsmen.

My purpose here is to speak to souls that are advanced in devotion. For you must know that we have in this town a congregation of maidens and widows who, having retired from the world, live with one mind in God's service, under the protection of his most holy Mother, and as their purity and piety of spirit have oftentimes given me great consolation, so have I striven to return them the like by a frequent distribution of the holy word, which I have announced to them as well in public sermons as in spiritual conferences, and this almost always in presence of some religious men and people of great piety. Hence I have often had to treat of the most delicate sentiments of piety, passing beyond that which I had said to Philothea: and I owe a good part of that which now I communicate to you to this blessed Society because she who is the mother of them and rules them, knowing that I was writing upon this subject, and yet that scarcely was I able to accomplish it without God's very special assistance, and their continual urging, took a constant care to pray and get prayers for this end, and holily conjured me to pick out all the little morsels of leisure which she judged might be spared here and there from the press of my hindrances and to employ them in this. And because this soul is in that considera-tion with me which God knows, she has had no little power to animate me in this occasion. I began indeed long ago to think of writing on holy love, but that thought came far short of what this occasion has made me produce, an occasion which I declare to you thus simply and in good faith, in imitation of the ancients, that you may know that I write only as I get the chance and opportunity, and that I may find you more favourable. It is said amongst the Pagans that Phidias never represented anything so perfectly as the gods, nor Apelles as Alexander. One is not always equally successful : if I fall short in this treatise, let your goodness make progress and God will bless your reading.

To this end I have dedicated this work to the Mother of dilec-tion and to the Father of cordial love, as I dedicated the *Intro-duction* to the Divine child who is the Saviour of lovers and the love of the saved. And as women, while they are strong and able to bring forth their children with ease, choose commonly their worldly friends to be godfathers, but when their feebleness and indisposition make their delivery hard and dangerous invoke the saints of heaven, and vow to have their children stood to by some poor body or by some devout soul in the name of S. Joseph, S. Francis of Assisi, S. Francis of Paula, S. Nicholas, or some other of the blessed, who may obtain of God their safe delivery and that the child may be born alive :—so I, while I was not yet bishop, having more leisure and less fears for my writings, dedicated my little works to princes of the earth, but now being weighed down with my charge, and having a thousand difficulties in writing, I consecrate all to the princes of heaven, that they may obtain for me the light requisite, and that if such be the Divine will, these my writings may be fruitful and profitable to many.

Thus my dear reader I beseech God to bless you and to enrich you with his love. Meanwhile from my very heart I submit all my writings, my words and actions to the correction of the most holy Catholic, Apostolic, and Roman Church, knowing that she is the *pillar and ground of truth*,* wherein she can neither be deceived nor deceive us, and that none can have God for his father who will not have this Church for his mother.

* 1 Tim. iii. 15.

Annecy, the day of the most loving Apostles
S. Peter and S. Paul. 1616.

BLESSED BE GOD.

THE LOVE OF GOD.

BOOK I.

CONTAINING A

PREPARATION FOR THE WHOLE TREATISE.

CHAPTER I.

THAT FOR THE BEAUTY OF HUMAN NATURE GOD HAS GIVEN THE
GOVERNMENT OF ALL THE FACULTIES OF THE SOUL TO THE WILL.

Union in distinction makes order; order produces agreement; and proportion and agreement, in complete and finished things, make beauty. An army has beauty when it is composed of parts so ranged in order that their distinction is reduced to that proportion which they ought to have together for the making of one single army. For music to be beautiful, the voices must not only be true, clear, and distinct from one another, but also united together in such a way that there may arise a just consonance and harmony which is not unfitly termed a discordant harmony or rather harmonious discord.

Now as the angelic S. Thomas, following the great S. Denis, says excellently well, beauty and goodness though in some things they agree, yet still are not one and the same thing: for good is that which pleases the appetite and will, beauty that which pleases the understanding or knowledge; or, in other words, good is that which gives pleasure when we enjoy it, beauty that which gives pleasure when we know it.   For which cause in proper speech we only attribute corporal beauty to the objects of those two senses which are the most intellectual and most in the service of the understanding—namely, sight and hearing, so that we do not say, these are beautiful odours or beautiful tastes : but we rightly say, these are beautiful voices and beautiful colours.

The beautiful then being called beautiful, because the knowledge thereof gives pleasure, it is requisite that besides the union and the distinction, the integrity, the order, and the agreement of its parts, there should be also splendour and brightness that it may be knowable and visible.   Voices to be beautiful must be clear and true ; discourses intelligible ; colours brilliant and shining. Obscurity, shade and darkness are ugly and disfigure all things, because in them nothing is knowable, neither order, distinction, union nor agreement ; which caused S. Denis to say, that " God as the sovereign beauty is author of the beautiful harmony, beautiful lustre and good grace which is found in all things, making the distribution and decomposition of his one ray of beauty spread out, as light, to make all things beautiful," willing that to compose beauty there should be agreement, clearness and good grace.

Certainly, Theotimus, beauty is without effect, unprofitable and dead, if light and splendour do not make it lively and effective, whence we term colours lively when they have light and lustre.

But as to animated and living things their beauty is not complete without good grace, which, besides the agreement of perfect parts which makes beauty, adds the harmony of move-ments, gestures and actions, which is as it were the life and soul of the beauty of living things.   Thus, in the sovereign beauty of our God, we acknowledge union, yea, unity of essence in the distinction of persons, with an infinite glory, together with an incomprehensible harmony of all perfections of actions and motions, sovereignly comprised, and as one would say excellently joined and adjusted, in the most unique and simple perfection of the pure divine act, which is God Himself, immu-table and invariable, as elsewhere we shall show.

God, therefore, having a will to make all things good and beautiful, reduced the multitude and distinction of the same to a perfect unity, and, as man would say, brought them all under a monarchy, making a subordination of one thing to another and of all things to himself the sovereign Monarch. He reduces all our members into one body under one head, of many persons he forms a family, of many families a town, of many towns a province, of many provinces a kingdom, putting the whole kingdom under the government of one sole king. So, Theotimus, over the innumerable multitude and variety of actions, motions, feelings, inclinations, habits, passions, faculties and powers which are in man, God has established a natural monarchy in the will, which rules and commands all that is found in this little world : and God seems to have said to the will as Pharao said to Joseph : *Thou shalt be over my house, and at the command-ment of thy mouth all the people shall obey.** This dominion of the will is exercised indeed in very various ways.

CHAPTER II.

HOW THE WILL VARIOUSLY GOVERNS THE POWERS OF THE SOUL.

A FATHER directs his wife, his children and his servants by his ordinances and commandments, which they are obliged to obey though they are able not to obey ; but if he have servants and slaves, he rules them by force which they have no power to contradict ; his horses, oxen and mules he manages by industry, binding, bridling, goading, shutting in, or letting out.

Now the will governs the faculty of our exterior motion as a serf or slave : for unless some external thing hinder, it never fails to obey. We open and shut our mouth, move our tongue, our hands, feet, eyes, and all the members to which the power of this movement refers, without resistance, according to our wish and will.

But as for our senses and the faculties of nourishing, growing,

* Gen. xli. 40.

and producing, we cannot with the same ease govern them, but we must employ industry and art. If a slave be called he comes, if he be told to stop, he stops; but we must not expect this obedience from a sparrowhawk or falcon: he that desires it should return to the hand must show it the lure; if he would keep it quiet he must hood it. We bid our servant turn to the right or left hand and he does it, but to make a horse so turn we must make use of the bridle. We must not, Theotimus, command our eyes not to see, our ears not to hear, our hands not to touch, our stomach not to digest, or our body not to grow, for these faculties not having intelligence are not capable of obedience. No one can add a cubit to his stature. We often eat without nourishing ourselves or growing; he that will prevail with these powers must use industry. A physician who has to do with a child in the cradle commands him nothing, but only gives orders to the nurse to do such and such things, or else perchance he prescribes for the nurse to eat this or that meat, to take such and such medicine. This infuses its qualities into the milk which enters the child's body, and the physician accomplishes his will in this little weakling who has not even the power to think of it. We must not give the orders of abstinence, sobriety or continency unto the palate or stomach, but the hands must be commanded only to furnish to the mouth meat and drink in such and such a measure, we take away from or give our faculties their object and subject, and the food which strengthens them, as reason requires. If we desire our eyes not to see we must turn them away, or cover them with their natural hood, and shut them, and by these means we may bring them to the point which the will desires. It would be folly to command a horse not to wax fat, not to grow, not to kick,—to effect all this, stop his corn; you must not command him, you must simply make him do as you wish.

The will also exercises a certain power over the understanding and memory, for of many things which the understanding has power to understand and the memory has power to remember, the will determines those to which she would have her faculties apply themselves, or from which divert themselves. It is true she cannot manage or range them so absolutely as she does the hands, feet or tongue, on account of the sensitive faculties, especially the fancy, which do not obey the will with a prompt and infallible obedience, and which are necessarily required for the operations of the understanding and memory : but yet the will moves, employs and applies these faculties at her pleasure though not so firmly and constantly that the light and variable fancy does not often divert and distract them, so that as the Apostle cries out : *I do not the good which I desire, but the evil which I hate.** So we are often forced to complain that we think not of the good which we love, but the evil which we hate.

CHAPTER III.

HOW THE WILL GOVERNS THE SENSUAL APPETITE.

THE will then, Theotimus, bears rule over the memory, understanding and fancy, not by force but by authority, so that she is not infallibly obeyed any more than the father of a family is always obeyed by his children and servants. It is the same as regards the sensitive appetite, which, as S. Augustine says, is called in us sinners concupiscence, and is subject to the will and understanding as the wife to her husband, because as it was said to the woman : *Be under thy husband, and he shall have dominion over thee,*† so was it said to Cain, *that the lust of sin should be under him and he should have dominion over it.*‡ And this *being under* means nothing else than being submitted and subjected to him. " O man," says S. Bernard, " it is in thy power if thou wilt to bring thy enemy to be thy servant so that all things may go well with thee; thy appetite is under thee and thou shalt domineer over it. Thy enemy can move in thee the feeling of temptation, but it is in thy power if thou wilt to give or refuse consent. In case thou permit thy appetite to carry thee away to sin, then thou shalt be under it, and it shall domineer over thee, for *whosoever sinneth is made the servant of sin,* but before thou sinnest, so long as sin gets

* Rom. vii. 15.   † Gen. iii. 16.   ‡ Ib. iv. 7.

not entry into thy consent, but only into thy sense, that is to say, so long as it stays in the appetite, not going so far as thy will, thy appetite is subject unto thee and thou lord over it." Before the Emperor is created he is subject to the electors' dominion, in whose hands it is to reject him or to elect him to the imperial dignity; but being once elected and elevated by their means, henceforth they are under him and he rules over them.   Before the will consents to the appetite, she rules over it, but having once given consent she becomes its slave.

To conclude, this sensual appetite in plain truth is a rebellious subject, seditious, restive, and we must confess we cannot so defeat it that it does not rise again, encounter and assault the reason; yet the will has such a strong hand over it that she is able, if she please, to bridle it, break its designs and repulse it, since not to consent to its suggestions is a sufficient repulse. We cannot hinder concupiscence from conceiving, but we can from bringing forth and accomplishing, sin.

Now this concupiscence or sensual appetite has twelve movements, by which as by so many mutinous captains it raises sedition in man.   And because ordinarily they trouble the soul and disquiet the body; insomuch as they trouble the soul, they are called perturbations, insomuch as they disquiet the body they are named passions, as S. Augustine declares.   They all place before themselves good or evil, the former to obtain, the latter to avoid.   If good be considered in itself according to its natural goodness it excites love, the first and principal passion; if good be regarded as absent it provokes us to desire; if being desired we think we are able to obtain it we enter into hope; if we think we cannot obtain it we feel despair; but when we possess it as present, it moves us to joy.

On the contrary, as soon as we discover evil we hate it, if it be absent we fly it, if we cannot avoid it we fear it; if we think we can avoid it we grow bold and courageous: but if we feel it as present we grieve; and then anger and wrath suddenly rush forth to reject and repel the evil or at least to take vengeance for it.   If we cannot succeed we remain in grief.   But if we repulse or avenge it we feel satisfaction and satiation, which is a pleasure of triumph, for as the possession of good gladdens the heart, so the victory over evil exalts the spirits.   And over all this multitude of sensual passions the will bears empire, rejecting their suggestions, repulsing their attacks, hindering their effects, or at the very least sternly refusing them consent, without which they can never harm us, and by refusing which they remain vanquished, yea in the long run broken down, weakened, worn out, beaten down, and if not altogether dead, at least deadened or mortified.

And Theotimus, this multitude of passions is permitted to reside in our soul for the exercise of our will in virtue and spiritual valour; insomuch that the Stoics who denied that passions were found in wise men greatly erred, and so much the more because they practised in deeds what in words they denied, as S. Augustine shows, recounting this agreeable history. Aulus Gellius having gone on sea with a famous Stoic, a great tempest arose, at which the Stoic being frightened began to grow pale, to blench and to tremble so sensibly that all in the boat perceived it, and watched him curiously, although they were in the same hazard with him.   In the meantime the sea grew calm, the danger passed, and safety restoring to each the liberty to talk and even to rally one another, a certain voluptuous Asiatic reproached him with his fear, which had made him aghast and pale at the danger, whereas the other on the contrary had remained firm and without fear.   To this the Stoic replied by relating what Aristippus, a Socratic philosopher, had answered a man, who for the same reason had attacked him with the like reproach; saying to him : As for thee, thou hadst no reason to be troubled for the soul of a wicked rascal : but I should have done myself wrong not to have feared to lose the life of an Aristippus. And the value of the story is, that Aulus Gellius, an eye-witness, relates it.   But as to the Stoic's reply contained therein, it did more commend his wit than his cause, since bringing forward this comrade in his fear, he left it proved by two irreproachable witnesses, that Stoics were touched with fear, and with the fear which shows its effects in the eyes, face and behaviour, and is consequently a passion.

A great folly, to wish to be wise with an impossible wisdom Truly the Church has condemned the folly of that wisdom which

certain presumptuous Anchorites would formally have introduced, against which the whole Scripture but especially the
great Apostle, cries out : *We have a law in our body which
resisteth the law of our mind.** " Amongst us Christians," says
the great S. Augustine, " according to holy Scripture and sound
doctrine, the citizens of the sacred city of God, living according to God, in the pilgrimage of this world fear, desire, grieve,
rejoice." Yea even the sovereign King of this city has feared,
desired, has grieved and rejoiced, even to tears, wanness,
trembling, sweating of blood ; though in him as these were
not the motions of passions like ours, the great S. Jerome, and
after him the School durst not use the name, *passions*, for
reverence of the person in whom they were, but the respectful
name, *pro-passions*. This was to testify that sensible movements in Our Saviour held the place of passions, though they
were not such indeed, seeing that he suffered or endured nothing
from them except what seemed good to him and as he pleased,
which we sinners cannot do, who suffer and endure these
motions with disorder, against our wills, to the great prejudice
of the good estate and polity of our soul.

CHAPTER IV.

THAT LOVE RULES OVER ALL THE AFFECTIONS, AND PASSIONS, AND
EVEN GOVERNS THE WILL, ALTHOUGH THE WILL HAS ALSO
A DOMINION OVER IT.

LOVE being the first complacency which we take in good, as we
shall presently show, it of course precedes desire ; and indeed
what other thing do we desire, but that which we love? It
precedes delectation, for how could we rejoice in the enjoyment
of a thing if we loved it not? It precedes hope, for we hope
only for the good which we love : it precedes hatred, for we
hate not evil, except for the love we have for good : nor is evil
evil but because it is contrary to good. And, Theotimus, it is

* Rom. vii. **23**.

the same with all the other passions and affections; for they all proceed from love, as from their source and root.

For which cause the other passions and affections, are good or bad, vicious or virtuous, according as the love whence they proceed is good or bad; for love so spreads over them her own qualities, that they seem to be no other than this same love. S. Augustine reducing all these passions and affections to four, as did also Boetius, Cicero, Virgil, with the greatest part of the ancients :—"Love," says he, "tending to the possession of what it loves, is termed concupiscence or desire; having and possessing it it is called joy; flying that which is contrary to it, it is named fear; but if this really seizes it and it feels it, love is named grief, and consequently these passions are evil if the love be evil, good if it be good. The citizens of the heavenly city fear, desire, grieve, love, and because their love is just, all their affections are also just. Christian doctrine subjects the reason to God that he may guide and help it, and subjects all these passions to the spirit, that it may bridle and moderate them and so convert them to the service of justice and virtue. The right will is good love, the bad will is evil love;"* that is to say, in a word, Theotimus, love has such dominion over the will as to make it exactly such as it is itself.

The wife ordinarily changes her condition into that of her husband, becoming noble if he be noble, queen if he be king, duchess if he be duke. The will also changes her condition according to the love she espouses; if this be carnal she becomes carnal, if this be spiritual she is spiritual, and all the affections of desire, joy, hope, fear, grief, as children born of the marriage between love and the will, consequently receive their qualities from love. In short, Theotimus, the will is only moved by her affections, amongst which love, as the *primum mobile* and first affection, gives motion to all the rest, and causes all the other motions of the soul.

But it does not follow hence that the will does not also rule over love, seeing that the will only loves while willing to love, and that of many loves which present themselves she can apply

* De Civ. Dei, xiv. **ix.**

herself to which she pleases, otherwise there would be no love either forbidden or commanded. She is then mistress over her loves as a maiden over her suitors, amongst whom she may make election of which she pleases. But as after marriage she loses her liberty and of mistress becomes subject to her husband's power, remaining taken by him whom she took, so the will which at her own pleasure made election of love, after she has chosen one remains subject to it. And as the wife is always subject to the husband whom she has chosen as long as he lives, and if he die regains her former liberty to marry another, so while a love lives in the will it reigns there, and the will is subject to its movements, but if this love die she can afterwards take another. And again there is a liberty in the will which the wife has not, and it is that the will can reject her love at her pleasure, by applying her understanding to motives which make it displeasing, and by taking a resolution to change the object. For thus, to make divine love live and reign in us, we kill self-love, and if we cannot entirely annihilate it at least we weaken it in such a way that though it lives yet it does not reign in us. As, on the contrary, in forsaking divine love we may adhere to that of creatures, which is the infamous adultery with which the Divine lover so often reproaches sinners.

CHAPTER V.

OF THE AFFECTIONS OF THE WILL.

THERE are no fewer movements in the intellectual or reasonable appetite which is called the will, than there are in the sensitive or sensual, but the first are customarily named affections, the latter passions. The philosophers and pagans did in some manner love God, the state, virtue, sciences; they hated vice, aspired after honours, despaired of escaping death or calumny, were desirous of knowledge, yea even of beatitude after death. They encouraged themselves to surmount the difficulties which cross the way of virtue, dreaded blame, avoided some faults, avenged public injuries, opposed tyrants, without any self-interest. Now all these movements were seated in the reasonable part, since the senses, and consequently, the sensual appetite, are not capable of being applied to these objects, and therefore these movements were affections of the intellectual or reasonable appetite, not passions of the sensual.

How often do we feel passions in the sensual appetite or concupiscence, contrary to the affections which at the same time we perceive in the reasonable appetite or will? How clearly was shown at one and the same time the action of the pleasure of the senses and the displeasure of the will, in that young martyr mentioned by S. Jerom, who, forced to bear the attacks of sensuality, bit off a piece of his tongue and spat it in his tempter's face? How often do we tremble amidst the dangers to which our will carries us and in which it makes us remain? How often do we hate the pleasure in which the sensual appetite takes delight, and love the spiritual good with which that is disgusted? In this consists the war which we daily experience between the spirit and the flesh: between our exterior man, which is under the senses, and the interior which is under the reason; between the old Adam who follows the appetites of his Eve, or concupiscence, and the new Adam who follows heavenly wisdom and holy reason.

The Stoics, as S. Augustine remarks,* denying that the wise man can have passions, appear to have confessed that he has affections, which they term *eupathies,* or good passions, or, as Cicero called them, constancies: for they said the wise man did not covet but desired, had not glee but joy; that he had no fear, but only foresight and precaution, so that he was not moved except by reason and according to reason: for this cause they peremptorily denied that a wise man could ever be sorrowful, that being caused by present evil, whereas no evil can befal a wise man, since no man is hurt but by himself, according to their maxim. And truly, Theotimus, they were not wrong in holding that there are eupathies and good affections in the reasonable part of man, but they erred much in saying that there were no passions in the sensitive part, and that sorrow did not touch a wise man's heart: for omitting the fact that they

* De Civ. Dei, xiv.

themselves were troubled in this kind (as was just said), how could it be that wisdom should deprive us of pity, which is a virtuous sorrow and which comes into our hearts in order to make them desire to deliver our neighbour from the evil which he endures ?   And the wisest man of all paganism, Epictetus, did not hold this error that passions do not rise in the wise man, as S. Augustine witnesses, showing further that the Stoics' difference with other philosophers on this subject was but a mere dispute of words and strife of language.

Now these affections which we feel in our reasonable part are more or less noble and spiritual, according as their objects are more or less sublime, and as they are in a more eminent department of the spirit : for there are affections in us which proceed from conclusions gained by the experience of our senses ; others by reasonings from human sciences ; others from principles of faith ; and finally there are some which have their origin from the simple sentiment of the truth of God, and acquiescence in his will.   The first are called natural affections, for who is he that does not naturally desire health, his provision of food and clothing, sweet and agreeable conversation ? The second class of affections are named reasonable, as being altogether founded upon the spiritual knowledge of the reason, by which our will is excited to seek tranquillity of heart, moral virtues, true honour, the contemplation of eternal things.   The third sort of affections are termed Christian, because they issue from reasonings founded on the doctrine of Our Lord, who makes us love voluntary Poverty, perfect Chastity, the glory of heaven. But the affections of the supreme degree are named divine and supernatural because God himself spreads them abroad in our spirits, and because they regard God and aim at him, without the medium of any reasoning, or any light of nature, as it will be easy to understand from what we shall say afterwards about the acquiescences and affections which are made in the sanctuary of the soul.   And these supernatural affections are principally three : the love of the mind for the beautiful in the mysteries of faith, love for the useful in the goods which are promised us in the other life, and love for the sovereign good of the most holy and eternal divinity.

CHAPTER VI.

HOW THE LOVE OF GOD HAS DOMINION OVER OTHER LOVES.

THE will governs all the other faculties of man's soul, yet it is governed by its love which makes it such as its love is. Now of all loves that of God holds the sceptre, and has the authority of commanding so inseparably united to it and proper to its nature, that if it be not master it ceases to be and perishes.

Ismael was not co-heir with Isaac his younger brother, Esau was appointed to be his younger brother's servant, Joseph was adored, not only by his brothers, but also by his father, yea, and by his mother also, in the person of Benjamin, as he had foreseen in the dreams of his youth. Truly it is not without mystery that the younger of these brethren thus bear away the advantage from the elder. Divine love is indeed the last begotten of all the affections of man's heart, for as the Apostle says: *That which is animal is first; afterwards that which is spiritual:**—but this last born inherits all the authority, and self-love, as another Esau is deputed to his service; and not only all the other motions of the soul as his brethren adore him and are subject to him, but also the understanding and will which are to him as father and mother. All is subject to this heavenly love, who will either be king or nothing, who cannot live unless he reign, nor reign if not sovereignly.

Isaac, Jacob and Joseph were supernatural children; for their mothers, Sarah, Rebecca and Rachel, being sterile by nature, conceived them by the grace of the divine goodness, and for this cause they were established masters of their brethren. Similarly, divine love is a child of miracle, since man's will cannot conceive it if it be not poured into our hearts by the Holy Ghost. And as supernatural it must rule and reign over all the affections, yea, even over the understanding and will.

And although there are other supernatural movements in the soul,—fear, piety, force, hope,—as Esau and Benjamin were supernatural children of Rachel and Rebecca, yet is divine love

* 1 Cor. xv. 46.

still master, heir and superior, as being the son of promise, since in virtue of it heaven is promised to man. Salvation is shown to faith, it is prepared for hope, but it is given only to charity. Faith points out the way to the land of promise as a pillar of cloud and of fire, that is, light and dark; hope feeds us with its manna of sweetness, but charity actually introduces us into it, as the Ark of alliance, which makes for us the passage of the Jordan, that is, of the judgment, and which shall remain amidst the people in the heavenly land promised to the true Israelites, where neither the pillar of faith serves as guide nor the manna of hope is used as food.

Divine love makes its abode in the most high and sublime region of the soul, where it offers sacrifice and holocausts to the divinity as Abraham did, and as our Saviour sacrificed himself upon the top of Calvary, to the end that from so exalted a place it may be heard and obeyed by its people, that is, by all the faculties and affections of the soul. These he governs with an incomparable sweetness, for love has no convicts nor slaves, but brings all things under its obedience with a force so delightful, that as nothing is so strong as love nothing also is so sweet as its strength.

The virtues are in the soul to moderate its movements, and charity, as first of all the virtues, governs and tempers them all, not only because the first in every species of things serves as a rule and measure to the rest, but also because God, having created man to his image and likeness, wills that as in himself so in man all things should be ordered by love and for love.

CHAPTER VII.

DESCRIPTION OF LOVE IN GENERAL.

THE will has so great a sympathy with good that as soon as she perceives it she turns towards it to delight therein as in her most agreeable object, to which she is so closely allied that her nature cannot be explained except by the relation she has thereto, just as one cannot show the nature of what is good except by the affinity it has with the will. For, tell me,

Theotimus, what is good but that which every one wills. And what is the will, if not the faculty which bears us towards and makes us tend to good or what the will believes to be such?

The will then perceiving and feeling the good, by the help of the understanding which proposes it, feels at the same time a sudden delight and complacency at this meeting, which sweetly yet powerfully moves her towards this pleasing object in order to unite herself with it, and makes her search out the means most proper to attain this union.

The will then has a most close affinity with good; this affinity produces the complacency which the will takes in feeling and perceiving good; this complacency moves and spurs the will forward to good; this movement tends to union; and in fine the will moved and tending to union searches out all the means necessary to get it.

And in truth, speaking generally, love comprises all this together, as a beautiful tree, whose root is the correspondence which the will has to good, its foot is the complacency, its trunk is the movement, its seekings, its pursuits, and other efforts are the branches, but union and enjoyment are its fruits. Thus love seems to be composed of these five principal parts under which a number of other little pieces are contained as we shall see in the course of this work.

Let us consider, I pray you, the exercise of an insensible love between the loadstone and iron; for it is the true image of the sensible and voluntary love of which we speak. Iron, then, has such a sympathy with the loadstone that as soon as it feels the power thereof, it turns towards it; then it suddenly begins to stir and quiver with little throbbings, testifying by this the complacency it feels, and then it advances and moves towards the loadstone striving by all means possible to be united to it. Do you not see all the parts of love well represented in these lifeless things?

But to conclude, Theotimus, the complacency and the movement towards, or effusion of the will upon, the thing beloved is properly speaking love; yet in such sort that the complacency is but the beginning of love, and the movement or effusion of the heart which ensues is the true essential love, so that the one

and the other may truly be named love, but in a different
sense : for as the dawning of day may be termed day, so
this first complacency of the heart in the thing beloved may
be called love because it is the first feeling of love. But
as the true heart of the day is measured from the end of dawn
till sunset, so the true essence of love consists in the movement
and effusion of the heart which immediately follows complacency and ends in union. In short, complacency is the first
stirring or emotion which good causes in the will, and this
emotion is followed by the movement and effusion by which the
soul runs towards and reaches the thing beloved, which is the
true and proper love. We may express it thus : the good
takes, grasps and ties the heart by complacency, but by love it
draws, conducts and conveys it to itself, by complacency it
makes it start on its way, but by love it makes it achieve the
journey. Complacency is the awakener of the heart, but love is
its action; complacency makes it get up, but love makes it
walk. The heart spreads its wings by complacency but love is
its flight. Love then, to speak distinctly and precisely, is no
other thing than the movement, effusion and advancement of
the heart towards good.

Many great persons have been of opinion that love is no other
thing than complacency itself, in which they have had much
appearance of reason. For not only does the movement of love
take its origin from the complacency which the heart feels at
the first approach of good, and find its end in a second complacency which returns to the heart by union with the thing
beloved,—but further, it depends for its preservation on this
complacency, and can only subsist through it as through its
mother and nurse ; so that as soon as the complacency ceases
love ceases. And as the bee being born in honey, feeds
on honey, and only flies for honey, so love is born of
complacency, maintained by complacency, and tends to complacency. It is the weight of things which stirs them, moves
them, and stays them ; it is the weight of the stone that
stirs it and moves it to its descent as soon as the obstacles are
removed; it is the same weight that makes it continue its
movement downwards ; and finally it is the same weight that

makes it stop and rest as soon as it has reached its place. So it is with the complacency which excites the will : this moves it, and this makes it repose in the thing beloved when it has united itself therewith. This motion of love then having its birth, preservation, and perfection dependent on complacency, and being always inseparably joined thereto, it is no marvel that these great minds considered love and complacency to be the same, though in truth love being a true passion of the soul cannot be a simple complacency, but must needs be the motion proceeding from it.

Now this motion caused by complacency lasts till the union or fruition. Therefore when it tends to a present good, it does no more than push the heart, clasp it, join, and apply it to the thing beloved, which by this means it enjoys, and then it is called love of complacency, because as soon as ever it is begotten of the first complacency it ends in the second, which it receives in being united to its present object. But when the good towards which the heart is turned, inclined, and moved is distant, absent or future, or when so perfect a union cannot yet be made as is desired, then the motion of love by which the heart tends, makes and aspires towards this absent object, is properly named desire, for desire is no other thing than the appetite, concupiscence, or cupidity for things we have not, but which however we aim at getting.

There are yet certain other motions of love by which we desire things that we neither expect nor aim at in any way, as when we say :—Why am I not now in heaven ! I wish I were a king ; I would to God I were younger ; how I wish I had never sinned, and the like. These indeed are desires, but imperfect ones, which, to speak properly, I think, might be called wishings (*souhaits*). And indeed these affections are not expressed like desires, for when we express our true desires we say : I desire (*Je desire*) : but when we signify our imperfect desires we say : I should or I would desire (*je desirerois*), or I should like. We may well say : I would desire to be young ; but we do not say : I desire to be young ; seeing that this is not possible ; and this motion is called a wishing, or as the Scholastics term it a *velleity,* which is nothing else but a commencement of willing, not followed out, because the will, by reason of impossibility or extreme difficulty, stops her motion, and ends it in this simple affection of a wish. It is as though she said : this good which I behold and cannot expect to get is truly very agreeable to me, and though I cannot will it nor hope for it, yet so my affection stands, that if I could will or desire it, I would desire and will it gladly.

In brief, these wishings or velleities are nothing else but a little love, which may be called love of simple approbation, because the soul approves the good she knows, and being unable to effectually desire she protests she would willingly desire it, and that it is truly to be desired.

Nor is this all, Theotimus, for there are desires and velleities which are yet more imperfect than those we have spoken of, forasmuch as their motions are not stayed by reason of impossibility or extreme difficulty, but by their incompatibility with other more powerful desires or willings; as when a sick man desires to eat mushrooms or melons ;—though he may have them at his order, yet he will not eat them, fearing thereby to make himself worse; for who sees not that there are two desires in this man, the one to eat mushrooms, the other to be cured ? But because the desire of being cured is the stronger, it blocks up and suffocates the other and hinders it from producing any effect. Jephte wished to preserve his daughter, but this not being compatible with his desire to keep his vow, he willed what he did not wish, namely, to sacrifice his daughter, and wished what he did not will, namely, to preserve his daughter. Pilate and Herod wished, the one to deliver our Saviour, the other his precursor : but because these wishes were incompatible with the desires, the one to please the Jews and Cæsar, the other, Herodias and her daughter, these wishes were vain and fruitless. Now in proportion as those things which are incompatible with our wishes are less desirable, the wishes are more imperfect, since they are stopped and, as it were, stifled by contraries so weak. Thus the wish which Herod had not to behead S. John was more imperfect than that of Pilate to free our Saviour. For the latter feared the calumny and indignation of the people and of Cæsar; the other feared to disappoint one woman alone.

And these wishes which are hindered, not by impossibility, but by incompatibility with stronger desires, are called indeed wishes and desires, but vain, stifled and unprofitable ones. As to wishes of things impossible, we say: I wish, but cannot; and of the wishes of possible things we say: I wish, but will not.

CHAPTER VIII.

WHAT KIND OF AFFINITY (*CONVENANCE*) IT IS WHICH EXCITES LOVE.

WE say the eye sees, the ear hears, the tongue speaks, the understanding reasons, the memory remembers, the will loves: but still we know well that it is the man, to speak properly, who by divers faculties and different organs works all this variety of operations. Man also then it is who by the affective faculty named the will tends to and pleases himself in good, and who has for it that great affinity which is the source and origin of love. Now they have made a mistake who have believed that resemblance is the only affinity which produces love. For who knows not that the most sensible old men tenderly and dearly love little children, and are reciprocally loved by them; that the wise love the ignorant, provided they are docile, and the sick their physicians. And if we may draw any argument from the image of love which is found in things without sense, what resemblance can draw the iron towards the loadstone? Has not one loadstone more resemblance with another or with another stone, than with iron which is of a totally different species? And though some, to reduce all affinities to resemblance, assure us that iron draws iron and the loadstone the loadstone, yet they are unable to explain why the loadstone draws iron more powerfully than iron does iron itself. But I pray you what similitude is there between lime and water? or between water and a sponge? and yet both of them drink water with a quenchless desire, testifying an excessive insensible love towards it. Now it is the same in human love; for sometimes it takes more strongly amongst persons of contrary qualities, than

among those who are very like.   The affinity then which causes
love does not always consist in resemblance, but in the proportion,
relation or correspondence between the lover and the thing
loved.   For thus it is not resemblance which makes the doctor
dear to the sick man, but a correspondence of the one's necessity
with the other's sufficiency, in that the one can afford the
assistance which the other stands in need of : as again the
doctor loves the sick man, and the master his apprentice because
they can exercise their powers on them.   The old man loves
children, not by sympathy, but because the great simplicity,
feebleness and tenderness of the one exalts and makes more
apparent the prudence and stability of the other, and this dis-
similitude is agreeable.   On the other hand, children love old
men because they see them busy and careful about them, and by
secret instinct they perceive they have need of their direction.
Musical concord consists in a kind of discord, in which unlike
voices correspond, making up altogether one single multiplex
proportion, as the unlikeness of precious stones and flowers
makes the agreeable composition of enamel and diapry.   Thus
love is not caused always by resemblance and sympathy, but by
correspondence and proportion, which consists in this that by
the union of one thing to another they mutually receive one
another's perfection, and so become better.   The head certainly
does not resemble the body, nor the hand the arm, yet they have
such a correspondence and join so naturally together that by
their conjunction they excellently perfect one the other.
Wherefore, if these parts had each one a distinct soul they
would have a perfect mutual love, not by resemblance, for they
have none, but by their correspondence towards a mutual perfection.   For this cause the melancholy and the joyous, the sour and
the sweet, have often a correspondence of affection, by reason of
the mutual impressions which they receive one of another by
which their humours are reciprocally moderated.

But when this mutual correspondence is joined with
resemblance, love without doubt is engendered much more
efficaciously ; for resemblance being the true image of unity,
when two like things are united by a proportion to the same
end it seems rather to be unity than union.

The affinity then of the lover and the thing loved is the first source of love, and this affinity consists in correspondence, which is nothing else than a mutual relation, which makes things apt to unite in order to communicate to one another some perfection. But this will be understood better in the progress of our discourse.

CHAPTER IX.

THAT LOVE TENDS TO UNION.

THE great Solomon describes, in an admirably delicious manner, the loves of the Saviour and the devout soul, in that divine work which for its excellent sweetness is named the Canticle of Canticles. And to raise ourselves by a more easy flight to the consideration of this spiritual love which is exercised between God and us by the correspondence of the movements of our hearts with the inspirations of his divine majesty, he makes use of a perpetual representation of the loves of a chaste shepherd and a modest shepherdess. Now making the spouse or bride begin first by manner of a certain surprise of love, he first puts into her mouth this ejaculation: *Let him kiss me with the kiss of his mouth.** Notice, Theotimus, how the soul, in the person of this shepherdess, has but the one aim, in the first expression of her desire, of a chaste union with her spouse, protesting that it is the only end of her ambition and the only thing she aspires after; for, I pray you, what other thing would this first sigh intimate? *Let him kiss me with the kiss of his mouth.*

A kiss from all ages as by natural instinct has been employed to represent perfect love, that is, the union of hearts, and not without cause: we express and make known our passions and the movements which our souls have in common with the animals, by our eyes, eyebrows, forehead and the rest of our countenance. *Man is known by his look,*† says the Scripture,

* Cant. i. 1.   † Eccli. xix. 26.

and Aristotle giving a reason why ordinarily it is only the faces of great men that are portrayed,—it is, says he, because the face shows what we are.

Yet we do not utter our discourse nor the thoughts which proceed from the spiritual portion of our soul, which we call reason, and by which we are distinguished from beasts, except by words, and consequently by help of the mouth; insomuch that to pour out our soul and open out our heart is nothing else but to speak. *Pour out your hearts before God,** says the Psalmist, that is, express and turn the affections of your hearts into words. And Samuel's pious mother pronouncing her prayers so softly that one could hardly discern the motion of her lips: *I have poured out my soul before the Lord,†* said she. And thus one mouth is applied to another in kissing to testify that we would desire to pour out one soul into the other, to unite them reciprocally in a perfect union. For this reason, at all times and amongst the most saintly men the world has had, the kiss has been a sign of love and affection, and such use was universally made of it amongst the ancient Christians as the great S. Paul testifies, when, writing to the Romans and Corinthians, he says, *Salute one another in a holy kiss.‡* And as many declare, Judas in betraying Our Saviour made use of a kiss to manifest him, because this divine Saviour was accustomed to kiss his disciples when he met them; and not only his disciples but even little children, whom he took lovingly in his arms; as he did him by whose example he so solemnly invited his disciples to the love of their neighbour, whom many think to have been S. Martial, as the Bishop Jansenius§ says.

Thus then the kiss being a lively mark of the union of hearts, the spouse who has no other aim in all her endeavours than to be united to her beloved, *Let him kiss me,* says she, *with the kiss of his mouth;* as if she cried out:—so many sighs and inflamed darts which my love throws out will they never impetrate that which my soul desires? I run—Ah! shall I never gain the prize towards which I urge myself, which is to be united heart

* lxi. 9.   † 1 Kings i. 15.   ‡ Rom. xvi. 16; 1 Cor. xvi. 20.
§ Of Ghent, uncle of the heretic, but himself an orthodox and esteemed writer. (Tr.)

to heart, spirit to spirit, to my God, my spouse my life ? When will the hour come in which I shall pour my soul into his heart, and he will pour his heart into my soul, and thus happily united we shall live inseparable.

When the Holy Ghost would express a perfect love, he almost always employs words expressing union or conjunction. *And the multitude of believers,* says S. Luke, *had but one heart and one soul.** Our Saviour prayed for all the faithful *that they all may be one.*† S. Paul warns us to be *careful to preserve the unity of the spirit in the bond of peace.*‡ These unities of heart, of soul, and of spirit signify the perfection of love which joins many souls in one. So it is said that Jonathan's soul was knit to David's, that is to say, as the Scripture adds, *He loved him as his own soul.*§ The great Apostle of France (S. Denis) as well according to his own sentiment as when giving that of his Hierotheus, writes a hundred times, I think, in a single chapter of the *De Nominibus Divinis,* that love is unifying, uniting, drawing together, embracing, collecting and bringing all things to unity! S. Gregory Nazianzen and S. Augustine say that their friends and they had but one soul, and Aristotle approving already in his time this manner of speech : " When," says he, " we would express how much we love our friends, we say his and my soul is but one." Hatred separates us, and love brings us into one. The end then of love is no other thing than the union of the lover and the thing loved.

CHAPTER X.

THAT THE UNION TO WHICH LOVE ASPIRES IS SPIRITUAL.

WE must, however, take notice that there are natural unions, as those of similitude, consanguinity, and of cause and effect; and others which not being natural may be termed voluntary; for though they be according to Nature yet they are only made

---

* Acts iv. 32. † John xvii. 21. ‡ Eph. iv. 3.
§ 1 Kings xviii. 1.

at our will : like that union which takes its origin from benefits—
which undoubtedly unite him that receives them to the giver,—
that of conversation, society and the like.   Now natural union
produces love, and the love which it produces inclines us to
another and voluntary union, perfecting the natural.   Thus the
father and son, the mother and daughter, or two brothers, being
joined in a natural union by the participation of the same blood,
are excited by this union to love, and by love are borne towards
a union of will and spirit which may be called voluntary, because
although its foundation is natural, yet is its action deliberate.
In these loves produced by natural union we need look for no
other affinity than the union itself, by which Nature preventing
the will, obliges it to approve, to love, and to perfect the union
it has already made.   But as to voluntary unions, which follow
love, love is indeed their effective cause, but they are its final
cause, as being the only end and aim of love.   So that as love
tends to union, even so union very often extends and augments
love : for love makes us seek the society of the beloved, and this
often nourishes and increases love ; love causes a desire of nuptial
union, and this union reciprocally preserves and increases love,
so that in every sense it is true that love tends to union.

But to what kind of union does it tend ?   Did you not note,
Theotimus, that the sacred spouse expressed her desire of being
united to her spouse by the kiss, and that the kiss represents
the spiritual union which is caused by the reciprocal communication of souls ?   It is indeed the man who loves, but he
loves by his will, and therefore the end of his love is of the
nature of his will : but his will is spiritual, and consequently
the union which love aims at is spiritual also, and so much
the more because the heart, which is the seat and source of love,
would not only not be perfected by union with corporal things,
but would be degraded.

It will not hence be inferred that there are not certain
passions in man which, as mistleto comes on trees by manner of
excrescence and over-growth, sprout up indeed amongst and
about love.   Nevertheless they are neither love, nor any
part of love, but excrescences and superfluities thereof,
which are so far from being suited to maintain or perfect

love, that on the contrary they greatly harm it, weaken it, and at last, if they be not cut away, utterly ruin it: and here is the reason.

In proportion to the number of operations to which the soul applies herself (whether of the same or of a different kind) she does them less perfectly and vigorously: because being finite, her active virtue is also finite, so that furnishing her activity to divers operations it is necessary that each one of them have less thereof. Thus a man attentive to several things is less attentive to each of them : we cannot quietly consider a person's features with our sight, and at the same time give an exact hearing to the harmony of a grand piece of music, nor at the same instant be attentive to figure and to colour: if we are talking earnestly, we cannot attend to anything else.

I am not ignorant of what is said concerning Cæsar nor incredulous about what so many great persons testify of Origen,—that they could apply their attention at the same time to several objects; yet every one confesses that according to the measure they applied it to more objects it became less for each one of them. There is then a difference between seeing, hearing and understanding more, and seeing, hearing, and understanding better, for he that sees better, sees less, and he that sees more, sees not so well: it is rare for those who know much to know well what they know, because the virtue and force of the understanding being scattered upon the knowledge of divers things is less strong and vigorous than when it is restrained to the consideration of one only object. Hence it is that when the soul employs her forces in divers operations of love, the action so divided is less vigorous and perfect. We have three sorts of actions of love, the spiritual, the reasonable, and the sensitive ; when love exerts its forces through all these three operations, doubtless it is more extended but less intense, but when through one operation only, it is more intense though less extended. Do we not see that fire, the symbol of love, forced to make its way out by the mouth of the cannon alone, makes a prodigious flash, which would have been much less if it had found vent by two or three passages? Since then love is an act of our will, he that desires to have it, not only noble and generous, but also very vigorous and active, must contain the virtue and force of it within the limits of spiritual operations, for he that would apply it to the operations of the sensible or sensitive part of our soul, would so far forth weaken the intellectual operations, in which essential love consists.

The ancient philosophers have recognized that there are two sorts of ecstasies, of which the one raises us above ourselves, the other degrades us below ourselves : as though they would say that man was of a nature between angels and beasts : in his intellectual part sharing the angelical nature, and in his sensitive the nature of beasts ; and yet that he could by the acts of his life and by a continual attention to himself, deliver and emancipate himself from this mean condition, and habituating himself much to intellectual actions might bring himself nearer to the nature of angels than of beasts. If however he did much apply himself to sensible actions, he descended from his middle state and approached that of beasts : and because an ecstasy is no other thing than a going out of oneself, whether one go upwards or downwards he is truly in an ecstasy. Those then who, touched with intellectual and divine pleasures, let their hearts be carried away by those feelings, are truly out of themselves, that is, above the condition of their nature, but by a blessed and desirable out-going, by which, entering into a more noble and eminent estate, they are as much angels by the operation of their soul as men by the substance of their nature, and are either to be called human angels or angelic men. On the contrary, those who, allured by sensual pleasures give themselves over to the enjoying of them, descend from their middle condition to the lowest of brute beasts, and deserve as much to be called brutal by their operations as men by nature : miserable in thus going out of themselves only to enter into a condition infinitely unworthy of their natural state.

Now according as the ecstasy is greater, either above us or below us, by so much more it hinders the soul from returning to itself, and from doing operations contrary to the ecstasy in which it is. So those angelic men who are ravished in God and heavenly things, lose altogether, as long as their ecstasy lasts, the use and attention of the senses, movement, and all exterior actions, because their soul, in order to apply its power and activity more entirely and attentively to that divine object, retires and withdraws them from all its other faculties, to turn them in that direction.   And in like manner brutish men give up all the use of their reason and understanding to bury themselves in sensual pleasure.   The first mystically imitate Elias taken up in the fiery chariot amid the angels : the others Nabuchodonosor brutalized and debased to the rank of savage beasts.

Now I say that when the soul practises love by actions which are sensual, and which carry her below herself, it is impossible that thereby the exercise of her superior love, should not be so much the more weakened.   So that true and essential love is so far from being aided and preserved by the union to which sensual love tends, that it is impaired, dissipated and ruined by it. Job's oxen ploughed the ground, while the useless asses fed by them, eating the pasture due to the labouring oxen.   While the intellectual part of our soul is employed in honest and virtuous love of some worthy object, it comes to pass oftentimes that the senses and faculties of the inferior part tend to the union which they are adapted to, and which is their pasture, though union only belongs to the heart and to the spirit, which also is alone able to produce true and substantial love.

Eliseus having cured Naaman the Syrian was satisfied with having done him a service, and refused his gold, his silver and the goods he offered him, but his faithless servant Giezi, running after him, demanded and took, against his master's pleasure, that which he had refused.   Intellectual and cordial love, which certainly either is or should be master in our heart, refuses all sorts of corporal and sensible unions, and is contented with goodwill only, but the powers of the sensitive part, which are or should be the handmaids of the spirit, demand, seek after and take that which reason refused, and without leave make after their abject and servile love, dishonouring, like Giezi, the purity of the intention of their master, the spirit.   And in proportion as the soul turns herself to such gross and sensible unions, so far does she divert herself from the delicate, intellectual and cordial union.

You see then plainly, Theotimus, that these unions which
tend to animal complacency and passions are so far from producing or preserving love that they greatly hurt it and render it
extremely weak.

Basil, rosemary, marigold, hyssop, cloves, chamomile, nutmeg,
lemon, and musk, put together and incorporated, yield a truly
delightful odour by the mixture of their good perfume; yet not
nearly so much as does the water which is distilled from them,
in which the sweets of all these ingredients separated from their
bodies are mingled in a much more excellent manner, uniting
in a most perfect scent, which penetrates the sense of smelling
far more strongly than it would do if with it and its water the
bodies of the ingredients were found mingled and united. So
love may be found in the unions proper to the sensual powers,
mixed with the unions of intellectual powers, but never so excellently as when the spirits and souls alone, separated from all
corporeal affections but united together, make love pure and
spiritual. For the scent of affections thus mingled is not only
sweeter and better, but more lively, more active and more
essential.

True it is that many having gross, earthly and vile hearts
rate the value of love like that of gold pieces, the most massive
of which are the best, and most current; for so their idea is
that brutish love is more strong, because it is more violent and
turbulent, more solid, because more gross and terrene, greater,
because more sensible and fierce :—but on the contrary, love is
like fire, which is of clearer and fairer flame as its matter is more
delicate, which cannot be more quickly extinguished than by
beating it down and covering it with earth; for, in like manner,
by how much more exalted and spiritual the subject of love is,
by so much its actions are more lively, subsistent and permanent :
nor is there a more easy way to ruin love than to debase it to
vile and earthly unions. "There is this difference," says S.
Gregory, "between spiritual and corporal pleasures, that
corporal ones beget a desire before we obtain them, and a
disgust when we have obtained them; but spiritual ones, on the
contrary, are not cared for when we have them not, but are
desired when we have them."

CHAPTER XI.

THAT THERE ARE TWO PORTIONS IN THE SOUL, AND HOW.

WE have but one soul, Theotimus, and an indivisible one; but in that one soul there are various degrees of perfection, for it is living, sensible and reasonable; and according to these different degrees it has also different properties and inclinations by which it is moved to the avoidance or to the acceptance of things. For first, as we see that the vine hates, so to speak, and avoids the cabbage, so that the one is pernicious to the other; and, on the contrary, is delighted in the olive:—so we perceive a natural opposition between man and the serpent, so great that a man's fasting spittle is mortal to the serpent: on the contrary, man and the sheep have a wondrous affinity, and are agreeable one to the other. Now this inclination does not proceed from any knowledge that the one has of the hurtfulness of its contrary, or of the advantage of the one with which it has affinity, but only from a certain occult and secret quality which produces this insensible opposition and antipathy, or this complacency and sympathy.

Secondly, we have in us the sensitive appetite, whereby we are moved to the seeking and avoiding many things by the sensitive knowledge we have of them; not unlike to the animals, some of which have an appetite to one thing, some to another, according to the knowledge which they have that it suits them or not. In this appetite resides, or from it proceeds, the love which we call sensual or brutish, which yet properly speaking ought not to be termed love but simply appetite.

Thirdly, inasmuch as we are reasonable, we have a will, by which we are led to seek after good, according as by reasoning we know or judge it to be such. Now in our soul, taken as reasonable, we manifestly observe two degrees of perfection, which the great S. Augustine, and after him all the doctors, have named two portions of the soul, inferior and superior. That is called inferior which reasons and draws conclusions according to what it learns and experiences by the senses; and that is called superior, which reasons and draws conclusions according to an intellectual knowledge not grounded upon the experience of sense, but on the discernment and judgment of the spirit. This superior part is called the spirit and mental part of the soul, as the inferior is termed commonly, sense, feeling, and human reason.

Now this superior part can reason according to two sorts of lights; either according to natural light, as the philosophers and all those who have reasoned by science did; or according to supernatural light, as do theologians and Christians, since they establish their reasoning upon faith and the revealed word of God, and still more especially those whose spirit is conducted by particular illustrations, inspirations, and heavenly motions. This is what S. Augustine said, namely, that it is by the superior portion of the soul that we adhere and apply ourselves to the observance of the eternal law.

Jacob, pressed by the extreme necessity of his family, let Benjamin be taken by his brethren into Egypt, which yet he did against his will, as the sacred History witnesses. In this he shows two wills, the one inferior, by which he grieved at sending him, the other superior, by which he took the resolution to part with him. For the reason which moved him to disapprove his departure was grounded on the pleasure which he felt in his presence and the pain he would feel in his absence, which are grounds that touch the senses and the feelings, but the resolution which he took to send him, was grounded upon the reason of the state of his family, from his foreseeing future and imminent necessities. Abraham, according to the inferior portion of his soul spoke words testifying in him a kind of diffidence when the angel announced unto him the happy tidings of a son. *Shall a son, thinkest thou, be born to him that is a hundred years old ?** but according to his superior part he believed in God *and it was reputed to him unto justice.*† According to his inferior part, doubtless he was in great anguish when he was commanded to sacrifice his son : but according to his superior part he resolved courageously to sacrifice him.

* Gen. xvii. 17.   † Ib. xv. 6.

We also daily experience in ourselves various contrary wills. A father sending his son either to court or to his studies, does not deny tears to his departure, testifying, that though according to his superior part, for the child's advancement in virtue, he wills his departure, yet according to his inferior part he has a repugnance to the separation. Again, though a girl be married to the contentment of her father and mother, yet when she takes their blessing she excites their tears, in such sort that though the superior will acquiesces in the departure, yet the inferior shows resistance. We must not hence infer that a man has two souls or two natures, as the Manicheans dreamed. No, says S. Augustine, in the 8th book, 10th chapter, of his Confessions, "but the will inticed by different baits, moved by different reasons, seems to be divided in itself while it is pulled two ways, until, making use of its liberty, it chooses the one or the other: for then the more efficacious will conquers, and gaining the day, leaves in the soul the feeling of the evil that the struggle caused her, which we call reluctance (*contrecœur*)."

But the example of our Saviour is admirable in this point, and being considered it leaves no further doubt touching the distinction of the superior and inferior part of the soul. For who amongst theologians knows not that he was perfectly glorious from the instant of his conception in his virgin-mother's womb, and yet at the same time he was subject to sadness, grief, and afflictions of heart. Nor must we say he suffered only in the body, or only in the soul as sensitive, or, which is the same thing, according to sense: for he attests himself that before he suffered any exterior torment, or saw the tormentors near him, his *soul* was *sorrowful even unto death*. For which cause he prayed that the cup of his passion might pass away from him, that is, that he might be excused from drinking it; in which he manifestly shows the desire of the inferior portion of his soul; which, dwelling upon the sad and agonizing objects of the passion which was prepared for him (the lively image whereof was represented to his imagination), he desired, by a most reasonable consequence, the deliverance and escape from them, which he begs from his

Father. By this we clearly see that the inferior part of the soul is not the same thing as the sensitive degree of it, nor the inferior will the same with the sensitive appetite; for neither the sensitive appetite, nor the soul insomuch as it is sensitive, is capable of making any demand or prayer, these being acts of the reasonable power; and they are, specially, incapable of speaking to God, an object which the senses cannot reach, so as to make it known to the appetite. But the same Saviour, having thus exercised the inferior part, and testified that according to it and its considerations his will inclined to the avoidance of the griefs and pains, showed afterwards that he had the superior part, by which inviolably adhering to the eternal will, and to the decree made by his heavenly Father, he willingly accepted death, and in spite of the repugnance of the inferior part of reason, he said: Ah! no, *my Father, not my will, but thine be done.* When he says *my will,* he speaks of his will according to the inferior portion, and inasmuch as he says it voluntarily, he shows that he has a superior will.

CHAPTER XII.

THAT IN THESE TWO PORTIONS OF THE SOUL THERE ARE FOUR DIFFERENT DEGREES OF REASON.

THERE were three courts in Solomon's temple. One was for the Gentiles and strangers who, wishing to have recourse to God, went to adore in Jerusalem; the second for the Israelites, men and women (the separation of men from women not being made by Solomon); the third for the priests and Levites; and in fine, besides all this, there was the sanctuary or sacred house, which was open to the high priest only, and that but once a year. Our reason, or, to speak better, our soul in so far as it is reasonable, is the true temple of the great God, who there takes up his chief residence. "I sought thee," says S. Augustine, "outside myself, but I found thee not, because thou art within me." In this mystical temple there are also three courts, which are three different degrees of reason; in the first we reason according to the experience of sense, in the second according to human sciences, in the third according to faith: and in fine, beyond this, there is a certain eminence or supreme point of the reason and spiritual faculty, which is not guided by the light of argument or reasoning, but by a simple view of the understanding and a simple movement of the will, by which the spirit bends and submits to the truth and the will of God.

Now this extremity and summit of our soul, this highest point of our spirit, is very naturally represented by the sanctuary or holy place. For, first, in the sanctuary there were no windows to give light: in this degree of the soul there is no reasoning which illuminates. Secondly, all the light entered by the door; in this degree of the soul nothing enters but by faith, which produces, like rays, the sight and the sentiment of the beauty and goodness of the good pleasure of God. Thirdly, none entered the sanctuary save the high priest; in this apex of the soul reasoning enters not, but only the high, universal and sovereign feeling that the divine will ought sovereignly to be loved, approved and embraced, not only in some particular things but in general for all things, nor generally in all things only, but also particularly in each thing. Fourthly, the high priest entering into the sanctuary obscured even that light which came by the door, putting many perfumes into his thurible, the smoke whereof drove back the rays of light to which the open door gave entrance: and all the light which is in the supreme part of the soul is in some sort obscured and veiled by the renunciations and resignations which the soul makes, not desiring so much to behold and see the goodness of the truth and the truth of the goodness presented to her, as to embrace and adore the same, so that the soul would almost wish to shut her eyes as soon as she begins to see the dignity of God's will, to the end that not occupying herself further in considering it, she may more powerfully and perfectly accept it, and by an absolute complacency perfectly unite and submit herself thereto. Fifthly, to conclude, in the sanctuary was kept the ark of alliance, and in that, or at least adjoining to it, the tables of the law, manna in a golden vessel, and Aaron's rod which in one night bore flowers and fruit: and in this highest point of the soul are found : 1. The light of faith, figured by the manna hidden in its vessel, by which we acquiesce in the truths of the mysteries which we do not understand. 2. The utility of hope, represented by Aaron's flowering and fruitful rod, by which we acquiesce in the promises of the goods which we see not. 3. The sweetness of holy charity, represented by God's commandments which charity contains, by which we acquiesce in the union of our spirit with God's, which we scarcely perceive.

For although faith, hope and charity spread out their divine movements into almost all the faculties of the soul, as well reasonable as sensitive, reducing and holily subjecting them to their just authority, yet their special residence, their true and natural dwelling, is in this supreme region of the soul, from whence as from a happy source of living water, they run out by divers conduits and brooks upon the inferior parts and faculties.

So that, Theotimus, in the superior part of reason there are two degrees of reason. In the one those discourses are made which depend on faith and supernatural light, in the other the simple acquiescings of faith, hope and charity. Saint Paul's soul found itself pressed by two different desires, the one to be delivered from his body, so as to go to heaven with Jesus Christ, the other to remain in this world to labour in the conversion of souls : both these desires were without doubt in the superior part, for they both proceeded from charity, but his resolution to follow the latter proceeded not from reasoning but from a simple sight, seeing and loving his master's will, in which the superior point alone of the spirit acquiesced, putting on one side all that reasoning might conclude.

But if faith, hope and charity be formed by this holy acquiescence in the point of the spirit, how can reasonings which depend on the light of faith be made in the inferior part of the soul? As, Theotimus, we see that barristers dispute with many arguments on the acts and rights of parties to a suit, and that the high parliament or senate settles all the strife by a positive sentence, though even after this is pronounced the advocates and auditors do not give up discoursing among themselves the motives parliament may have had:—even so, after reasoning, and above all the grace of God have persuaded the point and highest part of the spirit to acquiesce, and make the act of faith after the manner of a sentence or judgment, the understanding does not at once cease discoursing upon that same act of faith already conceived, to consider the motives and reasons thereof. But always the arguments of theology are stated at the pleading place and bar of the superior portion of the soul, but the acquiescence is given above, on the bench and tribunal of the point of the spirit. Now, because the knowledge of these four degrees of the reason is much required for understanding all treatises on spiritual things, I have thought well to explain it rather fully.

CHAPTER XIII.

ON THE DIFFERENCE OF LOVES.

LOVE is divided into two species, whereof one is called love of benevolence (or goodwill) the other of cupidity (*convoitise*). The love of cupidity is that by which we love something for the profit we expect from it. Love of benevolence is that by which we love a thing for its own good. For what other thing is it to have the love of benevolence for any one than to wish him good.

If he to whom we wish good have it already and possesses it, then we wish it him by the pleasure and contentment which we have to see him possessed of it, and hence springs the love of complacency, which is simply an act of the will by which it is joined and united to the pleasure, content and good of another. But in case he to whom we wish good have not yet obtained it we desire it him, and hence that love is termed love of desire.

When the love of benevolence is exercised without correspondence on the part of the beloved, it is called the love of simple benevolence; but when it is practised with mutual correspondence, it is called the love of friendship. Now mutual correspondence consists in three things; friends must love one another, know that they love one another, and have communication, intimacy and familiarity with one another.

If we love a friend without preferring him before others, the friendship is simple ; if we prefer him, then this friendship will be called dilection, as if we said love of election, because we choose this from amongst many things we love, and prefer it.

Again, when by this dilection we do not much prefer one friend before others it is called simple dilection, but when, on the contrary, we much more esteem and greatly prefer one friend before others of his kind, then this friendship is called dilection by excellence.

If the esteem and preference of our friend, though great and without equal, do yet enter into comparison and proportion with others, the friendship will be called eminent dilection, but if the eminence of it be, beyond proportion and comparison, above every other, then it is graced with the title of incomparable, sovereign and supereminent dilection, and in a word it will be charity, which is due to the one God only. And indeed in our language the words *cher, cherement, encherir,** represent a certain particular esteem, prize or value, so that as amongst the people the word *man* is almost appropriated to the male-kind as to the more excellent sex, and the word adoration is almost exclusively kept for God as for its proper object, so the name of Charity has been kept for the love of God as for supreme and sovereign dilection.

CHAPTER XIV.

THAT CHARITY MAY BE NAMED LOVE.

ORIGEN says somewhere† that in his opinion the Divine Scripture wishing to hinder the word love from giving occasion of evil thoughts to the weak, as being more proper to signify a carnal passion than a spiritual affection, instead of this name of

---

* Meaning *dear, dearly,* to *endear.* The Saint's argument cannot be given in English. It rests on the connection between *cher* and *charité,* like the Latin *carus* and *caritas.* (Tr.)

† Hom. I. in Can.

love has used the words charity and dilection, which are more honest. But S. Augustine having deeply weighed the use of God's word clearly shows that the name love is no less sacred than the word dilection, and that the one and the other signify sometimes a holy affection and sometimes also a depraved passion, alleging to this purpose different passages of Holy Scripture. But the great S. Denis, as excelling doctor of the proper use of the divine names, goes much further in favour of the word love, teaching that theologians, that is, the Apostles and their first disciples (for this saint knew no other theologians) to disabuse the common people, and break down their error in taking the word love in a profane and carnal sense, more willingly employed it in divine things than that of dilection; and, though they considered that both might be used for the same thing, yet some of them were of opinion that the word love was more proper and suitable to God than the word dilection. Hence the divine Ignatius wrote these words: "My love is crucified." And as these ancient theologians made use of the word love in divine things to free it from the taint of impurity of which it was suspected according to the imagination of the world, so to express human affections they liked to use the word dilection as exempt from all suspicion of impropriety. Wherefore one of them, as S. Denis reports, said: "Thy dilection has entered into my soul like the dilection of women."* In fine the word love signifies more fervour, efficacy, and activity than that of dilection, so that amongst the Latins dilection is much less significative than love: "Clodius," says their great orator, "bears me dilection, and to say it more excellently, he loves me." Therefore the word love, as the most excellent, has justly been given to charity, as to the chief and most eminent of all loves; so that for all these reasons, and because I intend to speak of the acts of charity rather than of its habit, I have entitled this little work, A Treatise of the Love of God.

* De Div. Nom. iv. § 12. The reference, of course, is to 2 Kings i. 26. S. Francis is careful to quote S. Denis, who used the Septuagint text, ἀγάπησις. The Vulgate does not mark the difference. (Tr.)

CHAPTER XV.

OF THE AFFINITY THERE IS BETWEEN GOD AND MAN.

As soon as man thinks with even a little attention of the divinity, he feels a certain delightful emotion of the heart, which testifies that God is God of the human heart; and our understanding is never so filled with pleasure as in this thought of the divinity, the smallest knowledge of which, as says the prince of philosophers, is worth more than the greatest knowledge of other things; as the least beam of the sun is more luminous than the greatest of the moon or stars, yea is more luminous than the moon and stars together. And if some accident terrifies our heart, it immediately has recourse to the Divinity, protesting thereby that when all other things fail him, It alone stands his friend, and that when he is in peril, It only, as his sovereign good, can save and secure him.

This pleasure, this confidence which man's heart naturally has in God, can spring from no other root than the affinity there is between this divine goodness and man's soul, a great but secret affinity, an affinity which each one knows but few understand, an affinity which cannot be denied nor yet be easily sounded. We are created to the image and likeness of God :—what does this mean but that we have an extreme affinity with his divine majesty ?

Our soul is spiritual, indivisible, immortal; understands and wills freely, is capable of judging, reasoning, knowing, and of having virtues, in which it resembles God. It resides whole in the whole body, and whole in every part thereof, as the divinity is all in all the world, and all in every part thereof. Man knows and loves himself by produced and expressed acts of his understanding and will, which proceeding from the understanding and the will, and distinct from one another, yet are and remain inseparably united in the soul, and in the faculties from whence they proceed. So the Son proceeds from the Father as his knowledge expressed, and the Holy Ghost as love breathed forth and produced from the Father and the Son, both the Persons being distinct from one another and from the

Father, and yet inseparable and united, or rather one same, sole, simple, and entirely one indivisible divinity.

But besides this affinity of likenesses, there is an incomparable correspondence between God and man, for their reciprocal perfection : not that God can receive any perfection from man, but because as man cannot be perfected but by the divine goodness, so the divine goodness can scarcely so well exercise its perfection outside itself, as upon our humanity : the one has great want and capacity to receive good, the other great abundance and inclination to bestow it. Nothing is so agreeable to poverty as a liberal abundance, nor to a liberal abundance as a needy poverty, and by how much the good is more abundant, by so much more strong is the inclination to pour forth and communicate itself. By how much more the poor man is in want, so much the more eager is he to receive, as a void is to fill itself. The meeting then of abundance and indigence is most sweet and agreeable, and one could scarcely have said whether the abounding good have a greater contentment in spreading and communicating itself, or the failing and needy good in receiving and in drawing to itself, until Our Saviour had told us that *it is more blessed to give than to receive.** Now where there is more blessedness there is more satisfaction, and therefore the divine goodness receives greater pleasure in giving than we in receiving.

Mothers' breasts are sometimes so full that they must offer them to some child, and though the child takes the breast with great avidity, the nurse offers it still more eagerly, the child pressed by its necessity, and the mother by her abundance.

The sacred spouse wished for the holy kiss of union : O, said she, *let him kiss me with the kiss of his mouth.*† But is there affinity enough, O well-beloved spouse of the well-beloved, between thee and thy loving one to bring to the union which thou desirest ? Yes, says she : give me it ; this kiss of union, O thou dear love of my heart : *for thy breasts are better than wine, smelling sweet of the best ointment.* New wine works

---

* Acts xx. 35.　　　　　　　† Cant. i. 1.

and boils in itself by virtue of its goodness, and cannot be contained within the casks; but thy breasts are yet better, they press thee more strongly, and to draw the children of thy heart to them, they spread a perfume attractive beyond all the scent of ointments. Thus, Theotimus, our emptiness has need of the divine abundance by reason of its want and necessity, but God's abundance has no need of our poverty but by reason of the excellency of his perfection and goodness; a goodness which is not at all bettered by communication, for it acquires nothing in pouring itself out of itself, on the contrary it gives: but our poverty would remain wanting and miserable, if it were not enriched by the divine abundance.

Our soul then seeing that nothing can perfectly content her, and that nothing the world can afford is able to fill her capacity, considering that her understanding has an infinite inclination ever to know more, and her will an insatiable appetite to love and find the good;—has she not reason to cry out: Ah! I am not then made for this world, there is a sovereign good on which I depend, some infinite workman who has placed in me this endless desire of knowing, and this appetite which cannot be appeased! And therefore I must tend and extend towards Him, to unite and join myself to the goodness of Him to whom I belong and whose I am! Such is the affinity between God and man's soul.

CHAPTER XVI.

THAT WE HAVE A NATURAL INCLINATION TO LOVE GOD ABOVE ALL THINGS.

IF there could be found any men who were in the integrity of original justice in which Adam was created, though otherwise not helped by another assistance from God than that which he affords to each creature, in order that it may be able to do the actions befitting its nature, such men would not only have an inclination to love God above all things but even naturally would be able to put into execution so just an inclination. For as this heavenly author and master of nature co-operates with and lends his strong hand to fire to spring on high, to water to flow towards the sea, to earth to sink down to its centre and stay there—so having himself planted in man's heart a special natural inclination not only to love good in general but to love in particular and above all things his divine goodness which is better and sweeter than all things—the sweetness of his sovereign providence required that he should contribute to these blessed men of whom we speak as much help as should be necessary to practise and effectuate that inclination. This help would be on the one hand natural, as being suitable to nature, and tending to the love of God as author and sovereign master of nature, and on the other hand it would be supernatural, because it would correspond not with the simple nature of man, but with nature adorned, enriched and honoured by original justice, which is a supernatural quality proceeding from a most special favour of God. But as to the love above all things which such help would enable these men to practise, it would be called natural, because virtuous actions take their names from their objects and motives, and this love of which we speak would only tend to God as acknowledged to be author, lord and sovereign of every creature by natural light only, and consequently to be amiable and estimable above all things by natural inclination and tendency.

And although now our human nature be not endowed with that original soundness and righteousness which the first man had in his creation, but on the contrary be greatly depraved by sin, yet still the holy inclination to love God above all things stays with us, as also the natural light by which we see his sovereign goodness to be more worthy of love than all things; and it is impossible that one thinking attentively upon God, yea even by natural reasoning only, should not feel a certain movement of love which the secret inclination of our nature excites in the bottom of our hearts, by which at the first apprehension of this chief and sovereign object, the will is taken, and perceives itself stirred up to a complacency in it.

It happens often amongst partridges that one steals away

another's eggs with intention to sit on them, whether moved by greediness to become a mother, or by a stupidity which makes them mistake their own, and behold a strange thing, yet well supported by testimony !—the young one which was hatched and nourished under the wings of a stranger partridge, at the first call of the true mother, who had laid the egg whence she was hatched, quits the thief-partridge, goes back to the first mother, and puts herself in her brood, from the correspondence which she has with her first origin. Yet this correspondence appeared not, but remained secret, shut up and as it were sleeping in the bottom of nature, till it met with its object; when suddenly excited, and in a sort awakened, it produces its effect, and turns the young partridge's inclination to its first duty. It is the same, Theotimus, with our heart, which though it be formed, nourished and bred amongst corporal, base and transitory things, and in a manner under the wings of nature, notwithstanding, at the first look it throws on God, at its first knowledge of him, the natural and first inclination to love God which was dull and imperceptible, awakes in an instant, and suddenly appears as a spark from amongst the ashes, which touching our will gives it a movement of the supreme love due to the sovereign and first principle of all things.

CHAPTER XVII.

THAT WE HAVE NOT NATURALLY THE POWER TO LOVE GOD ABOVE ALL THINGS.

EAGLES have a great heart, and much strength of flight, yet they have incomparably more sight than flight, and extend their vision much quicker and further than their wings. So our souls animated with a holy natural inclination towards the divinity, have far more light in the understanding to see how lovable it is than force in the will to love it. Sin has much more weakened man's will than darkened his intellect, and the rebellion of the sensual appetite, which we call concupiscence, does indeed disturb the understanding, but still it is against the will that it principally stirs up sedition and revolt: so that the poor will, already quite infirm, being shaken with the continual assaults which concupiscence directs against it, cannot make so great progress in divine love as reason and natural inclination suggest to it that it should do.

Alas! Theotimus, what fine testimonies not only of a great knowledge of God, but also of a strong inclination towards him, have been left by those great philosophers, Socrates, Plato, Trismegistus, Aristotle, Hippocrates, Seneca, Epictetus? Socrates, the most highly praised amongst them, came to the clear knowledge of the unity of God, and felt in himself such an inclination to love him, that as S. Augustine testifies, many were of opinion that he never had any other aim in teaching moral philosophy than to purify minds that they might better contemplate the sovereign good, which is the simple unity of the Divinity. And as for Plato, he sufficiently declares himself in his definition of philosophy and of a philosopher; saying that to do the part of a philosopher is nothing else but to love God, and that a philosopher is no other thing than a lover of God. What shall I say of the great Aristotle, who so efficaciously proves the unity of God and has spoken so honourably of it in so many places?

But, O eternal God! those great spirits which had so great an inclination to love it, were all wanting in force and courage to love it well. By visible creatures they have known the invisible things of God, yea even *his eternal power also and divinity*, says the Apostle, *so that they are inexcusable. Because that, when they knew God, they have not glorified him as God, or given thanks.** They glorified him indeed in some sort, attributing to him sovereign titles of honour, yet they did not glorify him as they ought, that is, they did not glorify him above all things; not having the courage to destroy idolatry, but communicating with idolators, *detaining the truth which they knew in injustice,* prisoner in their hearts, and preferring the honour and vain repose of their lives before the honour due unto God, *they grew vain in their knowledge.*

* Rom. i. 20.

Is it not a great pity, Theotimus, to see Socrates, as Plato reports, speak upon his deathbed concerning the gods as though there had been many, he knowing so well that there was but one only ? Is it not a thing to be deplored that Plato who understood so clearly the truth of the divine unity should ordain that sacrifice should be offered to many gods ? And is it not a lamentable thing that Mercury Trismegistus should so basely lament and grieve over the abolition of idolatry, who on so many occasions had spoken so worthily of the divinity ? But above all I wonder at the poor good man Epictetus, whose words and sentences are so sweet in our tongue, in the translation which the learned and agreeable pen of the R. F. D. John of S. Francis, Provincial of the Congregation of the Feuillants in the Gauls, has recently put before us. For what a pity it is, I pray you, to see this excellent philosopher speak of God sometimes with such relish, feeling, and zeal that one would have taken him for a Christian coming from some holy and profound meditation, and yet again from time to time talking of gods after the Pagan manner ! Alas ! this good man, who knew so well the unity of God, and had so much delight in his goodness, why had he not the holy jealousy of the divine honour, so as not to stumble or dissemble in a matter of so great consequence ?

In a word, Theotimus, our wretched nature spoilt by sin, is like palm-trees in this land of ours, which indeed make some imperfect productions and as it were experiments of fruits, but to bear entire, ripe and seasoned dates—that is, reserved for hotter climates. For so our human heart naturally produces certain beginnings of God's love, but to proceed so far as to love him above all things, which is the true ripeness of the love due unto this supreme goodness,—this belongs only to hearts animated and assisted with heavenly grace, and which are in the state of holy charity. This little imperfect love of which nature by itself feels the stirrings, is but a will without will, a will that would but wills not, a sterile will, which does not produce true effects, a will sick of the palsy, which sees the healthful pond of holy love, but has not the strength to throw itself into it. To conclude, this will is an abortion of good will, which has not the life of generous strength necessary to effectually prefer God before all things. Whereupon the Apostle speaking in the person of the sinner, cries out: *To will good is present with me, but to accomplish that which is good I find not.**

CHAPTER XVIII.

THAT THE NATURAL INCLINATION WHICH WE HAVE TO LOVE GOD IS NOT USELESS.

But seeing we have not power naturally to love God above all things, why have we naturally an inclination to it? Is not nature vain to incite us to a love which she cannot bestow upon us? Why does she give us a thirst for a precious water of which she cannot give us to drink? Ah! Theotimus, how good God has been to us! The perfidy which we committed in offending him deserved truly that he should have deprived us of all the marks of his benevolence, and of the favour which he deigned to our nature when he imprinted upon it the light of his divine countenance, and gave to our hearts the joyfulness of feeling themselves inclined to the love of the divine goodness: so that the angels seeing this miserable man would have had occasion to say in pity: *Is this the creature of perfect beauty, the joy of all the earth?*†

But this infinite clemency could never be so rigorous to the work of his hands; he saw that we were clothed with flesh *a wind which goeth and returneth not,*‡ and therefore according to the bowels of his mercy he would not utterly ruin us, nor deprive us of the sign of his lost grace, in order that seeing this, and feeling in ourselves this alliance, and this inclination to love him, we should strive to do so, that no one might justly say: *Who showeth us good things ?*§ For though by this sole natural inclination we cannot be so happy as to love God as we ought, yet if we employed it faithfully, the sweetness of the divine piety would afford us some assistance, by means of which we might make progress, and if we second this first assistance the paternal goodness of God would bestow upon us another greater, and

---

* Rom. vii. 18.   † Lam. ii. 15.   ‡ Ps. lxxvii. 39.   § Ps. iv. 6.

conduct us from good to better in all sweetness, till he brought
us to the sovereign love, to which our natural inclination impels
us : since it is certain that to him who is faithful in a little, and
who does what is in his power, the divine benignity never denies
its assistance to advance him more and more.

This natural inclination then which we have to love God
above all things is not left for nothing in our hearts : for on
God's part it is a handle by which he can hold us and draw us
to himself ;—and the divine goodness seems in some sort by this
impression to keep our hearts tied as little birds in a string, by
which he can draw us when it pleases his mercy to take pity
upon us—and on our part it is a mark and memorial of our first
principle and Creator, to whose love it moves us, giving us a
secret intimation that we belong to his divine goodness ; even as
harts upon whom princes have had collars put with their arms,
though afterwards they cause them to be let loose and run at
liberty in the forest, do not fail to be recognized by any one
who meets them not only as having been once taken by the
prince whose arms they bear, but also as being still reserved for
him. And in this way was known the extreme old age of a hart
which according to some historians was taken three hundred
years after the death of Cæsar ; because there was found on
him a collar with Cæsar's device upon it, and these words :
Cæsar let me go.

In truth the honourable inclination which God has left in our
hearts testifies as well to our friends as to our enemies that we
did not only sometime belong to our Creator, but furthermore,
though he has left us and let us go at the mercy of our free will,
that we still appertain to him, and that he has reserved the right
of taking us again to himself, to save us, according as his holy
and sweet providence shall require. Hence the royal prophet
terms this inclination not only a *light*, in that it makes us see
whither we are to tend, but also a joy and *gladness*,* for it comforts us when we stray, giving us a hope that he who engraved
and left in us this clear mark of our origin intends also and desires
to reduce and bring us back thither, if we be so happy as to let
ourselves be retaken by his divine goodness.

* *Ibid.* 7.

THE SECOND BOOK.

THE HISTORY OF THE GENERATION AND HEAVENLY BIRTH OF DIVINE LOVE.

CHAPTER I.

THAT THE DIVINE PERFECTIONS ARE ONLY A SINGLE BUT INFINITE PERFECTION.

When the sun rises red and soon after looks black, or hollow and sunk; or again when it sets wan, pale, and dull, we say it is a sign of rain. Theotimus, the sun is not red, nor black, nor grey, nor green: that great luminary is not subject to these vicissitudes and changes of colour, having for its sole colour its most clear and perpetual light which, unless by miracle, is invariable. But we use this manner of speaking, because it seems such to us, according to the variety of vapours interposed between him and our eyes, which make him appear in different ways.

In like manner we discourse of God, not so much according to what he is in himself, as according to his works, by means of which we contemplate him; for according to our various considerations we name him variously, even as though he had a great multitude of different excellences and perfections. If we regard him inasmuch as he punishes the wicked, we term him just; if as he delivers sinners from their misery, we proclaim him merciful; since he has created all things and done many wonders, we name him omnipotent; as exactly fulfilling his promises we call him true; as ranging all things in so goodly an order we call him most wise; and thus, con-

tinuing and following the variety of his works, we attribute
unto him a great diversity of perfections. But, all the time,
in God there is neither variety, nor any difference whatever of
perfections. He is himself one most sole, most simple and most
indivisible, unique perfection : for all that is in him is but
himself, and all the excellences which we say are in him in so
great diversity are really there in a most simple and pure unity.
And as the sun has none of the colours which we ascribe unto
it, but one sole most clear light surpassing all colour, and giving
colour to all colours,—so in God there is not one of those
perfections which we imagine, but an only most pure excellence,
which is above all perfection and gives perfection to all that is
perfect. Now to assign a perfect name to this supreme
excellence, which in its most singular unity comprehends, yea
surmounts, all excellence, is not within the reach of the creature,
whether human or angelic; for as is said in the Apocalypse :
Our Lord has *a name which no man knoweth but himself :**
because as he only perfectly knows his own infinite perfection
he also alone can express it by a suitable name. Whence
the ancients have said that no one but God is a true theologian,
as none but he can reach the full knowledge of the infinite
greatness of the divine perfection, nor, consequently, represent
it in words. And for this cause, God, answering by the angel
Samson's father who demanded his name, said : *Why asketh thou
my name which is wonderful ?*† As though he had said : My
name may be admired, but never pronounced by creatures; it
must be adored, but cannot be comprehended save by me, who
alone can pronounce the proper name by which truly and to the
life I express my excellence. Our thoughts are too feeble to
form a conception which should represent an excellence so
immense, which comprehends in its most simple and most sole
perfection, distinctly and perfectly, all other perfections in a
manner infinitely excellent and eminent, to which our thoughts
cannot raise themselves. We are forced, then, in order to speak
in some way of God, to use a great number of names, saying
that he is good, wise, omnipotent, true, just, holy, infinite,

---

* Apoc. xix. 12. † Judges xiii. 18.

immortal, invisible ;—and certainly we speak truly ; God is all
this together, because he is more than all this, that is to say, he
is all this in so pure, so excellent and so exalted a way, that in
one most simple perfection he contains the virtue, vigour and
excellence of all perfection.

In the same way, the manna was one meat, which, containing
in itself the taste and virtue of all other meats, might have been
said to have the taste of the lemon, the melon, the grape, the
plum and the pear. Yet one might have said with still greater
truth that it had not all these tastes, but one only, which was
its own proper one, but which contained in its unity all that was
agreeable and desirable in all the diversity of other tastes : like
the herb *dodecatheos,* which, says Pliny, while curing all
diseases, is nor rhubarb, nor senna, nor rose, nor clove, nor
bugloss, but one simple, which in its own proper simplicity
contains as much virtue as all other medicaments together. O
abyss of the divine perfections ! How admirable art thou, to
possess in one only perfection the excellence of all perfection in
so excellent a manner that none can comprehend it but thyself !

We shall say much, says the Scripture, *and yet shall want
words : but the sum of our words is : He is all. What shall we be
able to do to glorify him, for the Almighty himself is above all
his works ? The Lord is terrible, and exceeding great, and his
power is admirable. Glorify the Lord as much as ever you can,
for he will yet far exceed, and his magnificence is wonderful.
Blessing the Lord, exalt him as much as you can : for he is above
all praise. When you exalt him put forth all your strength, and
be not weary : for you can never go far enough.** No, Theotimus,
we can never comprehend him, since, as St. John says, *he is
greater than our heart.*† Nevertheless, *let every spirit praise the
Lord,* calling him by all the most eminent names which may be
found, and for the greatest praise we can render unto him let us
confess that never can he be sufficiently praised ; and for the
most excellent name we can attribute unto him let us protest
that his name surpasses all names, nor can we worthily name
him.

---

* Ecclus. xliii. 29   † 1 John iii. 20.

CHAPTER II.

THAT IN GOD THERE IS BUT ONE ONLY ACT, WHICH IS HIS OWN DIVINITY.

THERE is in us great diversity of faculties and habits, which produce also a great variety of actions, and those actions an incomparable multitude of works. Thus differ the faculties of hearing, seeing, tasting, touching, moving, feeding, understanding, willing; and the habits of speaking, walking, playing, singing, sewing, leaping, swimming: as also the actions and works which issue from these faculties and habits are greatly different.

But it is not the same in God; for in him there is one only most simple infinite perfection, and in that perfection one only most sole and most pure act: yea to speak more holily and sagely, God *is* one unique and most uniquely sovereign perfection, and this perfection is one sole most purely simple and most simply pure act, which being no other thing than the proper divine essence, is consequently ever permanent and eternal. Nevertheless, poor creatures that we are, we talk of God's actions as though daily done in great number and variety, though we know the contrary. But our weakness, Theotimus, forces us to this; for our speech can but follow our understanding, and our understanding the customary order of things with us. Now, as in natural things there is hardly any diversity of works without diversity of actions, when we behold so many different works, such great variety of productions, and the innumerable multitude of the effects of the divine might, it seems to us at first that this diversity is caused by as many acts as we see different effects, and we speak of them in the same way, in order to speak more at our ease, according to our ordinary practice and our customary way of understanding things. And indeed we do not in this violate truth, for though in God there is no multitude of actions, but one sole act which is the divinity itself, yet this act is so perfect that it comprehends by excellence the force and virtue of all the acts which would seem requisite to the production of all the different effects we see.

God spoke but one word, and in virtue of that in a moment were made the sun, moon and that innumerable multitude of stars, with their differences in brightness, motion and influence. *He spoke and they were made.** A single word of God's filled the air with birds, and the sea with fishes, made spring from the earth all the plants and all the beasts we see. For although the sacred historian, accommodating himself to our fashion of understanding, recounts that God often repeated that omnipotent word : *Let there be :* according to the days of the world's creation, nevertheless, properly speaking, this word was singularly one ; so that David terms it a breathing or *spirit of the divine mouth ;*† that is, one single act of his infinite will, which so powerfully spreads its virtue over the variety of created things, that it makes us conceive this act as if it were multiplied and diversified into as many differences as there are in these effects, though in reality it is most simply and singularly one. Thus S. Chrysostom remarks that what Moses said in many words describing the creation of the world, the glorious S. John expressed in a single word, saying that *by the word*, that is by that eternal word who is the Son of God, *all things were made.*‡

This word then, Theotimus, whilst most simple and most single, produces all the distinction of things ; being invariable produces all fit changes, and, in fine, being permanent in his eternity gives succession, vicissitude, order, rank and season to all things.

Let us imagine, I pray you, on the one hand, a painter making a picture of Our Saviour's birth (and I write this in the days dedicated to this holy mystery). Doubtless he will give a thousand and a thousand touches with his brush, and will take, not only days, but weeks and months, to perfect this picture, according to the variety of persons and other things he wants to represent in it. But on the other hand, let us look at a printer of pictures, who having spread his sheet upon the plate which has the same mystery of the Nativity cut in it, gives but

* Ps. cxlviii. 5.　　Ps. xxxii. 6.　　‡ John i. 3.

a single stroke of the press : in this one stroke, Theotimus, he will do all his work, and instantly he will draw off a picture representing in a fine engraving all that has been imagined, as sacred history records it.   Now though with one movement he performed the work, yet it contains a great number of person-ages, and other different things, each one well distinguished in its order, rank, place, distance and proportion : so that one not acquainted with the secret would be astonished to see proceed from one act so great a variety of effects.   In the same way, Theotimus, nature as a painter multiplies and diversifies her acts according as the works she has in hand are various, and it takes her a great time to finish great effects, but God, like the printer, has given being to all the diversity of creatures which have been, are, or shall be, by one only stroke of his omnipotent will.   He draws from his idea as from a well cut plate, this admirable difference of persons and of things, which succeed one another in seasons, in ages, and in times, each one in its order, as they were to be.   For this sovereign unity of the divine act is opposed to confusion and disorder, and not to distinction and variety ; these on the contrary it purposely uses, to make beauty from them, by reducing all differences and diversities to proportion, proportion to order, and order to the unity of the world, which comprises all things created, visible and invisible.   All these together are called the universe, perhaps because all their diversity is reduced to unity as though one said " unidiverse," that is, one and diverse, one with diversity and diverse with unity.

To sum up, the sovereign divine unity diversifies all, and his permanent eternity gives change to all things, because the per-fection of this unity being above all difference and variety, it has wherewith to furnish all the diversities of created per-fections with their beings, and contains a virtue to produce them ; in sign of which the Scripture having told us that God in the beginning said : *Let there be lights made in the firma-ment of heaven, to divide the day and the night, and let them be for signs, and for seasons and for days and years,**—we see

---

* Gen. i. 14.

even to this day a perpetual revolution and succession of times and seasons which shall continue till the end of the world. So we learn that as *he spoke and they were made,* so the single eternal will of his divine Majesty extends its force from age to age, yea to ages of ages, to all that has been, is, or shall be eternally; and nothing at all has existence save by this sole most singular, most simple, and most eternal divine act, to which be honour and glory.   Amen.

CHAPTER III.

OF THE DIVINE PROVIDENCE IN GENERAL.

GOD, then, Theotimus, needs not many acts, because one only divine act of his all-powerful will, by reason of its infinite perfection, is sufficient to produce all the variety of his works. But we mortals must treat them after the method and manner of understanding which our small minds can attain to; according to which, to speak of divine providence, let us consider, I pray you, the reign of the great Solomon, as a perfect model of the art of good government.

This great king then, knowing by divine inspiration that the commonwealth is to religion as the body to the soul, and religion to the commonwealth as the soul to the body, disposed with himself all the parts requisite as well for the establishment of religion as of the commonwealth. As to religion, he determined that a temple must be erected of such and such length, breadth, and height, so many porches and courts, so many windows, and thus of all the rest which belonged to the temple; then so many sacrificers, so many singers and other officers of the temple. And as for the commonwealth he determined to make a royal palace and court for his majesty, and in this so many stewards, so many gentlemen and other courtiers; and, for the people, judges, and other magistrates who were to execute justice further, for the assurance of the kingdom, and securing of the public peace which it enjoyed, he arranged to have in time of peace a powerful preparation for war, and to this effect two hundred and fifty commanders in various charges, forty thousand horses, and all that great equipage which the Scripture and historians record.

Now having disposed and arranged in his mind all the principal things requisite for his kingdom, he came to the act of providing them, and thought out all that was necessary to construct the temple, to maintain the sacred officers, the royal ministers and magistrates, and the soldiers whom he intended to appoint, and resolved to send to Hiram for fit timber, to begin commerce with Peru* and Ophir, and to take all convenient means to procure all things requisite for the fulfilment and success of his undertaking. Neither stayed he there, Theotimus, for having made his project and deliberated with himself about the proper means to accomplish it, coming to the practice, he actually created officers as he had disposed, and by a good government caused provision to be made of all things requisite to carry out and to accomplish their charges. So that having the knowledge of the art of reigning well, he put it into practice, executed that disposition which he had made in his mind for the creation of officers of every sort, and provided in effect what he had seen it necessary to provide; and so his art of government which consisted in disposition, and in providence or foresight, was put into practice by the creation of officers and by actual government and good management. But inasmuch as the disposing is useless without the creation of officers, and creation also vain without that provident foresight which looks after what is needed to maintain the officers created or appointed; and since this maintaining by good government is nothing more than a providence put into effect, therefore not only the disposition but also the creation and good government of Solomon were called by the name of providence, nor do we indeed say that a man is provident unless he govern well.

Now, Theotimus, speaking of heavenly things according to the impression we have gained by the consideration of human things, we affirm that God, having had an eternal and most perfect

---

* According to the opinion not uncommon in S. Francis's day.   (Tr.)

knowledge of the art of making the world for his glory, disposed
before all things in his divine understanding all the principal
parts of the universe which might render him honour ; to wit,
angelic and human nature,—and in the angelic nature the variety
of hierarchies and orders, as the sacred Scripture and holy doctors
teach us ; as also among men he ordained that there should be
that great diversity which we see.   Further, in this same eternity he provided and determined in his mind all the means
requisite for men and angels to come to the end for which he had
ordained them, and so made the act of his providence; and not
stopping there, he, in order to effect what he had disposed, really
created angels and men, and to effect his providence he did and
does by his government furnish reasonable creatures with all
things necessary to attain glory, so that, to say it in a word,
sovereign providence is no other thing than the act whereby God
furnishes men or angels with the means necessary or useful for
the obtaining of their end.   But because these means are of
different kinds we also diversify the name of providence, and say
that there is one providence natural, another supernatural, and
that the latter again is general, or special, or particular.

And because hereafter, Theotimus, I shall exhort you to
unite your will to God's providence, I would, while on this part
of my subject, say a word about natural providence.   God then,
willing to provide men with the natural means necessary for
them to render glory to the divine goodness, produced in their
behalf all the other animals and the plants, and to provide for
the other animals and the plants, he has produced a variety of
lands, seasons, waters, winds, rains ; and, as well for man as
for the other things appertaining to him, he created the elements,
the sky, the stars, ordaining in an admirable manner that almost
all creatures should mutually serve one another.   Horses carry
us, and we care for them ; sheep feed and clothe us, and we
feed them ; the earth sends vapours to the air, and the air
rain to the earth ; the hand serves the foot, and the foot the
hand.   O ! he who should consider this general commerce and
traffic which creatures have together, in so perfect a correspondence—with how strong an amorous passion for this sovereign
wisdom would he be moved, crying out: *Thy providence O*

*great and eternal Father governs all things !** S. Basil and S. Ambrose in their Hexaemerons, the good Louis of Granada in his introduction to the Creed, and Louis Richeome in many of his beautiful works, will furnish ample motives to loving souls profitably to employ this consideration.

Thus, dear Theotimus, this providence reaches all, reigns over all, and reduces all to its glory. There are indeed fortuitous cases and unexpected accidents, but they are only fortuitous or unexpected to us, and are of course most certain to the divine providence, which foresees them, and directs them to the general good of the universe. These accidents happen by the concurrence of various causes, which having no natural alliance one with the other, produce each of them its particular effect, but in such a way that from their concourse there issues another effect of a different nature, to which though one could not foresee it, all these different causes contributed. For example, it was reasonable to chastise the curiosity of the poet Æschylus, who being told by a diviner that he would perish by the fall of some house, kept himself all that day in the open country, to escape his fate, and as he was standing up bareheaded, a falcon which held in its claws a tortoise, seeing this bald head, and thinking it to be the point of a rock, let the tortoise fall upon it, and behold Æschylus dies immediately, crushed by the house and shell of a tortoise. This was doubtless a fortuitous accident, for this man did not go into the country to die, but to escape death, nor did the falcon dream of crushing a poet's head, but the head and shell of a tortoise to make itself master of the meat within: yet it chanced to the contrary, for the tortoise remained safe and poor Æschylus was killed. According to us this chance was unexpected, but in respect of the Divine providence which looked from above and saw the concurrence of causes, it was an act of justice punishing the superstition of the man. The adventures of Joseph of old were admirable in their variety and the way they passed from one extreme to the other. His brethren who to ruin him had sold him, were amazed to see that he had become viceroy, and were mightily appre-

* Wisdom xiv. 3.

hensive that he remained sensible of the wrong they had done him : but no said he : *Not by your counsel was I sent hither, but by the will of God.   You thought evil against me, but God turned it into good.** You see, Theotimus, the world would have termed this a chance, or fortuitous event, which Joseph called a design of the sovereign providence, which turns and reduces all to its service.   It is the same with all things that happen in the world yea, even with monstrosities, whose birth makes complete and perfect works more esteemed, begets admiration, provokes discussion, and many good thoughts ; in a word they are in the world as the shades in pictures, which give grace and seem to bring out the colours.

CHAPTER IV.

OF THE SUPERNATURAL PROVIDENCE WHICH GOD USES TOWARDS REASONABLE CREATURES.

ALL God's works are ordained to the salvation of men and angels; and the order of his providence is this, as far as, by attention to the Holy Scriptures and the doctrine of the Fathers, we are able to discover and our weakness permits us to describe it.

God knew from all eternity that he could make an innumerable multitude of creatures with divers perfections and qualities, to whom he might communicate himself, and considering that amongst all the different communications there was none so excellent as that of uniting himself to some created nature, in such sort that the creature might be engrafted and implanted in the divinity, and become one single person with it, his infinite goodness, which of itself and by itself tends towards communication, resolved and determined to communicate himself in this manner.   So that, as eternally there is an essential communication in God by which the Father communicates all his infinite and indivisible divinity to the Son in producing him, and the Father and the Son together producing the Holy Ghost

* Gen. xlv. 8; l. 20.

communicate to him also their own singular divinity;—so this sovereign sweetness was so perfectly communicated externally to a creature, that the created nature and the divinity, retaining each of them its own properties, were notwithstanding so united together that they were but one same person.

Now of all the creatures which that sovereign omnipotence could produce, he thought good to make choice of the same humanity which afterwards in effect was united to the person of God the Son; to which he destined that incomparable honour of personal union with his divine Majesty, to the end that for all eternity it might enjoy by excellence the treasures of his infinite glory. Then having selected for this happiness the sacred humanity of our Saviour, the supreme providence decreed not to restrain his goodness to the only person of his well-beloved Son, but for his sake to pour it out upon divers other creatures, and out of the mass of that innumerable quantity of things which he could produce, he chose to create men and angels to accompany his Son, participate in his graces and glory, adore and praise him for ever. And inasmuch as he saw that he could in various manners form the humanity of this Son, while making him true man, as for example by creating him out of nothing, not only in regard of the soul but also in regard of the body; or again by forming the body of some previously existing matter as he did that of Adam and Eve, or by way of ordinary human birth, or finally by extraordinary birth from a woman without man, he determined that the work should be effected by the last way, and of all the women he might have chosen to this end he made choice of the most holy virgin Our Lady, through whom the Saviour of our souls should not only be man, but a child of the human race.

Furthermore the sacred providence determined to produce all other things as well natural as supernatural in behalf of Our Saviour, in order that angels and men might, by serving him, share in his glory; on which account, although God willed to create both angels and men with free-will, free with a true freedom to choose evil or good, still, to show that on the part of the divine goodness they were dedicated to good and to glory, he created them all in original justice, which is no other thing than a most sweet love, which disposed, turned and set them forward towards eternal felicity.

But because this supreme wisdom had determined so to temper this original love with the will of his creatures that love should not force the will but should leave it in its freedom, he foresaw that a part, yet the less part, of the angelic nature, voluntarily quitting holy love, would consequently lose glory. And because the angelic nature could only commit this sin by an express malice, without temptation or any motive which could excuse them, and on the other hand the far greater part of that same nature would remain constant in the service of their Saviour,—therefore God, who had so amply glorified his mercy in the work of the creation of angels, would also magnify his justice, and in the fury of his indignation resolved for ever to abandon that woful and accursed troop of traitors, who in the fury of their rebellion had so villanously abandoned him.

He also clearly foresaw that the first man would abuse his liberty and forsaking grace would lose glory, yet would he not treat human nature so rigorously as he determined to treat the angelic. It was human nature of which he had determined to take a blessed portion to unite it to his divinity. He saw that it was a feeble nature, *a wind which goeth and returneth not,** that is, which is dissipated as it goes. He had regard to the surprise by which the malign and perverse Satan had taken the first man, and to the greatness of the temptation which ruined him. He saw that all the race of men was perishing by the fault of one only, so that for these reasons he beheld our nature with the eye of pity and resolved to admit it to his mercy.

But in order that the sweetness of his mercy might be adorned with the beauty of his justice, he determined to save man by way of a rigorous redemption. And as this could not properly be done but by his Son, he settled that he should redeem man not only by one of his amorous actions, which would have been perfectly sufficient to ransom a million million of worlds : but also by all the innumerable amorous actions and dolorous passions which he would perform or suffer till death,

* Ps. lxxvii. 39.

and the death of the cross, to which he destined him. He willed that thus he should make himself the companion of our miseries to make us afterwards companions of his glory, showing thereby the riches of his goodness, by this copious, abundant, superabundant, magnificent and excessive redemption, which has gained for us, and as it were reconquered for us, all the means necessary to attain glory, so that no man can ever complain as though the divine mercy were wanting to any one.

CHAPTER V.

THAT HEAVENLY PROVIDENCE HAS PROVIDED MEN WITH A MOST ABUNDANT REDEMPTION.

Now when saying, Theotimus, that God had seen and willed first one thing and then secondly another, observing an order in his wills : I meant this in the sense I declared before, namely, that though all this passed in a most singular and simple act, yet in that act the order, distinction and dependence of things were no less observed than if there had been indeed several acts in the understanding and will of God. And since every well-ordered will which determines itself to love several objects equally present, loves better and above all the rest that which is most lovable ; it follows that the sovereign Providence, making his eternal purpose and design of all that he would produce, first willed and preferred by excellence the most amiable object of his love which is Our Saviour ; and then other creatures in order, according as they more or less belong to the service, honour, and glory of him.

Thus were all things made for that divine man, who for this cause is called *the first-born of every creature :** possessed* by the divine majesty *in the beginning of his ways, before he made anything from the beginning.†   For in him were all things created in heaven, and on earth, visible, and invisible, whether thrones, or dominations, or principalities, or powers : all things were created*

* Col. i. 15.   † Prov. viii. 22.

by him and in him : And he is the head of the body, the church,
who is the beginning, the first-born from among the dead: that in
*all things he may hold the primacy.** The principal reason of
planting the vine is the fruit, and therefore the fruit is the first
thing desired and aimed at, though the leaves and the buds are
first produced. So our great Saviour was the first in the divine
intention, and in that eternal project which the divine providence made of the production of creatures, and in view of this
desired fruit the vine of the universe was planted, and the
succession of many generations established, which as leaves or
blossoms proceed from it as forerunners and fit preparatives for
the production of that grape which the sacred spouse so much
praises in the Canticles, and the juice of which rejoices God
and men.

But now, my Theotimus, who can doubt of the abundance of
the means of salvation, since we have so great a Saviour, in
consideration of whom we have been made, and by whose merits
we have been ransomed. For he died for all because all were
dead, and his mercy was more salutary to buy back the race of
men than Adam's misery was to ruin it. Indeed Adam's sin
was so far from overwhelming the divine benignity that on the
contrary it excited and provoked it. So that by a most sweet
and most loving reaction and struggle, it received vigour from
its adversary's presence, and as if re-collecting its forces for
victory, it made *grace to superabound where sin had abounded.**
Whence the holy Church by a pious excess of admiration cries
out upon Easter-eve: " O truly necessary sin of Adam which
was blotted out by the death of Jesus Christ ! O blessed fault,
which merited to have such and so great a Redeemer !" Truly,
Theotimus, we may say as did he of old, " we were ruined had
we not been undone :" that is, ruin brought us profit, since in
effect human nature has received more graces by its Saviour
redeeming, than ever it would have received by Adam's innocence, if he had persevered therein.

For though the divine Providence has left in man deep marks
of his severity, yea, even amidst the very grace of his mercy,

* Col. i. 16.   † Rom. v. 20.

as for example the necessity of dying, diseases, labours, the
rebellion of sensuality,—yet the divine favour floating as it were
over all this, takes pleasure in turning these miseries to the
greater profit of those who love him, making patience spring
from labours, contempt of the world from the necessity of death,
a thousand victories from out of concupiscence; and, as the
rainbow touching the thorn *aspalathus* makes it more odoriferous than the lily, so Our Saviour's Redemption touching our
miseries, makes them more beneficial and worthy of love than
original innocence could ever have been. *I say to you*, says Our
Saviour, *there shall be joy in heaven upon one sinner that doth
penance, more than upon ninety-nine just who need not penance,**
and so the state of redemption is a hundred times better than that
of innocence. Verily by the watering of Our Saviour's blood
made with the hyssop of the cross, we have been replaced in a
whiteness incomparably more excellent than the snow of innocence. We come out, like Naaman, from the stream of salvation
more pure and clean than if we had never been leprous, to the
end that the divine Majesty, as he has ordained also for us, should
not *be overcome by evil, but overcome evil by good,*† *that mercy*
(as a sacred oil) should keep *itself above judgment,*‡ and *his
tender mercies be over all his works.*§

CHAPTER VI.

OF CERTAIN SPECIAL FAVOURS EXERCISED BY THE DIVINE PROVIDENCE IN THE REDEMPTION OF MAN.

GOD indeed shows to admiration the incomprehensible riches of
his power in this great variety of things which we see in nature,
yet he makes the infinite treasures of his goodness still more
magnificently appear in the incomparable variety of the goods
which we acknowledge in grace. For, Theotimus, he was not
content, in the holy excess of his mercy, with sending to his

* Luke xv. 7.   † Rom. xii. 21.   ‡ James ii. 13.
§ Ps. cxliv. 9.

people, that is, to mankind, a general and universal redemption, by means whereof every one might be saved, but he has diversified it in so many ways, that while his liberality shines in all this variety, this variety reciprocally embellishes his liberality.

And thus he first of all destined for his most holy Mother a favour worthy of the love of a Son who, being all wise, all mighty, and all good, wished to prepare a mother to his liking; and therefore he willed his redemption to be applied to her after the manner of a preserving remedy, that the sin which was spreading from generation to generation should not reach her. She then was so excellently redeemed, that though when the time came, the torrent of original iniquity rushed to pour its unhappy waves over her conception, with as much impetuosity as it had done on that of the other daughters of Adam; yet when it reached there it passed not beyond, but stopped, as did anciently the Jordan in the time of Josue, and for the same respect : for this river held its stream in reverence for the passage of the Ark of Alliance ; and original sin drew back its waters, revering and dreading the presence of the true Tabernacle of the eternal alliance. In this way then God *turned away all captivity* from his glorious Mother, giving her the blessing of both the states of human nature; since she had the innocence which the first Adam had lost, and enjoyed in an excellent sort the redemption acquired for her. Whence as a garden of election which was to bring forth the fruit of life, she was made to flourish in all sorts of perfections ; this son of eternal love having thus clothed his mother *in gilded clothing, surrounded with variety*,* that she might be the queen of his right hand, that is to say, the first of all the elect to enjoy *the delights of God's right hand :*† so that this sacred mother as being altogether reserved for her son, was by him redeemed not only from damnation but also from all peril of damnation, he giving her grace and the perfection of grace, so that she went like a lovely dawn, which, beginning to break, increases continually in brightness till perfect daylight. Admirable redemption ! master-piece of the redeemer ! and first of all redemptions ! by which the son with a

* Ps. xliv. 10.   † Ps. xv. 11.

truly filial heart *preventing* his mother with the *blessings of sweetness*, preserved her not only from sin as he did the angels, but also from all danger of sin and from everything that might divert or retard her in the exercise of holy love. And he protests that amongst all the reasonable creatures he has chosen, this mother is his *one dove*, his *all perfect one*, his all dear love, beyond all likeness and all comparison.

God also appointed other favours for a small number of rare creatures whom he would preserve from the peril of damnation, as is certain of S. John Baptist and very probable of Jeremias and some others, whom the Divine providence seized upon in their mother's womb, and thereupon established them in the perpetuity of his grace, that they might remain firm in his love, though subject to checks and venial sins, which are contrary to the perfection of love though not to love itself. And these souls in comparison with others, are as queens, ever crowned with charity, holding the principal place in the love of their Saviour next to his mother, who is queen of queens, a queen crowned not only with love but with the perfection of love, yea, what is yet more, crowned with her own Son, the sovereign object of love, since children are the crown of their father and mother.

There are yet other souls whom God determined for a time to leave exposed to the danger, not of losing their salvation, but yet of losing his love ; yea he permitted them actually to lose it, not assuring them love for the whole time of their life, but only for the end of it and for a certain time preceding. Such were the Apostles, David, Magdalen and many others, who for a time remained out of God's grace, but in the end being once for al converted were confirmed in grace until death ; so that though from that time they continued subject to some imperfections, yet were they exempt from all mortal sin, and consequently from danger of losing the divine love, and were sacred spouses of the heavenly bridegroom. And they were indeed adorned with a wedding garment of his most holy love, yet they were not crowned, because a crown is an ornament of the head, that is, of the chief part of a person ; now the first part of the life of this rank of souls having been subject to earthly love, they were not to be adorned with the crown of heavenly love, but it is suffi-

cient for them to wear the robe, which fits them for the marriage bed of the heavenly spouse, and for being eternally happy
with him.

CHAPTER VII.

HOW ADMIRABLE THE DIVINE PROVIDENCE IS IN THE DIVERSITY OF GRACES GIVEN TO MEN.

THERE was then in the eternal providence an incomparable
privilege for the queen of queens, *mother of fair love,* and most
singularly all perfect. There were also for certain others some
special favours. But after this the sovereign goodness poured
an abundance of graces and benedictions over the whole race of
mankind and upon the angels, with which all were watered
as with a *rain that falleth on the just and unjust,* all were illuminated as with a light that enlighteneth every man coming into
this world ; every one received his portion as of seed, which falls
not only upon the good ground but upon the highway, amongst
thorns, and upon rocks, that all might be inexcusable before the
Redeemer, if they employ not this most abundant redemption for
their salvation.

But still, Theotimus, although this most abundant sufficiency
of grace is thus poured out over all human nature, and although
in this we are all equal that a rich abundance of benedictions is
offered to us all, yet the variety of these favours is so great, that
one cannot say whether the greatness of all these graces in so great
a diversity, or the diversity in such greatness, is more admirable.
For who sees not that the means of salvation amongst Christians
are greater and more efficacious than amongst barbarians,
and again that amongst Christians there are people and towns
where the pastors get more fruit, and are more capable ?
Now to deny that these exterior means were benefits of the
divine providence, or to doubt whether they did avail to the
salvation and perfection of souls, were to be ungrateful to the
divine goodness, and to belie certain experience, by which we see
that ordinarily where these exterior helps abound, the interior
are more efficacious and succeed better.

In truth, as we see that there are never found two men perfectly resembling one another in natural gifts, so are there never found any wholly equal in supernatural ones. The angels, as the great S. Augustine and S. Thomas assure us, received grace according to the variety of their natural conditions; now they are all either of a different species or at least of a different condition, since they are distinguished one from another; therefore as many angels as there are, so many different graces are there. And though grace is not given to men according to their natural conditions, yet the divine sweetness rejoicing, and as one would say exulting, in the production of graces, infinitely diversifies them, to the end that out of this variety the fair enamel of his redemption and mercy may appear: whence the church upon the feast of every Confessor and Bishop sings " There was not found the like to him." And as in heaven no one knows the new name, save him that receives it,* because each one of the blessed has his own apart, according to the new being of glory which he acquires; similarly on earth every one receives a grace so special that all are different. Our Saviour also compares his grace to pearls, which as Pliny says are otherwise called unities, because each one of them is so singular in its qualities that two of them are never found perfectly alike; *and as one star differeth from another in glory*,† so shall men be different from one another in glory, an evident sign that they will have been so in grace. Now this variety in grace, or this grace in variety, composes a most sacred beauty and most sweet harmony, rejoicing all the holy city of the heavenly Jerusalem.

But we must be very careful never to make inquiry why the supreme wisdom bestows a grace rather upon one than another, nor why it makes its favours abound rather in one behalf than another. No, Theotimus, never enter into this curiosity, for having all of us sufficiently, yea abundantly, that which is requisite to salvation, what reason can any creature living have to complain if it please God to bestow his graces more amply upon one than another? If one should ask why God made melons larger than strawberries, or lilies larger than violets, why the

* Apoc. ii. 17.   † 1 Cor. xv. 41.

rosemary is not a rose, or why the pink is not a marigold, why the peacock is more beautiful than a bat, or why the fig is sweet and the lemon acid,—one would laugh at his question, and say: poor man, since the beauty of the world requires variety it is necessary there should be difference and inequality in things, and that the one should not be the other. That is why some things are little, others big, some bitter, others sweet, the one more, the other less beautiful. Now it is the same in supernatural things. *Every one hath his proper gift from God; one after this manner, and another after that,* * says the Holy Ghost. It is then an impertinence to search out why S. Paul had not the grace of S. Peter, or S. Peter that of S. Paul; why S. Antony was not S. Athanasius, or S. Athanasius S. Jerome; for one would answer to these inquiries that the church is a garden diapered with innumerable flowers; it is necessary then they should be of various sizes, various colours, various odours, in fine of different perfections. All have their price, their charm and their colour, and all of them in the collection of their differences make up a most grateful perfection of beauty.

CHAPTER VIII.

HOW MUCH GOD DESIRES WE SHOULD LOVE HIM.

ALTHOUGH our Saviour's redemption is applied to us in as many different manners as there are souls, yet still, love is the universal means of salvation, which mingles with everything, and without which nothing is profitable, as we shall show elsewhere. The Cherubim were placed at the gate of the earthly paradise with their flaming sword, to teach us that no one shall enter into the heavenly paradise who is not pierced through with the sword of love. For this cause, Theotimus, the sweet Jesus who bought us with his blood, is infinitely desirous that we should love him that we may eternally be saved, and desires we may be saved that we may love him eternally, his love tending to our salvation

* 1 Cor. vii. 7.

and our salvation to his love.　Ah ! said he : *I am come to cast fire on the earth ; and what will I but that it be kindled ?** But to set out more to the life the ardour of this desire, he in admirable terms requires this love from us.　*Thou shalt love the Lord thy God with thy whole heart, and with thy whole soul, and with thy whole mind.　This is the greatest and the first commandment.*†　Good God ! Theotimus, how amorous the divine heart is of our love.　Would it not have sufficed to publish a permission giving us leave to love him, as Laban permitted Jacob to love his fair Rachel, and to gain her by services ?　Ah no ! he makes a stronger declaration of his passionate love of us, and commands us to love him with all our power, lest the consideration of his majesty and our misery, which make so great a distance and inequality between us, or some other pretext, might divert us from his love.　In this, Theotimus, he well shows that he did not leave in us for nothing the natural inclination to love him, for to the end it may not be idle, he urges us by this general commandment to employ it, and that this commandment may be effected, he leaves no living man without furnishing him abundantly with all means requisite thereto.　The visible sun touches everything with its vivifying heat, and as the universal lover of inferior things, imparts to them the vigour requisite to produce, and even so the divine goodness animates all souls and encourages all hearts to its love, none being excluded from its heat.　Eternal *wisdom*, says Solomon, *preacheth abroad, she uttereth her voice in the streets : At the head of multitudes she crieth out, in the entrance of the gates of the city she uttereth her words, saying : O children, how long will you love childishness, and fools covet those things which are hurtful to themselves, and the unwise hate knowledge ?　Turn ye at my reproof : behold I will utter my spirit to you, and will show you my words.*‡ And the same wisdom continues in Ezechiel saying : *Our iniquities and our sins are upon us, and we pine away in them : how then can we live ?　Say to them : As I live, saith the Lord God, I desire not the death of the wicked, but that the wicked turn from his way, and live.*§

---

* Luke xii. 49.　　† Matt. xxii. 37, 38.　　‡ Prov. i. 20, 21, 22, 23.
§ Ezech. xxxiii. 10, 12.

Now to live according to God is to love, and *he that loveth not abideth in death.** See now, Theotimus, whether God does not desire we should love him!

But he is not content with announcing thus publicly his extreme desire to be loved, so that every one may have a share in his sweet invitation, but he goes even from door to door, knocking and protesting that, *if any man shall hear my voice, and open to me the door, I will come in to him, and will sup with him, and he with me :*† that is, he will testify all sorts of good will towards him.

Now what does all this mean, Theotimus, except that God does not only give us a simple sufficiency of means to love him, and in loving him to save ourselves, but also a rich, ample and magnificent sufficiency, and such as ought to be expected from so great a bounty as his. The great Apostle speaking to obstinate sinners : *Despisest thou,* says he, *the riches of his goodness, and patience, and long-suffering ? Knowest thou not that the benignity of God leadeth thee to penance ? But according to thy hardness and impenitent heart, thou treasurest up to thyself wrath, against the day of wrath and revelation of the just judgment of God.*‡ My dear Theotimus, God does not therefore employ a simple sufficiency of remedies to convert the obstinate, but uses to this end the riches of his goodness. The Apostle, as you see, opposes the riches of God's goodness against the treasures of the impenitent heart's malice, and says that the malicious heart is so rich in iniquity that he despises even the riches of the mildness by which God leads him to repentance; and mark that the obstinate man not only contemns the riches of God's goodness, but also the riches which lead to penance, riches whereof one can scarcely be ignorant. Verily this rich, full and plenteous sufficiency of means which God freely bestows upon sinners to love him appears almost everywhere in the Scriptures. Behold this divine lover at the gate, he does not simply knock, but stands knocking; he calls the soul, *come, arise, make haste, my love,*§ and puts his hand into the lock to try whether he cannot open it. If he uttereth his voice in

---

* 1 John iii. 14.   † Apoc. iii. 20.   ‡ Rom. ii. 4, 5.
§ Cant. ii. 16.

the streets he does not simply utter it, but he goes crying out, that is, he continues to cry out. When he proclaims that every one must be converted, he thinks he has never repeated it sufficiently. *Be converted, do penance, return to me, live, why dost thou die, O house of Israel?** In a word this heavenly Saviour forgets nothing to show that his mercies are above all his works, that his mercy surpasses his judgment, that his redemption is copious, that his love is infinite, and, as the Apostle says, that he is *rich in mercy,* and consequently he *will have all men to be saved; not willing that any should perish.*†

CHAPTER IX.

HOW THE ETERNAL LOVE OF GOD PREVENTS OUR HEARTS WITH HIS INSPIRATIONS IN ORDER THAT WE MAY LOVE HIM.

I have loved thee with an everlasting love, therefore have I drawn thee, taking pity on thee. And I will build thee again, and thou shalt be built, O virgin of Israel.‡ These are the words of God, by which he promises that the Saviour coming into the world shall establish a new kingdom in his Church, which shall be his virgin-spouse, and true spiritual Israelite.

Now as you see, Theotimus, it was *not by the works of justice, which we have done, but according to his mercy he saved us,*§ by that ancient, yea, eternal, charity which moved his divine Providence to draw us unto him. *No man can come to me except the Father, who hath sent me, draw him.*‖ For if the Father had not drawn us we had never come to the Son, our Saviour, nor consequently to salvation.

There are certain birds, Theotimus, which Aristotle calls *apodes,*¶ because having extremely short legs, and feeble feet, they use them no more than if they had none. And if ever they light upon the ground they must remain there, so that they can never take flight again of their own power, because having

---

* Ezech. xviii. 30.   † 1 Tim. ii. 4.   ‡ Jerem. xxxi. 3.
§ Titus iii. 5.   ‖ John vi. 44.   ¶ *i.e.,* Footless. [Tr.]

no use of their legs or feet, they have therefore no power to move and start themselves into the air : hence they remain there motionless, and die, unless some wind, propitious to their impotence, sending out its blasts upon the face of the earth, happen to seize upon and bear them up, as it does many other things. If this happen, and they make use of their wings to correspond with this first start and motion which the wind gives them, it also continues its assistance to them, bringing them by little and little into flight.

Theotimus, the angels are like to those birds, which for their beauty and rarity are called birds-of-paradise, never seen on earth but dead. For those heavenly spirits had no sooner forsaken divine love to attach themselves to self-love, than suddenly they fell as dead, buried in hell, seeing that the same effect which death has on men, separating them everlastingly from this mortal life, the same had the angels' fall on them, excluding them for ever from eternal life. But we mortals rather resemble apodes : for if it chance that we, quitting the air of holy divine love, fall upon earth and adhere to creatures, which we do as often as we offend God, we die indeed, yet not so absolute a death but that there remains in us a little movement, besides our legs and feet, namely, some weak affections, which enable us to make some essays of love, though so weakly, that in truth we are impotent of ourselves to detach our hearts from sin, or start ourselves again in the flight of sacred love, which, wretches that we are, we have perfidiously and voluntarily forsaken.

And truly we should well deserve to remain abandoned of God, when with this disloyalty we have thus abandoned him. But his eternal charity does not often permit his justice to use this chastisement, but rather, exciting his compassion, it provokes him to reclaim us from our misery, which he does by sending us the favourable wind of his most holy inspirations, which, blowing upon our hearts with a gentle violence, seizes and moves them, raising our thoughts, and moving our affections into the air of divine love.

Now this first stirring or motion which God causes in our hearts to incite them to their own good, is effected indeed in us but not by us; for it comes unexpectedly, before we have either thought of it or been able to think of it, *seeing we are not suffi-cient to think anything* towards our *salvation of ourselves as of ourselves, but our sufficiency is from God,** who did not only love us before we were, but also to the end we might be, and might be saints. For which cause he prevents us with the blessings of his fatherly sweetness, and excites our souls, in order to bring them to holy repentance and conversion. See, I pray you, Theotimus, the prince of the Apostles, stupefied with sin in the sad night of his Master's passion; he no more thought of sorrow-ing for his sin, than though he had never known his heavenly Saviour. And as a miserable apode fallen to earth, he would never have been raised, had not the cock, as an instrument of divine providence, struck his ears with its voice, at the same instant in which his sweet Redeemer casting upon him a gracious look, like a dart of love, transpierced that heart of stone, which afterwards sent forth water in such abundance, like the ancient rock smitten by Moses in the desert. But look again and see this holy Apostle sleeping in Herod's prison, bound with two chains: he is there in quality of a martyr, and nevertheless he represents the poor man who sleeps amid sin, prisoner and slave to Satan. Alas! who will deliver him? The angel descends from heaven, and striking the great Saint Peter, the prisoner, upon the side, awakens him, saying: *Arise quickly!* So the inspiration comes from heaven like an angel, and striking upon the poor sinner's heart, stirs him up to rise from his iniquity. Is it not true then, my dear Theotimus, that this first emotion and shock which the soul perceives, when God, preventing it with love, awakens it and excites it to forsake sin and return unto him, and not only this shock, but also the whole awakening, is done in us, and for us, but not by us? We are awake, but have not awakened of ourselves, it is the inspiration which has awakened us, and to awaken us has shaken and moved us. *I slept,* says that devout spouse, *but* my beloved, who is *my heart, watched.* Ah! see that it is he who awakens me, calling me by the name of our loves, and I know well by his voice that it is he. It is un-awares and unexpectedly that God calls and awakens us by his

* 2 Cor. iii. 5.

holy inspiration, and in this beginning of grace we do nothing but feel the touch which God gives, in us, as S. Bernard says, but without us.

———

CHAPTER X.

HOW WE OFTENTIMES REPULSE THE INSPIRATION AND REFUSE TO LOVE GOD.

Wo to thee, Corozain, wo to thee, Bethsaida : for if in Tyre and Sidon had been wrought the miracles that have been wrought in you, they had long ago done penance in sackcloth and ashes.* Such is the word of Our Saviour. Hark I pray you, Theotimus, how the inhabitants of Corozain and Bethsaida, instructed in the true religion, and having received favours so great that they would effectually have converted the pagans themselves, remained nevertheless obstinate, and never willed to use them, rejecting this holy light by an incomparable rebellion. Certainly at the day of judgment the Ninivites and the Queen of Saba will rise up against the Jews, and will convict them as worthy of damnation : because, as to the Ninivites, though idolators and barbarians, at the voice of Jonas they were converted and did penance ; and as to the Queen of Saba, she, though engaged in the affairs of a kingdom, yet having heard the renown of Solomon's wisdom, forsook all, to go and hear him. Yet the Jews, hearing with their ears the heavenly wisdom of the true Solomon, the Saviour of the world ; seeing with their eyes his miracles ; touching with their hands his virtues and benefits ; ceased not for all that to be hardened, and to resist the grace which was proffered them. See then again, Theotimus, how they who had less attractions are brought to penance, and those who had more remain obdurate : those who have less occasion to come, come to the school of wisdom, and those who have more, stay in their folly.

Thus will be made the judgment of comparison, as all doctors have remarked, which can have no foundation save in this, that

———

* Matt. xi. 21.

notwithstanding some have had as many calls as others have, or more, they will have denied consent to God's mercy, whereas others, assisted with the like, yea even lesser helps, will have followed the inspiration, betaking themselves to holy penance. For how could one otherwise reasonably reproach the impenitent with their impenitence, in comparison with such as are converted ?

Certainly Our Saviour clearly shows, and all Christians in simplicity understand, that in this just judgment the Jews shall be condemned in comparison with the Ninivites, because those have had many favours and yet no love, much assistance and no repentance, these less favour and more love, less assistance and much penitence.

The great S. Augustine throws a great light on this reasoning, by his own arguments in Book XII. of the ' City of God,' Chapters vi., vii., viii., ix. For though he refers particularly to the angels, still he likens men to them in this point.

Now, after having taken, in the sixth chapter, two men, entirely equal in goodness and in all things, attacked by the same temptation, he presupposes that one resists, the other gives way to the enemy; then in the ninth chapter, having proved that all the angels were created in charity, stating further as probable that grace and charity were equal in them all, he asks how it came to pass that some of them persevered, and made progress in goodness even to the attaining of glory, while others forsook good to embrace evil unto damnation, and he answers that no other answer can be rendered, than that the one company persevered by the grace of their Creator in the chaste love which they received in their creation, the other, having been good, made themselves bad by their own sole will.

But if it is true, as S. Thomas extremely well proves, that grace was different in the angels in proportion and according to their natural gifts, the Seraphim must have had a grace incomparably more excellent than the simple angels of the last order. How then did it happen that some of the Seraphim, yea even the first of all, according to the common and most probable opinion of the ancients, fell, while an innumerable multitude of other angels, inferior in nature and grace, excellently and courageously persevered? How came it to pass that Lucifer, so excellent by nature and so superexcellent by grace, fell, while so many angels with less advantages remained upright in their fidelity? Truly those who persevered ought to render all the praise thereof to God, who of his mercy created and maintained them good. But to whom can Lucifer and all his crew ascribe their fall, if not, as S. Augustine says, to their own will, which by their liberty divorced them from God's grace that had so sweetly prevented them? *How art thou fallen from heaven, O Lucifer, who didst rise in the morning?** Who didst come out into this invisible world clothed with original charity as with the beginning of the brightness of a fair day, which was to increase unto the mid-day of eternal glory? Grace did not fail thee, for thou hadst it, like thy nature, the most excellent of all, but thou wast wanting to grace. God did not deprive thee of the operation of his love, but thou didst deprive his love of thy co-operation. God would never have rejected thee if thou hadst not rejected his love. O all-good God! thou dost not forsake unless forsaken, thou never takest away thy gifts till we take away our hearts.

We rob God of his right if we attribute to ourselves the glory of our salvation, but we dishonour his mercy if we say he failed us. If we do not confess his benefits we wrong his liberality, but we blaspheme his goodness if we deny that he has assisted and succoured us. In fine, God cries loud and clear in our ears: *Destruction is thy own, O Israel: thy help is only in me.†*

CHAPTER XI.

THAT IT IS NO FAULT OF THE DIVINE GOODNESS IF WE HAVE NOT A MOST EXCELLENT LOVE.

O God! Theotimus, if we received divine inspirations to the full extent of their virtue, in how short a time should we make a great progress in sanctity? Be the fountain ever so copious,

* Isa. xiv. 12.   † Osee xiii. 9.

its streams enter not into a garden according to their plenty, but according to the littleness or greatness of the channel by which they are conducted thither. Although the Holy Ghost, as a spring of living water, flows up to every part of our heart to spread his graces in it, yet as he will not have them enter without the free consent of our will, he will only pour them out according to his good pleasure and our own disposition and co-operation, as the Holy Council says, which also, by reason, as I suppose, of the correspondence between our consent and grace, calls the reception thereof a voluntary reception.

In this sense S. Paul *exhorts us not to receive God's grace in vain.** For as a sick man, who having received a draught in his hand did not take it into his stomach, would truly have received the potion, yet without receiving it, that is, he would have received it in a useless and fruitless way, so we receive the grace of God in vain, when we receive it at the gate of our heart, and not within the consent of our heart; for so we receive it without receiving it, that is, we receive it without fruit, since it is nothing to feel the inspiration without consenting unto it. And as the sick man who had the potion given into his hand, if he took it not wholly but only partly, would also have the operation thereof in part only, and not wholly,—so when God sends a great and mighty inspiration to move us to embrace his holy love, if we consent not according to its whole extent it will but profit us in the same measure. It happens that being inspired to do much we consent not to the whole inspiration but only to some part thereof, as did those good people in the Gospel, who upon the inspiration which Our Lord gave them to follow him wished to make reservations, the one to go first and bury his father, the other to go to take leave of his people.

As long as the poor widow had empty vessels, the oil which Eliseus had by prayer miraculously multiplied never left off running, but when she had no more vessels to receive it, it ceased to flow. In the same measure in which our heart dilates itself, or rather in the measure in which it permits itself to be enlarged and dilated, keeping itself empty by the simple

* 2 Cor. vi. 1.

fact of not refusing consent to the divine mercy, this ever pours forth and ceaselessly spreads its sacred inspirations, which ever increase and make us increase more and more in heavenly love ; but when there is no more room, that is, when we no longer give consent, it stops.

How comes it then that we are not so advanced in the love of God as S. Augustine, S. Francis, S. Catharine of Genoa or S. Frances ? Theotimus, it is because God has not given us the grace. But why has he not given us the grace ? Because we did not correspond with his inspirations as we should have done. And why did we not correspond ? Because being free we have herein abused our liberty. But why did we abuse our liberty ? Ah! Theotimus, we must stop there, for, as S. Augustine says, the depravation of our will proceeds from no cause, but from some deficiency in the agent (*cause*) who commits the sin. And we must not expect to be able to give a reason of the fault which occurs in sin, because the fault would not be a sin if it was not without reason.

The devout Brother Rufinus upon a certain vision which he had of the glory which the great S. Francis would attain unto by his humility, asked him this question : My dear father, I beseech you, tell me truly what opinion you have of yourself ? The Saint answered : Verily I hold myself to be the greatest sinner in the world, and the one who serves Our Lord least. But, Brother Rufinus replied, how can you say this in truth and conscience, seeing that many others, as we manifestly see, commit many great sins from which, God be thanked, you are exempt. To which S. Francis answered : If God had favoured those others of whom you speak with as great mercy as he has favoured me, I am certain, be they ever so bad now, they would have acknowledged God's gifts far better than I do, and would serve him much better than I do, and if my God abandoned me I should commit more wickedness than any one else.

You see, Theotimus, the opinion of this man, who indeed was scarcely man, but a seraph upon earth. I know it was humility that moved him to speak thus of himself, yet nevertheless he believed for a certain truth that an equal grace granted by an equal mercy might be more faithfully employed by one sinner than by another. Now I hold for an oracle the sentiment of this great doctor in the science of the saints, who, brought up in the school of the Crucifix, breathed nothing but the divine inspirations. And this maxim has been praised and repeated by all the most devout who have followed him, many of whom are of opinion that the great Apostle S. Paul said in the same sense that he was *the chief of all sinners.**

The Blessed Mother (S.) Teresa of Jesus, also, in good truth, a quite angelic virgin, speaking of the prayer of quiet, says these words:—"There are divers souls who come up to this perfection, but those who pass beyond are a very small number: I know not the cause of it, certainly the fault is not on God's side, for since his divine majesty aids us and gives us the grace to arrive at this point, I believe that he would not fail to give us still more if it were not for our fault, and the impediment which we on our part place." Let us therefore, Theotimus, be attentive to advance in the love which we owe to God, for that which he bears us will never fail us.

CHAPTER XII.

THAT DIVINE INSPIRATIONS LEAVE US IN FULL LIBERTY TO FOLLOW OR REPULSE THEM.

I WILL not here speak, my dear Theotimus, of those miraculous graces which have almost in an instant transformed wolves into shepherds, rocks into waters, persecutors into preachers. I leave on one side those all-powerful vocations, and holily violent attractions by which God has brought some elect souls from the extremity of vice to the extremity of grace, working as it were in them a certain moral and spiritual transubstantiation: as it happened to the great Apostle, who of Saul, vessel of persecution, became suddenly Paul, *vessel of election.*† We must give a particular rank to those privileged souls in regard of whom it

---

* 1 Tim. i. 15.   † Acts ix. 15.

pleased God to make not the mere outflowing, but the inundation —to exercise, if one may so say, not the simple liberality and effusion, but the prodigality and profusion of his love. The divine justice chastises us in this world with punishments which, as they are ordinary, so they remain almost always unknown and imperceptible ; sometimes, however, he sends out deluges and abysses of punishments, to make known and dreaded the severity of his indignation. In like manner his mercy ordinarily converts and graces souls so sweetly, gently and delicately, that its movement is scarcely perceived; and yet it happens sometimes that this sovereign goodness, overflowing its ordinary banks (as a flood swollen and overcharged with the abundance of waters and breaking out over the plain) makes an outpouring of his graces so impetuous, though loving, that in a moment he steeps and covers the whole soul with benedictions, in order that the riches of his love may appear, and that as his justice proceeds commonly by the ordinary way and sometimes by the extraordinary, so his mercy may exercise liberality upon the common sort of men in the ordinary way, and on some also by extraordinary ways.

But what are then the ordinary cords whereby the divine providence is accustomed to draw our hearts to his love ? Such truly as he himself marks, describing the means which he used to draw the people of Israel out of Egypt, and out of the desert, unto the land of promise. *I will draw them*, says he by Osee, *with the cords of Adam, with the bands of love,** and of friendship. Doubtless, Theotimus, we are not drawn to God by iron chains, as bulls and wild oxen, but by enticements, sweet attractions, and holy inspirations, which, in a word, are the *cords of Adam*, and of humanity, that is, proportionate and adapted to the human heart, to which liberty is natural. The *band* of the human will is delight and pleasure. We show nuts to a child, says S. Augustine, and he is drawn by his love, he is drawn by the cords, not of the body, but of the heart. Mark then how the Eternal Father draws us: while teaching, he delights us, not imposing upon us any necessity ; he casts into our hearts delec-

* Osee xi. 4.

tations and spiritual pleasures as sacred baits, by which he sweetly draws us to take and taste the sweetness of his doctrine.

In this way then, dearest Theotimus, our free-will is in no way forced or necessitated by grace, but notwithstanding the all-powerful force of God's merciful hand, which touches, surrounds and ties the soul with such a number of inspirations, invitations and attractions, this human will remains perfectly free, enfranchised and exempt from every sort of constraint and necessity. Grace is so gracious, and so graciously seizes our hearts to draw them, that she noways offends the liberty of our will; she touches powerfully but yet so delicately the springs of our spirit that our free will suffers no violence from it. Grace has power, not to force but to entice the heart; she has a holy violence not to violate our liberty but to make it full of love; she acts strongly, yet so sweetly that our will is not overwhelmed by so powerful an action ; she presses us but does not oppress our liberty ; so that under the very action of her power, we can consent to or resist her movements as we list. But what is as admirable as it is veritable is, that when our will follows the attraction, and consents to the divine movement, she follows as freely as she resists freely when she does resist, although the consent to grace depends much more on grace than on the will, while the resistance to grace depends upon the will only. So sweet is God's hand in the handling of our hearts ! So dexterous is it in communicating unto us its strength without depriving us of liberty, and in imparting unto us the motion of its power without hindering that of our will ! He adjusts his power to his sweetness in such sort, that as in what regards good his might sweetly gives us the power, so his sweetness mightily maintains the freedom of the will. *If thou didst know the gift of God*, said our Saviour to the Samaritan woman, *and who he is that saith to thee, give me to drink ; thou perhaps wouldst have asked of him, and he would have given thee living water.** Note, I pray you, Theotimus, Our Saviour's manner of speaking of his attractions. *If thou didst know*, he means, *the gift of God*, thou wouldst without doubt be moved and attracted to ask the

* John iv. 10.

water of eternal life, and *perhaps* thou wouldst ask it. As though he said : Thou wouldst have power and wouldst be provoked to ask, yet in no wise be forced or constrained ; but only *perhaps thou wouldst have asked*, for thy liberty would remain to ask it or not to ask it. Such are our Saviour's words according to the ordinary edition, and according to S. Augustine upon S. John.

To conclude, if any one should say that our free-will does not co-operate in consenting to the grace with which God prevents it, or that it could not reject and deny consent thereto, he would contradict the whole Scripture, all the ancient Fathers, and experience, and would be excommunicated by the sacred Council of Trent. But when it is said that we have power to reject the divine inspirations and motions, it is of course not meant that we can hinder God from inspiring us or touching our hearts, for as I have already said, that is done in us and yet without us. These are favours which God bestows upon us before we have thought of them, he awakens us when we sleep, and consequently we find ourselves awake before we have thought of it ; but it is in our power to rise, or not to rise, and though he has awakened us without us, he will not raise us without us. Now not to rise, and to go to sleep again, is to resist the call, seeing we are called only to the end we should rise. We cannot hinder the inspiration from taking us, or consequently from setting us in motion, but if as it drives us forwards we repulse it by not yielding ourselves to its motion, we then make resistance. So the wind, having seized upon and raised our apodes, will not bear them very far unless they display their wings and co-operate, raising themselves aloft and flying in the air, into which they have been lifted. If, on the contrary, allured may be by some verdure they see upon the ground, or benumbed by their stay there, in lieu of seconding the wind they keep their wings folded and cast themselves again upon the earth, they have received indeed the motion of the wind, but in vain, since they did not help themselves thereby. Theotimus, inspirations prevent us, and even before they are thought of make themselves felt, but after we have felt them it is ours either to consent to them so as to second and follow their attractions, or else to dissent and repulse them.

They make themselves felt by us without us, but they do not make us consent without us.

———

CHAPTER XIII.

OF THE FIRST SENTIMENTS OF LOVE WHICH DIVINE INSPIRATIONS CAUSE IN THE SOUL BEFORE SHE HAS FAITH.

THE wind that raises the apodes blows first upon their feathers, as the parts most light and most susceptible of its agitation, by which it gives the beginning of motion to their wings, extending and displaying them in such sort that they give a hold by which to seize the bird and waft it into the air. And if they, thus raised, do contribute the motion of their wings to that of the wind, the same wind that took them will still aid them more and more to fly with ease. Even so, my dear Theotimus, when the inspiration, as a sacred gale, comes to blow us forward into the air of holy love, it first takes our will, and by the sentiment of some heavenly delectation it moves it, extending and unfolding the natural inclination which the will has to good, so that this same inclination serves as a hold by which to seize our spirit. And all this, as I have said, is done in us without us, for it is the divine favour that prevents us in this sort. But if our will thus holily prevented, perceiving the wings of her inclination moved, displayed, extended, stirred, and agitated, by this heavenly wind, contributes, be it never so little, its consent—Ah! how happy it is, Theotimus. The same favourable inspiration which has seized us, mingling its action with our consent, animating our feeble motions with its vigour, and vivifying our weak co-operation by the power of its operation, will aid, conduct, and accompany us, from love to love, even unto the act of most holy faith requisite for our conversion.

True God! Theotimus, what a consolation it is to consider the secret method by which the Holy Ghost pours into our hearts the first rays and feelings of his light and vital heat! O Jesus! how delightful a pleasure it is to see celestial love, which is the sun of virtues, as little by little with a progress

which insensibly becomes sensible, it displays its light upon a
soul, and stops not till it has it all covered with the splendour
of its presence, giving it at last the perfect beauty of love's day !
O how cheerful, beautiful, sweet and agreeable this daybreak is !
Nevertheless true it is that break of day is either not day,
or if it be day, it is but a beginning day, a rising of the day,
and rather the infancy of the day than the day itself. In like
manner without doubt these motions of love which forerun the
act of faith required for our justification are either not love
properly speaking, or but a beginning and imperfect love. They
are the first verdant buds which the soul, warmed with the
heavenly sun, begins, as a mystical tree, to put forth in spring-
time, rather presages of fruit than fruit itself.

S. Pachomius then a young soldier and without knowledge of
God, enrolled under the colours of the army which Constantine
had levied against the tyrant Maxentius, came, with the troop
to which he belonged, to lodge nigh a little town not far distant
from Thebes, where he, and indeed the whole army, were in
extreme want of victuals. The inhabitants of the little town
having understood this, being by good fortune of the faithful of
Jesus Christ, and consequently friendly and charitable to their
neighbours, immediately succoured the soldiers in their necessities, but with such care, courtesy and love, that Pachomius was
struck with admiration thereat, and asking what nation it was
that was so good, amiable and gracious, it was answered him
that they were Christians ; and inquiring again what law and
manner of life were theirs, he learned that they believed in
Jesus Christ the only Son of God, and did good to all sorts of
people, with a firm hope of receiving from God himself an
ample recompense. Alas! Theotimus, the poor Pachomius,
though of a good natural disposition, was as yet asleep in the
bed of his infidelity, and behold how upon a sudden God was
present at the gate of his heart, and by the good example of
these Christians, as by a sweet voice, he calls him, awakens him,
and gives him the first feelings of the vital heat of his love.
For scarcely had he heard, as I have said, of the sweet law of
Our Saviour, than, all filled with a new light and interior consolation, having retired apart, and mused for a space, he lifted

up his hands towards heaven, and with a profound sigh he said : Lord God, who hast made heaven and earth, if thou deign to cast thine eyes upon my baseness and misery, and to give me the knowledge of thy divinity, I promise to serve thee, and obey thy commandments all the days of my life! After this prayer and promise, the love of the true good and of piety so increased in him, that he ceased not to practise a thousand thousand acts of virtue.

Methinks I see in this example a nightingale which, awaking at the peep of day, begins to stir, and to stretch itself, unfold its plumes, skip from branch to branch in its grove, and little by little warble out its delicious wood-music. For did you not note, how the good example of the charitable Christians excited and awakened with a sudden start the blessed Pachomius? Truly this astonished admiration he had was nothing else than his awakening, in which God touched him, as the sun touches the earth, with a ray of his brightness, which filled him with a great feeling of spiritual pleasure. For which cause Pachomius shakes himself loose from distractions, to the end he may with more attention and facility gather together and relish the grace he has received, withdrawing himself to think thereupon. Then he extends his heart and hands towards heaven, whither the inspiration is drawing him, and beginning to display the wings of his affections, flying between diffidence of himself, and confidence in God, he entones in a humbly amorous air the canticle of his conversion. He first testifies that he already knows one only God Creator of heaven and earth : but withal he knows that he does not yet know him sufficiently to serve him as he ought, and therefore he petitions that a more perfect knowledge may be imparted to him, that thereby he may come to the perfect service of his divine majesty.

Behold, therefore, I pray you, Theotimus, how gently God moves, strengthening by little and little the grace of his inspiration in consenting hearts, drawing them after him, as it were step by step, upon this Jacob's ladder. But what are his drawings? The first, by which he prevents and awakens us, is done by him in us and without our action; all the others are also done by him and in us, but not without our action.   *Draw me* : says the sacred spouse, *we will run after thee to the odour of thy ointments,** that is, begin thou first : I cannot awake of myself, I cannot move unless thou move me ; but when thou shalt once have given motion, then, O dear spouse of my heart, *we run,* we two, thou runnest before me drawing me ever forward, and, as for me, I will follow thee in thy course consenting to thy drawing.   But let no one think that thou draggest me after thee like a forced slave, or a lifeless wagon. Ah ! no, thou drawest me by the *odour of thy ointments ;* though I follow thee, it is not that thou trailest me but that thou enticest me ; thy drawing is mighty, but not violent, since its whole force lies in its sweetness.   Perfumes have no other force to draw men to follow them than their sweetness, and sweetness —how could it draw but sweetly and delightfully ?

CHAPTER XIV.

OF THE SENTIMENT OF DIVINE LOVE WHICH IS HAD BY FAITH.

WHEN God gives us faith he enters into our soul and speaks to our spirit, not by manner of discourse, but by way of inspiration, proposing in so sweet a manner unto the understanding that which ought to be believed, that the will receives therefrom a great complacency, so great indeed that it moves the understanding to consent and yield to truth without any doubt or distrust, and here lies the marvel : for God proposes the mysteries of faith to our souls amidst obscurities and darkness, in such sort that we do not see the truths but we only half-see them.†   It is like what happens sometimes when the face of the earth is covered with mist so that we cannot see the sun, but only see a little more brightness in the direction where he is.   Then, as one would say, we see it without seeing it ; because on the one hand we see it not so well that we can truly say we see it, yet again we see it not so little that we can say we

* Cant. i. 3.
† *Nous ne voyons pas, ains seluement nous entrevoyons.*

do not see it; and this is what we call half-seeing. And yet, when this obscure light of faith has entered our spirit, not by force of reasoning or show of argument, but solely by the sweetness of its presence, it makes the understanding believe and obey it with so much authority that the certitude it gives us of the truth surpasses all other certitudes, and keeps the understanding and all its workings in such subjection that they get no hearing in comparison with it.

May I, Theotimus, have leave to say this? Faith is the chief beloved of our understanding, and may justly speak to human sciences which boast that they are more evident and clear than she, as did the sacred spouse to the other shepherdesses. *I am black but beautiful*,*—O human reasonings, O acquired knowledge! *I am black*, for I am amidst the obscurities of simple revelation, which have no apparent evidence, and which make me look *black*, putting me well-nigh out of knowledge: yet I am *beautiful* in myself by reason of my infinite certainty; and if mortal eyes could behold me such as I am by nature they would find me *all fair*. And must it not necessarily follow that in effect I am infinitely to be loved, since the gloomy darkness and thick mists, amid which I am—not seen but only half-seen, cannot hinder me from being so dearly loved, that the soul, prizing me above all, cleaving the crowd of all other knowledges, makes them all give place to me and receives me as his queen, placing me on the highest throne in his palace, from whence I give the law to all sciences, and keep all argument and all human sense under? Yea, verily, Theotimus, even as the commanders of the army of Israel taking off their garments, put them together and made a royal throne of them, on which they placed Jehu, and said: *Jehu is king* :† so on the arrival of faith, the understanding puts off all discourse and arguments, and laying them underneath faith, makes her sit upon them, acknowledging her as Queen, and with great joy cries out : Long live faith !

Pious discourses and arguments, the miracles and other advantages of the Christian religion, make it extremely credible

---

* Cant. i. 4.   † 4 Kings ix. 13.

and knowable, but faith alone makes it believed and acknow-ledged, enamouring men with the beauty of its truth, and making them believe the truth of its beauty, by means of the sweetness faith pours into their wills, and the certitude which it gives to their understanding. The Jews saw the miracles and heard the marvellous teachings of Our Saviour, but being indis-posed to receive faith, that is, their will not being susceptible of the gentle sweetness of faith, on account of the bitterness and malice with which they were filled, they persisted in their infi-delity. They perceived the force of the argument, but they relished not the sweetness of the conclusion, and therefore did not acquiesce in its truth. But the act of faith consists in this very acquiescence of our spirit, which having received the grateful light of truth, accepts it by means of a sweet, yet powerful and solid assurance and certitude which it finds in the authority of the revelation which has been made to her.

You have heard, Theotimus, that in general councils there are great disputations and inquiries made about truth by discourse, reasons and theological arguments, but the matters being dis-cussed, the Fathers, that is, the bishops, and especially the Pope who is the chief of the bishops, conclude, resolve and determine; and the determination being once pronounced, every one fully accepts it and acquiesces in it, not in consideration of the reasons alleged in the preceding discussion and inquisition, but in virtue of the authority of the Holy Ghost, who, presiding invisibly in councils, has judged, determined and concluded, by the mouth of his servants whom he has established pastors of Christianity. The inquisition then and the disputation are made in the priests' court by the doctors, but the resolution and acquiescence are formed in the sanctuary, where the Holy Ghost who ani-mates the body of his Church, speaks by the mouth of its chiefs, as Our Lord has promised. In like manner the ostrich lays her eggs upon the sands of Libya, but the sun alone hatches her young ones; and doctors by their inquiry and discourse propose truth, but only the beams of the sun of justice give certainty and acquiescence. To conclude then, Theotimus, this assurance which man's reason finds in things revealed and in the mysteries of faith, begins by an amorous sentiment of complacency which the will receives from the beauty and sweetness of the proposed truth; so that faith includes a beginning of love, which the heart feels towards divine things.

CHAPTER XV.

OF THE GREAT SENTIMENT OF LOVE WHICH WE RECEIVE BY HOLY HOPE.

As when exposed to the rays of the sun at mid-day, we hardly see the brightness before we suddenly feel the heat; so the light of faith has no sooner spread the splendour of its truths in our understanding, but immediately our will feels the holy heat of heavenly love. Faith makes us know by an infallible certitude that God is, that he is infinite in goodness, that he can communicate himself unto us, and not only that he can, but that he will; so that by an ineffable sweetness he has provided us with all things requisite to obtain the happiness of immortal glory. Now we have a natural inclination to the sovereign good, by reason of which our heart is touched with a certain inward anxious desire and continual uneasiness, not being able in any way to quiet itself, or to cease to testify that its perfect satisfaction and solid contentment are wanting to it. But when holy faith has represented to our understanding this lovely object of our natural inclination,—Oh! Theotimus, what joy! what pleasure! how our whole soul is thrilled, and, all amazed at the sight of so excellent a beauty, it cries out with love: *Behold, thou art fair, my beloved, behold thou art fair !* *

Eliezer sought a wife for the son of his master Abraham; how could he tell whether he should find her beautiful and gracious as he desired? But when he had found her at the fountain, and saw her so excellent in beauty and so perfect in sweetness, and especially when he had obtained her, he adored God, and blessed him with thanksgiving, full of incomparable joy. Man's heart tends to God by its natural inclination, with-

* Cant. i. 14.

out fully knowing what he is; but when it finds him at the
fountain of faith, and sees him so good, so lovely, so sweet and
gracious to all, and so ready to give himself, as the sovereign
good, to all who desire him,—O God! what delight! and what
sacred movements in the soul, to unite itself for ever to this
goodness so sovereignly amiable! I have found, says the soul
thus inspired, I have at last found that which my heart desired,
and now I am at rest. And as Jacob, having seen the fair
Rachel, after he had holily kissed her, melted into tears of
sweetness for the happiness he experienced in so desirable a
meeting, so our poor heart, having found God, and received of
him the first kiss, the kiss of holy faith, it dissolves forthwith
in sweetness of love for the infinite good which it presently
discovers in that sovereign beauty.

We sometimes experience in ourselves a certain joyousness
which comes as it were unexpectedly, without any apparent
reason, and this is often a presage of some greater joy; whence
many are of opinion that our good angels, foreseeing the good
which is coming unto us, give us by this means a foretaste
thereof, as on the contrary they give us certain fears and terrors
amidst dangers we are not aware of, to make us invoke God's
assistance and stand upon our guard. Now when the presaged
good arrives, we receive it with open arms, and reflecting upon
the joyousness we formerly felt without knowing its cause, we
only then begin to perceive that it was a forerunner of the
happiness we now enjoy. Even so, my dear Theotimus, our
heart having had for so long a time an inclination to its
sovereign good, knew not to what end this motion tended: but
so soon as faith has shown it, then man clearly discerns that this
was what his soul coveted, his understanding sought, and his
inclination tended towards. Certainly, whether we wish or wish
not, our soul tends towards the sovereign good. But what is
this sovereign good? We are like those good Athenians who
sacrificed unto the true God, although he was unknown to
them, till the great S. Paul taught them the knowledge of him.
For so our heart, by a deep and secret instinct, in all its actions
tends towards, and aims at, felicity, seeking it here and there, as
it were groping, without knowing where it resides, or in what it

consists, till faith shows and describes the infinite marvels thereof. But then, having found the treasure it sought for,—ah! what a satisfaction to this poor human heart! What joy, what complacency of love! O I have met with him, whom my heart sought for without knowing him! O how little I knew whither my aims tended, when nothing contented me of all I aimed at, because, in fact, I knew not what I was aiming at. I was seeking to love and knew not what to love, and therefore my intention not finding its true love, my love remained ever in a true but ignorant intention. I had indeed sufficient foretaste of love to make me seek, but not sufficient knowledge of the goodness I had to love, to actually practise love.

CHAPTER XVI.

HOW LOVE IS PRACTISED IN HOPE.

MAN's understanding then, being properly applied to the consideration of that which faith represents to it touching its sovereign good, the will instantly conceives an extreme complacency in this divine object, which, as yet absent, begets an ardent desire of its presence, whence the soul holily cries out: *Let him kiss me with the kiss of his mouth.** *My soul panteth after thee, O God.*†

And as the unhooded falcon having her prey in view suddenly launches herself upon the wing, and if held in her leash struggles upon the hand with extreme ardour; so faith, having drawn the veil of ignorance, and made us see our sovereign good, whom nevertheless we cannot yet possess, detained by the condition of this mortal life,—Ah! Theotimus, we then desire it in such sort that, *as the hart panteth after the fountains of waters; so my soul panteth after thee, O God! My soul hath thirsted after the strong living God; when shall I come and appear before the face of God?* ‡

This desire is just, Theotimus, for who would not desire so desirable a good? But it would be a useless desire, and would be but a continual torment to our heart if we had not assur-

* Cant. i. 1.   † Ps. xli. 1.   ‡ Ibid. 1, 2.

ance that we should at length satiate it.   He who on account of
the delay of this happiness, protests that his tears were *his*
ordinary *bread day and night*, so long as his God was absent,
and his enemies demanded : *where is thy God ?**—Alas ! what
would he have done if he had not had some hope of one day
enjoying this good, after which he sighed.   The divine spouse
goes *weeping and languishing with love,*† because she does not at
once find the well-beloved she is searching for.   The love of
the well-beloved had bred in her a desire, that desire begot an
ardour to pursue it, and that ardour caused in her a languishing
which would have consumed and annihilated her poor heart, unless
she had hoped at length to meet with what she sought after.
So then, lest the unrest and dolorous languor which the efforts
of desiring love cause in our souls should make us fail in
courage or reduce us to despair, the same sovereign good which
moves in us so vehement a desire, also by a thousand thousand
promises made in his Word and his inspirations, gives us
assurance, that we may with ease obtain it, provided always that
we will to employ the means which he has prepared for us, and
offers us to this effect.

Now these divine promises and assurances, by a particular
marvel, increase the cause of our disquiet, and yet, while they
increase the cause, they undo and destroy the effects.   Yea,
verily, Theotimus ; for the assurance which God gives us that
paradise is ours, infinitely strengthens the desire we have to
enjoy it, and yet weakens, yea altogether destroys, the trouble
and disquiet which this desire brought unto us ; so that our
hearts by the promises which the divine goodness has made us,
remain quite calmed, and this calm is the root of the most holy
virtue which we call hope.   For the will, assured by faith that
she has power to enjoy the sovereign good by using the means
appointed, makes two great acts of virtue : by the one she
expects from God the fruition of his sovereign goodness, by the
other she aspires to that holy fruition.

And indeed, Theotimus, between hoping and aspiring (*esperer
et aspirer*) there is but this difference, that we hope for those

* Ps. xli. 4.   † Cant. v. 8.

things which we expect to get by another's assistance, and we aspire unto those things which we think to reach by means that lie in our own power. And since we attain the fruition of our sovereign good, which is God, by his favour, grace and mercy, and yet the same mercy will have us co-operate with his favour, by contributing the weakness of our consent to the strength of his grace; our hope is thence in some sort mingled with aspiring, so that we do not altogether hope without aspiring, nor do we ever aspire without entirely hoping. Hope then keeps ever the principal place, as being founded upon divine grace, without which, as we cannot even so much as think of our sovereign good in the way required to reach it, so can we never without this grace aspire towards our sovereign God in the way required to obtain it.

Aspiration then is a scion of hope, as our co-operation is of grace: and as those that would hope without aspiring, would be rejected as cowardly and negligent; so those that should aspire without hoping, would be rash, insolent and presumptuous. But when hope is seconded with aspiration, when, hoping we aspire and aspiring we hope, then, dear Theotimus, hope by aspiration becomes a courageous desire, and aspiration is changed by hope into a humble claim, and we hope and aspire as God inspires us. But both are caused by that desiring love which tends to our sovereign good, to that good which the more surely it is hoped for, the more it is loved; yea hope is no other thing than the loving complacency we take in the expecting and seeking our sovereign good. All that is there is love, Theotimus. As soon as faith has shown me my sovereign good, I have loved it; and because it was absent I have desired it, and having understood that it would bestow itself upon me, I have loved and desired it yet more ardently; for indeed its goodness is so much more to be beloved and desired by how much more it is disposed to communicate itself. Now by this progress love has turned its desire into hope, seeking and expectation, so that hope is an expectant and aspiring love; and because the sovereign good which hope expects is God, and because also she expects it from God himself, to whom and by whom she hopes and aspires, this holy virtue of hope, abutting everywhere on God, is by consequence a divine or theological virtue.

CHAPTER XVII.

THAT THE LOVE WHICH IS IN HOPE IS VERY GOOD, THOUGH IMPERFECT.

THE love which we practise in hope goes indeed to God, Theotimus, but it returns to us; its sight is turned upon the divine goodness, yet with some respect to our own profit; it tends to that supreme perfection, but aiming at our own satisfaction. That is to say, it bears us to God, not because he is sovereignly good in himself, but because he is sovereignly good to us, in which as you see there is something of the *our* and the *us*, so that this love is truly love, but love of cupidity and self-interest. Yet I do not say that it does in such sort return to ourselves that it makes us love God only for the love of ourselves; O God! no : for the soul which should only love God for the love of herself, placing the end of the love which she bears to God in her own interest, would, alas! commit an extreme sacrilege. If a wife loved her husband only for the love of his servant, she would love her husband as a servant, and his servant as a husband : and the soul that only loves God for love of herself, loves herself as she ought to love God, and God as she ought to love herself.

But there is a great difference between this expression: *I love God for the good which I expect from him,* and this : *I only love God for the good which I expect from him :* as again it is a very different thing to say: *I love God for myself :* and *I love God for the love of myself.* For when I say I love God for myself, it is as if I said : I love to have God, I love that God should be mine, should be my sovereign good; which is a holy affection of the heavenly spouse, who a hundred times in excess of delight protests: *My beloved to me, and I to him, who feedeth among the lilies.** But to say : I love God for love of myself, is as if one should say : the love which I bear to myself is the end for which I love God ; in such sort that the love of God would

---

* Cant. ii. 16.

be dependent, subordinate, and inferior to self-love, to our love for ourselves, which is a matchless impiety.

This love, then, which we term hope, is a love of cupidity, but of a holy and well-ordered cupidity, by means whereof we do not draw God to us nor to our utility, but we adjoin ourselves unto him as to our final felicity. By this love we love ourselves together with God, yet not preferring or equalizing ourselves to him ; in this love the love of ourselves is mingled with that of God, but that of God floats on the top ; our own love enters indeed, but as a simple motive, not as a principal end ; our own interest has some place there, but God holds the principal rank. Yes, without doubt, Theotimus : for when we love God as our sovereign good, we love him for a quality by which we do not refer him to us but ourselves to him. We are not his end, aim, or perfection, but he is ours ; he does not appertain to us, but we to him ; he depends not on us but we on him ; and, in a word, by the quality of sovereign good for which we love him, he receives nothing of us, but we receive of him. He exercises towards us his affluence and goodness, and we our indigence and scarcity ; so that to love God under the title of sovereign good is to love him under an honourable and respectful title, by which we acknowledge him to be our perfection, repose and end, in the fruition of which our felicity consists. Some goods there are which we use for ourselves when we employ them, as our slaves, servants, horses, clothes : and the love which we bear unto them is a love of pure cupidity, since we love them only for our own profit. Other goods there are which we possess, but with a possession which is reciprocal and equal on each side, as in the case of our friends : for the love we have unto them inasmuch as they content us is indeed a love of cupidity, yet of an honest cupidity, by which they are ours and we similarly theirs, they belong to us and we equally to them. But there are yet other goods which we possess with a possession of dependence, participation and subjection, as we do the benevolence, or presence, or favour of our pastors, princes, father, mother : for the love which we bear unto them is then truly a love of cupidity, when we love them in that they are *our* pastors, *our* princes, *our* fathers, *our* mothers, since it is not precisely the quality of pastor, nor of prince, nor of father, nor of mother, which is the cause of our affection towards them, but the fact that they are so to us and in our regard. Still this cupidity is a love of respect, reverence and honour; for we love our father, for example, not because he is ours but because we are his; and after the same manner it is that we love and aspire to God by hope, not to the end he may become our good, but because he is it; not to the end he may become ours, but because we are his; not as though he existed for us, but inasmuch as we exist for him.

And note, Theotimus, that in this love, the reason why we love (that is, why we apply our heart to the love of the good which we desire) is because it is our good; but the measure and quantity of this love depend on the excellence and dignity of the good which we love. We love our benefactors because they are such to us, but we love them more or less as they are more or less our benefactors. Why then do we love God, Theotimus, with this love of cupidity? Because he is our good. But why do we sovereignly love him? Because he is our sovereign good.

But when I say we love God sovereignly, I do not therefore say that we love him with sovereign love. Sovereign love is only in charity, whereas in hope love is imperfect, because it does not tend to his infinite goodness as being such in itself, but only because it is such to us. Still, because in this kind of love there is no motive more excellent than that which proceeds from the consideration of the sovereign good, we say that by it we love sovereignly, though in real truth no one is able by virtue of this love either to keep God's commandments, or obtain life everlasting, because it is a love that yields more affection than effect, when it is not accompanied with charity.

CHAPTER XVIII.

THAT LOVE IS EXERCISED IN PENITENCE, AND FIRST, THAT
THERE ARE DIVERS SORTS OF PENITENCE.

To speak generally, penitence is a repentance whereby a man
rejects and detests the sin he has committed, with the resolution
to repair as much as in him lies the offence and injury done to
him against whom he has sinned. I comprehend in penitence
a purpose to repair the offence, because that repentance does
not sufficiently detest the fault which voluntarily permits the
principal effect thereof, to wit the offence and injury, to subsist;
and it permits it to subsist, so long as, being able in some sort
to make reparation, it does not do so.

I omit here the penitence of certain pagans, who, as Tertullian witnesses, had some appearances of it amongst them, but so
vain and fruitless that they often had penitence for having done
well; for I speak only of virtuous penitence, which according to
the different motives whence it proceeds is also of various
species. There is one sort purely moral and human, as was that
of Alexander the Great, who having slain his dear Clitus determined to starve himself to death, so great, says Cicero, was the
force of penitence : or that of Alcibiades, who, being convinced
by Socrates that he was not a wise man, began to weep bitterly,
being sorrowful and afflicted for not being what he ought to
have been, as S. Augustine says. Aristotle also, recognising
this sort of penitence, assures us that the intemperate man who
of set purpose gives himself over to pleasures is wholly incor-
rigible, because he cannot repent, and he that is without repentance is incurable.

Certainly, Seneca, Plutarch and the Pythagoreans, who so
highly commend the examen of conscience, but especially the
first, who speaks so feelingly of the torment which interior remorse excites in the soul, must have understood that there was
a repentance; and as for the sage Epictetus, he so well describes
the way in which a man should reprehend himself that it could
scarcely be better expressed.

There is yet another penitence which is indeed moral, yet religious too, yea in some sort divine, proceeding from the natural knowledge which we have of our offending God by sin. For certainly many philosophers understood that to live virtuously was a thing agreeable to the divinity, and that consequently to live viciously was offensive to him. The good man Epictetus makes the wish to die a true Christian (as it is very probable he did), and amongst other things he says he should be content if dying he could lift up his hands to God and say unto him : For my part I have not dishonoured Thee : and, further, he will have his philosopher to make an admirable oath to God never to be disobedient to his divine Majesty, nor to question or blame anything coming from him, nor in any sort to complain thereof; and in another place he teaches that God and our good angel are present during our actions. You see clearly then, Theotimus, that this philosopher, while yet a pagan, knew that sin offended God, as virtue honoured him, and consequently he willed that it should be repented of, since he even ordained an examen of conscience at night, about which, with Pythagoras, he lays down this maxim :

> If thou hast ill done, chide thyself bitterly,
> If thou hast well done, rest thee contentedly.

Now this kind of repentance joined to the knowledge and love of God which nature can give, was a dependence of moral religion. But as natural reason bestowed more knowledge than love upon the philosophers, who did not glorify God in proportion to the knowledge they had of him, so nature has furnished more light to understand how much God is offended by sin, than heat to excite the repentance necessary for the reparation of the offence.

But although religious penitence may have been in some sort recognized by some of the philosophers, yet this has been so rarely and feebly, that those who were reputed the most virtuous amongst them, to wit the Stoics, maintained that the wise man was never grieved, whereupon they framed a maxim as contrary to reason, as the proposition on which it was grounded was contrary to experience, namely, that the wise man sinned not.

We may therefore well say, Theotimus, that penitence is a virtue wholly Christian, since on the one side it was so little known to the pagans, and, on the other side, it is so well recognized amongst true Christians, that in it consists a great part of the evangelical philosophy, according to which whosoever affirms that he sins not, is senseless, and whosoever expects without penitence to redress his sin is mad ; for it is our Saviour's exhortation of exhortations : *Do penance.** And now let me give a brief description of the progress of this virtue.

We enter into a profound apprehending of the fact that, as far as is in us, we offend God by our sins, despising and dishonouring him, giving way to disobedience and rebellion against him ; and he also on his part considers himself as offended, irritated, and despised; for he dislikes, reproves and abominates iniquity. From this true apprehension there spring several motives, which all, or several together, or each one apart, may carry us to this repentance.

For we consider sometimes how God who is offended has established a rigorous punishment in hell for sinners, and how he will deprive them of the paradise prepared for the good. And as the desire of paradise is extremely honourable, so the fear of losing it is an excellent fear ; and not only so, but the desire of paradise being very worthy of esteem, the fear of its contrary, which is hell, is good and praiseworthy. Ah ! who would not dread so great a loss, so great a torment ! And this double fear—the one servile, the other mercenary—greatly bears us on towards a repentance for our sins, by which we have incurred them. And to this effect in the Holy Word this fear is a hundred and a hundred times inculcated. At other times we consider the deformity and malice of sin, according as faith teaches us; for example, because by it the likeness and image of God which we have, is defiled and disfigured, the dignity of our soul dishonoured, we are made like brute beasts, we have violated our duty towards the Creator of the world, forfeited the good of the society of the angels, to associate and subject ourselves to the devil, making ourselves slaves of our

* Matt. iv. 17.

passions, overturning the order of reason, offending our good angels to whom we have so great obligations.

At other times we are provoked to repentance by the beauty of virtue, which brings as much good with it as sin does evil; further we are often moved to it by the example of the saints; for who could ever have cast his eyes upon the exercises of the incomparable penitence of Magdalen, of Mary of Egypt, or of the penitents of the monastery called *Prison*, described by S. John Climacus, without being moved to repentance for his sins, since the mere reading of the history incites to it such as are not altogether insensible.

CHAPTER XIX.

THAT PENITENCE WITHOUT LOVE IS IMPERFECT.

Now all these motives are taught us by faith and the Christian religion, and therefore the repentance which results from them is very laudable though imperfect. Laudable certainly it is, for neither Holy Scripture nor the Church would stir us up by such motives if the penitence thence proceeding were not good, and we see manifestly that it is a most reasonable thing to repent of sin for these considerations, yea, that it is impossible that he who considers them attentively should not repent. Yet still it is an imperfect repentance, because divine love is not as yet found in it. Ah! do you not see, Theotimus, that all these repentances are made for the sake of our own soul, of its felicity, of its interior beauty, its honour, its dignity, and in a word for love of ourselves, although a lawful, just and well-ordered love.

And note, that I do not say that these repentances reject the love of God, but only that they do not include it; they do not repulse it, yet they do not contain it; they are not contrary to it, but as yet are without it; it is not forbidden entrance, and yet it is not in. The will which simply embraces good is very good, yet if it so embrace this as to reject the better, it is truly ill-ordered, not in accepting the one but in repulsing the other. So the vow to give alms this day is good, yet the vow to give only this day is bad, because it would exclude the better, which is to give both to-day, to-morrow, and every day when we are able.   Certainly it is good, and this cannot be denied, to repent of our sins in order to avoid the pains of hell and obtain heaven, but he that should make the resolution never to be willing to repent for any other motive, would wilfully shut out the better, which is to repent for the love of God, and would commit a great sin.   And what father would not be ill pleased that his son was willing indeed to serve him, yet never with love, or by love?

The beginning of good things is good, the progress better, the end the best.   At the same time, it is as a beginning that the beginning is good, and as progress that progress is good: and to wish to finish the work by its beginning or in its progress would be to invert the order of things.   Infancy is good, but to desire to remain always a child would be bad; for the child of a hundred years old is despised.   It is laudable to begin to learn, yet he that should begin with intention never to perfect himself would go against all reason.   Fear, and those other motives of repentance of which I spoke, are good for the beginning of Christian wisdom, which consists in penitence; but he who deliberately willed not to attain to love which is the perfection of penitence, would greatly offend him who ordained all to his love, as to the end of all things.

To conclude: the repentance which excludes the love of God is infernal like to that of the damned.   The repentance which does not reject the love of God, though as yet it be without it, is a good and desirable penitence, but imperfect, and it cannot give salvation until it attain love and is mingled therewith.   So that as the great Apostle said that though he should *deliver his body to be burned, and all his goods to the poor, wanting charity it would profit him nothing,** so we may truly say, that though our penitence were so great that it should cause our eyes to dissolve in tears, and our hearts to break with sorrow, yet if we have not the holy love of God, all this would profit nothing for eternal life.

* 1 Cor. xiii. 3.

CHAPTER XX.

HOW THE MINGLING OF LOVE AND SORROW TAKES PLACE IN CONTRITION.

NATURE, as far as I know, never converts fire into water, though some waters turn into fire. Yet God did it once by miracle. For as it is written in the Book of Machabees,* when the children of Israel were conducted into Babylon, in the time of Sedecias, the priests, by the counsel of Jeremias, hid the holy fire in a valley, in a dry well, and upon their return, the children of those that had hid it went to seek it, following the direction their fathers had given them, and they found it converted into a thick water, which being drawn by them, and poured upon the sacrifices, as Nehemias commanded, was, when the sunbeams touched it, converted into a great fire.

Theotimus, amongst the tribulations and remorse of a lively repentance God often puts in the bottom of our heart the sacred fire of his love, this love is converted into the water of tears, they by a second change into another and greater fire of love. Thus the famous penitent lover first loved her Saviour, her love was converted into tears, and these tears into an excellent love ; whence Our Saviour told her that many sins were pardoned her because she *had loved much.*† And as we see fire turns wine into a certain water which is called almost everywhere *aquavitæ*, which so easily takes and augments fire that in many places it is also termed *ardent ;* so the amorous consideration of the goodness which, while it ought to have been sovereignly loved, has been offended by sin, produces the water of holy penitence ; and from this water the fire of divine love issues, thence properly termed *water of life* or *ardent.* Penitence is indeed a *water* in its substance, being a true displeasure, a real sorrow and repentance ; yet is it *ardent*, in that it contains the virtue and properties of love, as arising from a motive of love, and by this property it gives the life of grace. So that perfect penitence has two different effects ; for in virtue of its sorrow and detesta-

* 2 Mach. i.   † Luke vii. 47.

tion it separates us from sin and the creature, to which delectation had attached us ; but in virtue of the motive of love, whence it takes its origin, it reconciles us and reunites us to our God, from whom we had separated ourselves by contempt: so that it at once reclaims us from sin in quality of repentance, and reunites us to God in quality of love.

But I do not mean to say that the perfect love of God, by which we love him above all things, always precedes this repentance, or that this repentance always precedes this love.   For though it often so happens, still at other times, as soon as divine love is born in our hearts, penitence is born within the love, and oftentimes penitence entering into our heart, love enters in penitence.   And as when Esau was born, Jacob his twin brother held him by the foot, that their births might not only follow the one the other, but also might cleave together and be intermingled; so repentance, rude and rough in regard of its pain, is born first, as another Esau; and love, gentle and gracious as Jacob, holds him by the foot, and cleaves unto him so closely that their birth is but one, since the end of the birth of repentance is the beginning of that of perfect love.   Now as Esau first appeared, so repentance ordinarily makes itself to be seen before love, but love, as another Jacob, although the younger, afterwards subdues penitence, converting it into consolation.

Mark, I pray you, Theotimus, the well-beloved Magdalen, how she weeps with love : *They have taken away my Lord,* says she, melting into tears ; *and I know not where they have laid him,** but having with sighs and tears found him, she holds and possesses him by love.   Imperfect love desires and runs after him, penitence seeks and finds him; perfect love holds and clasps him.   It is with it as is said to be with Ethiopian rubies, whose fire is naturally very faint, but when they are dipped in vinegar it sparkles out and casts a most brilliant lustre: for the love which goes before repentance is ordinarily imperfect ; but being steeped in the sharpness of penitence, it gains strength and becomes excellent love.

It even happens sometimes that repentance, though perfect,

* John xx. 13.

contains not in itself the proper action of love, but only the virtue and property of it. You will ask me, what virtue or property of love can repentance have, if it have not the action? Theotimus, God's goodness is the motive of perfect repentance, which it displeases us to have offended: now this motive is a motive only because it stirs us and gives us movement. But the movement which the divine goodness gives unto the heart which considers it, can be no other than the movement of love, that is, of union. And therefore true repentance, though it seem not so, and though we perceive not the proper effect of love, yet ever takes the movement of love, and the unitive quality of love, by which it re-unites and re-joins us to the divine goodness. Tell me, I pray:—it is the property of the loadstone to draw and unite iron unto itself; but do we not see that iron touched with the loadstone, without having either it or its nature, but only its virtue and attractive quality, can draw and unite to itself another iron? So perfect repentance, touched with the motive of love, is not without the virtue and quality thereof, that is, the movement of union to re-join and re-unite our hearts to the divine will. But you will reply, what difference is there between this movement of penitence, and the proper action of love? Theotimus, the action of love is indeed a movement of union, but it is made by complacency, whereas the movement of union which is in penitence is not made by way of complacency, but by displeasure, repentance, reparation, reconciliation. Forasmuch therefore as this motive unites, it has the quality of love; inasmuch as it is bitter and dolorous it has the quality of penitence, and in fine, by its natural condition it is a true movement of penitence, but one which has the virtue and uniting quality of love.

So *Theriacum*-wine is not so named because it contains the proper substance of Theriacum, for there is none at all in it; but it is so called because the plant of the vine having been steeped in Theriacum, the grapes and the wine which have sprung from it have drawn into themselves the virtue and operation of Theriacum against all sorts of poison. We must not therefore think it strange if penitence, according to the Holy Scripture, blots out sin, saves the soul, makes her grateful to

God and justifies her, which are effects appertaining to love, and which apparently should only be attributed to love: for though love itself be not always found in perfect penitence, yet its virtue and properties are always there, having flowed into it by the motive of love whence it springs.

Nor must we wonder that the force of love should be found in penitence before love be formed in it, since we see that by the reflection of the rays of the sun beating upon a mirror, heat, which is the virtue and the proper quality of fire, grows by little and little so strong that it begins to burn before it has yet well produced the fire, or at least before we have perceived it. For so the Holy Ghost casting into our understanding the consideration of the greatness of our sins, in that by them we have offended so sovereign a goodness, and our will receiving the reflection of this knowledge, repentance by little and little grows so strong, with a certain affective heat and desire to return into grace with God, that in fine this movementcomes to such a height, that it burns and unites even before the love be fully formed, though love, as a sacred fire, is always at once lighted, at this point. So that repentance never comes to this height of burning and re-uniting the heart to God, which is her utmost perfection, without finding herself wholly converted into fire and flame of love, the end of the one giving the other a beginning; or rather, the end of penitence is within the commencement of love, as Esau's foot was within Jacob's hand; in such sort that while Esau was ending his birth, Jacob was beginning his, the end of the one's birth being joined and fastened to, yea, what is more, included in, the beginning of the other's: for so the beginning of perfect love not only follows the end of penitence but even cleaves and ties itself to it; and to say all in one word, this beginning of love mingles itself with the end of penitence, and in this moment of mingling, penitence and contrition merit life everlasting.

Now because this loving repentance is ordinarily practised by elevations and raisings of the heart to God, like to those of the ancient penitents: *I am thine, save thou me. Have mercy on me, O God, have mercy on me: for my soul trusteth in thee! Save me, O God; for the waters are come in even unto my soul! Make*

*me as one of thy hired servants!   O God be merciful to me a
sinner!*—it is not without reason that some have said, that
prayer justifies; for the repentant prayer, or the suppliant
repentance, raising up the soul to God and re-uniting it to his
goodness, without doubt obtains pardon in virtue of the holy
love, which gives it the sacred movement.   And therefore we
ought all to have very many such ejaculatory prayers, made in
the sense of a loving repentance and of sighs which seek our
reconciliation with God, so that by these laying our tribulation
before Our Saviour, we may pour out our souls before and
within his pitiful heart, which will receive them to mercy.

CHAPTER XXI.

HOW OUR SAVIOUR'S LOVING ATTRACTIONS ASSIST AND ACCOMPANY US TO FAITH AND CHARITY.

BETWEEN the first awaking from sin or infidelity to the final
resolution of a perfect belief, there often runs a good deal of
time in which we are able to pray, as we have seen S. Pachomius did, and as that poor lunatic's father, who, as S. Mark
relates, giving assurance that he believed, that is, that he began
to believe, knew at the same time that he did not believe sufficiently; whence he cried out: *I do believe, Lord help my unbelief,* * as though he would say : I am no longer in the obscurity
of the night of infidelity, the rays of your faith already
enlighten the horizon of my soul : but still I do not yet believe
as I ought ; it is a knowledge as yet weak and mixed with
darkness ; Ah! Lord, help me.   And the great S. Augustine
solemnly pronounces these remarkable words: " But listen, O
man ! and understand.   Art thou not drawn ? pray, in order
that thou mayest be drawn."   In which words his intention is
not to speak of the first movement which God works in us without us, when he excites and awakens us out of the sleep of sin :

* Mark ix. 23.

for how could we ask to be awakened seeing no man can pray before he be awakened? But he speaks of the resolution which we make to be faithful, for he considers that to believe is to be drawn, and therefore he admonishes such as have been excited to believe in God, to ask the gift of faith. And indeed no one could better know the difficulties which ordinarily pass between the first movement God makes in us, and the perfect resolution of believing fully, than S. Augustine, who having had so great a variety of attractions by the words of the glorious S. Ambrose, by the conference he had with Politian, and a thousand other means, yet made so many delays and had so much difficulty in resolving. For more truly to him than to any other might have been applied that which he afterwards said to others: Alas! Augustine, if thou be not drawn, if thou believe not, pray that thou mayest be drawn, and that thou mayest believe.

Our Saviour draws hearts by the delights that he gives them, which make them find heavenly doctrine sweet and agreeable, but, until this sweetness has engaged and fastened the will by its beloved bonds to draw it to the perfect acquiescence and consent of faith, as God does not fail to exercise his greatness upon us by his holy inspirations, so does not our enemy cease to practise his malice by temptations. And meantime we remain in full liberty, to consent to the divine drawings or to reject them; for as the sacred Council of Trent has clearly decreed: "If any one should say that man's freewill, being moved and incited by God, does not in any way co-operate, by consenting to God, who moves and calls him that he may dispose and prepare himself to obtain the grace of justification, and that he is unable to refuse consent though he would," truly such a man would be excommunicated, and reproved by the Church. But if we do not repulse the grace of holy love, it dilates itself by continual increase in our souls, until they are entirely converted; like great rivers, which finding open plains spread themselves, and ever take up more space.

But if the inspiration, having drawn us to faith, find no resistance in us, it draws us also to penitence and charity. S. Peter, as an *apode*, raised by the inspiration which came from the eyes of his master, freely letting himself be moved and carried by this gentle wind of the Holy Ghost, looks upon those life-giving eyes which had excited him ; he reads as in the book of life the sweet invitation to pardon which the divine clemency offers him; he draws from it a just motive of hope; he goes out of the court, considers the horror of his sin, and detests it ; he weeps, he sobs, he prostrates his miserable heart before his Saviour's mercy, craves pardon for his faults, makes a resolution of inviolable loyalty, and by this progress of movements, practised by the help of grace which continually conducts, assists, and helps him, he comes at length to the holy remission of his sins, and passes so from grace to grace: according to what S. Prosper lays down, that without grace a man does not run to grace.

So then to conclude this point, the soul, prevented by grace, feeling the first drawings, and consenting to their sweetness, as if returning to herself after a long swoon, begins to sigh out these words: Ah! my dear spouse, my friend ! Draw me, I beseech thee, and take hold of me under my arms, for otherwise I am not able to walk : but if thou draw me we run, thou in helping me by the odour of thy perfumes, and I corresponding by my weak consent, and by relishing thy sweetnesses which strengthen and reinvigorate me, till the balm of thy sacred name, that is the salutary ointment of my justification be poured out over me. Do you see, Theotimus, she would not pray if she were not excited; but as soon as she is, and feels the attractions, she prays that she may be drawn ; being drawn she runs, nevertheless she would not run if the perfumes which draw her and by which she is drawn did not inspirit her heart by the power of their precious odour; and as her course is more swift, and as she approaches nearer her heavenly spouse, she has ever a more delightful sense of the sweetnesses which he pours out, until at last he himself flows out in her heart, like a spread balm, whence she cries, as being surprised by this delight, not so quickly expected, and as yet unlooked for: O my spouse, thou art as balm poured into my bosom; it is no marvel that young souls cherish thee dearly.

In this way, my dear Theotimus, the divine inspiration comes to us, and prevents us, moving our wills to sacred love. And if we do not repulse it, it goes with us and keeps near us, to incite us and ever push us further forwards; and if we do not abandon it, it does not abandon us, till such time as it has brought us to the haven of most holy charity, performing for us the three good offices which the great angel Raphael fulfilled for his dear Tobias : for it guides us through all our journey of holy penitence, it preserves us from dangers and from the assaults of the devil, and it consoles, animates, and fortifies us in our difficulties.

CHAPTER XXII.

A SHORT DESCRIPTION OF CHARITY.

BEHOLD at length, Theotimus, how God, by a progress full of ineffable sweetness, conducts the soul which he makes leave the Egypt of sin, from love to love, as from mansion to mansion, till he has made her enter into the land of promise, I mean into most holy charity, which to say it in one word, is a friendship, and a disinterested love, for by charity we love God for his own sake, by reason of his most sovereignly amiable goodness. But this friendship is a true friendship, being reciprocal, for God has loved eternally all who have loved him, do, or shall love him temporally. It is shown and acknowledged mutually, since God cannot be ignorant of the love we bear him, he himself bestowing it upon us, nor can we be ignorant of his love to us, seeing that he has so published it abroad, and that we acknowledge all the good we have, to be true effects of his benevolence. And in fine we have continual communications with him, who never ceases to speak unto our hearts by inspirations, allurements, and sacred motions; he ceases not to do us good, or to give all sorts of testimonies of his most holy affection, having openly revealed unto us all his secrets, as to his confidential friends. And to crown his holy loving intercourse with us, he has made himself our proper food in the most holy Sacrament of the Eucharist; and as for us, we have freedom to treat with him at all times when we please in holy prayer, having our whole life, movement and being not only with him, but in him and by him.

Now this friendship is not a simple friendship, but a friendship of dilection, by which we make election of God, to love him with a special love. He is *chosen,* says the sacred spouse, *out of thousands**—she says *out of thousands,* but she means out of all, whence this love is not a love of simple excellence, but an incomparable love; for charity loves God by a certain esteem and preference of his goodness so high and elevated above all other esteems, that other loves either are not true loves in comparison of this, or if they be true loves, this love is infinitely more than love; and therefore, Theotimus, it is not a love which the force of nature either angelic or human can produce, but the Holy Ghost gives it and *pours it abroad in our hearts.*† And as our souls which give life to our bodies, have not their origin from the body but are put in them by the natural providence of God, so charity which gives life to our hearts has not her origin from our hearts, but is poured into them as a heavenly liquor by the supernatural providence of his divine Majesty.

For this reason, and because it has reference to God and tends unto him not according to the natural knowledge we have of his goodness, but according to the supernatural knowledge of faith, we name it supernatural friendship. Whence it, together with faith and hope, makes its abode in the point and summit of the spirit, and, as a queen of majesty, is seated in the will as on her throne, whence she conveys into the soul her delights and sweetnesses, making her thereby all fair, agreeable and amiable to the divine goodness. So that if the soul be a kingdom of which the Holy Ghost is king, charity is the queen *set at his right hand in gilded clothing surrounded with variety;*‡ if the soul be a queen, spouse to the great king of heaven, charity is her crown, which royally adorns her head; and if the soul with the body be a little world, charity is the sun which beautifies all, heats all, and vivifies all.

Charity, then, is a love of friendship, a friendship of dilection, a dilection of preference, but a preference incomparable, sovereign, and supernatural, which is as a sun in the whole soul to

* Cant. v. 10.   † Rom. v. 5.
‡ Ps. xliv. 10.

enlighten it with its rays, in all the spiritual faculties to perfect them, in all the powers to moderate them, but in the will as on its throne, there to reside and to make it cherish and love its God above all things.   O how happy is the soul wherein this holy love is poured abroad, since *all good things come together with her !**

* Wisdom vii. 11.

BOOK III.

PROGRESS AND PERFECTION OF LOVE.

———◆———

CHAPTER I.

THAT HOLY LOVE MAY BE AUGMENTED STILL MORE AND MORE IN EVERY ONE OF US.

THE sacred Council of Trent assures us, that the friends of God, proceeding from virtue to virtue, are day by day renewed, that is, they increase by good works in the justice which they have received by God's grace, and are more and more justified, according to those heavenly admonitions; *He that is just let him be justified still : and he that is holy, let him be sanctified still.** And : *Be not afraid to be justified even to death.*† *The path of the just, as a shining light, goeth forwards and increaseth even to perfect day.*‡ *Doing the truth in charity, let us in all things grow up in him who is the head, even Christ.*§ And finally : *This I pray, that your charity may more and more abound in knowledge and in all understanding.*‖ All these are sacred words out of David, S. John, Ecclesiasticus, and S. Paul.

I never heard of any living creature whose growth was not bounded and limited, except the crocodile, who from an extremely little beginning never ceases to grow till it comes to its end, representing equally in this the good and the wicked : *For the pride of them that hate thee ascendeth continually,*¶ says

---

* Apoc. xxii. 11. † Ecclus. xviii. 22. ‡ Prov. iv. 18.
§ Eph. iv. 15. ‖ Phil. i. 9. ¶ Ps. lxxiii. 23.

127

the great king David; and the good increase as the break of day, from brightness to brightness. And to remain at a stand-still is impossible; he that gains not, loses in this traffic; he that ascends not, descends upon this ladder; he that vanquishes not in this battle, is vanquished : we live amidst the dangers of the wars which our enemies wage against us, if we resist not we perish; and we cannot resist unless we overcome, nor overcome without triumph. For as the glorious S. Bernard says: " It is written in particular of man that *he never con-tinueth in the same state ;** he necessarily either goes forward or returns backward. *All run indeed but one obtains the prize, so run that you may obtain.†* Who is the prize but Jesus Christ ? And how can you take hold on him if you follow him not ? But if you follow him you will march and run continually, for he never stayed, but continued his course of love and obedience until death and the death of the cross."

Go then, says S. Bernard ; go, I say with him ; go, my dear Theotimus, and admit no other bounds than those of life, and as long as it remains run after this Saviour. But run ardently and swiftly : for what better will you be for following him, if you be not so happy as to take hold of him ! Let us hear the Prophet : *I have inclined my heart to do thy justifications for ever :‡* he does not say that he will do them for a time only, but for ever, and because he desires eternally to do well, he shall have an eternal reward. *Blessed are the undefiled in the way, who walk in the law of the Lord.§* Accursed are they who are defiled, who walk not in the law of the Lord : it is only for the devil to say that he will *sit in the sides of the north.‖* Detestable one, wilt thou *sit ?* Ah ! knowest thou not that thou art upon the way, and that the way is not made to sit down but to go in, and it is so made to go in, that going is called making way. And God speaking to one of his greatest friends says : *Walk before me and be perfect.¶*

True virtue has no limits, it goes ever further; but especially holy charity, which is the virtue of virtues, and which, having an

---

* Job xiv. 2.   † 1 Cor. ix. 24.   ‡ Ps. cxviii. 112.
§ *Ibid.* 1.   ‖ Is. xiv. 13.   ¶ Gen. xvii. 1.

infinite object, would be capable of becoming infinite if it could meet with a heart capable of infinity. Nothing hinders this love from being infinite except the condition of the will which receives it, and which is to act by it : a condition which prevents any one loving God as much as God is amiable, as it prevents them from seeing him as much as he is visible. The heart which could love God with a love equal to the divine goodness would have a will infinitely good, which cannot be but in God. Charity then in us may be perfected up to the infinite, but exclusively; that is, charity may become more and more, and ever more, excellent, yet never infinite. The Holy Ghost may elevate our hearts, and apply them to what supernatural actions it may please him, so they be not infinite. Between little and great things, though the one exceed the other never so much, there is still some proportion, provided always that the excess of the thing which exceeds be not an infinite excess : but between finite and infinite there is no proportion, and to make any, it would be necessary, either to raise the finite and make it infinite, or to lower the infinite and make it finite, which is impossible.

So that even the charity which is in our Redeemer, as he is man, though greater than Angels or men can comprehend, yet is not infinite of itself and in its own being, but only in regard to its value and merit, as being the charity of a divine Person, who is the eternal Son of the omnipotent Father.

Meanwhile it is an extreme honour to our souls that they may still grow more and more in the love of their God, as long as they shall live in this failing life : *Ascending by steps from virtue to virtue.**

CHAPTER II.

HOW EASY OUR SAVIOUR HAS MADE THE INCREASE OF LOVE.

Do you see, Theotimus, that glass of water or that piece of bread which a holy soul gives to a poor body for God's sake; it is a small matter, God knows, and in human judgment hardly worthy

* Ps. lxxxiii. 6.

of consideration: God, notwithstanding, recompenses it, and forthwith gives for it some increase of charity. The goat's-hair which was anciently presented to the Tabernacle was received in good part, and had place amongst the holy offerings; and the little actions which proceed from charity are agreeable to God, and have their place among merits. For as in Araby the Blest, not only the plants which are by nature aromatic, but even all the others, are sweet, gaining a share in the felicity of that soil; so in a charitable soul, not only the works which are excellent of their own nature, but also the little actions, smell of the virtue of holy love, and have a good odour before the majesty of God, who in consideration of them increases charity. And I say God does it, because Charity does not produce her own increase as a tree does, which by its own virtue produces and throws out, one from another, its boughs: but as Faith, Hope and Charity are virtues which have their origin from the divine goodness, so thence also they draw their increase and perfection, not unlike bees, which, having their extraction from honey, have also their food from it.

Wherefore, as pearls are not only bred of dew but fed also with it, the mother-pearls to this end opening their shells towards heaven to beg, as it were, the drops which the freshness of the air makes fall at the break of day, so we, having received Faith, Hope and Charity from the heavenly bounty, ought always to turn our hearts and keep them turned towards it, thence to obtain the continuation and augmentation of the same virtues. " O, Lord," does holy Church our mother teach us to say, "give us the increase of faith, hope and charity." And this is in imitation of those that said to Our Saviour: *Lord increase our faith,** and following the counsel of S. Paul, who assures us that: *God alone is able to make all grace abound in* us.†

It is God therefore that gives this increase, in consideration of the use we make of his grace, as it is written; *For he that hath,* that is, who uses well the favours received, *to him shall be given, and he shall abound.‡* Thus is Our Saviour's exhortation practised: *Lay up to yourselves treasures in heaven :§* as though

---

* Luke xvii. 5.   † 2 Cor. ix. 8.   ‡ Matt. xiii. 12.   § Matt. vi. 20.

he said : add ever new good works to the former ones ; for fasting, prayer and alms-deeds are the coins whereof your treasures are to consist.   Now as amongst the treasures of the temple, the poor widow's mite was much esteemed, and as indeed, by the addition of many little pieces treasures become great, and their value increases, so the least little good works, even though performed somewhat coldly, and not according to the whole extent of the charity which is in us, are agreeable to God, and esteemed by him; in such sort that though of themselves they cannot cause any increase in the existing love, being of less force than it, yet the divine Providence, counting, and out of his goodness, valuing them, forthwith rewards them with increase of charity for the present, and assigns to them a greater heavenly glory for the future.

Theotimus, bees make the delicious honey which is their chief work ; but the wax, which they also make, does not therefore cease to be of some worth, or to make their labour valuable. The loving heart ought to endeavour to bring forth works full of fervour, and of high value, that it may powerfully augment charity : yet if it bring forth some of lesser value, it shall not lose its recompense ; for God will be pleased by these, that is to say he will love us ever a little more for them.   Now God never loves a soul more without bestowing also upon her more charity, our love towards him being the proper, and special effect, of his love towards us.

The more attentively we regard our image in a looking-glass, the more attentively it regards us again ; and the more lovingly God casts his gracious eyes upon our soul, which is made to his image and likeness, our soul in return, with so much the more attention and fervour is fixed upon the divine goodness, answering, according to her littleness, every increase which this sovereign sweetness makes of his divine love towards her.   The Council of Trent says thus : " If any say that justice received is not preserved, yea that it is not augmented, by good works in the sight of God, but that works are only the fruits and signs of justification acquired, and not the cause of its increase, let him be anathema."   Do you see, Theotimus, the justification wrought by charity is augmented by good works, and, which

is to be noted, by good works without exception: for, as
S. Bernard says excellently well on another subject, nothing is
excepted where nothing is distinguished. The Council speaks
of good works indifferently, and without reservation, giving us
to understand, that not only the great and fervent, but also the
little and feeble works cause the increase of holy Charity, but
the great ones greatly, and the little much less.

Such is the love which God bears to our souls, such his desire
to make us increase in the love which we owe to him. The
divine sweetness renders all things profitable to us, takes all to
our advantage, and turns all our endeavours, though never so
lowly and feeble, to our gain.

In the action of moral virtues little works bring no increase
to the virtue whence they proceed, yea, if they be very little,
they impair it: for a great liberality perishes if it occupies
itself in bestowing things of small value, and of liberality becomes
niggardliness. But in the actions of those virtues which issue
from God's mercy, and especially of charity, every work gives
increase. Nor is it strange that sacred love, as King of virtues,
has nothing either great or small which is not loveable, since
the balm tree, prince of aromatic trees, has neither bark nor
leaf that is not odoriferous: and what could love bring forth
that were not worthy of love, or did not tend to love?

CHAPTER III.

HOW A SOUL IN CHARITY MAKES PROGRESS IN IT.

LET us make use of a parable, Theotimus, seeing that this method
was so agreeable to the sovereign Master of the love which we
are teaching. A great and brave King, having espoused a most
amiable young princess, and having on a certain day led her into
a very retired cabinet, there to converse with her more at his
pleasure, after some discourse saw her by a certain sudden
accident fall down as dead at his feet. Alas! he was extremely
disturbed at this, and it well nigh put him also into a swoon; for
she was dearer to him than his own life. Yet the same love that

gave him this assault of grief, gave him an equal strength to sustain it, and set him into action to remedy, with an incomparable promptitude, the evil which had happened to the dear companion of his life. Therefore rapidly opening a sideboard which stood by, he takes a cordial-water, infinitely precious, and having filled his mouth with it, by force he opens the lips and the set teeth of his well-beloved princess, then breathing and spurting the precious liquor which he held in his mouth, into that of his poor lifeless one who lay in a swoon, and pouring what was left in the phial about the nostrils, the temples, and the heart, he made her return to herself and to her senses again; that done, he helps her up gently, and by virtue of remedies so strengthens and revives her, that she begins to stand and walk very quietly with him; but in no sort without his help, for he goes assisting and sustaining her by her arm, till at length he lays to her heart an *epithem* so precious and of so great virtue, that finding herself entirely restored to her wonted health, she walks all alone, her dear spouse not now sustaining her so much, but only holding her right hand softly between his, and his right arm folded over hers on to her bosom. Thus he went on treating her, and fulfilling to her in all this four most agreeable offices : for 1. He gave testimony that his heart was lovingly careful of her. 2. He continued ever a little nursing her. 3. If she had felt any touch of her former faintness he would have sustained her. 4. If she had lighted on any rough and difficult place in her walking he would have been her support and stay : and in accidents, or when she would make a little more haste, he raised her and powerfully succoured her. In fine he stayed by her with this heartfelt care till night approached, and then he assisted to lay her in her royal bed.

The soul is the spouse of Our Saviour when she is just ; and because she is never just but when she is in charity, she is also no sooner spouse than she is led into the cabinet of those delicious perfumes mentioned in the Canticles. Now when the soul which has been thus honoured commits sin, she falls as if dead in a spiritual swoon; and this is in good truth a most unlooked-for accident : for who would ever think that a creature could forsake her Creator and sovereign good for things so trifling as the allurements of sin ? Truly the heavens are astonished at it, and if God were subject to passions he would fall down in a swoon at this misfortune, as when he was mortal he died upon the cross for our redemption. But seeing it is not now necessary that he should employ his love in dying for us, when he sees the soul overthrown by sin he commonly runs to her succour, and by an unspeakable mercy, lays open the gates of her heart by the stings and remorses of conscience which come from the divers lights and apprehensions which he casts into our hearts, with salutary movements, by which, as by odorous and vital liquors, he makes the soul return to herself, and brings her back to good sentiments. And all this, Theotimus, God works in us without our action,* by his all-amiable Goodness which prevents us with its sweetness. For even as our bride, having fainted, would have died in her swoon, if the King had not assisted her; so the soul would remain lost in her sin if God prevented her not. But if the soul thus excited add her consent to the solicitation of grace, seconding the inspiration which prevents her, and accepting the required helps provided for her by God; he will fortify her, and conduct her through various movements of faith, hope and penitence, even till he restore her to her true spiritual health, which is no other thing than charity. And while he thus makes her walk in the virtues by which he disposes her to this holy love, he does not conduct her only, but in such sort sustains her, that as she for her part goes as well as she is able, so he on his part supports and sustains her; and it is hard to say whether she goes or is carried; for she is not so carried that she goes not, and yet her going is such that if she were not carried she could not go. So that, to speak apostolically, she must say : I walk, *not I* alone, *but the grace of God with me.*†

But the soul being entirely restored to her health by the excellent *epithem* of charity which the Holy Ghost infuses into her heart, she is then able to walk and keep herself upon her feet of herself, yet by virtue of this health and this sacred epithem of holy love. Wherefore though she is able to walk of herself, yet is she to render the glory thereof to God, who has

In nobis sine nobis (S. Aug.) † 1 Cor. xv. 10.

bestowed upon her a health so vigorous and strong : for whether the Holy Ghost fortify us by the motions which he enables our heart to make, or sustain us by the charity which he infuses into them, whether he succour us by manner of assistance in raising and carrying us, or strengthen our hearts by pouring into them fortifying and quickening love, we always live, walk, and work, in him and by him.

And although by means of charity poured into our hearts, we are able to walk in the presence of God, and make progress in the way of salvation, yet still it is the goodness of God which ever helps the soul to whom he has given his love, continually holding her with his holy hand ; for so 1. He doth better make appear the sweetness of his love towards her. 2. He ever animates her more and more. 3. He supports her against depraved inclinations and evil habits contracted by former sins. 4. And finally, he supports her and defends her against temptations.

Do we not often see, Theotimus, that sound and robust men must be provoked to employ their strength and power well; and, as one would say, must be drawn by the hand to the work ? So God having given us his charity, and by it the force and the means to gain ground in the way of perfection, his love does not permit him to let us walk thus alone, but makes him put himself upon the way with us, urges him to urge us, and solicits his heart to solicit and drive forward ours to make good use of the charity which he has given us, repeating often, by means of his inspirations, S. Paul's admonitions : *See that you receive not the grace of God in vain.** *Whilst we have time, let us work good to all men.†* *So run that you may obtain.‡* So that we are often to think that he repeats in our ears the words which he used to the good father Abraham : *Walk before me and be perfect.§*

But principally the special assistance of God to the soul endowed with charity is required in sublime and extraordinary enterprises ; for though charity, however weak it be, gives us enough inclination, and, as I think, enough power, to do the

---

* 2 Cor. vi. 1.   † Gal. vi. 10.   ‡ 1 Cor. ix. 24.
§ Gen. xvii. 1.

works necessary for salvation, yet, to aspire to and undertake excellent and extraordinary actions, our hearts stand in need of being pushed and raised by the hand and motion of this great heavenly lover; as the princess in our parable, although restored to health, could not ascend nor go fast, unless her dear spouse raised and strongly supported her. Thus S. Antony and S. Simeon Stylites were in the grace of God and charity when they designed so exalted a life; as also the B. Mother (S.) Teresa when she made her particular vow of obedience, S. Francis and S. Louis, when they undertook their journey beyond-seas for the advancement of God's glory, the Blessed Francis Xavier, when he consecrated his life to the conversion of the Indians, S. Charles, in exposing himself to serve the plague-stricken, S. Paulinus, when he sold himself to redeem the poor widow's child; yet still never would they have struck such mighty and generous blows, unless God, to that charity which they had in their hearts, had added special inspirations, invitations, lights and forces, whereby he animated and pushed them forward to these extraordinary exploits of spiritual valour.

Do you not mark the young man of the gospel, whom Our Saviour loved, and who, consequently, was in charity? Certainly, he never dreamed of selling all he had to give it to the poor, and following Our Saviour: nay though Our Saviour had given him such an inspiration, yet had he not the courage to put it into execution. For these great works, Theotimus, we need not only to be inspired, but also to be fortified, in order to effect what the inspiration inclines us to. As again, in the fierce assaults of extraordinary temptations, a special and particular presence of heavenly succour is absolutely necessary. For this cause holy church makes us so frequently cry out: "Excite our hearts O Lord:" "Prevent our actions by thy holy inspirations and further them with thy continual help:" "O Lord, make haste to help us:" and the like, in order by such prayers to obtain grace to be able to effect excellent and extraordinary works, and more frequently and fervently to do ordinary ones: as also more ardently to resist small temptations, and boldly to combat the greatest. S. Antony was assailed by a hideous legion of devils, and having long sustained their attacks, not without incredible pain and torment, at length saw the roof of his cell burst open, and a heavenly ray enter the breach, which made the black and darksome troop of his enemies vanish in a moment, and delivered him from all the pain of the wounds received in that battle; whence he perceived God's particular presence, and fetching a profound sigh towards the vision—" where wast thou, O good Jesus," said he, " where wast thou? Why wast thou not here from the beginning to have relieved my pain? It was answered him from above. Antony, I was here: but I awaited the event of thy combat: and since thou didst behave thyself bravely and valiantly, I will be thy continual aid." But in what did the valour and courage of this brave spiritual combatant consist? He himself declared it another time when, being set upon by a devil who acknowledged himself to be the spirit of fornication, this glorious saint after many words worthy of his great courage began to sing the 7th verse of the 117th Psalm : *The Lord is my helper : and I will look over my enemies.*

And Our Saviour revealed to S. Catharine of Sienna, that he was in the midst of her heart in a cruel temptation she had, as a captain in the midst of a fort to hold it; and that without his succour she would have been lost in that battle. It is the same in all the great assaults which our enemy makes against us : and we may well say with Jacob that it is *the angel that delivereth* us *from all evil,** and may sing with the great King David : *The Lord ruleth me : and I shall want nothing. He hath set me in a place of pasture. He hath brought me up, on the water of refreshment : he hath converted my soul.* So that we ought often to repeat this exclamation and prayer : *And thy mercy will follow me all the days of my life.*†

* Gen. xlviii. 16. †Ps. xxii.

CHAPTER IV.

OF HOLY PERSEVERANCE IN SACRED LOVE.

EVEN as a tender mother, leading with her her little babe, assists and supports him as need requires, letting him now and then venture a step by himself in less dangerous and very smooth places, now taking him by the hand and steadying him, now taking him up in her arms and bearing him, so Our Lord has a continual care to conduct his children, that is such as are in charity ; making them walk before him, reaching them his hand in difficulties, and bearing them himself in such travails, as he sees otherwise insupportable unto them.   This he declared by Isaias saying : *I am the Lord thy God, who take thee by the hand, and say to thee : fear not, I have helped thee.** So that with a good heart we must have a firm confidence in God, and his assistance, for if we fail not to second his grace, he will accomplish in us the good work of our salvation, which he also began, working in us *both to will and to accomplish,*† as the holy Council of Trent assures us.

In this conduct which the heavenly sweetness makes of our souls, from their entry into charity until their final perfection, which is not finished but in the hour of death, consists the great gift of perseverance, to which our Saviour attaches the greatest gift of eternal glory, according to his saying : *He that shall persevere unto the end, he shall be saved :*‡ for this gift is no other thing than the combination and sequence of the various helps, solaces and succours, whereby we continue in the love of God to the end : as the education, bringing up and supporting of a child is no other thing, than the many cares, aids, succours, and other offices necessary to a child, exercised and continued towards him till he grow to years in which he no longer needs them.

But the continuance of succours and helps is not equal in all those that persevere.   In some it is short ; as in such as were converted a little before their death : so it happened to the Good Thief ; so to that officer, who seeing the constancy of S. James

---

* Is. xli. 13.   † Phil. ii. 13.   ‡ Matt. x. 22.

made forthwith profession of faith, and became a companion of the martyrdom of this great Apostle ; so to the blessed gaoler who guarded the forty martyrs at Sebaste, who seeing one of them lose courage, and forsake the crown of martyrdom, put himself in his place and became Christian, martyr and glorious all at once; so to the notary of whom mention is made in the life of S. Antony of Padua, who having all his life been a false villain yet died a martyr : and so it happened to a thousand others of whom we have seen and read that they died well, after an ill-spent life. As for these, they stand not in need of a great variety of succours, but unless some great temptation cross their way, they can make this short perseverance solely by the charity given them, and by the aids by which they were converted. For they arrive at the port without voyaging, and finish their pilgrimage in a single leap, which the powerful mercy of God makes them take so opportunely that their enemies see them triumph before seeing them fight : so that their conversion and perseverance are almost the same thing. And if we would speak with exact propriety, the grace which they received of God whereby they attained as soon the issue, as the beginning of their course, cannot well be termed perseverance, though all the same, because actually it holds the place of perseverance in giving salvation, we comprehend it under the name of perseverance. In others, on the contrary, perseverance is longer, as in S. Anne the prophetess, in S. John the Evangelist, S. Paul the first hermit, S. Hilarion, S. Romuald, S. Francis of Paula;—and they stood in need of a thousand sorts of different assistances, according to the variety of the adventures of their pilgrimage and the length of it.

But in any case, perseverance is the most desirable gift we can hope for in this life, and the one which, as the Council of Trent says, we cannot have but from the hand of God, who alone can assure him that stands, and help him up that falls : wherefore we must incessantly demand it, making use of the means which Our Saviour has taught us to the obtaining of it ; prayer, fasting, alms-deeds, frequenting the sacraments, intercourse with the good, the hearing and reading of holy words.

Now since the gift of prayer and devotion is liberally granted to all those who sincerely will to consent to divine inspirations, it is consequently in our power to persevere. Not of course that I mean to say that our perseverance has its origin from our power, for on the contrary I know it springs from God's mercy, whose most precious gift it is, but I mean that though it does not come from our power, yet it comes within our power, by means of our will, which we cannot deny to be in our power: for though God's grace is necessary for us, to will to persevere, yet is this will in our power, because heavenly grace is never wanting to our will, and our will is not wanting to our power. And indeed according to the great S. Bernard's opinion, we may all truly say with the Apostle that: *Neither death, nor life, nor Angels, nor principalities, nor powers, nor things present, nor things to come, nor might, nor height, nor depth, nor any other creature, shall be able to separate us from the love of God, which is in Christ Jesus Our Lord.** Yes, indeed, for no creature can take us away by force from this holy love; we only can forsake and abandon it by our own will, except for which there is nothing to be feared in this matter.

So, Theotimus, following the advice of the holy Council, we ought to place our whole hope in God, who will perfect the work of our salvation which he has begun in us, if we be not wanting to his grace: for we are not to think that he who said to the paralytic: Go, and do not will to sin again:† gave him not also power to avoid that willing which he forbade him: and surely he would never exhort the faithful to persevere, if he were not ready to furnish them with the power. *Be thou faithful until death,* said he to the bishop of Smyrna, *and I will give thee the crown of life.‡ Watch ye, stand fast in the faith, do manfully, and be strengthened. Let all your actions be done in charity.§ So run that you may obtain.‖* We must often then with the great King demand of God the heavenly gift of perseverance, and hope that he will grant it us. *Cast me not off in the time of old age; when my strength shall fail, do not thou forsake me.¶*

---

* Rom. viii. 38–9   † John v. 14.   ‡ Apoc. ii. 10.
§ 1 Cor. xvi. 13.   ‖ 1 Cor. ix. 24.   ¶ Ps. lxx. 9.

CHAPTER V.

THAT THE HAPPINESS OF DYING IN HEAVENLY CHARITY IS A SPECIAL GIFT OF GOD.

In fine, the heavenly King having brought the soul which he loves to the end of this life, he assists her also in her blessed departure, by which he draws her to the marriage-bed of eternal glory, which is the delicious fruit of holy perseverance. And then, dear Theotimus, this soul, wholly ravished with the love of her well-beloved, putting before her eyes the multitude of favours and succours wherewith she was prevented and helped while she was yet in her pilgrimage, incessantly kisses this sweet helping hand, which conducted, drew and supported her in the way; and confesses, that it is of this divine Saviour that she holds her felicity, seeing he has done for her all that the patriarch Jacob wished for his journey, when he had seen the ladder to heaven. O Lord, she then says, thou wast with me, and didst guide me in the way by which I came. Thou didst feed me with the bread of thy sacraments, thou didst clothe me with the wedding garment of charity, thou hast happily conducted me to this mansion of glory, which is thy house, O my eternal Father. Oh! what remains, O Lord, save that I should protest that thou art my God for ever and ever! Amen.

Thou hast held me by my right hand; and by thy will thou hast conducted me, and with thy glory thou hast received me.* Such then is the order of our journey to eternal life, for the accomplishment of which the divine providence ordained from all eternity the number, distinction and succession of graces necessary to it, with their dependence on one another.

He willed, first, with a true will, that even after the sin of Adam all men should be saved, but upon terms and by means agreeable to the condition of their nature, which is endowed with free-will; that is to say he willed the salvation of all those who would contribute their consent, to the graces and favours which he would prepare, offer and distribute to this end.

* Ps. lxxii. 24.

Now, amongst these favours, his will was that vocation should be the first, and that it should be so accommodated to our liberty that we might at our pleasure accept or reject it: and such as he saw would receive it, he would furnish with the sacred motions of penitence, and to those who would second these motions he determined to give charity, those again who were in charity, he purposed to supply with the helps necessary to persevere, and to such as should make use of these divine helps he resolved to impart final perseverance, and the glorious felicity of his eternal love.

And thus we may give account of the order which is found in the effects of that Providence which regards our salvation, descending from the first to the last, that is from the fruit, which is glory, to the root of this fair tree, which is Our Saviour's redemption. For the divine goodness gives glory after merits, merits after charity, charity after penitence, penitence after obedience to vocation, obedience to vocation after vocation itself, vocation after Our Saviour's redemption, on which rests all this mystical ladder of the great Jacob, as well at its heavenly end, since it rests in the bosom of the eternal Father, in which he receives and glorifies the elect, as also at its earthly end, since it is planted upon the bosom and pierced side of Our Saviour, who for this cause died upon Mount Calvary.

And that this order of the effects of Providence was thus ordained, with the same dependence which they have on one another in the eternal will of God, holy Church, in the preface of one of her solemn prayers, witnesses in these words: " O eternal and Almighty God, who art Lord of the living and the dead, and art merciful to all those who thou foreknowest will be thine by faith and good works :" as though she were declaring that glory, which is the crown and the fruit of God's mercy towards men, has only been ordained for those, of whom the divine wisdom has foreseen that in the future, obeying the vocation, they will attain the living faith which works by charity.

Finally, all these effects have an absolute dependence on Our Saviour's redemption, who merited them for us in rigour of justice by the loving obedience which he exercised even till death and the death of the cross, which is the root of all the graces which we receive; we who are the spiritual grafts engrafted on his stock. If being engrafted we remain in him, we shall certainly bear, by the life of grace which he will communicate unto us, the fruit of glory prepared for us. But if we prove broken sprigs and grafts upon this tree, that is, if by resistance we interrupt the progress and break the connection of the effects of his clemency, it will not be strange, if in the end we be wholly cut off, and be thrown into eternal fire, as fruitless branches.

God, doubtless, prepared heaven for those only who he foresaw would be his. Let us be his then, Theotimus, by faith and works, and he will be ours by glory. Now it is in our power to be his: for though it be a gift of God to be God's, yet is it a gift which God denies no one, but offers to all, to give it to such as freely consent to receive it.

But mark, I pray you, Theotimus, how ardently God desires we should be his, since to this end he has made himself entirely ours; bestowing upon us his death and his life; his life, to exempt us from eternal death, his death, to possess us of eternal life. Let us remain therefore in peace and serve God, to be his in this mortal life, and still more his in the eternal.

CHAPTER VI.

THAT WE CANNOT ATTAIN TO PERFECT UNION WITH GOD IN THIS MORTAL LIFE.

ALL the rivers flow incessantly, and, as the wise man says: *Unto the place from whence they come they return to flow again.** The sea which is the place whence they spring, is also the place of their final repose; all their motion tends no farther than to unite themselves to their fountain. "O God," says S. Augustine, "thou hast created my heart for thyself, and it can never repose but in thee." *For what have I in heaven, and besides thee what do I desire upon earth? Thou art the God of my heart, and the*

Eccles. i. 7.

God that is my portion for ever.*   Still the union which our
heart aspires to cannot attain to its perfection in this mortal life;
we can commence our loves in this, but we can consummate them
only in the other.

The heavenly Spouse makes a delicate expression of this. *I
found him whom my soul loveth*, says she, *I held him, and I will
not let him go, till I bring him into my mother's house, and into the
chamber of her that bore me.*† She finds him then, this well-
beloved, for he makes her feel his presence by a thousand consolations; she holds him, for these feelings cause in her strong
affections, by which she clasps and embraces him, protesting
that she will never let him go,—O no! for these affections turn
into eternal resolutions; yet she cannot consider that she kisses
him with the nuptial kiss till she meet with him in her mother's
house, which is the heavenly Jerusalem, as S. Paul says. But
see, Theotimus, how this spouse thinks of nothing less than of
keeping her beloved at her mercy as a slave of love; whence she
imagines to herself that it is hers to lead him at her will, and to
introduce him into her mother's happy abode; though in reality
it is she who must be conducted thither by him, as was Rebecca
into Sara's chamber by her dear Isaac. The spirit urged by
amorous passion always gives itself a little advantage over what
it loves; and the spouse himself confesses: *Thou hast wounded
my heart, my sister, my spouse, thou hast wounded my heart with
one of thy eyes, and with one hair of thy neck:*‡ acknowledging
himself her prisoner by love.

This perfect conjunction then of the soul with God, shall only
be in heaven, where, as the Apocalypse says, the Lamb's marriage
feast shall be made. In this mortal life the soul is truly espoused
and betrothed to the immaculate Lamb, but not as yet married
to him: the troth is plighted, and promise given, but the execution
of the marriage is deferred: so that we have always time, though
never reason, to withdraw from it; our faithful spouse never
abandons us unless we oblige him to it by our disloyalty and
unfaithfulness. But in heaven the marriage of this divine union
being celebrated, the bond which ties our hearts to their sovereign
principle shall be eternally indissoluble.

* Ps. lxxii. 25-6.   † Cant. iii. 4.   ‡ *Ibid.* iv. 9.

It is true, Theotimus, that while we await this great kiss of indissoluble union which we shall receive from the spouse there above in glory, he gives us some kisses by a thousand feelings of his delightful presence : for unless the soul were kissed she would not be drawn, nor would she run in the odour of the beloved's perfumes. Whence, according to the original Hebrew text and the Seventy interpreters, she desires many kisses. *Let him kiss me*, says she, *with the kisses of his mouth.* But because these little kisses of this present life all refer to the eternal kiss of the life to come, the sacred Vulgate edition has holily reduced the kisses of grace to that of glory, expressing the desires of the spouse in this manner : *Let him kiss me with the kiss of his mouth,** as though she said : of all the kisses, of all the favours that the friend of my heart, or the heart of my soul has provided for me, ah ! I only breathe after and aspire to this great and solemn marriage-kiss which remains for ever, and in comparison of which the other kisses deserve not the name of kisses, being rather signs of the future union between my beloved and me than union itself.

CHAPTER VII.

THAT THE CHARITY OF SAINTS IN THIS MORTAL LIFE EQUALS, YEA SOMETIMES SURPASSES, THAT OF THE BLESSED.

WHEN after the labours and dangers of this mortal life, good souls arrive at the port of the eternal, they ascend to the highest and utmost degree of love to which they can attain ; and this final increase being bestowed upon them in recompense of their merits, it is distributed to them, not only in good measure, but *in a measure which is pressed down and shaken together and running over*,† as Our Saviour says ; so that the love which is given for reward is greater in every one than that which was given for meriting.

Now, not only shall each one in particular have a greater love

* Cant. i. 1.   † Luke vi. 38.

in heaven than ever he had on earth, but the exercise of the
least charity in heaven, shall be much more happy and excellent, generally speaking, than that of the greatest which is, or
has been, or shall be, in this failing life : for there above, all the
saints incessantly, without any intermission, exercise love ; while
here below God's greatest servants, drawn away and tyrannized
over by the necessities of this dying life, are forced to suffer a
thousand and a thousand distractions, which often take them off
the practice of holy love.

In heaven, Theotimus, the loving attention of the blessed is
firm, constant, inviolable, and cannot perish or decrease ; their
intention is pure and freed from all mixture of any inferior intention : in short, this felicity of seeing God clearly and loving
him unchangeably is incomparable.   And who would ever equal
the pleasure, if there be any, of living amidst the perils, the
continual tempests, the perpetual agitations and viscissitudes
which have to be gone through on sea, with the contentment
there is of being in a royal palace, where all things are at every
wish, yea where delights incomparably surpass every wish ?

There is then more content, sweetness and perfection in the
exercise of sacred love amongst the inhabitants of heaven, than
amongst the pilgrims of this miserable earth.   Yet still there
have been some so happy in their pilgrimage that their charity
has been greater than that of many saints already enjoying the
eternal fatherland : for certainly it were strange if the charity
of the great S. John, of the Apostles and Apostolic men, were
not greater, even while they were detained here below, than
that of little children, who, dying simply with the grace of
baptism, enjoy immortal glory.

It is not usual for shepherds to be more valiant than soldiers ;
and yet David, when a little shepherd, coming to the army of
Israel, while he found every one more expert in the use of arms
than himself, yet he was more valiant than all.   So it is not
an ordinary thing for mortals to have more charity than the
immortals, and yet there have been some mortals, inferior
to the immortals in the exercise of love, who, notwithstanding,
have surpassed them in charity and the habit of love.   And
as, when comparing hot iron and a burning lamp, we say the

iron has more fire and heat, the lamp more flame and light; so if we parallel a child in glory with S. John while yet prisoner, or S. Paul yet captive, we must say that the child in heaven has more brightness and light in the understanding, more flame and exercise of love in the will, but that S. John or S. Paul had even on earth more fire of charity, and heat of love.

CHAPTER VIII.

OF THE INCOMPARABLE LOVE WHICH THE MOTHER OF GOD, OUR BLESSED LADY, HAD.

BUT always and everywhere, when I make comparisons, I intend not to speak of the most holy virgin-mother, Our Blessed Lady. O my God—no indeed! For she is the daughter of incomparable dilection, the one only dove, the all-perfect spouse. Of this heavenly Queen, from my heart I pronounce this thought, amorous but true, that, at least towards the end of her mortal days, her charity surpassed that of the Seraphim, for *many daughters have gathered together riches : thou hast surpassed them all.** The Saints and Angels are but compared to stars, and the first of them to the fairest of the stars : but she is fair as the moon, as easy to be chosen and discerned from all the Saints as the sun from the stars. And going on further I think again that as the charity of this Mother of love excels in perfection that of all the Saints in heaven, so did she exercise it more perfectly, I say even in this mortal life. She never sinned venially, as the church considers ; she had then no change nor delay in the way of love, but by a perpetual advancement ascended from love to love. She never felt any contradiction from the sensual appetite, and therefore her love, as a true Solomon, reigned peaceably in her soul and made all its acts at its pleasure. The virginity of her heart and body was more worthy and honourable than that of the Angels. So that her spirit, not divided or separated, as S. Paul says, *was solicitous for the things that belong to the Lord how* it *might please God.†* And, in fine, maternal

* Prov. xxxi. 29.   † 1 Cor. vii. 32.

love, the most pressing, the most active and the most ardent of all, what must it not have worked in the heart of such a Mother and for the heart of such a Son?

Ah! do not say, I pray you, that this virgin was subject to sleep; no, say not this to me, Theotimus: for do you not see that her sleep is a sleep of love? So that even her spouse wishes that she should sleep as long as she pleases. Ah! take heed, *I adjure you*, says he, *that you stir not up nor make the beloved to awake till she please.** No, Theotimus, this heavenly Queen never slept but with love, since she never gave repose to her precious body, but to reinvigorate it, the better afterwards to serve her God, which is certainly a most excellent act of charity. For, as the great S. Augustine says, charity obliges us to love our bodies properly, insomuch as they are necessary to good works, as they make a part of our person, and as they shall be sharers in our eternal felicity. In good truth, a Christian is to love his body as a living image of Our Saviour incarnate, as having issued from the same stock, and consequently belonging to him in parentage and consanguinity; especially after we have renewed the alliance, by the real reception of the divine body of Our Redeemer, in the most adorable sacrament of the Eucharist, and when by Baptism, Confirmation and other Sacraments we have dedicated and consecrated ourselves to the sovereign goodness.

But as to the Blessed Virgin,—O God, with what devotion must she have loved her virginal body! Not only because it was a sweet, humble, pure body, obedient to divine love, and wholly embalmed with a thousand sweetnesses, but also because it was the living source of Our Saviour's, and belonged so strictly to him, by an incomparable appurtenance. For which cause when she placed her angelic body in the repose of sleep: Repose then now, would she say, O Tabernacle of Alliance, Ark of Sanctity, Throne of the Divinity, ease thyself a little of thy weariness, and repair thy forces, by this sweet tranquillity.

Besides, dear Theotimus, do you not know that bad dreams, voluntarily procured by the depraved thoughts of the day, are

* Cant. ii. 7.

in some sort sins, inasmuch as they are consequences and execution of the malice preceding? Even so the dreams which proceed from the holy affections of our waking time, are reputed virtuous and holy. O God! Theotimus, what a consolation it is to hear S. Chrysostom recounting on a certain day to his people the vehemence of his love towards them. " The necessity of sleep," said he, " pressing our eyelids, the tyranny of our love towards you excites the eyes of our mind : and many a time while I sleep methinks I speak unto you, for the soul is wont to see in a dream by imagination what she thinks in the daytime. Thus while we see you not with the eyes of the flesh, we see you with the eyes of charity." O sweet Jesus! what dreams must thy most holy Mother have had when she slept, while her heart watched? Did she not dream that she had thee yet in her womb, or hanging at her sacred breasts and sweetly pressing those virginal lilies? Ah! what sweetness was in this soul. Perhaps she often dreamed that as Our Saviour had formerly slept in her bosom, as a tender lambkin upon the soft flank of its mother, so she slept in his pierced side, as a white dove in the cave of an assured rock : so that her sleep was wholly like to an ecstasy as regards the spirit, though as regards the body it was a sweet and grateful unwearying and rest. But if ever she dreamed, as did the ancient Joseph, of her future greatness, —when in heaven she should be *clothed with the sun, crowned with stars and having the moon under her feet,** that is, wholly environed with her Son's glory, crowned with that of the Saints, and having the universe under her—or if ever, like Jacob, she saw the progress and fruit of the redemption made by her Son, for the love of the angels and of men ;—Theotimus, who could ever imagine the immensity of so great delights? O what conferences with her dear child! What delights on every side!

But mark, I pray you, that I neither say nor mean to say that this privileged soul of the Mother of God was deprived of the use of reason in her sleep. Many are of opinion that Solomon in that beautiful dream, though really a dream, in which he demanded and received the gift of his incomparable

* Gen. xxxvii.; Apoc. xii. I.

wisdom, had the true use of his free-will, on account of the judicious eloquence of the discourse he made, of his choice full of discretion, and of the most excellent prayer which he used, the whole without any mixture of inconsistency or distraction of mind. But how much more probability is there then that the mother of the true Solomon had the use of reason in her sleep, that is to say, as Solomon himself makes her say, that her heart watched while she slept? Surely it was a far greater marvel that S. John had the exercise of reason in his mother's womb, and why then should we deny a less to her for whom, and to whom, God did more favours, than either he did or ever will do for all creatures besides?

To conclude, as the precious stone, *asbestos*, does by a peerless propriety preserve for ever the fire which it has conceived, so the Virgin Mother's heart remained perpetually inflamed with the holy love which she received of her Son: yet with this difference, that the fire of the asbestos, as it cannot be extinguished, so it cannot be augmented, but the Virgin's sacred flames, since they could neither perish, diminish, nor remain in the same state, never ceased to take incredible increase, even as far as heaven the place of their origin: so true it is that this Mother is the *Mother of fair love*, that is, as the most amiable, so the most loving, and as the most loving, so the most beloved Mother of this only Son; who again is the most amiable, most loving, and most beloved Son of this only Mother.

———

CHAPTER IX.

A PREPARATION FOR THE DISCOURSE ON THE UNION OF THE BLESSED WITH GOD.

THE triumphant love which the blessed in heaven exercise, consists in the final, invariable and eternal union of the soul with its God. But this union—what is it?

By how much more agreeable and excellent are the objects our senses meet with, so much more ardently and greedily they give themselves to the fruition of them. By how much more fair, delightful to the view, and duly set in light they are, so much the more eagerly and attentively does the eye regard them : and by how much more sweet and pleasant voices or music are, so much the more is the attention of the ear drawn to them. So that every object exercises a powerful but grateful violence upon the sense to which it belongs, a violence more or less strong as the excellence is greater or less ; provided always that it be proportionable to the capacity of the sense which desires to enjoy it ; for the eye which finds so much pleasure in light cannot, however, bear an extreme light, nor fix itself upon the sun, and be music never so sweet, if loud and too near, it importunes and offends our ears. Truth is the object of our understanding, which consequently has all its content in discovering and knowing the truth of things ; and according as truths are more excellent, so the understanding applies itself with more delight and attention to the consideration of them. How great was the pleasure, think you, Theotimus, of those ancient philosophers who had such an excellent knowledge of so many beautiful truths of Nature ? Verily they reputed all pleasures as nothing in comparison with their well-beloved philosophy, for which some of them quitted honours, others great riches, others their country : and there was such a one as deliberately plucked out his eyes, depriving himself for ever of the enjoyment of the fair and agreeable corporal light, that he might with more liberty apply himself to consider the truth of things by the light of the spirit. This we read of Democritus : so sweet is the knowledge of truth ! Hence Aristotle has very often said that human felicity and beatitude consists in wisdom, which is the knowledge of the eminent truths.

But when our spirit, raised above natural light, begins to see the sacred truths of faith, O God ! Theotimus, what joy ! The soul melts with pleasure, hearing the voice of her heavenly spouse, whom she finds more sweet and delicious then the honey of all human sciences.

God has imprinted upon all created things his traces, trail, or footsteps, so that the knowledge we have of his divine Majesty by creatures seems no other thing than the sight of the feet of

God, while in comparison of this, faith is a view of the very face of the divine Majesty. This we do not yet see in the clear day of glory, but as it were in the breaking of day ; as it happened to Jacob near to the ford of Jaboc; for though he saw not the angel with whom he wrestled, save in the weak light of daybreak, yet this was enough to make him cry out, ravished with delight : *I have seen God face to face, and my soul has been saved.** O ! how delightful is the holy light of faith, by which we know, with an unequalled certitude, not only the history of the beginning of creatures, and their true use, but even that of the eternal birth of the great and sovereign divine Word, for whom and by whom all has been made, and who with the Father and the Holy Ghost is one only God, most singular, most adorable, and blessed for ever and ever ! Amen. Ah ! says S. Jerome to his Paulinus : " The learned Plato never knew this, the eloquent Demosthenes was ignorant of it." *How sweet are thy words, O Lord, to my palate,* said that great king, *more than honey to my mouth !*† *Was not our burning within us, whilst he spoke in the way ?*‡ said those happy pilgrims of Emmaus, speaking of the flames of love with which they were touched by the word of faith. But if divine truths be so sweet, when proposed in the obscure light of faith, O God, what shall they be when we shall contemplate them in the light of the noonday of glory !

The Queen of Saba, who at the greatness of Solomon's renown had left all to go and see him, having arrived in his presence, and having heard the wonders of the wisdom which he poured out in his speeches, as one astonished and lost in admiration, cried out that what she had learnt by hearsay of this heavenly wisdom was not half the knowledge which sight and experience gave her.

Ah ! how beautiful and dear are the truths which faith discovers unto us by hearing ! But when having arrived in the heavenly Jerusalem, we shall see the great Solomon, the King of Glory, seated upon the thrown of his wisdom, manifesting by an incomprehensible brightness the wonders and eternal secrets

---

* Gen. xxxii. 30. † Ps. cxviii. 103. ‡ Luke xxiv. 32.

of his sovereign truth, with such light that our understanding will actually see what it had believed here below—Ah ! then, dearest Theotimus, what raptures ! what ecstasies ! what admiration ! what love ! what sweetness ! No, never (shall we say in this excess of sweetness) never could we have conceived that we should see truths so delightsome. We believed indeed all the glorious things that were said of thee, *O great city of God*, but we could not conceive the infinite greatness of the abysses of thy delights.

CHAPTER X.

THAT THE PRECEDING DESIRE WILL MUCH INCREASE THE UNION OF THE BLESSED WITH GOD.

THE desire which precedes enjoyment, sharpens and intensifies the feeling of it, and by how much the desire was more urgent and powerful, by so much more agreeable and delicious is the possession of the thing desired. Oh ! my dear Theotimus, what pleasure will man's heart take in seeing the face of the Divinity, a face so much desired, yea a face the only desire of our souls ? Our hearts have a thirst which cannot be quenched by the pleasures of this mortal life, whereof the most esteemed and highest prized if moderate do not satisfy us, and if extreme suffocate us. Yet we desire them always to be extreme, and they are never such without being excessive, insupportable, hurtful. We die of joy as well as of grief : yea, joy is more active to ruin us than grief. Alexander, having swallowed up, in effect or in hope, all this lower world, heard some base fellow say, that there were yet many other worlds, and like a little child, who will cry if one refuse him an apple, this Alexander, whom the world styles the great, more foolish notwithstanding than a little child, began bitterly to weep, because there was no likelihood that he should conquer the other worlds, not having as yet got the entire possession of this. He that did more fully enjoy the world than ever any other did, is yet so little satisfied with it that he weeps for sorrow that he cannot have the other worlds which the foolish persuasion of a wretched babbler made him imagine to exist. Tell me, I pray you, Theotimus, does he not show that the thirst of his heart cannot be slaked in this life, and that this world is not sufficient to quench it? O wonderful yet dear unrest of man's heart! Be, be ever, my soul, without any rest or tranquillity on this earth, till thou shalt have met with the fresh waters of the immortal life and the most holy Divinity, which alone can satisfy thy thirst and quiet thy desire.

Now, Theotimus, imagine to yourself with the Psalmist, that hart which, hard set by the hounds, has neither wind nor legs; how greedily he plunges himself into the waters which he panted after, and with what ardour he rolls into and buries himself in that element. One would think he would willingly be dissolved and converted into water, more fully to enjoy its coolness. Ah! what a union of our hearts shall there be with God there above in heaven, where, after these infinite desires of the true good never assuaged in this world, we shall find the living and powerful source thereof. Then, truly, as we see a hungry child closely fixed to his mother's breast, greedily press this dear fountain of most desired sweetness, so that one would think that either it would thrust itself into its mother's breast, or else suck and draw all that breast into itself; so our soul, panting with an extreme thirst for the true good, when she shall find that inexhaustible source in the Divinity,—O good God! what a holy and sweet ardour to be united and joined to the plentiful breasts of the All-goodness, either to be altogether absorbed in it, or to have it come entirely into us!

CHAPTER XI.

OF THE UNION OF THE BLESSED SPIRITS WITH GOD, IN THE VISION OF THE DIVINITY.

WHEN we look upon anything, though it is present to us, it is not itself united to our eyes, but only sends out to them a certain representation or picture of itself, which is called its *sensible species*, by means of which we see. So also when we contemplate or understand anything, that which we understand is not united to our understanding otherwise than by another representation and most delicate and spiritual image, which is called *intelligible species.* But further, these species, by how many windings and changes do they get to the understanding! They arrive at the exterior senses, thence pass to the interior, then to the imagination, then to the active understanding, and come at last to the passive understanding, to the end that passing through so many strainers and under so many files they may be purified, subtilised and perfected, and of sensible become intelligible.

Thus, Theotimus, we see and understand all that we see and understand in this mortal life, yea even things of faith ; for, as the mirror contains not the thing we see in it but only the representation and species of it (which representation, stayed by the mirror, produces another in the beholding eye), so the word of faith does not contain the things which it announces, but only represents them, and this representation of divine things which is in the word of faith produces another representation of them, which our understanding, helped by God's grace, accepts and receives as a representation of holy truth, and our will takes delight in it, and embraces it, as an honourable, profitable, lovely and excellent truth. Thus the truths signified in God's word are by it represented to the understanding as things expressed in the mirror are by the mirror represented to the eye : whence the great Apostle said that to believe is to *see as in a glass.**

But in heaven, Theotimus,—Ah! my God, what a favour !— The Divinity will unite itself to our understanding without the mediation of any species or representation at all, but it will itself apply and join itself to our understanding, making itself in such sort present unto it, that that inward presence shall be instead of a representation or species. O God! what sweetness shall it be for man's understanding to be united for ever to its sovereign object, receiving not its representation but its presence, not the picture or species, but the very essence of its divine truth and majesty. We shall be there as most happy

* 1 Cor. xiii. 12.

children of the divinity, and shall have the honour to be fed
with the divine substance itself, taken into our soul by the mouth
of our understanding, and what surpasses all sweetness is, that
as mothers are not contented with feeding their babes with
their milk, which is their own substance, if they do not also
put the breast into their mouth, that these may receive their
substance, not in a spoon or other instrument, but even in, and
by this same substance (so that this maternal substance serves
as well for food, as for a conduit to convey it to the dear little
suckling);—so God our Father is not contented to make us
receive his proper substance in our understanding, that is, to
make us see his divinity, but by an abyss of his sweetness, wills
himself to apply his substance to our soul, to the end that we
may no longer understand it by species or representation but in
itself and by itself; so that his fatherly and eternal substance
is both species and object to our understanding. Then these
divine promises shall be fulfilled in an excellent manner : *I will
lead her into the wilderness, and I will speak to her heart,** and
give her suck. *Rejoice with Jerusalem and be glad with her.
That you may suck and be filled with the breasts of her consolations,
that you may milk out, and flow with delights from the abundance
of her glory : you shall be carried at the breasts, and upon the
knees they shall caress you.†

Infinite bliss, Theotimus, and one which has not been promised
only, but of which we have a pledge in the Blessed Sacrament,
that perpetual feast of Divine Grace. For in it we receive the
blood of Our Saviour in his flesh, and his flesh in his blood;
his blood being applied unto us by means of his flesh, his substance by his substance to our very corporal mouth; that we may
know that so he will apply unto us his divine essence in the
eternal feast of his glory. True it is, this favour is done unto
us here really but covertly, under Sacramental species and
appearances, whereas in heaven, the Divinity will give himself
openly, and we shall see him face to face as he is.

* Osee. ii. 14.   † Is. lxvi. 10, 11, 12.

CHAPTER XII.

OF THE ETERNAL UNION OF THE BLESSED SPIRITS WITH GOD, IN THE VISION OF THE ETERNAL BIRTH OF THE SON OF GOD.

O HOLY and Divine Spirit, eternal Love of the Father and the Son, be propitious to mine infancy. Our understanding then shall see God, Theotimus; yes, it shall see God Himself face to face, contemplating with a view of true and real presence, the divine essence Itself, and in It, the infinite beauties thereof, all-power, all-goodness, all-wisdom, all-justice, and the rest of this abyss of perfections.

It shall see clearly then, shall this understanding, the infinite knowledge which God the Father had from all eternity of His own beauty, for the expression of which in Himself, He pronounced and said eternally the Word, the *Verbum,* or the most singular and most infinite speech and diction, which, comprising and representing all the perfection of the Father, can be but one same God, entirely one with Him, without division or separation. We shall thus then see that eternal and admirable generation of the Divine Word and Son, by which He was eternally born to the image and likeness of the Father, a lively and natural image and likeness, not representing any accidents or external thing ; since in God all is substance, nor can there be any accident, all is interior, nor can there be any exterior ; but an image representing the proper substance of the Father so perfectly, so naturally, so essentially and substantially, that therefore it can be no other thing than the same God with Him, without distinction or difference at all either in essence or substance, and with only the distinction of Persons. For how could this Divine Son be the true, truly perfect and truly natural image, resemblance and figure of the infinite beauty and substance of the Father, if this image did not represent absolutely to the life and according to nature, the infinite perfections of the Father ? And how could it infinitely represent infinite perfections if it were not itself infinitely perfect ? And how could it be infinitely perfect if it were not God, and how could it be God if it were not one same God with the Father ?

This Son then, the infinite image and figure of His infinite Father, is with His Father one sole, most unique, and infinite God, there being no difference of substance between Them, but only the distinction of persons. This distinction of persons, as it is certainly required, so also it is absolutely sufficient, to effect that the Father pronounces, and the Son is the Word pronounced; that the Father speaks, and the Son is the Word, or the diction; that the Father expresses, and the Son is the image, likeness or figure expressed, and, in short, that the Father is Father, and the Son, Son—two distinct persons, but one only Essence or Divinity; so that God Who is sole is not solitary, for He is sole in His most singular and simple Deity, yet is not solitary, because He is Father and Son in two persons. O Theotimus, what joy, what jubilee to celebrate this eternal birth, kept *in the brightness of the Saints,** to celebrate it in seeing it, and to see it in celebrating it!

The most sweet S. Bernard, as yet a little boy at Chastillon-sur-Seine, was waiting in Church on Christmas night for the divine office to begin, and whilst waiting the poor child fell into a light slumber, during which (O God what sweetness!) he saw in spirit, yet in a vision very distinct and clear, how the Son of God, having espoused human nature, and becoming a little child in His Mother's most pure womb, was with a humble sweetness mingled with a celestial majesty, virginally born of her:—*As a bridegroom coming out of his bride-chamber* :†—a vision, Theotimus, which so replenished the loving heart of the little Bernard with gladness, jubilation and spiritual delights, that he had all his life an extreme sense of it, and therefore, though afterwards as a sacred bee he ever culled out of all the divine mysteries the honey of a thousand sweet and heavenly consolations, yet had he a more particular sweetness in the solemnity of the Nativity, and spoke with a singular relish of this birth of his Master. But Ah! I beseech thee, Theotimus, if a mystical and imaginary vision of the temporal and human birth of the Son of God, by which he proceeded man from a woman, virgin from a virgin, ravishes and so highly delights a

---

* Ps. cix. 3.   † Ps. xviii. 6.

child's heart, what shall it be when our spirits, gloriously illuminated with the light of glory, shall see this eternal birth by which the Son proceeds, God from God, Light from Light, true God from true God, divinely and eternally! Then shall our spirit be joined by an incomprehensible complacency to this object of delight, and by an unchangeable attention remain united to it for ever.

CHAPTER XIII.

OF THE UNION OF THE BLESSED WITH GOD IN THE VISION OF THE PRODUCTION OF THE HOLY GHOST.

THE eternal Father seeing the infinite goodness and beauty of His own essence, so perfectly, essentially and substantially expressed in His Son, and the Son seeing reciprocally that His same essence, goodness and beauty is originally in His Father as in its source and fountain, ah! can it possibly be that this Divine Father and His Son should not mutually love one another with an infinite love, since Their will by which They love, and Their goodness for which They love are infinite in each of Them.

Love not finding us equal, equalizes us, not finding us united, unites us. Now the Father and the Son finding Themselves not only equal and united, but even one same God, one same goodness, one same essence and one same unity, how much must They needs love one another. But this love does not act like the love which intellectual creatures have amongst themselves, or towards their Creator; for created love is exercised by many and various movements, aspirations, unions and joinings which immediately succeed one another, and make a continuation of love with a grateful vicissitude of spiritual movements, but the divine love of the eternal Father towards His Son is practised in one only spiration (*souspir*) mutually from Them both, Who in this sort remain united and joined together. Yes, Theotimus; for the goodness of the Father and Son being but one sole most perfectly singular goodness, common to Them both, the love of this goodness can be but one only love; for though there be two lovers, to wit, the Father and the Son, yet seeing it is only Their most singular goodness common to Them both which is loved, and Their most unique will which loves, it is therefore but one love exercised by one amorous spiration. The Father breathes this love and so does the Son ; but because the Father only breathes this love by means of the same will and for the same goodness which is equally and singularly in Him and His Son : the Son again only breathes this spiration of love for this same goodness and by this same will,—therefore this spiration of love is but one spiration, or one only spirit breathed out by two breathers.

And because the Father and the Son Who breathe, have an infinite essence and will by which They breathe, and because the goodness for which They breathe is infinite, it is impossible Their breathing should not be infinite ; and forasmuch as it cannot be infinite without being God, therefore this Spirit breathed from the Father and the Son is true God : and since there neither is, nor can be, more than one only God, He is one only true God with the Father and the Son. Moreover, as this love is an act which proceeds mutually from the Father and the Son, it can neither be the Father, nor the Son, from whom it proceeds, though it has the same goodness and substance of the Father and the Son, but must necessarily be a third person, Who with the Father and the Son is one only God. And because this love is produced by manner of breathings or spirations, it is called the Holy Spirit.

Now, Theotimus, King David, describing the sweetness of the friendship of God's servants, cries out : *Behold how good and how pleasant it is for brethren to dwell together in unity : like the precious ointment on the head, that ran down upon the beard, the beard of Aaron, which ran down to the skirt of his garment : as the dew of Hermon, which descendeth upon Mount Sion.**

But, O God ! if human friendship be so agreeably lovely, and spread so delicious an odour on them that contemplate it, what shall it be, my well-beloved Theotimus, to behold the sacred

* Ps. cxxxii.

exercise of mutual love between the eternal Father and the Son. S. Gregory Nazianzen recounts that the incomparable love which existed between him and S. Basil the Great was famous all through Greece, and Tertullian testifies, that the Pagans admired the more than brotherly love which reigned amongst the primitive Christians. Oh! with what celebration and solemnity, with what praises and benedictions, should be kept, with what admirations should be honoured and loved, the eternal and sovereign friendship of the Father and the Son! What is there to be loved and desired if friendship is not? And if friendship is to be loved and desired, what friendship can be so in comparison with that infinite friendship which is between the Father and the Son, and Which is one same most sole God with them? Our heart, Theotimus, will sink lost in love, through admiration of the beauty and sweetness of the love, that this eternal Father and this incomprehensible Son practise divinely and eternally.

CHAPTER XIV.

THAT THE HOLY LIGHT OF GLORY WILL SERVE FOR THE UNION OF THE BLESSED SPIRITS WITH GOD.

THE created understanding then shall see the divine essence, without any medium of species or representation; yet not without a certain excellent light which disposes, elevates, and strengthens it, to raise its view so high, and to an object so sublime and resplendent. For as the owl has a sight strong enough to bear the sombre light of a clear night, but not strong enough to stand the mid-day light, which is too brilliant to be borne by eyes so dim and weak; so our understanding, which is strong enough to consider natural truths by its discourse, yea even the supernatural things of grace by the light of faith, is not yet able, by the light of either nature or faith, to attain unto the view of the divine substance in itself. Wherefore the sweetness of the eternal wisdom determined not to apply His essence to our understanding till He had prepared, strengthened and fitted it to receive a sight so eminent, and so disproportionate to its natural condition as is the view of the Divinity. So the sun, the sovereign object of our corporal eyes amongst natural things, does not present itself unto our view without sending first its rays, by means whereof we may be able to see it, so that we only see it by its light.   Yet there is a difference between the rays which the sun casts upon our corporal eyes and the light which God will create in our understandings in heaven : for the sun's rays do not fortify our corporal eyes when they are weak and unable to see, but rather blind them, dazzling and confounding their infirm vision : whereas, on the contrary, this sacred light of glory, finding our understandings unapt and unable to behold the Divinity, raises, strengthens and perfects them so excellently, that by an incomprehensible marvel they behold and contemplate the abyss of the divine brightness in itself with a fixed and direct gaze, not being dazzled or beaten back by the infinite greatness of its splendour.

In like manner, therefore, as God has given us the light of reason, by which we may know Him as Author of nature, and the light of faith by which we consider Him as source of grace, so will He bestow upon us the light of glory by which we shall contemplate Him as the fountain of beatitude and eternal life : but a fountain, Theotimus, which we shall not contemplate afar off as we do now by faith, but which we shall see by the light of glory while plunged and swallowed up in it.

Divers, who, fishing for precious stones, go down into the water, take oil, says Pliny, in their mouths, that by scattering it, they may have more light to see in the waters where they swim.   Theotimus, a blessed soul having entered and plunged into the ocean of the divine essence, God will pour into its understanding the sacred light of glory, which will enlighten it in this abyss of inaccessible light, that so by the light of glory we may see the light of the Divinity.   *For with Thee is the fountain of life; and in Thy light we shall see light.**

* Ps. xxxv. 10.

CHAPTER XV.

THAT THERE SHALL BE DIFFERENT DEGREES OF THE UNION OF THE BLESSED WITH GOD.

Now this light of glory, Theotimus, shall be the measure of the sight and centemplation of the Blessed; and according as we shall have less or more of this holy splendour, we shall see more or less clearly, and consequently with more or less happiness, the most holy Divinity, which as it is beholden diversely so it will make us diversely glorious. All the spirits indeed in this heavenly Paradise see all the divine essence, yet it is not seen and cannot be seen entirely by any one of them or by all of them together. No, Theotimus, for God being most singularly one, and most simply indivisible, we cannot see Him without seeing Him all: but being infinite, without limit, without bounds or measure at all in His perfection, there neither is, nor can be, any capacity out of Himself which can ever totally comprehend or penetrate the infinity of His goodness, infinitely essential and essentially infinite.

This created light of the visible sun, which is limited and finite, is in such sort all seen by those that behold it that it is never totally seen by any one of them nor by all together. It is in a manner so with all our senses. Amongst many that hear excellent music, though all of them hear it all, yet some hear it not so well, nor with so much delight as others, according as their ears are more or less delicate. The manna was all tasted by each one that ate it, yet differently, according to the different appetites of those who ate it, and was never wholly tasted, for it had more tastes of different kinds than the Israelites had varieties of tasting power. Theotimus, we shall see and taste in heaven all the Divinity, but no one of the Blessed nor all together shall ever see or taste it totally. This infinite Divinity shall still have infinitely more excellences than we sufficiency and capacity; and we shall have an unspeakable content to know that after we have satiated all the desires of our heart, and fully replenished its capacity in the fruition of the infinite good which is God, nevertheless there will remain in this infinity, infinite perfections to be seen, enjoyed and possessed, which His divine Majesty knows and sees, it alone comprehending itself.

So fishes enjoy the incredible vastness of the ocean; but not any fish, nor yet all the multitude of fishes, ever saw all the shores of the sea or wetted their fins in all its waters. Birds sport in the open air at their pleasure, but not any bird, nor yet all the flocks of birds together, did ever beat with their wings all the regions of the air, or arrive at the supreme region of the same. Ah! Theotimus, our souls shall freely and according to the full extent of their wishes swim in the ocean and soar in the air of the Divinity, rejoicing eternally to see that this air is so infinite, this ocean so vast, that it cannot be measured by their wings, and that enjoying without reserve or exception all this infinite abyss of the Divinity, yet shall they never be able to equalize their fruition to this infinity, which remains still infinitely infinite beyond their capacity.

And at this the Blessed Spirits are ravished with two admirations, first for the infinite beauty which they contemplate, secondly for the abyss of the infinity which remains to be seen in this same beauty. O God! how admirable is that which they see! But, O God! how much more admirable is that which they see not! And yet, Theotimus, since the most sacred beauty which they see is infinite, it entirely satisfies and satiates them, and being content to enjoy it according to the rank which they hold in heaven, because God's most amiable providence has so determined, they convert the knowledge they have of not possessing and of not being able totally to possess their object, into a simple complacency of admiration, in which they have a sovereign joy to see that the beauty they love is so infinite that it cannot be totally known but by itself. For in this consists the Divinity of this infinite beauty or the beauty of this infinite Divinity.

BOOK IV.

DECAY AND RUIN OF CHARITY.

———◆◆◆———

CHAPTER I.

THAT AS LONG AS WE ARE IN THIS MORTAL LIFE WE MAY LOSE THE LOVE OF GOD.

WE do not now speak of those great elect souls whom God by a most special favour so maintains and confirms in his love, that they run no hazard of losing it. We speak for the rest of mortals, to whom the Holy Ghost addresses these warnings: *He that thinketh himself to stand, let him take heed lest he fall.** *Hold fast that which thou hast, that no man take thy crown.*† *Labour the more that by good works you may make sure your calling and election.*‡ Whence he makes them make this prayer: *Cast me not away from thy face; and take not thy holy spirit from me.*§ *And lead us not into temptation:* that they may *work out their salvation with* a holy *trembling*, and a sacred *fear,*‖ knowing that they are not more constant and strong to preserve God's love than were the first angel with his followers and Judas, who receiving it lost it, and losing it lost themselves for ever; nor than Solomon, who, having once left it, holds the whole world in doubt of his damnation; nor than Adam and Eve, David, S. Peter, who being children of salvation, fell yet for a space from the love without which there is no salvation. Alas! Theotimus, who shall then have assurance of preserving

---

* I Cor. x. 12.   † Apoc. iii. 11.   ‡ 2 Peter i. 10.
          § Ps. l. 13.   ‖ Phil. ii. 12.

sacred love in the navigation of this mortal life, since, as well on earth as in heaven, so many persons of incomparable dignity have suffered such cruel shipwrecks?

But, O eternal God! how is it possible, will one say, that a soul that has the love of God can ever lose it; for where love is it resists sin, and how comes it to pass then that sin gets entry there, since *love is strong as death, hard* in fight *as hell?** How can the forces of death or hell, that is, of sins, vanquish love, which at least equals them in strength, and surpasses them in helps and in right? And how can it be that a reasonable soul which has once relished so great a sweetness as is that of heavenly love, can ever willingly swallow the bitter waters of offence? Children, though children, being fed with milk, abhor the bitterness of wormwood and of aloes, and cry themselves into convulsions when they are made to take them. Ah! then, O true God! Theotimus, how can the soul, once joined to the goodness of the Creator, forsake him to follow the vanity of the creature?

My dear Theotimus, *the heavens themselves are astonished, their gates become desolate* with fear,† and the angels of peace are lost in amazement at this prodigious misery of man's heart, abandoning a good so worthy of love, to join itself to things so unworthy. But have you never seen that little marvel which every one knows, though every one does not know the reason of it? When a very full barrel is broached, the wine will not run unless it have air given from above, which yet happens not to barrels in which there is already a void, for they are no sooner open but the wine runs. Truly in this mortal life though our souls abound with heavenly love yet they are never so full of it but that by temptation this love may depart: in heaven, however, when the sweetness of God's beauty shall occupy all our understanding, and the delights of his goodness shall wholly satiate our wills, so that there shall be nothing which the fulness of his love shall not replenish, no object, though it penetrate even to our hearts, can ever draw or make run out one sole drop of the precious liquor of our heavenly love. And to expect to give air above, that is, to deceive

* Cant. viii. 6. † Jer. ii. 12.

or surprise the understanding, shall no more be possible; for it shall be immovable in the apprehension of the sovereign truth.

So wine well purified and separated from the lees is easily kept from turning and getting thick; that which is on its lees is in continual danger; and we, so long as we are in this world, have our souls upon the lees or tartar of a thousand moods and miseries, and consequently easy to change and spoil in their love. But once in heaven, where, as in the great feast described by Isaias, we shall have wine purified from all lees, we shall be no longer subject to change, but be inseparably united by love to our sovereign good. Here in the twilight of dawning we are afraid that in lieu of the spouse we may meet some other object, which may engage and deceive us, but when we shall find Him above, where He feeds and reposes in the mid-day, there will be no chance of being deceived, for His light will be too clear, and His sweetness will bind us so closely to His goodness, that we shall no longer have the power to will to unfasten ourselves.

We are like the coral, which in the sea, the place of its origin, is a pale-green, weak, drooping and pliable tree, but being drawn from the bottom of the sea, as from its mother's womb, it becomes almost a stone, firm and unbending, while it changes its pale-green into a lively red. For so we being as yet amidst the sea of this world the place of our birth, are subject to extreme vicissitudes, liable to be bent on every side; to the right, which is heavenly love, by inspiration, to the left, which is earthly love, by temptation. But if, being once drawn out of this mortality, we have changed the pale-green of our trembling hopes into the bright red of assured fruition, we shall never more be movable, but make a settled abode for ever in eternal love.

It is impossible to see the Divinity and not love it, but here below where we do not see it, but only have a glimpse of it through the clouds of faith, as in a mirror, our knowledge is not yet so perfect as not to leave an opening for the surprises of other objects and apparent goods, which through the obscurities which are mixed with the certainty and verity of faith, steal in unperceived, like little fox cubs, and demolish our flourishing vineyard. To conclude, Theotimus, when we have charity our free-will is clothed with her wedding garment, which, as she can still keep it on if she please by well-doing, so she can put off if she please by offending.

———

CHAPTER II.

HOW THE SOUL GROWS COLD IN HOLY LOVE.

THE soul is often grieved and troubled in the body, even so far as to desert many of its members, which remain deprived of motion and feeling, while it never forsakes the heart, wherein it fully remains till the very end of life. So charity is sometimes weakened and depressed in the affections till it seems to be scarcely in exercise at all, and yet it remains entire in the supreme region of the soul. This happens when, under the multitude of venial sins as under ashes, the fire of holy love remains covered, and its flame smothered, though it is not dead or extinguished. For as the presence of the diamond hinders the exercise and action of that property which the adamant has of drawing iron, and yet does not take it away, as it acts immediately this obstacle is removed, so the presence of venial sins in no sort deprives charity of its force and power to work, yet as it were benumbs it and deprives it of the use of its activity, so that charity remains without action, sterile and unfruitful. It is true that neither venial sin, nor even the affection to it, is contrary to the essential resolution of charity, which is to prefer God before all things ; because by this sin we love something outside reason but not against reason, we defer a little too much, and more than is fit, to creatures, yet we do not prefer them before the Creator, we occupy ourselves more than we ought in earthly things, yet do we not for all that forsake heavenly things. In fine, this kind of sin impedes us in the way of charity, but does not put us out of it, and therefore venial sin, not being contrary to charity, never destroys charity either wholly or partially.

God signified to the Bishop of Ephesus that he had *forsaken his first charity,** where he does not say that he was without

* Apoc. ii. 4.

charity, but only that it was not such as in the beginning; that is, that it was not now prompt, fervent, growing in love, or fruitful: as we are wont to say of him who from being bright, cheerful and blithe, becomes sad, heavy and sullen, that he is not now the same man he was; for our meaning is not that he is not the same in substance, but only in his actions and exercises. And thus Our Saviour says that in the latter days *the charity of many shall grow cold,** that is, it shall not be so active and courageous, by reason of fear and sadness which shall oppress men's hearts. Certain it is that *when concupiscence hath conceived it bringeth forth sin.*† The sin however, though sin indeed, does not always beget the death of the soul, but then only when it is complete in malice, and when it is consummate and accomplished, as S. James says. And he here establishes so clearly the difference between mortal and venial sin, that it is strange that some in our age have had the temerity to deny it.

However, venial sin is sin, and consequently troubles charity, not as a thing that is contrary to charity itself, but contrary to its operations and progress, and even to its intention. For as this intention is that we should direct all our actions to God, it is violated by venial sin, which directs the actions by which we commit it, not indeed against God yet outside God and his will. And as we say of a tree rudely visited and stripped by a tempest that nothing is left, because though the tree be entire yet it is left without fruit, so when our charity is shaken by the affection we have to venial sin, we say it is diminished and weakened; not because the habit of love is not entire in our hearts, but because it is without the works which are its fruits.

The affection to great sins did so make *truth prisoner to injustice* amongst the pagan philosophers, that, as the great Apostle says: *Knowing God they honoured him not* according to that knowledge;‡ so that though this affection did not banish natural light, yet it made it profitless. So the affection to venial sin does not abolish charity, but it holds it as a slave, tied hand and foot, hindering its freedom and action. This affection, attaching us too closely to the enjoyment of creatures, deprives us of the spiritual intimacy between God and us, to which

---

* Matt. xxiv. 12.   † James i. 15.   ‡ Rom. i. 21.

charity, as true friendship, excites us; consequently this affection
makes us lose the interior helps and assistances which are as it
were the vital and animating spirits of the soul, in default of
which there follows a certain spiritual palsy, which in the end,
if it be not remedied, brings us to death. For, after all, charity
being an active quality cannot be long without either acting or
dying: it is, say our Ancients, of the nature of Rachel, who
also represented it. *Give me*, said she to her husband, *children,
otherwise I shall die;** and charity urges the heart which she
has espoused to make her fertile of good works; otherwise she
will perish.

We are rarely in this mortal life without many temptations.
Now low and slothful hearts, and such as are given to exterior
pleasures, not being accustomed to fight nor exercised in spiritual warfare, never preserve charity long, but let themselves
ordinarily be surprised by mortal sin, which happens the more
easily because the soul is more disposed by venial sin to mortal.
For as that man of old, having continued to carry every day
the same calf, bore him also when he was grown to be a great
ox, custom having by little and little made insensible the increase
of so heavy a burden; so he that accustoms himself to play for
pence will in the end play for crowns, pistoles and horses, and
after his stud all his estate.† He that gives the reins to little
angers becomes in the end furious and unbearable; he that
addicts himself to lying in jest, is in great peril of lying with
calumny.

In fine, Theotimus, we are wont to say that such as have a
very weakly constitution have no life, that they have not an
ounce, or not a handful of it, because that which is quickly to
have an end seems indeed already not to be. And those good-
for-nothing souls who are addicted to pleasure and set upon
transitory things, may well say that they no longer have charity,
for if they have it they are in the way soon to lose it.

* Gen. xxx. I.   † *Apres ses chevaux toute sa chevance.*

CHAPTER III.

HOW WE FORSAKE DIVINE LOVE FOR THAT OF CREATURES.

THIS misery of quitting God for the creature happens thus. We do not love God without intermission, because in this mortal life charity is in us as a simple habit, which, as philosophers have remarked, we use when we like and never against our liking. When then we do not make use of the charity which is in us, that is, when we are not applying our spirit to the exercises of holy love, but, when (keeping it busied in some other affair, or it being idle in itself) it remains useless and negligent, then, Theotimus, it may be assaulted by some bad object and surprised by temptation. And though the habit of charity be at that instant in the bottom of our hearts and perform its office, inclining us to reject the bad suggestion, yet it only urges us or leads us to the action of resistance according as we second it, as is the manner of habits; and therefore, charity leaving us in our freedom, it happens often that the bad object having cast its allurements deeply into our hearts, we attach ourselves unto it by an excessive complacency, which when it comes to grow, we can hardly get rid of, and like thorns, according to the saying of Our Saviour, it in the end stifles the seed of grace and heavenly love. So it fell out with our first mother Eve, whose overthrow began by a certain amusement which she took in discoursing with the serpent, receiving complacency in hearing it talk of her advancement in knowledge, and in seeing the beauty of the forbidden fruit, so that the complacency growing with the amusement and the amusement feeding itself in the complacency, she found herself at length so entangled, that giving away to consent, she committed the accursed sin into which afterwards she drew her husband.

We see that pigeons, touched with vanity, display themselves (*se pavonnent*) sometimes in the air, and sail about hither and thither, admiring the variety of their plumage, and then the tercelets and falcons that espy them fall upon them and seize them, which they could never do if the pigeons had been flying their proper flight, as they have a stronger wing than have birds of prey. Ah! Theotimus, if we did not amuse ourselves with the vanity of fleeting pleasures, especially in the complacency of self-love, but if having once got charity we were careful to fly straight thither whither it would carry us, suggestion and temptation should never catch us, but because as doves seduced and beguiled by self-esteem we look back upon ourselves, and engage our spirits too much with creatures, we often find ourselves seized by the talons of our enemies, who bear away and devour us.

God does not will to hinder temptations from attacking us, to the end that by resistance our charity may be more exercised, that by fighting we may gain the victory, and by victory obtain the triumph. But for us to have any kind of inclination to delight ourselves in the temptation—this rises from the condition of our nature, which so earnestly loves good that it is subject to be enticed by anything that has a show of good, and temptation's hook is ever baited with this kind of bait: for, as holy Writ teaches, there is either some good honourable in the world's sight to move us to the *pride of* a worldly *life,* or a good delightful to sense to carry us to *concupiscence of the flesh,* or a good tending towards wealth, to incite us to the *concupiscence* and avarice *of the eyes.** But if we kept our faith, which can discern between the true good we are to pursue and the false which we are to reject, sharply attentive to its office, without doubt it would be a trusty sentinel to charity, and would give intelligence of that evil which approaches the heart under pretext of good, and charity would immediately repulse it. But because ordinarily we keep our faith either asleep or less attentive than is requisite for the preservation of our charity, we are often surprised by temptation, which, seducing our senses, while our senses incite the inferior part of our soul to rebellion, often brings to pass that the superior part of reason yields to the violence of this revolt, and by committing sin loses charity.

Such was the progress of the sedition which the disloyal Absalom stirred up against his good father David; for he put forward propositions which were good in appearance, which

* 1 John ii. 16.

being once received by the poor Israelites whose prudence was put to sleep and smothered, he solicited them in such sort that he wrought them to a complete rebellion; so that David was constrained to depart from Jerusalem with all his most faithful friends, leaving there no men of distinction save Sadoc and Abiathar, priests of the Eternal, with their children : now Sadoc was a seer, that is to say a prophet.*

For so, most dear Theotimus, self-love, finding our faith without attention and drowsy, presents unto us vain yet apparent goods, seduces our senses, our imagination and the faculties of our souls, and lays so hard at our free-wills that it brings them to an entire revolt against the holy love of God, which then, as another David, departs from our heart with all its train, that is with the gifts of the Holy Ghost and the other heavenly virtues, which are the inseparable companions of charity, if not her properties and faculties. Nor does there remain in the Jerusalem of our soul any virtue of importance saving Sadoc the seer, that is the gift of faith which can make us see eternal truths, with the exercise of it, and with him Abiathar, that is the gift of hope with its action ; both these remain much afflicted and sorrowful, yet maintain in us the ark of alliance, that is the quality and title of Christian purchased by baptism.

Alas ! Theotimus, what a pitiful spectacle it is to the angels of peace to see the Holy Ghost and his love depart in this manner out of our sinful souls ! Verily I think if they could weep they would pour out infinite tears, and, with a mournful voice lamenting our misery, would sing the sad canticle which Jeremias took up, when sitting upon the threshold of the desolate temple he contemplated the ruin of Jerusalem in the time of Sedecias : *How doth the city sit solitary that was full of people ! How is the mistress of the Gentiles become as a widow : the princess of provinces made tributary !*†

* 2 Kings xv.   † Jer. Lam. i. 1.

CHAPTER IV.

THAT HEAVENLY LOVE IS LOST IN A MOMENT.

THE love of God, which brings us as far as contempt of self, makes us citizens of the heavenly Jerusalem; self-love, which pushes us forward to the contempt of God, makes us slaves of the infernal Babylon. It is true that only little by little we come to despise God, but we have no sooner done it than instantly, in a moment, holy charity forsakes us, or rather wholly perishes. Yes, Theotimus, for in this contempt of God does mortal sin consist, and one only mortal sin banishes charity from the soul, inasmuch as it breaks the connection and union with God, which is obedience and submission to his will: and as man's heart cannot live divided, so charity, which is the heart of the soul and the soul of the heart, can never be wounded without being slain: as they say of pearls, which being conceived of heavenly dew perish if any drop of salt water get within the shell that holds them. Our soul, as you know, does not go out of our body by little and little, but in a moment, when the indisposition of the body is so great that it can no longer exercise the actions of life in it: even so, the very instant the heart is so disordered by passions that charity can no longer reign there, she quits and abandons it: for she is so noble, that she cannot cease to reign without ceasing to be.

Habits acquired by our human actions alone do not perish by one single contrary act: for a man is not said to be intemperate for one single act of intemperance, nor is a painter held an unskilful master for having once failed in his art; but, as all such habits are acquired by the influence of a series of acts, so we lose them by a long cessation from their acts or by many contrary acts. But charity, Theotimus, which in a moment the Holy Ghost pours into our hearts as soon as the conditions requisite for this infusion are found in us, is also in an instant taken from us, as soon as, diverting our will from the obedience we owe to God, we complete our consent to the rebellion and disloyalty to which temptation excites us.

It is true that charity increases by degrees and goes from

perfection to perfection according as by our works or by the frequenting of the sacraments we make place for it, yet it does not decrease by a lessening of its perfection, for we never lose any least part of it but we lose it all. In which it resembles the masterpiece of Phidias so famous amongst the ancients; for they say that this great sculptor made at Athens an ivory statue of Minerva, twenty-six cubits high, and in the buckler which she held, wherein he had represented the battles of the Amazons and Giants, he carved his own face with so great art that one could not take away one line of it, says Aristotle, without destroying the whole statue, so that this work, though it had been brought to perfection by adding piece to piece, yet would have perished in an instant if one little parcel of the workman's likeness had been removed. In like manner, Theotimus, though the Holy Ghost having infused charity into a soul increases it by adding one degree to another and one perfection of love to another, yet still, the resolution of preferring God's will before all things being the essential point of sacred love, and that wherein the image of eternal love, that is of the Holy Ghost, is represented, one cannot withdraw one single piece of it but presently charity wholly perishes.

This preference of God before all things is the dear child of charity. And if Agar, who was but an Egyptian, seeing her son in danger of death had not the heart to stay by him, but would have left him, saying: *Ah! I will not see the child die,** is it strange then that charity, the daughter of heavenly sweetness and delight, cannot bear to behold the death of her child, which is the resolution never to offend God? So that while free-will is resolving to consent to sin and is thereby putting to death this holy resolution, charity dies with it, saying in its last sigh: Ah! no, never will I see this child die. In fine, Theotimus, as the precious stone called *prassius* loses its lustre in the presence of any poison, so in an instant the soul loses her splendour, grace and beauty, which consist in holy love, upon the entry and presence of any mortal sin;—whence it is written that *the soul that sinneth, the same shall die.*†

* Gen. xxi. 16.   † Ezech. xviii. 4.

CHAPTER V.

THAT THE SOLE CAUSE OF THE DECAY AND COOLING OF CHARITY IS IN THE CREATURE'S WILL.

As it would be an impious effrontery to attribute the works of holy love done by the Holy Ghost in and with us to the strength of our will, it would be a shameless impiety to lay the defect of love in ungrateful men, on the failure of heavenly assistance and grace. For the Holy Ghost cries everywhere, on the contrary, that our ruin is from ourselves : *Destruction is thine own, O Israel! thy help is only in me :** that Our Saviour brought *the fire* of love, and *desires nothing but that it should be enkindled* in our hearts :† that *salvation is prepared before the face of all peoples : a light to the revelation of the Gentiles and the glory of Israel :*‡ that the divine goodness is *not willing that any should perish,*§ *but that all should come to the knowledge of the truth : and will have all men to be saved,*‖ their Saviour being come into the world, *that he might redeem them who were under the law, that we might receive the adoption of sons.*¶ And the wise man clearly warns us, *Say not : it is through God that she (wisdom) is not with me.*** And the sacred Council of Trent divinely inculcates upon all the children of holy Church, that the Grace of God is never wanting to such as do what they can, invoking the divine assistance ; that God never abandons such as he has once justified unless they abandon him first ; so that, if they be not wanting to grace they shall obtain glory.

In fine, Theotimus, Our Saviour is *the true light which enlighteneth every man that cometh into this world.*†† Some travellers, one summer's day about noontide, lay down to repose under the shade of a tree, but while their weariness and the coolness of the shadow kept them asleep, the sun advancing on them threw just upon their eyes his strongest light, which by its glittering brightness gave glimpses of itself like little flashes of lightning about the pupils of these sleepers' eyes, and by the heat which pierced their eyelids, forced them by a gentle violence

---

* Osee xiii. 9. † Luke xii. 49. ‡ Luke ii. 32. § 2 Peter iii. 9.
‖ 1 Tim. ii. 4. ¶ Gal. iv. 5. ** Eccli. xv. 11. †† John i. 9.

to awake. Some of them being awakened get up, and making way get happily to their lodging, the rest not only do not rise, but turning their backs to the sun and pressing their hats over their eyes, spend their day there in sleeping, till surprised by night and yet being desirous to make towards their lodging, they stray, one here, one there, in the forest, at the mercy of wolves, wild-boars, and other savage beasts. Now tell me, I pray, Theotimus, those that arrived, ought they not to give all their thanks for their good success to the sun, or to speak like a Christian, to the sun's Creator? Yes surely; for they thought not of waking when it was time : the sun did them this good office, and by the gentle invitation of his light and heat came lovingly to call them up. 'Tis true they resisted not his call, but he also helped them much even in that; for he spread his light fairly upon them, giving them a half-sight of himself through their eyelids, and by his heat as it were by his love he unsealed their eyes, and urged them to see his day.

On the contrary, those poor strangers, what right had they to cry in that wood : Alas! what have we done to the sun that he did not make us see his light, as he did our companions, that we might have arrived at our lodgings and not have wandered in this hideous darkness? For who would not undertake the sun's or rather God's cause, my dear Theotimus, to answer these wretches. What is there, miserable beings, that the sun could really do for you and did not? His favours were equal to all ye that slept : he approached you all with the same light, touched you with the same rays, spread over you a like heat, but unhappy ye, although you saw your risen companions take their pilgrim's staff to gain way, ye turned your backs to the sun and would not make use of his light, nor be conquered by his heat.

Now, Theotimus, see here what I would say. We are all pilgrims in this mortal life; almost all of us have voluntarily slept in sin; God the sun of justice darts upon us most suffi-ciently, yea abundantly, the beams of his inspirations, warms our hearts with his benedictions, touching every one with the allurements of his love. Ah! how comes it then that these allurements allure so few and draw yet fewer? Ah! certainly such as, first allured, afterwards drawn, follow the inspiration, have great occasion to rejoice, but not to glorify themselves for it. Let them rejoice because they enjoy a great good; yet let them not glorify themselves therein, because it is by God's pure goodness, who, leaving them the profit of their good works, reserves to himself the glory of them. But concerning them that remain in the sleep of sin: Oh! what good reason they have to lament, groan, weep, and say: woe the day! for they are in the most lamentable of cases; yet have they no reason to grieve or complain, save about themselves, who despised, yea rebelled against, the light; who were untractable to invitations, and obstinate against inspirations; so that it is their own malice alone they must ever curse and reproach, since they themselves are the sole authors of their ruin, the sole workers of their damnation. So the Japanese, complaining to the Blessed Francis Xavier, their Apostle, that God who had had so much care of other nations, seemed to have forgotten their predecessors, not having given them the knowledge of himself, for want of which they must have been lost: the man of God answered them that the divine natural law was engraven in the hearts of all mortals, and that if their forerunners had observed it, the light of heaven would without doubt have illuminated them, as, on the contrary, having violated it, they deserved damnation. An apostolic answer of an apostolic man, and resembling the reason given by the great Apostle of the loss of the ancient Gentiles, whom he calls inexcusable, for that having known good they followed evil; for it is in a word that which he inculcates in the first chapter of his epistle to the Romans. Misery upon misery to those who do not acknowledge that their misery comes from their malice!

CHAPTER VI.

THAT WE OUGHT TO ACKNOWLEDGE ALL THE LOVE WE BEAR TO GOD TO BE FROM GOD.

THE love of men towards God takes its being, progress and perfection from the eternal love of God towards men. This is the universal sense of the Church our mother, who with an ardent jealousy will have us to acknowledge our salvation and the means thereof, to proceed solely from Our Saviour's mercy, to the end that on earth as in heaven to him alone may be honour and glory.

What hast thou that thou hast not received? says the divine Apostle, speaking of the gifts of knowledge, eloquence, and other like qualities of Church-pastors; *and if thou hast received, why dost thou glory as if thou hadst not received.** It is true; we have received all from God, but especially the supernatural goods of holy love. And if we have received them, why should we take the glory of them?

Certainly if any one would extol himself for having made progress in the love of God: Alas! wretched man, should we say unto him, thou wast aswoon in thy iniquity, having neither force nor life left in thee to rise (as it happened to the princess in our parable),† and God of his infinite goodness ran to thy succour, and crying with a loud voice: *Open the mouth* of thy attention *and I will fill it*‡, he himself put his fingers between thy lips and unlocked thy teeth, casting into thy heart his holy inspiration, and thou didst receive it; and when thou wast brought back to thy senses, he went on by divers movements and various means to strengthen thy heart, till at length he infused into it his charity, as thy vital and perfect health.

Well then, tell me now, miserable creature, what hast thou done in all this of which thou canst boast? Thou didst consent, I know it well; the motion of thy will did freely follow that of heavenly grace. But all this, what is it more than to receive the divine operation without resistance? And what is there in this, that thou hast not received? Yea, poor wretch that thou art, thou didst receive the receiving in which thou gloriest, and the consent which thou vauntest: for tell me, I pray thee, wilt thou not grant me, that if God had not prevented thee, thou wouldst never have perceived his goodness, and consequently never have consented to his love? No, nor yet hadst thou thought a single good thought of him. His movement gave

---

* 1 Cor. iv. 7.   † See Book iii. 3.   ‡ Ps. lxxx. 11.

being and life to thine, and if his liberty had not animated, excited and provoked thy liberty, by the powerful invitations of his sweetness, thy liberty had been for ever unprofitable to thy salvation. I confess thou didst co-operate with the inspiration by consenting, but, if thou knowest it not, I teach thee that thy co-operation took being from the operation of grace and thy free-will together, yet so, that if grace had not prevented and filled thy heart with its operation, never had thy heart had either power or will to co-operate.

But tell me again, I beseech thee, vile and abject man, is it not ridiculous of thee to think that thou hast a share in the glory of thy conversion because thou didst not repel the inspiration? Is not this a frenzy of robbers and tyrants, to pretend they give life to those from whom they do not take it? And is it not a frantic impiety to think that thou gavest holy efficacy and living activity to the divine inspiration, because by resistance thou didst not take it away? We can hinder the effects of inspiration, but we cannot give it any; it takes its force and virtue from the divine goodness which is the place of its starting, and not from man's will the place of its arrival. Should we not be moved to wrath, to hear the princess of our parable boast that it was she that gave virtue and power to the cordial waters and other medicines, or that she cured herself, because if she had not received the remedies which the king gave her and poured into her mouth (at such time as being half dead there remained hardly any sense in her), they had had no operation? Yes, might one say to her: ungrateful that thou art, thou mightest have obstinately refused to receive the remedies, thou mightest, after thou hadst received them into thy mouth, have cast them out again, yet for all that it is not true that thou gavest them force and virtue. This they had as their natural property, thou didst only consent to receive them, and let them operate; and besides, thou wouldst never have consented, if the King had not first rein-vigorated thee, and then solicited thee to take them; never hadst thou received them, had not he assisted thee to receive them, opening thy very mouth with his fingers, and pouring the potion into it   Art thou not then a monster of ingratitude to wish to attribute to thyself a benefit which by so many titles thou owest to thy dear spouse ?

The curious little fish, called *echeneis*, or *remora*, has indeed the power to stay or not to stay a ship sailing on the high sea under full sail : but it has not the power to make it set sail, or proceed or arrive; it can hinder motion, but cannot give it. Our free-will can stay and hinder the course of the inspiration, and when the favourable gale of God's grace swells the sails of our soul it is in our power to refuse consent, and thereby to hinder the effect of the wind's favour : but when our spirit sails along, and makes its voyage prosperously, it is not we that make the gale of the inspiration blow for us, nor we that make our sails swell with it, nor we that give motion to the ship of our heart; but we simply receive the gale sent from heaven, consent to its motion, and let our ship sail under it, not hindering it by the remora of our resistance. It is the inspiration then which impresses on our free-will the happy and sweet influence whereby it not only makes it see the beauty of good, but also heats, helps, and strengthens it, and moves it so sweetly that it thus turns and freely flows out towards what is good.

The heavens in spring time prepare the fresh dewdrops, and shower them down upon the face of the sea, and the mother-pearls that open their shells receive these drops, which are converted into pearls : but, on the contrary, the mother-pearls which keep their shells shut do not hinder the dews from falling upon them, yet they hinder them from falling into them. Now have not the heavens sent their dew and their influence as much upon the one as the other mother-pearl ? Why then did the one in effect produce its pearl and the others not ? The heavens were as bountiful to that one which remained sterile as was requisite to empearl and impregnate it with its fair unity,* but it hindered the effect of the heavens' favour, by keeping itself closed and covered. And as for that which conceived the pearl on receiving the dew, it has nothing in that work which it did not receive from heaven, not even its opening whereby it received the dew ; for without the touches of the morning's rays, which did gently excite it, it had not risen up to the surface of

* *i.e.* pearl. See p. 82 [Tr.]

the sea, nor yet opened its shell. Theotimus, if we have any
love for God, his be the honour and glory, who did all in us,
and without whom nothing were done; ours be the profit and
obligation. This is the division his divine goodness makes with
us; he leaves us the fruits of his benefits, and reserves to himself
the honour and praise of them; and verily since we are
nothing but by his grace, we ought to be nothing but for his
glory.

<hr>

CHAPTER VII.

THAT WE MUST AVOID ALL CURIOSITY, AND HUMBLY ACQUIESCE IN GOD'S MOST WISE PROVIDENCE.

THE human spirit is so weak that when it would look too
curiously into the causes and reasons of God's will it embarrasses
and entangles itself in the meshes of a thousand difficulties, out
of which it has much to do to deliver itself; it resembles smoke,
for as smoke ascends it gets more subtle, and as it grows more
subtle it vanishes. In striving to raise our reasonings too high
in divine things by curiosity we grow vain or empty in our
thoughts, and instead of arriving at the knowledge of truth, we
fall into the folly of our vanity.

But above all we are unreasonable towards Divine providence
in regard to the diversity of the means which he bestows upon
us to draw us to his holy love, and by his holy love to glory.
For our temerity urges us ever to inquire why God gives more
means to one than to another; why he did not amongst the
Tyrians and Sidonians the miracles which he did in Corozain
and Bethsaida, seeing they would have made as good use of
them; and, in fine, why he draws one rather than another to
his love.

O Theotimus! my friend, never, no never, must we permit
our minds to be carried away by this mad whirlwind, nor expect
to find a better reason of God's will than his will itself, which is
sovereignly reasonable, yea, the reason of all reasons, the rule of
all goodness, the law of all equity. And although the Holy

Ghost, speaking in the Holy Scripture, gives reason in divers places of almost all we can wish to know of what this divine providence does in conducting men to holy love and eternal salvation, yet on various occasions he shows that we must in no wise depart from the respect which is due to his will, whose purpose, decree, good-pleasure, and sentence we are to adore; and he being sovereign judge and sovereignly equitable, it is not reasonable that at the end he manifest his motives, but it is sufficient that he say simply—*for reasons.* And if charity obliges us to bear so much respect to the decrees of sovereign courts, composed of corruptible judges, of the earth and earthly, as to believe that they were not made without motives, though we know these not— ah ! Lord God, with what a loving reverence ought we to adore the equity of thy supreme providence which is infinite in justice and goodness !

So in a thousand places of the holy Word we find the reason why God has reprobated the Jews. *Because,* say S. Paul and S. Barnabas, *you reject the word of God, and judge yourselves unworthy of eternal life, behold we turn to the Gentiles.**
And he that shall consider in tranquillity of heart Chapters IX. X. and XI. of the Epistle to the Romans, shall clearly see that God's will did not without reason reject the Jews ; nevertheless, this reason must not be sought out by man's spirit, which, on the contrary, is obliged to be satisfied with purely and simply reverencing the divine decree, admiring it with love as infinitely just and upright, and loving it with admiration as impenetrable and incomprehensible. So that the divine Apostle thus concludes the long discourse which he had made concerning it : *O the depth of the riches of the wisdom and of the knowledge of God ! How incomprehensible are his judgments, and how unsearchable his ways ! For who hath known the mind of the Lord ? Or who hath been his counsellor ?†* By which exclamation he testifies that God does all things with great wisdom, knowledge and reason ; yet so, that, as man has not entered into the divine counsels, whose judgments and designs are placed infinitely above our reach, we ought devoutly to adore

---

* Acts xiii. 46.   † Rom. xi. 33, 34.

his decrees as most just, without searching out their motives. These he keeps in secret to himself, in order to keep our understanding in respect and humility to ourself.

S. Augustine in a hundred places teaches us this practice. " No one cometh to Our Saviour," says he, " if not drawn ;— whom he draws, and whom he draws not, why he draws this one and not that,—do not wish to judge if you do not wish to err. Listen once for all and understand. Art thou not drawn, pray that thou mayst be drawn." " Verily it is sufficient for a Christian living as yet by faith, and not seeing that which is perfect, but only knowing in part, to know and believe that God delivers none from damnation, but by his free mercy, through our Lord Jesus Christ ; and that he condemns none but by his most just truth, through the same Lord Jesus Christ. But to know why he delivers this one rather than the other—let that man sound so great a depth of God's judgments who is able, but let him beware of the precipice." " These judgments are not therefore unjust because they are hidden." " But why then does he deliver this man rather than that ? We say again, *O man, who art thou that repliest against God ?** His judgments are incomprehensible, and his ways unknown, and let us add this : *Seek not the things that are too high for thee, and search not into things above thy ability.*"† " Now he granteth not them mercy, to whom, by a truth most secret and furthest removed from men's thoughts, he judges it not fit to communicate his favours and mercy."

We see sometimes twins, of whom one is born alive and receives Baptism, the other in his birth loses his temporal life, before being regenerated to the eternal, and consequently the one is heir of heaven, the other is deprived of the inheritance. Now why does divine providence give such different fates to one equal birth ? Truly it might be answered that ordinarily God's providence does not violate the laws of nature, so that one of these twins being strong, and the other too feeble to support the labour of his delivery, the latter died before he could be baptized, the other lived ; divine providence not willing to stop the course of natural causes, which on this occasion were the reason why

---

* Rom. ix. 20. † Eccli. iii. 22.

the one was deprived of Baptism.   And truly this is a perfectly solid answer.   But, following the advice of the divine S. Paul, and of S. Augustine, we ought not to busy our thoughts in this consideration, which, though it be good, yet in no respect enters into comparison with many others which God has reserved to himself, and will show us in heaven. " Then," says S. Augustine, " the secret shall end why rather the one than the other was received, the causes being equal as to both, and why miracles were not done amongst those who in case they had been done would have been brought to repentance, and were done amongst such as would will not to believe them."   And in another place the same saint, speaking of sinners, some of whom God leaves in their iniquity while others he raises, says : " Now why he retains the one and not the other, it is not possible to comprehend, nor lawful to inquire, since it is enough to know that it is by him we stand and that it is not by him we fall."   And again : " This is hidden and far removed from man's understanding, at least from mine."

Behold, Theotimus, the most holy way of philosophising on this subject.   Wherefore I have always considered that the learned modesty and most wise humility of the seraphic Doctor S. Bonaventure were greatly to be admired and loved, in the discourse which he makes of the reason why divine providence ordains the elect to eternal life.   " Perhaps," says he, " it is by a foresight of the good works which will be done by him that is drawn, insomuch as they proceed in some sort from the will : but distinctly to declare which good works being foreseen move God's will, I am not able, nor will I make inquiry thereupon : and there is no other reason than some sort of congruity, so that we might assign one while it might be another. Wherefore we cannot with assurance point out the true reason nor the true motive of God's will in this : for as S. Augustine says : 'Although the truth of it is most certain, yet is it far removed from our thoughts.'   So that we can say nothing assuredly of it unless by the revelation of him who knows all things.   And whereas it was not expedient for our salvation that we should have knowledge of these secrets, but on the contrary, it was more profitable that we should be ignorant of them, to keep us in humility, God would not reveal them, yea the holy Apostle did not dare to inquire about them, but testified the insufficiency of our understanding in this matter when he cried out : *O the depth of the riches of the wisdom and of the knowledge of God !*"   Could one speak more holily Theotimus of so holy a mystery ?   Indeed these are the words of a most saintly and prudent Doctor of the Church.

CHAPTER VIII.

AN EXHORTATION TO THE AMOROUS SUBMISSION WHICH WE OWE TO THE DECREES OF DIVINE PROVIDENCE.

LET us love then, Theotimus, and adore in humility of spirit this depth of God's judgments, which, as S. Augustine says, the holy Apostle discovers not, but admires, when he cries out : *O the depth of God's judgments !*   "Who can count the sands of the sea, and the drops of rain, or measure the depths of the abyss," says that excellent understanding S. Gregory Nazianzen :*   "and who can sound the depth of the Divine Wisdom by which it has created all things, and governs them as it pleases and judges fit.   For indeed it suffices that, after the example of the Apostle, we admire it without stopping at the difficulty and obscurity of it.   *O the depth of the riches of the wisdom and of the knowledge of God !   How incomprehensible are his judgments, and how unsearchable his ways !   For who hath known the mind of the Lord ?   Or who hath been his counsellor ?*   Theotimus, the reasons of God's will cannot be penetrated by our intelligence till we see the face of *him who reacheth from end to end mightily and ordereth all things sweetly ;*† doing all that he doth *in measure, and number, and weight ;*‡ and to whom the Psalmist says, *Lord, thou hast made all things in wisdom.*"§

How often does it happen that we are ignorant why and how even the works of men are done?   And therefore, says the

* Orat. xiv. : On Love of the Poor.
† Wis. viii. 1.   ‡ Ibid. xi, 21.   § Ps. ciii. 24.

same holy Bishop of Nazianzus, "as the artist is not ignorant of his art, so the things of this world are not carelessly and unskilfully made, though we know not the reasons of them." Entering into a clockmaker's shop, we shall sometimes find a clock no greater than an orange, which yet has in it a hundred or two hundred pieces, of which some serve to show the time, others to strike the hour or give the morning alarm; we shall see in it little wheels, some turning to the right, others to the left, one by the top, another by the bottom; and the balance which with measured beats keeps rising and falling on either side. We wonder how art could join together such a number of pieces, with so just a correspondence, not knowing what each little piece serves for, nor why it is made so, unless the master tell us; knowing only in general that all serve either to point out or to strike the hour. It is reported that the good Indians will stand whole days musing upon a clock, to hear it strike at the times fixed, and not being able to guess how it is done, they do not therefore say that it is without art or reason, but are taken with love and respect towards those who regulate the clocks, admiring them as more than men. Theotimus, we see in this manner the universe, but specially human nature, to be a sort of clock, composed with so great a variety of actions and movements that we cannot but be astonished at it. And we know in general that these so diversely ordered pieces serve all, either to point out, as on a dial-plate, God's most holy justice or as by a bell of praise, to sound the triumphant mercy of his goodness. But to know the particular use of every piece, how it is ordered to the general end, or why it is so, we cannot conceive, unless the sovereign Workman instruct us. Now he conceals his art from us, to the end that with more reverence we may admire it, till in heaven he shall ravish us with the sweetness of his wisdom, where in the abundance of his love he will discover unto us the reasons, means and motives of all that shall have passed in the world towards our eternal salvation.

"We resemble," says yet again the great Nazianzen, "those, who are troubled with giddiness or turning of the head. They think that all about them is turning upside down, though it be but their brain and imagination which turn, and not the things;

so we, when we meet with any events of which the causes are unknown to us, fancy that the world is governed without reason, because we are ignorant of it. Let us believe then that as God is the maker and father of all things, so he takes care of all things by his providence, which embraces and sustains all the machine of creatures. But especially let us believe that he rules our affairs, (ours who know him) though our life be tossed about in so great contrariety of accidents. Of these we know not the reasons, to the end, perhaps, that not being able to attain this knowledge we may admire the sovereign reason of God which surpasses all things: for with us things easily known are easily despised; but that which surpasses the highest powers of our spirit, by how much it is harder to be known, by so much it excites a greater admiration in us. Truly the reasons of divine providence were low placed if our small capacities could reach unto them; they would be less lovable in their sweetness and less admirable in their majesty if they were set at a less distance from our capacity !"

Let us cry out then, Theotimus, on all occurrences, but let it be with an entirely amorous heart towards the most wise, most prudent, and most sweet providence of our eternal Father : *O the depth of the riches of the wisdom and of the knowledge of God !* O Saviour Jesus, Theotimus, how excessive are the riches of the Divine goodness ! His love towards us is an incomprehensible abyss, whence he has provided for us a rich sufficiency, or rather a rich abundance of means proper for our salvation; and sweetly to apply them he makes use of a sovereign wisdom, having by his infinite knowledge foreseen and known all that was requisite to that effect. Ah ! what can we fear, nay rather, what ought not we to hope for, being the children of a Father so rich in goodness to love and to will to save us; who knows so well how to prepare the means suitable for this, and is so wise to apply them ; so good to will, so clear-sighted to ordain, and so prudent to execute ?

Let us never permit our minds to flutter with curiosity about God's judgments, for, like little butterflies, we shall burn our wings, and perish in this sacred flame. These judgments are incomprehensible, or, as S. Gregory Nazianzen says, inscrutable, that is, one cannot search out and sound their motives; the means and ways by which he executes and brings them to perfection cannot be discerned and recognized : and, clever as we may be, yet we shall find ourselves thrown out at every turn and lose the scent. *For who hath known the mind,* the meaning and the intention of God ? *Who hath been his counsellor,* to know his purposes and their motives ? *Or who hath first given to him ?* Is it not he, on the contrary, who presents us with the benedictions of his grace to crown us with the felicity of his glory ? Ah ! Theotimus, *all things are from him,* as being their Creator; all things are *by him,* as being their Governor; all things are *in him,* as being their Protector ; *to him be honour and glory for ever and ever,* Amen !* Let us walk in peace, Theotimus, in the way of holy love, for he that shall have divine love in dying, after death shall enjoy love eternally.

CHAPTER IX.

OF A CERTAIN REMAINDER OF LOVE THAT OFTENTIMES RESTS IN THE SOUL THAT HAS LOST HOLY CHARITY.

THE life of a man who, spent out, lies dying little by little on his bed, hardly deserves to be termed life, since, though it be life, it is so mingled with death that it is hard to say whether it is a death yet living or a life dying. Alas ! how pitiful a spectacle it is, Theotimus ! But far more lamentable is the state of a soul ungrateful to her Saviour, who goes backward step by step, withdrawing herself from God's love by certain degrees of indevotion and disloyalty, till at length, having quite forsaken it, she is left in the horrible obscurity of perdition. This love which is in its decline, and which is fading and perishing, is called imperfect love, because, though it be entire in the soul, yet seems it not to be there entirely ; that is, it hardly stays in the soul any longer, but is upon the point of forsaking it. Now,

* Rom. xi.

charity being separated from the soul by sin, there frequently
remains a certain resemblance of charity which may deceive
us and vainly occupy our minds, and I will tell you what
it is. Charity while it is in us produces many actions of love
towards God, by the frequent exercise of which our soul gets a
habit and custom of loving God, which is not charity, but only
a bent and inclination which the multitude of the actions has
given to our hearts.

After a long habit of preaching or saying Mass with deliberation, it happens often that in dreaming we utter and speak
the same things which we should say in preaching or celebrating ; in the same manner the custom and habit acquired by
election and virtue is, in some sort, afterwards practised without
election or virtue, since the actions of those who are asleep have,
generally speaking, nothing of virtue save only an apparent
image, and are only the similitudes or representations thereof.
So charity, by the multitude of acts which it produces, imprints
in us a certain facility in loving which it leaves in us even after
we are deprived of its presence. When I was a young scholar,
I found that in a village near Paris, in a certain well, there was
an echo, which would repeat several times the words that we pronounced in it : and if some simpleton without experience had heard
these repetitions of words, he would have thought there was
some one at the bottom of the well who did it. But we knew
beforehand by philosophy that it was not any one in the well
who repeated our words, but simply that there were cavities, in
one of which our voices were collected, and not finding a passage
through, they, lest they might altogether perish, and not employ
the force that was left to them, produced second voices, and
these gathering together in another concavity produced a third,
the third a fourth, and so consecutively up to eleven, so that
those voices in the well were no longer our voices, but resem-
blances and images of them. And indeed there was a great difference between our voices and those : for when we made a long
continuance of words, they only repeated some, they shortened
the pronunciation of the syllables, which they uttered very
rapidly, and with tones and accents quite different from ours ; nor
did they begin to form these words until we had quite finished

pronouncing them. In fine, they were not the words of a living man, but, so to say, of a hollow and empty rock, which notwithstanding so well counterfeited man's voice whence they sprang, that an ignorant person would have been misled and beguiled by them.

Now this is what I would say. When holy charity meets a pliable soul in which she long resides, she produces a second love, which is not a love of charity, though it issues from charity ; it is a human love which is yet so like charity, that though afterwards charity perish in the soul it seems to be still there, inasmuch as it leaves behind it this its picture and likeness, which so represents charity that one who was ignorant would be deceived therein, as were the birds by the painting of the grapes of Zeuxis, which they deemed to be true grapes, so exactly had art imitated nature. And yet there is a great difference between charity and the human love it produces in us : for the voice of charity declares, impresses, and effects all the commandments of God in our hearts ; the human love which remains after it does indeed sometimes declare and impress all the commandments, yet it never effects them all, but some few only. Charity pronounces and puts together all the syllables, that is, all the circumstances of God's commandments ; human love always leaves out some of them, especially that of the right and pure intention ; and as for the tone, charity keeps it always steady, sweet, and full of grace, human love takes it always too high in earthly things, or too low in heavenly, and never sets upon its work until charity has ended hers. For so long as charity is in the soul, she uses this human love which is her creature and employs it to facilitate her operations ; so that during that time the works of this love, as of a servant, belong to charity its mistress : but when charity is gone, then the actions of this love are entirely its own, and have no longer the price and value of charity. For as the staff of Eliseus, in his absence, though in the hand of Giezi who received it from him, wrought no miracle, so actions done in the absence of charity, by the simple habit of human love, are of no value or merit to eternal life, though this human love learned from charity to do them, and is but charity's servant. And this so comes about because this human love, in the absence of charity, has no supernatural strength to raise the soul to the excellent action of the love of God above all things.

CHAPTER X.

HOW DANGEROUS THIS IMPERFECT LOVE IS.

ALAS! my Theotimus, behold, I pray you, the poor Judas after he had betrayed his Master, how he goes to return the money to the Jews, how he acknowledges his sin, how honourably he speaks of the blood of this immaculate Lamb. These were effects of imperfect love, which former charity, now past, had left in his heart. We descend to impiety by certain degrees, and hardly any one arrives in an instant at the extremity of malice.

Perfumers, though out of their shops, bear about with them for a long time the scent of the perfumes which they have handled. In like manner, those who have been in the cabinet of heavenly ointments, that is in holy charity, keep for some time afterwards the scent of it.

Where the hart has lodged by night, there, the morning after, is a fresh scent or vent of him; towards night it is harder to perceive; and as his strain grows older and harder, the hounds lose it more and more. When charity has reigned for a time in the soul, one may find there its path, marks, strain or scent for a time after it has departed, but little by little all this quite vanishes, and a man loses all knowledge that charity was ever there.

I have seen certain young people, well brought up in the love of God, who, putting themselves out of that path, remained for some time during their miserable decay still giving great signs of their past virtue, and, the habit acquired in time of charity resisting present vice, scarcely could one for some months discern whether they were out of charity or not, and whether they were virtuous or vicious, till such time as the course of things made it clear that these virtuous exercises proceeded not from present charity but from past, not from perfect but from imperfect love, which charity had left behind her, as a sign that she had lodged in those souls.

Now this imperfect love, Theotimus, is good in itself, for being a creature of holy charity, and as it were one of her retinue, it cannot but be good; and indeed it did faithfully serve charity, while she sojourned in the soul, as it is still ready to serve upon her return. Nor is it to be contemned because it cannot do actions of perfect love, the condition of its nature being such; as stars, which in comparison with the sun are very imperfect, are yet extremely beautiful beheld alone, and, having no worth in the presence of the sun, have some in his absence.

At the same time though this imperfect love be good in itself, yet it is perilous for us; for oftentimes we are contented with it alone, because having many exterior and interior marks of charity, we, thinking we have charity, deceive ourselves and think we are holy, while, in this vain persuasion, the sins which deprived us of charity increase, grow great, and multiply so fast that in the end they make themselves masters of our heart.

Self-love deceives us, as Laban did Jacob between Rachel and Lia. We leave charity for a moment, and this imperfect habit of human love is thrust on us, and we content ourselves with it as if it were true charity, till some clear light shows us that we have been deceived.

Ah! my God! is it not a great pity to see a soul flattering herself in the imagination of being holy, and remaining in repose as though she were possessed of charity, only to find in the end that her holiness is a fiction, her rest a lethargy, and her joy a madness.

CHAPTER XI.

A MEANS TO DISCERN THIS IMPERFECT LOVE.

BUT, you will ask me, what means is there to discern whether it be Rachel or Lia, charity or imperfect love, which gives me the feelings of devotion wherewith I am touched? If when you examine in particular the objects of the desires, affections and designs which you have at the time, you find any one for which you would go against the will and good-pleasure of God by sinning mortally, it is then beyond doubt that all the feeling, all the facility and promptitude which you have in God's service, issue from no other source than human and imperfect love : for if perfect love reigned in us—Ah ! it would break every affection, every desire, every design, the object of which was so pernicious, and it would not endure that your heart should behold it.

But note that I said this examination must be made upon the affections you have at the time, for it is not requisite that you should imagine to yourself such as may arise hereafter, since it is sufficient that we be faithful in present occurrences, according to the diversity of times, and since each season has quite enough labour and pain of its own.

Yet if you were desirous to exercise your heart in spiritual valour, by the representation of divers encounters and assaults, you might profitably do so, provided that after the acts of this imaginary valour which your heart may have made, you esteem not yourself more valiant : for the children of Ephraim, who did wonders with their bows and arrows in their warlike games at home, when it came indeed to the push upon the day of battle, turned their backs, and had not so much as the courage to lay their arrows on the string, or to face the points of those of their enemies. *They have turned back in the day of battle.**

When therefore we practise this valour about future occur- rences, or such as are only possible, if we find a good and faithful feeling we are to thank God for it, for this feeling is good as far as it goes : still we are to keep ourselves with humility between confidence and diffidence, hoping that by God's grace we should do, on occasion, that which we imagined, and still fearing that according to our ordinary misery we should perhaps do nothing and lose heart. But if the diffidence should become so excessive, that we should seem to ourselves to have neither force nor courage, and therefore feel a despair

* Ps. lxxvii. 9.

with regard to imaginary temptations, as though we were not in God's charity and grace, then in despite of our feeling of discouragement we must make a resolution of great fidelity in all that may occur up to the temptation which troubles us, hoping that when it comes, God will multiply his grace, redouble his succours, and afford us all necessary assistance; and while he gives us not the force for an imaginary and unnecessary war, he will give it us when it comes to the need. For as many in the assault have lost courage, so many have also lost fear, and have taken heart and resolution in the presence of danger and difficulty which without this they could never have done. And so, many of God's servants, representing to themselves absent temptations, have been affrighted at them even almost to the losing of courage, while when they saw them present, they behaved themselves courageously. Finally in those fears which arise from the representation of future assaults, when our heart seems to fail us, it is sufficient that we desire courage, and trust that God will bestow it upon us at the necessary time. Samson had not his strength always, but we are told in the Scripture that the lion of the vines of Thamnatha, coming towards him, *raging and roaring, the spirit of the Lord came upon him:* that is, God gave him the movement of a new force and a new courage, *and he tore the lion as he would have torn a kid in pieces.**   And the same happened when he defeated the thousand Philistines, who thought they would have overthrown him in the field of Lechi. So, my dear Theotimus, it is not necessary for us to have always the feeling and movement of courage requisite to overcome *the roaring lion which goeth about seeking whom he may devour:* this might cause us vanity and presumption. It is sufficient that we have a good desire to fight valiantly, and a perfect confidence that the Holy Ghost will assist us with his helping hand, when occasion shall present itself.

* Judges xiv.

BOOK V.

TWO PRINCIPAL EXERCISES OF HOLY LOVE WHICH CONSIST IN COMPLACENCY AND BENEVOLENCE.

———

CHAPTER I.

OF THE SACRED COMPLACENCY OF LOVE; AND FIRST OF WHAT IT CONSISTS.

LOVE, as we have said, is no other thing than the movement and outflowing of the heart towards good by means of the complacency which we take in it; so that complacency is the great motive of love, as love is the great movement of complacency.

Now this movement is practised towards God in this manner. We know by faith that the Divinity is an incomprehensible abyss of all perfection, sovereignly infinite in excellence and infinitely sovereign in goodness. This truth which faith teaches us we attentively consider by meditation, beholding that immensity of goods which are in God, either all together by assembling all the perfections, or in particular by considering his excellences one after another; for example, his all-power, his all-wisdom, his all-goodness, his eternity, his infinity. Now when we have brought our understanding to be very attentive to the greatness of the goods that are in this Divine object, it is impossible that our will should not be touched with complacency in this good, and then we use the liberty and power which we have over ourselves, provoking our own heart to redouble and strengthen its first complacency by acts of approbation and rejoicing.

" Oh !" says the devout soul then, "how beautiful art thou, my beloved, how beautiful art thou! Thou art all desirable, yea, thou art desire itself ! *Such is my beloved and he is my friend, O ye daughters of Jerusalem.** O blessed be my God for ever because he is so good ! Ah! whether I die or whether I live, too happy am I in knowing that my God is so rich in all goodness, his goodness so infinite, and his infinity so good !"

Thus approving the good which we see in God, and rejoicing in it, we make the act of love which is called complacency ; for we please ourselves in the divine pleasure infinitely more than in our own, and it is this love which gave so much content to the Saints when they could recount the perfections of their well-beloved, and which caused them to declare with so much delight that God was God. *Know ye,* said they, *that the Lord he is God. O God,* my God, my God, *thou art my God. I have said to the Lord : Thou art my God. Thou art the God of my heart, and my God is my portion for ever.*† He is the God of our heart by this complacency, since by it our heart embraces him and makes him its own : he is our inheritance, because by this act, we enjoy the goods which are in God, and, as from an inheritance, we draw from it all pleasure and content : by means of this complacency we spiritually drink and eat the perfections of the Divinity, for we make them our own and draw them into our hearts.

Jacob's ewes drew into themselves the variety of colours which they observed. So a soul, captivated by the loving complacency which she takes in considering the Divinity, and in it an infinity of excellences, draws into her heart the colours thereof, that is to say, the multitude of wonders and perfections which she contemplates, and makes them her own by the pleasure which she takes in them.

O God ! what joy shall we have in heaven, Theotimus, when we shall see the well-beloved of our hearts as an infinite sea, whose waters are perfection and goodness ! Then as stags, long and sorely chased, putting their mouths to a clear and cool stream draw into themselves the coolness of its fair waters, so our

* Cant. v. 16.   † Ps. xcix. xv. lxxii.

hearts, after so many languors and desires meeting with the
mighty and living spring of the Divinity, shall draw by their
complacency all the perfections of the well-beloved, and shall
have the perfect fruition of them by the joy which they shall take
in them, replenishing themselves with his immortal delights; and
in this way the dear spouse will enter into us as into his nuptial bed, to communicate his eternal joy unto our souls, according as he himself says, that if we keep the holy law of his
love he will come and *dwell within us.* Such is the sweet and
noble robbery of love, which, without uncolouring the well-beloved colours itself with his colours; without disrobing him
invests itself with his robes, without taking from him takes all
that he has, and without impoverishing him is enriched with
all his wealth; as the air takes light, not lessening the original
brightness of the sun, and the mirror takes the grace of the
countenance, not diminishing that of him who looks in it.

They became abominable, as those things were which they loved,*
said the Prophet, speaking of the wicked; so might one say of
the good, that they are become lovely as the things they have
loved. Behold, I beseech you, the heart of S. Clare of Montefalco: it so delighted in our Saviour's passion and in meditating on the most holy Trinity, that it drew into itself all the
marks of the passion, and an admirable representation of the
Trinity, being made such as the things it loved. The love which
the great Apostle S. Paul bore to the life, death and passion of
our divine Saviour was so great that it drew the very life, death,
and passion of this divine Saviour into his loving servant's
heart; whose will was filled with it by dilection, his memory by
meditation, and his understanding by contemplation. But by
what channel or conduit did the sweet Jesus come into the heart
of S. Paul? By the channel of complacency, as he himself
declares, saying: *God forbid that I should glory, save in the cross
of our Lord Jesus Christ.*† For if you mark well, there is no
difference between glorying in a person and taking complacency in
him, between glorying and delighting in, save that he who glories
in a thing, to pleasure adds honour; honour not being without

* Osee ix. 10.   † Gal. vi. 14.

pleasure, though pleasure can be without honour. This soul, then, had such complacency, aud esteemed himself so much honoured in the divine goodness which appears in the life, death and passion of our Saviour, that he took no pleasure but in this honour. And it is this that made him say, *God forbid that I should glory save in the cross of our Lord Jesus Christ;* as he also said that he lived not himself but Jesus Christ lived in him.

CHAPTER II.

HOW BY HOLY COMPLACENCY WE ARE MADE AS LITTLE INFANTS AT OUR SAVIOUR'S BREASTS.

O GOD! how happy the soul is who takes pleasure in knowing and fully knowing that God is God, and that his goodness is an infinite goodness! For this heavenly spouse, by this gate of complacency, enters into us and sups with us and we with him. We feed ourselves with his sweetness by the pleasure which we take therein, and satiate our heart in the divine perfections by the delight we take in them: and this repast is a supper by reason of the repose which follows it, complacency making us sweetly rest in the sweetness of the good which delights us, and with which we feed our heart; for as you know, Theotimus, the heart is fed with that which delights it, whence in our French tongue we say that such a one is fed with honour, another with riches, as the wise man said that *the mouth of fools feedeth on foolishness,** and the sovereign wisdom protests that *his meat,* that is his pleasure, *is to do the will of him that sent him.*† In conclusion the physician's aphorism is true—what is relished, nourishes : and the philosophers—what pleases, feeds.

Let my beloved come into his garden, said the sacred spouse, *and eat the fruit of his apple-trees.*‡ Now the heavenly spouse comes into his garden when he comes into the devout soul, for seeing his *delight is to be with the children of men,* where can he

* Prov. xv. 14.   † John iv. 34.   ‡ Cant. v. 1.

better lodge than in the country of the spirit, which he made to
his image and likeness. He himself plants in this garden the
loving complacency which we have in his goodness, and which
we feed on ; as, likewise, his goodness takes his pleasure and
repast in our complacency ; so that, again, our complacency is
augmented in perceiving that God is pleased to see us pleased in
him. So that these reciprocal pleasures cause the love of an incomparable complacency, by which our soul, being made the
garden of her spouse, and having from his goodness the apple
trees of his delights, renders him the fruit thereof, since she is
pleased that he is pleased in the complacency she takes in him.
Thus do we draw God's heart into ours, and he spreads in it
his precious balm, and thus is that practised which the holy
bride spoke with such joy. *The king hath brought me into his
store-rooms : we will be glad and rejoice in thee, remembering thy
breasts more than wine; the righteous love thee.** For I pray
you, Theotimus, what are the store-rooms of this king of love
but his breasts, which abound in the variety of sweetness and
delights. The bosom and breasts of the mother are the store-
room of the little infant's treasures : he has no other riches
than those, which are more precious unto him than gold or the
topaz, more beloved than all the rest of the world.

The soul then which contemplates the infinite treasures of
divine perfections in her well-beloved, holds herself too happy
and rich in this that love makes her mistress by complacency of
all the perfections and contentments of this dear spouse. And
even as a baby makes little movements towards his mother's
breasts, and dances with joy to see them discovered, and as the
mother again on her part presents them unto him with a love
always a little forward, even so the devout soul feels the
thrillings and movements of an incomparable joy, through the content which she has in beholding the treasures of the perfections
of the king of her holy love; but especially when she sees that
he himself discovers them by love, and that amongst them that
perfection of his infinite love excellently shines. Has not this
fair soul reason to cry : O my king how lovable are thy riches

* Cant. i. 3.

and how rich thy loves! Oh! which of us has more joy, thou that enjoyest it, or I who rejoice thereat! *We will be glad and rejoice in thee remembering thy breasts** so abounding in all excellence of sweetness! I because my well-beloved enjoys it, thou because thy well-beloved rejoices in it; we both enjoy it, since thy goodness makes thee enjoy my rejoicing, and my love makes me rejoice in thy enjoying. *Ah ! the righteous* and the good *love thee*, and how can one be good and not love so great a goodness! Worldly princes keep their treasures in the cabinets of their palaces, their arms in their arsenals, but the heavenly Prince keeps his treasures in his bosom, his weapons within his breast, and because his treasure is his goodness, as his weapons are his loves, his breast and bosom resemble those of a tender mother, who has her breasts like two cabinets rich in the trea-sures of sweet milk, armed with as many weapons to conquer the dear little baby as it makes its attacks in sucking.

Nature surely lodges the breasts in the bosom to the end that, since the heat of the heart there concocts the milk, as the mother is the child's nurse, so her heart may be his foster-father, and the milk may be a food of love, better a hundred times than wine. Note, meantime, Theotimus, that the com-parison of milk and wine seems so proper to the holy spouse that she is not content to have said once that the breasts of her beloved *are better than wine,*† but she repeats it thrice. Wine, Theotimus, is the milk of grapes, and milk is the wine of the breasts, and the sacred spouse says that her well-beloved is to her a cluster of grapes, but of Cyprian grapes,‡ that is, of an excellent odour. Moses said that the Israelites might drink the most pure and excellent blood of the grape, and Jacob describ-ing to his son Juda the fertility of the portion which he should have in the land of promise, prophesied under this figure the true felicity of Christians, saying that the Saviour would *wash his robe*, that is, his holy Church, *in the blood of the grape,*§ that is in his own blood. Now blood and milk are no more different

* Cant. i. 3. † Cant. i. 1.
‡ *Botrus Cypri.* Our version wrongly translates this as *a cluster of Cypress* [Tr.] § Gen. xlix. 11.

than verjuice and wine, for as verjuice ripening by the sun's heat changes its colour, becomes a grateful wine, and is made good for food, so blood tempered by the heat of the heart takes a fair white colour, and becomes a food most suited for infants.

Milk, which is a food provided by the heart and all of love, represents mystical science and theology, that is, the sweet relish which proceeds from the loving complacency taken by the spirit when it meditates on the perfections of the divine goodness. But wine signifies ordinary and acquired science, which is squeezed out by force of speculation under the press of divers arguments and discussions. Now the milk which our souls draw from the breasts of our Saviour's charity is incomparably better than the wine which we press out from human reasoning; for this milk flows from heavenly love, who prepares it for her children even before they have thought of it; it has a sweet and agreeable taste, and the odour thereof surpasses all perfumes; it makes the breath fresh and sweet as that of a sucking child; it gives joy without immoderation, it inebriates without stupefying, it does not excite the senses but elevates them (*ne leve pas mais releve*).

When the holy Isaac embraced and kissed his dear child Jacob, he smelt the good odour of his garments, and at once, filled with an extreme pleasure, he said: *Behold the smell of my son is as the smell of a plentiful field which the Lord hath blessed.** The garment and perfumes were Jacob's, but Isaac had the complacency and enjoyment of them. Ah! the soul which by love holds her Saviour in the arms of her affections, how deliciously does she smell the perfumes of the infinite perfections which are found in him, with what complacency does she say in herself: behold how the scent of my God is as the sweet smell of a flowery garden, ah! how precious are his breasts, spreading sovereign perfumes.

So the soul of the great S. Augustine, stayed in suspense between the sacred contentment which he had in considering on the one side the mystery of his Master's birth, on the other the

* Gen. xxvii. 27.

mystery of his passion, cried out, ravished in this complacency : "I know not whither to turn my heart. On the one side the Mother's breast offers me its milk, on the other the life-giving wound of the Son gives me to drink of his blood."

CHAPTER III.

THAT HOLY COMPLACENCY GIVES OUR HEART TO GOD, AND MAKES US FEEL A PERPETUAL DESIRE IN FRUITION.

THE love which we bear to God starts from the first complacency which our heart feels on first perceiving the divine goodness, when it begins to tend towards it. Now when by the exercise of love we augment and strengthen this first complacency, as we have explained in the preceding chapters, we then draw into our hearts the divine perfections and enjoy the divine goodness by rejoicing in it, practising the first part of the amorous content- ment of love expressed by the sacred spouse, saying: *My beloved to me.** But because this amorous complacency being in us who have it, ceases not to be in God in whom we have it, it gives us reciprocally to his divine goodness; so that by this holy love of complacency we enjoy the goods which are in God as though they were our own; but because the divine perfections are stronger than our spirit, entering into it they possess it reci- procally, insomuch that we not only say God is ours by this complacency but also that we are *to Him.**

The herb *aproxis* (as we have said elsewhere) has so great a correspondence with fire, that though at a distance from it, as soon as it sees it, it draws the flame and begins to burn, conceiving fire not so much from the heat as from the light of the fire presented to it. When then by this attraction it is united to the fire, if it could speak, might it not well say : my well- beloved fire is mine since I draw it to me and enjoy its flames, but I am also its, for though I drew it to me it reduced me into it as more strong and noble; it is my fire and I am its herb : I

* Cant. ii. 2.

draw it and it sets me on fire.　So our heart being brought into the presence of the divine goodness, and having drawn the perfections thereof by the complacency it takes in them, may truly say : God's goodness is all mine since I enjoy his excellences, and I again am wholly his, seeing that his delights possess me.

By complacency our soul, like Gideon's fleece, is wholly filled with heavenly dew, and this dew belongs to the fleece because it falls upon it, and again the fleece is the dew's because it is steeped in it and receives virtue from it.　Which belongs more to the other, the pearl to the oyster or the oyster to the pearl ? The pearl is the oyster's because she drew it to her, but the oyster is the pearl's because it gives her worth and value. Complacency makes us possessors of God, drawing into us his perfections, but it makes us also possessed of God, applying and fastening us to his perfections.

Now in this complacency we satiate our soul with delights in such a manner that we do not yet cease to desire to be satiated, and relishing the divine goodness we desire yet to relish it ; while satiating ourselves we would still eat, as whilst eating we feel ourselves satisfied.　The chief of the Apostles, having said in his first epistle that the ancient prophets had manifested the graces which were to abound amongst Christians, and amongst other things our Saviour's passion, and the glory which was to follow it (as well by the resurrection of his body as also by the exaltation of his name), in the end concludes that the very angels desire to behold the mysteries of the redemption in this divine Saviour : *On whom*, says he, *the angels desire to look*.*　But how can this be understood, that the angels who see the Redeemer and in him all the mysteries of our salvation, do yet desire to see him ?　Theotimus, verily they see him continually, but with a view so agreeable and delightsome that the complacency they take in it satiates them without taking away their desire, and makes them desire without removing their satiety ; the fruition is not lessened by desire, but perfected, as their desire is not cloyed but intensified by fruition.

The fruition of a thing which always contents never lessens,

<hr>

* 1 Pet. i. 12.

but is renewed and flourishes incessantly; it is ever agreeable, ever desirable. The perpetual contentment of heavenly lovers produces a desire perpetually content, as their continual desire begets in them a contentment perpetually desired. Good which is finite in giving the possession ends the desire, and in giving the desire takes away the possession, being unable to be at once possessed and desired. But the infinite good makes desire reign in possession and possession in desire, finding a way to satiate desire by a holy presence, and yet to make it live by the greatness of its excellence, which nourishes in all those that possess it a desire always content and a content always full of desire.

Consider, Theotimus, such as hold in their mouth the herb *sciticum;* according to report they are never hungry nor thirsty, it is so satisfying, and yet never lose their appetite, it nourishes them so deliciously. When our will meets God it reposes in him, taking in him a sovereign complacency, yet without staying the movement of her desire, for as she desires to love so she loves to desire, she has the desire of love and the love of desire. The repose of the heart consists not in immobility but in needing nothing, not in having no movement but in having no need to move.

The damned are in eternal movement without any mixture of rest; we mortals who are yet in this pilgrimage have, now movement, now rest, in our affections; the Blessed ever have repose in their movements and movement in their repose; only God has repose without movement, because he is sovereignly a pure and substantial act. Now although according to the ordinary condition of this mortal life we have not repose in movement, yet still, when we practise the acts of holy love, we find repose in the movement of our affections, and movement in the repose of the complacency which we take in our well-beloved, receiving hereby a foretaste of the future felicity to which we aspire.

If it be true that the chameleon lives on air, wheresoever he goes in the air he finds food, and though he move from one place to another, it is not to find wherewith to be filled, but to exercise himself within that element which is also his food, as fishes do in the sea. He who desires God while possessing him, does not desire him in order to seek him, but in order to exercise this affection within the very good which he enjoys; for the heart does not make this movement of desire as aiming at the enjoyment of a thing not had, since it is already had, but as dilating itself in the enjoyment which it has; not to obtain the good, but to recreate and please itself therein; not to gain the enjoyment of it but to take enjoyment in it. So we walk and move to go to some delicious garden, where, being arrived, we cease not to walk and exercise ourselves, not now to get there, but being there to walk and pass our time therein: we walk in order to go and enjoy the pleasantness of the garden, being there we walk to take our pleasure in the enjoyment of it. *Seek ye the Lord and be strengthened, seek his face evermore.** We always seek him whom we always love, says the great S. Augustine: love seeks that which it has found, not to have it but to have it always.

Finally, Theotimus, the soul which is in the exercise of the love of complacency cries continually in her sacred silence: It suffices me that God is God, that his goodness is infinite, that his perfection is immense; whether I die or whether I live matters little to me since my dear well-beloved lives eternally an all-triumphant life. Death itself cannot trouble a heart which knows that its sovereign love lives. It is sufficient for a heart that loves that he whom it loves more than itself is replenished with eternal happiness, seeing that it lives more in him whom it loves than in him whom it animates; yea, that it lives not itself, but its well-beloved lives in it.

* Ps. civ. 4.

CHAPTER IV.

OF THE LOVING CONDOLENCE BY WHICH THE COMPLACENCY OF
LOVE IS STILL BETTER DECLARED.

COMPASSION, condolence, commiseration, or pity, is no other
thing than an affection which makes us share in the suffering
and sorrow of him whom we love, drawing the misery which he
endures into our heart; whence it is called *misericorde*, or, as it
were, *misere de cœur:* as complacency draws into the lover's
heart the pleasures and contentments of the thing beloved. It
is love that works both effects, by the virtue it has of uniting
the heart which loves to the thing loved, thus making the
goods and the evils of friends common; and what happens in
compassion much illustrates what regards complacency.

Compassion takes its greatness from the love which produces
it. Thus the condolence of mothers in the afflictions of their
only children is great, as the Scripture often testifies. How
great was the sorrow of Agar's heart upon the pains of her
Ismael, whom she saw well-nigh perish with thirst in the
desert! How much did David's soul commiserate the misery
of his Absalom! Ah! do you not mark the motherly heart of
the great Apostle, sick with the sick, burning with zeal for such
as were scandalized, having a continual sorrow for the ruin of
the Jews, and daily dying for his dear spiritual children. But
especially consider how love draws all the pains, all the torments, travails, sufferings, griefs, wounds, passion, cross and
very death of our Redeemer into his most sacred mother's
heart. Alas! the same nails that crucified the body of this
divine child, also crucified the soul of this all-sweet mother;
she endured the same miseries with her son by commiseration,
the same dolours by condolence, the same passions by compassion, and, in a word, the sword of death which transpierced the
body of this best beloved Son, struck through the heart of this
most loving mother,* whence she might well have said that he
was to her as *a bundle of myrrh between her breasts,†* that is,

* Luke ii. 35.   † Cant. i. 12.

in her bosom and in the midst of her heart. You see how
Jacob, hearing the sad though false news of the death of his
dear Joseph, is afflicted with it. *Ah !* said he, *I will go down
mourning into hell,* that is to say, to Limbo into Abraham's
bosom, *to my son.**

Condolence is also great according to the greatness of the
sorrows which we see those we love suffering; for how little
soever the friendship be, if the evils which we see endured be
extreme, they cause in us great pity. This made Cæsar weep
over Pompey, and the daughters of Jerusalem could not
refrain from weeping over our Saviour, though the greater
number of them were not greatly attached to him; as also the
friends of Job, though wicked friends, made great lamentation
in beholding the dreadful spectacle of his incomparable misery.
And what a stroke of grief was it in the heart of Jacob to
think that his dear child had died by a death so cruel as that of
being devoured by a savage beast. But, besides all this, commiseration is much strengthened by the presence of the object
which is in misery; this caused poor Agar to go away from her
dying son, to disburden herself in some sort of the compassionate
grief which she felt, saying: *I will not see the boy die;†*
as on the contrary our Saviour weeps seeing the sepulchre of
his well-beloved Lazarus and regarding his dear Jerusalem; and
our good Jacob is beside himself with grief when he sees the
bloody coat of his poor little Joseph.

Now the same causes increase complacency. In proportion
as a friend is more dear to us we take more pleasure in his contentment, and his good enters more deeply into our heart. If
the good is excellent, our joy is also greater. But if we see our
friend enjoying it, our rejoicing becomes extreme. When the
good Jacob knew that his son lived,—O God! What joy! His
spirit returned to him, he lived once more, he, so to speak,
rose again from death. But what does this mean,—he revived
or returned to life? Theotimus, spirits die not their own
death but by sin, which separates them from God, their true
supernatural life, yet they sometimes die another's death; and

* Gen. xxxvii. 35.　　　　　　　† Gen. xxi. 16.

this happened to the good Jacob of whom we speak, for love, which draws into the heart of the lover the good and evil of the thing beloved, the one by complacency, the other by commiseration, drew the death of the beloved Joseph into the loving Jacob's heart, and, by a miracle impossible to any other power than love, the spirit of this good father was full of the death of him that was living and reigning, for affection having been deceived ran before the effect.

But, on the contrary, as soon as he knew that his son was alive, love which had so long kept the supposed death of the son in the spirit of the good father, seeing that it had been deceived, speedily rejected this imaginary death, and made enter in its place the true life of the same son. Thus then he returned to a new life, because the life of his son entered into his heart by complacency, and animated him with an incomparable contentment: with which finding himself satisfied, and not esteeming any other pleasure in comparison of this: *It is enough for me,* said he, *if Joseph my son be yet living.** But when with his own eyes he saw by experience the truth of the grandeur of this dear child in Gessen, falling upon his neck and embracing him, he wept saying: *Now shall I die with joy because I have seen thy face and leave thee alive.†* Ah! what a joy, Theotimus, and how excellently expressed by this old man! For what would he say by these words, *now shall I die with joy because I have seen thy face,* but that his content was so great, that it was able to render death itself joyful and agreeable, even death, which is the most grievous and horrible thing in the world. Tell me, I pray you, Theotimus, who has more sense of Joseph's good, he who enjoys it or Jacob who rejoices in it. Certainly, if good be not good but in respect of the content which it affords us, the father has as much as the son, yea more, for the son, together with the viceroy's dignity of which he is possessed, has consequently much care and many affairs, but the father enjoys by complacency, and purely possesses all that is good in this greatness and dignity of his son, without charge, care or trouble. *Now shall I die with joy,* says he. Ah! who does not see his contentment? If even death cannot trouble his joy, who can

* Gen. xlv. 28.   † Gen. xlvi. 30.

ever change it ?   If his content can live amidst the distresses of
death, who can ever bereave him of it ?   *Love is strong as death,*
and the joys of love surmount the sorrows of death, for death
cannot kill but enlivens them ; so that, as there is a fire which
is marvellously kept alive in a fountain near Grenoble (as we
know for certain and the great S. Augustine attests), so holy
charity has strength to nourish her flames and consolations in
the most grievous anguishes of death, and the waters of tribulations cannot quench her fire.

————

CHAPTER V.

OF THE CONDOLENCE AND COMPLACENCY OF LOVE IN THE PASSION OF OUR LORD.

WHEN I see my Saviour on the Mount of Olives with his *soul
sorrowful even unto death :*—Ah ! Lord Jesus, say I, what can
have brought the sorrows of death into the soul of life except
love, which, exciting commiseration, drew thereby our miseries
into thy sovereign heart ?   Now a devout soul, seeing this abyss
of heaviness and distress in this divine lover, how can she be
without a holily loving sorrow ?   But considering, on the other
hand, that all the afflictions of her well-beloved proceed from no
imperfection or want of strength, but from the greatness of his
dearest love, she cannot but melt away with a holy sorrowful
love.   So that she cries : *I am black* with sorrow by compassion,
but beautiful with love by complacency ; the anguish of my
well-beloved *has changed my colour :* for how could a faithful
lover behold such torments in him whom she lòves more than
her life, without swooning away and becoming all wan and
wasted with grief.   The tents of nomads, perpetually exposed
to the injuries of weather and war, are almost always ragged
and covered with dust ; and I, ever exposed to the griefs which
by condolence I receive from the immeasurable travails of my
divine Saviour, I am all covered with distress, and rent with
sorrow.   But because the pains of him I love come from his
love, in what measure they afflict me by compassion, they de-

light me by complacency; for how could a faithful lover not take an extreme content to see herself so loved by her heavenly spouse? Wherefore the beauty of love is in the ill-favour of sorrow. And if I wear mourning for the passion and death of my King, all swarthy and black with grief, I cease not to have an incomparable sweetness in seeing the excess of his love amid his travails and his sorrows; and the tents of Solomon, all embroidered and worked in an admirable variety of decorations, were never so lovely as I am content, and, consequently, sweet, amiable and agreeable, in the variety of the sentiments of love which I have amid those griefs. Love equalizes lovers: Ah! I see him, this dear lover—he is a fire of love burning in a thorny bush of sorrow, and I am the same: I am all inflamed with love amid the thorny bushes of my griefs, I am *a lily among thorns.* Ah! do not even look at the horrors of my poignant sorrows, but see the beauty of my agreeable love. Alas! he suffers insupportable pains, this well-beloved divine lover: it is this which grieves me and makes me faint with anguish; but he takes pleasure in suffering, he loves his torments, and dies with joy at dying with pain for me: wherefore as I am sorrowing over his pains, so I am all ravished with joy at his love; not only do I grieve with him, but I glorify myself in him.

It was this love, Theotimus, which brought upon the seraphic S. Francis the stigmata, and upon the loving angelic S. Catharine of Siena the burning wounds of the Saviour, amorous complacency having sharpened the points of dolorous compassion; as honey makes more penetrating and sensible the bitterness of wormwood, whilst on the contrary the sweet smell of roses is intensified by the neighbourhood of garlic planted near the trees. For, in the same way, the loving complacency we have taken in the love of our Saviour makes the compassion we feel for his pains infinitely stronger: as reciprocally, passing back from the compassion for his pains to complacency in love, the pleasure of this is far more ardent and exalted. Then are practised pain in love and love in pain; then amorous condolence and dolorous complacency, as another Esau and another Jacob, struggling as to which shall make the greater effort, put the soul in incredible convulsions and agonies, and there takes place an ecstasy lovingly sorrowful and sorrowfully loving. So those great souls of S. Francis and S. Catharine felt matchless love in their pains, and incomparable pains in their love, when they were stigmatized, relishing that joyous love of suffering for a beloved one, which their Saviour exercised in the supreme degree on the tree of the cross. Thus is born the precious union of our heart with its God, which, like a mystical Benjamin, is the child of pain and joy both together.

It cannot be declared, Theotimus, how strongly the Saviour desires to enter into our souls by this love of sorrowing complacency. Ah! says he, *Open to me, my sister, my love, my dove, my undefiled; for my head is full of dew, and my locks of the drops of the night.** What is this dew, and what are the drops of the night but the afflictions and pains of his passion? Pearls, in sooth (as we have said often enough), are nothing but drops of dew, which the freshness of night rains over the face of the sea, received into the shells of oysters or pearl-mothers. Ah! this divine lover of the soul would say, I am laden with the pains and sweats of my passion, almost all of which passed either in the darkness of the night, or in the night of the darkness which the obscured sun made in the very brightness of its noon. Open then thy heart towards me as the pearl-mothers open their shells towards the sky, and I will shed upon thee the dew of my passion, which will be changed into pearls of consolation.

CHAPTER VI.

OF THE LOVE OF BENEVOLENCE WHICH WE EXERCISE TOWARDS OUR SAVIOUR BY WAY OF DESIRE.

In the love which God exercises towards us he always begins by benevolence, willing and effecting all the good that is in us, in which afterwards he takes complacency. He made David according to his heart by benevolence, then he found him according to his heart by complacency. He first created the

---

* Cant. v. 2.

universe for man, and man in the universe, giving to each thing such a measure of goodness as was proportionable to it, out of his pure benevolence, then he approved all that he had done, finding that all was very good, and by complacency rested in his work.

But, on the contrary, our love towards God begins from the complacency which we have in the sovereign goodness and infinite perfection which we know is in the Divinity, then we come to the exercise of benevolence; and as the complacency which God takes in his creatures is no other thing than a continuation of his benevolence towards them, so the benevolence which we bear towards God is nothing else but an approbation of and perseverance in the complacency we have in him.

Now this love of benevolence towards God is practised in this sort. We cannot, with a true desire, wish any good to God, because his goodness is infinitely more perfect than we can either wish or think : desire is only of a future good, and no good is future to God, since all good is so present to him that the presence of good in his divine Majesty is nothing else but the Divinity itself. Not being able then to make any absolute desire for God, we make imaginary and conditional ones, in this manner : *I have said to the Lord, thou art my God,* who being full of thine own infinite goodness, *hast no need of my goods,** nor of anything whatever, but if, by imagination of a thing impossible, I could think thou hadst need of anything, I would never cease to wish it thee, even with the loss of my life, of my being, and of all that is in the world. And if, being what thou art, and what thou canst not but still be, it were possible that thou couldst receive any increase of good,—O God ! what a desire would I have that thou shouldst have it ! I would desire, O eternal Lord ! to see my heart converted into a wish, and my life into a sigh, to desire thee such a good ! Ah ! yet would I not for all this, O thou sacred well-beloved of my soul, desire to be able to wish any good to thy Majesty, yea I delight with all my heart in this supreme degree of goodness which thou hast, to which nothing can be added, either by desire or yet by thought. But if such

* Ps. xv. 2.

a desire were possible, O infinite Divinity, O divine Infinity! my soul would be that desire and nothing else, so intensely would she be desirous to desire for thee that which she is infinitely pleased that she cannot desire ; seeing that her powerlessness to make this desire proceeds from the infinite infinity of thy perfection, which outstrips all desire and all thought. Ah! O my God! how dearly I love the impossibility of being able to desire thee any good, since this comes from the incomprehensible immensity of thy abundance. That is so sovereignly infinite, that if there were an infinite desire it would be infinitely satiated by the infinity of thy goodness, which would convert it into an infinite complacency. This desire then, by imagination of impossibilities, may be sometimes profitably practised amidst great and extraordinary feelings and fervours. We are told that the great S. Augustine often made such, pouring out in an excess of love these words: " Ah! Lord, I am Augustine and thou art God, but still, if that, which neither is nor can be, were, that I were God and thou Augustine, I would, changing my condition with thee, become Augustine to the end that thou mightest be God!"

It is yet another kind of benevolence towards God, when feeling we cannot exalt him in himself, we strive to do it in ourselves, that is, still more and more to increase the complacency we take in his goodness. And then, Theotimus, we desire not the complacency for the pleasure it yields us, but purely because this pleasure is in God. For as we desire not the compassion for the pain it brings to our heart, but because this sorrow unites and associates us to our well-beloved, who is in pain ; so we do not love the complacency because it brings us pleasure, but because this pleasure is taken in union with the pleasure and good which is in God, to be more united to which, we would desire to exercise a complacency infinitely greater, in imitation of the most holy Queen and Mother of love, whose sacred soul continually magnified and exalted God. And that it might be known that this magnifying was made by the complacency which she took in the divine goodness, she declares; *My spirit hath* exultingly *rejoiced in God my Saviour.**

* Luke i. 47.

CHAPTER VII.

HOW THE DESIRE TO EXALT AND MAGNIFY GOD SEPARATES US FROM
INFERIOR PLEASURES, AND MAKES US ATTENTIVE TO THE DIVINE
PERFECTIONS.

THE love of benevolence, then, causes in us a desire, more and
more to increase the complacency which we take in the divine
goodness; and to effect this increase, the soul sedulously deprives
herself of all other pleasure that she may give herself more entirely to taking pleasure in God. A religious man asked the
devout Brother Giles, one of the first and most holy companions
of S. Francis, in what work he could be most agreeable to God:
he answered by singing: " One to one," which he afterwards
explained, saying, " Give ever your whole soul which is one, to
God who is one." The soul pours itself out by pleasures, and the
diversity of these dissipates and hinders her from being able to
apply herself attentively to the pleasure which she ought to take
in God. The glorious S. Paul reputed all things as dung and
dirt in comparison of his Saviour. And the sacred spouse is
wholly for her well-beloved only: *My beloved to me and I to
him.* And if the soul that stands thus holily affected meet with
creatures never so excellent, yea though they were angels, she
makes no delay with them, save only what she needs for the
help and furtherance of her desire. Tell me then, says she to
them, tell me, I conjure you, *have you seen him whom my soul
loveth?** The glorious lover Magdalen met the angels at the
sepulchre, who doubtless spoke to her angelically, that is most
sweetly, but she, on the contrary, wholly ruthful, could take no
content, either in their sweet words or in the glory of their
garments, or in the all-heavenly grace of their deportment, or in
the most delightsome beauty of their faces, but all steeped in
tears: *They have taken away my Lord,* says she, *and I know not
where they have laid him :†* and, turning about, she saw her sweet
Saviour, but in form of a gardener, with whom her heart cannot
be satisfied, for full of the love of the death of her Master,

* Cant. iii. 3.   † John xx. 13.

flowers she will have none, nor consequently gardeners; she has within her heart the cross, the nails, the thorns; she seeks her crucified. Ah! my dear sir gardener, says she, if perchance you have planted my well-beloved deceased Lord amongst your flowers, as a crushed and withered lily, tell me quickly and I, I will carry him away. But no sooner had he called her by her name, than, wholly melting with delight, O God! says she, my Master! Nothing can content her, nor angels' company delight her, no nor yet her very Saviour's, unless he appear in that form in which he had stolen her heart. The kings could not content themselves either in the beauty of Jerusalem or in the magnificence of Herod's court, or in the brightness of the star; their heart seeks the little cave and the little child of Bethlehem. The mother of fair loving and the spouse of most holy love cannot stay among their kinsfolks and acquaintance; they still walk on in grief, seeking after the only object of their delight. The desire to increase holy complacency cuts off all other pleasure, to the end that it may more actively practise that to which the divine benevolence excites it.

Now still more to magnify this sovereign well-beloved, the soul goes ever seeking his face: that is, with an attention more and more careful and fervent, she keeps noting every particular of the beauties and perfections which are in him, making a continual progress in this sweet searching out of motives, which may perpetually urge her to a greater complacency in the incomprehensible goodness which she loves. So David in many of his heavenly psalms recites one by one the works and wonders of God, and the sacred spouse ranges, in her divine canticles, as a well-ranked army, all the perfections of her beloved, one after another, to provoke her soul to most holy complacency, thereby more highly to magnify his excellence, and also to subject all other spirits to the love of her beloved so dear.

CHAPTER VIII.

HOW HOLY BENEVOLENCE PRODUCES THE PRAISE OF THE DIVINE WELL-BELOVED.

HONOUR, my dear Theotimus, is not in him who is honoured, but in him who honours: for how often it happens that he whom we honour knows nothing of it, nor has so much as thought about it. How often we praise such as know us not, or who are sleeping; and yet according to the common estimation of men, and their ordinary manner of conceiving, it seems that we do one some good when we do him honour, and that we give him much when we give him titles and praises, and we find no difficulty in saying that a man is rich in honour, glory, reputation, praise, though indeed we know that all this is outside the person who is honoured. He oftentimes receives no manner of profit therefrom, according to a saying ascribed to the great S. Augustine: O poor Aristotle, thou art being praised where thou art not, and where thou art, thou art being burned. What fruit, I pray you, do Cæsar and Alexander the Great reap from so many vain words which some vain souls employ in their praise?

God being replenished with a goodness which surpasses all praise and honour, receives no advantage nor increase by all the benedictions which we give him. He is neither richer nor greater, nor more content or happy by them, for his happiness, his content, his greatness, and his riches neither are nor can be any other thing than the divine infinity of his goodness. At the same time, since, according to our ordinary estimation, honour is held one of the greatest effects of our benevolence towards others, and since by it we not only do not imply any indigence in those we honour, but rather protest that they abound in excellence, we therefore make use of this kind of benevolence towards God, who not only approves it, but exacts it, as suitable to our condition, and so proper to testify the respectful love we bear him, that he has ordained we should render and refer all honour and glory unto him.

Thus then the soul who has taken a great complacency in God's infinite perfection, seeing that she cannot wish him any increase of goodness, because he has infinitely more than she can either wish or conceive, desires at least that his name may be blessed, exalted, praised, honoured and adored ever more and more. And beginning with her own heart, she ceases not to provoke it to this holy exercise, and, as a sacred bee, flies hither and thither amongst the flowers of the divine works and excellences, gathering from them a sweet variety of complacencies, from which she works up and composes the heavenly honey of benedictions, praises, and confessions of honour, by which, as far as she is able, she magnifies and glorifies the name of her well-beloved : in imitation of the great Psalmist, who having gone round, and as it were in spirit run over the wonders of the divine goodness, immolated on the altar of his heart the mystic victim of the utterances of his voice, by canticles and psalms of admiration and benediction : *I have gone round, and have offered up in his tabernacle a sacrifice of jubilation : I will sing, and recite a psalm to the Lord.** But, Theotimus, this desire of praising God which holy benevolence excites in our hearts is insatiable, for the soul that is touched with it would wish to have infinite praises to bestow upon her well-beloved, because she finds his perfections more than infinite : so that, finding herself to fall far short of being able to satisfy her desire, she makes extreme efforts of affection to praise at least in some measure this goodness all worthy of praise, and these efforts of benevolence are marvellously augmented by complacency : for in proportion as the soul finds God good, relishing more and more his sweetness, and taking complacency in his infinite goodness, she would also raise higher the benedictions and praises she gives him. And again, as the soul grows warm in praising the incomprehensible sweetness of God, she enlarges and dilates the complacency she takes in him, and by this enlargement she more strongly excites herself to his praise. So that the affection of complacency and that of praise, by these reciprocal movements and mutual inclinations, advance one another with great and continual increase.

* Ps. xxvi. 6.

So nightingales, according to Pliny, take such complacency in their songs, that, by reason of this complacency, for fifteen days and fifteen nights they never cease warbling, forcing themselves to sing better in emulous striving with one another; so that when they sing the best, they take a greater complacency, and this increase of complacency makes them force themselves to greater efforts of trilling, augmenting in such sort their complacency by their song and their song by their complacency, that it is often found that they die and their throats burst with their singing. Birds worthy the fair name of philomel, since they die thus, of and for the love of melody!

O God! my Theotimus, how the soul ardently pressed with affection to praise her God, is touched with a dolour most delicious and a delight most dolorous, when after a thousand efforts of praise she comes so short. Alas! she would wish, this poor nightingale, to raise her accents ever higher, and perfect her melody, the better to sing the praises of her well-beloved. By how much more she praises, by so much more is she delighted in praising: and by how much greater her delight in praising is, by so much her pain is greater that she cannot yet more praise him; still, to find what content she can in this passion, she makes all sorts of efforts, and in the midst of them faints and fails, as it happened to the most glorious S. Francis, who amidst the pleasure he had in praising God and singing his canticles of love, shed a great abundance of tears, and often let fall through feebleness, what he might be holding in his hands: being like a sacred nightingale all outspent, and often losing respiration through the effort of aspiration after the praises of him whom he could never praise sufficiently.

But hear an agreeable similitude upon this subject, drawn from the name which this loving Saint gave his religious; for he called them *Cicalas,* by reason of the nightly praises they sang to God. Cicalas, Theotimus, as though they were nature's *organs,* have their breasts set with pipes; and to sing the better they live only on dew, which they take not by the mouth, for they have none, but suck it by a certain little tongue they have on the breast, by which they utter their cries with so much noise that they seem to be nothing but voice. Now this is the

state of the sacred lover ; for all the faculties of her soul are
as so many pipes which she has in her breast, to repeat the
canticles and praises of the well-beloved. Her devotion in the
midst of all these is the tongue of her heart, according to S.
Bernard, by which she receives the dew of the divine perfections,
sucking and drawing them to her, as her food, by the most holy
complacency which she takes in them ; and by the same tongue
of devotion she utters all her voices of prayer, praise, canticles,
psalms, benedictions, according to the testimony of one of the
most glorious spiritual cicalas that was ever heard, who sang
thus : *Bless the Lord, O my soul : and let all that is within me
bless his holy name.** For is it not as though he had said, I am
a mystical cicala, my soul, my spirit, my thoughts, all the
faculties that are collected within me, are organ pipes. Let all
these for ever bless the name and sound the praises of my God.
*I will bless the Lord at all times, his praise shall be always in
my mouth. In the Lord shall my soul be praised; let the meek
hear and rejoice.**

CHAPTER IX.

HOW BENEVOLENCE MAKES US CALL ALL CREATURES TO THE PRAISE OF GOD.

THE heart that is taken and pressed with a desire of praising
the divine goodness more than it is able, after many endeavours
goes oftentimes out of itself, to invite all creatures to help it in
its design. As did the three children in the furnace, in that
admirable canticle of benedictions, by which they excite all
that is in heaven, on earth and under the earth, to render
thanks to the eternal God, by blessing and praising him
sovereignly. So the glorious Psalmist, quite mastered by holily
disordered passion moving him to praise God, goes without
order, leaping from heaven to earth, and from earth to heaven
again, invoking angels, fishes, mountains, waters, dragons,
birds, serpents, fire, hail, mists, assembling by his desires

* Ps. cii. 1.   † Ps. xxxiii. 1, 2.

all creatures,—to the end that they all may conspire to lovingly magnify their Creator, some in their own persons celebrating the divine praise, others affording matter of praise by the wonders of their different properties, which manifest their Maker's power ; so that this divine royal Psalmist, having composed a great number of psalms with this inscription: *Praise God :* after he had run through all creatures, holily inviting them to bless the divine Majesty, and gone over a great variety of means and instruments proper for the celebration of the praises of this eternal goodness, in the end, as falling down through lack of breath, closes his sacred song with this ejaculation: *Let every spirit praise the Lord ;* that is, let all that has life, neither live nor breathe but to bless its Creator, according to the invitation he had elsewhere given : *O magnify the Lord with me ; and let us extol his name together.*†

So the great S. Francis sang the canticle of the sun, and a hundred other excellent benedictions, to invoke creatures to help his heart, all fainting because he could not satisfy himself in the praises of the dear Saviour of his soul. So the heavenly spouse perceiving herself almost to faint away amid the violent efforts she made to bless and magnify the well-beloved king of her heart, Ah ! she cried out to her companions, this divine spouse *has led me* by contemplation *into his wine-cellar*, making me taste the incomparable delights of the perfections of his excellence, and I have so steeped and holily inebriated myself in the holy complacency which I have taken in this abyss of beauty, that my soul languishes, wounded with a lovingly mortal desire, which urges me everlastingly to praise so exalted a goodness. Ah! come, I beseech you, to the assistance of my poor heart, which is upon the point of falling down dead. For pity sustain it, and *stay me up with flowers ;* strengthen me *and compass me about with apples*, or I fall lifeless. Complacency draws the divine sweetnesses into her heart, which so ardently fills itself therewith that it is overcharged. But the love of benevolence makes our heart pass out of itself, and exhale itself in vapours of delicious perfumes, that is, in all kinds of holy praises. And

* Ps. cl. 6.   † Ps. xxxiii. 4.

yet not being able to produce as many as it would wish: Oh! it says, let all creatures come and contribute the flowers of their benedictions, the apples of their thanksgivings, honours and adorations, so that on every side we may smell odours poured out to the glory of him whose infinite sweetness surpasses all honour, and whom we can never right worthily magnify.

It is this divine passion that brings forth so many discourses, sends through all hazards a Xavier, a Berzée, an Anthony, that multitude of Jesuits, Capuchins, and religious and ecclesiastics of all kinds, to the Indies, Japan, Marañon, that the holy name of Jesus may be known, acknowledged, and adored throughout those immense nations. It is this holy passion which causes so many books of piety to be written, so many churches, altars, pious houses to be erected, and in a word which makes many of God's servants watch, labour, and die amid the flames of zeal which consume and spend them.

CHAPTER X.

HOW THE DESIRE TO PRAISE GOD MAKES US ASPIRE TO HEAVEN.

THE amorous soul, perceiving that she cannot satiate the desire she has to praise her well-beloved while she lives in this world, and knowing that the praises which are given in heaven to the divine goodness are sung to an incomparably more delightful air,—O God! says she, how much to be praised are the praises which are poured forth by those blessed spirits before the throne of my heavenly king; how blessed are their blessings! O what a happiness is it to hear this melody of the most holy eternity, in which by the sweetest concurrence of dissimilar and varied tones, are made those admirable accords—all the parts mingling together with a continued sequence and marvellous linking of progressive movements—by which perpetual Alleluias do resound on every side.

Voices which for their loudness are compared to thunders, to trumpets, to the noise of the waves of a troubled sea; yet voices which, for their incomparable softness and sweetness, are compared to the melody of harps, delicately and delightfully touched by hands of the most skilful players; and voices all of which unite to sing the joyous Paschal canticle : *Alleluia,* praise God, *Amen,* praise God. For know, Theotimus, that a voice goes out from the divine throne which ceases not to cry to the happy inhabitants of the glorious heavenly Jerusalem : *Praise God, O you that are his servants, and you that fear him great and little :** at which all the innumerable multitude of saints,—the choirs of angels and the choirs of assembled men,—answer, singing with all their force : *Alleluia,* praise God. But what is this admirable voice, which issuing out from the divine throne entones the Alleluias of the elect, except most holy complacency, which being received into the heart, makes them feel the sweetness of the divine perfections, whereupon a loving benevolence, the source of heavenly praises, is bred in them ? So that complacency coming from the throne, declares to the blessed the grandeurs of God, and benevolence excites them to pour out in their turn the perfumes of praise before the throne. Wherefore by way of answer they eternally sing: *Alleluia,* that is, praise God. The complacency comes from the throne into the heart, and benevolence goes from the heart to the throne.

O how worthy of love is this temple, wholly resounding with praise! O what content have such as live in this sacred dwelling, where so many heavenly philomels and nightingales sing with this holy strife of love, the canticles of eternal delight!

The heart, then, that in this world can neither sing nor hear the divine praises to its liking, enters into unutterable desires of being delivered from the bonds of this life to pass to the other, where the heavenly well-beloved is so perfectly praised : and these desires having taken possession of the heart, often become so strong and urgent in the breast of sacred lovers, that banishing all other desires they cause disgust of all earthly things, and render the soul languishing and lovesick: yea, sometimes the holy passion goes so far, that, God permitting, one dies of it.

So that glorious and seraphical lover S. Francis, having been long torn with this strong affection for praising God, in the end, in his last years, after he had had assurance, by a special revela-

* Apoc. xix.

tion, of his eternal salvation, could not contain his joy, but wasted daily, as if his life and soul had burnt away like incense, upon the fire of the ardent desires which he had to see his Master, incessantly to praise him : so that these ardours taking every day a fresh increase, his soul left his body by a passionate movement which he made towards heaven; for the divine Providence thought good that he should die pronouncing these sacred words: *Bring my soul out of prison, that I may praise thy name : the just wait for me, until thou reward me.** Behold, Theotimus, I beseech you, this soul, who, as a heavenly nightingale shut up in the cage of his body, in which he cannot at will sing the benedictions of his eternal love, knows that he could better trill and practise his delicious song if he could gain the air, to enjoy his liberty and the society of other philomels, amongst the gay and flowery hills of the land of the blessed ; wherefore he cries: Alas ! O Lord of my life, ah ! by thy sweet goodness, deliver poor me from the cage of my body, free me from this little prison, to the end that released from this bondage I may fly to my dear companions, who expect me there above in heaven, to make me one of their choirs, and environ me with their joy. There, Lord, according my voice to theirs, I with them will make up a sweet harmony of delicious airs and words, singing, praising, and blessing thy mercy. This admirable Saint, as an orator who would end and conclude all he had said in some short sentence, put this happy ending to all his wishes and desires, whereof these last words were an abridgment ; words to which he so firmly attached his soul, that in breathing them he breathed his last. My God, Theotimus, what a sweet and dear death was this ! a happily loving death, a holily mortal love.

CHAPTER XI.

HOW WE PRACTISE THE LOVE OF BENEVOLENCE IN THE PRAISES WHICH OUR SAVIOUR AND HIS MOTHER GIVE TO GOD.

WE mount then in this holy exercise from step to step, by the creatures which we invite to praise God, passing from the insensible to the reasonable and intellectual, and from the

* Ps. cxli. 8.

Church militant to the triumphant, in which we rise through the angels and the saints, till above them all we have found the most sacred virgin, who in a matchless air praises and magnifies the divinity more highly, holily and delightfully than all other creatures together can ever do.

Being two years ago at Milan, whither the veneration of the recent memory of the great Archbishop S. Charles had drawn me, with some of our clergy, we heard in different churches many sorts of music : but in a monastery of women we heard a religious whose voice was so admirably delightful that she alone created an impression more agreeable, beyond comparison, than all the rest together, which though otherwise excellent, yet seemed to serve only to bring out and raise the perfection and grace of this unique voice. So, Theotimus, amongst all the choirs of men and all the choirs of angels, the most sacred virgin's clear voice is heard above all the rest, giving more praise to God, than do all the other creatures. And indeed the heavenly King in a particular manner invites her to sing : *Show me thy face,* says he, my well-beloved, *let thy voice sound in my ears : for thy voice is sweet, and thy face comely.**

But these praises which this mother of honour and fair love, together with all creatures, gives to the divinity, though excellent and admirable, come so infinitely short of the infinite merit of God's goodness, that they bear no proportion to it : and therefore, although they greatly please the sacred benevolence which the loving heart has for its well-beloved, yet do they not satiate it. Wherefore it goes forward and invites our Saviour to praise and glorify his eternal Father with all the benedictions which a Son's love can furnish him with. And then, Theotimus, the spirit comes unto a place of silence, for we can no longer do aught but wonder and admire. O what a canticle is this of the Son to his Father ! O how fair this dear well-beloved is amongst all the children of men ! O how sweet is his voice, as issuing from the lips upon which the fulness of grace was poured ! All the others are perfumed, but he is

* Cant. ii. 14.

perfume itself; the others are embalmed, but he is balm poured out; the Eternal receives others' praises, as scents of particular flowers, but perceiving the odour of the praises which our Saviour gives him, doubtless he cries out : *Behold the smell of* the praises of *my Son is as the smell of a plentiful field, which* I have *blessed !** Yes, my dear Theotimus, all the benedictions which the Church militant and triumphant offers to God are angelical and human benedictions; for, although they are addressed to the Creator, yet they proceed from the creature; but those of the Son are divine, for they not only tend to God, as the others, but they flow from God : the Redeemer being true God, they are not only divine in respect of their end but also of their origin; divine, because they tend to God ; divine, because they issue from God. To others God gives his inspiration and sufficient grace, for the utterance of praise; but that of the Redeemer, he, who is God, himself produces, and therefore it is infinite.

He who, on a morning, having heard for some good space of time in the neighbouring woods the sweet chanting of finches, linnets, goldfinches, and such like little birds, should in the end hear a master-nightingale, which in perfect melody filled the air and ear with its admirable voice, doubtless would prefer this one woodland singer before the whole flock of the others. So, having heard all the praises which so many different sorts of creatures, in emulation of one another, render unanimously to their Creator, when at length we listen to the praise our Saviour gives, we find in it a certain infinity of merit, of worth, of sweetness, which surpasses all the hope and expectation of the heart: and the soul, as if awakened out of a deep sleep, is then instantly ravished with the extreme sweetness of such melody. Ah! I hear it: Oh! the voice, the voice of my well-beloved! the king-voice of all voices, a voice, in comparison with which all other voices are but a dumb and gloomy silence! See how this dear love springs forward, see how he comes leaping upon the highest mountains, transcending the hills : his voice is heard above the Seraphim, and all other creatures; he has the eyes of a roe to pene-trate deeper than any other into the beauty of the sacred object which he desires to praise. He loves the melody of the glory

* Gen. xxvii. 27.

and praise of his Father more than all others do, and therefore he takes his Father's praises and benedictions in a strain above them all. Ah ! behold him, this divine love of the beloved, how he stands behind the wall of his humanity, making himself to be seen through the wounds of his body and the opening of his side, as by windows, and as by a lattice through which he looks out on us.*

Yea, truly, Theotimus, divine love being seated upon our Saviour's Heart as upon his royal throne, beholds by the cleft of his pierced side all the hearts of the sons of men : for this Heart being the King of hearts keeps his eyes ever fixed upon hearts. But as those that look through a lattice see others clearly, and are but half-seen themselves, so the divine love of this Heart, or rather this Heart of divine love, continually sees our hearts clearly and regards them with the eyes of his love, but we do not see him, we only half-see him. For, O God ! if we could see him as he is, we should die of love for him, so long as we are mortal ; as he himself died for us while he was mortal, and as he would yet die, if he were not immortal. O when we hear this divine Heart, as it sings with a voice of infinite sweetness the canticle of praise to the divinity, what joy, Theotimus, what efforts of our hearts to spring up to heaven that we may ever hear it ! And verily this dear friend of our hearts invites us to this. *Arise, make haste,* leave thyself and take thy flight towards me, *my dove, my beautiful,* unto this heavenly abode, where all is joy and nought is heard but praises and benedictions. All is flowers, all is sweetness and perfume ; *the turtles,* the most silent of all birds, yet there take up their songs. *Come, my well-beloved* and all-dear ; and to see me more clearly, come to the same windows by which I see thee : come and behold my heart *in the clefts of* the opening in my side, which was made when my body, like a house in ruins, was so pitifully broken down on the tree of the cross : come, *show me thy face.* Ah ! I see it now without thy showing it, but then I shall see it, and thou shalt show it me, for thou shalt see that I see thee : *let thy voice sound in my ears,* for I would join it with mine : thus shall *thy voice be sweet and thy face comely.* O what a

* Cant. ii.

delight will it be to our hearts, when, our voices being tuned and accorded to our Saviour's, we shall take part in the infinite sweetness of the praises which the well-beloved Son gives to his eternal Father!

CHAPTER XII.

OF THE SOVEREIGN PRAISE WHICH GOD GIVES UNTO HIMSELF, AND HOW WE EXERCISE BENEVOLENCE IN IT.

ALL our Saviour's human actions are of an infinite merit and value, by reason of the person who produces them, who is the same God with the Father and the Holy Ghost, yet they are not infinite by nature and essence. For as, being in a chamber, we receive not light according to the greatness of the brightness of the sun which sends it out, but according to the greatness of the window, by which it is communicated,—so our Saviour's human actions are not infinite, though indeed they are of infinite value; for although they are the actions of a divine person, yet they are not done according to the extent of his infinity, but according to the finite greatness of his humanity by which he does them. So that, as the human actions of our sweet Saviour are infinite compared to ours, so are they only finite in comparison with the essential infinity of the divinity. They are infinite in value, estimation and dignity, as proceeding from a person who is God; yet are they finite by nature and essence, as being done by God according to his human nature and substance, which is finite; and therefore the praises which are given by our Saviour, as he is man, not being in all respects infinite, cannot fully correspond to the infinite greatness of the divinity, to which they are directed.

Wherefore after the first ravishment of admiration which seizes us, when we meet with a praise so glorious as is that which our Saviour renders to his Father, we fail not to recognise that the divinity is yet infinitely more deserving of praise than it can be praised, either by all creatures, or by the very humanity of the eternal Son.

If a man were praising the sun for its light, the more he lifted himself towards it in praising it, the more praiseworthy he would find it, because he would still discover more and more brightness in it. And if, as is very probable, it be the beauty of this light which provokes larks to sing, it is no marvel that, as they fly more loftily, they sing more clearly, equally raising their voice and their flight, till such time as hardly being able to sing any more, they begin to fall in voice and body, bringing down by little and little their flight and their voice. So, Theotimus, while by benevolence we are rising towards the divinity to intone and hear his praises, we see ever that he is above all praise. And finally, we learn that he cannot be praised according to his worth save only by himself, who alone can worthily match his sovereign goodness with sovereign praise. Hereupon we cry out : " Glory be to the Father, and to the Son, and to the Holy Ghost :" and that every one may know that it is not the glory of created praises which we wish God by this ejaculation, but the essential and eternal glory that is in himself, by himself, of himself, and which is himself, we add : " As it was in the beginning, is now, and ever shall be, world without end. Amen." As though we expressed a wish that God should be glorified for ever with the glory which he had before all creatures, in his infinite eternity and eternal infinity. For this we add the verse *Gloria* to every psalm and canticle, according to the ancient custom of the Eastern Church, which the great S. Jerome begged Pope S. Damasus to institute here in the Western ; to protest, that all the praises of men and angels are too low to praise worthily the divine goodness, and that, to be worthily praised, itself must be its own glory, praise and benediction.

O God ! what complacency, what a joy to the soul who loves, when she has her desire satisfied, in seeing her beloved infinitely praise, bless and magnify himself ! But from this complacency there springs a new desire of praise : for the soul would gladly praise this so worthy a praise given to God by himself, thanking him profoundly for it, and calling again all things to her assistance, to come and glorify the glory of God with her, to bless his infinite benedictions, and praise his eternal praises ; so that by this return and repetition of praises upon praises, she engages herself, between complacency and benevolence, in a most happy labyrinth of love, being wholly lost in this immense sweetness, sovereignly praising the divinity in that it cannot be sufficiently praised but by itself. And though in the beginning, the amorous soul had conceived a certain desire of being able to praise God sufficiently, yet reflecting upon herself again, she protests that she would not wish to have power to praise him sufficiently, but remains in a most humble complacency, to perceive that the divine goodness is so infinitely praiseworthy, that it cannot be sufficiently praised save by its own infinity alone.

And here the soul, ravished with admiration, sings the song of sacred silence : *A hymn becometh thee, O Lord, in Sion, and a vow shall be paid to thee in Jerusalem.**

For so the seraphim of Isaias, adoring and praising God, veiled their faces and feet, confessing therein their want of ability to contemplate or serve him properly; for our feet, by which we go, signify service: but still they fly with two wings in the sweet unrest of complacency and benevolence, their love reposing in that delightful unrest.

Man's heart is never so much disquieted as when the motion by which it continually opens and shuts itself is hindered, never so quiet as when its motions are free ; so that the heart's quiet consists in its motion. Now it is the same with the love of the Seraphim and seraphical men; for this has its repose in its continual movement of complacency, by which it draws God into itself, as if shutting itself, and of benevolence, by which it opens itself and throws itself entirely into God. This love then desires to behold the infinite wonders of God's goodness, yet it spreads its wings over its face, confessing that it cannot succeed in this : it would also present some worthy service, but it folds this desire over its feet, confessing that it has not power to perform it, nor does anything remain save the two wings of complacency and benevolence, by which it flies and darts towards God.

* Ps. lxiv. I.

BOOK VI.

EXERCISES OF HOLY LOVE IN PRAYER.

———◆◆◆———

CHAPTER I.

A DESCRIPTION OF MYSTICAL THEOLOGY, WHICH IS NO OTHER THING THAN PRAYER.

WE have two principal exercises of our love towards God, the one affective, the other effective, or, as S. Bernard calls it, active; by that we affect or love God and what he loves, by this we serve God and do what he ordains; that joins us to God's goodness, this makes us execute his will: the one fills us with complacency, benevolence, yearnings, desires, aspirations and spiritual ardours, causing us to practise the sacred infusions and minglings of our spirit with God's; the other establishes in us the solid resolution, the constancy of heart, and the inviolable obedience requisite to effect the ordinances of the divine will, and to suffer, accept, approve and embrace, all that comes from his good-pleasure; the one makes us pleased in God, the other makes us please God: by the one we conceive, by the other we bring forth: by the one we *place* God *upon* our *heart*, as a standard of love, around which all our affections are ranged, by the other we *place* him *upon* our *arm*, as a sword of love whereby we effect all the exploits of virtue.

Now the first exercise consists principally in prayer; in which so many different interior movements take place that to express them all is impossible, not only by reason of their number, but also for their nature and quality, which being spiritual, they

cannot but be very rarefied, and almost imperceptible to our
understanding. The cleverest and best trained hounds are often
at fault ; they lose the strain and scent by the variety of sleights
which the stag uses, who makes doubles, puts them on a wrong
scent, and practises a thousand arts to escape the cry; and we
oftentimes lose the scent and knowledge of our own heart in the
infinite diversity of motions by which it turns itself, in so many
ways and with such promptitude, that one cannot discern its
track.

God alone is he, who, by his infinite wisdom, sees, knows and
penetrates all the turnings and windings of our hearts : he understands our thoughts from afar, he finds out our traces, doubles
and turnings; his knowledge therein is admirable, surpassing
our capacity and reach.   Certainly if our spirits would turn
back upon themselves by reflections, and by reconsiderations of
their acts, we should enter into labyrinths from which we should
find no outgate ; and it would require an attention quite beyond
our power, to think what our thoughts are, to consider our considerations, to observe all our spiritual observations, to discern
that we discern, to remember that we remember,—these acts
would be mazes from which we could not deliver ourselves.
This treatise, then, is difficult, especially to one who is not a
man of great prayer.

We take not here the word prayer (*oraison*) only for the
petition (*priere*) or demand for some good, poured out by the
faithful before God, as S. Basil calls it, but as S. Bonaventure
does, when he says that prayer, generally speaking, comprehends
all the acts of contemplation ; or as S. Gregory Nazianzen, who
teaches that prayer is a conference or conversation of the soul
with God; or again as S. Chrysostom, when he says that prayer
is a discoursing with the divine Majesty; or finally as S. Augustine
and S. Damascene, who term prayer an ascent or raising of the
soul to God.   And if prayer be a colloquy, a discourse or a
conversation of the soul with God, by it then we speak to God,
and he again speaks to us; we aspire to him and breathe in him,
and he reciprocally inspires us and breathes upon us.

But of what do we discourse in prayer ? What is the subject
of our conference?   Theotimus, in it we speak of God only :

for of what can love discourse and talk but of the well-beloved ?
And therefore prayer, and mystical theology, are one same thing.
It is called theology, because, as speculative theology has God
for its object, so this also treats only of God, yet with three
differences : for, 1. The former treats of God as God, but the
latter treats of him as sovereignly amiable ; that is, the former
regards the Divinity of the supreme goodness, and the latter the
supreme goodness of the Divinity.   2. The speculative treats of
God with men and amongst men, the mystical speaks of God with
God, and in God himself.   3. The speculative tends to the
knowledge of God, and the mystical to the love of God ; that,
therefore, makes its scholars wise, and learned, and theologians,
but this makes its scholars fervent, and affectionate, lovers of God,
a *Philotheus* or a *Theophilus.*

Now it is called mystical, because its conversation is altogether
secret, and there is nothing said in it between God and the
soul save only from heart to heart, by a communication incom-
municable to all but those who make it.   Lovers' language is
so peculiar to themselves that none but themselves understand
it.   *I sleep*, said the holy spouse, *and my heart watcheth.*   Ah !
hark !   *The voice of my beloved knocking.** Who would have
guessed that this spouse being asleep could yet talk with her
beloved ?   But where love reigns, the sound of exterior words
is not necessary, nor the help of sense to entertain and to hear
one another.   In fine, prayer and mystical theology is nothing
else but a conversation in which the soul amorously entertains
herself with God concerning his most amiable goodness, to unite
and join herself thereto.

Prayer is a manna, for the infinity of delicious tastes and
precious sweetnesses which it gives to such as use it, but it is
hidden,† because it falls before the light of any science, in the
mental solitude where the soul alone treats with her God alone.
Who is she, might one say of her, *that goeth up by the desert, as
a pillar of smoke of aromatical spices, of myrrh, and frankin-
cense, and of all the powders of the perfumer ?‡*   And it was the
desire of secrecy that moved her to make this petition to her

---

* Cant. v. 2.   † Apoc. ii. 17.   ‡ Cant. iii. 6.

love: *Come, my beloved, let us go forth into the field, let us abide in the villages.** For this reason the heavenly spouse is styled a turtle, a bird which is delighted in shady and solitary places, where she makes no other use of her song but for her only mate, either in life wooing him or after his death plaining him. For this reason, in the Canticles, the divine lover and the heavenly spouse describe their loves by a continual conversing together; and if their friends sometimes speak during their conference, it is but casually, and without interrupting their colloquy. Hence the Blessed Mother (S.) Teresa of Jesus found at first more profit in the mysteries where our Saviour was most alone; as in the Garden of Olives, and where he was awaiting the Samaritan woman, for she fancied that he being alone would more readily admit her into his company.

Love desires secrecy; yea, though lovers may have nothing secret to say, yet they love to say it secretly: and this is partly, if I am not mistaken, because they would speak only for themselves, whereas when they speak out loud it seems no longer to be for themselves alone; partly because they do not say common things in a common manner, but with touches which are particular, and which manifest the special affection with which they speak. The language of love is common, as to the words, but in manner and pronunciation it is so special that none but lovers understand it. The name of a friend uttered in public is no great thing, but spoken apart, secretly in the ear, it imports wonders, and the more secretly it is spoken the more delightful is its signification. O God! what a difference there is between the language of the ancient lovers of the Divinity,—Ignatius, Cyprian, Chrysostom, Augustine, Hilary, Ephrem, Gregory, Bernard,—and that of less affectionate theologians! We use their very words, but with them the words were full of fire and of sweets of amorous perfumes; with us they are cold and have no scent at all.

Love speaks not only by the tongue, but by the eyes, by sighs, and play of features; yea, silence and dumbness are words for it. *My heart hath said to thee, my face hath sought thee: thy face, O*

* Cant. vii. 11.

*Lord, will I still seek.** *My eyes have failed for thy word, saying :
When wilt thou comfort me ?† Hear my prayer, O Lord, and my
supplication : gwe ear to my tears.‡ Let not the apple of thy
eye cease,§* said the desolate heart of the inhabitants of Jerusalem
to their own city. Do you mark, Theotimus, how the silence
of afflicted lovers speaks by the apple of their eye, and by tears ?
Truly the chief exercise in mystical theology is to speak to God
and to hear God speak in the bottom of the heart ; and because
this discourse passes in most secret aspirations and inspirations,
we term it a silent conversing. Eyes speak to eyes, and heart
to heart, and none understand what passes save the sacred lovers
who speak.

CHAPTER II.

OF MEDITATION—THE FIRST DEGREE OF PRAYER OR MYSTICAL THEOLOGY.

THIS word is much used in the holy Scriptures, and means simply
an attentive and reiterated thought, proper to produce good or
evil affections. In the first Psalm, the man is said to be blessed :
*Whose will is in the way of the Lord, and who in his law shall
meditate day and night.* But in the second Psalm : *Why did the
Gentiles rage, and the people meditate vain things?* Meditation
therefore is made as well for evil as for good. Yet whereas in
the holy Scripture, the word meditation is ordinarily applied to
the attention which we have to divine things to stir us up to love
them, it has, as one might say, been canonized by the common consent of theologians, like the name, angel, and, zeal ; as on the contrary the words, craft (*dol*), and, demon, have been stigmatized :
so that now when we say, meditation, we mean that which is
holy, and that by which we begin mystical theology.

Every meditation is a thought, but every thought is not
meditation. For we have thoughts to which our mind is
carried without any design or aim, by way of simple musing,
as we see common flies flying from from one flower to another,

---

* Ps. xxvi. 8.　　† Ps. cxviii. 82.　　‡ Ps. xxxviii. 13.
§ Jer. Lam. ii. 18.

without drawing anything from them. And be this kind of
thought as attentive as it may, it can never bear the name of
meditation, but should simply be called thought.   Sometimes
we consider a thing attentively to learn its causes, its effects,
its qualities, and this thought is named study; in which the
mind acts as locusts do, which promiscuously fly upon flowers
and leaves, to eat them and nourish themselves therewith.   But
when we think of divine things, not to learn, but to make ourselves love them, this is called meditating, and this exercise,
Meditation; in which our spirit, not as a fly for simple amusement, nor as a locust to eat and be filled, but as a sacred bee,
moves over the flowers of holy mysteries, to extract from them
the honey of divine love.

Thus many persons are always dreaming, and engaged in
unprofitable thoughts, almost without knowing what they are
thinking about; and, which is noteworthy, they are only
attentive to these thoughts inadvertently, and would wish
not to have them; witness him who said : *My thoughts are
dissipated, tormenting my heart :** many also study, and by a most
laborious occupation fill themselves with vanity, not being able
to resist curiosity : but there are few who meditate to inflame
their heart with holy heavenly love.   In fine, thoughts and
study may be upon any subject, but meditation, in our present
sense, has reference only to those objects whose consideration
tends to make us good and devout.   So that meditation is no
other thing than an attentive thought, voluntarily reiterated or
entertained in the mind, to excite the will to holy and salutary
affections and resolutions.

The holy Word explains in a truly admirable manner, and
by an excellent similitude, in what holy meditation consists.
Ezechias wishing to express in his canticle the attentive consideration which he makes of his evil : *I will cry*, says he, *like
a young swallow, I will meditate like a dove.*†   For, my dear
Theotimus, if ever you took notice of it, the young swallows
open their beaks very wide in their chirping, and, on the
contrary, doves, above all birds, make their murmuring with

* Job xvii. 11.   † Is. xxxviii. 14.

their beaks close shut up, keeping their voices in their throat
and breast, nothing passing outward but a certain resonant,
echo-like sound; and this little murmuring equally serves them
to express their griefs and to declare their loves. Ezechias,
then, to show that in his calamity he made many vocal prayers,
says: *I will cry like a young swallow,* opening my mouth, to
utter before God many lamentable cries; and to testify also that
he made use of holy mental prayer, he adds: *I will meditate like
a dove,* turning and doubling my thoughts within my heart by
an attentive consideration, to excite myself to bless and praise
the sovereign mercy of my God, who has brought me back
from death's gate, taking compassion on my misery. So Isaias
says: *We shall roar all of us like bears, and shall lament,
meditating like doves,** where the roaring of bears refers to
the exclamations which we utter in vocal prayer, and the
mourning of doves to holy meditation. But to make it appear
that doves use their cooing on occasions not only of grief but
also of love and joy, the sacred lover, describing the natural
spring-time in order to express the beauties of the spiritual
spring-time, says: *The voice of the turtle is heard in our land,*†
because in the spring the turtle begins to glow with love, which
she testifies by her more frequent song; and presently after:
*My dove, shew me thy face, let thy voice sound in my ears: for
thy voice is sweet, and thy face comely.*‡ He means, Theotimus,
that the devout soul is very agreeable unto him when she
presents herself before him, and meditates to inflame herself
with holy spiritual love. So he who had said, *I will meditate like
a dove:* putting his conception into other words: *I will think
over again for thee,* said he, *all my years in the bitterness of my
soul.*§ For to meditate, and to think over again in order to
move the affections, is the same thing. Hence Moses, exhorting the people to recall to mind the benefits received of God,
adds this reason: *That thou shouldst keep the commandments of
the Lord thy God, and walk in his ways, and fear him.*‖ And
Our Lord himself gave this command to Josue: *Let not the*

---

* Is. lix. 11.   † Cant. ii. 12.   ‡ Cant. ii. 14.
  § Is. xxxviii. 15.   ‖ Deut. viii. 6.

*book of this law depart from thy mouth : but thou shalt meditate
on it day and night, that thou mayest observe and do all things that
are written in it.** What in one of the passages is expressed by
the word, meditate, is declared in the other by, think over again,
and to show that reiterated thought and meditation tend to
move us to affections, resolutions and actions, it is said, as well
in the one as the other passage, that we must think over again,
and meditate in, the law, to observe and practise it. In this
sense the apostle exhorts us thus: *Think diligently upon him
that endured such opposition from sinners against himself ; that
you be not wearied, fainting in your minds.*† When he says
think diligently, it is as though he said *meditate*. But why
would he have us to meditate the holy passion ? Not that we
should become learned, but that we should become patient and
constant in the way of heaven. *O how have I loved thy law, O
Lord!* says David: *It is my meditation all the day.*‡ He meditates on the law because he loves it, and he loves it because he
meditates on it.

Meditation is the mystical rumination§ required for not being
unclean, to which one of the devout shepherdesses who followed
the sacred Sulamitess invites us : for she assures us that holy
writ is as a precious wine, worthy not only to be drunk, by
pastors and doctors, but also to be diligently relished, and, so to
speak, ruminated and turned over and over. *Thy throat*, says
she (in which the holy words are formed) is *like the best wine,
worthy for my beloved to drink, and for his lips and his teeth to
ruminate.*‖ So the blessed Isaac, as a chaste and pure lamb,
went forth into the field, the day being now well spent, to make
his retirement, his conference, and his exercise of spirit with
God, that is, to pray and *to meditate.*¶

The bee flies from flower to flower in the spring-time, not at
hazard but of set purpose, not only to be recreated in the verdant
diapering of the meadows, but to gather honey ; which having
found, she sucks it up, and loads herself with it ; then carrying
it to her hive, she treats it skilfully, separating from it the wax,

---

* Josue i. 8.   † Heb. xii. 3.   ‡ Ps. cxviii. 97.
§ Lev. xi. 3.   ‖ Cant. vii. 9.   ¶ Gen. xxiv. 63.

of which she makes comb, to store the honey for the ensuing
winter. Such is the devout soul in meditation. She passes
from mystery to mystery, not at random, or only to solace herself in viewing the admirable beauty of those divine objects,
but deliberately and of set purpose, to find out motives of love
or of some heavenly affection; and having found them she
draws them to her, she relishes them, she loads herself with
them, and having brought them back and put them within her
heart, she lays up what she sees most useful for her advancement, by finally making resolutions suitable for the time of
temptation. Thus in the Canticle of Canticles the heavenly
spouse, as a mystical bee, settles, now on the eyes, now on the
lips, on the cheeks, on the hair of her beloved, to draw thence
the sweetness of a thousand passions of love, noting in particular whatever she finds best for this. So that, inflamed with
holy love, she speaks with him, she questions him, she listens
to him, sighs, aspires, admires him, as he on his part fills her
with delight, inspiring her, touching and opening her heart, and
pouring into it brightness, lights and sweetnesses without end,
but in so secret a manner that one may rightly say of this holy
conversation of the soul with God, what the holy text says of
God's with Moses: that Moses being alone upon the top of the
mountain *spoke* to God, *and God answered him.**

CHAPTER III.

A DESCRIPTION OF CONTEMPLATION, AND OF THE FIRST DIFFERENCE
THAT THERE IS BETWEEN IT AND MEDITATION.

THEOTIMUS, contemplation is no other thing than a loving,
simple and permanent attention of the spirit to divine things;
which you may easily understand by comparing meditation
with it.

Little bees are called nymphs or *schadons* until they make

* Ex. xix. 19.

honey, and then they are called bees: so prayer is named Meditation until it has produced the honey of devotion, and then it is converted into Contemplation. For as the bees fly through their meadows, settling here and there and gathering honey, which having heaped together, they work in it for the pleasure they take in its sweetness, so we meditate to gather the love of God, but having gathered it we contemplate God, and are attentive to his goodness, by reason of the sweetness which love makes us find in it. The desire we have to obtain divine love makes us meditate, but love obtained makes us contemplate; for by love we find so agreeable a sweetness in the thing beloved, that we can never satiate our spirits in seeing and considering it.

Behold, Theotimus, how the queen of Saba,—regarding the proofs of Solomon's wisdom in his answers, in the beauty of his house, in the magnificence of his table, in his servants' lodgings, in the order that his courtiers kept while executing their charges, in their apparel and behaviour, in the multitude of holocausts which were offered in the Temple,—was taken with an ardent love, which changed her meditation into contemplation, in which, being rapt out of herself, she uttered divers words of extreme satisfaction. The sight of so many wonders begot in her heart an exceeding love, and that love enkindled a new desire, to see still more and enjoy the presence of him whose they were; whence she cried: *Blessed are thy servants who stand before thee always, and hear thy wisdom.** In like manner we sometimes begin to eat to get an appetite, but our appetite being excited, we continue eating to content it. And in the beginning we consider the goodness of God to excite our will to love him, but love being formed in our hearts, we consider the same goodness to content our love, which cannot be satiated in seeing continually what it loves. In conclusion, Meditation is the mother, and Contemplation the daughter of love, and for this reason I called Contemplation a loving attention, for children are named after their fathers, and not fathers after their children.

It is true, Theotimus, that as Joseph of old was the crown

* 3 Kings x. 8.

and glory of his father, greatly increased his honours and contentment, and made him young in his old age, so contemplation crowns its father which is love, perfects him, and gives him the crown of excellence; for love having excited in us contemplative attention, that attention breeds reciprocally a greater and more fervent love, which at last is crowned with perfection when it enjoys what it loves. Love makes us take pleasure in the sight of our well-beloved, and the sight of our well-beloved makes us take pleasure in his divine love, so that by this mutual movement, from love to sight, and from sight to love, as love renders the beauty of the thing beloved more beautiful, so the sight of it makes love more loving and delightful. Love by an imperceptible power makes the beauty which we love appear more fair, and sight likewise refines love, to make it find beauty more amiable. Love urges the eyes continually to behold the beloved beauty more attentively, and sight forces the heart to love it ever more ardently.

CHAPTER IV.

THAT LOVE IN THIS LIFE TAKES ITS ORIGIN BUT NOT ITS EXCELLENCE FROM THE KNOWLEDGE OF GOD.

BUT which has the more force, I pray you; love, to make us look upon the well-beloved, or the sight to make us love him? Knowledge, Theotimus, is required for the production of love, for we can never love what we do not know; and according as the attentive knowledge of good is augmented, love is also augmented, provided there is nothing to hinder its activity. Yet it happens often, that knowledge having produced holy love, love does not stay within the limits of the knowledge which is in the understanding, but goes forward and passes very far beyond it; so that in this life we are able to have more love than knowledge of God: whence the great S. Thomas assures us, that oftentimes the most simple women abound in devotion, and are ordinarily more capable of heavenly love than clever and learned men.

The famous Abbot of S. Andrew's at Vercelli, master of S. Antony of Padua, in his commentaries upon S. Denis, often repeats that love penetrates where exterior knowledge cannot reach, and says that many bishops of old, though not very learned, have penetrated the mystery of the Trinity; admiring in this point his scholar S. Antony of Padua, who, without earthly knowledge, had so profound a grasp of mystical theology, that, like another S. John Baptist, one might have called him *a burning and a shining light.* The Blessed Brother Giles, one of the first companions of S. Francis, said one day to S. Bonaventure: " O how happy you learned men are, for you understand many things whereby you praise God, but what can we idiots do?" And S. Bonaventure replied: "The grace to be able to love God is sufficient." "Nay, but Father," replied Brother Giles, " can an ignorant man love God as well as a learned?" "Yes," said S. Bonaventure, "and further, a poor simple woman may love God as much as a doctor of divinity." Then Brother Giles cried out in fervour: " O poor simple woman, love thy Saviour, and thou shall be as great as Brother Bonaventure." And upon this he remained for the space of three hours in a rapture.

The will only perceives good by means of the understanding, but having once perceived it she has no more need of the understanding to practise love, for the force of pleasure which she feels, or expects to feel, from union with her object, draws her powerfully to the love and to the desire of enjoying it; so that the knowledge of good gives birth, but not measure, to love; as we see the knowledge of an injury starts anger, which, if not suppressed, almost always becomes greater than the subject deserves. The passions do not follow the knowledge which moves them, but very often, leaving this quite in the rear, they make towards their object without any measure or limit.

Now this happens still more strongly in holy love, inasmuch as our will is not applied to it by a natural knowledge, but by the light of faith, which assuring us of the infinite goodness that is in God, gives us sufficient cause to love him with all our force. We dig the earth to find gold and silver, employing a present labour for a good which as yet is only hoped for; so that an uncertain knowledge sets us upon a present and certain labour, and as we more discover the vein of the mineral, we search and search more earnestly. Even a cold scent serves to move the hound to the game, so, dear Theotimus, a knowledge obscure and involved in clouds, like that of faith, most powerfully stirs our affection to love the goodness which it makes us perceive. O how true it is, according to S. Augustine's exclamation, that the unlearned bear away heaven, while many of the wise are swallowed up in hell!

In your opinion, Theotimus, which of the two would love the light more—the one born blind, who might know all the discourses that philosophers make of it and the praises they give it, or the ploughman, who by a clear sight feels and realizes the agreeable splendour of the fair rising sun ? The first has more knowledge of it, but the second more fruition, and that fruition produces a love far more lively and affective than a simple knowledge by reasons ; for the experience of good makes it infinitely more agreeable than all the science which can be had of it. We begin our love by the knowledge which faith gives us of God's goodness, which afterwards we relish and taste by love ; love whets our taste and our taste heightens our love, so that, as we see the waves, under the stress of winds, roll against one another and swell up, as if contact forced each to strive to outdo the rest, so the taste of good strengthens our love of it, and increases our relish for it, according to that oracle of the divine Wisdom : *They that eat me, shall yet hunger : and they that drink me shall yet thirst.** Which of the two I pray you loved God more, the theologian Occam, held by some to be the most subtle of mortals, or S. Catharine of Genoa, an unlearned woman ? He knew God better by science, she by experience ; and her experience conducted her deep into seraphic love, while he with his knowledge remained far remote from this excellent perfection.

We extremely love the sciences, even before we fully know them, says S. Thomas, from such confused and general knowledge as we may have of them : in the same way, it is the know-

* Ecclus. xxiv. 29.

ledge of God's goodness which makes our will begin to love, but as soon as it is set going, love increases of itself, by the pleasure which the will takes in being united to this sovereign good. Before children have tasted honey and sugar it is difficult to make them receive them into their mouth; but after they have tasted their sweetness, they love them much more than we wish, and eagerly seek to get them always.

We must admit, however, that the will, attracted by the delectation which it takes in its object, is much more forcibly drawn to unite itself therewith, when the understanding on its side excellently proposes the goodness thereof; for it is then at once both drawn and pushed; pushed by knowledge, drawn by delight : so that knowledge is not of itself contrary, but very useful to devotion, and meeting together they marvellously assist one another; though it often happens through our misery that knowledge hinders the birth of devotion, because *knowledge puffeth up* and makes us proud, and pride, which is contrary to all virtue, is the total ruin of devotion. Without doubt, the eminent science of a Cyprian, an Augustine, a Hilary, a Chrysostom, a Basil, a Gregory, a Bonaventure, a Thomas,—has not only much recommended but greatly improved their devotion, as again their devotion has not only raised but eminently perfected their science.

CHAPTER V.

THE SECOND DIFFERENCE BETWEEN MEDITATION AND CONTEMPLATION.

MEDITATION considers in detail, and as it were piece by piece, the objects calculated to move us, but contemplation takes a very simple and collected view of the object which it loves, and the consideration thus brought to a point causes a more lively and strong movement. One may behold the beauty of a rich crown two ways; either by looking upon all its ornaments, and all the precious stones of which it is composed, one after the other; or again, having considered all the particular parts, by beholding all the work of it together in one single and simple view. The first kind resembles meditation, in which, for example, we consider the effects of God's mercy to excite us to his love; but the second is like to contemplation, in which we consider with one single steady regard of our mind, all the variety of the same effects as a single beauty, composed of all these pieces, making up a single splendid brilliant. In meditating, we as it were count the divine perfections which we find in a mystery, but in contemplating we sum up their total. The companions of the sacred spouse had asked her what manner of one was her well-beloved, and she makes answer in an admirable description of all the parts of his perfect beauty: *My beloved is white and ruddy, his head is as the finest gold, his locks as branches of palm trees, black as a raven, his eyes as doves, his cheeks are as beds of aromatical spices, set by the perfumers, his lips are as lilies dropping choice myrrh, his hands are turned and as of gold full of hyacinths, his legs as pillars of marble.* Thus she goes on, meditating this sovereign beauty in detail, till at length she concludes by way of contemplation, putting all the beauties into one: *His throat is most sweet, and he is all lovely: such is my beloved, and he is my friend.**

Meditation reminds of one who smells a pink, a rose, rosemary, thyme, jessamine, orange-flower, separately one after the other; but contemplation is like to one smelling the perfumed water distilled from all those flowers: for the latter in one smell receives all the scents together, which the other had smelt divided and separated; and there is no doubt that this one scent alone, arising from the mingling together of all these scents, is more sweet and precious by itself than the scents of which it is composed, smelt separately one after another. Hence it is that the heavenly lover so prizes the being seen by his well-beloved with one of her eyes, and that her hair is so well plaited that it seems to be but one hair; for what is this beholding the spouse with one eye only, except the beholding him with a single attentive view without multiplying looks?

* Cant. v.

And what is it to have her hair thus plaited together, except the not scattering her thoughts in the multiplicity of considerations. Oh! how happy are they who, having run over the multitude of motives which they have to love God, reducing all their looks to one only look, and all their thoughts to one conclusion, stay their mind in the unity of contemplation; after the example of S. Augustine or S. Bruno, pronouncing secretly in their soul in a permanent admiration: " O Goodness! Goodness! Goodness, ever old and ever new!" or after the example of the great S. Francis, who, kneeling in prayer passed the whole night in these words: "O God, thou art my God and my All!" repeating the same continually, as the Blessed Brother Bernard of Quintaval relates who had heard it with his own ears.

Look at S. Bernard, Theotimus: he had meditated all the passion point by point; then of all the principal points put together he made a nosegay of loving grief, and putting it upon his breast to change his meditation into contemplation, he cried out: *A bundle of myrrh is my beloved to me.**

But again look with still greater devotion at the Creator of the world, how in the creation he first meditated the goodness of his works severally, one by one, as he saw them produced. *He saw*, says the Scripture, *that the light was good*, that the heavens and the earth were good, and so the herbs and plants, the sun, moon and stars, the living beasts, and in fine all the rest of creatures as he created them one after another: till at length, all the universe being accomplished, the divine meditation is changed as it were into contemplation: for viewing all the goodness that was in his works with one only look—*He saw*, says Moses, *all the things that he had made, and they were very good.*† The different parts considered severally by manner of meditation were *good*, but beheld in one only regard all together in form of contemplation, they were found *very good*: as many little brooks running together make a river, which carries greater freights than the multitude of the same brooks separately could do.

After we have excited a great many different pious affections

* Cant. i. 12. † Gen. i. 31.

by the multitude of considerations of which meditation is
composed, we in the end gather together the virtue of all these
affections, from which, by the pouring together and mixture of
their forces, springs a certain quintessence of affection, and of
affection more active and powerful than all the affections whence
it proceeds, because, though it be but one, yet it contains the
virtue and property of all the others, and is called contemplative
affection.

So it is an opinion amongst divines that the angels who are
higher in glory have a knowledge of God and creatures much
more simple than the inferior have, and that the species or
ideas by which they see are more universal, so that what the
less perfect angels see by various species and various regards,
the more perfect see by fewer species and fewer acts of regard.
And the great S. Augustine, followed by S. Thomas, says that
in heaven we shall not have these vicissitudes, varieties, changes
and returns of thoughts and cogitations, which come and go
from object to object and from one thing to another, but with
one sole thought we shall be able to attend to the diversity of
many things, and receive the knowledge of them. The further
water runs from its source, the more does it divide itself, and
waste its waters, unless it is kept in with a great care; and
perfections separate and divide themselves according as they are
more remote from God their source; but approaching near
him they are united, until they are lost in the abyss of that
sole sovereign perfection, which is the necessary unity and *the
better part*, which Magdalen chose and which shall not be taken
away from her.

CHAPTER VI.

THAT CONTEMPLATION IS MADE WITHOUT LABOUR, WHICH IS THE
THIRD DIFFERENCE BETWEEN IT AND MEDITATION.

Now the simple view of contemplation is performed in one of
these three ways. Sometimes we regard only some one of God's
perfections, as for example his infinite goodness, not thinking of

his other attributes or virtues; like a bridegroom, who simply
stays his eye upon the beautiful complexion of his bride, and
by this means truly sees all her countenance, forasmuch as her
colour is spread over almost all the parts of it, and who yet at
the same time would not be attending to the features, expression,
and other points of beauty: for, in like manner, sometimes the
mind, considering the sovereign goodness of the divinity, although
withal it sees in it justice, wisdom, power, yet is only attentive
to its goodness, to which the simple view of its contemplation is
addressed. Sometimes also we attentively behold in God several
of his infinite perfections, yet with a simple view and without
distinction, as he who with one glance, passing his eyes from the
head to the feet of his richly dressed spouse, would attentively
have seen all in general, and nothing in particular, not well
discerning what neck-jewels, or gown, she wore, nor what countenance she bore, nor what expression she had, nor what her
eyes were saying, but only that all was fair and agreeable: for
so in contemplation we often cast one single regard of simple
contemplation over several divine greatnesses and perfections
together, and we could not describe anything in particular, but
only say that all is perfectly good and lovely. And finally we
at other times consider neither many nor only one of the divine
perfections, but only some divine action or work, to which we
are attentive; as for example to the act of mercy by which God
pardons sins, or the act of creation, or the resurrection of Lazarus,
or the conversion of S. Paul: as a bridegroom who might not
regard the eyes, but only the sweetness of the looks which
his spouse casts upon him, nor take notice of her mouth, but
only of the sweetness of the words uttered by it. And here,
Theotimus, the soul makes a certain outburst of love, not only
upon the actions she considers, but upon him from whom they
proceed: *Thou art good; and in thy goodness teach me thy
justifications.** *His throat* (that is, the word which comes from
it) *is most sweet, and he is all lovely.*† Ah! *How sweet are thy
words to my palate, more than honey to my mouth:*‡ or with

---

* Ps. cxviii. 68.   † Cant. v. 16.

‡ Ps. cxviii. 103.

S. Thomas : *My Lord and my God ;* and with S. Magdalen :
" Rabboni, Ah ! my master !"

But take which of these three ways you will, contemplation has
still this excellency that it is made with delight, for it supposes
that we have found God and his holy love, that we enjoy it and
delight in it, saying : *I found him whom my soul loveth : I held
him : and I will not let him go.** In which it differs from
meditation, which almost always is performed with difficulty,
labour and reasoning ; our mind passing in it from consideration to consideration, searching in many places either the well-
beloved of her love, or the love of her well-beloved. Jacob
labours in meditation to obtain Rachel, but in contemplation he
rejoices with her, forgetting all his labour. The divine lover
like a shepherd, and indeed he is one, prepared a sumptuous
banquet according to the country fashion for his sacred spouse,
which he so described that mystically it represented all the
mysteries of man's redemption. *I am come into my garden,* said
he, *O my sister, my spouse, I have gathered my myrrh, with aromatical spices ; I have eaten the honey-comb with my honey, I
have drunk my wine with my milk ; eat, O friends, and drink,
and be inebriated, my dearly beloved !*† Theotimus, Ah ! when
was it, I pray you, that our Saviour came into his garden, if
not when he came into his mother's purest, humblest and
sweetest womb, replenished with all the flourishing plants of
holy virtues ? And what is meant by our Saviour's gathering
his myrrh with his perfumes, except that he joined suffering to
suffering until death, *even the death of the cross,* heaping by that
means merit upon merit and treasures upon treasures, to enrich
his spiritual children ? And how did he eat his honey-comb
with his honey, but when he lived a new life, reuniting his soul,
more sweet than honey, to his pierced and wounded body, with
more holes than a honeycomb ? And when ascending into
heaven he took possession of all the surroundings and depen-
dencies of his divine glory, what other thing did he if not mix
the exhilarating wine of the essential glory of his soul, with the
delightful milk of the perfect felicity of his body, in a more
excellent manner than hitherto he had done ?

* Cant. iii. 4.   † Cant. v. 1.

Now in all these divine mysteries, which contain all others, there is food provided for dear *friends to eat and drink* well, and for *dearest friends to be inebriated.* Some eat and drink, but they eat more than they drink and so are not inebriated: the others eat and drink, but drink more than they eat, and those are they who are inebriated. Now to eat is to meditate, for in meditating a man doth chew, turning his spiritual meat hither and thither between the teeth of consideration, to bruise, break and digest it, which is not done without some labour. To drink is to contemplate, which we do without labour or difficulty, yea with pleasure and tranquillity. But to be inebriated is to contemplate so frequently and so ardently as to be quite out of self to be wholly in God. O holy and sacred inebriation, which, contrarily to corporal inebriation, does not alienate us from the spiritual sense, but from the corporal senses; does not dull or besot us, but *angelicizes* and in a sort deifies us; putting us out of ourselves, not to abase us and rank us with beasts, as terrestrial drunkenness does, but to raise us above ourselves and range us with angels, so that we may live more in God than in ourselves, being attentive to and occupied in seeing his beauty and being united to his goodness by love!

Now whereas to attain unto contemplation we stand ordinarily in need of hearing the word of God, of having spiritual discourse and conference with others, like the ancient anchorites, of reading, praying, meditating, singing canticles, conceiving good thoughts,—for this reason, holy contemplation being the end and aim of all these exercises, they are all reduced to it, and those who practise them are called contemplatives, as also the occupation itself is called a contemplative life. This is on account of the action of our understanding, by which we regard the truth of the divine beauty and goodness with an amorous attention, that is, with a love which makes us attentive, or, with an attention which proceeds from love, and augments the love which we have for the infinite sweetness of our Lord.

CHAPTER VII.

OF THE LOVING RECOLLECTION OF THE SOUL IN CONTEMPLATION.

I SPEAK not here, Theotimus, of the recollection by which such as are about to pray, place themselves in God's presence, entering into themselves, and as one would say bringing their soul into their hearts, there to speak with God ; for this recollection is made by love's command, which, provoking us to prayer, moves us to take this means of doing it well, so that we ourselves make this withdrawing of our spirit. But the recollection of which I mean to speak is not made by love's command but by love itself, that is, we do not make it by free choice, for it is not in our power to have it when we please, and does not depend on our care, but God at his pleasure works it in us by his most holy grace. The Blessed Mother (S.) Teresa of Jesus says : " He who has written that the prayer of recollection is made as when a hedgehog or tortoise draws itself within itself, said well, saving that these beasts draw themselves in when they please, whereas recollection is not in our will, but comes to us only when it pleases God to do us this grace."

Now it comes thus. Nothing is so natural to good as to draw and unite unto itself such things as are sensible of it ; as our souls do, which continually draw towards them and give themselves to their treasure, that is, what they love. It happens then sometimes that our Lord imperceptibly infuses into the depths of our hearts a certain agreeable sweetness, which testifies his presence, and then the powers, yea the very exterior senses of the soul, by a certain secret contentment, turn in towards that most interior part where is the most amiable and dearest spouse. For as a new swarm of bees when it would take flight and change country, is recalled by a sound softly made on metal basins, by the smell of honied wine, or by the scent of some odoriferous herbs, being stayed by the attraction of these agreeable things, and entering into the hive prepared for it :—so our Saviour,—pronouncing some secret word of his love, or pouring out the odour of the wine of his dilection, more delicious than honey, or letting stream the perfumes of his garments, that is, feelings of his heavenly consolations in our hearts, and thereby making them perceive his most welcome presence,—draws unto him all the faculties of our soul, which gather about him and stay themselves in him as in their most desired object. And as he who should cast a piece of loadstone amongst a number of needles would instantly see them turn all their points towards their well-beloved adamant, and join themselves to it, so when our Saviour makes his most delicious presence to be felt in the midst of our hearts, all our faculties turn their points in that direction, to be united to this incomparable sweetness.

O God! says then the soul in imitation of S. Augustine, whither was I wandering to seek thee! O most infinite beauty! I sought thee without, and thou wast in the midst of my heart. All Magdalen's affections, and all her thoughts, were scattered about the sepulchre of her Saviour, whom she went seeking hither and thither, and though she had found him, and he spoke to her, yet leaves she them dispersed, because she does not perceive his presence; but as soon as he had called her by her name, see how she gathers herself together and entirely attaches herself to his feet: one only word puts her into recollection.

Propose to yourself, Theotimus, the most holy Virgin, our Lady, when she had conceived the Son of God, her only love. The soul of that well-beloved mother did wholly collect itself about that well-beloved child, and because this heavenly dear one was harboured in her sacred womb, all the faculties of her soul gathered themselves within her, as holy bees into their hive, wherein their honey is; and by how much the divine greatness was, so to speak, straitened and contracted within her virginal womb, by so much her soul did more increase and magnify the praises of that infinite loving-kindness, and her spirit within her body leapt with joy (as S. John in his mother's womb) in presence of her God, whom she felt. She launched not her affections out of herself, since her treasure, her loves and her delights were in the midst of her sacred womb. Now the same contentment may be practised by imitation, among those who, having communicated, feel by the certainty of faith that which, not flesh and blood, but the Heavenly Father has revealed, that their Saviour is body and soul present, with a most real presence, to their body and to their soul, by this most adorable sacrament. For as the pearl-mother, having received the drops of the fresh dew of the morning, closes up, not only to keep them pure from all possible mixture with the water of the sea, but also for the pleasure she feels in relishing the agreeable freshness of this heaven-sent germ :—so does it happen to many holy and devout of the faithful, that having received the Divine Sacrament which contains the dew of all heavenly benedictions, their heart closes over It, and all their faculties collect themselves together, not only to adore this sovereign King, but for the spiritual consolation and refreshment, beyond belief, which they receive in feeling by faith this divine germ of immortality within them. Where you will carefully note, Theotimus, that to say all in a word this recollection is wholly made by love, which perceiving the presence of the well-beloved by the attractions he spreads in the midst of the heart, gathers and carries all the soul towards it, by a most agreeable inclination, a most sweet turning, and a delicious bending of all the faculties towards this well-beloved, who attracts them unto him by the force of his sweetness, with which he ties and draws hearts, as bodies are drawn by material ropes and bands.

But this sweet recollection of our soul in itself is not only made by the sentiment of God's presence in the midst of our heart, but also by any means which puts us in this sacred presence. It happens sometimes that all our interior powers close and withdraw themselves into themselves by the extreme reverence and sweet fear which seizes upon us in the consideration of his sovereign Majesty who is present with us and beholds us; just as, however distracted we may be, if the Pope or some great prince should appear we return to ourselves, and bring back our thoughts upon ourselves, to keep ourselves in good behaviour and respect. The blue lily, otherwise called the flag, is said to draw its flowers together at the sight of the sun, because they close and unite while the sun shines, but in its absence they spread out and keep open all the night. The like happens in this kind of recollection which we speak of; for at the simple presence of God, or the simple feeling that he sees us, either from heaven or from any other place outside us (even if we are not remembering the other sort of presence by which he is in us), our powers and faculties assemble and gather together within us, out of respect to his divine Majesty, which love makes us fear with a fear of honour and respect.

Indeed I know a soul who, as soon as she heard mention of some mystery or sentence which put her a little more expressly in mind of the presence of God than usual, whether in confession or private conference, would so deeply enter into hersel that she could hardly recover herself to speak and make answer, so that outwardly she remained as one deprived of life, and with all her senses benumbed, till her spouse permitted her to quit that state : which was sometimes pretty soon, and other times more slowly.

CHAPTER VIII.

OF THE REPOSE OF A SOUL RECOLLECTED IN HER WELL-BELOVED.

THE soul, then, being thus inwardly recollected in God or before God, now and then becomes so sweetly attentive to the goodness of her well-beloved, that her attention seems not to her to be attention, so purely and delicately is it exercised : as it happens to certain rivers, which glide so calmly and smoothly that beholders, and such as float upon them, seem neither to see nor feel any motion, because the waters are not seen to ripple or flow at all. And it is this admirable repose of the soul which the Blessed Virgin (S.) Teresa of Jesus names prayer of quiet, not far different from that which she also calls the sleep of the powers, at least if I understand her right.

Even human lovers are content, sometimes, with being near or within sight of the person they love without speaking to her, and without even distinctly thinking of her or her perfections, satiated, as it were, and satisfied to relish this dear presence, not by any reflection they make upon it, but by a certain gratification and repose which their spirit takes in it. *A bundle of myrrh is my beloved to me, he shall abide between my breasts. My beloved to me, and I to him, who feedeth among the lilies, till the day break, and the shadows retire. Shew me, O thou whom my soul loveth, where thou feedest, where thou liest in the mid-day.** Do you see, Theotimus, how the holy Sulamitess is contented with knowing that her well-beloved is with her, whether in her bosom, or in her gardens, or elsewhere, so she know where he is. And indeed she is the Sulamitess, wholly peaceable, calm, and at rest.

Now this repose sometimes goes so deep in its tranquillity, that the whole soul and all its powers fall as it were asleep, and make no movement nor action whatever, except the will alone, and even this does no more than receive the delight and satisfaction which the presence of the well-beloved affords. And what is yet more admirable is, that the will does not even perceive the delight and contentment which she receives, enjoying it insensibly, being not mindful of herself but of him whose presence gives her this pleasure, as happens frequently when, surprised by a light slumber, we only hear indistinctly what our friends are saying around us, or feel their caresses almost imperceptibly, not feeling that we feel.

However, the soul who in this sweet repose enjoys this delicate sense of the divine presence, though she is not conscious of the enjoyment, yet clearly shows how dear and precious this happiness is unto her, if one offer to deprive her of it or divert her from it; for then the poor soul complains, cries out, yea sometimes weeps, as a little child awakened before it has taken its full sleep, who, by the sorrow it feels in being awakened, clearly shows the content it had in sleeping. Hereupon the heavenly shepherd adjures the daughters of Jerusalem, *by the roes and harts of the fields, not to make the beloved awake until she please,*† that is, to let her awake of herself. No, Theotimus, a soul thus recollected in her God would not change her repose for the greatest goods in the world.

Such, or little different from it, was the quiet of most holy Magdalen, when sitting at her Master's feet she heard his holy

* Cant. i.   † Cant. ii. 7.

word. Behold her, I beseech you, Theotimus; she is in a profound tranquillity, she says not a word, she weeps not, she sobs
not, she sighs not, she stirs not, she prays not. Martha full of
business passes and repasses through the hall: Mary notices her
not. And what then is she doing? She is doing nothing, but only
hearkening. And what does this mean—she hearkens? It means
that she is there as a vessel of honour, to receive drop by drop
the myrrh of sweetness which the lips of her well-beloved distilled into her heart; and this divine lover, jealous of this love-
sleep and repose of this well-beloved, chid Martha for wanting
to awaken her: *Martha, Martha, thou art careful, and art
troubled about many things. But one thing is necessary, Mary hath
chosen the best part, which shall not be taken away from her.*[*]
But what was Mary's portion or part? To remain in peace,
repose, and quiet, near unto her sweet Jesus.

The well-beloved S. John is ordinarily painted, in the Last
Supper, not only lying but even sleeping in his Master's bosom,
because he was seated after the fashion of the Easterns (*Levantins*),
so that his head was towards his dear lover's breast: and as he
slept no corporal sleep there,—what likelihood of that?—so I
make no question but that, finding himself so near the breasts
of the eternal sweetness, he took a profound mystical sleep,
like a child of love which locked to its mother's breast sucks
while sleeping. Oh! what a delight it was to this Benjamin,
child of his Saviour's joy, to sleep in the arms of that father,
who the day after, recommended him, as the Benoni, child of
pain, to his mother's sweet breasts. Nothing is more desirable
to the little child, whether he wake or sleep, than his father's
bosom and mother's breast.

Wherefore, when you shall find yourself in this simple and
pure filial confidence with our Lord, stay there, my dear Theotimus, without moving yourself to make sensible acts, either of the
understanding or of the will; for this simple love of confidence,
and this love-sleep of your spirit in the arms of the Saviour,
contains by excellence all that you go seeking hither and thither
to satisfy your taste: it is better to sleep upon this sacred breast
than to watch elsewhere, wherever it be.

* Luke x. 41, 42.

CHAPTER IX.

HOW THIS SACRED REPOSE IS PRACTISED.

HAVE you never noted, Theotimus, with what ardour little children sometimes cleave to their mother's breast when hungry? You will see them, with a deep soft murmur, hold and squeeze it with their mouths, sucking so eagerly that they even put their mother to pain; but after the freshness of the milk has in some sort allayed the urgent heat of their little frame, and the agreeable vapours which it sends to the brain begin to lull them to sleep, Theotimus, you will see them softly shut their little eyes, and little by little give way to sleep; yet without letting go the breast, upon which they make no action saving a slow and almost insensible movement of the lips, whereby they continually draw the milk which they swallow imperceptibly.   This they do without thinking of it, yet not without pleasure; for if one draw the teat from them before they fall sound asleep, they awake and weep bitterly, testifying by the sorrow which they show in the privation that their content was great in the possession.   Now it fares in like manner with the soul who is in rest and quiet before God: for she sucks in a manner insensibly the delights of his presence, without any discourse, operation or motion of any of her faculties, save only the highest part of the will, which she moves softly and almost imperceptibly, as the mouth by which enter the delight and insensible satiety she finds in the fruition of the divine presence.   But if one trouble this poor little babe, or offer to take from it its treasure because it seems to sleep, it will plainly show then that though it sleep to all other things yet not to that; for it perceives the trouble of this separation and grieves over it, showing thereby the pleasure which it took, though without thinking of it, in the good which it possessed.   The Blessed Mother (S.) Teresa having written that she found this a fit similitude, I have thought good to make use of it.

And tell me, Theotimus, why should the soul recollected in its God be disquieted?   Has she not reason to be at peace and to remain in repose?   For indeed what should she seek?   She has found him whom she sought, what remains now for her but to say : *I found him whom my soul loveth : I held him and I will not let him go*.* She has no need to trouble herself with the discourse of the understanding, for she sees her spouse present with so sweet a view that reasonings would be to her unprofitable and superfluous. And even if she do not see him by the understanding she cares not, being content to feel his presence by the delight and satisfaction which the will receives from it. Ah! the mother of God, our Blessed Lady and Mistress, while she did not see her divine child but felt him within her,—Ah! my God! what content had she therein! And did not S. Elizabeth admirably enjoy the fruits of our Saviour's divine presence without seeing him, upon the day of the most holy Visitation? Nor does the soul in this repose stand in need of the memory, for she has her lover present. Nor has she need of the imagination, for why should we represent in an exterior or interior image him whose presence we are possessed of? So that, to conclude, it is the will alone that softly, and as it were tenderly sucking, draws the milk of this sweet presence; all the rest of the soul quietly reposing with her by the sweetness of the pleasure which she takes.

Honied wine is used not only to withdraw and recall bees to their hives, but also to pacify them. For when they stir up sedition and mutiny amongst themselves with mutual slaughter and destruction, their keeper has no better remedy than to throw honied wine amidst this enraged little people; because, when they perceive this sweet and agreeable odour, they are pacified, and giving themselves up to the fruition of this sweetness, they remain quieted and tranquil. O Eternal God! When by thy sweet presence thou dost cast odoriferous perfumes into our hearts, perfumes more pleasing than delicious wine and honey, all the powers of our soul enter into so delightful a repose and so absolute a rest, that there is no movement save of the will, which, as the spiritual sense of smell, remains delightfully engaged in enjoying, without adverting to it, the incomparable good of having its God present.

* Cant. iii. 4.

CHAPTER X.

OF VARIOUS DEGREES OF THIS REPOSE, AND HOW IT IS TO BE PRESERVED.

THERE are souls active, fertile and abounding in considerations. There are souls who readily double and bend back on themselves, who love to feel what they are doing, who wish to see and scrutinize what passes in them, turning their view ever on themselves to discover the progress they make. And there are yet others who are not content to be content unless they feel, see, and relish their contentment ; these are like to persons who being well protected against the cold would not believe it if they knew not how many garments they had on, or who, seeing their cabinets full of money, would not esteem themselves rich unless they knew the number of their coins.

Now all these spirits are ordinarily subject to be troubled in prayer, for if God deign them the sacred repose of his presence, they voluntarily forsake it to note their own behaviour therein, and to examine whether they are really in content, disquieting themselves to discern whether their tranquillity is really tranquil, and their quietude quiet : so that instead of sweetly occupying their will in tasting the sweets of the divine presence, they employ their understanding in reasoning upon the feelings they have ; as a bride who should keep her attention on her wedding-ring without looking upon the bridegroom who gave it her. There is a great difference, Theotimus, between being occupied with God who gives us the contentment, and being busied with the contentment which God gives us.

The soul, then, to whom God gives holy, loving quiet in prayer, must abstain as far as she is able from looking upon herself or her repose, which to be preserved must not be curiously observed ; for he who loves it too much loses it, and the right rule of loving it properly is not to love it too anxiously.* And as a child who, to see where his feet are, has taken his head

* *La juste reigle de le bien affectionner, c'est de ne point l'affecter.*

from his mother's breast, immediately returns to it, because he
dearly loves it; so if we perceive ourselves distracted, through
a curiosity to know what we are doing in prayer, we must replace
our hearts in the sweet and peaceable attention to God's presence
from whence we strayed. Yet we are not to apprehend any
danger of losing this sacred repose by actions of body or mind
which are not done from lightness or indiscretion. For, as the
Blessed Mother (S.) Teresa says, it were a superstition to be so
jealous of this repose as not to cough, spit or breathe, for fear
of losing it, since God who gives this peace does not withdraw
it for such necessary movements, nor yet for those distractions
and wanderings of the mind which are not voluntary : and the
will having once tasted the divine presence does not cease to
relish the sweetness thereof, though the understanding or memory
should make an escape and slip away after foreign and useless
thoughts.

It is true the repose of the soul is not then so great as when
the understanding and memory conspire with the will, yet is it a
true spiritual tranquillity, since it continues to reign in the will,
which is the mistress of all the other faculties. Indeed we have
seen a soul most strongly fixed and united to her God, who yet
had her understanding and memory so free from all interior
occupation, that she understood very distinctly all that was said
around her, and perfectly remembered it, though she could not
answer, or loose herself from God, to whom she was fastened by
the application of her will. And so attached, I tell you, that she
could not be withdrawn from this sweet entertainment without
experiencing a great grief, which provoked her to sighs : these
indeed she gave in the very deepest of her consolation and quiet ;
as we see young children murmur and make little plaints when
they have ardently desired the milk, and begin to suck ; or as
Jacob did, who, in kissing the fair and chaste Rachel, *lifting up
his voice wept,** through the vehemence of the consolation and
tenderness which he felt. This soul, then, whom I speak of,
having only her will engaged, but her understanding, memory,
hearing and imagination free, resembled, I think, the little child

---

* Gen. xxix. 11.

who, while sucking, might see and hear and even move his arms, without quitting the dear breast.

However, the peace of the soul would be much greater and sweeter if there were no noise around her, nor occasion given of stirring herself either in body or mind, for she would greatly wish to be solely occupied in the sweetness of this divine presence ; however, being sometimes unable to hinder distractions in her other faculties, she preserves peace in the will at least, which is the faculty whereby she receives the enjoyment of good. And note, that then the will being retained in quiet by the pleasure which it takes in the divine presence, does not move itself to bring back the other powers which are straying; because by undertaking this she would lose her repose, separating herself from her dearly beloved ; and she would lose her labour if she ran hither and thither to catch these volatile powers, which also can never be better brought to their duty than by the perseverance of the will in holy quiet : for little by little all the faculties are attracted by the pleasure which the will receives, and of which she gives them a certain perception like perfumes which excite them to draw near her, to participate in the good which she enjoys.

CHAPTER XI.

A CONTINUATION OF THE DISCOURSE TOUCHING THE VARIOUS DE-
GREES OF HOLY QUIET, AND OF AN EXCELLENT ABNEGATION
OF SELF WHICH IS SOMETIMES PRACTISED THEREIN.

ACCORDING then to what we have said, holy quiet has divers degrees. For sometimes it is in all the powers of the soul joined and united to the will; sometimes it is in the will only, and there sometimes sensibly at other times imperceptibly : because it happens sometimes that the soul takes an incomparable delight in feeling by certain interior sweetnesses that God is present with her (as happened to S. Elizabeth when our Blessed Lady visited her) : and at other times the soul has a certain ardent sweetness in being in God's presence, which for the moment is imperceptible to her, as happened to the pilgrim-disciples, who walking with our Saviour did not fully perceive the agreeable pleasure with which they were thrilled, till such time as they had arrived and had known him in the divine breaking of the bread.* Sometimes the soul not only perceives God's presence, but hears him speak, by certain inward illuminations and interior persuasions which stand in place of words. Sometimes she perceives him, and in her turn speaks to him, but so secretly, sweetly and delicately, that it does not make her lose her holy peace and quiet, so that without awaking she watches with him; that is, she wakes and speaks to her well-beloved's heart, with as sweet tranquillity and grateful repose as though she sweetly slumbered. At other times she hears the beloved speak, but she cannot speak to him, because the delight she has to hear him, or the reverence she bears him, keeps her in silence, or, perhaps, because she is in dryness, and is so languid in spirit that she has only strength to hear and not to speak; as is sometimes the case in corporeal matters with those who are going to sleep, or who are greatly weakened by some malady.

But, finally, sometimes she neither hears nor speaks to her well-beloved, nor yet feels any sign of his presence, but simply knows that she is in the presence of her God, to whom it is pleasing that she should be there. Suppose, Theotimus, that the glorious Apostle S. John had slept with a bodily sleep in the bosom of his dear Master at the Last Supper, and that he had slept by his commandment; verily in that case he would have been in his Master's presence without in any way feeling it. And mark, I pray you, that there is more care required to place oneself in God's presence, than to remain there when placed: for, to place oneself there it is requisite to apply the mind and render it actually attentive to this presence (as I explain in the Introduction.†) But being placed in this presence, we keep ourself there by many other means, so long as, whether by understanding or by will, we do anything in God or for God: as, for example, by beholding him, or anything for love of him;

* Luke xxiv.   † II. 2.

by hearing him, or those that speak for him; by speaking to him, or to some one for love of him; and by doing any work whatsoever for his honour and service. Yea, one may continue in God's presence not only by hearing him, seeing him, or speaking to him, but also by waiting to see if it may please him to look at us, to speak to us, or to make us speak to him: or yet again, by doing nothing of all this, but by simply staying where it pleases him for us to be, and because it pleases him for us to be there. But if to this simple fashion of staying before him, it pleases him to add some little feeling that we are all his, and he all ours—O God! how desirable and precious is our privilege!

My dear Theotimus, let us further take the liberty to frame this imagination. If a statue which the sculptor had niched in the gallery of some great prince were endowed with understanding, and could reason and talk; and if it were asked: O fair statue, tell me now, why art thou in that niche?—It would answer,—Because my master placed me there. And if one should reply,—But why stayest thou there without doing anything?—Because, would it say, my master did not place me here to do anything, but simply that I should be here motionless. But if one should urge it further, saying: But, poor statue, what art thou the better for remaining there in that sort? Well! would it say, I am not here for my own interest and service, but to obey and accomplish the will of my master and maker; and this suffices me. And if one should yet insist thus: Tell me then, statue, I pray, not seeing thy master how dost thou find contentment in contenting him? No, verily, would it confess; I see him not, for I have not eyes for seeing, as I have not feet for walking; but I am too contented to know that my dear master sees me here, and takes pleasure in seeing me here. But if one should continue the dispute with the statue, and say unto it: But wouldst thou not at least wish to have power to move that thou mightest approach near thy maker, to afford him some better service? Doubtless it would answer, No, and would protest that it desired to do nothing but what its master wished. Is it possible then, would one say at last, that thou desirest nothing but to be an immovable statue there within that hollow niche? Yes, truly, would that wise statue answer in conclusion; I desire to be nothing but a statue and ever in this niche, so long as my master pleases, contenting myself to be here, and thus, since such is the contentment of him whose I am, and by whom I am what I am.

O true God! how good a way it is of remaining in God's presence to be, and to will to be, ever and for ever, at his good-pleasure! For so, I consider, in all occurrences, yea, in our deepest sleep, we are still more deeply in the most holy presence of God. Yea, verily, Theotimus: for if we love him we sleep not only in his sight, but at his pleasure, and not only by his will, but also according to his will. And meseems it is himself, our Creator and heavenly sculptor, who lays us there on our beds as statues in their niches, that we may settle there as birds nestle in their nests. Then at our waking, if we reflect upon it, we find that God was ever present with us, and that we were in no wise absent or separated from him. We have then been there in the presence of his good-pleasure, though without seeing or noticing him, so that we might say in imitation of Jacob:* Indeed I have slept by my God and in the arms of his divine presence and providence, *and I knew it not!*

Now this quiet, in which the will works not save only by a simple acquiescence in the divine good-pleasure, willing to be in prayer without any other aim than to be in the sight of God according as it shall please him, is a sovereignly excellent quiet, because it has no mixture of self-interest, the faculties of the soul taking no content in it, nor even the will save by its supreme point, in which its contentment is to admit no other contentment but that of being without contentment for the love of the contentment and good-pleasure of its God, in which it rests. For in fine the height of love's ecstasy is to have our will not in its own contentment but in God's, or, not to have our contentment in our own will, but in God's.

* Gen. xxviii. 16.

CHAPTER XII.

OF THE OUTFLOWING (*escoulement*) OR LIQUEFACTION OF THE
SOUL IN GOD.

MOIST and liquid things easily receive the figures and limits
which may be given them, because they have no firmness or
solidity which stops or limits them in themselves. Put liquid
into a vessel, and you will see it remain bounded within the
limits of the vessel, and according as this is round or square
the liquid will be the same, having no other limit or shape than
that of the vessel which contains it.

The soul is not so by nature, for she has her proper shapes
and limits: she takes her shape from her habits and inclinations,
her limits from her will; and when she is fixed upon her own
inclinations and wills, we say she is hard, that is, self-willed,
obstinate. *I will take away*, says God, *the stony heart out of
your flesh, and will give you a heart of flesh.** To change the
form of stones, iron, or wood, the axe, hammer and fire are
required. We call that a heart of iron, or wood, or stone,
which does not easily receive the divine impressions, but lives
in its own will, amidst the inclinations which accompany our
depraved nature. On the contrary, a gentle, pliable and
tractable heart, is termed a melting and liquefied heart. *My
heart*, said David, speaking in the person of our Saviour upon
the cross, *is become like wax melting in the midst of my bowels !*†
Cleopatra, that infamous Queen of Egypt, striving to outvie
Mark Antony in all the excesses and dissolutions of his banquets,
at the end of a feast which she made in her turn, called for a
vial of fine vinegar, and dropped into it one of the pearls which
she wore in her ears, valued at two hundred and fifty thousand
crowns, which being dissolved, melted and liquefied, she
swallowed it, and would further have buried, in the sink of
her vile stomach, the pearl which she wore in her other ear,
if Lucius Plautus had not prevented her. Our Saviour's heart,
the true oriental pearl, singularly unique and priceless, thrown

---

* Ezech. xxxvi. 26.   † Ps. xxi. 15.

into the midst of a sea of incomparable bitternesses in the day
of his passion, melted in itself, dissolved, liquefied, gave way
and flowed out in pain, under the press of so many mortal
anguishes; but love, *stronger than death*, mollifies, softens and
melts hearts far more quickly than all the other passions.

My heart, said the holy spouse, *melted when he spoke.** And
what does *melted* mean save that it was no longer contained
within itself, but had flowed out towards its divine lover? God
ordered that Moses should speak to the rock, and that it should
produce waters: no marvel then if he himself melted the heart
of his spouse when he spoke to her in his sweetness. Balm is
so thick by nature that it is not fluid or liquid, and the longer
it is kept the thicker it grows, and in the end grows hard,
becoming red and transparent: yet heat dissolves it and makes
it fluid. Love had made the beloved fluid and flowing, whence
the spouse calls him *oil poured out;* and now she tells us that
she herself is all melted with love. *My soul*, said she, *melted
when he spoke.* The love of her spouse was in her heart and
breast as a strong new wine which cannot be contained in the
tun; for it overflowed on every side; and, because the soul
follows its love, after the spouse had said: *Thy breasts are better
than wine, smelling sweet of the best ointments,* she adds: *Thy
name is as oil poured out.*† And as the beloved had poured
out his love and his soul into the heart of the spouse, so the
spouse reciprocally pours her soul into the heart of her beloved;
and as we see a honeycomb touched with the sun's ardent rays
goes out of itself, and forsakes its form, to flow out towards
that side where the rays touch it, so the soul of this lover
flowed out towards where the voice of her beloved was heard,
going out of herself and passing the limits of her natural
being, to follow him that spoke unto her.

But how does this sacred outflowing of the soul into its well-
beloved take place? An extreme complacency of the lover in
the thing beloved begets a certain spiritual powerlessness, which
makes the soul feel herself no longer able to remain in herself.
Wherefore, as melted balm, that no longer has firmness or

* Cant. v. 6.　　　　　　　† Cant. i. 1, 2.

solidity, she lets herself pass and flow into what she loves : she does not spring out of herself as by a sudden leap, nor does she cling as by a joining and union, but gently glides as a fluid and liquid thing, into the divinity whom she loves. And as we see that the clouds, thickened by the south wind, melting and turning to rain, cannot contain themselves, but fall and flow downwards, and mix themselves so entirely with the earth which they moisten that they become one thing with it, so the soul which, though loving, remained as yet in herself, goes out by this sacred outflowing and holy liquefaction, and quits herself, not only to be united to the well-beloved, but to be entirely mingled with and steeped in him.

You see then clearly, Theotimus, that the outflowing of a soul into her God is a true ecstasy, by which the soul quite transcends the limits of her natural form of existence (*maintien*) being wholly mingled with, absorbed and engulfed in, her God. Hence it happens that such as attain to these holy excesses of heavenly love, afterwards, being come to themselves, find nothing on the earth that can content them, and living in an extreme annihilation of themselves, remain much weakened in all that belongs to the senses, and have perpetually in their hearts the maxim of the Blessed Mother (S.) Teresa : " What is not God is to me nothing." And it seems that such was the loving passion of that great friend of the well-beloved, who said: *I live, now not I ; but Christ liveth in me,*[*] and : *Our life is hid with Christ in God.*[†] For tell me, I pray you, Theotimus, if a drop of common water, thrown into an ocean of some priceless essence, were alive, and could speak and declare its condition, would it not cry out with great joy : O mortals! I live indeed, but I live not myself, but this ocean lives in me, and my life is hidden in this abyss ?

The soul that has flowed out into God dies not, for how can she die by being swallowed up in life ? But she lives without living in herself, because, as the stars without losing their light still do not shine in the presence of the sun, but the sun shines in them and they are hidden in the light of the sun, so the

* Gal. ii. 20.   † Col. iii. 3.

soul, without losing her life, lives not herself when mingled with God, but God lives in her. Such, I think, were the feelings of the great Blessed (SS.) Philip Neri and Francis Xavier, when, overwhelmed with heavenly consolations, they petitioned God to withdraw himself for a space from them, since his will was that their life should a little longer appear unto the world; which could not be while it was wholly hidden and absorbed in God.

CHAPTER XIII.

OF THE WOUND OF LOVE.

ALL these terms of love are drawn from the resemblance there is between the affections of the mind and the passions of the body. Grief, fear, hope, hatred, and the rest of the affections of the soul, only enter the heart when love draws them after it. We do not hate evil except because it is contrary to the good which we love : we fear future evil because it will deprive us of the good we love. Though an evil be extreme yet we never hate it except in so far as we love the good to which it is opposed. He who does not much love the commonwealth is not much troubled to see it ruined : he who scarcely loves God, scarcely also hates sin. Love is the first, yea the principle and origin, of all the passions, and therefore it is love that first enters the heart; and because it penetrates and pierces down to the very bottom of the will where its seat is, we say it wounds the heart. " It is sharp," says the apostle of France,* " and enters into the spirit most deeply." The other affections enter indeed, but by the agency of love, for it is this which piercing the heart makes a passage for them. It is only the point of the dart that wounds, the rest only increases the wound and the pain.

Now, if it wound, it consequently gives pain. Pomegranates, by their vermilion colour, by the multitude of their seeds, so close set and ranked, and by their fair crowns, vividly represent,

---

* S. Denis (Tr.)

as S. Gregory says, most holy charity, all red by reason of its ardour towards God, loaded with all the variety of virtues, and alone bearing away the crown of eternal rewards: but the juice of pomegranates, which as we know is so agreeable both to the healthy and to the sick, is so mingled of sweet and sour that one can hardly discern whether it delights the taste more because it has a sweet tartness or because it has a tart sweetness. Verily, Theotimus, love is thus bitter-sweet, and while we live in this world it never has a sweetness perfectly sweet, because it is not perfect, nor ever purely satiated and satisfied : and yet it fails not to be of very agreeable taste, its tartness correcting the lusciousness of its sweetness, as its sweetness heightens the relish of its tartness. But how can this be ? You shall see a young man enter into a company, free, hearty, and in the best of spirits, who, being off his guard, feels, before he goes away, that love, making use of the glances, the gestures, the words, yea even of the hair of a silly and weak creature, as of so many darts, has smitten and wounded his poor heart, so that there he is, all sad, gloomy and depressed. Why I pray you is he sad ? Without doubt because he is wounded. And what has wounded him ? Love. But love being the child of complacency, how can it wound and give pain ? Sometimes the beloved object is absent, and then, my dear Theotimus, love wounds the heart by the desire which it excites; this it is which, being unable to satiate itself, grievously torments the spirit.

If a bee had stung a child, it were to poor purpose to say to him: Ah! my child, the bee that stung you is the very same that makes the honey you are so fond of. For he might say : it is true, that its honey is very pleasant to my taste, but its sting is very painful, and while its sting remains in my cheek I cannot be at peace, and do you not see that my face is all swollen with it ? Theotimus, love is indeed a complacency, and consequently very delightful, provided that it does not leave in our heart the sting of desire ; for when it leaves this, it leaves therewith a great pain. True it is this pain proceeds from love, and therefore is a loveable and beloved pain. Hear the painful yet love-full ejaculations of a royal lover. *My soul hath thirsted after the strong living God ; when shall I come and*

*appear before the face of God? My tears have been my bread
day and night, whilst it is said to me daily: where is thy
God?** And the sacred Sulamitess, wholly steeped in her
dolorous loves, speaking to the daughters of Jerusalem: *Ah!*
says she, *I adjure you, O daughters of Jerusalem, if you find my
beloved, that you tell him that I languish with love.† Hope that
is deferred afflicteth the soul.‡*

Now the painful wounds of love are of many sorts. 1. The
first strokes we receive from love are called wounds, because the
heart which appeared sound, entire and all its own before it
loved, being struck with love begins to separate and divide itself
from itself, to give itself to the beloved object. Now this separation cannot be made without pain, seeing that pain is nothing
but the division of living things which belong to one another.
2. Desire incessantly stings and wounds the heart in which it is,
as we have said. 3. But, Theotimus, speaking of heavenly
love, there is in the practice of it a kind of wound given by
God himself to the soul which he would highly perfect. For
he gives her admirable sentiments of and incomparable attractions for his sovereign goodness, as if pressing and soliciting her
to love him; and then she forcibly lifts herself up as if to soar
higher towards her divine object; but stopping short, because
she cannot love as much as she desires:—O God! she feels a
pain which has no equal. At the same time that she is powerfully drawn to fly towards her dear well-beloved, she is also
powerfully kept back and cannot fly, being chained to the base
miseries of this mortal life and of her own powerlessness: she
desires *the wings of a dove that* she *may fly away and be at rest,§*
and she finds not. There then she is, rudely tormented between
the violence of her desires and her own powerlessness. *Unhappy man that I am*, said one of those who had experienced
this torture, *who shall deliver me from the body of this death?‖*
In this case, if you notice, Theotimus, it is not the desire of a
thing absent that wounds the heart, for the soul feels that her
God is present; he has already led her into his wine-cellar, he

---

* Ps. xli. 3.   † Cant. v. 8.   ‡ Prov. xiii. 12.
        § Ps. liv. 7.   ‖ Rom. vii. 24.

has planted upon her heart the banner of love : but still, though already he sees her wholly his, he urges her, and from time to time casts a thousand thousand darts of his love, showing her in new ways, how much more he is lovable than loved. And she, who has not so much force to love as love to force herself, seeing her forces so weak in respect of the desire she has to love worthily him whom no force of love can love enough,—Ah ! she feels herself tortured with an incomparable pain ; for, as many efforts as she makes to fly higher in her desiring love, so many thrills of pain does she receive.

This heart in love with its God, desiring infinitely to love, sees notwithstanding that it can neither love nor desire sufficiently. And this desire which cannot come to effect is as a dart in the side of a noble spirit; yet the pain which proceeds from it is welcome, because whosoever desires earnestly to love, loves also earnestly to desire, and would esteem himself the most miserable man in the universe, if he did not continually desire to love that which is so sovereignly worthy of love. Desiring to love, he receives pain ; but loving to desire, he receives sweetness.

My God ! Theotimus, what am I going to say ? The blessed in heaven seeing that God is still more lovable than they are loving, would fail and eternally perish with a desire to love him still more, if the most holy will of God did not impose upon theirs the admirable repose which it enjoys : for they so sovereignly love this sovereign will, that its willing stays theirs, and the divine contentment contents them, they acquiescing to be limited in their love even by that will whose goodness is the object of their love. If this were not so, their love would be equally delicious and dolorous, delicious by the possession of so great a good, dolorous through an extreme desire of a greater love. God therefore continually drawing arrows, if we may say so, out of the quiver of his infinite beauty, wounds the hearts of his lovers, making them clearly see that they do not love him nearly as much as he is worthy to be beloved. That mortal who does not desire to love the divine goodness more, loves him not enough; sufficiency in this divine exercise is not sufficient, when a man would stay in it as though it sufficed him.

CHAPTER XIV.

OF SOME OTHER MEANS BY WHICH HOLY LOVE WOUNDS THE HEART.

NOTHING so much wounds a loving heart as to perceive another wounded with the love of it. The pelican builds her nest upon the ground, wherefore serpents often sting her young ones. Now when this happens, the pelican, as an excellent physician, with the point of her beak wounds these poor chicks all over, to cause the poison which the serpents' sting had spread through all the parts of their bodies to flow out with the blood; and to get out all the poison she lets out all the blood, and thus consequently, permits this little pelican-brood to perish. But seeing them dead she wounds herself, and spreading her blood over them she vivifies them with a new and purer life. Her love wounded them, and forthwith by the same love she wounds herself. Never do we wound a heart with the wound of love but we ourselves are wounded with the same. When the soul sees her God wounded by love for her sake, she immediately receives from it a reciprocal wound. *Thou hast wounded my heart,** said the heavenly lover to the Sulamitess, and the Sulamitess cries out: *Tell my beloved that I languish with love.*† Bees never wound without being themselves wounded to death. And we, seeing the Saviour of our souls wounded to death by love of us, *even to the death of the cross,*—how can we but be wounded for him, but wounded with a wound as much more dolorously amorous as his was amorously dolorous, and a wound as great as is our inability to love him as much as his love and death require? It is, again, another wound of love, when the soul feels truly that she loves God, and yet he treats her as if he knew not that she loved him, or as if he were distrustful of her love: for then, my dear Theotimus, the soul is put into an extreme anguish, as it is insupportable to her to see and feel even the mere pretence God makes of distrusting her. The poor S. Peter had and felt his heart all filled with love for his

* Cant. iv. 9. † Cant. v. 8.

master, and Our Lord, hiding his knowledge of it : *Peter,* said he, *dost thou love me more than these ?* Ah ! *Lord,* said the Apostle, *thou knowest that I love thee.* But, *Peter, lovest thou me,* replied Our Saviour. My dear Master, said the Apostle, truly I love thee, *thou knowest* it. But this sweet master to prove him, and as if showing a diffidence of his love : *Peter,* said he, *dost thou love me?* Ah ! Lord, thou woundest this poor heart, which greatly afflicted cries out, amorously yet dolorously : *Lord thou knowest all things : thou knowest that I love thee.** It happened once that a possessed person was being exorcised, and the wicked spirit being urged to tell his name : I am, said he, that miserable being deprived of love : and S. Catharine of Genoa who was there present suddenly perceived her whole frame disturbed and disordered, merely from having heard the words, privation of love, pronounced : for as the devils so hate divine love that they quake when they see its sign, or hear its name, that is, when they see the cross, or hear the name of Jesus pronounced, so those who dearly love Our Lord thrill with pain and horror when they see some sign or hear some word, that refers to the privation of this holy love.

S. Peter was quite sure that Our Lord, knowing all things, could not be ignorant how much he was loved by him, yet because the repetition of this demand : *Peter, dost thou love me ?* had some appearance of distrust, S. Peter is greatly grieved by it. Alas! that poor soul who feels that she is resolved rather to die than offend her God, and yet feels not a spark of fervour, but on the contrary an extreme coldness, which so benumbs and weakens her that at every step she falls into very sensible imperfections,—this soul I say, Theotimus, is all wounded : for her love is exceedingly in pain to see that God lets himself look as if he did not see how much she loves him, leaving her as a creature not belonging to him ; and she fancies that amid her failings, her distractions and coldness, Our Lord smites her with this reproach : How canst thou say that thou lovest me, seeing thy soul is not with me ? And this is a dart of pain through her heart, but a dart of pain which proceeds from love ; for if

* John xxi. 19.

she loved not, she would not be afflicted with the fear that she loved not.

Sometimes this wound of love is made merely by the remembrance we have that there was a time in which we loved not our God. " Oh! too late have I loved thee, beauty ever ancient and ever new," said that saint who for thirty years was a heretic. The past life is an object of horror to the present life of him who has passed his previous life without loving the sovereign goodness.

Sometimes love wounds us with the mere consideration of the multitude of those who contemn the love of God; so that we faint away with grief for this, as did he who said: *My zeal hath made me pine away: because my enemies forgot thy words.** And the great S. Francis, thinking he was not heard, upon a day wept, sobbed and lamented so pitifully, that a good man hearing him ran as if to the succour of one who was going to be slain, and finding him all alone asked him : why dost thou cry so hard, poor man ? Alas! said he, I weep to think that Our Lord endured so much for love of us and no one thinks of it : and having said thus he took to his tears again, and this good man sobbed and wept with him.

But, however it be, there is this admirable in the wounds received from the divine love that their pain is delightful, and all that feel it consent to it, and would not change this pain for all the pleasures of the world. There is no pain in love, or if there is pain it is well-beloved pain. Once a Seraph, holding a golden arrow, from the head of which issued a little flame, darted it into the heart of the Blessed Mother (S.) Teresa; and when he would draw it out, it seemed to this virgin that he was tearing out her very entrails, the pain being so excessive that she had only strength to utter low and feeble moans; but yet a pain so dear that she would have wished never to be delivered from it. Such was the arrow of love that God sent into the heart of the great S. Catharine of Genoa in the beginning of her conversion, after which she became another woman, dead to the world and things created, to live only to her Creator.

* Ps. cxviii. 139.

The well-beloved is a bundle of bitter myrrh, and this bitter bundle again is well-beloved, which *abides* dearly placed *between the breasts,** that is, the best-beloved of all the well-beloved.

CHAPTER XV.

OF THE AFFECTIONATE LANGUISHING OF THE HEART WOUNDED WITH LOVE.

IT is a thing very well known that human love not only wounds the heart, but even makes the body sick unto death; because, as the passion and temperament of the body have great power to incline the soul and draw her after it, so the affections of the soul have great force to stir the humours and change the qualities of the body. But besides this, love when it is violent bears away the soul to the thing beloved with such impetuosity, and so strongly possesses her, that she fails in all her other operations, be they sensitive or intellectual; so that to feed and second this love, the soul seems to abandon all other care, all other exercises, yea and herself too, whence Plato said that love was poor, ragged, naked, barefoot, miserable, houseless, that it lies without doors upon the hard ground, always in want. It is poor, because it makes one quit all for the thing beloved; it is houseless, because it urges the soul to leave her own habitation to follow continually him who is loved; it is miserable, pale, lean and broken down, because it makes one lose sleep, meat and drink; it is naked and barefoot, since it makes one forsake all other affections to embrace those of the thing beloved; it lies without upon the hard ground because it causes the heart that is in love to lie open, making it manifest its passion by sighs, plaints, praises, suspicions, jealousies; it lies along at the gate like a beggar, because it makes the lover perpetually attentive to the eyes and mouth of the thing which it loves, keeping continually to the ears thereof to speak to it and beg favours, wherewith love is never satiated; now the eyes, ears, and mouth

* Cant. i. **12.**

are the gates of the soul. In fine the condition of its life is to be ever indigent, for if ever it is satiated it is no longer ardent, nor, consequently, love.

True it is, Theotimus, that Plato spoke thus of the abject, vile and miserable love of worldlings; yet the same properties fail not to be found in heavenly and divine love. For turn your eyes a little upon those first masters of Christian doctrine, I mean those first doctors of holy evangelical love, and mark what one of them who had laboured the most said: *Even unto this hour,* says he, *we both hunger, and thirst, and are naked, and are buffeted, and have no fixed abode. And we labour working with our own hands: we are reviled, and we bless: we are persecuted, and we suffer it. We are blasphemed, and w entreat: we are made as the refuse of this world, the off-scouring,* and as it were the parings, *of all even until now.** As though he had said we are so abject that if the world be a palace we are held the sweepings thereof, if the world be an apple we are its parings. What I pray you had brought them to this state but love? It was love that threw S. Francis naked before his bishop, and made him die naked upon the ground; it was love that made him a beggar all his life; it was love that sent the great S. Francis Xavier poor, needy, ragged, through the Indies and amongst the Japanese; it was love that brought the great Cardinal S. Charles, Archbishop of Milan, to that extremity of poverty amidst the riches which his birth and dignity gave him, that, as says the eloquent orator of Italy, Master (*Monseigneur*) Pancirola, he was as a dog in his master's house, eating but a bit of bread, drinking but a drop of water, and lying upon a little straw.

Let us hear, I beseech you, the holy Sulamitess, who cries lmost in this manner: Although by reason of a thousand consolations which my love gives me I be more fair than the rich tents of my Solomon (I mean more fair than heaven, which is the inanimate pavilion of his royal majesty, while I am his animated pavilion), yet am I all black, rent, dust-worn, and all spoilt by so many wounds and blows given me by the same love.

* 1 Cor. iv. 11.

Ah ! regard not my hue, for truly I am brown, because my beloved, who is my sun, has darted the rays of his love upon me ; rays which by their light illuminate, but which by their heat have made me sunburnt and swarthy, and touching me with their splendour they have bereft me of my colour. The passion of love has made me too happy in giving me a spouse such as is my king, but the same passion which is a mother to me (seeing she alone gave me in marriage, and not my merits), has other children which fiercely assault and trouble me, bringing me to such a languor, that as, on the one hand, I am like to a queen who is beside her king, so on the other hand I am as a vineyard-keeper who, in a miserable hut, looks to a vineyard, and a vineyard that is not his own.

Truly, Theotimus, when the wounds and strokes of love are frequent and strong they put us into a languor, and into love's well-beloved sickness. Who could ever describe the loving languors of the SS. Catharine of Siena and Genoa, or of a S. Angela of Foligno, or S. Christina, or the Blessed Mother (S.) Teresa, a S. Bernard, a S. Francis. And as for this last, his life was nothing but tears, sighs, plaints, languors, wastings, love-trances. But in all this nothing is so wonderful as that admirable communication which the sweet Jesus made him of his loving and precious pains, by the impression of his wounds and stigmata. Theotimus, I have often pondered this wonder, and have made this conception of it. That great servant of God, a man wholly seraphical, beholding the lively picture of his crucified Saviour, represented in a shining seraph, who appeared unto him upon Mount Alverno, was touched beyond what could be imagined, being taken with a sovereign consolation and compassion, in beholding this bright mirror of love, which the angels cannot satisfy themselves in beholding. Ah ! he as it were swooned away with sweetness and contentment. But seeing also the lively representation of the marks and wounds of his Saviour crucified, he felt in his soul the merciless sword which transfixed the sacred breast of the virgin-mother on the day of the passion, with as much interior pain as though he had been crucified with his dear Saviour. O God ! Theotimus, if the picture of Abraham holding the death-stroke over his dear only-begotten, to sacrifice him, a picture drawn by mortal hand, had the power to touch and make weep the great S. Gregory, Bishop of Nyssa, as often as he beheld it,—Ah! how extreme was the tenderness of the great S. Francis when he beheld the picture of our Saviour sacrificing himself upon the cross, a picture which not a mortal hand, but the master-hand of a heavenly seraph, had drawn and traced from its very original, representing to the life and to nature the divine king of angels, bruised, wounded, pierced, broken, crucified.

This soul then being thus mollified, softened and almost melted away in this love-full pain, was thereby extremely disposed to receive the impressions and marks of the love and pain of his sovereign lover; for his memory was wholly steeped in the remembrance of this divine love, his imagination forcibly applied to represent unto himself the wounds and livid bruises which his eyes then saw so perfectly expressed in the picture before him; the understanding received those most vivid images which the imagination furnished to it; and, finally, love employed all the forces of the will to enter into and conform itself to the passion of her well-beloved; whence without doubt the soul found herself transformed into a second crucified. Now the soul, as the form and mistress of the body, exercising her authority over it, impressed the pains of the wounds with which she was struck, on the parts corresponding to those wherein her beloved had endured them. Love is admirable in sharpening the imagination to penetrate to the exterior. In Laban's ewes the imagination had a corporal effect upon the lambs, and the imagination of human mothers affects their children. A strong imagination makes a man become grey in one night, and disturbs his health and all his humours. Love then drove the interior torment of this great lover S. Francis to the exterior, and wounded the body with the same dart of pain with which it had wounded the heart; but love being within could not well make the holes in the flesh without, and therefore the burning seraph coming to its help, darted rays of so penetrating a light, that it really made in the flesh the exterior wounds of the crucified, which love had imprinted interiorly in the soul. So the seraph seeing that Isaias did not dare to speak, because he perceived his lips defiled, came in the name of God to touch and purify his lips with a burning coal taken from off the altar, seconding in this sort his desire. The myrrh tree brings forth its gum and first liquor by way of sweat and tran-spiration, but that it may let out all its juice, it must be helped by incision. In the same way the divine love of S. Francis appeared in his whole life, after the manner of a sweating, for in all his actions he showed nothing but this sacred affection; but to make the incomparable abundance of it plainly appear, the divine seraph came to make the incision and wounds. And to the end it might be known that these wounds were wounds of Heaven's love, they were made not with the steel, but with rays of light. O true God! Theotimus, what amorous dolours and dolorous loves! For not only at that instant, but also his whole life after, this poor Saint went pining and languishing, as sick with very love.

The Blessed (S.) Philip Neri, at fourscore years of age, had such an inflammation of heart through divine love, that the heat making the ribs give way to it, greatly enlarged them, and broke the fourth and fifth, that the heart might receive air and be re-freshed. B. (S.) Stanislaus Kotska, a youth of fourteen years, was so assaulted by the love of his Saviour that he often fainted away and fell down, and he was constrained to apply linen steeped in cold water to his breast, to moderate the violence of the burning which he felt.

To conclude, Theotimus, how do you think that a soul which has once tasted divine consolations at all freely, can live in this world so full of miseries, without an almost continual pain and languishing? That great man of God, Francis Xavier, was often heard lifting up his voice to Heaven, when he thought himself all alone, in this sort: Ah! my God, do not, for pity, do not bear me down with so great abundance of consolations; or if through thy infinite goodness it please thee to make me so abound in delights, draw me then into Paradise; for he who has once tasted thy sweetness must necessarily live in bitterness while he does not enjoy thee.   And therefore when God has somewhat largely bestowed his heavenly sweetnesses upon a soul, and afterwards withdraws them, he wounds her by this privation, and she afterwards is left pining ; sighing out with David: *My soul hath thirsted after the strong living God ; when shall I come and appear before the face of God ?**   And with the great Apostle: *Unhappy man that I am, who shall deliver me from the body of this death ?*†

* Ps. xli. 3.   † Rom. vii. 24.

BOOK VII.

UNION OF THE SOUL WITH HER GOD, WHICH IS PERFECTED IN PRAYER.

————

CHAPTER I.

HOW LOVE EFFECTS THE UNION OF THE SOUL WITH GOD IN PRAYER.

WE speak not here of the general union of the heart with its God, but of certain particular acts and movements which the soul, recollected in God, makes by way of prayer, to be more and more united and joined to his divine goodness : for there is truly a difference between joining or uniting one thing to another, and clasping or pressing one thing against or upon another; because to join or unite there is only required an application of one thing to the other, so that they may touch, and be together, as we join vines to elms, and jessamine to the trellis-work of the arbours which are made in gardens. But to squeeze and press together, a strong application must be made, which increases and augments the union; so that to clasp together is to join strongly and closely, as we see ivy joined to trees, which is not united only, but pressed and clasped so hard to them that it even penetrates and enters into their bark.

We must not drop the comparison of the love of little children towards their mothers, because of its innocence and purity. Regard, then, that sweet little child, to whom the seated mother presents her breast. It casts itself into her arms,

281

gathering and folding its little body in this bosom and on this beloved breast. And see the mother, reciprocally, how, receiving it she clasps it, and as it were glues it to her bosom, and joining her mouth to its mouth kisses it. But see again this little babe, allured with its mother's caresses, how for its part it concurs in this union between its mother and itself: for it also, as much as it possibly can, squeezes and presses itself to its mother's breast and face, as though it would wholly dive into, and hide itself in that beloved being from whom it came. Now, Theotimus, in this moment union is perfect; which being but one, proceeds notwithstanding from the mother and the child, yet so, that it has its whole dependence upon the mother. For she drew the child to her, she first locked it in her arms, and pressed it to her breast; nor had the babe strength enough to clasp and keep itself so tight to its mother. Yet the poor little one does for its part what it can, and joins itself with all its strength to its mother's bosom, not consenting only to the delightful union which its mother makes, but contributing, with all its heart, its feeble endeavours: and I say its feeble endeavours, because they are so weak that they rather resemble efforts after union than actual union.

Thus then, Theotimus, our Saviour, showing the most delightful breast of his divine love to the devout soul, draws her wholly to himself, gathers her up, and as it were folds all her powers in the bosom of his more than motherly sweetness, and then burning with love, he clasps the soul, joins, presses and glues her on his lips of sweetness, and to his delicious breast, kissing her with the sacred *kiss of his mouth,* and making her relish *his breasts more sweet than wine.** Then the soul, allured with the delights of these favours, not only consents, and yields herself to the union which God makes, but with all her power co-operates, forcing herself to join and clasp herself closer and closer to the divine goodness; yet in such a way that she fully acknowledges her union and attachment to this sovereign sweetness to be wholly dependent upon God's operation, without which she could not make the least effort in the world to be united unto him.

* Cant. i. 1.

When we see an exquisite beauty beheld with great ardour, or an excellent melody heard with great attention, or a rare discourse listened to with great satisfaction, we are wont to say that this beauty rivets the eyes of the spectators, this music takes the ears, and this discourse captivates the hearts, of the auditors.   What does this mean—to rivet the eyes and ears, or to captivate the heart—save to unite and most closely join these senses and powers to their objects ?   The soul then closely joins herself to, and presses herself upon, her object, when she exercises her affection towards it with great intensity; for pressure is nothing more than the progress and advancement of the union and conjunction.   We make use of this word, according to our language, even in moral matters : he presses me to do this, or he presses me to stay, that is, he does not merely use his persuasion and prayer, but does it with earnestness and entreaty, as did the pilgrims in Emmaus, who not only petitioned our Saviour, but even pressed and forcibly urged him, and compelled him by a loving violence to remain in their lodging with them.

Now in prayer this union is often made by manner of little yet frequent flights and advancings of the soul towards God : and if you take notice of little children united and joined to their mothers' breasts, you will see that ever and anon they press and clasp closer, with little movements which the pleasure they take in sucking makes them give : so the heart united to God in prayer often makes certain renewals of union, by movements which press and join it more closely to the divine sweetness.   As for example, the soul having long dwelt in the feeling of the union whereby she sweetly tastes how happy she is to belong to God, in fine, augmenting this union by an amorous pressing and moving forwards : Yea, Lord, will she say, I am thine, all, all, all, without reserve; or : Ah Lord! I am so indeed, and will be daily ever more ; or, by way of prayer : O sweet Jesus! Ah! draw me still more deeply into thy heart, that thy love may devour me, and that I may be swallowed up in its sweetness.

But at other times the union is made not by repeated movements, but by way of a continued insensible pressing and

advancing of the heart in the divine goodness. For as we see
a great and heavy mass of lead, brass or stone, though not
forced down, so work itself, sink down, and press itself, into the
earth where it lies, that at length it is found buried, by reason
of the effect of its weight, which makes it incessantly tend to
the centre;—so our heart, being once joined to God, if without
being drawn away it remain in this union, sinks still deeper by
an insensible progress of union, till it is wholly in God, by
reason of the sacred inclination given it by love to unite itself
ever more and more to the sovereign goodness. For as the
great apostle of France says: "Love is a unitive virtue:" that
is, it carries us to perfect union with the sovereign good. And
since it is an undoubted truth that divine love, while we are in
this life, is a movement, or at least a habit active and tending to
movement; even after it has attained simple union, it ceases
not to act, though imperceptibly, in order more and more to
increase and perfect it.

So trees that require transplanting, as soon as they are moved
spread their roots and lodge them deeply in the bosom of the
earth, which is their element and their aliment, nor do any
perceive it while it is doing, but only after it is done. And
man's heart, transplanted out of the world into God by celestial
love, if it earnestly practise prayer, will certainly ever extend itself,
and will fasten itself to the Divinity, uniting itself more and more
to his goodness, but by imperceptible advances, whose progress
one can hardly see while it is doing, but only when it is done.
If you drink any exquisite water, for instance, imperial water,
the simple union of it with you is instantly made upon your
receiving it; for the receiving and union is all one in this case;
but afterwards by little and little this union is increased, by a
progress imperceptibly sensible: for the virtue of this water
penetrating to all parts, will strengthen the brain, invigorate
the heart, and extend its influence through all your humours.
In like manner, a feeling of love—as for example: How good
God is!—having got entrance into the heart, at first causes union
with this goodness; but being entertained for some fairly long
time, as a precious perfume it penetrates every part of the soul,
pours out and dilates itself in our will, and, as it were, incor-

porates itself with our spirit, joining and fastening itself on
every side more and more closely to us, and uniting us to it.
And this is what the great David teaches us, when he compares
the sacred words to honey; for who knows not that the sweetness of honey is united more and more to our sense by a
continual increase of savour, when, keeping it a good while in
our mouth, or swallowing it slowly, the relish thereof more
deeply penetrates our sense of taste. In the same way that
sentiment of the divine goodness, expressed in those words of
S. Bruno: O Goodness! or those of S. Thomas: My Lord
and my God! or those of S. Magdalen: Ah! my Master! or
those of S. Francis: My God and my All!—this sentiment, I
say, having been kept some while within a loving heart,
dilates itself, spreads itself, and sinks into the spirit by an intimate penetration, and more and more steeps it all in its savour.
This is nothing else than to increase union; as does precious
ointment or balm, which, falling upon cotton-wool, so sinks into
it and unites itself to it more and more, little by little, that in
the end one cannot easily say whether the wool is perfumed or
perfume, or, whether the perfume is wool, or the wool perfume.
Oh! how happy is the soul who in the tranquillity of her heart
lovingly preserves the sacred feeling of God's presence! For
her union with the divine goodness will have continual though
imperceptible increase, and will thoroughly steep the spirit of
such a one in infinite sweetness. Now when I speak here of
the sacred sentiment of the presence of God, I do not mean to
speak of a sensible feeling, but of that which resides in the
summit and supreme point of the spirit, where heavenly love
reigns and conducts its principal exercises.

CHAPTER II.

OF THE VARIOUS DEGREES OF THE HOLY UNION WHICH IS MADE
IN PRAYER.

SOMETIMES the union is made without our co-operation, save
only by a simple following (*suite*), permitting ourselves to be
united to the divine goodness without resistance, as a little child,
in love with its mother's breasts, and yet so feeble that it cannot
move itself towards them, nor cleave to them when there; only
it is—Ah! so happy, to be taken and drawn within its mother's
arms, and to be pressed by her to her bosom.

Sometimes we co-operate, when, being drawn, *we willingly
run*,* to second the force of God's goodness which draws us and
clasps us to him by love.

Sometimes we seem to begin to join and fasten ourselves to
God before he joins himself to us, because we feel the action of
the union on our part, without perceiving what God is doing on
his side, who, however, there is no doubt, always acts first on
us, though we do not always perceive his action: for unless he
united himself to us we should never unite ourselves to him;
he always chooses and lays hold of us, before we choose or lay
hold of him.   But when, following his imperceptible attractions,
we begin to unite ourselves to him, he sometimes makes the
continuation of our union, assisting our weakness, and joining
himself perceptibly to us, insomuch that we feel him enter and
penetrate our hearts with an incomparable sweetness.   And
sometimes also, as he drew us insensibly to the union, he continues insensibly to aid and assist us.   And we know not indeed
how so great a union is made, yet know we well that our forces
are not able to make it, wherefore we justly argue that some
secret power is working insensibly in us: as skippers with a
cargo of iron perceiving their ships move apace with a very
light breeze, know that they are near mountains of loadstone,
which draw them imperceptibly, and thus they perceive a sensible
and perceptible advancement caused by an insensible and im-

* Cant. i. 3.

perceptible means.   For so when we see our spirit unite itself ever closer and closer to God, during the little efforts which our will makes, we rightly judge that we have too little wind to sail so fast, and that it must needs be that the loadstone of our souls draws us by the secret influence of his grace : which he would leave imperceptible, that it may be more admirable, and that undistracted by the sense of his drawings, we may with more purity and simplicity be occupied in uniting ourselves to his goodness.

Sometimes this union is made so insensibly that our heart neither perceives the divine operation in her, nor yet her own co-operation, but finds simply the union itself insensibly effected, like Jacob, who found himself married to Lia without thinking of it : or rather, like another Samson, but more happy, the heart finds itself netted and tied in the bands of holy union, without having ever perceived it.

At other times we feel the embraces, the union being made by sensible actions as well on God's side, as on ours.

Sometimes the union is made by the will only, and in the will only ; and sometimes the understanding has its part therein, because the will draws it after it and applies it to its object, making it take a special pleasure in being fastened down to the consideration thereof; as we see that love causes in our corporal eyes a profound and special attention, to rivet them on the sight of what we love.

Sometimes this union is made by all the faculties of the soul, which gather about the will, not to be united to God themselves, not being all capable of it, but to give more convenience to the will to make its union ; for if the other faculties were applied each to its proper object, the soul working in them, could not so perfectly give herself to the action by which the union with God is made.   Such is the variety of unions.

Look at S. Martial (for he was, they say, the blessed child mentioned in S. Mark): Our Saviour took him, lifted him up, and held him for a good while in his arms.   O lovely little Martial, how happy thou art to be laid hold of, taken up and carried, to be united, joined and clasped to the heavenly bosom of our Saviour, and kissed with his sacred mouth, without any co-operation of thine, save that thou didst not resist the receiving of those divine caresses! On the contrary, S. Simeon embraces our Saviour, and clasps him to his bosom, our Saviour giving no sign of co-operating in this union, though, as the holy Church sings: "The old man carried the child, but the child was governing the old man." S. Bonaventure, touched with a holy humility, did not only not unite himself to our Saviour, but withdrew himself from his real presence, that is, from the holy sacrament of the altar, when, hearing Mass one day, our Saviour came to unite himself with him, bringing him his holy sacrament. But this union being made,—Ah! Theotimus, think with what fervour this holy soul locked his Saviour in his heart! On the contrary S. Catharine of Siena ardently desiring our Saviour in the holy communion, pressing and advancing her soul and affection towards him—he came and joined himself unto her, entering into her mouth with a thousand benedictions. So that our Saviour began the union with S. Bonaventure, and S. Catharine seemed to begin that which she had with her Saviour. The sacred spouse in the Canticles speaks as having practised both sorts of unions. *I to my beloved, and his turning is towards me :** which is as much as if she had said: I am united to my dear love, and he likewise turns towards me, to the end that uniting himself more and more unto me he may become wholly mine. *A bundle of myrrh is my beloved to me, he shall abide between my breasts.†* *My soul*, says David, *hath stuck close to thee: thy right hand hath received me.‡* But in another place she confesses that she is first taken, saying: *My beloved to me and I to him.§* We make a holy union, by which he joins himself to me and I join myself to him. And yet to show that the whole union is ever made by God's grace, which draws us unto it, and by its attractions moves our soul and animates the movement of our union towards him, she cries out, as being wholly powerless: *Draw me :* yet to testify that she will not let herself be drawn as a stone or a galley-slave, but that on her side she will concur and will mingle her feeble movements with the mighty drawings of her lover : *We will*

* Cant. vii. 10.   † Cant. i. 12.   ‡ Ps. lxii. 9.   § Cant. ii. 16.

run after thee, she says, *to the odour of thy ointments.** And to make it known that if she is strongly drawn by the will, all the powers of the soul will make towards the union : Draw *me*, says she, and *we* will run ; the spouse draws but one, and many run to the union. It is the will only that God desires, but all the other powers run after it to be united to God with it.

To this union the divine Shepherd of souls provoked his dear Sulamitess. *Put me*, says he, *as a seal upon thy heart, as a seal upon thy arm.*† To impress properly a signet upon wax, one not only applies it, but presses it hard down : so he desires that we should be united unto him by a union so strict and close, that we should remain marked with his seal.

The charity of Christ presses us.‡ O God! what an example of excellent union ! He was united to our human nature by grace, as a vine to its elm, to make it in some sort participate in his fruit; but seeing this union undone by Adam's sin, he made another more close and pressing union in the Incarnation, whereby human nature remains for ever joined in personal unity to the Divinity ; and to the end that not human nature only, but that every man might be intimately united with his goodness, he instituted the Sacrament of the most holy Eucharist, in which every one may participate, to unite his Saviour to himself really and by way of food. Theotimus, this sacramental union urges and aids us towards the spiritual, of which we speak.

CHAPTER III.

OF THE SOVEREIGN DEGREE OF UNION BY SUSPENSION AND RAVISHMENT.

WHETHER, therefore, the union of our soul with God be made perceptibly or imperceptibly, God is always the author thereof; for none can be united to him, but by going unto him, nor can any one go unto him, unless he be drawn by him, as the heavenly

* Cant. i. 3.   † Cant. viii. 6.   ‡ 2 Cor. v. 14.

lover testifies, saying : *No man can come to me, except the Father, who hath sent me, draw him.** Which his holy spouse also protests, saying : *Draw me; we will run after thee to the odour of thy ointments.*†

Now the perfection of this union consists in two points; in being pure, and in being strong.   May I not approach a person to speak to him, to see him better, to obtain something of him, to smell the perfumes which are about him, to lean on him? And then I certainly go towards him and join myself unto him : yet the approach and union is not my principal intention, and I only make this a means and way to the obtaining of another thing.   But if I approach and join myself to him for no other end than to be near him, and to enjoy this proximity and union, it is then an approach of pure and simple union.

Thus many approach our Saviour : some to hear him as Magdalen; some to be cured by him, as she that had the issue of blood; others to adore him, as the three kings; others to serve him, as Martha; others to overcome their unbelief, as S. Thomas; others to embalm him, as Magdalen, Joseph, Nicodemus; but his divine Sulamitess seeks him to find him, and having found him, desires no other thing than to hold him fast, and holding him, never to quit him.   *I held him,* says she, *and will not let him go.*‡   Jacob, says S. Bernard, having fast hold of God, will let him go, provided he receive his benediction; but the Sulamitess will not let him depart for all the benedictions he can give her; for she wills not the benedictions of God, but the God of benedictions, saying with David : *What have I in heaven, and besides thee what do I desire upon earth?   Thou art the God of my heart, and the God that is my portion for ever.*§

Thus was the glorious Mother at the foot of her Son's cross. Ah! what dost thou seek, O Mother of life, on this mount of Calvary, in this place of death?   I am seeking, would she have said, my child, who is the life of my life.   And why dost thou seek him?   To be close by him.   But now he is amidst the sorrows of death.   Ah! it is not joy I seek, it is himself, and my

* John vi. 44.   † Cant. i. 3.   ‡ Cant. iii. 4.
§ Ps. lxxii. 25, 26.

heart, full of love, makes me seek alway to be united to that amiable child, my tenderly beloved one. In a word, the intention of the soul in this union is nothing, save to be with her lover.

But when the union of the soul with God is most specially strict and close, it is called by theologians inhesion or adhesion, because by it the soul is caught up, fastened, glued and affixed to the divine majesty, so that she cannot easily loose or draw herself back again. Regard, I pray you, that man caught and pressed by attention to the delight of an harmonious music, or mayhap (which is extravagant) to the folly of a game at cards: you would draw him from it, but cannot; what business soever is waiting for him at home, there is no forcing him thence; even meat and drink are forgotten for it. O God! Theotimus, how much more ought the soul which is in love with its God to be held and fast locked, being united to the divinity of the infinite sweetness, and taken and wholly possessed by this object of incomparable perfections? Such was the soul of the great vessel of election who cried out: *That I may live to God, with Christ I am nailed to the Cross :** and he protests that nothing, no not death itself can separate him from his master. This effect of love was also produced between David and Jonathan, for it is said that: *The soul of Jonathan was knit with the soul of David.*† And it is an axiom celebrated amongst the ancient Fathers, that friendship which can end was never true friendship, as I have said elsewhere.

See, I beseech you, Theotimus, this little child cleaving to the breast and neck of his mother; if one offer to take him thence to lay him in his cradle, it being high time, he struggles and disputes as far as he is able, in order not to leave that beloved bosom, and if he is made to let go with one hand, with the other he grapples, and if he is carried quite off, he falls a weeping; and keeping his heart and his eyes where he cannot keep his body, he continues crying out for his dear mother, till by rocking he is brought to sleep. So the soul who by the exercise of union has come as far as to be taken and fastened to the divine good-

* Gal. ii. 19.   † 1 Kings xviii. 1.

ness, can hardly be drawn from it save by force and with much pain. It is not possible to make her loose hold; if one divert her imagination she ceases not to keep hold by her understanding, and if one loose her understanding she cleaves by the will; or if by some violent distraction one make her abandon it with her will, she turns back every instant towards her dear object, from which she cannot be entirely untied, but, striving all she can to link together again the sweet bonds of her union with him by the frequent returns which she makes, as by stealth, she experiences S. Paul's distress :* for she is pressed with two desires; to be freed from all exterior employment in order to remain with Jesus Christ in her interior, and yet to proceed to the work of obedience which the very union with Jesus Christ teaches her to be necessary.

Now the Blessed Mother (S.) Teresa says excellently, that when union arrives at this perfection of keeping us held by and fastened to our Saviour, it is not distinguished from a rapture, trance, or suspension of the spirit; but that it is called only union, trance or suspension, when it is short; and when it is long, ecstasy or rapture, because the soul which is so firmly and closely united to her God that she cannot easily be drawn from him, is actually no longer in herself but in God; as a crucified body belongs not to itself but to the cross, and as ivy which grasps a wall, is no longer its own, but of the wall.

But to avoid all ambiguity, know, Theotimus, that charity is a bond, *and a bond of perfection ;*† and he that has more charity is more closely united and fastened unto God. But we have not been speaking of that union which is permanent in us by manner of habit, whether we be sleeping or waking, but of the union made by action, and which is one of the exercises of love and charity. Imagine then that S. Paul, S. Denis, S. Augustine, S. Bernard, S. Francis, SS. Catharine of Genoa and Siena, are again in this world, and have fallen asleep, wearied with their many labours, undertaken for the love of God. Represent to yourself on the other side some good soul, yet not so holy as they are, who is in the prayer of union at the same time : I ask you, Theotimus,

* Phil. i. 23.   † Col. iii. 14.

who is more united, clasped and fastened to God,—is it these great saints who sleep, or that soul who prays? Without doubt, these admirable lovers; for they have more charity, and their affections, though in some sort asleep, are so engaged and tied to their master that they cannot be separated from him. But, you will say to me, how can it be, that a soul in the prayer of union, even unto ecstasy, should be less united unto God than such as sleep, be they never so saintly? Mark what I tell you, Theotimus; that soul is more advanced in the exercise of union, those in the union itself: these *are* united, they are not *being* united, as they are asleep: and that one is *being* united, that is, she is in the actual practice and exercise of union.

For the rest, this exercise of union with God may even be practised by short and passing, yet frequent, movements of our heart to God, by way of ejaculatory prayer made for this intention. Ah Jesus! Who will give me the grace to be one spirit with thee! At last, Lord, rejecting the multiplicity of creatures, I desire thine only unity! O God, thou art the only one and only unity necessary for my soul! Alas! dear love of my heart, unite my poor one soul, to thy one singular goodness! Ah! thou art wholly mine, when shall I be wholly thine? The adamant draws and unites iron unto it; O Lord, my lover, be my draw-heart, clasp, press and unite my heart for ever unto thy fatherly breast! Ah! since I am made for thee, why am I not in thee? Swallow up, as a single drop, this spirit which thou hast bestowed upon me, into the sea of thy goodness from whence it proceeds. Ah Lord! seeing that thy heart loves me, why does it not force me to itself, since I truly will it? Draw me, and I will run after thy drawings, to cast myself into thy fatherly arms, to leave them no more for ever and ever. Amen.

CHAPTER IV.

OF RAPTURE, AND OF THE FIRST SPECIES OF IT.

AN ecstasy is called a rapture inasmuch as God does thereby rapt us, and raise us up to himself, and a rapture is termed an ecstasy, because by it we go and remain out of, and above, ourselves, to be united to God. And although the attractions by which God draws us be admirably pleasing, sweet and delicious, yet on account of the force which the divine beauty and goodness have to draw unto them the attention and application of the spirit, it seems that it not only raises us but that it ravishes and bears us away. As, on the contrary, by reason of the most free consent and ardent motion, by which the ravished soul goes out after the divine attractions, she seems not only to mount and rise, but also to break out of herself and cast herself into the very divinity. Similarly the soul may be ravished out of itself by the infamous ecstasy of sensual pleasure, by which however it is not raised up, but is degraded below itself.

But, my dear Theotimus, as to sacred ecstasies, they are of three kinds; the one of them belongs to the understanding, another to the affection, and the third to action. The one is in splendour, the other in fervour, the third in works: the one is made by admiration, the other by devotion, and the third by operation. Admiration is caused in us by the meeting with a new truth, which we neither knew, nor yet expected to know; and if the new truth we meet with be accompanied by beauty and goodness, the admiration which proceeds from it is very delicious. So the Queen of Saba finding more true wisdom in Solomon than she had imagined, became filled with admiration. And the Jews, acknowledging in our Saviour more knowledge than they could ever have believed, were taken with a great admiration. When therefore it pleases the divine goodness to illuminate our heart with some special light, whereby it is raised to an extraordinary and sublime contemplation of heavenly mysteries, then, discovering more beauty in them than it could have imagined, it falls into admiration.

Now admiration of things that cause pleasure closely fixes and glues the spirit to the thing admired, as well by reason of the excellent beauty which it causes to be found therein, as by the novelty of this excellence, the understanding being unable to delight itself enough in seeing what it never saw before, and what is so agreeable to the view. Sometimes also besides this, God imparts to the soul a light not only clear but growing, like the daybreak; and then, as those who have found a gold-mine continually break more earth, ever to find more of the wished-for metal, so the understanding ever buries itself deeper and deeper in the consideration and admiration of its divine object: for even as admiration has produced philosophy, and the attentive study of natural things, so it has also caused contemplation and mystical theology; and as this admiration when it is strong, keeps us out of ourselves and above ourselves by a lively attention and application of our understanding to heavenly things, it carries us consequently into ecstasy.

CHAPTER V.

OF THE SECOND SPECIES OF RAPTURE.

GOD draws men's spirits unto him by his sovereign beauty and incomprehensible goodness, which two excellences are however but one supreme divinity, at once most singularly beautiful and good. Every thing is done for the good and for the beautiful, all things look towards them, are moved and stayed by them. The good and beautiful are desirable, agreeable, and dear to all, for them all things do and will whatsoever they do and will. And as for the beautiful, because it draws and recalls all things to itself, the Greeks give it a name which signifies recalling.*

In like manner, as to good, its true image is light, especially because light collects, reduces and turns all things towards itself,

* τὸ καλόν [Tr.]

whence the sun is named amongst the Greeks from a word* which
shows that its influence causes all things to be drawn together
and united, bringing together things dispersed; as goodness
turns all things unto itself, being not only the sovereign unity,
but sovereignly unitive, since all things desire it, as their principle, their preservation and their last end.   So that in conclusion, the good and the beautiful is but one and the same thing,
because all things desire the good and the beautiful.

   This discourse, Theotimus, is almost entirely composed of the
words of the divine S. Denis the Areopagite; and certainly it
is true that the sun, the source of corporeal light, is the true
image of the good and the beautiful; for amongst merely
corporeal creatures there is neither goodness nor beauty equal
to that of the sun.   Now the beauty and goodness of the sun
consist in his light, without which nothing would be beautiful,
nothing good, in this corporeal world.   As beautiful he
illuminates all, as good he heats and quickens all: insomuch as
he is beautiful and bright, he draws unto himself all seeing
eyes in the world; insomuch as he is good and gives heat, he
gains unto himself all the appetites and inclinations of the
corporeal world.   For he extracts and draws up the exhalations
and vapours, he draws and makes rise from their originals
plants and living creatures; nor is there any production to
which the vital heat of this great luminary does not contribute.
So God, Father of all light, sovereignly good and beautiful,
draws our understanding by his beauty to contemplate him, and
draws our will by his goodness to love him.   As beautiful,
replenishing our understanding with delight, he pours his love
into our wills; as good, filling our wills with his love, he excites
our understanding to contemplate him,—love provoking us to
contemplation, and contemplation to love: whence it follows
that ecstasies and raptures depend wholly on love, for it is love
that carries the understanding to contemplation and the will to
union: so that, finally, we must conclude with the great
S. Denis, that divine love is ecstatic, not permitting lovers to
live to themselves, but to the thing beloved: for which cause the

* ἥλιος [Tr.]

admirable Apostle S. Paul, being possessed of this divine love, and participating in its ecstatic power, said with divinely inspired mouth : *I live, now not I, but Christ liveth in me.** As a true lover gone out of himself into God, he lived now not his own life, but the life of his beloved, as being sovereignly to be loved.

Now this rapture of love happens in the will thus. God touches it with the attractions of his sweetness, and then, as the needle touched by the loadstone turns and moves towards the pole, forgetful of its insensible condition, so the will touched with heavenly love moves forward and advances itself towards God, leaving all its earthly inclinations, and by this means enters into a rapture, not of knowledge, but of fruition ; not of admiration but of affection ; not of science but of experience ; not of sight but of taste and relish. It is true, as I have already signified, the understanding enters sometimes into admiration, seeing the sacred delight which the will takes in her ecstasy, as the will often takes pleasure to perceive the understanding in admiration, so that these two faculties interchange their ravishments ; the view of beauty making us love it, and the love thereof making us view it. Rarely is a man warmed by the sunbeams without being illuminated, or illuminated without being warmed. Love easily makes us admire, and admiration easily makes us love. Still the two ecstasies, of the understanding and of the will, are not so essential to one another that the one may not very often be without the other ; for as philosophers have had more knowledge than love of the Creator, so good Christians often have more love than knowledge, and consequently exceeding knowledge is not always followed by exceeding love, as I have remarked elsewhere. Now if the ecstasy of admiration be alone, we are not made better by it, according to what he said of it who had been lifted up in ecstasy into the third heaven. *If I should know,* said he, *all mysteries, and all knowledge,—and have not charity, I am nothing ;*† and therefore the evil spirit can put into an ecstasy, if we may so say, and ravish the understanding by proposing unto it

---

* Gal. ii. 20   † 1 Cor. xiii. 2.

wonders which hold it suspended and elevated above its natural forces, and further, by such lights he can give the will some kind of vain, soft, tender and imperfect love, by way of sensible complacency, satisfaction and consolation. But to give the true ecstasy of the will, whereby it is solely and powerfully joined unto the divine goodness, appertains only to that sovereign Spirit by whom the charity of God is *spread abroad in our hearts.**

CHAPTER VI.

OF THE SIGNS OF GOOD RAPTURE, AND OF THE THIRD SPECIES OF THE SAME.

INDEED, Theotimus, there have been many in our age who believed, and others with them, that they were very frequently ravished by God in ecstasy, and yet in the end it was discovered that all were but diabolical illusions and operations. A certain priest in S. Augustine's time put himself into ecstasies whenever he pleased, singing or getting sung certain mournful and melancholy airs, and this only to content the curiosity of those who desired to view this spectacle. But what is most wonderful is, that his ecstasy went so far that he did not feel fire which was applied to him, till after he was come to himself; and yet if any one spoke somewhat loudly, and with a clear voice, he heard them as if from afar, and he had no respiration. The philosophers themselves acknowledged certain species of natural ecstasies, caused by a vehement application of the spirit to the consideration of high things : wherefore we must not think it strange if the devil, to play the ape, to beguile souls, to scandalize the weak, and to transform himself into an angel of light, cause raptures in certain souls who are not solidly instructed in solid piety.

To the end, then, that one might discern divine ecstasies

* Rom. v. 5.

from human and diabolical, God's servants have left many teachings: but for my part, it will suffice for my purpose to propose to you two marks of the good and holy ecstasy. The one is, that sacred ecstasy never so much takes and affects the understanding as it does the will, which it moves, warms and fills with a powerful affection towards God. So that, if the ecstasy be more beautiful than good, more bright than warm, more speculative than affective, it is very doubtful, and deserving of suspicion. I do not say that one may not have raptures, yea prophetical visions, without charity: for, as I know well one may have charity without being ravished, or prophesying, so one may also be ravished and may prophesy without having charity: but I affirm that he who in his rapture has more light in the understanding to admire God, than heat in the will to love him, is to stand upon his guard; for it is to be feared that this ecstasy may be false, and may rather puff up the spirit than edify it, putting him indeed as Saul, Balaam, and Caiphas, amongst the prophets, yet still leaving him amongst the reprobate.

The second mark of true ecstasy consists in the third species of ecstasy which we mentioned above, an ecstasy all holy, all worthy of love, the crown of the two others,—the ecstasy of act and life. The entire observance of God's commandments is not within the bounds of human strength, yet is it within the stretch of the instinct of the human spirit, as being most conformable to natural light and reason: so that living according to God's commandments, we are not therefore outside our natural inclination. Yet besides God's commandments, there are certain heavenly inspirations to the effecting of which it is not only requisite that God should raise us above our own strength, but also that he should draw us above our natural instincts and inclinations, because although these inspirations are not opposite to human reason, yet they exceed it, surpass it, and are placed above it, so that then we live not only a civil, honest, and Christian life, but a supernatural, spiritual, devout and ecstatic life, that is, a life which is in every way beyond and above our natural condition.

Not to steal, not to lie, not to commit impurity, to pray to God, not to swear in vain, to love and honour one's father, not to kill,—is to live according to man's natural reason : but to forsake all our goods, to love poverty, to call her and to consider her a most delightful mistress, to repute reproaches, contempts, abjections, persecutions, martyrdoms, as felicities and beatitudes, to contain oneself within the terms of a most absolute chastity, and in fine to live, amidst the world and in this mortal life, contrary to all the opinions and maxims of the world, and against the current of the river of this life, by habitual resignations, renunciations, and abnegations of ourselves ;— this is not to live in ourselves, but out of and above ourselves; and because no one is able to go out of himself in this manner above himself unless the eternal *Father draw him,* hence it is that this kind of life is a perpetual rapture, and a continual ecstasy of action and operation.

You are dead, said the great Apostle to the Colossians, *and your life is hid with Christ in God.** Death's effect is that the soul no longer lives in its body nor in the limits thereof. What then do these words of the Apostle mean, Theotimus : *you are dead ?* it is as though he said : you no longer live in your- selves nor in the limits of your natural condition ; your soul does not now live according to herself but above herself. The true nature of the phœnix lies in this, that by the help of the sunbeams, she annihilates her own life, to have a life more desirable and vigorous, hiding, as it were, her life under ashes. Silkworms change their being, and from worms become butter- flies ; bees are born worms, then become nymphs crawling on their feet, and at last they become flying bees. We do the same, Theotimus, if we are spiritual : for we forsake our natural life to live a more eminent life above ourselves, hiding all this new life in God with Jesus Christ, who alone sees, knows and bestows it. Our new life is heavenly love, which quickens and animates our soul, and this love is wholly hidden in God and divine things with Jesus Christ: for since (as the sacred Gospel text says), after our Saviour had shown himself for a little to his disciples as he rose up to heaven, thither above, he was at length environed with a cloud which took him and hid

* Col. iii. 3.

him from their view,—therefore Jesus Christ is hidden in heaven in God.   Now Jesus Christ is our love, and our love is the life of our soul : therefore *our life is hidden in God with Jesus Christ;* and *when Jesus Christ,* who is our love, and consequently our spiritual life, *shall appear,* in the day of Judgment, we *also shall appear with him in glory;* that is, Jesus Christ our love will glorify us, communicating to us his felicity and splendour.

CHAPTER VII.

HOW LOVE IS THE LIFE OF THE SOUL, AND CONTINUATION OF THE DISCOURSE ON THE ECSTATIC LIFE.

THE soul is the first act and principle of all the vital movements of man, and, as Aristotle expresses it, the principle whereby we live, feel and understand : whence it follows, that we know the different kinds of life from the difference of movements ; so much so, indeed, that animals when entirely without movement are entirely without life.   Even so, Theotimus, love is the first act or principle of our devout or spiritual life, by which we live, feel and move : and our spiritual life is such as the movements of our love are, and a heart that has no movement nor affection, has no love ; as on the contrary a heart possessed of love is not without affective movement.   As soon therefore as we have set our affection upon Jesus Christ, we have consequently placed in him our spiritual life.   But he is now hidden in God in heaven, as God was hidden in him while he was here below.   Our life therefore is hidden in him, and when he shall appear in glory, our life and our love shall likewise appear with him in God. Hence S. Ignatius (Martyr) as S. Denis relates, said that his love was crucified, as though he would say : my natural and human love, with all the passions that depend on it, is nailed to the cross ; I have put it to death as a mortal love, which made my heart live a mortal life ; and as my Saviour was crucified

and died according to his mortal life, so did I die with him upon
the cross according to my natural love, which was the mortal
life of my soul, to the end that I might rise again to the supernatural life of a love which, because it can be exercised in
heaven, is consequently also immortal.

When therefore we see a soul that has raptures in prayer, by
which she goes out from and mounts above herself in God, and
yet has no ecstasy in her life, that is, leads not a life elevated and
united to God, by abnegation of worldly concupiscences, by
mortification of natural wills and inclinations, by an interior
sweetness, simplicity, humility, and above all by a continual
charity;—believe, Theotimus, that all these raptures are
exceedingly doubtful and dangerous; these are raptures fit to
stir up men to admiration, but not to sanctify them. For what
can it profit the soul to be ravished unto God by prayer, while
in her life and conversation she is ravished by earthly, base and
natural affections; to be above herself in prayer and below
herself in life and operation, to be angelic in meditation and
brutish in conversation? It is to *halt on two sides,** to swear by
the Lord and swear by Melchom.*† In a word it is a true mark
that such raptures and ecstasies are but operations and deceits
of the evil spirit. Blessed are they who live a superhuman
and ecstatic life, raised above themselves, though they may not
be ravished above themselves in prayer. There are many
saints in heaven who were never in ecstasy or rapture of contemplation. For how many martyrs and great saints do we see
in history never to have had other privilege in prayer than that
of devotion and fervour. But there was never saint who had
not the ecstasy and rapture of life and operation, overcoming
himself and his natural inclinations.

And who sees not, I pray you, Theotimus, that it is the
ecstasy of life and operation that the great Apostle principally
speaks of when he says: *I live now, not I, but Christ liveth in
me ;*‡ for he himself explains it in other terms to the Romans,
saying that: *Our old man is crucified with him,*§ that we are

---

* 3 Kings xviii. 21.   † Soph. i. 5.   ‡ Gal. ii. 20.
    § Rom. vi. 6.

dead to sin with him, and that we are also risen with him to *walk in newness of life, that we may serve sin no longer.* Behold, Theotimus, how two men are represented in each of us, and consequently two lives; the one of the old man, which is an old life; like, they say, the eagle's, which having grown into old age can but drag its wings along, and is unable to take flight: the other is the life of the new man, which also is a new life, like that of the eagle, which, being disburdened of its old feathers, now shaken off into the sea, takes new ones, and having grown young again, flies in the newness of its strength.

In the first life we live according to the old man, that is, according to the failings, weaknesses and infirmities contracted by the sin of our first father, Adam; and therefore we live to Adam's sin, and our life is a mortal life, yea death itself. In the second life we live according to the new man, that is, according to the graces, favours, ordinances and wills of our Saviour, and consequently, we live to salvation and redemption, and this new life is a lively, living and life-giving life. But whosoever would attain the new life, must make his way by the death of the old, *crucifying his flesh with the vices and concupiscences** thereof, burying it under the waters of holy baptism or penance: as Naaman drowned and buried in the waters of Jordan his leprous and infected old life, to live a new, sound, and spotless life; for one might well have said of him, that he was not now the old, leprous, corrupt, infected Naaman, but a new, clean, sound, and honourable Naaman, because he was dead to leprosy and was living to health and cleanness.

Now whosoever is raised up again to this new life of our Saviour, neither lives to himself, nor for himself, but to his Saviour, in his Saviour, and for his Saviour. *So you also reckon, says S. Paul, that you are dead to sin but alive unto God, in Christ Jesus our Lord.*†

* Gal. v. 24.   † Rom. vi. 11.

CHAPTER VIII.

BUT finally, methinks S. Paul makes the most forcible, pressing and admirable argument that ever was made, to urge us all to the ecstasy and rapture of life and operation. Hear, Theotimus, I beseech you; be attentive and weigh the force and efficacy of the ardent and heavenly words of this Apostle, ravished and transported with the love of his Master. Speaking then of himself (and the like is to be said of everyone), *the charity,* says he, *of Christ presseth us.** Yes, Theotimus, nothing so much presses man's heart as love; if a man know that he is beloved, be it by whom it may, he is pressed to love in his turn. But if a common man be beloved by a great lord, he is much more pressed; and if by a great monarch, how much more yet? And now, I pray you, knowing well that Jesus Christ, the true eternal God omnipotent, has loved us even to suffering death for us, *and the death of the cross*——is not this, O my dear Theotimus, to have our hearts under the press, and to feel them strongly pressed, and to feel love pressed out of them by violence and constraint, which is so much the more violent by how much it is more lovable and beloved! But how does this divine lover press us? *The charity of Christ presseth us,* says his holy Apostle, *judging this.* What means that *judging this?* It means that our Saviour's charity presses us then especially when we judge, consider, ponder, meditate, and attend to, the resolution of this question which faith gives. And what resolution? Mark, my good Theotimus, how he proceeds, graving, fixing and stamping his conception on our hearts. *Judging this,* says he; and what? *That if one died for all, then all were dead, and Jesus Christ died for all.* It is true, indeed: if one Jesus Christ died for all, all then are dead in the person of this only Saviour who died for them, and his death is to be imputed

* 2 Cor. v. 14.

unto them, since it was endured for them and in consideration of them.

But what follows from this? Methinks I hear that apostolic mouth, as with a peal of thunder startling the ears of our hearts! *That* follows then, O Christians, which Jesus Christ dying for us desired of us. And what did he desire of us but that we should be conformed unto him, to the end, says the Apostle, *that those who live may not now live to themselves, but unto him who died for them, and rose again.* True God! Theotimus, how powerful a consequence is this in the matter of love! Jesus Christ died for us; by his death he has given us life; we only live because he died; he died for us, as ours, and in us; our life then is no more ours, but his who has purchased it for us by his death: we are therefore no more to live to ourselves but to him, nor in ourselves but in him, nor for ourselves but for him. A maiden of the Isle of Sestos had brought up a young eagle with the care children are wont to bestow upon such affairs; the eagle being come to its full growth began little by little to fly and to chase birds, according to its natural instinct; then getting more strength it seized upon wild beasts, never failing faithfully to take home the prey to its dear mistress, as in acknowledgment of the bringing up which it had had from her. Now it happened upon a day that this young damsel died, while the poor eagle was on the hunt, and her body, according to the custom of that time and country, was publicly placed upon the funeral pile to be burnt; when even as the flame began to seize upon her the eagle came up with strong and eager flight, and, when it beheld this unlooked-for and sad spectacle, pierced with grief, it opened its talons, let fall its prey, and spread itself upon its poor beloved mistress; and covering her with its wings, as it were to defend her from the fire, or for pity's sake to embrace her, it remained there constant and immovable, courageously dying and burning with her; the ardour of its affection not giving way to flames and ardours of fire, that so it might become the victim and holocaust of its brave and prodigious love, as its mistress was of death and fire.

O Theotimus! To what a high flight this eagle moves us! Our Saviour has bred us up from our tender youth, yea he formed us and received us as a loving nurse into the arms of his divine Providence, even from the instant of our conception.

> Not being yet, thy holy hand did make me ;
> Scarce born, into thy arms thy love did take me.

He made us his own by Baptism, and tenderly nourishes both our soul and our body with an incomprehensible love; to purchase us life he suffered death, he has fed us with his own flesh and blood. Ah! what remains then, my dear Theotimus, what conclusion are we to draw from this, except *that those who live should live no more to themselves but to him that died for them :* that is to say, that we should consecrate all the moments of our life to the divine love of our Saviour's death, bringing home to his glory all our prey, all our conquests, all our actions, all our thoughts, and all our affections. Let us behold him, Theotimus, this heavenly Redeemer, extended upon the cross as upon a funeral pile of honour, where he dies of love for us, yea of a love more dolorous than death itself, or a death more amorous than love itself. Ah! why do we not spiritually cast ourselves upon him to die upon the cross with him, who has truly willed to die for love of us? I will hold him, should we say, if we had the eagle's generosity, and will never depart from him. I will die with him and burn in the flames of his love, one and the same fire shall consume this divine Creator and his poor creature. My Jesus is wholly mine, and I am wholly his: I will live and die upon his breast, nor life nor death shall ever separate me from him. Thus then is made the holy ecstasy of true love, when we live not according to human reason and inclinations, but above them, following the inspirations and instincts of the divine Saviour of our souls.

CHAPTER IX.

OF THE SUPREME EFFECT OF AFFECTIVE LOVE, WHICH IS THE DEATH
OF THE LOVERS ; AND FIRST, OF SUCH AS DIED IN LOVE.

*Love is strong as death.** Death separates the soul of him who
dies from the body, and from all the things of the world ; sacred
love separates the soul of the lover from his body and from all
the things of the world: nor is there any other difference, saving
that death does that in effect, which love ordinarily does only in
affection. I say ordinarily, Theotimus, because holy love is
sometimes so violent that it even actually causes a separation
between the body and the soul ; making the lovers die a most
happy death, better than a hundred lives.

As it is the special character of the reprobate that they die in
sin, so of the elect it is that they die in the love and grace of
God. But still this happens in different ways. The just man never
dies unprovidedly ; for to have persevered in Christian justice
even to the end, is to have well provided for death ; but he does
sometimes die of   unexpected or sudden death. For this
cause the all-wise Church does not make us pray in her Litanies
that we may simply be delivered from sudden death, but from
sudden and unprovided death. It is no worse for being sudden,
if it be not also unprovided. If weak and ordinary souls had
seen the fire from heaven fall upon the great S. Simeon Stylites's
head and kill him, what would they have thought but thoughts
of scandal? Yet ought we to have no other thought than that
this great saint, having most perfectly immolated himself to God
in his heart, and being already wholly consumed with love, the
fire came from heaven to perfect the holocaust and entirely
consume it ; for the Abbot Julian, being a day's journey off,
saw his soul ascend to heaven, and thereupon caused incense to
be offered in thanksgiving to God. The Blessed Homobonus of
Cremona, on a certain day hearing Mass on his knees with
extreme devotion, rose not at the Gospel according to custom,

* Cant. viii. 6.

whence those that were about him, looked at him, and perceived that he was dead. There have been in our time men most famous for virtue and learning, found dead, some in a confessional, others while hearing a sermon : yea some have been seen to fall down dead at their going out of the pulpit, where they had preached with great fervour ; and all these deaths were sudden, yet not unprovided. And how many good people do we see die in apoplexy, in a lethargy, and a thousand other ways, very suddenly ? And others die in delirium and madness, out of the use of reason ; and all these, together with children who are baptized, die in grace and consequently in the love of God. But how could they die in the love of God, since they did not even think of God at the time of their departure ?

Learned men, Theotimus, lose not their knowledge while they are asleep; otherwise they would be unlearned at their awaking, and have to return to school. The like it is in all the habits of prudence, temperance, faith, hope and charity; they are ever within the just man's heart, though they are not always in action. While a man sleeps it seems that all his habits sleep with him, and when he awakes awake with him; so a just man dying suddenly, whether crushed by a house falling upon him, or killed by thunder, or stifled by an effusion on the lungs, or dying out of his senses by the violence of a burning fever, dies not indeed in the exercise of holy love, yet he dies in the habit thereof. Whereupon the wise man says : *The just man, if he be prevented with death, shall be in rest :** for to obtain eternal life it suffices to die in the state and habit of love and charity.

Many saints, however, have departed this life not only in charity and with the habit of heavenly love, but even in the act and practice thereof. S. Augustine died in the exercise of holy contrition, which cannot be without love : S. Jerome exhorting his dear children to the love of God, of their neighbour, and of virtue : S. Ambrose in a rapture, sweetly discoursing with his Saviour, immediately after he had received the holy Sacrament of the altar : S. Antony of Padua after he had recited a hymn to the glorious Virgin-mother, and while talking joyously with

* Wis. iv. 7.

our Saviour : S. Thomas Aquinas joining his hands, elevating his eyes towards heaven, raising his voice very high, and pronouncing by way of ejaculation with great fervour, these words of the Canticles (the last which he had expounded) : *Come my beloved, let us go forth into the field, let us abide in the villages.** All the Apostles and almost all the Martyrs died in prayer. The Blessed and Venerable Bede having foreknown by revelation the time of his departure, went to Vespers (and it was Ascension day), and standing upright, leaning only on the elbows of his stall, without any disease at all, ended his life at the same instant that he ended his singing of Vespers, as it were directly to follow his Master ascending unto heaven, there to enjoy the fair morning of eternity, which has no Vesper.† John Gerson, Chancellor of the University of Paris, a man so learned and pious that, as Sixtus Senensis says, one can hardly discern whether his learning surpassed his piety, or his piety his learning, having expounded the fifty properties of divine love mentioned in the Canticle of Canticles, three days afterwards, having a face and heart full of life, expired pronouncing and repeating many times, by way of ejaculatory prayer, these holy words, drawn out of the same Canticles : O God ! thy *love is strong as death.* S. Martin, as everyone knows, died so attentive to the exercise of devotion, that more could not be. S. Louis, that great king amongst saints, and great saint amongst kings, being struck with the plague, never ceased to pray ; and then, having received the divine Viaticum, spreading out his arms in form of a cross, his eyes fixed upon heaven, yielded up the ghost, ardently sighing out these words with a perfect confidence of love : *I will come into thy house ; I will worship towards thy holy temple and I will give glory to thy name.*‡ S. Peter Celestine, being wholly steeped in cruel afflictions which can scarce be described, having reached the end of his days, began to sing, as a sacred swan, the last of the psalms, and ended his song and his life with these amorous words : *Let every spirit praise the*

* Cant. vii. 11.

† S. Francis's account of this blessed death is not strictly according to history. We cannot ascertain what Life of Venerable Bede he used (Tr.).

‡ Pss. v. 8 ; cxxxvii. 2.

Lord. The admirable S. Eusebia, surnamed the stranger, died
on her knees and in fervent prayer: S. Peter Martyr, writing
with his finger and in his own blood the confession of the faith
for which he died, and uttering these words: Lord, *into thy
hands I commend my spirit:* and the great Apostle of the
Japanese, S. Francis Xavier, holding and kissing the image of
the crucifix, and repeating at every kiss these ejaculations of
his soul: " O Jesus ! the God of my heart !"

CHAPTER X.

OF THOSE WHO DIED BY AND FOR DIVINE LOVE.

ALL the Martyrs, Theotimus, died for the love of God; for
when we say that some of them died for the faith, we mean not
that they died for a dead faith, but for the living faith, that is,
quickened by charity. And again the confession of faith is not
so much an act of the understanding and of faith, as an act of the
will and of the love of God. And this is why the great S. Peter,
keeping the faith in his soul on the day of the passion, yet lost
charity, refusing in words to profess him to be his Master, whom
in his heart he acknowledged to be such. But there were yet
other Martyrs who died expressly for charity alone, as our
Saviour's great Precursor, who was martyred for fraternal
correction ; and the glorious princes of the Apostles, S. Peter
and S. Paul, and particularly S. Paul, died for having reclaimed
those women to a pious and pure life whom the infamous Nero
had led into sin. The holy Bishops Stanislaus and Thomas of
Canterbury were slain for a matter that touched not faith, but
charity. In fine a great part of the sacred Virgin-martyrs were
slain for the zeal they had to preserve their chastity, which
charity had caused them to dedicate to their heavenly spouse.

But some sacred lovers so absolutely give themselves over
to the exercises of divine love, that this holy fire wastes and
consumes their life. Grief does sometimes so long hinder the

afflicted from eating, drinking, or sleeping, that in the end weakened and wasted they die; whence it is commonly said that such die of grief: but it is not so indeed; for they die through failure of strength, and inanition. Yet since this failure came through grief, we must allow that though they died not of grief, they died by reason of grief and by grief. So, my dear Theotimus, when the fervour of holy love is great, it gives so many assaults to the heart, so often wounds it, causes in it so many languors, melts it so habitually, and puts it so frequently into ecstasies and raptures, that by this means, the soul, almost entirely occupied in God, not being able to afford sufficient assistance to nature to effect digestion and nourish itself properly, the animal and vital spirits begin little by little to fail, life is shortened, and death takes place.

O God! Theotimus, how happy this death is! How delightful is this love-dart, which, wounding us with the incurable wound of heavenly love, makes us for ever pining and sick, with so strong a beating of the heart, that at length we must yield to death. How much, do you think, did these sacred languors and labours undergone for charity, advance the days of the divine lovers S. Catharine of Siena, S. Francis, young Stanislaus Kotska, S. Charles, and many hundreds more who died so young? Verily, as for S. Francis, from the time that he received the holy stigmata of his master, he had such violent and sharp pains, pangs, convulsions and illnesses, that he became mere skin and bone, and he seemed rather to be a skeleton, or a picture of death, than a man yet living and breathing.

CHAPTER XI.

HOW SOME OF THE HEAVENLY LOVERS DIED ALSO OF LOVE.

ALL the elect then, Theotimus, died in the habit of holy love; but further, some died even in the exercise of it, others for this love, and others by this same love. But what belongs to the sovereign degree of love is, that some die of love; and then it is that love not only wounds the soul, so as to make her languish, but even pierces her through, delivering its blow right in the middle of the heart, and so fatally, that it drives the soul out of the body;—which happens thus. The soul, powerfully drawn by the divine sweetness of her beloved, to correspond on her side with his sweet attractions, forcibly and to the best of her power springs out towards this longed-for beloved who attracts her, and, not being able to draw her body after her, rather than stay with it in this miserable life, she quits it and gets clear; flying alone, as a fair dove, into the delicious bosom of her heavenly spouse. She throws herself upon her beloved, and her beloved draws and ravishes her to himself. And as the bridegroom leaves father and mother to cleave to his dearly beloved, so this chaste bride forsaketh the flesh to unite herself to her beloved. Now this is the most violent effect of love in a soul, and one which requires first a great offstripping of all such affections as keep the heart attached either to the world or to the body, so that as fire, having by little and little separated an essence from its mass, and wholly purified it, at length brings out the quintessence,—even so holy love having withdrawn man's heart from all humours, inclinations, and passions, as far as may be, does at length urge out the soul, to the end that by this death, precious in the divine eyes, she may pass to eternal glory.

The great S. Francis, who in this subject of heavenly love ever returns before my eyes, could not possibly escape dying by love, because of the manifold and great languors, ecstasies and faintings which his love of God gave him; but besides this, God, who had set him forth to the view of the whole world as a miracle of love, willed that he should not only die for love but also of love. For consider, I beseech you, Theotimus, his death. Perceiving himself upon the point of his departure, he caused himself to be laid naked upon the ground, where having received as an alms a habit which they put on him, he discoursed to his brethren, animating them to the love of God and the Church, had our Saviour's passion read, and then with an extreme fervour began Psalm cxli. : *I cried to the Lord with my voice ; with my voice I made supplication to the Lord;* and having pronounced these last words: *Bring my soul out of prison, that I may praise thy name ; the just wait for me, until thou reward me,* he died,—in his forty-fifth year. Who sees not, I beseech you, Theotimus, that this seraphical man who had so earnestly desired to be martyred and to die for love, died in the end of love, as in another place I have described?

S. Magdalen having for the space of thirty years lived in a cave which is yet to be seen in Provence, having seven times each day had raptures and been borne up in the air by angels, as though she went to sing the seven canonical hours in their choir; in the end, upon a Sunday, she came to Church, where her dear Bishop, S. Maximin, finding her in contemplation, her eyes full of tears and her arms stretched out, communicated her, and soon afterwards she delivered up her blessed soul, which once again, for good and all, went to her Saviour's feet, to enjoy *the better part*, which she had already made choice of here below.

S. Basil had contracted a strict friendship with a physician, a Jew by nation and religion, with the intention of bringing him to the faith of Jesus Christ, which nevertheless he could not effect till such time as, worn out with fastings, watchings and labours, being upon the point of dying, he inquired of the physician what opinion he had of him, conjuring him to speak frankly. The physician did so, and having felt his pulse :— there is no further remedy, said he ; before the sun sets you will depart this life. But what will you say, replied the patient, if to-morrow I shall be alive? I will become a Christian, I promise you, said the physician. With this the saint prayed to God, and obtained a prolongation of his own temporal life, for the good of his physician's spiritual life, who having seen this miracle was converted, and S. Basil rising courageously out of his bed, went to the Church and baptized him with all his family, then returning to his chamber and to his bed, having entertained himself a good space with our Saviour in prayer, he holily exhorted the assistants to serve God with their whole heart, and finally, seeing the angels approach, and pronouncing with an extreme delight these words : O God I recommend unto thee my soul, and restore it

into thy hands; he died.   But the poor converted physician
seeing him thus pass away, embracing him, and melting into
tears over him :—" O great Basil, said he, indeed if thou hadst
willed thou wouldst no more have died to-day than yesterday."
Who does not see that this death was wholly of love?   And the
Blessed Mother (S.) Teresa of Jesus revealed after her death
that she died of an impetuous assault of love, which had been so
violent that nature not being able to support it, the soul had
departed towards the beloved object of its affections.

CHAPTER XII.

MARVELLOUS HISTORY OF THE DEATH OF A GENTLEMAN WHO DIED OF LOVE ON MOUNT OLIVET.

BESIDES what I have said, I have found a history which to
sacred lovers is none the less credible for being wonderful, since,
as the holy Apostle says : *Charity* willingly *believeth all things;**
that is, it is not quick to believe that any one is lying, and if
there are no apparent marks of falsehood in things which are
told, it makes no difficulty about believing them ; but above all
when they are things which exalt and magnify the love of God
towards men, or the love of men towards God, for charity,
which is sovereign queen of the virtues, rejoices in the things
which contribute to the glory of its empire and domination.
And although the account I am about to give is not so fully
published nor so well witnessed as the greatness of the marvel
which it contains would require, it does not therefore lose its
truth; for, as S. Augustine excellently says, miracles, magnificent as they may be, are scarcely known in the very place
where they are worked ; and even when they are related by those
who have seen them, they are with difficulty believed, but they
do not therefore cease to be true; and, in matter of religion,

---

* I Cor. xiii. 7.

good souls have more sweetness in believing things in which there is more difficulty and admiration.

Upon a time, then, a very illustrious and virtuous knight went beyond seas to Palestine, to visit the holy places in which Our Lord had done the works of our redemption; and, properly to begin this holy exercise, before everything he worthily confessed and communicated. Then he went first to the town of Nazareth, where the angel announced to the most holy Virgin the most sacred Incarnation, and where the most adorable conception of the Eternal Word took place; and there this good pilgrim set himself to contemplate the abyss of the heavenly goodness, which had deigned to take human flesh in order to withdraw men from perdition. Thence he passed to Bethlehem, to the place of the Nativity, and one could not say how many tears there he shed, contemplating those with which the Son of God, little infant of the Virgin, had watered that holy stable, kissing and kissing again a hundred times that sacred earth, and licking the dust on which the first infancy of the divine Babe had been received. From Bethlehem he went to Bethabara, and passed as far as the little place of Bethania, when, remembering that Our Lord had unclothed himself to be baptized, he also unclothed himself, and entering into the Jordan, and bathing in it, and drinking of the waters thereof, it seemed to him as if he saw his Saviour receiving baptism from the hand of his precursor, and the Holy Ghost descending upon him in the form of a dove, with the heavens yet opened, while from them seemed to him to come the voice of the Eternal Father, saying: *This is my beloved Son in whom I am well pleased.* From Bethania he goes into the desert, and there sees with the eyes of his Spirit the Saviour fasting, and fighting and conquering the enemy, then the angels ministering to him admirable meats. Thence he goes up to Mount Thabor, where he sees the Saviour transfigured, then to Mount Sion, where he seems to see Our Lord still on his knees in the supper-room, washing the disciples' feet, and afterwards distributing to them his divine body in the sacred Eucharist. He passes the torrent of Cedron, and goes to the Garden of Gethsemani, where his heart melts into the tears of a most loving sorrow, while he there represents to himself

his dear Saviour sweating blood, in that extreme agony, which
he suffered there, to be soon afterwards bound fast with cords
and led into Jerusalem; whither he goes also, following everywhere the footprints of his beloved, and in imagination sees
him dragged hither and thither, to Annas, to Caiphas, to Pilate,
to Herod, scourged, blindfolded, spat upon, crowned with
thorns, presented to the people, condemed to death, loaded with
his cross—which he carries, and while carrying it has the
pitiful meeting with his mother all steeped in grief, and with
the daughters of Jerusalem who weep over him. He ascends
at last, this devout pilgrim, to Mount Calvary, when he sees in
spirit the cross laid upon the earth, and our Saviour, stript
naked, thrown down and nailed hands and feet upon it, most
cruelly. He contemplates then how they raise the cross and
the Crucified into the air, and the blood which streams from all
parts of this ruined divine body. He regards the poor sacred
Virgin, quite transpierced with the sword of sorrow ; then he
turns his eyes on the crucified Saviour, whose seven words he
hears with a matchless love, and at last he sees him dying, then
dead, then receiving the lance-stroke, and showing by the
opening of the wound his divine heart, then taken down from
the cross and carried to the sepulchre, whither he follows him,
shedding a sea of tears on the places moistened with the blood
of his Redeemer. And so he enters into the sepulchre and
buries his heart by the body of his divine Master ; then, rising
again with him, he goes to Emmaus, and sees all that passes
between the Lord and the two disciples; and at last returning
to Mount Olivet, where the mystery of the Ascension took
place, and there seeing the last marks and vestiges of the feet of
the Divine Saviour, prostrate upon them, and kissing them a
thousand thousand times, with sighs of an infinite love, he
began to draw up to himself all the forces of his affections, as
an archer draws the string of his bow when he wishes to shoot
his arrow, then rising, his eyes and his hands turned to heaven:
O Jesus! said he, my sweet Jesus! I know no more where to
seek and follow thee on earth: Ah! Jesus, Jesus, my love,
grant then to this heart that it may follow thee and go after
thee thither above. And with these ardent words, he at the

same moment shot his soul into heaven, a sacred arrow which as an archer of God he directed into the central-white of his most blessed mark. But his companions and servants who saw this poor lover fall suddenly thus as if dead, amazed at this accident, ran instantly for the doctor, who coming found that he had really passed away : and to make a safe judgment on the causes of so unexpected a death, he inquires of what temperament, of what manners, and of what feelings, the deceased might be; and he learned that he was of a disposition very sweet, very amiable, wondrously devout, and most ardent in the love of God. Whereupon the doctor said : Without doubt, then, his heart has broken with excess and fervour of love. And in order the better to confirm his decision, he would have him opened, and found that glorious heart open, with this sacred word engraved within it : *Jesus my love!* Love, then, did in this heart the office of death, separating the soul from the body, no other cause concurring. And it is S. Bernardine of Siena, a very wise and very holy doctor, who makes this relation in the first of his Sermons on the Ascension.

Indeed, another author of nearly the same age, who has concealed his name out of humility, but who is worthy to be named, in a book which he has entitled : *Mirror of Spiritual Persons*, relates a history even more admirable. For he says that in the parts of Provence there was a nobleman entirely devoted to the love of God and to the devotion of the Most Holy Sacrament of the Altar. Now one day, being extremely afflicted with a malady which caused him continual vomitings, the divine communion was brought him; and not daring to receive it on account of the danger of casting it up again, he begged his pastor to apply it at least to his breast, and with it to make the sign of the cross over him. This was done, and in a moment his breast, inflamed with holy love, was cleft, and drew into itself the heavenly food wherein his beloved was contained, and at the same instant gave up its breath. I see in good truth that this history is extraordinary, and would deserve a more weighty testimony : yet after the true history of the cleft heart of S. Clare of Montefalco, which all the world may see even to this day, and that of the stigmata of S. Francis, which is most certain, my soul finds nothing hard to be believed amongst the effects of divine love.

CHAPTER XIII.

THAT THE MOST SACRED VIRGIN MOTHER OF GOD DIED
OF LOVE FOR HER SON.

ONE can hardly well doubt that the great S. Joseph died before the passion and death of our Saviour, who otherwise would not have commended his mother to S. John. And how can one then imagine that the dear child of his heart, his beloved foster-child, did not assist him at the hour of his departure? *Blessed are the merciful for they shall obtain mercy.* Ah! how much sweetness, charity and mercy, did this good foster-father use towards our Saviour, when he was born a little child in the world! And who can then believe but that, at his departure out of it, this divine child rendered him the like a hundred-fold, filling him with heavenly delights? Storks are the true representation of the mutual piety of children towards their parents and of parents towards their children: for, being birds of passage, they bear their old parents with them in their journey, as their parents had borne them while they were yet young, on the like occasions. While our Saviour was yet a little child, the great S. Joseph his foster-father, and the most glorious Virgin his mother, had many times carried him, but especially in their journey from Judea to Egypt, and from Egypt to Judea. Ah! who then can doubt that this holy father being come to the end of his days, was reciprocally carried by his divine foster-child, in the passage from this to another life, into Abraham's bosom, to be translated thence into his own, into glory, on the day of his Ascension? A saint who had loved so much in his life, could not die but of love; for his heart not being able to love his dear Jesus as much as he desired while he continued amongst the distractions of this life, and having already performed the duty which was required in the childhood of Jesus, what remained but that he should say to the eternal Father : O Father, *I have finished the work which thou gavest me to do :* and then to the Son, O my child! as thy heavenly Father put thy tender body into my hands the day of thy coming into this world, so do I render up my soul into thine, this day of my departure out of the world.

Such, as I conceive, was the death of this great patriarch, a man elected to perform the most tender and loving offices that ever were or shall be performed to the Son of God, save those that were done by his sacred spouse, the true natural mother of the said Son. Now of her it is not possible to imagine that she died of any other kind of death than of love, the noblest of deaths, and consequently due to the noblest life that ever was amongst creatures : a death of which the very angels would desire to die, if die they could. If the primitive Christians were said to have but one heart and one soul, by reason of their perfect mutual love, if S. Paul lived not in himself, but Jesus Christ lived in him, by reason of the close union of his heart to his Master's, whereby his soul was as it were dead in his heart which it animated, to live in the heart of the Saviour which it loved,—O true God! how much more really had the sacred virgin and her son but one soul, one heart and one life, so that this heavenly mother, living, lived not, but her son lived in her ! 'Twas a mother the most loving and the most beloved that ever could be, yea loving and beloved with a love incomparably more eminent than that of all the orders of angels and men, as the names of mother-only and only-son, are names passing all other names in matter of love. And I say mother-only and only-son, because all the other sons of men divide the acknowledgment of their production between their father and mother ; but in this son, as all his human birth depended on his mother alone, who alone contributed that which was requisite to the virtue of the Holy Ghost for the conception of this heavenly child, so to her alone all the love which sprang from that production was due and rendered : wherefore this son and this mother were united in a union by so much more excellent, as

* John xvii. 4.

her name is excellent in love above all other names. For which of all the seraphim can say to our Saviour: Thou art my true son, and I love thee as my true son ? And to which of all his creatures did our Saviour ever say : Thou art my true mother, and as my true mother I love thee: thou art my true mother, entirely mine, and I am thy true son wholly thine ? If then a loving servant durst say, and did say, that he had no other life than his master's—Ah ! how confidently and fervently might this mother exclaim : I have no life but the life of my son, my life is wholly in his, and his wholly in mine ; for it was no longer union but unity of hearts between this mother and this son.

And if this mother lived her son's life, she also died her son's death. The phœnix, as report goes, grown very aged, gathers together on the top of a mountain a quantity of aromatical wood, upon which, as upon its bed of honour, it goes to end its days: for when the sun, being at its highest, pours out its hottest beams, this sole bird, to contribute an increase of activity to the ardour of the sun, ceases not to beat with its wings upon its bed, till it has made it take fire, and burning with it is consumed, and dies in those odoriferous flames. In like manner, Theotimus, the virgin-mother, having collected in her spirit all the most beloved mysteries of the life and death of her son by a most lively and continual memory of them, and withal, ever receiving directly the most ardent inspirations which her child, the sun of justice, has cast upon human beings in the highest noon of his charity ; and besides, making on her part also, a perpetual movement of contemplation, at length the sacred fire of this divine love consumed her entirely as a holocaust of sweetness, so that she died thereof, the soul being wholly ravished and transported into the arms of the dilection of her son. O, death, amorously life-giving ! O, love, vitally death-giving !

Several sacred lovers were present at the death of the Saviour, amongst whom those who had the most love had the most sorrow ; for love was then all steeped in sorrow, and sorrow in love ; and all they who for their Saviour were impassioned with love were in love with his passion and sorrow. But the sweet Mother, who loved more than all, was more than all transfixed with the sword of sorrow. The sorrow of the Son at that time was a piercing sword, which passed through the heart of the Mother, because that Mother's heart was glued, joined and united to her Son, with so perfect a union that nothing could wound the one without inflicting a lively torture upon the other. Now this maternal bosom, being thus wounded with love, not only did not seek a cure for its wound, but loved her wound more than all cure, dearly keeping the shafts of sorrow she had received, on account of the love which had shot them into her heart, and continually desiring to die of them, since her Son died of them, who, as say all the Holy Scriptures and all Doctors, died amidst the flames of his charity, a perfect holocaust for all the sins of the world.

CHAPTER XIV.

THAT THE GLORIOUS VIRGIN DIED BY AN EXTREMELY SWEET AND TRANQUIL DEATH.

It is said on the one side that Our Lady revealed to S. Mechtilde that the malady of which she died was no other thing than an impetuous assault of divine love; but S. Bridget and S. John Damascene testify that she died an extremely peaceful death: and both statements are true, Theotimus.

The stars are marvellously beautiful to see, and send forth a fair light; but, if you have taken notice, it is by flushes of light, by sparks and flashes, that they produce their rays, as if they brought forth light with effort, at distinct intervals; whether it is because their feebler light cannot so continuously shine with evenness, or because our weak eyes do not allow us a constant and firm view of them, on account of the great distance there is between them and our eyes. In the same way, generally speaking, the saints who died of love felt a great variety of accidents and symptoms of love, before it brought them to death; many sudden movements, many assaults, many ecstasies, many languors, many agonies; and it seemed that their love with many renewed efforts brought forth their blessed death: this happened on account of the weakness of their love, not yet absolutely perfect, which could not continue its loving with an even fervour.

But it was quite otherwise with the most holy Virgin. For, as we see the lovely dawning of day grow, not at intervals and by shocks, but by a certain dilating and continuous brightening, which is almost insensibly perceptible, so that we truly see it grow in clearness, but so evenly that no one perceives any interruption, separation or discontinuance in its growing;— thus divine love grew at each moment in the virginal heart of our glorious Lady, but by sweet, peaceable and continuous growths, without any agitation, or shock, or violence. Ah ! no, Theotimus, we must not suppose an impetuosity of agitation in this celestial love of the maternal heart of the Virgin; for love, of itself, is sweet, gracious, peaceful and tranquil. If it sometimes deliver assaults, if it give shocks to the spirit, this is because it finds resistance there : but when the passages of the soul are opened to it without opposition or contradiction, it makes its progress peaceably, with an incomparable sweetness. It was so, then, that holy love employed its force in the virginal heart of the sacred Mother, without effort of violent impetuosity, because it found no resistance or hindrance whatever. For as we see great rivers boil and leap, with a mighty roaring, in rough places where the rocks make shoals and reefs to oppose and prevent the flowing of the waters, but, on the contrary, finding themselves on the plain, sweetly glide and flow without effort ;—so divine love, finding in human souls some hindrance and resistance (as in truth all have in some degree, though differently), does violence there, combating bad inclinations, striking the heart, pushing the will by divers agitations and various efforts to get room for itself, or at least to pass these obstacles. But in the sacred Virgin, everything favoured and seconded the course of heavenly love; its progress and increase were incomparably greater than in all other creatures, yet a progress infinitely sweet, peaceful and tranquil. No, she swooned not away, either with love or with compassion, by the cross of her Son, although she then experienced the most ardent and painful attack of love that can be imagined : for although the attack was extreme, yet, at the same time, it was at once equally strong and gentle, mighty and tranquil, active and peaceful, consisting in a heat which was sharp but sweet.

I am not saying, Theotimus, that in the soul of the most holy Virgin there were not two portions, aud consequently two appetites, one according to the spirit and superior reason, the other according to the senses and inferior reason, so that she could feel repugnances and contradictions of the one to the other appetite, for this burden was felt even by her Son;—but I say that in this celestial Mother all the affections were so well ranged and ordered, that divine love exercised in her its empire and domination most peaceably, without being troubled by the diversity of wills and appetites, or by the contradiction of the senses, because neither the repugnances of the natural appetite nor the movements of the senses ever went as far as sin, not even as far as venial sin; but, on the contrary, all was employed holily and faithfully in the service of holy love, for the exercise of the other virtues, which, for the most part, cannot be prac. tised save amid difficulties, oppositions and contradictions.

Thorns, according to the vulgar opinion, are not only different from, but even contrary to, flowers; and it seems as if things would go better if there were none in the world: which has made S. Ambrose think that but for sin there would be none. But still, as here they are, the good husbandman renders them useful, making from them, about his fields and young trees, hedges and enclosures which serve as defence and rampart against cattle. So the glorious Virgin, having had a part in all human miseries, saving such as directly tend to sin, employed them most profitably for the exercise and increase of the holy virtues of fortitude, temperance, justice and prudence, poverty, humility, patience and compassion : so that these were so far from hindering, that they even assisted and strengthened heavenly love by continual exercises and advancements. And, in her, Magdalen is not distracted from the attention wherewith she receives from her Saviour the impressions of love, by all Martha's ardour and solicitude. She has made choice of her Son's love, and nothing deprives her of it.

The loadstone, as every one knows, Theotimus, naturally draws iron unto it, by a secret and most wonderful virtue : yet five things there are which hinder this operation. 1°. A too great distance. 2°. A diamond interposed. 3°. If the iron be greased.

4°. If it be rubbed with an onion. 5°. If it be too weighty. Our
heart is made for God, who continually allures it, never ceasing
to throw into it the baits of his celestial love. But five things
hinder the operation of his holy attraction. 1°. Sin, which puts
us at a distance from God. 2°. Affection to riches. 3°. Sensual
pleasures. 4°. Pride and vanity. 5°. Self-love together with
the multitude of inordinate passions which it brings forth, and
which are to us an overcharging load which weighs us down.
But none of these hindrances had place in the glorious Virgin's
heart. 1°. She was ever preserved from all sin. 2°. Ever most
poor in spirit. 3°. Ever most pure. 4°. Ever most humble.
5°. Ever peaceful mistress of all her passions, and totally exempt
from the rebellion which self-love raises against the love of God.
And therefore as iron, if clear of all obstacles and freed from its
own weight, would be powerfully, yet gently and equably, drawn
by the loadstone, in such sort, however, that the attraction would
ever grow more active and forcible as they came nearer the one
to the other, and the motion nearer to its end :—so the most
holy Mother, having nothing in her which hindered the operation
of the divine love of her Son, was united unto him in an
incomparable union, by gentle ecstasies, without trouble or
travail, ecstasies in which the sensible powers ceased not to
perform their actions, without in any way disturbing the union
of the spirit, as again the perfect application of her spirit did
not much divert her senses. So that this Virgin's death was
more sweet than could be imagined, her Son sweetly drawing
her after the odour of his perfumes, and she most lovingly
flowing out after their sacred sweetness even into the bosom of
her Son's goodness. And although this holy soul extremely
loved her most holy, most pure, and most love-worthy body, yet she
forsook it without any pain or resistance ; as the chaste Judith,
though she greatly loved the weeds of penance and widowhood
yet forsook them and freely put them off, to put on her marriage
garments when she went to be victorious over Holofernes ; or
as Jonathan did when for the love of David he stripped himself
of his garments. Love had given at the foot of the cross to this
divine Spouse the supreme sorrows of death, and therefore it
was reasonable that at length death should give her the sovereign
delights of love.

BOOK VIII.

LOVE OF CONFORMITY, BY WHICH WE UNITE OUR WILL TO THE WILL OF GOD, SIGNIFIED UNTO US BY HIS COMMANDMENTS, COUNSELS AND INSPIRATIONS.

CHAPTER I.

OF THE LOVE OF CONFORMITY PROCEEDING FROM SACRED COMPLACENCY.

As good ground having received the seed renders it back in its season a hundredfold, so the heart which has taken complacency in God cannot hinder itself from wishing to offer another complacency to God. No one pleases us but we desire to please him. Cool wine cools for a while those who drink it, but, as soon as it grows warm within the receiver, it reciprocally warms him, and the more heat is given to it, the more it gives back. True love is never ungrateful, but strives to please those in whom it finds its pleasure; and hence comes that loving conformity, which makes us such as those we love. The most devout and most wise King Solomon, became idolatrous and foolish when he loved women who were foolish and idolatrous, and served as many idols as his wives had. For this cause the Scripture terms those men effeminate who passionately love women as such, because love metamorphoses them from men into women, in manners and humours.

Now this transformation is made insensibly by complacency, which having got entry into our heart brings forth another complacency, to give to him of whom we have received it. They say there is a little land animal in the Indies, which finds such pleasure with fishes and in the sea, that by often swimming with them it becomes a fish, and of an animal of the land becomes entirely an animal of the sea. So by often delighting in God we become conformed to God, and our will is transformed into that of the Divine Majesty, by the complacency which it takes therein. The example of those we love has a sweet and unperceived empire and insensible authority over us: it is necessary either to imitate or forsake them. He who, drawn by the sweetness of perfumes, enters a perfumer's shop, while receiving the pleasure which he takes in the smell of those odours, perfumes himself, and going out, communicates to others the pleasure which he has received, spreading amongst them the scent of perfumes which he has contracted. Our heart, together with the pleasure which it takes in the thing beloved, draws unto itself the quality thereof, for delight opens the heart, as sorrow closes it, whence the sacred holy Scripture often uses the word, dilate, instead of, rejoice. Now the heart being opened by pleasure, the impressions of the qualities on which the pleasure depends find easy passage into the spirit; and together with them such others also as are in the same subject, though disagreeable to us, creep in amid the throng of pleasures, as he that lacked his marriage garment got into the banquet amongst those that were adorned with it. So Aristotle's scholars took pains to stammer like him, and Plato's walked bent-backed in imitation of their master. In fine the pleasure which we take in a thing has a certain communicative power which produces in the lover's heart the qualities of the thing which pleases. And hence it is that holy complacency transforms us into God whom we love, and by how much greater the complacency, by so much the transformation is more perfect: thus the saints that loved ardently were speedily and perfectly transformed, love transporting and translating the manners and disposition of the one heart into the other.

A strange yet a true thing! Place together two lutes which are in unison, that is, of the same sound and accord, and let one of them be played on :—the other though not touched will not fail to sound like that which is played on, the affinity which is between them, as by a natural love, causing this correspondence. We have a repugnance to imitate those we hate even in good things, nor would the Lacedæmonians follow the good counsel of a wicked man, unless some good man pronounced it after him. On the contrary, we cannot help conforming ourselves to what we love. In this sense, as I think, the great Apostle said that *the law* was *not made for the just :** for in truth the just man is not just but insomuch as he has love, and if he have love there is no need to press him by the rigour of the law, love being the most pressing teacher and solicitor, to urge the heart which it possesses to obey the will and the intention of the beloved. Love is a magistrate who exercises his authority without noise, without pursuivants or sergeants, by that mutual complacency, by which, as we find pleasure in God, so also we desire to please him. Love is the abridgment of all theology ; it made the ignorance of a Paul, an Antony, an Hilarion, a Simeon, a Francis, most holily learned, without books, masters or art. In virtue of this love, the spouse may say with assurance: *My beloved is wholly mine,* by the complacency wherewith he pleases and feeds me ; and I, *I am wholly his,* by the benevolence wherewith I please and feed him again. My heart feeds on the pleasure it takes in him, and his on my taking pleasure in him for his own sake. As a holy shepherd he feeds me, his dear sheep, amidst the lilies of his perfections, in which I take pleasure; and I, as his dear sheep, feed him with the milk of my affections, by which I strive to please him. Whosoever truly takes pleasure in God desires faithfully to please God, and in order to please him, desires to conform himself to him.

CHAPTER II.

OF THE CONFORMITY OF SUBMISSION WHICH PROCEEDS FROM THE LOVE OF BENEVOLENCE.

COMPLACENCY then draws into us the traits of the divine perfections according as we are capable of receiving them, as the

* 1 Tim. i. 9.

mirror receives the sun's image, not according to the excellence and amplitude of that great and admirable luminary, but in proportion to the capacity and measure of its glass : so that we thus become conformed to God.

But besides this the love of benevolence brings us to this holy conformity by another way. The love of complacency draws God into our hearts, but the love of benevolence casts our hearts into God, and consequently all our actions and affections, most lovingly dedicating and consecrating them unto him : for benevolence desires to God all the honour, all the glory, and all the acknowledgment which it is possible to give him, as a certain exterior good which is due to his goodness.

Now this desire is practised according to the complacency which we take in God, as follows. We have had an extreme complacency in perceiving that God is sovereignly good, and therefore by the love of benevolence we desire that all the loves which we can possibly imagine be employed to love this goodness properly. We have taken delight in the sovereign excellency of God's perfection, and thereupon we desire that he be sovereignly loved, honoured and adored. We have rejoiced to consider how God is not only the first beginning but also the last end, author, preserver, and Lord of all things, for which reason we desire that all things be subject to him by a sovereign obedience. We see God's will sovereignly perfect, right, just and equitable ; and upon this consideration our desire is that it be the rule and sovereign law of all things, and that it be observed, kept and obeyed by all other wills.

But note, Theotimus, that I treat not here of the obedience due unto God as he is our Lord and Master, our Father and Benefactor, for this kind of obedience belongs to the virtue of justice, not to love. No, it is not this I speak of at present, for though there were no hell to punish the rebellious, nor heaven to reward the good, and though we had no kind of obligation or duty to God (be this said by imagination of a thing impossible and scarce imaginable), yet would the love of benevolence move us to render all obedience and submission to God by election and inclination, yea by a sweet violence of love, in consideration of the sovereign goodness, justice and rectitude of his divine will.

Do not we see, Theotimus, that a maiden by a free choice, which proceeds from the love of benevolence, subjects herself to her husband, to whom otherwise she owed no duty ; or that a gentleman submits himself to a foreign prince's command, or, perhaps, gives up his will into the hands of the superior of some religious order which he may join ? Even so is our heart conformed to God's, when by holy benevolence we throw all our affections into the hands of the divine will, to be turned and directed as it chooses, to be moulded and formed to its good liking. And in this point consists the profoundest obedience of love, which has no need to be spurred by menaces or rewards, nor by any law or any commandment ; for it foreruns all this, submitting itself to God solely for the most perfect goodness which is in God, whereby he deserves that all wills should be obedient, subject and submissive to him, conforming and uniting themselves for ever, in everything, and everywhere, to his divine intentions.

CHAPTER III.

HOW WE ARE TO CONFORM OURSELVES TO THAT DIVINE WILL, WHICH IS CALLED THE SIGNIFIED WILL.

We sometimes consider God's will as it is in itself, and finding it all holy and all good, we willingly praise, bless and adore it, and sacrifice our own and all other creatures' wills to its obedience, by that divine exclamation : *Thy will be done on earth as it is in heaven.* At other times we consider God's will in the particular effects of it, as in the events that touch us, and accidents that befall us, and finally in the declaration and manifestation of his intentions. And although God in reality has but one quite single and most simple will, yet we call it by different names, according to the variety of the means whereby we know it ; by which variety also we are, in various ways, obliged to conform ourselves to it.

Christian doctrine clearly proposes unto us the truths which God wills that we should believe, the goods he will have us hope for, the pains he will have us dread, what he will have us love, the commandments he will have us observe, and the counsels he desires us to follow.   And this is called God's *signi-fied will*, because he has signified and made manifest unto us that it is his will and intention that all this should be believed, hoped for, feared, loved and practised.

Now forasmuch as this signified will of God proceeds by way of desire, and not by way of absolute will, we have power either to follow it by obedience, or by disobedience to resist it; for to this purpose God makes three acts of his will: he wills that we should be able to resist, he desires that we should not resist, and yet allows us to resist if we please.   That we have power to resist depends on our natural condition and liberty; that we do resist proceeds from our malice; that we do not resist is according to the desire of the divine goodness.   And therefore when we resist, God contri-butes nothing to our disobedience, but leaving our will in the hands of its liberty permits it to make choice of evil; but when we obey, God contributes his assistance, his inspiration, and his grace.   For permission is an action of the will which of itself is barren, sterile and fruitless, and is as it were a passive action, which acts not but only permits action; desire on the contrary is an active, fruitful, fertile action, which excites, invites and urges.   Wherefore God, in his desire that we should follow his signified will, solicits, exhorts, excites, inspires, aids and succours us, but in permitting us to resist he does nothing but simply leave us to our own wills, ac-cording to our free election, contrary to his desire and inten-tion.   And yet this desire is a true desire, for how can one more truly express the desire that his friend should make good cheer, than by providing a good and excellent banquet, as did the king in the Gospel parable, and then, inviting, urg-ing, and in a manner compelling him, by prayers, exhortations and pressing messages, to come and sit down at the table and eat.   In truth, he that should by main force open his friend's mouth, cram meat into his throat, and make him swallow it, would not be giving courteous entertainment to his friend, but would be using him like a beast, and like a capon that has to be fattened.   This kind of favour requires to be offered by way of invitation, persuasion, and solicitation, not violently and forcibly thrust upon a man, and hence it is done by way of desire, not of absolute will.   Now it is the same with regard to the signified will of God; for in this, God desires with a true desire that we should do what he makes known, and to this end he provides us with all things necessary, exhorting and urging us to make use of them.   In this kind of favour one could desire no more, and as the sunbeams cease not to be true sunbeams when they are shut out and repulsed by some obstacle, so God's signified will remains the true will of God even if it be resisted, though it has not the effects which it would have if it were seconded.

The conformity then of our heart to the signified will of God consists in this, that we will all that the divine goodness signifies unto us to be of his intention,—believing according to his doctrine, hoping according to his promises, fearing according to his threats, loving and living according to his ordinances and admonitions, to which all the protestations which we make so often in the holy ceremonies of the Church do tend.   For on this account we stand while the Gospel is read, as being prepared to obey the holy signification of God's will contained therein ; hence we kiss the book at the place of the Gospel, in adoration of the sacred word which declares his heavenly will.   Hence many saints of the old time carried in their bosoms the Gospel written, as an *epithem* of love, as is related of S. Cecily, and S. Matthew's Gospel was actually found upon the heart of the dead S. Barnabas, written with his own hand.   Wherefore in the ancient councils, in the midst of the whole assembly of Bishops, there was erected a high throne, and upon it was placed the book of the holy Gospels, which represented the person of our Saviour,— King, Doctor, Director, Spirit and sole Heart of the Councils, and of the whole Church : so much did they reverence the signification of God's will expressed in that divine book.   Indeed that great mirror of the pastoral order, S. Charles, Archbishop of Milan, never studied the holy Scripture but bareheaded and upon his knees, to testify with what respect we are to read and hear the signified will of God.

CHAPTER IV.

OF THE CONFORMITY OF OUR WILL TO THE WILL WHICH GOD HAS TO SAVE US.

GOD has signified unto us by so many ways and means that his will is that we should all be saved, that none can be ignorant of it. To this purpose he made us to his own image and likeness by creation, and made himself to our image and likeness by his Incarnation; after which he suffered death to ransom and save all mankind, which he did with so much love that, as the great S. Denis, apostle of France, recounts, he said once to the holy man Carpus that he was ready to suffer another Passion to save mankind, and that this would be agreeable to him if it could be done without any man's sin.

And although all are not saved, yet is this will a true will of God's, who works in us according to the condition of his and of our nature. For his goodness moves him to liberally communicate unto us the succours of his grace in order to bring us to the felicity of his glory, but our nature requires that his liberality should leave us at liberty to make use of it to our salvation, or to neglect it to our damnation.

One thing I have asked of the Lord, said the prophet, *this will I seek after; . . . . that I may see the delight of the Lord and visit his temple.** But what is the delight of the sovereign goodness, save to pour out and communicate his perfections? Verily his *delights are to be with the children of men*, and to shower his graces upon them. Nothing is so agreeable and delightful to free agents as to do their own will. Our sanctification is the will of God, and our salvation his good-pleasure, nor is there any difference at all between good-pleasure and delight, nor, consequently, between the divine delight and the divine good will: yea the will which God has to do man good is called *good*,† because it is amiable, kind, favourable, agreeable, delicious, and as the Greeks, after S. Paul, said; it is a true *Philanthropy*, that is a benevolence or a will entirely loving towards men.

---

* Ps. xxvi. 4.   † Rom. xii. 2.

All the celestial temple of the triumphant and of the militant Church resounds on every side with the canticles of this sweet love of God towards us. And the most sacred body of our Saviour, as a most holy temple of his divinity, is all decorated with the marks and tokens of this benevolence. So that in visiting the divine temple we behold the loving delights which his heart takes in doing us favours.

Let us then a thousand times a day turn our eyes upon this loving will of God, and, making ours melt into it, let us devoutly cry out : O goodness infinitely sweet, how amiable is thy will, how desirable are thy favours! Thou hast created us for eternal life, and, thy maternal bosom, with its sacred swelling breasts of an incomparable love, abounds in the milk of mercy, whether it be to pardon sinners or to perfect the just. Ah! why do not we then fasten our wills to thine, as children fasten themselves on to their mother's breast, to draw the milk of thy eternal benedictions!

Theotimus, we are to will our salvation in such sort as God wills it; now he wills it by way of desire, and we also must incessantly desire it, following his desire. Nor does he will it only, but in effect gives us all necessary means to attain it : we then, in fulfilment of the desire we have to be saved, must not only will, but in effect accept all the graces which he has provided for us and offers unto us. It is enough to say.: I desire to be saved. But with regard to the means of salvation, it is not enough to say : I desire them ;—but we must, with an absolute resolution, will and embrace the graces which God presents to us : for our will must correspond with God's. And inasmuch as it gives us the means of salvation, we ought to receive them, as we ought to desire salvation in such sort as God desires it for us, and because he desires it.

But it often happens that the means of attaining salvation, considered in the gross and in general, are according to our hearts' liking, but considered piecemeal and in particular, are terrifying to us. For have we not seen poor S. Peter prepared to undergo in general all kind of torments, yea, death itself, to follow his master, and yet, when it came to the deed and performance, grow pale, tremble, and, at the word of a simple

maid, deny his master? Every one deems himself able to drink
our Saviour's chalice with him, but when it is in fact presented
to us, we fly, we give up all.   Things proposed in detail
make a more strong impression, and more sensibly wound the
imagination.   And for this reason we have advised in the Introduction that after general affections we should descend to particular ones in holy prayer.*   David accepted particular afflictions as an advancement towards his perfection, when he sang in
this wise: *O Lord, how good it is for me that thou hast humbled
me, that I might learn thy justifications!*†   So also were the
Apostles joyous in their tribulations, because they were held
worthy to endure ignominy for their Saviour's name.

CHAPTER V.

OF THE CONFORMITY OF OUR WILL TO THAT WILL OF GOD'S WHICH
IS SIGNIFIED TO US BY HIS COMMANDMENTS.

THE desire which God has to make us observe his commandments is extreme, as the whole Scripture witnesses.   And how
could he better express it, than by the great rewards which
he proposes to the observers of his law, and the awful punishments with which he threatens those who shall violate the
same! This made David cry out: *O Lord, thou hast commanded
thy Commandments to be kept most diligently.*‡

Now the love of complacency, beholding this divine desire,
wills to please God by observing it; the love of benevolence
which submits all to God, consequently submits our desires and
wills to that will which God has signified to us; and hence
springs not only the observance, but also the love of the commandments, which David extraordinarily extols in Psalm cxviii.,
which he seems only to have composed for this object: *O how
have I loved thy law, O Lord! It is my meditation all the day
. . . . . Therefore have I loved thy commandments above gold*

* II. 6.   † Ps. cxviii. 71.   ‡ Ps. cxviii. 4.

*and the topaz. . . . . How sweet are thy words to my palate,
more than honey to my mouth.**

But to stir up in us this holy and salutary love of the commandments, we must contemplate their admirable beauty : for, as
there are works which are bad because they are prohibited,
and others which are prohibited because they are bad; so there
are some that are good, because they are commanded, and others
that are commanded because they are good and very useful. So
that all of them are exceeding good and worthy of love, because
the commandment gives goodness to such as were not otherwise
good, and gives an increase of goodness to those others which
even if not commanded would not cease to be good. We do not
take good in good part, when it is presented by an enemy's hand.
The Lacedæmonians would not follow solid and wholesome
advice coming from a wicked person, till it was repeated to them
by a good man. On the contrary, a friend's present is always
grateful. The sweetest commandments become bitter when they
are imposed by a tyrannical and cruel heart; and they become
most amiable when ordained by love. Jacob's service seemed a
royalty unto him, because it proceeded from love. O how sweet
and how much to be desired is the yoke of the heavenly law,
established by so amiable a king !

Many keep the commandments as sick men take medicines,
more from fear of dying in a state of damnation, than from love
of living according to our Saviour's pleasure. But as some
persons have an aversion for physic, be it never so agreeable,
only because it bears the name of physic, so there are some souls
who abhor things commanded simply because they are commanded : and there was a certain man, 'tis said, who, having lived
quietly in the great city of Paris for the space of fourscore years
without ever going out of it, as soon as it was enjoined him by
the king that he should remain there the rest of his days, went
abroad to see the country, which in his whole lifetime before he
had not desired.

On the contrary, the loving heart loves the commandments ;
and the harder they are, the more sweet and agreeable it finds

* vv. 97, 127, 103.

them, because it more perfectly pleases the beloved, and gives him more honour. It pours forth and sings hymns of joy when God teaches it his commandments and justifications. And as the pilgrim who merrily sings on his way adds indeed the exertion of singing to that of walking, and yet actually, by this increase of labour, unwearies himself, and lightens the hardship of the way; even so the sacred lover finds such sweetness in the commandments, that nothing so much eases and refreshes him, as the gracious load of the precepts of his God. Whereupon the holy Psalmist cries out: *O Lord, thy justifications,* or commandments, *were the subject of my song in the place of my pilgrimage.** It is said that mules and horses laden with figs presently fall under their burden and lose all their strength : more sweet than figs is the law of our Lord, but brutal man who is become as *the horse and the mule which have no understanding,* loses courage and finds not strength to bear this dear burden. But as a branch of *Agnus Castus* keeps the traveller that bears it about him from being weary, so the cross, the mortification, the yoke, the law of our Saviour, who is the true *Chaste Lamb,* is a burden which unwearies, refreshes and recreates the hearts that love his divine Majesty. There is no labour where love is, or if there be any, it is a beloved labour. Labour mixed with love is a certain *bitter-sweet,* more pleasant to the palate than a thing purely sweet.

Thus then does heavenly love conform us to the will of God, and make us carefully observe his commandments, as being the absolute desire of his divine Majesty whom we will to please. So that this complacency with its sweet and amiable violence, foreruns that necessity of obeying which the law imposes upon us, converting this necessity into the virtue of love, and every difficulty into delight.

* Ps. cxviii. 54.

CHAPTER VI.

OF THE CONFORMITY OF OUR WILL TO THAT WILL OF GOD WHICH IS SIGNIFIED UNTO US BY HIS COUNSELS.

A COMMANDMENT testifies a most entire and absolute will in him who gives it, but counsel only represents a will of desire: a commandment obliges us, counsel only invites us; a commandment makes the transgressors thereof culpable; counsel only makes such as do not follow it less worthy of praise; those who violate commandments deserve damnation, those who neglect counsels deserve only to be less glorified. There is a difference between commanding and recommending: in commanding we use authority to oblige, but in recommending we use friendliness to induce and incite: a commandment imposes necessity, counsel and recommendation induce to what is of greater utility: commandments correspond to obedience, counsels to credence: we follow counsel with intention to please, and commandments lest we should displease. And thence it is that the love of complacency which obliges us to please the beloved, consequently urges us to follow his counsels, and the love of benevolence, which desires that all wills and affections should be subjected unto him, causes that we not only will what he ordains, but also what he counsels and exhorts to: as the love and respect which a good child bears to his father make him resolve to live not only according to the commandments which his father imposes, but also according to the desires and inclinations which he manifests.

A counsel is indeed given for the benefit of him who receives it, to the end that he may become perfect: *If thou wilt be perfect*, said our Saviour, *go sell all that thou hast, give it to the poor, and come, follow me.** But the loving heart does not receive a counsel for its utility, but to conform itself to the desire of him who gives the counsel, and to render him the homage due to his will. And therefore it receives not counsels but in such sort as God desires, nor does God desire that every one should observe all counsels, but such only as are suitable,

* Matt. xix. 21.

according to the diversity of persons, times, occasions, strengths, as charity requires: for she it is who, as queen of all the virtues, of all the commandments, of all the counsels, and, in short, of all Christian laws and works, gives to all of them their rank, order, season and worth.

If your assistance be truly necessary to your father or mother to enable them to live, it is no time then to practise the counsel of retiring into a monastery, for charity ordains that you presently put into execution its command of honouring, serving, aiding and succouring your father or your mother. You are perhaps a prince, by whose posterity the subjects of your crown are to be preserved in peace, and assured against tyranny, sedition, civil wars: the effecting, therefore, of so great a good, obliges you to beget lawful successors in a holy marriage. It is either not to lose chastity, or at least to lose it chastely, when for love of charity it is sacrificed to the public good. Are you weak and uncertain in your health, and does it require great support? Do not then voluntarily undertake actual poverty, for this is forbidden you by charity. Charity not only forbids fathers of families to sell all and give it to the poor, but also commands them honestly to gather together what is requisite for the support and education of wife, children and servants: as also it commands kings and princes to lay up treasures, which, being acquired by a laudible frugality, and not by tyrannical measures, serve as wholesome defences against visible enemies. Does not S. Paul counsel such as are married, that, the time of prayer being ended, they should return to the well-ordered course of their married life?*

The counsels are all given for the perfection of the Christian people, but not for that of each Christian in particular. There are circumstances which make them sometimes impossible, sometimes unprofitable, sometimes perilous, sometimes hurtful to some men, which is one of the reasons why Our Saviour said of one of the counsels, what he would have to be understood of them all: *He that can receive it, let him receive it :†* as though he had said, according to S. Jerome's exposition: he that can

* 1 Cor vii. 5. †   † Matt. xix. 11.

win and bear away the honour of chastity as a prize of renown, let him take it, for it is proposed to such as shall run valiantly. Not every one then is able, that is, it is not expedient for every one, to observe always all the counsels, for as they are granted in favour of charity, so is this the rule and measure by which they are put in practice.

When, therefore, charity so orders, monks and religious are drawn out of their cloisters to be made cardinals, prelates, parish-priests, yea sometimes they are even joined in matrimony for a kingdom's repose, as I have already said. And if charity make those leave their cloister that had bound themselves thereto by solemn vow,—for better reason, and upon less occasion, one may by the authority of the same charity, counsel many to live at home, to keep their means, to marry, yea to turn soldiers and go to war, which is so perilous a profession.

Now when charity draws some to poverty and withdraws others from it, when she directs some to marriage and others to continence, when she shuts one up in a cloister and makes another quit it, she is not bound to give account thereof to any one : for she has the plenitude of power in Christian laws, as it is written : *charity* can do *all things*; she has the perfection of prudence, according to that : *charity does nothing wrongly.** And if any would contest, and demand why she so does, she will boldly make answer : *The Lord hath need of it.*† All is made for charity, and charity for God. All must serve her and she none : no, she serves not her well-beloved, whose servant she is not, but his spouse, whom she does not serve, but love : for which cause we are to take our orders from her how to exercise counsels. To some she will appoint chastity without poverty, to others obedience and not chastity, to others fasting but not alms-deeds, to others alms-deeds and fasting, to others solitude and not the pastoral charge, to others intercourse with men and not solitude. In fine she is a sacred water, by which the garden of the church is fertilized, and though she herself have no colour that can be called colour, yet the flowers which she makes spring have each one its particular colour. She makes

---

* I Cor. xiii.   † Matt. xxi. 3.

Martyrs redder than the rose, Virgins whiter than the lily; some she dyes with the fine violet of mortification, others with the yellow of marriage-cares, variously employing the counsels, for the perfection of the souls who are so happy as to live under her conduct.

————

CHAPTER VII.

THAT THE LOVE OF GOD'S WILL SIGNIFIED IN THE COMMANDMENTS MOVES US TO THE LOVE OF THE COUNSELS.

O THEOTIMUS! how amiable is this Divine will! O how amiable and desirable it is! O law all of love and all for love! The Hebrews by the word, peace, understand the collection and perfection of all good things, that is, happiness: and the Psalmist cries out: *Much peace have they that love thy law; and to them there is no stumbling-block:** as though he would say: O Lord! what delights are in the love of thy sacred commandments! The heart that is possessed with the love of thy law is possessed of all delicious sweetness. Truly that great king whose heart was made according to the heart of God, did so relish the perfect excellence of the divine commandments, that he seems to be a lover captivated with the beauty of this law as with the chaste spouse and queen of his heart; as appears by his continual praises thereof.

When the heavenly spouse would express the infinite sweetness of her divine lover's perfumes: *Thy name*, says she unto him, *is as oil poured out:*† as though she said: thou art so excellently perfumed, that thou seemest to be all perfume, and thou art more fitly termed ointment and perfume, than anointed and perfumed. So the soul that loves God is so transformed into the divine will, that it merits rather to be called, God's will, than to be called, obedient and subject to his will. Whence God says by Isaias, that he will call the Christian church by a new name, which the mouth of the Lord will pronounce,

———

* Ps. cxviii. 165.   † Cant. i. 2.

imprint, and engrave, in the hearts of his faithful ; and then, explaining this name, he says it shall be : *My will in her :** as though he had said, that among such as are not Christians every one has his own will in the midst of his heart, but among the true children of our Saviour, every one shall forsake his own will, and shall have only one master-will, dominant and universal, which shall animate, govern and direct all souls, all hearts and all wills: and the name of honour amongst Christians shall be no other than *God's will in them,* a will which shal' rule over all wills, and transform them all into itself; so that the will of Christians and the will of Our Lord may be but one single will.   This was perfectly verified in the primitive Church, when, as says the glorious S. Luke : *In the multitude of the faithful there was but one heart and one soul :*† for he means not there to speak of the heart that keeps alive our bodies, nor of the soul which animates hearts with a human life, but he speaks of the heart which gives our souls heavenly life, and of the soul that animates our hearts with the supernatural life ; the one, the singularly one heart and soul of true Christians, which is no other thing than the will of God.   *Life,* says the Psalmist, *is in the will of God,*‡ not only because our temporal life depends on the divine pleasure, but also because our spiritual life consists in the execution of it, by which God lives and reigns in us, making us live and subsist in him.   On the contrary, *the wicked from of old* (that is, always) have *broken the yoke* of the law of God, and have said : *I will not serve.*§   Wherefore God says that he named them *transgressors* and rebels *from the womb ;*‖ and speaking to the king of Tyre, he reproaches him for having *set his heart as the heart of God :*¶ for the spirit of revolt will have its heart to be its own master, and its own will to be sovereign like the will of God ; it would not have the divine will to reign over it, but would be absolute and without any dependence.   O eternal Lord! suffer not this,—but effect that not my will but thine be done.   Yes, we are in this world not to do our own will, but the will of thy goodness which has placed us here.

---

* Is. lxii. 14.   † Acts iv. 32.   ‡ Ps. xxix. 6.   § Jer. ii. 20.
‖ Is. xlviii. 8.   ¶ Ezech. xxviii. 2.

It was written of thee, O Saviour of my soul, that thou didst
*the will of thy Eternal Father,** and by the first act of the will of
thy human soul, at the instant of thy conception, thou didst
lovingly embrace this law of the divine will, and didst place it
in the midst of thy heart there to reign and have dominion for
ever. Ah ! who will give my soul the grace of having no will
save the will of her God !

Now when our love is exceeding great towards God's will,
we are not content to do only the Divine will which is signified
unto us by the commandments, but we also put ourselves under
the obedience of the counsels, which are only given us for a
more perfect observing of the commandments, to which also
they have reference, as S. Thomas says excellently well. O how
well does he observe the prohibition of unlawful pleasures who
has even renounced the most just and legitimate delights ! How
far is he from coveting another man's goods who rejects even
such as he might holily have kept ! How far is he from preferring his own will before God's, who, to do God's will, submits
himself to that of a man !

David upon a day was in his camp, and the Philistine garrison
in Bethlehem.† *And David longed, and said : Oh ! that some
man would give me a drink of the water out of the cistern that
is in Bethlehem, by the gate !* And behold, he had no sooner
said the word than three valiant men set out, hand and head
lowered, break through the hostile camp, go to the cistern of
Bethlehem, draw water, and bring it to David, who, seeing the
hazard which these three knightly men had run to gratify his
longing, would not drink the water obtained at the peril of their
blood and life, but *poured it out in sacrifice* to the eternal God.
Ah ! mark, I beseech you, Theotimus, how great the ardour of
these cavaliers in the service and satisfaction of their master !
They fly, they break through the ranks of their enemies, they incur
a thousand dangers of destruction, to gratify only one simple
desire, which their king expresses before them. Our Saviour
when he was in this world declared his will in some cases by
way of commandment, and in many others he only signified it

* Ps. xxxix. 9.   † 2 Kings xxiii.

by way of desire: for he did highly commend chastity, poverty, obedience and perfect resignation, the abnegation of one's own will, widowhood, fasting, continual prayer; and what he said of chastity, that he who could win the prize should win it, he said sufficiently of all the other counsels. At this desire, the most valiant Christians have entered on the race, and overcoming all repugnances, concupiscences and difficulties, they have arrived at holy perfection, keeping themselves to the strict observance of their King's desires, and by this means bearing away the crown of glory.

Verily, as witnesses the divine Psalmist, God hears not only the prayers of his faithful, but even their very *desire and the* mere *preparation of their hearts* for prayer;* so inclined and forward is he to do the will of those who love him. And why shall not we then in return be so zealous in following God's holy will, as to do not only what he orders, but also what we know he likes and wishes. Noble souls need no other spur to the undertaking of a design than to know that their beloved desires it: *My soul,* said one of them, *melted when he spoke.*†

CHAPTER VIII.

THAT THE CONTEMPT OF THE EVANGELICAL COUNSELS IS A GREAT SIN.

THE words in which our Saviour exhorts us to tend towards and aim at perfection, are so forcible and so pressing, that we cannot dissemble the obligation we have to undertake to carry out that design. *Be holy,* says he, *because I am holy.*‡ *He that is holy, let him be sanctified still; and he that is just, let him be justified still.*§ *Be perfect, as your heavenly Father is perfect.*‖ For this cause, the great S. Bernard writing to the glorious S. Guerin, Abbot of Aulps, whose life and miracles have left so sweet an odour in this diocese: "The just man," says he, "never says it is enough; he still hungers and thirsts after justice."

Truly, Theotimus, in temporal matters nothing suffices him

---

* Ps. ix. 38.   † Cant. v. 6.   ‡ Levit. xi. 44.
§ Apoc. xxii. 11.   ‖ Matt. v. 48.

who is not satisfied with what is enough; for what can suffice him to whom sufficiency is not sufficient? But in spiritual goods he has not sufficient who is satisfied with what is enough, and sufficiency is not sufficient, because true sufficiency in divine things consists partly in the desire of affluence. God in the beginning commanded the earth to bring forth *the green herb, and such as may seed, and the fruit-tree yielding fruit after its kind, which has also seed in itself.**

And do we not see by experience, that plants and fruits are not come to their full growth and maturity till they bring forth their seeds and pips, whence other trees and plants of the same kind spring. Never do our virtues come to their full stature and measure, till such time as they beget in us desires of progress, which like spiritual seeds serve for the production of new degrees of virtue. And, methinks, the earth of our heart is commanded to bring forth the plants of virtue, which bear the fruits of good works, every one in its kind, and having the seeds of desires and resolutions of ever multiplying and advancing in perfection. And the virtue that bears not the seed of these desires is not yet come to its growth and maturity. "So then," says S. Bernard to the tepid man, "you do not want to advance in perfection? No. Nor yet grow worse? No, truly. What, then—you would neither grow better nor worse?—poor man, you would be what cannot be. Nothing, indeed, in the world is either stable or constant; but of man it is said even more specially that *he never remaineth in the same state.*† It is necessary then that he either go forward or backward."

Now I say not, any more than does S. Bernard, that it is a sin not to practise the counsels. No, in truth, Theotimus: for it is the very difference between commandments and counsels, that the commandment obliges us under pain of sin, and the counsel only invites us without pain of sin. Yet I distinctly say that to contemn the aiming after Christian perfection is a great sin, and that it is a still greater to contemn the invitation by which our Saviour calls us to it; but it is an insupportable

* Gen. i. 11. † Job xiv. 2.

impiety to contemn the counsels and means which our Saviour points out for the attainment of it. It were a heresy to say, that our Saviour had not given us good counsel, and a blasphemy to say to God : *Depart from us, we desire not the knowledge of thy ways:** but it is a horrible irreverence towards him who with so much love and sweetness invites us to perfection, to say : I will not be holy or perfect, nor have any larger portion of thy benevolence, nor follow the counsels which thou givest me to make progress in perfection.

We may indeed without sin not follow the counsels, on account of the affection we may have to other things : as for example, it is lawful for a man not to sell what he possesseth to give to the poor, because he has not the courage to make so entire a renunciation. It is also lawful to marry, because one loves, or because one has not strength of mind necessary to undertake the war which must be waged against the flesh. But to profess not to wish to follow the counsels, nor any one of them, cannot be done without contempt of him who gives them. Not to follow the counsel of virginity, and so to marry, is not wrong, but marrying as if putting marriage higher than chastity, as heretics do, that is a great contempt either of the counsellor or of his counsel. To drink wine against the doctor's advice when overcome with thirst or with a desire to drink, is not precisely to contemn the doctor nor his advice : but to say—I will not follow the doctor's advice—must necessarily proceed from some bad opinion one harbours of him. Now as regards men, one may often contemn their counsel, without contemning those who give it, because to think that a man may have erred is not to contemn him. But to reject and contemn God's counsel, can only spring from an idea that he has not counselled us well ; which cannot be thought but by a spirit of blasphemy, as though God were not wise enough to be able, or good enough to will, to give good advice. We may say the same of the counsels of the Church, which by reason of the continued assistance of the Holy Ghost, who instructs and conducts her in all truth, can never give evil advice.

* Job xxi. 14.

CHAPTER IX.

A CONTINUATION OF THE PRECEDING DISCOURSE. HOW EVERY ONE,
WHILE BOUND TO LOVE, IS NOT BOUND TO PRACTISE, ALL THE
EVANGELICAL COUNSELS, AND YET HOW EVERY ONE SHOULD
PRACTISE WHAT HE IS ABLE.

ALTHOUGH all the Evangelical Counsels cannot and should not
be practised by every Christian in particular, yet every one is
obliged to love them all, because they are all very good. If you
have a sick headache, and the smell of musk annoys you, will
you therefore deny that this smell is good and delightsome ? If
a robe of gold does not suit you, will you say that therefore it
is worth nothing ? Or will you throw a ring into the dirt
because it fits not your finger ? Praise therefore, Theotimus,
and dearly love, all the counsels that God has given unto men.

Oh ! blessed be the Angel of Great Counsel for ever, together
with all the counsels he gives and exhortations he makes to men !
Ointment and perfumes rejoice the heart, says Solomon, *and the
good counsels of a friend are sweet to the soul !** But of what
friend, and of what counsels, do we speak ? O God ! it is of the
friend of friends; and his counsels are more delightful than
honey: our friend is our Saviour, his counsels are to save us.
Let us rejoice, Theotimus, when we see others undertake to
follow those counsels, which we either cannot or must not
observe ; let us pray for them, bless, favour and assist them : for
charity obliges us not only to love what is good for ourselves,
but that also which is good for our neighbour.

We shall sufficiently testify our love for all the counsels,
when we devoutly observe such as are suitable to our calling.
For, as he that believes one article of faith because God has
revealed it by his Word (announced and declared by the Church),
cannot disbelieve the others: and as he who observes one commandment for the pure love of God is most ready to observe
the others when occasion offers :—so he that loves and prizes
one evangelical counsel because it came from God, must
necessarily love all the others, because they are also from God.

* Prov. xxvii. 9.

Now we may with ease practise some of them, though not all of them together ; for God has given many, in order that every one may observe some of them, and not a day passes without our having some opportunity of doing so.

If charity require that to assist your father or mother you must live with them, preserve at the same time the love and affection for your seclusion ; do not keep your heart in your father's house more than is required for doing what charity orders to be done there. Is it inexpedient for you, on account of your rank, to preserve perfect chastity ? Keep it at least, as much as you may without violating charity. Let him who cannot do all, at least do some part. You are not *obliged* to seek out him who has offended you, for it is his place to return to himself, and to come to you to give you satisfaction, since he began the injury and outrage : yet go, Theotimus, follow our Saviour's counsel, prevent him in good, render him good for evil, cast upon his head and heart the burning coals of signs of charity, that may wholly inflame him and force him to a reconciliation. You are not bound by rigour of law to give alms to all the poor you meet, but only to such as are in very great need of them : yet do not therefore cease to give willingly, according to our Saviour's counsel, to every poor person you find, so far as your condition and your real necessities may allow. You have no obligation to make any vow at all, yet make some, such as shall be judged fit by your ghostly father for your advancement in Divine love. You have liberty to use wine within the limits of propriety; yet following S. Paul's counsel to Timothy, take only so much as is requisite for your stomach's sake.

In counsels there are various degrees of perfection. To lend to such poor people as are not in extreme want is the first degree of the counsel of alms-deeds; to give it them is a degree higher ; higher still to give all; but the highest is to give oneself, dedicating our person to their service. Hospitality except in extreme necessity is a counsel. To entertain strangers is the first degree of it; but to stay by the wayside to invite them as Abraham did, is a degree higher ; and yet higher than that is it to live in places of danger, in order to rescue, help and wait upon travellers : in

this excelled that great S. Bernard of Menthon, a native of this
diocese, who, being a scion of a most noble house, did for many
years inhabit the precipices and peaks of our Alps, and there got
together many associates to wait for, lodge and rescue, and to
deliver from the danger of the storm, travellers and passers-by
who would often perish amidst the tempests, snow and colds,
were it not for the hospices which this great friend of God
erected and founded upon the two mountains, which, taking their
names from him, are called the Great S. Bernard, in the diocese
of Sion, and the Little S. Bernard, in the diocese of Tarentaise.
To visit the sick who are not in extreme necessity is a laudable
charity, to serve them is yet better, but to consecrate a man's
self to their service is the excellence of that counsel : this, by
their institute, the Clerks of the Visitation of the Sick
exercise; as do many ladies in various places ; in imitation of
the great S. Samson, a gentleman and physician of Rome, who
at Constantinople, where he was made priest, with a wonderful
charity devoted himself to the service of the sick in a hospital
which he began there, and which the Emperor Justinian erected
and finished : and in imitation of SS. Catharine of Siena and of
Genoa, S. Elizabeth of Hungary, and the glorious friends of God
S. Francis and the Blessed (S.) Ignatius of Loyola, who in the
beginning of their Orders performed this exercise with an incomparable fervour and spiritual profit.

Virtues have then a certain sphere of perfection, and commonly we are not obliged to practise them to the height of their
excellence.   It is sufficient to go so far in the practice of them
as really to enter upon them.   But to go farther, and to advance
in perfection, is a counsel, as the acts of heroic virtues are not
ordinarily commanded, but counselled only.   And if upon some
occasion we find ourselves obliged to exercise them, it is by
reason of some rare and extraordinary occurrence, which makes
them necessary for the preservation of God's grace.   The blessed
door-keeper of the prison of Sebaste, seeing one of the forty who
were then martyred lose courage and the crown of martyrdom,
took his place without being apprehended, and thus made up the
forty of those glorious and triumphant soldiers of Our Lord.
S. Adauctus seeing S. Felix led to martyrdom,—I, quoth he (no

one urging him), I also am as much a Christian as he, worshipping the same Saviour; and with that, kissing S. Felix, he walked with him to martyrdom and was beheaded.   Thousands of the ancient martyrs did the like, and having it equally in their power to avoid or undergo martyrdom without sin, they chose rather generously to undergo it than lawfully to avoid it.   In these, martyrdom was an heroic act of the fortitude and constancy which a holy excess of love gave them.   But when it is necessary to endure martyrdom or else to renounce the faith, of martyrdom does not cease to be martyrdom, and an excellent act love and valour, yet do I scarcely think it is to be termed an heroic act, not being chosen by any excess of love but by force of the law which in that case commands it.   Now in the practice of the heroic acts of virtue consists the perfect imitation of our Saviour, who, as the great S. Thomas says, had all the virtues in an heroic degree from the first instant of his conception; yea I would willingly say more than heroic, since he was not simply more than man but infinitely more than man, that is, true God.

CHAPTER X.

HOW WE ARE TO CONFORM OURSELVES TO GOD'S WILL SIGNIFIED UNTO US BY INSPIRATIONS, AND FIRST, OF THE VARIETY OF THE MEANS BY WHICH GOD INSPIRES US.

THE rays of the sun enlighten while heating and heat while enlightening.   Inspiration is a heavenly ray which brings into our hearts a light full of heat, by which it makes us see the good and inflames us with a desire to pursue it.   All that lives upon the face of the earth is dulled by the cold of winter, but, upon the return of the vital heat of spring, it all takes up its movement again.   The animals run more swiftly, birds fly more quickly and sing more merrily, and plants put forth their leaves and flowers most gladsomely.   Without inspiration our souls would lead an idle, sluggish and fruitless life, but on receiving the divine rays of inspiration we are sensible of a light mingled with a quickening heat, which illuminates our understanding, and which excites and animates our will, giving it the strength to will and effect the good which is necessary for eternal salvation. God having formed man's body of the slime of the earth, as Moses says, *breathed into his face the breath of life, and man became a living soul,* that is, a soul which gave life, motion and operation to the body; and the same eternal God breathes and infuses into our souls the inspirations of the supernatural life, to the end that, as says the great Apostle, they may become *a quickening spirit,** that is, a spirit which makes us live, move, feel, and work according to the movements of grace, so that he who gave us being gives us also operation. The breath of man warms the things it enters into; witness the child of the Sunamitess,† to whose mouth the prophet Eliseus having laid his, and breathed upon him, his flesh grew warm; and experience makes it evident. But with regard to the breath of God, it not only warms, but also gives a perfect light, his Spirit being an infinite light, whose vital breath is called inspiration, because by it the divine goodness breathes upon us and inspires us with the desires and intentions of his heart.

Now it uses countless means of inspiring. S. Antony, S. Francis, S. Anselm, and a thousand others, had frequent inspirations by the sight of creatures. The ordinary means is preaching, but sometimes those whom the word does not help are taught by tribulation, according to that of the Prophet: *And vexation alone shall make you understand what you hear :‡* that is, such as by hearing the heavenly menaces against the wicked do not amend, shall be taught the truth by the event and effects, and feeling affliction shall become wise. S. Mary of Egypt was inspired by the sight of a picture of Our Lady; S. Anthony, by hearing the Gospel read at Mass; S. Augustine, by hearing the history of S. Anthony's life; the Duke of Gandia (S. Francis Borgia), by looking upon the dead empress; S. Pachomius, by seeing an example of charity; the Blessed (S.) Ignatius of Loyola, by reading the lives of the Saints; S. Cyprian (not the great Bishop of Carthage but a

* I Cor. xv. 45.　　† 4 Kings iv. 34.　　‡ Is. xxviii. 19.

layman, yet a glorious martyr) was moved by hearing the devil confess his impotence against those that trust in God. When I was a youth at Paris, two scholars, one of whom was a heretic, passing the night in the Faubourg S. Jacques in debauchery, heard the Carthusians ring to Matins, and the heretic asking the other why they rang, he described to him with what devotion they celebrated the Divine office in that holy monastery : O God, quoth he, how different is the practice of those religious from ours ! They perform the office of angels, and we that of brute beasts : and desiring the day after to see by experience what he had learnt by his companion's relation, he found the fathers in their stalls, standing like a row of marble statues in their niches, motionless except for the chanting of the Psalms, which they performed with a truly angelic attention and devotion, according to the custom of this holy Order; so that this poor youth, wholly ravished with admiration, was taken with the exceeding consolation which he found in seeing God so well worshipped amongst Catholics, and resolved, what afterwards he effected, to put himself into the bosom of the Church, the true and only spouse of him who had visited him with his inspiration, in the infamous litter of abomination in which he had been.

Oh how happy are they who keep their hearts open to holy inspirations ! For these are never wanting to any, in so far as they are necessary for living well and devoutly, according to each one's condition of life, or for fulfilling holily the duties of his profession. For as God, by the ministry of nature, furnishes every animal with the instincts which are necessary for its preservation and the exercise of its natural powers, so if we resist not God's grace, he bestows on every one of us the inspirations necessary to live, to work, and to preserve our spiritual life. O Lord, said the faithful Eliezer, *the God of my master, Abraham, meet me to-day, I beseech thee, and shew kindness to my master, Abraham ! Behold, I stand nigh the spring of water, and the daughters of the inhabitants of this city will come out to draw water : now, therefore, the maid to whom I shall say : let down thy pitcher that I may drink : and she shall answer, drink, and I will give thy camels drink also : let it be the same whom thou*

*hast provided for thy servant Isaac.** Theotimus Eliezer does
not express any desire of water except for himself, but the fair
Rebecca, obeying the inspiration which God and her kindness
gave her, offers withal to water his camels; whence she became
holy Isaac's wife, daughter-in-law to the great Abraham, and a
grandmother to our Saviour. Truly, the souls which are not
contented with doing what the heavenly beloved requires at
their hands by his commandments and counsels, but also
promptly comply with sacred inspirations, are they whom the
Eternal Father has destined to be the spouses of his well-beloved
son. And, as regards Eliezer, since he cannot otherwise distinguish
amongst the daughters of Haran (the town of Nachor) which of
them was destined for his master's son, God reveals it unto him by
inspiration. When we are at a loss, and human help fails us in
our perplexities, God then inspires us, nor will he permit us to
err, as long as we are humbly obedient. But I will say no more
of these necessary inspirations, having often spoken of them in
this work, as also in the *Introduction to the Devout Life.*

CHAPTER XI.

OF THE UNION OF OUR WILL WITH GOD'S IN THE INSPIRATIONS
WHICH ARE GIVEN FOR THE EXTRAORDINARY PRACTICE OF
VIRTUES; AND OF PERSEVERANCE IN ONE'S VOCATION, THE
FIRST MARK OF INSPIRATION.

THERE are certain inspirations which tend only to an extraordinary perfection of the ordinary exercises of the Christian
life. Charity towards the sick poor is an ordinary exercise of
true Christians; but an ordinary exercise which was practised
by S. Francis and S. Catharine with an extraordinary perfection,
when they licked and sucked the ulcers of the leprous and the
cancerous; and by the glorious S. Louis, when bare-head and
upon his knees he served the sick;—at which a Cistercian abbot

---

* Gen. xxiv. 12, 13, 14.

was lost in admiration, seeing him in this posture handle and dress
the horrible and cancerous sores of a poor wretch.   And it was
also a very extraordinary exercise of this holy monarch to serve
the most abject and vile of the poor at his table, and to eat their
leavings.   S. Jerome entertaining in his hospital at Bethlehem
the pilgrims of Europe who fled from the persecution of the
Goths, did not only wash their feet, but descended even so low
as to wash and rub the legs of their camels, imitating Rebecca
whom we just mentioned, who not only drew water for Eliezer,
but for his camels also.   S. Francis was not only extreme in the
practice of poverty, as is known to all, but was equally so in the
practice of simplicity.   He redeemed a lamb which he feared
was going to be slaughtered, because it represented our Saviour.
He showed respect to almost all creatures, contemplating in them
their Creator, by an unusual yet most wise simplicity.   Sometimes
he would busy himself with removing worms from the road, lest
passers by should trample them under their feet, remembering
that our Saviour had compared himself to the worm.   He called
creatures his brothers and sisters, by a certain admirable consideration which love suggested unto him.   S. Alexius, a gentleman of very noble descent, practised in an excellent manner the
abjection of himself, living unknown for the space of seventeen
years in his father's house at Rome as a poor pilgrim.   All these
inspirations were for ordinary exercises, practised, however, with
extraordinary perfection.   Now, in this kind of inspiration we
are to observe the rules which we gave for desires in our *Introduction.**   We must not strive to practise many exercises at
once, and upon a sudden, for the enemy often tries to make us
undertake and begin many designs, to the end that overwhelmed
with the multiplicity of business we may accomplish nothing,
but leave all unfinished : yea, sometimes he suggests the desire
of undertaking some excellent work which he foresees we shall
not accomplish, in order to turn us from prosecuting a work less
excellent which we should have performed ;   for he cares not how
many purposes, plans and beginnings be made, so long as nothing
is done.   He will not hinder the bringing forth of male children,

* III. 37.

any more than Pharao did, provided that before they grow they are slain. On the contrary, says the great S. Jerome, amongst Christians it is not so much the beginning as the end that is regarded. We must not swallow so much food as to be unable to digest what we take. The deceiving spirit makes us stay in beginnings, and content ourselves with the flowery spring-time, but the Divine Spirit makes us regard beginnings only in order to attain the end, and only makes us rejoice in the flowers of spring in the expectation of enjoying the ripe fruits of summer and autumn.

The great S. Thomas is of opinion that it is not expedient to consult and deliberate much concerning an inclination to enter a good and well-regulated religious Order ; for the religious life being counselled by our Saviour in the Gospel, what need is there of many consultations ? It is sufficient to make one good one, with a few persons who are thoroughly prudent and capable in such an affair, and who can assist us to make a speedy and solid resolution; but as soon as we have once deliberated and resolved, whether in this matter or in any other that appertains to God's service, we must be constant and immovable, not permitting ourselves to be shaken by any appearances of a greater good : for very often, says the glorious S. Bernard, the devil deludes us, and to draw us from the effecting of one good he proposes unto us some other good, that seems better; and after we have started this, he, in order to divert us from effecting it, presents a third, ready to let us make plenty of beginnings if only we do not make an end. We should not even go from one Order to another without very weighty motives, says S. Thomas, following the Abbot Nestorius cited by Cassian.

I borrow from the great S. Anselm (writing to Lanzo) a beautiful similitude. As a plant often transplanted can never take root, nor, consequently, come to perfection and return the expected fruit ; so the soul that transplants her heart from design to design cannot do well, nor come to the true growth of her perfection, since perfection does not consist in beginnings but in accomplishments. The sacred living creatures of Ezechiel *went whither the impulse of the spirit was to go, and they turned not when they went, and every one of them went straight forward :* we are to go whither the inspiration moves us, not turning about, nor returning back, but tending thither, whither God has turned our face, without changing our gaze. He that is in a good way, let him step out and get on. It happens sometimes that we forsake the good to seek the better, and that having forsaken the one we find not the other : better is the possession of a small treasure found, than the expectation of a greater which is to find. The inspiration which moves us to quit a real good which we enjoy in order to gain a better in the future, is to be suspected. A young Portuguese, called Francis Bassus, was admirable, not only in divine eloquence but also in the practice of virtue, under the discipline of the Blessed (S.) Philip Neri in the Congregation of the Oratory at Rome. Now he persuaded himself that he was inspired to leave this holy society, to place himself in an Order, strictly so called, and at last he resolved to do so. But the B. Philip, assisting at his reception into the Order of S. Dominic, wept bitterly ; whereupon being asked by Francis Marie Tauruse, afterwards Archbishop of Siena and Cardinal, why he shed tears : I deplore, said he, the loss of so many virtues. And in fact this young man, who was so excellently good and devout in the Congregation, after he became a religious was so inconstant and fickle, that agitated with various desires of novelties and changes, he gave afterwards great and grievous scandal.

If the fowler go straight to the partridge's nest, she will show herself, and counterfeit weakness and lameness, and, raising herself up as though she would take a great flight, will immediately tumble down, as if she were able to do no more, in order that the fowler being busied in looking after her, and expecting easily to take her, may not light on her little ones in the nest ; but when he has pursued her a while, and fancies he has her, she rises into the air and escapes. So our enemy, seeing a man by God's inspiration undertake a profession and manner of life fitted for his advancement in heavenly love, persuades him to enter into some other way, more perfect in appearance ; but having put him out of his first way, he makes him by little and

* Ezech. i. 12.

little apprehend the second way impossible, proposing a third; that so keeping him occupied in the continual inquiry for various and new means of perfecting himself, he may hinder him from making use of any, and consequently from attaining the end he seeks, which is perfection. Young hounds leave the pack at every new scent, and make after the fresh quarry; the old and well-scented hounds never change, but keep the scent they are on. Let every one then, having once found out God's holy will touching his vocation, keep to it holily and lovingly, practising therein its proper exercises, according to the order of discretion and with the zeal of perfection.

CHAPTER XII.

OF THE UNION OF MAN'S WILL WITH GOD'S IN THOSE INSPIRATIONS WHICH ARE CONTRARY TO ORDINARY LAWS; AND OF PEACE AND TRANQUILLITY OF HEART, SECOND MARK OF INSPIRATION.

THUS then, Theotimus, we are to behave ourselves in those inspirations which are only extraordinary in the sense that they move us to practise ordinary Christian exercises with an extraordinary fervour and perfection. But there are other inspirations which are called extraordinary, not only because they make the soul pass the bounds of ordinary actions, but also because they move it to actions contrary to the common laws, rules and customs of the most holy Church, and therefore are more admirable than imitable. The holy maiden named by historians Eusebia the Stranger, left Rome, her native city, with two other maidens, and taking male attire embarked on a sea-voyage, went to Alexandria, and thence to the Isle of Cos; there, finding herself safe, she put on again her woman's dress, and again taking ship went into Caria to the town of Mylassa, whither the great Paul, who had found her in Cos and had taken her under his spiritual direction, led her, and where afterwards, being made Bishop, he so holily directed her that she established a monastery and dedicated herself to serve the Church in the office of deaconess (as in those days it was called), with such fervour of charity that in the end she died a Saint, and by a number of miracles which God did by her relics and intercession, was recognized as such. To put on the attire belonging to the other sex, and thus disguised to expose oneself to a journey with men, does not only pass the ordinary rules of Christian modesty, but is even contrary to them. A certain young man, having given his mother a kick, touched with a lively repentance, confessed it to S. Anthony of Padua ; who, to imprint the horror of his sin more deeply in his heart, said to him, amongst other things : My child, the foot which was the instrument of your wickedness would deserve to be cut off for so great a trespass ; which the youth took in such good earnest, that having returned home to his mother, transported with the feeling of contrition, he cut off his foot. The words of the Saint would not have had such force, according to their ordinary meaning, unless God had added his inspiration thereunto ; but it was so extraordinary an inspiration that it must rather have been considered a temptation, if the miraculous restoration of his foot, effected by the Saint's benediction, had not warranted it. S. Paul the first hermit, S. Anthony, S. Mary of Egypt, did not bury themselves in those vast wildernesses—deprived of hearing Mass, of Communion, of Confession, and deprived, young as they were, of all direction and assistance,—without a strong inspiration. The great Simeon Stylites led a life that never mortal creature would have dreamt of or undertaken without heavenly instinct and assistance. S. John, bishop, surnamed the Silent, forsaking his diocese without the knowledge of any of his clergy, passed the rest of his days in the Monastery of Laura, nor was there afterwards any news heard of him. Was not this contrary to the rule of keeping holy residence ? And the great S. Paulinus, who sold himself to ransom a poor widow's son, how could he do it according to ordinary laws, since he was not his own, but, by his episcopal consecration, belonged to the Church and his people ? Those virgins and married women who, being pursued for their beauty, with voluntary wounds disfigured their faces, that under the mask of a holy deformity they might preserve their chastity, did they not do a thing, apparently, forbidden ?

Now one of the best marks of the goodness of all inspirations in general, and particularly of extraordinary ones, is the peace and tranquillity of the heart that receives them : for though indeed the Holy Ghost is violent, yet his violence is gentle, sweet and peaceful. He comes as a *mighty wind,** and as a heavenly thunder, but he does not overthrow the Apostles, he troubles them not ; the fear which they had in hearing the sound was of no continuance, but was immediately followed by a sweet assurance. That is why this fire *sits upon each of them*, taking and causing a sacred repose ; and as our Saviour is called a peaceful or pacific Solomon, so is his spouse called Sulamitess, calm and daughter of peace : and the voice, that is, the inspiration, of the bridegroom does not in any sort disquiet or trouble her, but draws her so sweetly that he makes her soul deliciously melt and, as it were, flow out into him : *My soul*, says she, *melted when my beloved spoke :†* and though she be warlike and martial, yet is she withal so peaceable, that amidst armies and battles she maintains the concord of an unequalled melody. *What shalt thou see*, saith she, *in the Sulamitess but the choirs of armies ?‡* Her armies are choirs, that is, harmonies of singers ; and her choirs are armies, because the weapons of the Church and of the devout soul, are only prayers, hymns, canticles and psalms. Thus it is that those servants of God who had the highest and sublimest inspirations were the most mild and peaceable men in the world, as Abraham, Isaac, Jacob : Moses is styled *the meekest of men ;* David is lauded for his mildness. On the contrary, the evil spirit is turbulent, rough, disturbing; and those who follow infernal suggestions, taking them to be heavenly inspirations, are as a rule easily known, because they are unquiet, headstrong, haughty, ready to undertake or meddle with all affairs, men who under the cloak of zeal turn everything upside down, censure every one, chide every one, find fault with everything ; they are persons who will not be directed, will not give in to any one, will bear nothing, but gratify the passions of self-love under the name of jealousy for God's honour.

* Acts ii. 2.　　　† Cant. v. 6.　　　‡ Cant. vii. 1.

CHAPTER XIII.

THIRD MARK OF INSPIRATION, WHICH IS HOLY OBEDIENCE TO
THE CHURCH AND SUPERIORS.

To peace and sweetness of heart is inseparably joined most holy
humility.   But I do not term humility, that ceremonious profusion of words, gestures, and kissings of the ground, obeisances,
inclinations,—when they are made, as often happens, without any
inward sense of our own abjection and of just esteem of our
neighbour : for all this is but a vain occupation of weak brains,
and is rather to be termed a phantom of humility, than
humility.

I speak of a noble, real, productive and solid humility, which
makes us supple to correction, pliable and prompt to obedience.
While the incomparable Simeon Stylites was yet a novice at
Teleda, he made himself indocile to the advice of his superiors,
who wished to hinder him from practising so many strange
austerities, which he did with an inordinate cruelty to himself ;
so that at length he was on this account turned out of the
monastery, as being too little capable of the mortification of the
heart, and too much addicted to that of the body.   But having
entered into himself and become more devout, and more prudent
in the spiritual life, he behaved quite differently, as he showed
in the following action.   When the hermits who were dispersed
through the deserts near Antioch knew the extraordinary life
which he led upon the pillar, in which he seemed to be either
an earthly angel or a heavenly man, they despatched a messenger
whom they ordered to speak thus to him from them : Why dost
thou, Simeon, leaving the highway trodden by so many great
and holy predecessors, follow another, unknown of men, and so
different from all that has been seen or heard to this day ?
Simeon, quit this pillar, and come amongst other men to live,
after the manner of life and way of serving God used by the
good Fathers who have gone before us.   In case Simeon,
yielding to their advice and giving in to their will, should
show himself ready to descend, they had charged the deputy

to leave him free to persevere in the manner of life he had begun, because by his obedience, said those good Fathers, it could well be known that he had undertaken this kind of life by the divine inspiration : but in case he should resist, and, despising their exhortations, follow his own will, it would be necessary to withdraw him thence by violence, and force him to forsake his pillar. The deputy then, being come to the pillar, had no sooner delivered his message, than the great Simeon, without delay, without reservation, without any reply, began to descend with an obedience and humility worthy of his rare sanctity. Which when the deputy saw : stay, said he, O Simeon! remain there, persevere with constancy, take courage, pursue thy enterprise valiantly; thy abiding upon this pillar is from God.

But mark, I pray you, Theotimus, how these ancient and holy anchorites in their general meeting, found no surer mark of a heavenly inspiration in so extraordinary a matter as was the life of this holy Stylite, than to find him simple, gentle, and tractable, under the laws of holy obedience ; and God, blessing the submission of this great man, gave him the grace to persevere thirty whole years upon the top of a pillar thirty-six cubits high, having previously passed seven years upon others of six, twelve, and twenty feet, and having before that been ten years on the peak of a little rock in the place called the Mandra. Thus this bird of paradise, living above in air, and not touching earth, was a spectacle of love to the angels, and of admiration to mortals.   In obedience all is secure, out of it all is to be suspected.

When God puts inspirations into a heart, the first he gives is obedience.   Was there ever a more illustrious and unmistakable inspiration than that which was given to the glorious S. Paul?   And the principal point of it was, that he should repair to the city, where he should learn from the mouth of Ananias what he was to do, and this Ananias, a very famous man, was, as S. Dorotheus says, the Bishop of Damascus.   Whosoever says he is inspired, and yet refuses to obey his superiors and follow their counsel, is an impostor.   All the Prophets and Preachers that ever were inspired by God, always loved the

Church, always adhered to her doctrine, always were approved by her, nor did they ever announce anything so distinctly as this truth, that the lips of the priest *shall keep wisdom, and they shall seek the law at his mouth.** So that extraordinary missions are diabolical illusions, not heavenly inspirations, unless they be acknowledged and approved by the pastors who have the ordinary mission. For thus Moses and the prophets are reconciled. S. Francis, S. Dominic, and the other Fathers of Religious Orders, were called to the service of souls by an extraordinary inspiration, but they did so much the more humbly and heartily submit themselves to the sacred Hierarchy of the Church. In conclusion, the three best and most assured marks of lawful inspirations, are perseverance, against inconstancy and levity; peace and gentleness of heart, against disquiet and solicitude; humble obedience, against obstinacy and extravagance.

And to conclude all that we have said touching the union of our will with that will of God which is called signified;—almost all the herbs which bear yellow flowers, yea, the chicory also which bears blue ones, ever turn them towards the sun, and thus follow its course: but the sunflower turns not only its flowers but also all its leaves, after the movements of this great luminary. In the same way all the elect turn the flower of their heart, which is obedience to the commandments, towards the Divine will, but souls entirely taken with holy love not only look towards this Divine goodness by obedience to the commandments, but also by the union of all their affections, following this heavenly sun in his round, in all that he commands, counsels and inspires, without reserve or exception whatever; whence they can say with the sacred Psalmist: *Lord, I am become as a beast before thee: and I am always with thee. Thou hast held me by my right hand; and by thy will thou hast conducted me, and with thy glory thou hast received me.*† For as a well-broken horse is easily, gently and exactly managed by his rider, in any way that is required, so the loving soul is so pliable to God's will that he does with her what he pleases.

* Mal. ii. 7.   † Ps. lxxii. 24, 23.

CHAPTER XIV.

A SHORT METHOD TO KNOW GOD'S WILL.

S. BASIL says that God's will is made clear unto us by his ordinances or commandments, and that then there is no deliberation to be made, for we are simply to do what is ordained ; but that for the rest we have freedom to choose what seems good according to our liking ; though we are not to do all that is lawful but only what is expedient, and to clearly discern what is expedient we are to follow the advice of our spiritual father.

But, Theotimus, I am to warn you of a troublesome temptation which often crosses the way of such souls as have a great desire to do what is most according to God's will. For the enemy at every turn puts them in doubt whether it is God's will for them to do one thing rather than another; as for example, whether they should eat with a friend or no, whether they should wear grey or black clothes, whether they should fast Friday or Saturday, whether they should take recreation or abstain from it; and in this they lose much time, and while they are busy and anxious to find out what is the better, they unprofitably let slip the time for doing many good things, the effecting of which would be far more to God's glory, than this distinguishing between the good and the better, which has taken up their time, could possibly be.

We are not accustomed to weigh little money, but only valuable pieces : trading would be too troublesome and would devour too much time, if we were to weigh pence, halfpence, farthings and half-farthings. So we are not to weigh every petty action to know whether it be of more value than others; yea there is often a kind of superstition in trying to make this examination ; for to what end should we puzzle to know whether it were better to hear Mass in one church than in another, to spin than to sew, to give alms to a man rather than a woman ? It is not good service to a master to spend as much time in considering what is to be done, as in doing the things which are to be done. We are to proportion our attention to the importance of what we undertake. It would be an ill-regulated carefulness to take as much trouble in deliberating over a journey of one day as over one of three or four hundred leagues.

The choice of one's vocation, the plan of some business of great consequence, of some work occupying much time, of some very great expenditure, the change of abode, the choice of society, and the like, deserve to be seriously pondered, in order to see what is most according to the will of God. But in little daily matters, in which even a mistake is neither of moment nor irreparable, what need is there to make a business of them, to scrutinize them, or to importunately ask advice about them? To what end should I put myself upon the rack to learn whether God would rather that I should say the Rosary or Our Lady's Office, since there can be no such difference between them, that a great examination need be held; that I should rather go to visit the sick in the hospital than to Vespers, that I should rather go to a sermon than to a church where there is an Indulgence? Commonly there is no such importance in the one more than the other that it is worth while to make any great deliberation. We must walk in good faith and without minute consideration in such matters, and, as S. Basil says, freely choose as we like, so as not to weary our spirit, lose our time, or put ourselves in danger of disquiet, scruples, and superstition. But I mean always where there is no great disproportion between the two works, and where there is nothing of consideration on one side more than on the other.

And even in matters of moment we are to use a great humility, and not to think we can find out God's will by force of examination and subtlety of discourse; but having implored the light of the Holy Ghost, applied our consideration to the seeking of his good-pleasure, taken the counsel of our director, and, perhaps, of two or three other spiritual persons, we must resolve and determine in the name of God, and must not afterwards question our choice, but devoutly, peacefully, and firmly keep and pursue it. And although the difficulties, temptations and the variety of circumstances which occur in the course of executing our design, might cause us some doubt as to whether we had made a good choice, yet we must remain settled, and not regard all this, but consider that if we had made another

choice we had perhaps been a hundred times worse; to say
nothing of our not knowing whether it be God's will that we
should be exercised in consolation or desolation, in peace or
war.   The resolution being once holily taken, we are never to
doubt of the holiness of the execution; for unless we fail it
cannot fail.   To act otherwise is a mark of great self-love, or of
childishness, weakness and silliness of spirit.

BOOK IX.

LOVE OF SUBMISSION, WHEREBY OUR WILL IS UNITED TO GOD'S GOOD-PLEASURE.

CHAPTER I.

OF THE UNION OF OUR WILL TO THAT DIVINE WILL WHICH IS
CALLED THE WILL OF GOOD-PLEASURE.

NOTHING, except sin, is done without that will of God which is
called absolute, or will of good-pleasure, which no one can
hinder, and which is only known to us by events : these show
us, by their very happening, that God has willed and intended
them.

Let us consider, in one view, Theotimus, all that has been, is,
and shall be, and ravished with amazement, we shall be forced
to cry out with the Psalmist : *I will praise thee, for thou art
fearfully magnified : wonderful are thy works, and my soul
knoweth right well. Thy knowledge is become wonderful to me :
it is high, and I cannot reach to it.** And from thence we pass
on to most holy complacency, rejoicing that God is so infinite
in wisdom, power and goodness, which are the three divine
attributes, of which the world is but a small evidence, or, as it
were, sample.

Let us behold men and angels and all the variety of nature,
of qualities, conditions, faculties, affections, passions, graces and
privileges, which the Divine Providence has established in the

---

* Ps. cxxxviii. 14, 6.

innumerable multitude of those heavenly intelligences and human creatures in whom God's justice and mercy are so admirably exercised, and we shall be unable to contain ourselves from singing, with a joy full of respect and loving dread : *Mercy and judgment I will sing to thee, O Lord.**

Theotimus, we are to take an exceeding complacency in seeing how God exercises his mercy in so many different benefits which he distributes amongst men and angels in heaven and on earth, and how he exerts his justice by an infinite variety of pains and chastisements : for his justice and mercy are equally amiable and admirable in themselves, since both of them are no other thing than one same most singular goodness and divinity. But the effects of his justice being sharp and full of bitterness to us, he always sweetens them with the mingling of his mercies, preserving the green olive amidst the waters of the deluge of his just indignation, and giving power to the devout soul, as to a chaste dove, to find it at last, provided always that after the fashion of doves she very lovingly ruminate in her mind. So death, afflictions, anguish, labours, whereof our life is full, and which by God's just ordinance are the punishments of sin, are also, by his sweet mercy, ladders to ascend to heaven, means to increase grace, and merits to obtain glory. Blessed are poverty, hunger, thirst, sorrow, sickness, death, persecution : for they are indeed the just punishments of our faults, yet punishments so steeped in, or, to use the physician's term, so aromatized with the Divine sweetness, benignity and clemency, that their bitterness is most delicious. It is a strange yet a true thing, Theotimus ; if the damned were not blinded by their obstinacy, and by their hatred for God, they would find consolation in their torments, and see the divine mercy admirably mingled with their eternally tormenting flames. Hence the Saints, considering on the one side the horrible and dreadful torments of the damned, praise the Divine justice therein, and cry out : *Thou art just, O Lord, and thy judgment is right :*† but seeing on the other side that these pains, though eternal and incomprehensible, come yet far short of the faults and crimes for which they were

---

* Ps. c. I.   † Ps. cxviii. 137.

inflicted—ravished with God's infinite mercy, they cry out : O Lord, how good thou art, since in the very heat of thy wrath thou canst not keep the torrent of thy mercies from pouring out its waters on the pitiless flames of hell!

> Mercy, O Lord, hath not thy soul forsaken,
> E'en while thy justice hath its vengeance taken
> In flames of hell ; nor could thine ire repress
> The torrent of thy wonted graciousness :
> In fiercest wrath thou still dost interlace
> Thy sternest justice with thine acts of grace.

Let us come, next, to ourselves in particular, and behold the multitude of interior and exterior goods, as also the very great number of interior and exterior pains, which the Divine Providence has prepared for us : and, as if opening the arms of our consent, let us most lovingly embrace all this, acquiescing in God's most holy will, and singing unto him as it were a hymn of eternal acquiescence : *Thy will be done on earth as it is in heaven :* yea, Lord, thy will be done on earth,—where we have no pleasure which is not mixed with some pain, no roses without thorns, no day without following night, no spring without preceding winter ; on earth, O Lord ! where consolations are thinly, and labours thickly, sown : yet, O God ! thy will be done, not only in carrying out thy commandments, counsels and inspirations, which are things to be done by us, but also in suffering the afflictions and pains which have to be borne by us; so that thy will may do by us, for us, in us, and with us, all that it pleases.

CHAPTER II.

THAT THE UNION OF OUR WILL WITH THE GOOD-PLEASURE OF GOD TAKES PLACE PRINCIPALLY IN TRIBULATIONS.

PAINFUL things cannot indeed be loved when considered in themselves, but viewed in their source, that is, in the Divine Will and Providence which ordains them, they are supremely delight-

ful.   Look at the rod of Moses upon the ground, and it is a
hideous serpent; look upon it in Moses's hand, and it is a wand
of miracles.   Look at tribulations in themselves, and they are
dreadful; behold them in the will of God, and they are love and
delights.   How often have we turned in disgust from remedies
and medicines when the doctor or apothecary offered them,
which, being offered by some well-beloved hand (love surmounting our loathing), we receive with delight.   In truth,
love either takes away the hardship of labour, or makes it dear
to us while we feel it.   It is said that there is a river in Bœotia
wherein the fish appear golden, but taken out of those their
native waters, they have the natural colour of other fishes:
afflictions are so; if we look at them outside God's will, they
have their natural bitterness, but he who considers them in that
eternal good-pleasure, finds them all golden, unspeakably lovely
and precious.

If Abraham had seen outside God's will the necessity of
slaying his son, think, Theotimus, what pangs and convulsions of
heart he would have felt, but seeing it in God's good-pleasure,
it appears all golden, and he tenderly embraces it.   If the martyrs had looked upon their torments outside this good-pleasure,
how could they have sung, in chains and flames?   The truly
loving heart loves God's good-pleasure not in consolations only
but in afflictions also; yea, it loves it better upon the cross in
pains and difficulties, because the principal effect of love is to
make the lover suffer for the thing beloved.

The Stoics, especially good Epictetus, placed all their
philosophy in abstaining and sustaining, bearing and forbearing;
in abstaining from and forbearing earthly delights, pleasures and
honours; in sustaining and bearing wrongs, labours and trials:
but Christian doctrine, which is the only true philosophy, has
three principles upon which it grounds all its exercises,—*abnegation of self*, which is far more than to abstain from pleasures,
carrying the cross, which is far more than tolerating or sustaining
it, *following Our Lord*, not only in renouncing our self and
bearing our cross, but also in the practice of all sorts of good
works.   But at the same time there is not so much love shown
in abnegation or in action, as in suffering.   The Holy Ghost in

Holy Scripture certainly signifies the death and passion which our Saviour suffered for us, to be the highest point of his love towards us.

1. To love God's will in consolations is a good love when it is indeed God's will that is loved, and not the consolation which is the form it takes : however, this is a love without contradiction, repugnance and effort : for who would not love so worthy a will in so agreeable a form ?   2. To love the will of God in his commandments, counsels and inspirations is a second degree of love, and much more perfect, for it leads us to the renouncing and quitting of our own will, and makes us abstain from and forbear some pleasures, though not all.   3. To love sufferings and afflictions for the love of God is the supreme point of most holy charity, for there is nothing therein to receive our affection save the will of God only ; there is great contradiction on the part of nature ; and we not only forsake pleasures, but embrace torments and labours.

Our mortal enemy knew well what was love's furthest and finest act, when having heard from the mouth of God that Job was just, righteous, fearing God, hating sin, and firm in innocence, he made no account of this, in comparison with bearing afflictions, by which he made the last and surest trial of the love of this great servant of God.   To make these afflictions extreme, he formed them out of the loss of all his goods and of all his children, abandonment by all his friends, an arrogant contradiction by his most intimate associates and his wife, a contradiction full of contempt, mockery and reproach ; to which he added the collection of almost all human diseases, and particularly a universal, cruel, offensive, horrible ulcer over all his body.

And yet behold the great Job, king as it were of all the miserable creatures of the world, seated upon a dunghill, as upon the throne of misery, adorned with sores, ulcers, and corruption, as with royal robes suitable to the quality of his kingship, with so great an abjection and annihilation, that if he had not spoken, one could not have discerned whether Job was a man reduced to a dunghill, or the dunghill a corruption in form of a man.   Now, I say, hear the great Job crying out : *If we have received good things from the hand of the Lord, why shall we not receive also*

evil?* O God! How this word is great with love! He
ponders, Theotimus, that it was from the hand of God that he
had received the good, testifying that he had not so much loved
goods because they were good, as because they came from the
hand of the Lord; whence he concludes that he is lovingly to
support adversities, since they proceed from the hand of the same
Lord, which is equally to be loved when it distributes afflictions
and when it bestows consolations. Every one easily receives
good things, but to receive evil is a work of perfect love, which
loves them so much the more, inasmuch as they are only lovable
in respect of the hand that gives them.

The traveller who is in fear whether he has the right way,
walks in doubt, viewing the country over, and stands in a muse
at the end of almost every field to think whether he goes not
astray, but he who is sure of his way walks on gaily, boldly, and
swiftly: even so the love that desires to walk to God's will
through consolations, walks ever in fear of taking the wrong
path, and of loving (in lieu of God's good-pleasure) the pleasure
which is in the consolation; but the love that strikes straight
through afflictions towards the will of God walks in assurance,
for affliction being in no wise lovable in itself, it is an easy
thing only to love it for the sake of him that sends it. The
hounds in spring-time are at fault at every step, finding hardly
any scent at all, because the herbs and flowers then smell so
freshly that their odour puts down that of the hart or hare: in
the spring-time of consolations love scarcely recognizes God's
good-pleasure, because the sensible pleasure of consolation so
allures the heart, that it troubles the attention which the heart
should pay to the will of God. S. Catharine of Siena, having
from our Saviour her choice of a crown of gold or a crown of
thorns, chose this latter, as better suiting with love: a desire
of suffering, says the Blessed (S.) Angela of Foligno, is an infallible mark of love: and the great Apostle cries out that he
glories only in the cross,† in infirmity, in persecution.

* Job ii. 10.   † Gal. vi. 14.

CHAPTER III.

OF THE UNION OF OUR WILL TO THE DIVINE GOOD-PLEASURE IN SPIRITUAL AFFLICTIONS, BY RESIGNATION.

THE love of the cross makes us undertake voluntary afflictions, as for example, fasting, watching, hair-shirts and other macerations of the flesh, and makes us renounce pleasures, honours and riches: and the love in these exercises is very delightful to the beloved. Yet it is still more so when we receive sweetly and contentedly pains, torments and tribulations, by reason of the Divine will which sends us them. But love is then at its height when we not only receive afflictions with patience and sweetness, but cherish, love, and embrace them for the sake of the Divine good-pleasure, whence they proceed.

Now of all the efforts of perfect love, that which is made by acquiescence of spirit in spiritual tribulations, is doubtless the purest and noblest. The Blessed (S.) Angela of Foligno makes an admirable description of the interior pangs which she sometimes felt, saying that her soul was tortured like to a man who being tied hand and foot, should be hung by the neck without being strangled, and should hang in this state betwixt life and death, without hope of help, and unable to support himself by his feet or assist himself with his hands, or to cry out, or even to sigh or moan. It is thus, Theotimus: the soul is sometimes so overcharged with interior afflictions, that all her faculties and powers are oppressed by the privation of all that might relieve her, and by the apprehension and feeling of all that can be grievous to her. So that in imitation of her Saviour she begins to be troubled, to fear, and to be dismayed, and at length to sadden with a sadness like to that of the dying. Whence she may rightly say : *My soul is sorrowful even unto death;* and with the consent of her whole interior, she desires, petitions, supplicates, that, if it be possible, this chalice may pass, having nothing left her save the very supreme point of her spirit, which cleaving hard to the divine will and good-pleasure, says in a most sincere submission : O eternal *Father,* Ah ! *not mine but thy will be done.*

And the main point is that the soul makes this resignation amidst such a world of troubles, contradictions, repugnances that she hardly even perceives that she makes it; at least it seems done so coldly as not to be done from her heart nor properly, since what then goes on for the divine good-pleasure is not only done without delight and contentment, but even against the pleasure and liking of all the rest of the heart, which is permitted by love to bemoan itself (if only for the reason that it may not bemoan itself) and to sigh out all the lamentations of Job and Jeremias, yet with the condition that a sacred peace be still preserved in the depths of the heart, in the highest and most delicate point of the spirit. But this submissive peace is not tender or sweet, it is scarcely sensible, though sincere, strong, unchangeable and full of love, and it seems to have betaken itself to the very end of the spirit as into the donjon-keep of the fort, where it remains in its high courage, though all the rest be taken and oppressed with sorrow : and in this case, the more love is deprived of all helps, and cut off from the aid of the powers and faculties of the soul, the more it is to be esteemed for preserving its fidelity so constantly.

This union or conformity with the divine good-pleasure is made either by holy Resignation or by most holy Indifference. Now resignation is practised with a certain effort of submission : one would willingly live instead of dying, yet since it is God's pleasure that die we must, we yield to it. We would willingly live, if it pleased God, yea, further, we wish that it was his pleasure to let us live : we die submissively, yet more willingly would we live ; we depart with a reasonably good will, yet we have a still stronger inclination to stay. Job in his afflictions made the act of resignation : *If we have received good things at the hand of God*, said he, *why should we not receive the evil,** why not sustain the pains and toils he sends us ? Mark, Theotimus, how he speaks of sustaining, supporting, enduring ; *As it hath pleased the Lord so is it done: blessed be the name of the Lord.*† These are words of resignation and acceptance, by way of suffering and patience.

* Job ii. 10.   † Job i. 21.

CHAPTER IV.

OF THE UNION OF OUR WILL TO THE GOOD-PLEASURE OF GOD BY INDIFFERENCE.

RESIGNATION prefers God's will before all things, yet it loves many other things besides the will of God. Indifference goes beyond resignation : for it loves nothing except for the love of God's will : insomuch that nothing can stir the indifferent heart, in the presence of the will of God. It is true that the most indifferent heart in the world may be touched with some affection, so long as it does not know where the will of God is. Eliezer being come to the fountain of Haran, saw the virgin Rebecca, and found her lovely and amiable beyond his expectation ; but yet he stayed in Indifference, till he knew by a sign from God, that the Divine will had prepared her for his master's son ; then he presented her with the earrings and bracelets of gold. On the contrary, if Jacob had only loved in Rachel the alliance with Laban, to which his father Isaac had obliged him, Lia would have been as dear unto him as Rachel, they being both Laban's daughters ; and consequently his father's will would have been as well fulfilled in the one as in the other. But because, besides his father's will, he desired to satisfy his own liking, charmed with the beauty and grace of Rachel, he disliked marrying Lia, and took her against his inclination, resignedly.

But the indifferent heart is not such ; for knowing that tribulation, though hard-favoured as another Lia, ceases not on that account to be daughter and well-beloved daughter to the Divine pleasure, it loves her as much as consolation, though the latter be in herself more amiable ;—yea, it loves tribulation more, because it sees nothing amiable in her save the mark of God's will. If I desire pure water only, what care I whether it be served in a golden vessel or in a glass, as in either case I take only the water : yea, I would rather have it in a glass, because this has no other colour than water itself, which thus I also see better. What matter whether God's will be presented to us in tribulation or in consolation, since I seek nothing in either of them but God's will, which is so much the better seen when there is no other beauty present save that of this most holy, eternal, good-pleasure.

Heroic, yea more than heroic, was the Indifference of the incomparable S. Paul. *I am straitened*, said he, *between two, having a desire to be dissolved and to be with Christ, a thing by far the better. But to abide still in the flesh is needful for you.** Wherein he was followed by the great Bishop S. Martin, who having come to the end of his life, pressed with an extreme desire to go to his God, did yet testify that he would most willingly remain amongst the labours of his charge, for the good of his flock, as if after having sung this canticle: *How lovely are thy tabernacles, O Lord of hosts! My soul longeth and fainteth for the courts of the Lord. My heart and my flesh have rejoiced in the living God:*†—he went on to make this exclamation: " Yet O Lord, if I am still necessary for the salvation of your people, I refuse not the labour,—your will be done." Admirable the Indifference of the Apostle, admirable that of this Apostolic man! They see heaven open for them, they see a thousand labours on earth, they are indifferent in the choice of either: nothing but the will of God can set their hearts at rest; heaven appears no more pleasant than worldly miseries, if God's good-pleasure be equally in them both: labours are a heaven if God's will be found in them, and heaven is unhappiness if it be not found therein; for as David said, they desire nothing in heaven or earth except to see God's good-pleasure accomplished. *What have I in heaven, and besides thee what do I desire upon earth?*‡

The indifferent heart is as a ball of wax in the hands of its God, receiving with equal readiness all the impressions of the Divine pleasure; it is a heart without choice, equally disposed for everything, having no other object of its will than the will of its God, and placing its affection not upon the things that God wills, but upon the will of God who wills them. Wherefore, when God's will is in various things, it chooses, at any cost, that

* Phil. i. 23.   † Ps. lxxxiii. 1.   ‡ Ps. lxxii. 25.

in which it appears most. God's will is found in marriage and in virginity, but because it is more in virginity, the indifferent heart makes choice of virginity though this cost it its life, as with S. Paul's dear spiritual daughter S. Thecla, with S. Cecily, S. Agatha, and a thousand others. God's will is found in the service of the poor and of the rich, but yet somewhat more in serving the poor; the indifferent heart will choose that side. God's will lies in moderation amid consolations, and in patience amid tribulations: the indifferent heart prefers the latter, as having more of God's will in it. To conclude, God's will is the sovereign object of the indifferent soul; wheresoever she sees it she runs after the odour of its perfumes, directing her course ever thither where it most appears, without considering anything else. She is conducted by the Divine will, as by a beloved chain; which way soever it goes, she follows it: she would prize hell more with God's will than heaven without it; nay she would even prefer hell before heaven if she perceived only a little more of God's good-pleasure in that than in this, so that if by supposition of an impossible thing she should know that her damnation would be more agreeable to God than her salvation, she would quit her salvation and run to her damnation.

CHAPTER V.

THAT HOLY INDIFFERENCE EXTENDS TO ALL THINGS.

INDIFFERENCE is to be practised in things belonging to the natural life, as in health, sickness, beauty, deformity, weakness, strength: in the affairs of the spiritual life, as in dryness, consolations, relish, aridity; in actions, in sufferings,—briefly, in all sorts of events. Job, in his natural life was struck with the most horrible sores that ever eye beheld, in his civil life he was scorned, reviled, contemned, and that by his nearest friends; in his spiritual life he was oppressed with languors, oppression, convulsions, anguish, darkness, and with all kinds of intolerable

interior griefs, as his complaints and lamentations bear witness.
The great Apostle proclaims to us a general Indifference; to
show ourselves the true servants of God, *in much patience, in
tribulation, in necessities, in distresses, in stripes, in prisons, in
seditions, in labours, in watchings, in fastings, in chastity; in knowledge, in long-suffering, in sweetness, in the Holy Ghost, in charity
unfeigned, in the word of truth, in the power of God; by the
armour of justice on the right hand and on the left, through
honour and dishonour, by evil report and good report: as de-
ceivers, and yet true; as unknown and yet known; as dying, and
behold we live; as chastised and not killed; as sorrowful, yet
always rejoicing: as needy, yet enriching many; as having nothing, and possessing all things.** *

Take notice, I pray you, Theotimus, how the life of the
Apostles was filled with afflictions: in the body by wounds, in
the heart by anguish, according to the world by infamy and
prisons, and in all these,—O God! what Indifference they had!
Their sorrow is joyous, their poverty rich, their death life-giving,
their dishonour honourable, that is, they are joyful for being sad,
content to be poor, strengthened with life amid the dangers of
death, and glorious in being made vile, because—such was the
will of God. And whereas the will of God was more recognized in sufferings than in the actions of virtues, he ranks the
exercise of patience first, saying: *But in all things let us exhibit ourselves as the ministers of God, in much patience, in tribulation, in necessities, in distresses:* and then, towards the end, *in
chastity, in knowledge, in long-suffering.*

In like manner our divine Saviour was incomparably
afflicted in his civil life, being condemned as guilty of treason
against God and man; beaten, scourged, reviled, and tormented
with extraordinary ignomy; in his natural life, dying in the
most cruel and sensible torments that heart could conceive; in
his spiritual life enduring sorrows, fears, terrors, anguish, abandonment, interior oppressions, such as never had, nor shall have,
their like. For though the supreme portion of his soul did
sovereignly enjoy eternal glory, yet love hindered this glory from

* 2 Cor. vi. 4–10.

spreading its delicious influence into the feelings, or the imagination, or the inferior reason, leaving thus his whole heart at the mercy of sorrow and distress.

Ezechiel saw the likeness of a hand, which took him by a single lock of the hairs of his head, lifting him up between heaven and earth;* in like manner our Saviour, lifted up on the cross between heaven and earth, seemed to be held in his Father's hand only by the very extremity of the spirit, and, as it were, by one hair of his head, which, touching the sweet hand of his eternal Father, received a sovereign affluence of felicity, all the rest being swallowed up in sorrow and grief: whereupon he cries out: *My God, why hast thou forsaken me?*

They say that the fish termed lantern-of-the-sea in the midst of the tempest thrusts out of the water her tongue, which is so luminous, resplendent and clear, that it serves as a light or beacon for mariners. So in the sea of passions by which Our Lord was overwhelmed, all the faculties of his soul were, so to say, swallowed up and buried in the whirlpool of so many pains, excepting only the point of his spirit, which, exempt from all trouble, remained bright and resplendent with glory and felicity. Oh how blessed is the love which reigns in the heights of the spirit of faithful souls, while they are tossed upon the billows and waves of interior tribulations!

CHAPTER VI.

OF THE PRACTICE OF LOVING INDIFFERENCE, IN THINGS BELONGING TO THE SERVICE OF GOD.

THE divine good-pleasure is scarcely known otherwise than by events, and as long as it is unknown to us, we must keep as close as possible to the will of God which is already declared or signified to us : but as soon as the Divine Majesty's pleasure appears, we must at once lovingly yield ourselves to its obedience.

* Ezech. viii. 3.

My mother (or it would be the same of myself) is ill in bed: how do I know whether God intends death to follow or not? Of course I cannot know; but I know well that while awaiting the event from his good-pleasure, he wills, by his declared will, that I use remedies proper to effect a cure. But if it be the Divine pleasure that the disease, victorious over the remedies, should at last bring death—as soon as ever I am certain of this by the actual event, I will amorously acquiesce, in the point of my spirit, in spite of all the opposition of the inferior powers of my soul. Yes, Lord, I will say, it is my will because thy good-pleasure is such; thus it has pleased thee, and so it shall please me, who am the most humble servant of thy will.

But if the Divine pleasure were declared to me before the event took place, as was to the great S. Peter the manner of his death, to the great S. Paul his chains and prisons, to Jeremias the destruction of his dear Jerusalem, to David the death of his son,—then we should have at the same instant to unite our will to God's in imitation of the great Abraham, and, like him, if we had such a command, we should have to undertake the execution of the eternal decree even in the slaying of our children: Oh admirable union of this patriarch's will to the will of God, when, believing that it was the Divine pleasure that he should sacrifice his child, he willed and undertook it so courageously! admirable that of the child, who so meekly submitted himself to his father's sword, to have God's good-pleasure performed at the price of his own death!

But note here, Theotimus, a mark of the perfect union of an indifferent heart with the Divine pleasure. Behold Abraham with the sword in his hand, his arm extended ready to give the deathblow to his dear only son: he is doing this to please the Divine will; and see at the same time an angel, who, on the part of this same will, suddenly stops him, and immediately he holds his stroke, equally ready to sacrifice or not to sacrifice his son; whose life and whose death are indifferent to him in the presence of God's will. When God gives him an order to sacrifice his son he does not grow sad, when God dispenses with the order given he does not rejoice, all is one to this great heart, so that God's will be fulfilled.

Yes, Theotimus, for God oftentimes to exercise us in this holy Indifference, inspires us with very high designs, which yet he will not have accomplished, and as then we are boldly, courageously and constantly to commence and to pursue the work as far as we can, so are we sweetly and quietly to acquiesce in such result of our enterprise as it pleases God to send us. S. Louis by inspiration passed the sea to conquer the Holy Land; the event answered not his expectation, he sweetly acquiesces. I more esteem the tranquillity of this submission than the magnanimity of his enterprise. S. Francis went into Egypt to convert the infidels, or amongst the infidels to die a martyr; such was the will of God: yet he returned without performing either, and that was also God's will. It was equally the will of God that S. Anthony of Padua desired martyrdom and that he obtained it not. Blessed (S.) Ignatius of Loyola having with such pains put on foot the Company of the name of Jesus, from which he saw so many fair fruits and foresaw many more in the time to come, had yet the nobility of soul to promise himself that though he should see it dissolved (which would be the bitterest pain that could befal him), within half an hour afterwards he would be stayed and tranquil in the will of God. John of Avila, that holy and learned preacher of Andalusia, having a design to form a company of reformed priests for the advancement of God's glory, and having already made good progress in the matter, as soon as he saw the Jesuits in the field, thinking they were enough for that time, immediately stopped his own undertaking, with an incomparable meekness and humility. Oh how blessed are such souls, bold and strong in the undertakings God proposes to them, and withal tractable and facile in giving them over when God so disposes! These are marks of a most perfect Indifference, to leave off doing a good when God pleases, and to return from half way when God's will, which is our guide, ordains it. Jonas was much to blame in being angry because God, as he considered, did not fulfil his prophecy upon Ninive. Jonas did God's will in announcing the destruction of Ninive; but he mingled his own interest and will with that of God; whence, seeing that God did not fulfil his prediction according to the rigour of the words he had used in announcing it, he was offended and shamefully murmured. Whereas if God's will had been the only motive of his actions, he would have been as well content to have seen it accomplished in remission of the penalty which Ninive had merited, as in punishment of the fault which Ninive had committed. We desire that what we undertake or manage should succeed, but it is not reasonable that God should do all after our liking. If God wills Ninive to be threatened, and yet not overthrown (since the threat is sufficient to correct it), why should Jonas think himself aggrieved?

But if this be so, we are then to care for (*affectionner*) nothing, but abandon our affairs to the mercy of events? Pardon me, Theotimus, we are to omit nothing which is requisite to bring the work which God has put into our hands to a happy issue, yet upon condition that, if the event be contrary, we should lovingly and peaceably embrace it. For we are commanded to have great care in what appertains to God's glory and to our charge, but we are not bound to, or responsible for, the event, because it is not in our power. *Take care of him*, was it said to the innkeeper, in the parable of the poor man who lay half-dead between Jerusalem and Jericho. It is not said, as St. Bernard remarks, cure him, but, *take care of him*. So the Apostles with most earnest affection preached first to the Jews, though they foresaw that in the end they would be forced to leave them as an unfruitful soil, and betake themselves to the Gentiles. It is our part to plant and water carefully, but to give increase—that belongs only to God.

The great Psalmist makes this prayer to our Saviour as by an exclamation of joy and with presage of victory: *O Lord in thy comeliness and thy beauty, bend thy bow, proceed prosperously and mount thy horse.** As though he would say that by the arrows of his heavenly love shot into human hearts, he made himself master of men, and then handled them at his pleasure, not unlike to a horse well trained. O Lord thou art the royal rider, who turnest the hearts of thy faithful lovers every way about: sometimes thou givest them the rein, and they run at full speed in the courses to which thou impellest them: and then, when it seems

* Ps. xliv. 6. According to the Septuagint and the Hebrew (Tr.)

good to thee, thou makest them stop in the midst of their career and at the height of their speed.

But further, if the enterprise begun by inspiration fail by the fault of those to whom it was committed, how can it then be said that a man is to acquiesce in God's will? For, some one will say to me, it is not God's will that hinders the success, but my fault. This is not caused by God's will, for God is not author of sin; but yet for all that, it is God's will that your fault should be followed by the overthrow and failure of your design, in punishment of your fault; for though his goodness cannot permit him to will your fault, yet does his justice make him will the punishment you suffer for it. So God was not the cause that David offended, yet it was God that inflicted upon him the pain due to his sin. He was not the cause of Saul's sin, but he was the cause that in punishment of it the victory fell from his hands.

When therefore it happens that in punishment of our fault our holy designs have not good success, we must equally detest the fault by a solid repentance, and accept its punishment; for as the sin is against the will of God, so the punishment is according to his will.

CHAPTER VII.

OF THE INDIFFERENCE WHICH WE ARE TO HAVE AS TO OUR ADVANCEMENT IN VIRTUES.

GOD has ordained that we should employ our whole endeavours to obtain holy virtues, let us then forget nothing which might help our good success in this pious enterprise. But after we have planted and watered, let us then know for certain that it is God who must give increase to the trees of our good inclinations and habits, and therefore from his Divine Providence we are to expect the fruits of our desires and labours, and if we find the progress and advancement of our hearts in devotion not such as we would desire, let us not be troubled, let us live in peace, let tranquillity always reign in our hearts.   It belongs to us diligently to cultivate our heart, and therefore we must faithfully attend to it, but as for the plenty of the crop or harvest, let us leave the care thereof to our Lord and Master.   The husbandman will never be reprehended for not having a good harvest, but only if he did not carefully till and sow his ground. Let us not be troubled at finding ourselves always novices in the exercise of virtues, for in the monastery of a devout life every one considers himself always a novice, and there the whole of life is meant as a probation; the most evident argument, not only that we are novices, but also that we are worthy of expulsion and reprobation, being, to esteem and hold ourselves professed. For according to the rule of this Order not the solemnity but the accomplishment of the vows makes the novices professed, nor are the vows ever fulfilled while there remains yet something to be done for their observance, and the obligation of serving God and making progress in his love lasts always until death. But after all, will some one say, if I know that it is by my own fault my progress in virtue is so slow, how can I help being grieved and disquieted?   I have said this in the *Introduction to a Devout Life*,* but I willingly say it again, because it can never be said sufficiently.   We must be sorry for faults with a repentance which is strong, settled, constant, tranquil, but not troubled, unquiet or fainthearted.   Are you sure that your backwardness in virtue has come from your fault?   Well then, humble yourself before God, implore his mercy, fall prostrate before the face of his goodness and demand pardon, confess your fault, cry him mercy in the very ear of your confessor, so as to obtain absolution ; but this being done remain in peace, and having detested the offence, embrace lovingly the abjection which you feel in yourself by reason of delaying your advancement in good.

Ah! my Theotimus, the souls in Purgatory are there doubtless for their sins, and for sins which they have detested and do supremely detest, but as for the abjection and pain which remain

* IV. 11.

from being detained in that place, and from being deprived for a space of the enjoyment of the blessed love which is in Paradise, they endure this lovingly, and they devoutly pronounce the canticle of the Divine justice : *Thou art just, O Lord, and thy judgment is right.** Let us therefore await our advancement with patience, and instead of disquieting ourselves because we have so little profited in the time past, let us diligently endeavour to do better in the time to come.

Behold, I beseech you, this good soul. She has greatly desired and endeavoured to throw off the slavery of anger ; and God has assisted her, for he has quite delivered her from all the sins which proceed from anger. She would die rather than utter a single injurious word, or let any sign of hatred escape her, and yet she is subject to the assaults and first motions of this passion, that is, to certain startings, strong movements and sallies of an angry heart, which the Chaldaic paraphrase calls stirrings (*tremoussements*), saying : Be stirred and sin not ;—where our sacred version says : *Be angry and sin not.*† In effect it is the same thing, for the prophet would only say that if anger surprise us, exciting in our hearts the first stirrings of sin, we should be careful not to let ourselves be carried further into this passion, for so we should offend. Now, although these first movements and stirrings be no sin, yet the poor soul that is often attacked by them, troubles, afflicts and disquiets herself, and thinks she does well in being sad, as if it were the love of God that provoked her to this sadness. And yet, Theotimus, it is not heavenly love that causes this trouble, for that is never offended except by sin ; it is our self-love that desires to be exempt from the pains and toils which the assaults of anger draw on us. It is not the offence that displeases us in these stirrings of anger, there being none at all committed, it is the pain we are put to in resisting which disquiets us.

These rebellions of the sensual appetite, as well in anger as in concupiscence, are left in us for our exercise, to the end that we may practise spiritual valour in resisting them. This is that Philistine, whom the true Israelites are ever to fight against but

---

* Ps. cxviii. 137.   † Ps. iv. 5.

never to put down; they may weaken him, but never annihilate
him. He only dies with us, and always lives with us. He is
truly accursed, and detestable, as springing from sin, and tending
towards sin : wherefore, as we are termed earth, because we are
formed of earth and shall return to earth, so this rebellion is
named sin by the great Apostle, as having sprung from sin and
tending to sin, though it never makes us guilty unless we second
and obey it.　Whereupon he exhorts us *that we permit it not to
reign in our mortal body to obey the concupiscence thereof.** He
prohibits not the sentiment of sin, but the consenting to it.　He
does not order us to hinder sin from coming into us and being
in us, but he commands that it should not reign in us.　It is in
us when we feel the rebellion of the sensual appetite, but it
does not reign in us unless we give consent unto it.　The physician will never order his feverish patient not to be athirst, for
that would be too great a folly ; but he will tell him that though
he be thirsty he must abstain from drinking.　No one will tell
a woman with child not to have a longing for extravagant things,
for this is not under her control, but she may well be told to
discover her longings, to the end that if she longs for hurtful
things one may divert her imagination, and not let such a fancy
get a hold on her brain.

　　The *sting of the flesh, an angel of Satan,* roughly attacked the
great S. Paul, in order to make him fall into sin.　The poor
Apostle endured this as a shameful and infamous wrong, and
on this account called it a buffeting and ignominious treatment,
and petitioned God to deliver him from it, but God answered
him : *Paul, my grace is sufficient for thee, for virtue is made
perfect in infirmity.*† Thereupon this great holy man said in
acquiescence :—*Gladly will I glory in my infirmities that the
power of Christ may dwell in me.* But take notice, I beseech
you, that there is sensual rebellion even in this admirable vessel
of election, who in running to the remedy of prayer teaches us
that we are to use the same arms against the temptations we
feel.　Note further that Our Lord does not always permit these
terrible revolts in man for the punishment of sin, but to manifest

---

　　* Rom. vi. 12.　　　　　　　† 2 Cor. xii. 9.

the strength and virtue of the Divine assistance and grace. Finally, note that we are not only not to be disquieted in our temptations and infirmities, but we are even *to glory in our infirmity that thereby God's virtue may appear in us,* sustaining our weakness against the force of the suggestion and temptation : for the glorious Apostle calls the stings and attacks of impurity which he endured his *infirmities,* and says that he glories in them, because, though he had the sense of them by his misery, yet through God's mercy he did not give consent to them.

Indeed, as I have said above, the church condemned the error of certain solitaries, who held that we might be perfectly delivered even in this world from the passions of anger, concupiscence, fear, and the like.   God wills us to have enemies, and it is also his will that we should repulse them.   Let us then behave ourselves courageously between the one and the other will of God, enduring with patience to be assaulted, and endeavouring with courage by resistance to make head against and resist our assailants.

CHAPTER VIII.

HOW WE ARE TO UNITE OUR WILL WITH GOD'S IN THE PERMISSION OF SINS.

GOD sovereignly hates sin, and yet he most wisely permits it, in order to let the reasonable creature act according to the condition of its nature ; and to make the good more worthy of commendation, when having power to transgress the law they do not transgress it.   Let us therefore adore and bless this holy permission, but since the Providence which permits sin infinitely hates it, let us also detest and hate it, desiring with all our power that sin permitted may not be committed, and according to this desire let us make use of all means possible to hinder the birth, growth and reign of sin.   Let us in this imitate our Saviour, who never ceases to exhort, promise, threaten, pro-

hibit, command and inspire us, in order to turn our will from
sin, so far forth as is possible without depriving us of liberty:
and when the sin is once committed let us endeavour what we
are able to have it blotted out, like our Saviour, who assured
Carpus, as was said above, that, if it were requisite, he was
ready to suffer death again to deliver a single soul from sin.
But if the sinner grow obstinate, let us weep, Theotimus, groan,
pray for him, before the Saviour of our souls, who having all his
lifetime shed an abundance of tears over sinners and over those
who represented all sinners, died in the end—his eyes full of
tears, his body all steeped in blood—lamenting the ruin of
sinners.   This affection touched David so to the quick that he
fell into a swoon over it: *A fainting*, said he, *hath seized me for
sinners abandoning thy law.** And the great Apostle protests
that he has *a continual sorrow in his heart*,† for the obstinacy of
the Jews.

Meanwhile, however obstinate sinners may be, let us never
desist from aiding and assisting them.   How do we know but
that they may do penance and be saved?   Happy is he that can
say to his neighbour as did S. Paul: *For three years I ceased
not with tears to admonish every one of you night and day. Wherefore I take you to witness this day that I am clear from the blood
of all men.   For I have not spared to declare unto you all the
counsel of God.*‡   So long as we are within the limits of hope
that the sinner will amend (which limits are always of the same
extent as those of his life), we must never reject him, but pray
for him and assist him as far as his misery will permit.

But, at last, after we have wept over the obstinate, and performed towards them the good offices of charity in trying to
reclaim them from perdition, we must imitate our Saviour and
the Apostles; that is, we must divert our spirit from thence
and place it upon other objects and employments which are
more to the advancement of God's glory.   *To you it behoved us
first* (said the Apostles to the Jews) *to speak the word of God:
but because you reject it, and judge yourselves unworthy of eternal
life, behold we turn to the Gentiles.*§ *The kingdom of God* (said our

* Ps. cxviii. 53.   † Rom. ix. 2.   ‡ Acts xx. 31, 26, 27.
§ Acts xiii. 46.

Saviour) *shall be taken from you, and shall be given to a nation yielding the fruits thereof.** For we cannot spend too long time in bewailing some, without losing time fit and necessary for procuring the salvation of others. The Apostle indeed says that the loss of the Jews is a continual sorrow to him, but this is said in the same sense that we say we praise God always; for we mean no other thing thereby than that we praise him very frequently, and on every occasion; and in the same manner the glorious St. Paul felt a continual grief in his heart on account of the reprobation of the Jews, in the sense that on every occasion he bemoaned their misfortune.

For the rest we must ever adore, love and praise God avenging and punishing justice as we love his mercy, being both daughters of his goodness; for by his grace he makes us good, being good, yea, sovereignly good, himself; by his justice he punishes sin because he hates it, and he hates it because, being sovereignly good, he hates the sovereign evil which is iniquity : and, in conclusion, note, that God never withdraws his mercy from us save by the just vengeance of his punishing justice, nor do we ever escape the rigour of his justice but by his justifying mercy : and always, whether punishing or favouring us, his good-pleasure is worthy of adoration, love and everlasting praise. So the just man who sings the praises of the mercy of God over such as shall be saved, will also rejoice when he shall see his vengeance. The blessed shall with joy approve the sentence of the damnation of the reprobate, as well as that of the salvation of the elect : and the angels, having exercised their charity towards those that they had in keeping, shall remain in peace, when they see them obstinate, yea even damned. We are therefore to submit ourselves to the Divine will, and kiss the right hand of his mercy and the left hand of his justice, with an equal love and reverence.

* Matt. **xxi.** 43.

CHAPTER IX.

HOW THE PURITY OF INDIFFERENCE IS TO BE PRACTISED IN THE ACTIONS OF SACRED LOVE.

ONE of the most excellent musicians in the world, who played perfectly upon the lute, became in time so extremely deaf that he entirely lost the use of his hearing, yet ceased he not for all that to sing and to handle his lute marvellous delicately, by reason of the great skill he had acquired, of which his deafness did not deprive him. But because he had no pleasure in his song, nor yet in the sound of his lute, inasmuch as, being deprived of his hearing he could not perceive its sweetness and beauty,—he no longer sang or played save only to content a prince whose native subject he was, and whom he had an extreme inclination, as well as an infinite obligation, to please, because brought up in his palace from childhood. Hence he took an incomparable delight in pleasing him, and when his prince showed that he was pleased with his music he was ravished with delight. But it happened sometimes that the prince, to make trial of this loving musician's love, gave him an order to sing, and then immediately leaving him there in his chamber, went to the chase. The desire which this singer had to accomplish his master's will, made him continue his music as attentively as though his prince had been present, though in very deed he had no content in singing. For he neither had the pleasure of the melody, whereof his deafness deprived him, nor the content of pleasing his prince, who being absent could not enjoy the sweetness of the beautiful airs he sang.

*My heart is ready, O God, my heart is ready: I will sing and rehearse a psalm. Arise, O my glory! Arise psaltery and harp: I will arise early.** Man's heart is the true chaunter of the canticle of sacred love, himself the harp and the psaltery. Now ordinarily this chaunter hears his own voice, and takes a great pleasure in the melody of his song. I mean that our heart, loving God, relishes the delights of this love, and takes an incomparable contentment in

---

* Ps. lvi. 8. 9.

loving so lovely an object. Notice, I pray you, Theotimus, what I mean. The young nightingales do first essay a beginning of song to imitate the old ones; but having got skill and become masters, they sing for the pleasure which they take in warbling, and they so passionately addict themselves to this delight, as I have said in another place, that by force of straining their voice, their throat bursts and they die. So our hearts in the beginning of their devotion love God that they may be united and become agreeable unto him, and imitate him in that he hath loved us for all eternity; but by little and little being formed and exercised in holy love, they are imperceptibly changed. In lieu of loving God in order to please God, they begin to love him for the pleasure they take in the exercises of holy love; and instead of falling in love with God they fall in love with the love they bear him, and stand affected to their own affections. They no longer take pleasure in God, but in the pleasure they find in his love. They content themselves with this love as being their own, in their spirit and proceeding from it : for though this sacred love be called the love of God because God is loved by it, yet it is also ours, because we are the lovers that love. And it is thus we make the change; for instead of loving this holy love because it tends to God who is the beloved, we love it because it proceeds from us who are the lovers. Now who does not see that in so doing we do not seek God, but turn home to ourselves, loving the love instead of loving the beloved ? Loving, I say, the love, not by reason of God's good-pleasure and liking, but for the pleasure and content we draw from it. This chaunter who in the beginning sang to God and for God, now rather sings to himself and for himself than for God; and the pleasure he takes in singing is not so much to please God's ear as his own. And forasmuch as the canticle of Divine love is of all the most excellent, he also loves it better, not by reason of the Divine excellence which is exalted therein, but because its music is more delicious and agreeable.

CHAPTER X.

MEANS TO DISCOVER WHEN WE CHANGE IN THE MATTER OF THIS HOLY LOVE.

You may easily discover this, Theotimus; for if this mystical nightingale sing to please God, she will sing the song which she knows to be most grateful to the Divine Providence, but if she sing for the delight which she herself takes in her melodious song, she will not sing the canticle which is most agreeable to the heavenly goodness, but that which she herself likes best, and from which she expects to draw the most contentment. Of two canticles which are both divine, it may well be that one may be sung because it is divine, and the other because it is pleasing. Rachel and Lia are equally wife of Jacob, but he loves one only in the quality of wife, the other in quality of beautiful. The canticle is divine, but the motive which moves us to sing it is the spiritual delectation which we expect from it.

Do you not see, we may say to a bishop, that God wills you to sing the pastoral song of his love among your flock, which, in virtue of holy love, he thrice commands you (in the person of S. Peter, the first of pastors) to feed? What is your answer? That at Rome or Paris there are more spiritual pleasures, and that there one may practise Divine love with more sweetness. O God! it is not then to please thee that this man desires to sing, it is for the pleasure he takes in it; it is not thou he seeks in his love, but the contentment which he receives in the exercises of this holy love. Religious men would sing the pastors' song, and married people that of religious, in order, as they say, to be able to love and serve God better. Ah! you deceive yourselves my dear friends: do not say that it is to love and serve God better: Oh no, no, indeed! It is to serve your own satisfaction better, you prefer this before God's. God's will is as much in sickness as in health, and ordinarily almost more so; wherefore if we love health better, let us never say that this is in order to serve God the better, for who sees not that it is health that we look for in God's will, not God's will in health.

It is hard, I confess, to behold long together and with delight the beauty of a mirror without casting an eye upon ourself, yea, without taking a complacency in ourself; yet there is a difference between the pleasure which we take in beholding the beauty of the mirror, and the complacency we take in seeing ourself in it. It is also without doubt very hard to love God and not withal love the pleasure which we take in his love, yet there is a notable difference between the pleasure which we take in loving God because he is beautiful, and that which we take in loving him because his love is agreeable to us. Now our task must be to seek in God only the love of his beauty, not the pleasure which is in the beauty of his love. He who in praying to God notices that he is praying, is not perfectly attentive to his prayer, for he diverts his attention from God to whom he prays, and turns it upon the prayer by which he prays. The very solicitude we have not to be distracted causes oftentimes a very great distraction; simplicity in spiritual actions is most to be commended. If you wish to contemplate God, contemplate him then, and that attentively: if you reflect and bring your eyes backwards upon yourself, to see how you look when you look upon him, it is not now he that you behold but your own behaviour —your self. He who prays fervently knows not whether he prays or not, for he is not thinking of the prayer which he makes but of God to whom he makes it. He that is in the heat of sacred love, does not turn his heart back upon himself to see what he is doing, but keeps it set and bent upon God to whom he applies his love. The heavenly chaunter takes such pleasure in pleasing God, that he has no pleasure in the melody of his voice, except in so far as God is pleased by it.

Why, Theotimus, did Amnon the son of David love Thamar so desperately that he even thought he should die of love? Do you think that it was she herself that he loved? You soon see it was not. Look at this man who prays, apparently, with such great devotion, and is so ardent in the practice of heavenly love. But stay a little, and you will discover whether it be God indeed whom he loves. Alas! as soon as the delight and satisfaction which he took in love departs, and dryness comes, he will stop short, and only casually pray. If it had been God

indeed whom he loved, why should he cease loving him, since
God is ever God? It was therefore the consolations of God
that he loved, not the God of consolation. In truth there are
many who take no delight in divine love unless it be candied in
the sugar of some sensible sweetness, and they would willingly
act like children, who, if they have a little honey spread upon
their bread, lick and suck off the honey, casting the bread away;
for if the delight could be separated from the love, they would
reject love and take the sweetness only. Wherefore as they
follow love for the sake of its sweetness, when they find not
this they make no account of love. But such persons are exposed to a great danger of either turning back as soon as they
miss their relish and consolations, or else of occupying themselves in vain sweetnesses, far remote from true love, and of
mistaking the honey of Heraclea for that of Narbonne.

CHAPTER XI.

OF THE PERPLEXITY OF A HEART WHICH LOVES WITHOUT KNOWING WHETHER IT PLEASES THE BELOVED.

THE musician of whom I have spoken having become deaf, had
no delight in his singing, save only that now and then he perceived his prince attentive to it and enjoying it. O how happy
is the heart that loves God without pretence of any other pleasure
than what it takes in pleasing God! For what more pure and
perfect pleasure can a soul ever take than that which is taken in
pleasing the Divinity? Yet this pleasure of pleasing God is not
properly Divine love, but the fruit thereof; which may be separated from it as the lemon from the lemon-tree. For, as I have
said, our musician always sang without reaping any contentment
from his song, because his deafness made him incapable of it:
and often also did he sing without having the pleasure of pleasing
his prince, who, after he had given him order to begin, would

withdraw, or go hunting, neither taking leisure nor pleasure to hear him.

While, O God, I see thy sweet face, which testifies unto me that thou art pleased in the song of my love, ah! how am I comforted. For is there any pleasure comparable to the pleasure of truly pleasing our God? But when thou turnest thine eyes from me, and I no longer perceive the sweet savour of the complacency which thou takest in my song—good God! what pangs my soul endures! But it ceases not, for all that, to love thee faithfully, or continually to sing the hymn of its dilection, not for any delight it finds therein, for it finds none at all, but for the pure love of thy will.

One may have seen a sick child bravely eat what his mother presents him (though with an incredible loathing) from the pure desire of giving her content. In this case he eats without taking any pleasure in his food, yet not without a pleasure of a higher order and value, which is the pleasure of pleasing his mother and of perceiving her content. But another who, without seeing his mother, from the mere knowledge he has of her desire, takes all that is sent him by her, eats without any pleasure at all. For he has neither the pleasure of eating, nor yet the contentment of seeing his mother pleased, but he eats purely and simply to do her will. The contentment of our prince present with us, or of any one whom we love tenderly, makes watchings, pains and labours delicious, and begets in us a love of peril: but nothing is so grievous as to serve a master who knows it not, or, if he know it, yet gives no sign that he is satisfied: love must be strong in such case, because it stands of itself, unsupported by any pleasure or any expectation.

So it comes to pass sometimes that we have no consolation in the exercises of holy love, because, like deaf singers, we hear not our own voices, nor enjoy the sweetness of our song; but on the contrary, besides this privation, are oppressed with a thousand fears, and frightened with a thousand false alarms which the enemy raises round about our heart; suggesting that perhaps we are not in grace with our master, and that our love is fruitless, yea, that it is false and vain, since it brings forth no comfort. And then, Theotimus, we labour not only without pleasure but with an exceeding distress, being neither able to discover the profit of our labours, nor the contentment of him for whom we labour.

But what in this case augments our trouble is that even the spirit and highest point of the reason cannot give any assuagement at all; for this poor superior portion of reason being beset round about with the suggestions of the enemy, is herself all troubled, and is fully engaged in keeping the guard, lest sin by surprise might get consent, so that she can make no sally to disengage the inferior part of her spirit, and although she has not lost heart, yet is she so desperately set at, that though she be free from fault yet is she not free from pain. Because, that her distress may be complete, she is deprived of the general consolation which ordinarily accompanies us through all the other calamities of this life, namely, the hope that they will not be of long continuance, but will have an end:—so that the heart in these spiritual distresses falls into a certain inability of thinking of their end, and consequently of being eased by hope. Faith indeed which resides in the supreme point of the spirit assures us that this trouble will have an end, and that one day we shall enjoy a true repose: but the loudness of the shouts and outcries which the enemy makes in the rest of the soul in the inferior reason, will scarcely permit the advice and remonstrances of faith to be heard; and there remains in the imagination only this sorrowful presage: Alas! joy I shall never have.

O God! my dear Theotimus, now it is that we are to show an invincible courage towards our Saviour, serving him purely for the love of his will, not only without pleasure, but amid this deluge of sorrows, horrors, distresses and assaults, as did his glorious Mother and St. John upon the day of his Passion. Amongst so many blasphemies, sorrows and deadly distresses, they remained constant in love, yea, even in that instant in which our Saviour, having withdrawn all his holy joy into the very summit of his spirit, left no joy or consolation at all in his Divine countenance, and when his eyes, languishing and covered with the dark veil of death, did only cast looks of sorrow, as the sun also shot forth rays of horror and frightful darkness.

CHAPTER XII.

HOW THE SOUL AMIDST THESE INTERIOR ANGUISHES KNOWS NOT
THE LOVE SHE BEARS TO GOD: AND OF THE MOST LOVE-
FULL DEATH OF THE WILL.

THE night before the great S. Peter was to suffer martyrdom,
an angel came to the prison and filled it with splendour, awoke
S. Peter, made him arise, made him gird himself, and put on his
shoes and clothes, freed him from his bonds and shackles, drew
him out of prison, and led him through the first and second
guard, till he came to the iron gate which gave on the town;
this of itself flew open before them, and having passed through
one street, the angel left the glorious S. Peter there in full
liberty. Behold a great variety of very corporeal actions, and
yet S. Peter, who was awake from the beginning, did not apprehend that what was done by the angel was done in deed, but
esteemed it a vision of the imagination. He was awake and yet
did not think so, he put on his clothes and shoes not knowing
that he had done it, he walked and yet thought he walked not,
he was delivered and believed it not, and all this because the
wonder of his deliverance was so great, and it engaged his heart
in such sort, that though he had sense and knowledge enough
to do what he did, yet had he not enough to discover that he did
it really and in good earnest. He saw indeed the angel, but he
did not discern that it was with a true and natural vision,
wherefore he took no consolation in his delivery till such time
as, coming to himself: *Now,* said he, *I know in very deed that
the Lord hath sent his Angel, and hath delivered me out of the hand
of Herod, and from all the expectation of the people of the Jews.**

Now, Theotimus, after the same manner it fares with a soul
which is overcharged with interior anguishes; for although she
has the power to believe, to trust, and to love her God, and in
reality does so, yet she has not the strength to see properly
whether she believes, hopes and loves, because her distress so

* Acts xii. 11.

engages her, and makes head against her so desperately, that she
can get no time to return into her interior and see what is going
on there.   And hence she thinks that she has no faith, nor
hope, nor charity, but only the shadows and fruitless impressions
of those virtues, which she feels in a manner without feeling
them, and as if foreign, instead of natural, to her soul.   And, if
you notice, you will find our souls always in this state when
they are strongly occupied by some violent passion, for they
perform many actions as though they were in a dream, with so
little sense of what they do that they can scarcely believe the
things actually happen.   Hence the sacred Psalmist expresses
the greatness of the consolation of the Israelites on their return
from the captivity of Babylon in these words: *When the Lord
brought back the captivity of Sion, we became like men comforted.**
And as the holy Latin version, following the Septuagint, has it:
facti sumis " sicut" consolati : that is, our wonder at the greatness of the good which came to us was so excessive, that it
hindered us from properly feeling the consolation which we
received, and it seemed to us that we were not truly comforted, nor had consolation in real truth, but only in a figure
and a dream.

Such then are the feelings of the soul which is in the midst
of spiritual anguishes.   These do exceedingly purify and refine
love, for being deprived of all pleasure by which its love might
be attached to God, it joins and unites us to God immediately,
will to will, heart to heart, without any intervention of satisfaction or desire.   Alas! Theotimus, how the poor heart is
afflicted when being as it were abandoned by love, she seeks
everywhere, and yet seems not to find it.   She finds it not in
the exterior senses, they not being capable of it; nor in the
imagination, which is cruelly tortured by conflicting impressions;
nor in the understanding, distracted with a thousand obscurities
of strange reasonings and fears; and though at length she finds
it in the top and supreme region of the spirit where it resides,
yet the soul does not recognize it, and thinks it is not love,
because the greatness of the distress and darkness hinders her

* Ps. cxxv. 1.

from perceiving its sweetness. She sees it without seeing it, meets it but does not know it, as though all passed in a dream only, or in a type. In this way Magdalen, having met with her dear Master, received no comfort from him, because she thought that it was not he indeed, but the gardener only.

But what is the soul to do that finds herself in this case? Theotimus, she knows not how to behave herself amidst so much anguish; nor has she any power save to let her will die in the hands of God's will; imitating her sweet Jesus, who being arrived at the height of the pains of the cross which his Father had ordained, and not being able any further to resist the extremity of his torments, did as the hart does,—which when it is run out of breath, and oppressed by the hounds, yielding itself up into the huntsman's hands, its eyes filled with tears, utters its last cries. For so this Divine Saviour, near unto his death, and giving up his last breath with a loud voice and abundance of tears—Alas! said he, *O Father, into thy hands I commit my spirit :*—a word, Theotimus, which was his very last, and the one by which the well-beloved Son gave the sovereign testimony of his love towards his Father. When therefore all fails us, when our troubles have come to their extremity, this word, this disposition, this rendering up of our soul into our Saviour's hands, can never fail us. The Son commended his spirit to his Father in this his last and incomparable anguish, and we, when the convulsions of spiritual pains shall bereave us of all other sort of solace and means of resistance, let us commend our spirit into the hands of this eternal Son who is our true Father, and bowing the head of our acquiescence in his good pleasure, let us make over our whole will unto him.

CHAPTER XIII.

HOW THE WILL BEING DEAD TO ITSELF LIVES ENTIRELY IN GOD'S WILL.

WE speak with a singular propriety of a man's death in our French tongue, for we call it an *overpassing (trèspas)* and the dead *the overpassers*, intimating that death amongst men is but a passing over from one life to another, and that to die is no other thing but to overpass the confines of this mortal life, to enter the immortal.   True it is, our will can no more die than our soul, yet does it sometimes go out of the limits of its ordinary life, to live wholly in the Divine will.   This is when it neither wills nor cares to desire any thing at all, but gives itself over totally and without reserve to the good pleasure of the Divine Providence, so mingling and saturating itself with this good pleasure, that itself is seen no more, but is all hidden with Jesus Christ in God, where it lives, not it, but the will of God lives in it.

What becomes of the light of the stars when the sun appears on our horizon?   Certainly it perishes not, but it is ravished into and absorbed in the sun's sovereign light, with which it is happily mingled and allied; and what becomes of man's will when it is entirely delivered up to God's pleasure?   It does not altogether perish, yet is it so lost and dispersed in the will of God that it appears not, and has no other will than the will of God.   Consider, Theotimus, the glorious and never sufficiently praised S. Louis, embarking and setting sail for beyond seas: and see the queen, his dear wife, embarking with his majesty. Now if any one had asked of this brave princess : Madam, whither are you going?   She would without doubt have replied, I go whither the king goes.—And if further asked : But do you know, Madam, whither the king goes?   She would also have made answer : He told me in general ; however, I care not for knowing, I only desire to accompany him.—And if one had replied : Why then, Madam, you have no design in this journey ? No, would she have said, I have none, except to be with my dear sovereign and husband.—Well then, it might have been said to her, he goes into Egypt to pass into Palestine; he will stay at Damietta, Acre, and many places besides,—do not you intend, Madam, to go thither also? To this she would have made answer : No, in truth, I have no intention save only to keep myself near my king ; as for the places whither he goes, they are all indifferent to me, and of no consideration whatever, except so far as he will be in them; for I have no affection for anything but the king's presence : it is therefore the king that goes, it is he that designs the journey, but, as for me, I do not go, I only follow : I desire not the journey, but solely the presence of the king ; the staying, the journeying, and all their circumstances being utterly indifferent to me.

Surely if we ask some servant who is in his master's train whither he is going, he ought not to answer that he is going to such a place, but simply that he follows his master, for he goes nowhere of his own accord, but at his master's pleasure only. In like manner, Theotimus, a will perfectly resigned to God's should have no will of its own, but simply follow that of God. And as he who is on ship does not move by his own motion, but leaves himself to be moved by the motion of the vessel in which he is, so the heart that is embarked in the Divine pleasure, ought to have no other will than that of permitting itself to be conducted by the Divine will. And then the heart does not as before say : *Thy will be done, not mine :*—for there is now no will to be renounced ; but it utters these words : *Lord I commend my will into thy hands,*—even as though it had not its will at its own disposition, but at the disposition of the Divine Providence. So that it is not exactly as with servants who follow their masters, for, in their case, although the journey be undertaken at their master's pleasure, yet their following comes from their own particular will, though a will following and serving, submitted and subjected to, that of their master : so that as the master and servant are two, the will of the master and the will of the servant are also two. But the will which is dead to herself that she may live in that of God, is without any particular will, remaining not only in conformity and subjection, but quite annihilated in herself, and cemented into God's, as one might speak of a little child who has not yet got the use of his will to love or desire anything save the bosom and face of his dear mother. For he does not think of willing to be on one side or on the other, or of anything else, except only to be in the arms of his mother, with whom he thinks himself to be one thing. He never troubles himself as to how he shall conform his will to his mother's, for he perceives not his own, nor does he think he has any, leaving all the care to his mother, to go, to do, and to will, what she judges profitable for him.

It is truly the highest perfection of our will to be thus united to that of our sovereign good, as was that saint's who said : *O Lord, thou hast conducted* and led me *at thy will.** For what did he mean but that he had made no use of his will to conduct himself, letting himself simply be led and guided by that of God.

CHAPTER XIV.

AN EXPLANATION OF WHAT HAS BEEN SAID TOUCHING THE DECEASE OF OUR WILL.

WE may well believe that the most sacred Virgin Our Lady received so much pleasure in carrying her little Jesus in her arms, that delight beguiled weariness, or at least made it agreeable; for if a branch of *agnus castus* can solace and unweary travellers, what solace did not the glorious Mother receive in carrying the immaculate Lamb of God? And though she permitted him now and then to run on foot by her, she holding him by the hand, yet this was not because she would not rather have had him hanging about her neck and on her breast, but it was to teach him to form his steps and walk alone. And we ourselves, Theotimus, as little children of the heavenly Father, may walk with him in two ways. For we may, in the first place, walk with the steps of our own will which we conform to

* Ps. lxxii. 24.

his, holding always with the hand of our obedience the hand of his divine intention, and following it wheresoever it leads,— which is what God requires from us by the signification of his will; for since he wills me to do what he ordains, he wills me to have the will to do it : God has signified that he wills me to keep holy the day of rest; since he wills me to do it, he wills then that I will to do it, and that for this end I should have a will of my own, by which I follow his, conforming myself and corresponding to his. But we may on other occasions walk with our Saviour without any will of our own, letting ourselves simply be carried at his divine good pleasure, as a little child in its mother's arms, by a certain kind of consent which may be termed union or rather unity of our heart with God's;—and this is the way that we are to endeavour to comport ourselves in God's will of good-pleasure, since the effects of this will of good-pleasure proceed purely from his Providence, and we do not effect them, but they happen to us. True it is we may will them to come according to God's will, and this willing is excellent; yet we may also receive the events of heaven's good pleasure by a most simple tranquillity of our will, which, willing nothing whatever, simply acquiesces in all that God would have done in us, on us, or by us.

If one had asked the sweet Jesus when he was carried in his mother's arms, whither he was going, might he not with good reason have answered : I go not, 'tis my mother that goes for me : And if one had said to him : But at least do you not go with your mother ? might he not reasonably have replied : No, I do not go, or if I go whither my mother carries me, I do not myself walk with her nor by my own steps, but by my mother's, by her, and in her : But if one had persisted with him, saying : But at least, O most dear divine child, you really will to let yourself be carried by your sweet mother ? No verily, might he have said, I will nothing of all this, but as my entirely good mother walks for me so she wills for me; I leave her the care as well to go as to will to go for me where she likes best; and as I go not but by her steps, so I will not but by her will; and from the instant I find myself in her arms, I give no attention either to willing or not willing, turning all other cares over to my mother, save only the care to be on her bosom, to suck her sacred breast, and to keep myself close clasped to her most beloved neck, that I may most lovingly kiss her with the kisses of my mouth. And be it known to you that while I am amidst the delights of these holy caresses which surpass all sweetness, I consider that my mother is a tree of life, and myself on her as its fruit; that I am her own heart in her breast, or her soul in the midst of her heart, so that as her going serves both her and me without my troubling myself to take a single step, so her will serves us both without my producing any act of my will about going or coming. Nor do I ever take notice whether she goes fast or slow, hither or thither, nor do I inquire whither she means to go, contenting myself with this, that go whither she please I go still locked in her arms, close laid at her beloved breasts, where I feed as amongst lilies. O divine child of Mary! Permit my poor soul these outbursts of love : Go then so, O most amiable dear little babe, or rather go not but stay, thus holily fastened to your sweet mother's breast; go always in her and never without her, while thou remainest a child! O *how blessed is the womb that bore thee, and the breasts that gave thee suck !** The Saviour of our souls had the use of reason from the instant of his conception in his Mother's womb, and could make all this discourse; so could even the glorious S. John his forerunner, from the day of the holy Visitation, and though both of them, as well in that time as all through their infancy, were possessed of liberty to will or not to will, yet, in what concerned their external conduct, they left to their mothers the care of doing and willing for them what was requisite.

Thus should we be, Theotimus, pliable and tractable to God's good-pleasure, as though we were of wax, not giving our thoughts leave to wander in wishing and willing things, but leaving God to will and do them for us as he pleases, *throwing upon him all our solicitude, because he hath care of us,*† as the holy Apostle says : and note that he says *all our solicitude*, that is, as well that which concerns the events, as that which pertains to willing or not willing, for he will have a care of the issue of our affairs, and of willing that which is best for us.

* Luke xi. 27. † 1 Pet. v. 7.

Meanwhile let us affectionately give our attention to blessing God in all his works, after the example of Job, saying : *The Lord gave and the Lord hath taken away, the name of the Lord be blessed!** No, Lord ; I will no events, for I leave you to will them for me at your pleasure, but instead of willing the events I will bless you because you have willed them.   O Theotimus ! what an excellent employment of our will is this, when it gives up the care of willing and choosing the effects of God's good-pleasure in order to praise and thank this good-pleasure for such effects.

CHAPTER XV.

OF THE MOST EXCELLENT EXERCISE WE CAN MAKE IN THE INTERIOR
AND EXTERIOR TROUBLES OF THIS LIFE, AFTER ATTAINING THE
INDIFFERENCE AND DEATH OF THE WILL.

To bless and thank God in all the events that his providence ordains, is in very deed a most holy exercise, yet if, while we leave the care to God of willing and doing in us, on us, and with us, what pleases him, without attending to what passes—though fully feeling it—we could divert our heart, and apply our attention to the divine goodness and sweetness—blessing it not in the effects or events it ordains, but in itself and in its own excellence—we should certainly practise a far more eminent exercise.   In the time that Demetrius was laying siege to Rhodes, Protogenes, who was in a little house in the suburbs, ceased not to work, and that with such assurance and repose of mind that though the enemies' sword was in a manner always at his throat, yet he executed the grand masterpiece and admirable representation of a Satyr amusing himself with playing upon a pipe.   O God ! how great are those souls who in all kinds of accidents keep their affections and attention ever upon the eternal goodness, honouring and loving it at all times.

* Job i. 21.

The daughter of an excellent physician and surgeon, being in a continual fever, and knowing that her father loved her entirely, said to one of her friends : I feel very great pain, but I do not think of remedies, for I do not know what might serve for my cure; I might desire one thing, and another be necessary for me. Do I not then gain more by leaving this care to my father, who knows, who can do, and who wills for me, all that is required for my health ? I should do wrong by willing anything, for he wills all that could be profitable to me. I will only wait to let him will to do what is expedient, and when he comes to me I will only look at him, testify my filial love for him, and show my perfect confidence. And on these words she fell asleep. Meanwhile her father, judging that it was fit to bleed her, disposed all that was necessary, and waking her up asked her if she were willing to suffer the operation. My father, she said, I am yours; I know not what to will for my cure; it is yours to will and do for me what seems good to you; it is enough for me to love and honour you with all my heart, as I do. So her arm is tied, and her father himself opens the vein. And while the blood flows, this loving daughter looks not at her arm nor at the spurting blood, but keeping her eyes fixed on her father's face, she says only, from time to time : My father loves me, and I, I am entirely his. And when all was done she did not thank him, but only repeated her words of filial confidence and love.

Now tell me, my friend Theotimus, did not this daughter show a more attentive and solid love for her father, than if she had taken great care to ask remedies for her malady, to watch the vein being opened, and the blood coming, and to say many words of thanks ? There is no doubt whatever about it. What could she have gained save useless solicitude by thinking for herself, since her father had care enough of her ; what but fear by looking at her arm ; and what virtue but gratitude would she have shown in thanking her father ? Did she not do best then in occupying herself entirely in the demonstration of her filial love, infinitely more agreeable to her father than every other virtue ?

My eyes are ever towards the Lord ; for he shall pluck my feet *out of the snare* and the nets.*   Have you fallen into the net of adversity?   Ah! look not upon your mishap, nor upon the snare in which you are taken : look upon God and leave all to him, he will have care of you : *Cast thy care upon the Lord and he shall sustain thee.*†   Why do you trouble yourself with willing or not willing the events and accidents of this world, since you are ignorant what were best for you to will, and since God will always will for you, without your putting yourself in trouble, all you could will for yourself?   Await therefore in peace of mind the effects of the divine pleasure, and let his willing suffice you, since it is always most good : for so he gave order to his well-beloved S. Catharine of Siena : Think in me, said he to her, and I will think for you.

It is very difficult to express exactly this extreme indifference of the human will, thus absorbed and dead in the will of God. For, meseems, we must not say it acquiesces in that of God, because acquiescence is an act of the soul which declares its consent.   We must not say it accepts or receives, because accepting and receiving are a sort of actions, which we might call in a certain sense passive actions, by which we embrace and take what happens : we must not say that it permits, as even permission is an act of the will, and hence is a certain inactive willing, which does not do and yet lets be done.   It seems to me the soul which is in this indifference, and which wills nothing, but lets God will what pleases him, should be said to have its will in a simple and general state of waiting (*attente*) : since waiting is not a doing or acting, but only the remaining prepared for some event.   And, if you take notice, this waiting of the soul is indeed voluntary, and yet it is not an action, but a simple disposition to receive whatsoever shall happen ; and as soon as the events come and are received, the waiting changes into consent or acquiescence, but, before they happen, the soul is truly in a state of simple waiting, indifferent to all that it shall please the divine will to ordain.

Our Saviour thus expresses the extreme submission of his human will to the will of his Eternal Father.   *The Lord God,*

* Ps. xxiv. 15.   † Ps. liv. 23.

he says, *hath opened my ear*, that is, he hath declared unto me his pleasure touching the multitude of the pains which I am to endure, and *I*, says he afterwards, *do not resist : I have not gone back.** What does this mean : *I do not resist : I have not gone back*, except this ? My will is in a simply waiting state, and is ready for all that God shall send; wherefore *I have given my body to the strikers, and my cheeks to them that plucked them : I have not turned away my face from them that rebuked me and spit upon me;* being prepared to let them exercise their pleasure upon me. But mark, I pray you, Theotimus, that even as our Saviour, after he had made his prayer of resignation in the garden of Olives, and after he was taken, left himself to be handled and dragged about at the will of them that crucified him, by an admirable surrender made of his body and life into their hands, so did he resign up his soul and will by a most perfect indifference into his Eternal Father's hands. For though he cries out : *My God, my God, why hast Thou forsaken me ?*— yet this was to let us understand the reality of the anguish and bitternesses of his soul, and not to detract from the most holy indifference in which it was ; as he showed very soon afterwards, concluding all his life and his passion with those incomparable words : *Father, into Thy hands I commend my spirit.*

CHAPTER XVI.

OF THE PERFECT STRIPPING OF THE SOUL WHICH IS UNITED TO GOD'S WILL.

LET us represent to ourselves, Theotimus, the sweet Jesus in Pilate's house, where for love of us he was divested of all his garments one after the other, by the soldiers, the ministers of death. And not content with that, they took his skin from him, tearing it with the blows of rods and whips; then afterwards his soul was bereft of his body, and his body of life, by the death which he endured upon the cross. But three days being

* Is. l. 5, 6.

run out, his soul, by the most holy Resurrection, put on again its glorious body, and his body its immortal skin, wearing sundry garments, now those of a gardener, now of a pilgrim, or other guise according as the salvation of man and the glory of God required. Love did all this, Theotimus, and it is love also which, entering into a soul to make it happily die to itself and live to God, bereaves it of all human desires, and of self-esteem which is as closely fixed to the spirit as the skin to the flesh, and strips her at length of her best beloved affections, such as those which she had to spiritual consolations, exercises of piety and the perfection of virtues, which seemed to be the very life of the soul.

Then, Theotimus, the soul may by good right cry out: *I have put off my garment, how shall I* find in my heart *to put it on? I have washed my feet,* from all sorts of affections, *how shall I defile them?* Naked came I out* of the hand of God, *and naked shall I return thither:* God gave me many desires and God hath taken them away: *As it hath pleased the Lord, so is it done: blessed be the name of the Lord.†* Yes, Theotimus, the same God who made us desire virtues in our beginning, and who makes us practise them on all occurrences, he it is that takes from us the affection to virtues and all spiritual exercises, that with more tranquillity, purity and simplicity, we should care for nothing but the divine Majesty's good pleasure. For as the fair and chaste Judith reserved indeed her costly festal robes in her cabinet, and yet placed not her affection upon them, nor yet ever wore them in the time of her widowhood, save only when by God's inspiration she went to overthrow Holofernes, so, though we have learnt the practice of virtue and the exercises of devotion, yet are we not to give our affection to them nor clothe our heart again with them, save only as far as we know that such is the good pleasure of God. Judith always wore mourning weeds except only on this occasion when God's will was that she should be in pomp; so are we peaceably to remain vested with our misery and abjection amidst our imperfections and infirmities, till God shall exalt us to the practice of excellent actions.

* Cant. v. 3. † Job i. 21.

We cannot long remain in this nakedness, despoiled of all sorts of affections. Wherefore, following the advice of the holy Apostle, as soon as we have put off the garments of the old Adam, we are to put on the habits of the new man, that is to say of Jesus Christ, for having renounced all,—yes, even the affection to virtues, neither desiring of these nor of other things a larger portion than God's will intends,—we must put on again divers affections, and perhaps the very same which we have renounced and resigned : but we must now put them on again not because they are agreeable, profitable, honourable to us, and proper to content the love we have for ourselves, but because they are agreeable to God, profitable to his honour, and destined to his glory.

Eliezer carried ear-jewels, bracelets and new attire for the maid whom God had provided for his master's son, and in effect he presented them to the virgin Rebecca, as soon as he knew it was she. New garments are required for our Saviour's spouse. If for the love of God she has stript herself of the ancient affection which she had to parents, country, home, friends, she must take quite new affections, loving all this in its order, not now according to human considerations, but because the heavenly spouse wills, commands, and intends it so, and has established this order in charity. If we have once put off our old affection to spiritual consolations, to exercises of devotion, to the practice of virtues, yea to our own advancement in perfection, we must put on another affection quite new, by loving all these graces and heavenly favours, not because they perfect and adorn our spirit, but because our Saviour's name is sanctified in them, his kingdom advanced, his good-pleasure glorified.

So did S. Peter vest himself in the prison, not at his own choice but at the angel's command. He puts on his girdle, then his sandals, and afterwards the rest of his garments. And the glorious S. Paul, stripped in a moment of all affections: *Lord,* said he, *what wilt thou have me do?* that is, what is it thy pleasure for me to love, now that throwing me to the ground thou hast made my own will to die? Ah! Lord, plant thy good-pleasure in the place of it, and, *teach me to do thy will, for thou art my God.** Theotimus, he who has forsaken all for God ought to resume nothing but according to God's good-pleasure. He feeds not his body but according to God's ordinance that it may be serviceable to the spirit; he only engages in studies in order to assist his neighbour and his own soul, according to the divine intention; he practises virtues not as being his own choice, but according to God's desire.

God commanded the prophet Isaias to strip himself naked; and he did so,† going and preaching in this way, for three days together as some hold, or for three years as others think, and then, the time prefixed by God having expired, he resumed his clothes. Even so are we to strip ourselves of all affections little and great, as also to make a frequent examination of our hearts to discover whether it be willing to divest itself, as Isaias did, of all its garments: then we must take up again, at proper times, the affections suitable to the service of charity, to the end that we may die with Our Saviour naked upon the cross, and rise again with him in newness of life. *Love is strong as death*‡ to make us quit all, it is magnificent as the Resurrection, to adorn us with honour and glory.

* Ps. cxlii. 10.   † Is. xx. 2.   ‡ Cant. viii. 6.

BOOK X.

OF THE

COMMANDMENT OF LOVING GOD ABOVE ALL THINGS.

———•◆•———

CHAPTER I.

OF THE SWEETNESS OF THE COMMANDMENT WHICH GOD HAS
GIVEN US OF LOVING HIM ABOVE ALL THINGS.

MAN is the perfection of the universe; the spirit is the perfection of man; love, that of the spirit; and charity, that of
love. Wherefore the love of God is the end, the perfection and
the excellence of the universe. In this, Theotimus, consists the
greatness and the primacy of the commandment of divine love,
which the Saviour calls *the first and greatest commandment.* This
commandment is as a sun which gives lustre and dignity to all
the sacred laws, to all the divine ordinances, and to all the Holy
Scriptures. All is done for this heavenly love, and all has reference to it. From the sacred tree of this commandment grow
all the counsels, exhortations, inspirations, and the other commandments, as its flowers, and eternal life as its fruit; and all
that does not tend to eternal love tends to eternal death. Grand
Commandment, the perfect fulfilment of which lasts through
eternal life, yea, is no other thing but eternal life!

But look, Theotimus, how amiable is this law of love. Ah!
Lord God, was it not enough for thee to permit us this divine
love, as Laban permitted Jacob that of Rachel, without the
necessity of inviting us to it by exhortations, or driving us to it

by commandments? But no, divine goodness, in order that neither thy greatness, nor our vileness, nor any pretext whatever should keep us from loving thee, thou dost command it to us. The poor Apelles, not able to keep from loving the beautiful Campaspe, yet dared not love her because she belonged to the great Alexander; but when he had leave to love her, how greatly obliged did he consider himself to him who gave this leave to him! He knew not whether he should more love that beautiful Campaspe whom so great an emperor had given up to him, or that great emperor who had given him so beautiful a Campaspe. Oh! if we were able to comprehend it, my dear Theotimus, what obligation should we have to this sovereign good, who not only permits but even commands us to love him! Ah! my God, I know not whether I ought more to love thine infinite beauty which so great a goodness orders me to love, or thy divine goodness which orders me to love so infinite a beauty! O beauty, how amiable thou art, being bestowed upon me by a goodness so immense! O goodness, how amiable thou art, in communicating unto me so eminent a beauty!

God at the Day of Judgment will imprint in the souls of the damned the knowledge of their loss, in a wondrous manner: for the divine majesty will make them clearly see the sovereign beauty of his face, and the treasures of his goodness; and at the sight of this abyss of infinite delights, the will with an extreme effort will desire to cast itself upon him, to be united unto him and enjoy his love. But all in vain, for it shall be as a woman, who in the pangs of childbirth, after having endured violent pains, cruel convulsions, and intolerable pangs, dies in the end without being delivered. For as soon as the clear and fair knowledge of the divine beauty shall have penetrated the understandings of those unhappy spirits, the divine justice shall in such sort deprive the will of its strength that it will be in no wise able to love this object which the understanding purposes to it, and represents to be so amiable; and the sight which should beget in the will so great a love, instead thereof shall engender an infinite sadness. This shall be made eternal by the memory of the sovereign beauty they saw, which shall for ever live in these lost souls; a memory void of all good, yea full of trouble, pains, torments and undying despair, because at the same time there shall be found in the will an impossibility of loving, yea a frightful and everlasting aversion and repugnance to loving this excellence so desirable. Thus the miserable damned shall live for ever in despairing rage—to know so sovereignly amiable a perfection, without being able ever to have the enjoyment or the love of it, because while they might have loved it they would not : they shall burn with a thirst so much the more violent as the remembrance of this fountain of waters of eternal life shall more inflame their ardour : they shall die immortally, *as dogs*,* of a famine as much more vehement, as their memory shall more sharpen its insatiable cruelty by the remembrance of the banquet of which they are deprived. *The wicked shall see, and shall be angry, he shall gnash with his teeth and pine away : the desire of the wicked shall perish.*† I would not indeed affirm for certain, that the view of God's beauty which the damned shall have, like a flash of lightning, will be as bright as that of the Blessed ; but still it will be clear enough to let them see *the Son of man in his majesty.*‡ *They shall look on him whom they pierced ;*§ and by the view of this glory shall learn the greatness of their loss. Ah ! if God had forbidden man to love him, what a torment would that have been to generous hearts ! What efforts would they not make to obtain permission to love him ? David braved the hazard of a most severe combat to gain the King's daughter,—and what did not Jacob do to espouse Rachel, and the Prince of Sichem to have Dina in marriage ? The damned would repute themselves blessed if they could entertain a hope of ever loving God : and the Blessed would esteem themselves damned, if they thought they could ever be deprived of this sacred love.

O good God ! Theotimus, how delicious is the sweetness of this commandment, seeing that if it pleased the divine will to give it to the damned, they would in a moment be delivered from their greatest misery, and seeing that the Blessed are only blessed by the practice of it ! O heavenly love, how lovely art

---

* Ps. lviii. 7.   † Ps. cxi. 10.   ‡ Matt. xxiv. 30.
§ John xix. 37.

thou to our souls! And blessed be the goodness of God for ever, who so earnestly commands us to love him, though this love is so desirable and so necessary to our happiness that without it we can but be miserable!

———

CHAPTER II.

THAT THIS DIVINE COMMANDMENT OF LOVE TENDS TO HEAVEN, YET IS GIVEN TO THE FAITHFUL IN THIS WORLD.

IF *the law is not made for the just man,** because, preventing the law and without the pressure of the law, he performs God's will by the instinct of charity which reigns in his soul; how free and exempt from all commandments must we consider the Blessed in Paradise to be, since from their enjoyment of the sovereign beauty and goodness of the well-beloved, a most sweet yet inevitable necessity in their spirits of loving eternally the most holy divinity, flows and proceeds. We shall love God in heaven, Theotimus, not as being tied and obliged by the law, but as being allured and ravished by the joy which this object, so perfectly worthy of love, shall yield to our hearts. Then the force of the commandment will cease, in order to give place to the force of contentment, which shall be the fruit and crown of the observance of the commandment. We are therefore destined to the contentment which is promised us in the immortal life, by this commandment which is given unto us in this mortal life, in which truly we are strictly bound to observe it, because it is the fundamental law which the King Jesus has given to the citizens of the militant Jerusalem, to make them merit the citizenship and joy of the triumphant Jerusalem.

There above in heaven we shall indeed have a heart quite free from passions, a soul purified from all distractions, a spirit liberated from contradictions, and powers exempt from opposition, and therefore we shall love God with a perpetual and never

* 1 Tim. i. 9.

interrupted affection, as it is said of those four living creatures, which, representing the Evangelists, continually praised the divinity, *not resting day or night.** O God! what joy, when, established in those eternal tabernacles, our spirits shall be in this perpetual movement, in which they shall enjoy the so much desired repose of their eternal loving. *Blessed are they that dwell in thy house, O Lord: they shall praise thee for ever and ever.*†

But we are not to expect this love so exceedingly perfect in this mortal life: for as yet we have neither the heart, nor the soul, nor the spirit, nor the forces of the Blessed. It is sufficient for us to love with all the heart and all the powers we have. While we are little children, we are wise like little children, we speak like little children, we love like little children, but when we shall come to our perfect growth, there above in heaven, we shall be freed from our state of infancy, and love God perfectly. Yet are we not for all this, Theotimus, during this infancy of our mortal life, to omit to do what in us lies according as we are commanded, since this is not only in our power, but is also very easy; the whole commandment being of love, and of the love of God, who as he is sovereignly good, so is he sovereignly amiable.

CHAPTER III.

HOW, WHILE THE WHOLE HEART IS EMPLOYED IN SACRED LOVE, YET ONE MAY LOVE GOD IN VARIOUS WAYS, AND ALSO MANY OTHER THINGS TOGETHER WITH HIM.

HE who says all, excludes nothing, and yet a man may be wholly God's, wholly his father's, wholly his mother's, wholly his prince's, wholly his commonwealth's, his children's, his friends': so that being all to each, yet he is all to all. This so happens because the duty by which a man is all to one, is not contrary to the duty by which a man is all to another.

* Apoc. **iv.**   † Ps. lxxxiii. 5.

Man gives himself wholly by love, and gives himself as much as he loves. He is therefore in a sovereign manner given to God when he loves the divine goodness sovereignly. And having once made this donation of himself, he is to love nothing that can remove his heart from God. Now never does any love take our hearts from God, save that which is contrary unto him.

Sara is not offended when she sees Ismael about her dear Isaac, so long as his play does not go on to striking and hurting the boy : and the divine goodness is not offended by seeing in us other loves besides his, so long as we preserve for him the reverence and submission due to him.

In heaven, Theotimus, God will truly give himself to us wholly, and not in part, since he is a whole that has no parts, yet will he give himself in different ways, and in as many different ways as there are blessed souls. This will so happen because, while giving himself all to all and all to each, he will never give himself wholly either to one in particular or to all in general. Now we shall give ourselves to him, according to the measure in which he gives himself to us : for we shall see him indeed face to face, as he is in his beauty ; and shall love him heart to heart, as he is in his goodness : yet all will not see him with an equal clearness, nor love him with an equal sweetness : but every one will see and love him, according to the particular measure of glory which the divine Providence has prepared for him. We shall all equally have the fulness of divine love, but still the fulnesses will be unequal in perfection. The honey of Narbonne is sweet, and so also is that of Paris : both of them are full of sweetness, but the one of a better, more delicate and richer sweetness : and though both of them are entirely sweet, yet neither contains all sweetness. I do homage to my sovereign prince, as also to my immediate superior : I engage then to each of them all my fealty, and I do not engage it to either of them totally : for in that which I give to the sovereign, I do not exclude that which I pay to the subaltern, and in that of the subaltern, I do not include that of the sovereign. Wherefore it is no wonder that, if in heaven (where these words, *Thou shalt love the Lord thy God with all thy heart*, shall be so excellently

practised) there are great differences in love, in this mortal life
there should be many.

Theotimus, among those who love God with all their heart
not only do some love him more and some less, but even one
and the same person often exceeds himself in this sovereign
exercise of loving God above all things.   Apelles did better one
time than another, sometimes he surpassed himself; for though
commonly he gave all his art and all his attention to painting
Alexander the Great, yet he did not always give them so totally
and entirely but that there remained other efforts to make, in
which he used not a greater art or a greater affection but used
them more actively and perfectly.   He always employed all his
genius to paint these pictures of Alexander well, because he used
it without reserve, yet sometimes he employed it more effectively
and happily.   Who knows not that in this holy love progress is
possible, and that the end of the Saints is crowned with a more
perfect love than their beginning ?

Now according to the expression of the holy Scriptures, to do
a thing with all one's heart means simply to do it with good
heart and without reserve.   *O Lord*, says David, *I have sought
thee with my whole heart.   I have cried with all my heart, O
Lord, hear me*,* and the holy Word testifies that he had truly
followed God with his whole heart ; and yet, notwithstanding
this, it affirms also of Ezechias, *that after him there was none like
him among all the kings of Judah*,† neither before nor after him,
that he was united to God and strayed not from him.   Afterwards treating of Josias it says that *there was no king before him
like unto him that returned to the Lord with all his heart, and
with all his soul, and with all his strength, according to all the
law of Moses, neither after him did there arise any like him.*‡
Mark then, I pray you, Theotimus, mark how David, Ezechias
and Josias, loved God with all their hearts, and yet not all three
equally, because no one of them had his like in this love, as the
sacred text says.   All three loved him, each of them with all his
heart ; yet, not one nor all together loved him totally, but each
one in his particular way ; so that as all the three were alike in

---

* Ps. cxviii.   † Kings xviii. 5.   ‡ Kings xxiii. 25.

this, that they gave each his whole heart, so were they unlike in their manner of giving it; yea, there is no doubt that David, to take him by himself, was far different from himself in this love; and that with his second *heart* which God *created* pure and *clean* in him, and with his *right spirit* which God *renewed* in his *bowels* by most holy penitence, he sang the canticle of his love far more melodiously than ever he had done with his first heart and his first spirit.

All true lovers are equal in this, that all give all their heart to God, and with all their strength, but they are unequal in this, that they give it diversely and in different manners, whence some give all their heart, with all their strength, less perfectly than others. This one gives it all by martyrdom, this, all by virginity, this, all by poverty, this, all by action, this, all by contemplation, this, all by the pastoral office; and whilst all give it all by the observance of the commandments, yet some give it with less perfection than others.

Yea, even Jacob who was called in Daniel the *holy one* of God,* and whom God declares himself to have loved, protests that he had served Laban with all his strength, and why did he serve Laban, but to obtain Rachel, whom he loved with all his strength? He serves Laban with all his strength, he serves God with all his strength; he loves Rachel with all his strength, he loves God with all his strength: yet withal he loves not Rachel as God, nor God as Rachel; he loves God as his God, above all things and more than himself; he loves Rachel as his wife, above all other women, and as himself. He loves God with an absolutely and sovereignly supreme love; and Rachel with a supreme nuptial love. Nor is the one love contrary to the other, since that of Rachel does not violate the privileges and sovereign prerogatives of the love of God.

So that our love to God, Theotimus, takes its worth from the eminence and excellence of the motive for which, and according to which, we love him; in that we love him for his sovereign infinite goodness, as God, and because he is God. Now one drop of this love is worth more, has more power, and deserves

---

* Dan. iii. 35.

more esteem, than all the other loves that can ever enter into the hearts of men or amongst the choirs of angels.   For while this love lives, it reigns and bears the sceptre over all the affections, making God to be preferred in its will before all things, indifferently, universally, and without reserve.

———

CHAPTER IV.

OF TWO DEGREES OF PERFECTION WITH WHICH THIS COMMANDMENT MAY BE KEPT IN THIS MORTAL LIFE.

WHILE the great King Solomon, possessing as yet the Spirit of God, was composing the sacred Canticle of Canticles, he had, according to the permission of those ages, a great variety of ladies and maidens attached to his service in different conditions and qualities.   For 1°. There was one, his singularly dear and wholly perfect one, most rare, as a singular dove, with whom the others entered not into comparison, and for this reason she was called by his own name, Sulamitess.*   2°. There were sixty, who, next to her, had the first rank of honour and estimation, and were called queens.   3°. There were, further, eighty ladies who were not indeed queens, but were in a recognized and honourable relation to him.   4°. There were young maidens without number, kept ready to be put in the place of the foregoing as was required.   Now under the figure of what passed in his palace, he described the various perfections of souls who in time to come were to adore, love and serve the great Pacific King Jesus Christ, our Saviour; amongst whom there are some, who being newly freed from their sins, and quite resolved to love God, are yet novices, apprentices, tender and feeble : so that they love indeed the divine sweetness, yet with such mixture of other affections that their sacred love being still as it were in its infancy, they love together with our Saviour, many superfluous, vain and dangerous things.   And as a phœnix newly hatched from out its ashes, having as yet but little, tender feathers and its first

* Spouse of Solomon [Tr.].

down, can only essay short flights, in which it should be said rather to leap than to fly; so these tender young souls, newly born from the ashes of their penance, cannot as yet soar on high, or fly in the broad air of sacred love, being held captives by the multitude of bad inclinations and evil habits which the sins of their past life have left them. Still they are living, they are animated with and possessed of love, yea and with true love too, else had they never forsaken sin; yet with a love still feeble and young, which, environed with a number of other loves, cannot produce fruit in such abundance as it would do if it had the full possession of the heart.

Such was the prodigal son, when, quitting the infamous company or the swine, amongst which he had lived, he returned into his father's arms, half-naked, unclean and bemired, and smelling most offensively of the filth which he had contracted in the company of those vile beasts. For what is it to forsake the swine, but to withdraw from sins? And what is it to return all ragged, tattered and unclean, but to have our affections engaged in the habits and inclinations which tend to sin? Yet still was he possessed of the life of the soul which is love; and as a phœnix rising out of its ashes, he found himself newly raised to life. *He was dead*, said his father, *and is come to life again*,* he has revived. And these souls are called young maidens in the Canticles, forasmuch as, having perceived the odour of the name of the beloved who breathes nothing but salvation and mercy, they love him with a true love, but a love, which is as themselves, in its tender youth. For even as young girls love their husbands properly if they have one, yet do not cease to greatly love rings and trifles, or their companions, with whom they amuse themselves extravagantly in playing, dancing and silliness, busying themselves with little birds, little dogs, squirrels and other such playthings;—so these young and novice-souls have truly an affection for the sacred lover, yet admit they with it a number of voluntary distractions and diversions : so that loving him above all things, they yet busy themselves in many things, which they love, not according to him but besides him, out of

* Luke xv. 32.

him, and without him. In truth, though little irregularities in words, in gestures, in apparel, in pastimes and follies, are not, properly speaking, against the will of God; yet are they not according to it, but out of it and without it.

But there are souls who, having already made some progress in the love of God, have also cut off all the love they had to dangerous things, and yet entertain dangerous and superfluous loves: because they love with excess, and with a love too tender and passionate, what God ordains they should love. It stood with God's pleasure that Adam should love Eve tenderly, yet not with such tenderness that, to content her, he should violate the order given him by his divine majesty. He loved not then a superfluous thing, nor a thing in itself dangerous, but he loved it superfluously and with danger. The love of our parents, friends and benefactors, is in itself according to God, yet we may love them with excess; as also our vocations, be they never so spiritual: our exercises also of devotion (which yet we ought so greatly to love) may be loved inordinately, as when we prefer them before obedience, or before a more general good; or when we love them as if they were our last end, while they are only means and furtherances to our final intention, which is the divine love. And these souls, who love nothing but what God would have them to love, and yet exceed in the manner of loving, love indeed the divine goodness above all things, yet not in all things: for the things, which, not only by permission but even by command, they are to love according to God, they love not only according to God, but for other causes and motives, which though indeed not contrary to God, yet are out of him. So that these souls resemble the phœnix, when, having got its first feathers and beginning to grow strong it already soars at large in the air, but has not yet strength enough to remain long on the wing, and often descends to earth to rest there. Such was the poor young man, who having from his tender age observed God's commandments, desired not his neighbour's goods, yet clung to his own over tenderly: so that when our Saviour counselled him to give them to the poor, he became sad and melancholy. He loved nothing but what he might lawfully love, yet he loved it with a superfluous and too attached a love.   It is plain, Theotimus, that these souls love too ardently and with superfluity; still, as they love not the superfluities, but only the thing, which may be loved, therefore they are entitled to the favours of the heavenly Solomon, namely, unions, recollections, and the repose of love, whereof we spoke in Books V. and VI.: but they do not enjoy them in quality of spouses, because the superfluity with which they love good things, hinders them from a frequent entry into these divine unions with the spouse; they are engaged in, and distracted by, loving that out of him and without him, which they ought not to love but in him and for him.

CHAPTER V.

OF TWO OTHER DEGREES OF GREATER PERFECTION, BY WHICH WE MAY LOVE GOD ABOVE ALL THINGS.

Now there are other souls who neither love superfluities, nor yet with superfluity, but love only that which God wills and as he wills :—blessed souls, who love God, their friends in God, and their enemies for God ; they love many things together with God, but none at all, save in God and for God : it is God that they love, not only above all things, but even in all things, and all things in God, resembling the phœnix when perfectly renewed in youth and strength, which is never seen but in the air, or upon the tops of mountains that are in high air : for so these souls love nothing but in God ; though indeed they love many things with God, and God with many things.   S. Luke recounts that our Saviour invited a young man to follow him, who indeed loved him dearly, but who had also a great affection for his father, and thereupon had a mind to return home to him.   But our Saviour cuts off this superfluity of love, and excites him to a love more pure, that he may not only love our Saviour more than his father, but not even love his father at all, but in our Saviour.   *Let the dead bury their dead: but* as for thee (who

hast met with life), *go thou, and preach the kingdom of God.**
And these souls, as you see, Theotimus, having so great a union
with the spouse, merit to share his rank, and to be queens, as he
is king; since they are entirely dedicated to him without any
division or separation, having no affections out of him, or without
him, but only in him and for him.

But, at last, above all these souls, there is yet one most only
one, who is the queen of queens, the most loving, the most
lovely, and the most beloved, of all the friends of the divine
beloved, who not only loves God above all things and in all
things, but also loves only God in all things, so that she loves
not many things, but one only thing, which is God himself. And
whereas it is God alone whom she loves in all that she loves,
she loves him indifferently in all things, according as his good-
pleasure may require, outside all things and without all things.
If it be only Esther that Assuerus loves, why should he love her
more when perfumed and adorned, than in her ordinary attire?
If it be my Saviour only that I love, why shall I not as much
love Mount Calvary as Mount Thabor, since he is as truly on the
one, as on the other? And why shall I not as affectionately in
one as in the other say : *It is good for us to be here.*† I love my
Saviour in Egypt, without loving Egypt; why shall I not love
him at the banquet of Simon the leper, without loving the banquet? And if I love him amidst the blasphemies which are
poured upon him, not loving the blasphemies, why shall I not
love him perfumed with Magdalen's ointment, without loving
either the ointment or its scent? It is the true sign that we love
only God in all things, when we love him equally in all things,
because he being always equal to himself, the inequality of our
love towards him must needs proceed from the consideration of
something that is not himself. Now this sacred loving one loves
no more her God with all the world, than if he were alone with-
ut the world : because all that is out of God, and is not God,
is nothing to her. She is an all-pure soul who loves not even
Paradise but because her beloved is loved there : and he is so
sovereignly beloved in his Paradise that if yet he had no Para-

* Luke ix. 60.　　　　　　† Matt. xvii. 4.

dise to bestow, he would neither appear less amiable, nor be less beloved of this generous loving heart, who cannot love the Paradise of her spouse but only her spouse of Paradise, and who puts no less price on Calvary while her spouse is there crucified, than upon Paradise where he is glorified. He that weighs one of the little balls of the heart of S. Clare of Montefalco, finds it as heavy as all the three together. So does perfect love find God as amiable all alone, as it finds all creatures together with him, since it loves all creatures only in God and for God.

Souls in this degree of perfection are so rare that each one is called *the only one of her mother*, who is divine Providence; she is called the *one dove*, for whom the love of her mate is all; she is termed *perfect*, because by love she is made the same thing with the sovereign Perfection, whence she may say with a most humble truth : *I to my beloved and his turning towards me.** Now there is no one save the most blessed Virgin our Lady, who has perfectly arrived at this height of excellence in the love of her dearly beloved : for she is a dove so singularly singular in love, that all the rest being compared to her are rather to be termed daws than doves. But leaving this peerless queen in her matchless eminence,—there have yet been other souls who have been in such estate of pure love that in comparison with others they might take the rank of queens, of only doves, of perfect friends of the spouse. For I pray you, Theotimus, what must he needs have been, who with all his heart sang to God : *What have I in heaven, and besides thee what do I desire upon earth ?*† And he that cried out : *I count all things but as dung that I may gain Christ ;*‡—did he not testify that he loved nothing out of his master, and that he loved his master without any other things ? And what must have been the feelings of that great lover, who sighed all the night : " My God is to me all things." Such were S. Augustine, S. Bernard, the two SS. Catharine, of Siena and of Genoa, and many others, in imitation of whom every one may aspire to this divine degree of love : rare and singular souls, who resemble no longer the birds of this world, no not the very phœnix itself, though so singularly rare ; but

* Cant. vii. 10.   † Ps. lxxii. 25.   ‡ Phil. iii. 8.

are only represented by that bird which, for its excellent beauty and nobleness is said not to be of this world, but of Paradise, of which it bears the name. For this fair bird disdaining the earth, never touches it, but lives above in the air; yea even when it desires to unweary itself, it will only cleave to the trees by little threads, hanging by them suspended in the air, out of which, or without which, it can neither fly nor repose. Even so these great souls do not, properly speaking, love creatures in themselves, but in their Creator, and their Creator in them. But if they cleave to any creature by the law of charity, it is only to repose in God, the single and final aim of their love. So that finding God in creatures, and creatures in God, they love God, not the creatures; as pearl-fishers, though they find the pearls in oysters, consider that they are simply fishing for pearls.

At the same time no mortal creature, as I think, ever loved the heavenly lover solely with this perfectly pure love, except that Virgin who was his spouse and mother both together; on the contrary, as regards the practice of these four differences of love, one can hardly live without passing from one of them to another. The souls which like young maidens are still entangled in some vain and dangerous affections are not, at times, without feelings of a purer and supreme love; but as these are but momentary and passing flashes, we cannot say that they raise them from the state of young novice, or apprentice, maidens. It happens also sometimes, to the souls who are in the degree of singular and perfect lovers, that they forget themselves and fail very sadly, even as far as to the committing great imperfections and grievous venial sins, as we see in various somewhat bitter dissensions which have occurred between great servants of God, yea even amongst some of the divine Apostles, who, as we cannot deny, fell into some imperfections; certainly charity was not violated by them, but the fervour of it was. Nevertheless, as these great souls ordinarily loved God with the perfectly pure love, we are not to say that they were not in the state of perfect love. For as we see that good trees never produce any hurtful fruit, yet sometimes bear green or defective and worm-eaten fruit, or mistletoe and moss; so great saints never produce any mortal sin, but still they produce some useless, immature, harsh, rough and ill-flavoured actions. In such cases we must allow that these trees are fruitful, otherwise they would not be good trees ; but still we must not deny that some of their fruits are fruitless. For who will deny that catkins and the mistletoe of trees are fruitless fruits ? And who also will deny that slight angers and little excesses of joy, of laughter, of vanity and of other similar passions, are unprofitable and unlawful movements ? Yet *the just man* brings them forth *seven times a day,* that is, very often.

CHAPTER VI.

THAT THE LOVE OF GOD ABOVE ALL THINGS IS COMMON TO ALL LOVERS.

Though there are so many degrees of love amongst true lovers, yet is there but one commandment of love, which universally and equally obliges every one, with an exactly like and entirely equal obligation, though it be observed differently and with an infinite variety of perfections ; there being perhaps no souls on earth, as there are no angels in heaven, who are perfectly equal to one another in their love. As one star differs from another in brightness, so shall it be with the Blessed in their resurrection, when each one sings a canticle of glory, and receives a name *which no man knoweth but he that receiveth it.** But what degree of love is it then, to which the divine commandment equally, universally and continually obliges all ?

It is an action of the providence of the Holy Ghost, that in our ordinary version, which his divine majesty has canonized and sanctified by the Council of Trent, the heavenly commandment of love is expressed by the word dilection rather than by the word love ; for although dilection is a kind of love, yet is it not a simple love, but a love of choice and election, which sense the word itself conveys, as the glorious S. Thomas notes : for

* Apoc. ii. 17.

this commandment enjoins us a love chosen out of thousands, the well-beloved object of this love being *chosen out of thousands*, according to that of the beloved Sulamitess in the Canticles.* It is a love which must prevail over all our loves, and reign over all our passions. And this is what God requires of us— that among all our loves his be the dearest, holding the first place in our hearts; the warmest, occupying our whole soul; the most general, employing all our powers; the highest, filling our whole spirit; and the strongest, exercising all our strength and vigour. And inasmuch as by this we choose and elect God for the sovereign object of our soul, it is a love of sovereign election, or an election of sovereign love. You are not ignorant, Theotimus, that there are various species of love, as for example, there is a fatherly love, a brotherly love, a filial love and a nuptial love; a love of society, of obligation, of dependence,— and a hundred more, which are all different in excellence, and are so proportioned to their objects that scarcely can they be applied or appropriated to any other. He who should love his father with the love of a brother only, would certainly not love him enough. He who should love his wife only like his father, would not love her properly; he who should love his servant with a filial love, would commit an impropriety. Love is like honour; for as honour is diversified according to the diversity of the excellences to which the honour is given, so loves are different according to the difference of the goodnesses for which we love. Sovereign honour is due to sovereign excellence, and sovereign love to sovereign goodness. The love of God is a love without peer, because the goodness of God is a peerless goodness. *Hear, O Israel, the Lord our God is one Lord*, and therefore, *Thou shalt love the Lord thy God with thy whole heart, and with thy whole soul, and with thy whole strength.*† For as God is the only Lord, his goodness is infinitely above all goodness, and he is to be loved with a love which is eminent, excellent, and mighty beyond all comparison. It is this supreme love which places God in such esteem in our souls, and makes us repute it so great a happiness to be agreeable in his sight,

---

* Cant. v. 10.   † Deut. vi. 4, 5.

that we prefer him and love him above all things. Now, Theotimus, do you not plainly see, that he who loves God in this sort has dedicated his whole soul and strength to God, since ever, and for ever, and in all occurrences, he will prefer the good grace of God to all things, and will be ever ready to forsake the whole world, in order to preserve the love which is due to the divine goodness. And, in a word, it is the love of excellence, or the excellence of love, which is commanded to all mortals in general, and to each one of them in particular as soon as they have the free use of reason: a love sufficient for each one, and necessary for salvation to all.

CHAPTER VII.

EXPLANATION OF THE PRECEDING CHAPTER.

WE do not always know, nor ever with perfect certainty (at least with certainty of faith), whether we have the true love of God which is required for salvation; still we have many marks of it, amongst which the most assured and almost infallible appears when some great love of creatures opposes itself to the designs of God's love; for then, if divine love is in the soul, it displays the greatness of the credit and authority which it has over the will, showing effectively, not only that it has no master, but that it has not even a companion, repressing and overthrowing all opposition, and making its intentions obeyed. When the unhappy troop of diabolic spirits, revolting from their Creator, essayed to draw to their faction the holy company of the blessed spirits, the glorious S. Michael, animating his comrades to the fidelity which they owed to their God, cried with loud voice (but in angelic sort) through the heavenly Jerusalem: "*Who is like to God?*" And by this word he overthrew that traitor Lucifer with his rout, who would have equalled themselves with the divine majesty ; and thence, as it is said, the name was given to S. Michael, since Michael simply means *Who is like to*

God? And when the loves of created things would draw our hearts to their party, to make us disobedient to the divine majesty, if the great divine love be found in the soul, it makes head against it, as another S. Michael, and establishes the powers and forces of the soul in God's service by this word of steadfastness: *Who is like to God?* What goodness is there in creatures which ought to draw the human heart into rebellion against the sovereign goodness of its God?

When the holy and noble Joseph perceived that the love of his mistress tended to the ruin of that which was due to his master: Ah! said he, be it far from me that I should violate the respect which I owe to my master, who reposes so much trust in me? *How then can I do this wicked thing, and sin against my God?** Mark, Theotimus, how there are three loves in the heart of this admirable Joseph, for he loves his mistress, his master, and God; but as soon as his mistress's love rises up against his master's, he suddenly forsakes it and flies, as he would also have forsaken his master's, if he had found it contrary to God's. Amongst all loves, God's is so to be preferred that we must always stand prepared in mind to forsake them all for that alone.

Abraham loved Sarai and Agar, and until Agar began to despise her mistress it could not well have been discerned which he loved the better. But when these two loves came into comparison with one another, the good Abraham made quite clear which was the stronger. For no sooner had Sarai complained that she was contemned by Agar, than he told her: *Behold thy handmaid is in thy own hand, use her as it pleaseth thee.*† Wherefore Sarai so afflicted the poor Agar that she was driven to run away. Divine love is willing for us to have other loves; nor can we easily discover which is the chief love of our heart: for this human heart often draws most affectionately into its complacency the love of creatures; yea, on many occasions it makes the acts of its affection for the creature far more numerous than that of its dilection for its Creator. Yet all the time sacred dilection ceases not to excel all the other loves, as the events show when the creature is opposed to the Creator; for then we take the part of sacred dilection, submitting unto it all our other affections.

* Gen. xxxix. 8.   † Gen. xvi. 6.

There is often a difference, among created things, between greatness and goodness. One of Cleopatra's pearls was worth more than our highest mountain; but the latter is much greater : the one has more bulk, the other more worth. It is made a question whether the honour which a prince achieves in war by feats of arms, or that which he merits by justice in time of peace be greater; and it seems to me that military glory is grander, and the other better; as, among instruments, drums and trumpets make more noise, lutes and virginals more melody; the sound of the one is stronger, of the other sweeter and more spiritual. An ounce of balm gives not so strong an odour as a pound of oil of lavender, but at the same time the smell of balm is better and more agreeable.

Truly, Theotimus, you will see a mother so busy about her child that she might seem to have no other love but that, having eyes only to see it, mouth to kiss it, breast to give it suck, care to bring it up; and one would think that her husband was nothing to her, in respect of her child; but if she had to make choice which she would lose, then would be plainly seen that she more values her husband, and that though the love of her child was more tender, more pressing and passionate, yet that other was the more excellent, stronger and better. So when a heart loves God in respect of his infinite goodness, with however little a portion of this excellent love, it will prefer God's will before all things, and in all the occasions that present themselves it will forsake everything, to preserve itself in grace with the sovereign goodness, and nothing whatever will divert it from this. So that, though this divine love does not always so sensibly affect and melt the heart as do the other loves; yet, on occasions, it performs actions so noble and excellent, that one of them only is better than ten millions of the others. Rabbits are incomparably fertile, elephants never have more than one calf; but this little elephant alone is of greater price than all the rabbits in the world. Our love towards creatures often abounds in the multitude of productions; but when sacred love acts its work is so eminent that it surpasses all: for it causes God to be preferred before all things, without reserve.

CHAPTER VIII.

A MEMORABLE HISTORY TO MAKE CLEARLY UNDERSTOOD IN WHAT
THE FORCE AND EXCELLENCE OF HOLY LOVE CONSIST.

How great an extent then, O my dear Theotimus, ought the force
of this sacred love of God above all things to have ? It must
surpass all affections, vanquish all difficulties, and prefer the
honour of God's good-will before all things; yea I say, before
all things absolutely, without any exception or reservation; and
I speak thus with such great distinctness, because there are
men who would courageously forsake their goods, honour, and
their own life for our Lord, who yet will not leave for his sake
things of much less consideration.

In the reign of the Emperors Valerianus and Gallus, there
lived in Antioch a priest named Sapricius, and a layman named
Nicephorus, who by reason of their long and exceeding great
friendship were considered as brothers : and yet it happened in
the end, I know not upon what occasion, that this friendship
failed, and according to custom was followed with a yet deeper
hatred, which reigned for a time between them, till at length
Nicephorus, acknowledging his fault, made three different at-
tempts to be reconciled with Sapricius, to whom, now by one of
their common friends, now by another, he sent words signifying
all the satisfaction and submission that heart could have wished.
But Sapricius, in no wise answering to his invitations, ever repulsed the reconciliation with as much contempt as Nicephorus
besought it with humility; insomuch that the poor Nicephorus,
thinking that if Sapricius saw him prostrate at his feet begging
pardon he would be more touched to the heart with it, goes and
finds him out and courageously casting himself down at his feet:
—Reverend Father, says he, Ah! pardon me, I beseech thee by
the bowels of our Saviour Jesus ; but even this humility was
disdained and rejected, together with his former endeavours.

Meanwhile, behold a hot persecution arose against the Christians, in which Sapricius with others being apprehended did
wonders in suffering a thousand thousand torments for the con-

fession of his faith,—especially when he was most roughly shaken and rolled in an instrument made purposely, after the manner of a wine-press—without ever losing his constancy. At this the Governor of Antioch being extremely irritated condemned him to death; whereupon he was publicly led out of prison towards the place where he was to receive the glorious crown of martyrdom. No sooner had Nicephorus learnt this, than immediately he ran, and having met Sapricius, throwing himself upon the ground : Alas! cried he, with a loud voice, O martyr of Jesus Christ, pardon me, for I have offended thee! But Sapricius taking no notice, the poor Nicephorus, getting again before him by a shorter way, came to him anew with the like humility, conjuring him to pardon him in these words : O martyr of Jesus Christ, pardon the offence which I have committed against thee, I who am but a man and subject to offend : for lo! a crown is already bestowed upon thee by our Saviour whom thou has not denied, yea thou hast confessed his holy name before many witnesses. But Sapricius continuing in his pride gave him not one word in answer ; until the very executioners, wondering at the perseverance of Nicephorus, said to him : We have never seen so foolish a man as thee; this fellow is going even at this moment to die, what dost thou want with his pardon? To whom Nicephorus answering : Thou knowest not, said he, what it is I demand of this confessor of Jesus Christ, but God knows. Meantime Sapricius arrived at the place of execution, where yet again Nicephorus, casting himself upon the ground before him : I beseech thee, said he, O martyr of Jesus Christ, that it would please thee to pardon me, for it is written : *Ask and it shall be granted thee :* words which could not in the least bend the caitiff and rebellious heart of the miserable Sapricius, who, obstinately denying mercy to his neighbour, was himself deprived by the just judgment of God of the most glorious palm of martyrdom. For the executioners commanding him to put himself on his knees, in order to behead him, he began to be daunted, and to parley with them, making in the end this deplorable and shameful submission : Oh! I pray you, behead me not : I will do what the Emperors order, and sacrifice to idols. Which the poor good Nicephorus hearing, with

tears in his eyes began to cry: Ah! my dear brother, do not,
do not, I beseech thee, transgress the law and deny Jesus Christ;
forsake him not, I beseech thee, lose not the crown of glory which
with so great labours and torments thou hast obtained! But
alas! this miserable priest coming to the altar of martyrdom
there to consecrate his life to the eternal God, had not called to
mind what the Prince of Martyrs had said: *If therefore thou
offer thy gift at the altar, and there thou remember that thy
brother hath anything against thee; leave there thy offering before
the altar, and go first to be reconciled to thy brother: and then
coming thou shalt offer thy gift.** Wherefore God rejected his
offering, and withdrawing his mercy from him, permitted him
not only to lose the sovereign happiness of martyrdom, but even
to fall headlong into the misery of idolatry; while the humble
and meek Nicephorus, perceiving this crown of martyrdom
vacant by the apostasy of the obdurate Sapricius, touched with
an excellent and extraordinary inspiration, boldly presses forward to obtain it, saying to the officers and executioners: I am
a Christian, my friends, I am in truth a Christian, and believe
in Jesus Christ, whom this man has denied: put me, therefore,
I beseech you, in his place, and cut off my head. At which the
officers being extremely astonished, carried the tidings to the
governor, who gave orders that Sapricius should be set at
liberty, and that Nicephorus should be put to death, which happened on the 9th of February, about the year of our salvation
260, as Metaphrastes and Surius relate. A terrible history, and
worthy of the gravest consideration in the subject we treat of!
For did you note, my dear Theotimus, this courageous Sapricius—
how bold and fervent he was in defence of his faith, how he
suffered a thousand torments, how constant and immovable he
was in the confession of our Saviour's name, while he was rolled
and crushed in that press-like machine, how ready he was to
receive the death-blow to fulfil the highest point of the divine
law, preferring God's honour before his own life? And yet,
because on the other side he prefers to the divine will the satisfaction which his cruel haughtiness takes in hating Nicephorus, he

* Matt. v. 23, 24.

stops short in his course, and when he is on the point of coming up to and attaining the prize of glory by martyrdom, he miserably falls and breaks his neck, falling headlong into idolatry.

It is therefore true, my Theotimus, that it is not enough for us to love God more than our own life, unless we also love him universally, absolutely, and without reserve, more than all we love or can love. But you will say to me, did not our Saviour assign the furthest point of our love towards him, when he said that *greater love than this no man hath, that a man lay down his life for his friends ?** It is true indeed, Theotimus, that amongst the particular acts and testimonies of divine love there is none so great as to undergo death for God's glory, yet it is also true that this is but one single act, and one single test ; it is indeed the masterpiece of charity, but besides it charity exacts many things at our hands, and so much more forcibly and instantly as they are acts more easy, common and ordinary with all lovers, and more generally necessary to the preservation of sacred love. O miserable Sapricius! Durst thou be bold to affirm that thou didst love God as was fitting, whilst thou didst not prefer the will of God before the passion of hatred and rancour entertained in thy heart against the poor Nicephorus ? To be willing to die for God is the greatest but not the only act of love which we owe to God ; and to will this act only, excluding the others,—this is not charity, it is vanity. Charity is not fanciful, which she would be in the highest degree, if being resolved to please the beloved in things of greatest difficulty, she would permit us to displease him in easier matters. How can he will to die for God who will not live according to God ?

A well-ordered mind that is resolved to die for a friend, would also without doubt undergo all other things ; for he that has once despised death ought to have despised everything. But the human spirit is weak, inconstant and humoursome, whence men sometimes rather choose to die than to undergo far slighter pains, and willingly give their life for extremely frivolous, childish, and vain satisfactions. Agrippina having learnt that the child she was bringing forth would be Emperor, indeed, but that he

* John xv. 13.

would put her to death : Let him kill me, said she, provided that
he reign.   Mark, I pray you, the disorder of this foolishly loving
mother's heart; she preferred her son's dignity before her own
life.   Cato and Cleopatra chose death rather than to see their
enemies exult and glory in their capture; and Lucretia chose to
put herself cruelly to death rather than to be unjustly branded
with the shame of a deed in which, it would seem, she was not
guilty.   How many are there who would willingly embrace
death for their friends, and yet would not live in their service, or
accomplish their other desires?   A man exposes his life, who
would not open his purse.   And though there may be found
many who engage their life for a friend's defence, yet scarcely
is there one found in a century who will imperil his liberty, or
lose an ounce of the most vain and unprofitable reputation or
renown in the world, be it for never so dear a friend.

CHAPTER IX.

A CONFIRMATION OF WHAT HAS BEEN SAID BY A NOTEWORTHY COMPARISON.

You know, Theotimus, what was Jacob's love for his Rachel.
And what did not he do to testify its greatness, force and fidelity,
from the hour he had saluted her at the well?   For from that
time he never ceased to love her, and to gain her in marriage
he served seven whole years with incredible devotion; yet he
considered that all this was nothing, so much did love sweeten
the pains which he supported for his beloved Rachel.   And when
he was, after all, disappointed of her, he served yet other seven
years to obtain her; so constant, loyal and courageous was he in
his affection; and having at length obtained her he neglected all
other affections, scarcely even taking any account of the duty he
had to Lia, his first spouse, a woman of great merit and very
worthy to be cherished, whom God himself compassionated for
the contempt she suffered, so remarkable was it.

But after all this, which was enough to bring down the haughtiest woman in the world to the love of so loyal a lover, it is verily a shame to see the weakness which Rachel showed in her affection to Jacob. The poor Lia had no tie of love with Jacob except the fact that she was the mother of his four sons. Reuben the first of these had gone into the fields at harvest-time and found some mandrakes, which he brought as a present to his mother.* Rachel asked for some of them, and when poor Lia said : *Dost thou think it a small matter that thou hast taken my husband from me, unless thou take also my son's mandrakes,—* Rachel sold, as it were, the favours and love of her husband for the mandrakes. But Jacob was distressed, and his heart sank, when he understood the weakness and inconstancy of Rachel, who for so trifling a thing sacrificed for a time the honour and pleasure of his special love. For, tell me truly, Theotimus— was it not a strange and most fickle levity in Rachel, to prefer a heap of little apples to the chaste company of so amiable a husband? If it had been for kingdoms, for monarchies!—but for a miserable handful of mandrakes!—Theotimus, what think you of it?

And yet, returning to ourselves, good God! how often do we make elections infinitely more shameful and wretched? The great S. Augustine upon a time took pleasure in leisurely viewing and contemplating mandrakes, the better to discern the cause why Rachel had so passionately coveted them, and he found that they were indeed pleasing to the sight, and of a delightful smell, yet altogether insipid and without flavour. Now Pliny relates that when the surgeons bring the juice of them to be drunk by those on whom they wish to make an incision, that they may not feel the operation, it happens often that the very smell works the effect and puts the patient sufficiently to sleep. Wherefore the mandrake is a bewitching plant, which enchants the eyes, and charms away pains, sorrows, and all passions by sleep. Besides, he who smells the scent of them too long turns mute, and he who drinks too much of them dies without remedy.

Theotimus, could worldly pomps, riches and delights be better

* Gen. xxx.

represented ? They have an attractive outside, but he who
bites this apple, that is, he who sounds their nature, finds neither
taste nor contentment in them, nevertheless they enchant us and
put us to sleep by the vanity of their smell; and the renown
which the children of the world attach to them, benumbs and
destroys those who give themselves up to them too intently, or
take them too abundantly. And it is for such mandrakes,
chimeras and phantoms of content, that we cast off the love of
the heavenly beloved; and how then can we say that we love him
above all things, since we prefer such empty vanities before his
grace ?

Is it not a marvel, but one worthy of tears, to see David, so
noble in surmounting hatred, so generous in pardoning injuries,
and yet so furiously unjust in love, that not content with possessing justly a great multitude of wives, he iniquitously usurps
and takes away the wife of poor Urias, and by an insupportable
cruelty causes the husband to be slain, that he may the better
enjoy the love of the wife? Who would not wonder at the
heart of a S. Peter, which was so bold amidst the armed soldiers
that he alone of all his master's company takes sword in hand and
strikes ; and yet a little afterwards he is so cowardly amongst
the women, that at the mere word of a maid he denies and
forswears his master ? And how can it seem so strange to us
that Rachel could sell the chaste favours of her Jacob for the
apples of the mandrake, since Adam and Eve actually forsook
grace for an apple which a serpent offers them to eat?

In fine, I say to you this word, worthy of note. Heretics
are heretics and bear the name, because out of the articles of
faith they choose at their taste and pleasure those which it seems
good to them to believe, rejecting and denying the others. And
Catholics are Catholics, because without any choice or election
they embrace, with an equal assurance and without exception,
all the faith of the Church. Now it is the same in the articles of
charity. It is a heresy in sacred love to make choice among
God's commandments, which to observe, and which to violate:
he who said: *Thou shalt not kill,* said also: *Thou shalt not
commit adultery.* If then thou kill not, but commit adultery,
it is not for love for God that thou killest not, but it is from

some other motive, which makes thee rather choose this commandment than the other ; a choice which makes heresy in
matter of charity. If a man told me that he would not cut off
my arm on account of his love for me, and yet proceeded to
pluck out my eye, to break my head, to run me through :—Ah !
should I cry, how do you say that it is for love you do not cut
off my arm, since you pluck out my eye which is no less precious
to me, or run my body through with your sword, which is still
more dangerous to me ? It is a maxim that good comes from an
entirely sound cause, evil from some defect. To make an act of
true charity, it must proceed from an entire, general and universal love, which extends to all the divine commandments, and
if we fail in any one commandment, love ceases to be entire and
universal, and the heart wherein it is cannot be called truly
loving, nor, consequently, truly good.

CHAPTER X.

THAT WE ARE TO LOVE THE DIVINE GOODNESS SOVEREIGNLY ABOVE OURSELVES.

ARISTOTLE was consistent in saying that good is indeed amiable,
but to each one his own good principally, so that the love which
we have for others proceeds from the love of ourselves :—for
how could a philosopher say otherwise who not only did not love
God, but hardly ever even spoke of the love of God ? As a
fact, however, this love of God precedes all love of ourselves,
even according to the natural inclination of our will, as I have
made clear in the first book.

In truth, the will is so dedicated, and, if we may say it, consecrated to goodness, that if an infinite goodness be clearly proposed unto it, it must, unless by miracle, sovereignly love this
goodness : yea, the Blessed are carried away and necessitated,
though not forced, to love God whose sovereign beauty they
clearly see; as the Scripture sufficiently shows in comparing
the contentment which fills the hearts of the glorious inhabitants

of the heavenly Jerusalem to a torrent and impetuous flood, whose waters cannot be kept from spreading over the plains it meets with.

But in this mortal life, Theotimus, we are not necessitated to love him so sovereignly, because we see him not so clearly. In heaven, where we shall see him face to face, we shall love him heart to heart; that is, as we shall all see the infinity of his beauty, each in our measure, with a sovereignly clear sight, so shall we be ravished, with the love of his infinite goodness in a sovereignly strong rapture, to which we shall neither desire, nor be able to desire, to make any resistance. But here below on earth, where we do not see this sovereign goodness in its beauty, but only have a half-sight of it amid our obscurities, we are indeed inclined and allured to love him more than ourselves;—yet we are not necessitated: on the contrary, though we have this holy natural inclination to love the divinity above all things, yet we have not the strength to put it in execution, unless the same divinity infuse its most holy charity supernaturally into our hearts.

Yet true it is that as the clear view of the divinity infallibly produces the necessity of loving it more than ourselves, so the half-view, that is, the natural knowledge, of the divinity, infallibly produces the inclination and tendency to love it more than ourselves; for, I pray you, Theotimus, since the will is wholly ordained unto the love of good, how can it know, ever so little, a sovereign good without being so far inclined to love it sovereignly? Of all goods which are not infinite, our will always prefers in its love that which is nearest to it, and chiefly its own; but there is so little proportion between the infinite and the finite, that our will having knowledge of an infinite good is without doubt moved, inclined and excited to prefer the friendship of this abyss of infinite goodness before every other sort of love, yea even the love of ourselves.

This inclination is strong principally because we are more in God than in ourselves, we live more in him than in ourselves, and are in such sort from him, by him, for him and belonging to him, that we cannot undistractedly consider what we are to him and he is to us, without being forced to exclaim: I am thine, Lord, and must belong to none but thee; my soul is thine, and ought not to live but by thee, my will is thine, and is only to tend to thee, I must love thee as my first principle since I have my being from thee, I must love thee as my end and centre since I am for thee, I must love thee more than my own being, since my being subsists by thee, I must love thee more than myself, since I am wholly thine and in thee.

And in case there were or could be some sovereign good whereof we were independent, we should also, supposing that we could unite ourselves unto it by love, be excited to love this more than ourselves, seeing that the infinity of its sweetness would be still sovereignly more powerful to draw our will to its love than all other goods, yea, even than our own good.

But if, by imagination of a thing impossible, there were an infinite goodness on which we had no dependence whatever, and with which we could have no kind of union or communication, we should indeed esteem it more than ourselves, for we should know that being infinite it would be more estimable and lovable than we; and consequently we should be able to make simple desires of being able to love it; yet, properly speaking, we should not love it, since love aims at union; and much less could we have charity towards it, since charity is a friendship, and friendship cannot be unless it be reciprocal, having for its groundwork communication, and for its end union. I speak thus for the benefit of certain fantastic and empty spirits, who very often on baseless imaginations revolve morbid thoughts to their own great affliction. But as for us, Theotimus, my dear friend, we see plainly that we cannot be true men without putting this inclination into effect. Let us love him more than ourselves who is to us more than all and more than ourselves. Amen, so it is.

CHAPTER XI.

HOW HOLY CHARITY PRODUCES THE LOVE OF OUR NEIGHBOUR.

As God created man to his own image and likeness, so did he appoint for man a love after the image and resemblance of the love which is due to his own divinity. *Thou shalt love the Lord thy God, with thy whole heart, and with thy whole soul, and with thy whole mind. This is the greatest, and the first commandment. And the second is like to this: Thou shalt love thy neighbour as thyself.* Why do we love God, Theotimus? "The cause for which we love God," says S. Bernard, "is God Himself;" as though he had said: we love God because he is the most sovereign and infinite goodness. And why do we love ourselves in charity? Surely because we are the image and likeness of God; and whereas all men are endowed with the same dignity, we love them also as ourselves, that is, as being holy and living images of the divinity. For it is on that account that we belong to God by so strict an alliance and so sweet a dependence of love, that he makes no difficulty to call himself our father, and to call us his children; it is on that account that we are capable of being united to his divine essence by the fruition of his sovereign goodness and felicity; it is on that account that we receive his grace, that our spirits are associated to his most Holy Spirit, and made in a manner participant of his divine nature, as S. Leo says. And therefore the same charity which produces the acts of the love of God, produces at the same time those of the love of our neighbour. And even as Jacob saw that one same ladder touched heaven and earth, serving the angels both for descending and ascending, so we know that one same charity extends itself to both the love of God and our neighbour, raising us to the union of our spirit with God, and bringing us back again to a loving society with our neighbours; always, however, on the understanding that we love our neighbour as being after the image and like-

* Matt. xxii. 37.

ness of God, created to have communication with the divine
goodness, to participate in his grace, and to enjoy his glory.

Theotimus, to love our neighbour in charity is to love God in
man, or man in God; it is to hold God alone dear for his own
sake and the creature for the love of him. The young Tobias,
accompanied by the angel Raphael, having met with Raguel his
relative, by whom, however, he was unknown,—Raguel had no
sooner set eyes upon him, says the Scripture, but turning himself
towards his wife: Anna, look, look, said he, *how like is this
young man to my cousin ?   And when he had spoken these words,
he said : whence are ye, young men our brethren ? But they said,
we are of the tribe of Nephthali, of the captivity of Ninive.   And
Raguel said to them : Do you know Tobias my brother ? And they
said, we know him.   And when he was speaking many good things
of him, the angel said to Raguel : Tobias concerning whom thou
nquirest is this young man's father.   And Raguel went to him,
and kissed him with tears, and weeping upon his neck, said : a
blessing be upon thee, my son, because thou art the son of a
virtuous man.   And Anna his wife and Sara their daughter wept,*
through tenderness of affection.   Do you not observe that
Raguel, without knowing the younger Tobias, embraces, caresses,
kisses him, and weeps for joy over him.   Whence proceeds this
love but from that which he had for the old Tobias, the father,
whom this child did so much resemble ? *A blessing be upon thee,*
said he ; but why ? certainly not because thou art a good youth,
for that as yet I know not, but because thou art son, and like, to
thy father, *a good and most virtuous man.*

Ah! then, Theotimus, when we see a neighbour who is created
to the image and likeness of God, ought we not to say one to
another : Observe and see this creature, how he resembles the
Creator ?   Might we not cast ourselves upon his neck, to caress
him and weep over him with love?   Should we not bless him
a thousand and a thousand times ?   And why?   For the love
of him ?   No verily : for we know not whether he be worthy
of love or hatred in himself; but wherefore then ? O Theotimus!
for the love of God, who has made him to his own image and

* Tobias vii. 2–8.

likeness, and consequently capable of participating in his good-ness, in grace and in glory. For the love of God, I say, from whom he is, whose he is, by whom he is, in whom he is, for whom he is, and whom he resembles in a most particular manner. Wherefore the love of God not only oftentimes commands the love of our neighbour, but itself produces this love and pours it into man's heart, as its resemblance and image : for even as man is the image of God, so the sacred love of man towards man, is the true image of the heavenly love of man towards God. But this subject of the love of our neighbour requires a treatise apart, which I beseech the sovereign lover of men to will to inspire into some one of his most excellent servants, since the supreme love of the divine goodness of the heavenly Father, consists in the perfection of the love of our brothers and companions.

CHAPTER XII.

HOW LOVE PRODUCES ZEAL.

As love tends towards the good of the thing beloved, either by taking delight in it if the beloved have it, or in desiring and pro-curing it for him if he have it not ; so it produces hatred, by which it flies the evil which is contrary to the thing beloved, either by desiring and seeking to remove it if it be there, or by keeping it off and preventing its coming if it be not there. But if evil can neither be hindered from approaching, nor be removed, love at least fails not to have it hated and detested. When love there-fore is fervent, and is come to that height that it would take away, remove and divert, what is opposite to the thing beloved, it is termed zeal. So that, to describe it properly, zeal is no other thing than love in its ardour, or rather the ardour that is in love. And therefore, such as the love is, such is the zeal, which is its ardour. If the love be good its zeal is good, if the love be bad its zeal is bad. Now when I speak of zeal, I mean to speak of jealousy too : for jealousy is a species of zeal, and if

I am not mistaken, there is but this difference between them, that zeal regards the whole good of the thing beloved, with the intention of removing the contrary evil from it, and jealousy regards the particular good of the friendship, that it may repulse all that opposes that.

When therefore we ardently love worldly and temporal things, beauty, honours, riches, rank,—this zeal, that is the ardour of this love, ends ordinarily in envy : because these base and vile things are so little, limited, particular, finite and imperfect, that being possessed by one, another cannot entirely possess them. So that being communicated to many, each one in particular has a less perfect communication of them. But when, in particular, we ardently love to be beloved, the zeal or ardour of this love turns into jealousy ; because human friendship, though otherwise a virtue, has this imperfection by reason of our weakness, that being divided amongst many, each one's part is less. Whereupon our ardour or zeal to be beloved will not permit rivals or companions ; and if we imagine we have any, we immediately enter into the passion of jealousy, which indeed in some sort resembles envy, but in reality is very different from it. 1°. Envy is always unjust, but jealousy is sometimes just, if it be moderate : for have not married people good reason to hinder their friendship from being diminished by being shared? 2°. Envy makes us sorry that our neighbour enjoys a greater good than, or a like good with, ourselves ; although he is taking from us nothing that we have ; and here envy is unreasonable, making us consider our neighbour's good to be our ill. But jealousy is not grieved at our neighbour's having some good provided that it is not our good : for the jealous man does not grieve at his fellow's being beloved by other women so long as he is not loved by the jealous man's wife ; indeed, properly speaking, one is not jealous of a rival until one belives that one has gained the friendship of the person loved : if there be any passion before that, it is not jealousy but envy. 3°. We do not presuppose any imperfection in the person we envy, but on the contrary we consider that he has the good which we envy in him : but we presuppose that the person of whom we are jealous is imperfect, fickle, changeable and easily led away. 4°. Jealousy proceeds from love, envy comes from the defect of love. 5°. Jealousy never happens but in matter of love, but envy is extended to all kinds of goods—honours, favours, beauty.   And if at any time one be envious of the affection which is borne to another, it is not for love, but for the fruits that spring from it.   The envious man is little troubled to see his fellow in favour with his prince, so that he be not on occasions graced and preferred by him.

CHAPTER XIII.

HOW GOD IS JEALOUS OF US.

GOD speaks thus : *I am the Lord thy God, a jealous God.** *The Lord his name is jealous.*† God is jealous then, Theotimus, but what is his jealousy ? Truly it seems at first to be a jealousy of cupidity such as is that of husbands for their wives : for he will have us so to be his, that he will in no sort have us to be any other's but his. *No man,* saith he, *can serve two masters.*‡ He demands all our heart, all our soul, all our mind, and all our strength ; for this very reason he calls himself our spouse, and our souls his spouses ; and names all sorts of separations from him, fornication, adultery. And high reason indeed has this great God, all singularly good, to exact most rigorously our whole heart : for ours is a little heart, which cannot supply love enough worthily to love the divine goodness.   Is it not therefore meet, that since we cannot give him such measure of love as were requisite, that at least we should give him all we can? The good which is sovereignly lovable, ought it not to be sovereignly loved ?   Now to love sovereignly, is to love totally.

However, God's jealousy of us is not truly a jealousy of cupidity, but of sovereign friendship : for it is not his interest that we should love him, but ours.   Our love is useless to him, but to us a great gain ; and if it be agreeable to him, it is because it is profitable to us : for being the sovereign good, he takes

---

* Deut. v. 9.   † Exod. xxxiv. 14.   ‡ Matt. vi. 24.

pleasure in communicating himself by love, without any kind of profit that can return to him thereby ; whence he cries out making his complaint of sinners by way of jealousy : *They have forsaken me, the fountain of living water, and have digged to themselves cisterns, broken cisterns, that can hold no water.** Consider a little, Theotimus, I pray you, how delicately this divine lover expresses the nobility and generosity of his jealousy : *They have left me*, says he, *who am the fountain of living water*. As if he said : I complain not that they have forsaken me because of any injury their forsaking can cause me, for what the worse is a living spring if men do not draw water at it ? Will it therefore cease to run, or to flow out on the earth ? But I grieve for their misfortune, that having left me, they have chosen for themselves wells that have no water. And if, by supposition of an impossible thing, they could have met with some other fountain of living water, I would lightly bear their departure from me, since I aim at nothing in their love, but their own good. But to forsake me to perish, to fly from me to fall headlong, is what astonishes and offends me in their folly. It is then for the love of us that he desires we should love him, because we cannot cease to love him without beginning to be lost, and whatever part of our affections we take from him we lose.

Put me, said the divine shepherd to the Sulamitess, *as a seal upon thy heart, as a seal upon thy arm.†* The Sulamitess had her heart quite full of the heavenly love of her dear lover, who, though he possess all, yet is not content with it, but by a holy distrust of jealousy will be set upon the heart which he possesses, and will seal it with himself, lest any of the love due to him escape, or anything get entry which might mingle with it. For he is not satisfied with the love with which the soul of his Sulamitess is filled, if it be not invariable, quite pure, quite solely his. And that he may not only enjoy the affections of our heart, but also the effects and operations of our hands, he will also be as a seal upon our right arm, that it may not be stretched out or employed save in the works of his service.

---

* Jer. ii. 13. † Cant. viii. 6.

And the reason of the divine lover's demand is, that as death is so strong that it separates the soul from all things, yea even from her own body, so sacred love which is come to the degree of zeal, divides and separates the soul from all other affections, and purifies her from all admixture ; since it is not only *strong as death,* but it is withal bitter, inexorable, *hard* and pitiless in punishing the wrong done unto it, when rivals are entertained with it, *as hell* is *hard* in punishing the damned. And even as hell, full of horror, rage and cruelty, admits no mingling of love, so jealous love tolerates no mixture of another affection, willing that all be for the well-beloved. Nothing is so gentle as the dove, yet nothing so merciless as he towards his mate, when he has some feeling of jealousy. If ever you have taken notice, Theotimus, you will have seen that this mild bird, returning from his flight, and finding his mate amongst his companions, is not able to suppress in himself a certain sense of distrust, which makes him churlish and ill-humoured, so that at their first accosting he circles about her, murmuring, fretting, treading upon her, and beating her with his wings, although he knows well that she is faithful, and that he sees her in the pure white of innocence.

One day S. Catharine of Siena was in a rapture which did not deprive her of the use of her senses, and while God was showing her wondrous things, one of her brothers passed by, and with the noise he made disturbed her attention, so that she turned and looked at him for a single little moment. This little distraction, so unforeseen and sudden, was neither sin, nor disloyalty, but only a shadow of sin and resemblance of disloyalty: and yet the most holy Mother of the heavenly lover did so earnestly chide her and the glorious S. Paul so put her to confusion for it, that she thought she should have melted away in tears. And David, re-established in grace by a perfect love, how was he treated for the simply venial sin which he had committed in numbering his people?

But, Theotimus, he who desires to see this jealousy delicately and excellently described, must read the instructions which the seraphic S. Catharine of Genoa has made to declare the properties of pure love, amongst which she inculcates and

strongly urges this;—that perfect love, namely, love which has
gone as far as zeal, cannot suffer any mediation, interposition,
or mingling of any other thing, not even of God's gifts, yea, up
to this extreme, that it permits not even the love of heaven,
except with intention to love more perfectly therein the goodness of him who gives it. So that the lamps of this pure love
have neither oil, wick, nor smoke, but are all fire and flame,
which nothing in the world can extinguish. And those who
carry these burning lamps in their hands, possess the most holy
fear of chaste spouses, not the fear which belongs to adulterous
women. Those have fear, and these also, but differently, says
S. Augustine; the chaste spouse fears the absence of her
husband, the adulterous, the presence of hers. The former
fears his departure, the latter his stay: the one is so deeply
amorous that she is extremely jealous; the other is not jealous,
because she is not amorous: the one fears to be punished, and
the other fears that she may not be loved enough;—yet in
sooth she does not precisely fear the not being loved enough, as
other jealous persons do, who love themselves and want to be
loved, but her fear is that she loves not him enough whom she
sees so love-worthy that none can love him according to the
greatness of the love which he deserves, as I have but just said.
Wherefore she is not jealous with a jealousy of self-interest, but
with a pure jealousy, which proceeds not from any cupidity, but
from a noble and simple friendship; a jealousy which, with the
love whence it proceeds, extends itself to our neighbour; for
since we love our neighbour as ourselves for God's sake, we are
also jealous of him, as of ourselves, for God's sake, so that we
would even die that he may not perish.

Now as zeal is an inflamed ardour, or an ardent inflaming of
love, it requires to be wisely and prudently practised; otherwise,
under the cloak of it, one would transgress the limits of moderation or discretion, and it would be easy to pass from zeal into
anger, and from a just affection to an unjust passion; wherefore,
this not being the proper place to put down the conditions of
zeal, my Theotimus, I tell you that for the practice of it you
must always have recourse to him whom God has given you for
your direction in the devout life.

CHAPTER XIV.

A GENTLEMAN desired a famous painter to paint him a horse running, and the painter having presented the horse to him on its back, and as it were rolling in the mire, the gentleman began to storm; whereupon the painter turning the picture upside down : Be not angry, sir, said he ; to change the position of a horse running into that of a horse rolling on its back, it is only necessary to reverse the picture. Theotimus, he who would clearly see what zeal or what jealousy we must have for God, has only to express properly the jealousy we have in human things, and then to turn it upside down, for such will that be which God requires from us for himself.

Imagine, Theotimus, what comparison there is between those who enjoy the brightness of the sun, and those who have only the paltry light of a lamp; the former are not jealous of one another, for they know well that that great light is abundantly sufficiently for all, that the one's enjoyment does not hinder the other's, and that, although all possess it in general, each one possesses it none the less than if he alone possessed it in particular. But as to the light of a lamp, since it is little, limited, and insufficient for many, each one desires to have it in his chamber, and he that has it is envied by the rest. The good of human things is so trifling and beggarly, that when one has it, another must be deprived of it; and human friendship is so limited and weak, that in proportion as it communicates itself to the one, it is weakened for the others : this is why we are jealous and angry when we have rivals and companions in it. The heart of God is so abounding in love, his good is so absolutely infinite, that all men may possess him without lessening each one's possession ; this infinity of goodness can never be drained, though it fill all the hearts of the universe ; for when everything has been filled with it to the brim, his infinity ever remains to him quite entire, without any diminution whatever. The sun shines no less upon a rose together with a thousand millions of other flowers, than though it shone but upon that alone. And God pours his love no less over one soul, though he loves with it an infinity of others, than if he loved that one only: the force of his love not decreasing by the multitude of rays which it spreads, but remaining ever quite full of his immensity.

But wherein consists the zeal or the jealousy which we ought to have for the divine goodness? Theotimus, its office is, first, to hate, fly, hinder, detest, reject, combat and overthrow, if one can, all that is opposed to God; that is, to his will, to his glory, and the sanctification of his name. *I have hated and abhorred iniquity,** said David, and : *Have I not hated them, O Lord, that hated thee: and pined away because of thy enemies.*† *My zeal hath made me pine away because my enemies forgot thy words.*‡ *In the morning I put to death all the wicked of the land ; that I might cut off all the workers of iniquity from the city of the Lord.*§ See, I pray you, Theotimus, with what zeal this great king is animated, and how he employs the passions of his soul in the service of holy jealousy! He does not simply hate iniquity but abhors it; upon the sight of it he pines away, he falls into a swoon and a failing of heart, he persecutes it, overthrows it, and exterminates it. So Phinees transported with a holy zeal ran his sword through that shameless Israelite and vile Madianite; so the zeal which consumed our Saviour's heart, made him cast out and instantly take vengeance on the irreverence and profanation which those buyers and sellers committed in the temple.

Secondly, zeal makes us ardently jealous of the purity of souls, which are the spouses of Jesus Christ, according to the word of the holy Apostle to the Corinthians : *I am jealous of you with the jealousy of God, for I have espoused you to one husband, that I may present you as a chaste virgin to Christ.*‖ Eliezer would have been stung with jealousy, if he had perceived the chaste and fair Rebecca, whom he was conducting to be espoused to his master's son, in any danger of being dishonoured; and doubtless he might have said to this holy maiden : I am jealous of you with the jealousy I have for my master, for I have es-

---

* Ps. cxviii. 163.   † Ps. cxxxviii. 21.   ‡ Ps. cxviii. 139.
§ Ps. c. 8.   ‖ 2 Cor. xi. 2.

poused you to one man, that I may present you a chaste virgin
to the son of my lord Abraham. So would the great S. Paul
say to his Corinthians: I was sent from God to your souls to
arrange the marriage of an eternal union between his Son our
Saviour, and you, and I have promised you to him to present
you as a chaste virgin to this divine lover; behold why I am
jealous, not with my own jealousy, but with the jealousy of God,
in whose behalf I have treated with you. It was this jealousy,
Theotimus, that caused this holy Apostle daily to die and swoon
away; *I die daily*, said he, *I protest by your glory.** *Who is
weak and I am not weak? Who is scandalized and I am not on
fire?*† Mark, say the ancients, mark what love, what care, and
what jealousy a mother-hen has for her chickens (for our
Saviour esteemed not this comparison unworthy of his Gospel).
The hen is a very hen, that is, a creature without any courage
or nobility, while she is not yet a mother, but with her mother-
ship she puts on a lion's heart: ever the head up, the eyes on
guard, and darting glances on every side, to espy the smallest
appearance of danger to her little ones. There is no enemy at
whose eyes she will not fly in defence of her dear brood, for
which she has a continual solicitude, making her ever run about
clucking and plaining. And if any of her chickens come to die,
—what grief, what anger! This is the jealousy of parents for
their children, of pastors for their flocks, of brothers for their
brethren. What was the zeal of the children of Jacob when
they knew that Dina had been insulted? What was the zeal of
Job from the apprehension and fear he had that his children
might have offended God? What was the zeal of a S. Paul for
his brethren according to the flesh, and for his children according to God, for whose sake he desired to be cast out as worthy
of anathema and excommunication? What the zeal of Moses
for his people, for whom he is willing, in a certain manner to be
struck out of the book of life?

Thirdly, in human jealousy we are afraid lest the thing beloved be possessed by some other, but our zeal for God makes
us on the contrary fear lest we should not be entirely enough

---

* 1 Cor. xv. 31.　　　　　† 2 Cor. xi. 29.

possessed by him. Human jealousy makes us fear not to be loved enough, Christian jealousy troubles us with the fear of not loving enough; whence the sacred Sulamitess cried out: *Show me, O thou whom my soul loveth, where thou feedest, where thou liest in the midday, lest I begin to wander after the flocks of thy companions.** Her fear is that she is not her sacred shepherd's own entirely, or that she may be led away, be it never so little, by those who wished to make themselves his rivals. For she will by no means permit that worldly pleasures, honours, or exterior goods shall take up a single particle of her love, which she has wholly dedicated to her dear Saviour.

CHAPTER XV.

ADVICE FOR THE DIRECTION OF HOLY ZEAL.

As zeal is an ardour and vehemence of love it stands in need of guidance; otherwise it would exceed the limits of moderation and discretion. Not indeed that divine love, however vehement, can be excessive in itself, or in the movements or inclinations which it gives to our spirit, but, inasmuch as it makes use of the understanding in the execution of its designs, ordering it to find out the means whereby they may be effected, and makes use of boldness or anger to surmount the difficulties which it meets with, the understanding often comes to propose and make us adopt courses too rough and violent, and anger or hardihood once aroused, and unable to contain itself within the limits of reason, carries away the heart into disorder, so that zeal is thus practised indiscreetly and inordinately; which makes it bad and blameworthy. David sent Joab with his army, against his disloyal and rebellious child, Absalom, whom he commanded them above all things not to injure, ordering that in all events they should take care to save him. But Joab being engaged, and being hot in the pursuit of the victory, with his own hand slew

* Cant. i. 6.

the poor Absalom, without regard to what the king had said to him. Even so, zeal employs anger against the evil, yet ever with express order, that in destroying wickedness and sin it should save, if possible, the sinner and the iniquitous : but it, once in its fury, like a hard-mouthed and wilful horse, runs away with its rider out of the lists, without stop or stay, while breath lasts.

That good man of the house whom our Saviour describes in the Gospel, knew well that hot and violent servants are wont to outrun their master's intention, for his servants presenting themselves unto him to go and weed his field in order to root out the cockle : *No*, said he, *lest perhaps gathering up the cockle you root up the wheat also together with it.** It is true, Theotimus, that anger is a servant who, being strong, courageous and of great undertakings, does also at first a great deal of work, but withal he is so ardent, so hotheaded, inconsiderate and impetuous, that he ordinarily does no good things without at the same time doing many evil. It is not good husbandry, say our countryfolk, to keep peacocks in the house ; for though they hunt spiders and rid the house of them, yet they so spoil the furniture and the buildings themselves that their usefulness is not comparable to the harm they do. Anger was given by Nature as a help to reason, and is employed by grace in the service of zeal, to put in execution its designs ; yet it is a dangerous help, and not greatly to be desired, for if it gets strength it becomes master, overturning the authority of reason ; and while it does no more than zeal would perform all alone, it keeps one in a well-founded fear that waxing strong it may take possession of the heart and of zeal, making them slaves to its tyranny, like a carefully disposed fire, which in an instant embraces a building, and which no one can extinguish. It were an act of despair to put foreign auxiliaries into a fortress, who may make themselves the strongest.

Self-love often deceives us and leads us away, gratifying its own passions under the name of zeal. Zeal has once made use of anger, and now anger in its turn uses the name of zeal, in order to keep its shameful disorder covered under this. And

* Matt. xiii. 29.

mark that I say it makes use of the name of zeal; for it can make no use of zeal itself, since it is the property of all virtues, but especially of Charity, whereof zeal is a dependence, to be so good that none can abuse them.

A notorious sinner, once went and threw himself at the feet of a good and worthy priest, protesting with much submission, that he came to find a cure for his disease, that is, to receive the holy absolution of his faults. A certain monk called Demophilus, considering that, in his opinion, this poor penitent came too nigh the holy altar, fell into so violent a fit of anger, that throwing himself upon him, he kicked and pushed him thence with his feet, railing at the good priest in an outrageous sort, who according to his duty had mildly received this poor penitent. And then running up to the altar he took off the holy things which were there, and carried them away, lest, as he would have men think, the place should have been profaned by the sinner's approach. Now having finished this fair exploit of zeal, he stayed not yet there, but made a great rejoicing about the matter to the great S. Denis the Areopagite in a letter which he wrote about it, to which he received an excellent answer, worthy of the apostolical spirit wherewith that great disciple of S. Paul was animated. For he made him clearly see that his zeal had been at once indiscreet, imprudent and impudent; because though the zeal for the honour due unto holy things were good and laudable, yet was it practised against all reason, without any consideration or judgment, since he had employed kicks, outrages, railing and reproaches, in a place, under circumstances, and against persons, whom and which he ought to have honoured, loved and respected; so that the zeal could not be good, being practised with such great disorder. But in this same answer, that great saint recounts another admirable example of a great zeal, proceeding from a very good soul, which was however spoilt and vitiated by the excess of anger which it had stirred up.

A pagan had led astray and made return to idolatry a Christian of Candia, recently converted to the faith. Carpus, a man eminent for purity and sanctity of life, who, as is very probable, was the bishop of Candia, conceived such an anger at it as he had never before entertained, and let himself be so far carried

away with this passion, that having risen at midnight to pray
according to his custom, he concluded with himself that it was
not reasonable that the wicked men should any longer live, with
great indignation beseeching the divine justice to strike down at
once with his thunderbolts these two sinners together, the pagan
seducer and the Christian seduced.   But hear, Theotimus, how
God corrected the bitterness of the passion which carried the
poor Carpus beyond himself.   First he made him, as another S.
Stephen, see the heavens open, and our Saviour Jesus Christ
seated upon a great throne, surrounded with a multitude of
angels, who attended him in human form; then he saw below,
the earth gaping as a horrid and vast gulf; and the two erring
ones, to whom he had wished so much evil, he saw upon the very
brink of this precipice, trembling and well-nigh paralysed with
fear, as being about to fall down it; on the one side they were
drawn by a multitude of serpents, which rising out of the gulf,
wrapped themselves about their legs, and with their tails gradu-
ally moved and provoked them to their fall; on the other side,
certain men pushed and beat them to make them tumble in, so
that they seemed on the point of being swallowed up in this
abyss.   Now consider, my Theotimus, the violence of the passion
of Carpus: for as he himself afterwards recounted to S. Denis,
he never thought of contemplating our Saviour and the angels,
who showed themselves in the heavens, such pleasure did he take
in seeing below them the frightful distress of those two miserable
wretches.   His only trouble was that they were so long perishing, and thereupon he endeavoured himself to precipitate them
down; and seeing he could not do it quite at once he was angry,
and began to curse them, until at length, lifting up his eyes to
heaven, he saw the sweet and most pitiful Saviour, who, moved
by an extreme pity and compassion at what was happening,
arising from his throne and descending to the place where the
two miserable beings were, stretched out to them his helping
hand, while the angels also, some on one side some on another,
caught hold of them to hinder them from falling into that dreadful gulf; and, at last the amiable and mild Jesus, turning himself
to the wrathful Carpus:—Nay, Carpus, said he, henceforth
wreak your anger on me : for I am ready to suffer once more to

save men, and it would be a joy to me to do so, if it could be without sin on man's part: at any rate, think which would be the better for thee, to be in that gulf with the serpents, or to live with angels who are such great friends of men. Theotimus, the holy man Carpus had just reason to enter into zeal concerning these two men, and his zeal had but rightly raised his anger against them, but anger being once moved left reason and zeal behind, transgressing all the terms and limits of holy love and consesequently of zeal, which is its fervour : anger had changed the hatred of sin into the hatred of the sinner, and most sweet charity into an outrageous cruelty.

Thus there are persons who think one cannot be very zealous unless one is very angry, thinking that unless they spoil all they can manage nothing, whereas on the contrary true zeal most rarely makes use of anger ; for as we never apply the lancet to the sick save when it cannot possibly be helped, so holy zeal does not employ anger save in extreme necessities.

CHAPTER XVI.

THAT THE EXAMPLE OF CERTAIN SAINTS WHO SEEM TO HAVE EXERCISED THEIR ZEAL WITH ANGER, MAKES NOTHING AGAINST THE DOCTRINE OF THE PRECEDING CHAPTER.

It is true, indeed, my friend Theotimus, that Moses, Phinees, Elias, Mathathias and many great servants of God made use of anger in the exercise of their zeal, on many remarkable occasions, yet note also, I pray you, that those were great souls, who could well handle their passions and regulate their anger ; like that brave captain of the Gospel who said to his soldiers : *go*, and they went, *come*, and they came :* but we, who are, all of us, but common little people, have no such power over our movements ; our horse is not so well broken in, that we can make him gallop or stop at our pleasure. Wise and well trained hounds run afield or

* Matt. viii. 9.

come back according to the huntsman's call, but untrained young hounds break away and are disobedient. Great saints who have made their passions tractable, mortifying them by the exercise of virtue, can also turn about their anger as they like, send it out and draw it back as seems good to them ; but we, who have unbridled passions, quite young, or at least mistaught, cannot let our anger go save at peril of great disorder, for being once loose we can no longer restrain or regulate it.

S. Denis speaking to this Demophilus who would have given the name of zeal to his rage and fury : " He that would correct others," said he, " must first have a care that anger do not turn reason out of the empire and dominion which God has given it in the soul, and that it do not stir up a revolt, sedition and confusion within ourselves; hence we in no sort approve your impetuosities (to which an indiscreet zeal urged you), though you should a thousand times recall Phinees and Elias; for similar words did not please Jesus Christ, when said to him by his disciples, who were not yet made partakers of that sweet and benign Spirit." Phinees, Theotimus, seeing a certain unhappy Israelite offend God with a Madianitess, slew them both : Elias foretold the death of Ochozias, who, indignant at this prediction, sent two captains one after another, each with fifty men, to take him : and the man of God made fire descend from heaven which devoured them.* Now one day that our Lord was journeying in Samaria, he sent into a town to take his lodging, but the inhabitants knowing that our Lord was a Jew by nation, and that he was going to Jerusalem, would not lodge him ; which S. John and S. James seeing, they said unto our Saviour : *Wilt thou that we command fire to come down from heaven and consume them ?* And our Lord *turning rebuked them, saying : you know not of what spirit you are. The Son of man came not to destroy souls but to save* them.† This it is then, Theotimus, that S. Denis would say to Demophilus, who alleged the example of Phinees and Elias : for S. John and S. James, who would have imitated Phinees and Elias in making fire descend from heaven upon men, were reprehended by our Lord, who gave them to

* 4 Kings i. 12. † Luke ix. 54.

know that his spirit and his zeal were sweet, mild and gracious, making use of indignation or wrath but very rarely, when there was no longer hope of doing good any other way. S. Thomas Aquinas, that great star of theology, being sick of the disease of which he died, at the Monastery of Fossanuova, of the order of Citeaux, the religious besought him to make them a short exposition of the Canticle of Canticles in imitation of S. Bernard, and he answered them : My dear fathers, give me S. Bernard's spirit and I will interpret this divine Canticle like S. Bernard. So verily, if it were said to one of us petty, miserable, imperfect and wretched Christians :—use anger and indignation in your zeal, as did Phinees, Elias, Mathathias, S. Peter and S. Paul : we ought to reply : give us the spirit of perfection and pure zeal, with the interior light which those great saints had, and we will arm ourselves with anger as they did. It is not the fortune of every one to know how to be angry when and as he ought.

Those great saints were immediately inspired by God, and therefore might boldly employ their anger without peril; for the same Spirit which animated them to these great acts also held the reins of their just wrath lest they might transgress the prescribed bounds. Anger which is inspired or excited by the Holy Ghost is no longer the anger of man, and it is man's wrath that we are to beware of, because, as S. James says : *The anger of man worketh not the justice of God.** And indeed, when those great servants of God made use of anger, it was on occurrences so solemn and for crimes so excessive, that there was no danger that the punishment would exceed the fault.

Are we, do you think, to take the liberty of abusing sinners, of blaming nations, of taking to task and censuring our directors and prelates, because S. Paul once calls the Galatians *senseless*, represents to the Candiots their bad inclinations, and *withstands to the face* the glorious S. Peter his superior ? Verily every one is not a S. Paul, to know how to do these things suitably : but bitter, harsh, presumptuous and reviling spirits, following their own inclinations, humours, aversions and arrogance, would throw the mantle of zeal over their iniquity ; and under the name of

* James i. 20.

this sacred fire every man permits himself to be burnt up with his own passions. It is zeal for the salvation of souls which makes the prelateship desired, if you will believe the ambitious man; which makes the monk, who is destined for the choir, run hither and thither, as the restless soul himself will tell you; which causes all those censures and murmurings against the prelates of the Church and temporal princes, if you will give ear to that arrogant man. You will hear from him of nothing but zeal, and you will see no zeal, but only opprobrious and railing speeches, anger, hatred and rancour, disquiet of spirit and of tongue.

Zeal may be practised in three ways. First in performing great actions of justice to repel evil; and this belongs only to those who have the public offices of correcting, censuring, and reprehending in quality of superiors, such as princes, prelates, magistrates, preachers: but since this office is honourable, every one undertakes it, every one will have to do with it. Secondly, one may use zeal by doing actions of great virtue in order to give good example, by suggesting remedies for evils, and exhorting men to apply them, by effecting the good that is opposite to the evil which we desire to banish. This belongs to every one, and yet few will to do it. Finally, the most excellent use of zeal lies in suffering and enduring much to hinder or divert evil, and scarce any will have this sort of zeal. A specious zeal is all our ambition; upon that, each one willingly spends his talent, never attending to the fact that it is not zeal indeed which is thereby sought but glory, the satisfaction of our pride, anger, annoyance and other passions.

Certainly our Saviour's zeal principally appeared in his death upon the cross to destroy death and sin in men: in which he was sovereignly imitated by that admirable vessel of election and dilection, as the great S. Gregory Nazianzen, in golden words, represents him; for speaking of this holy Apostle he says: " He fights for all, he prays for all, he is passionately jealous about all, he is inflamed for all, yea he has dared yet more for his brethren according to the flesh, so that if I may dare also to say it, he desires through charity that they may have his own place near Our Saviour. O excellence of courage and incredible fervour of spirit ! He imitates Jesus Christ, *who for us was made a curse,** *who took* on himself *our infirmities* and *carried our diseases.*† Or, that I may speak a little more soberly, he was the first after our Saviour who refused not to suffer and to be reputed wicked for their sake." Even so then, Theotimus, as our Saviour was whipped, condemned, crucified, as a man devoted, destined and set apart to bear and support all the reproaches, ignominies and punishments due to all the sinners in the world, and to be a general sacrifice for sin,—as he was made an anathema, was cast off and abandoned by his eternal Father, so, according to the true doctrine of this great Nazianzen, the glorious Apostle S. Paul desired to be filled with ignominy, to be crucified, cast off, abandoned and sacrificed for the sin of the Jews, that the curse and punishment which they deserved might fall upon him ; and as our Saviour took upon him the sins of the world, and was made a curse, sacrificed for sin and forsaken by his Father in such sense that he ceased not ever to be the well-beloved Son in whom his Father was well pleased,—so the holy Apostle desired indeed to be a curse, and to be separated from his master, to be left to the mercy of the reproaches and punishments due unto the Jews, yet he never desired to be deprived of charity and the grace of his Lord, from which, moreover, nothing could ever separate him; that is to say, he desired to be *treated* as a man cast off by God, but he did not desire actually to *be* cast off and deprived of his grace, for this cannot be holily desired. So the heavenly spouse declares, that though *love is strong as death,* which makes a separation between the body and soul, zeal, which is an ardent love, is yet stronger, for it resembles *hell,* which separates the soul from the sight of Our Lord ; but it is never said, nor can be said, that love or zeal was like to sin, which alone separates from the grace of God. And indeed how could the ardour of love possibly make one desire to be separated from grace, since love is grace itself, or at least cannot be without grace. And the zeal of the great S. Paul was in some sort practised by the little S. Paul, I mean S. Paulinus, who to deliver a slave out of bondage became himself a slave, sacrificing his own liberty to bestow it upon his neighbour.

* Gal. iii. 13.   † Matt. viii. 17.

" O how happy is he," says S. Ambrose, who knows how to discipline zeal!" " The devil will easily," says S. Bernard, "delude thy zeal, if thou neglect knowledge ; therefore let thy zeal be inflamed with charity, adorned with knowledge, established in constancy." True zeal is the child of charity as being its ardour ; wherefore, like to charity, it is *patient, is kind, envieth not, dealeth not perversely, seeketh not her own, is not provoked to anger, rejoiceth in the truth.** The ardour of true zeal resembles that of the huntsman, being diligent, careful, active, industrious, eager in pursuit, but without passion, anger or disquiet, for if the huntsman's work were done in anger, bad temper and vexation, it would not be so much loved and desired. Zeal in like manner has ardours which are extreme, but constant, solid, sweet, industrious, equally agreeable and untiring ; whereas on the contrary, false zeal is turbulent, troubled, insolent, arrogant, choleric, transient, equally impetuous and inconstant.

CHAPTER XVII.

HOW OUR LORD PRACTISED ALL THE MOST EXCELLENT ACTS OF LOVE.

HAVING spoken at large of the sacred acts of divine love, I present you, that you may more easily and holily preserve the memory of them, with a collection or abridgment of them. *The charity of Jesus Christ presseth us,*† says the great apostle. Yea truly, Theotimus, it forces and carries us away by its infinite sweetness, exercised in the whole work of our Redemption, in which appeared the benignity and love of God towards men : for what did not this divine lover do in matter of love ? 1. He loved us with a love of *Complacency,* for *his delights were to be with the children of men*‡ and to draw man to himself, making himself man. 2. He loved us with a love of *Benevolence,*

---

* 1 Cor. xiii.   † 2 Cor. v. 14.   ‡ Prov. viii. 31.

bestowing his own divinity upon man, so that man was God.
3. He united himself unto us by an incomprehensible *Union*,
whereby he adhered to our nature, and joined himself so closely,
indissolubly and supereminently to it, that never was anything
so strictly joined and bound to humanity as is now the most
holy divinity in the person of the Son of God. 4. He *flowed
out* into us, and as it were melted his greatness, to bring
it to the form and figure of our littleness, whence he is
styled a source of living water, dew and rain of heaven.
5. He loved us to *Ecstasy*, not only because, as S. Denis says,
by the excess of his loving goodness he goes in a certain
manner out of himself, extending his Providence to all things
and being in all things, but also because he has in a sort forsaken and emptied himself, dried up his greatness and glory,
resigned the throne of his incomprehensible majesty, and, if it
be lawful so to say, *annihilated himself* to stoop down to our
humanity, to fill us with his divinity, to replenish us with his
goodness, to raise us to his dignity, and bestow upon us the
divine being of children of God. And he of whom it is so
frequently written : *I live, saith the Lord ;* could afterwards
have said according to his apostle's language : *I live, now not
I,* but man *liveth in me.* To me *to live* is man, and *to die* for
man *is gain. My life is hidden* with man *in God.** He who
dwelt in himself dwells now in us, and he who was living from
all eternity in the bosom of his Eternal Father becomes mortal
in the bosom of his temporal Mother ; he who lived eternally by
his own divine life, lived with a human life, and he who from
eternity had been only God, shall be for all eternity man too :
so has the love of man ravished God, and drawn him into an
ecstasy ! 6. Love often led him to *admiration,* as of the Centurion
and Chanaanitess. 7. He *contemplated* the young man who had
till that hour kept the commandments, and desired to be taught
perfection. 8. He took a *loving quiet* in us, yea even with some
suspension of his senses, in his mother's womb and in his infancy.
9. He had wondrous movements of *Tenderness* towards
little children, whom he would take in his arms and lovingly

* Gal. ii. 20.

fondle; towards Martha and Magdalen, towards Lazarus, over whom he wept, as he wept also over the city of Jerusalem. 10. He was animated with an incomparable *Zeal*, which, as S. Denis says, changed into *Jealousy*, turning away, as much as possible, all evil from his beloved human nature, with hazard, yea with the price, of his own life; driving away the devil the prince of this world, who seemed to be his rival and companion. 11. He had a thousand thousand *Languors of love;* for whence could those divine words proceed: *I have a baptism, wherewith I am to be baptized: and how am I straightened until it be accomplished?** The hour in which he was baptized in his blood was not yet come, and he languished after it; the love which he bore unto us urging him thereunto, that he might by his death see us delivered from an eternal death. So he was sad, and sweated the blood of distress in the Garden of Olives, not only by reason of the exceeding sorrow which his soul felt in the inferior part of his reason, but also by reason of the singular love which he bore unto us in the superior portion thereof, sorrow causing in him a horror of death, and love giving him an extreme desire of the same; so that a most fierce combat and a cruel agony took place, between the desire and the dread of death, unto a mighty shedding of blood, which streamed down upon the earth as from a living spring.

12. Finally, Theotimus, this divine lover *died* amongst the flames and ardours of love, by reason of the infinite charity which he had towards us, and by the force and virtue of love: that is he died in love, by love, for love, and *of love*, for though his cruel torments were sufficient to have killed any one, yet could death never make entry into his life who keeps the keys of life and death, unless divine love, which handles those keys, had opened the gates to death, to let it ravage that divine body and despoil it of life. Love was not content to have only made him subject to death for us unless it made him dead. It was by choice, not by force of torment, that he died. *No man taketh my life away from me: but I lay it down of myself, and I have power to lay it down, and I have power to take it up again.*† *He*

---

* Luke xii. 50.　　　　† John x. 18.

was offered, says Isaias, *because it was his own will.** And therefore it is not said that his spirit went away, forsook him, or
separated itself from him, but, contrariwise, that he gave up his
spirit, breathed it out, yielded and commended it into the hands
of his eternal Father ; so that S. Athanasius remarks that he
bowed his head to die, that he might consent to and bend to
death's approach, which otherwise durst not have come near
him; and crying out with a loud voice he gives up his spirit into
his Father's hands, to show that as he had strength and breath
enough not to die, so had he love so great that he could no longer
live, but would by his death revive those who without it could
never escape death, nor have the chance of true life.   Wherefore
our Saviour's death was a true sacrifice, and a sacrifice of holocaust, which himself offered to his Father for our redemption :
for though the pains and dolours of his passion were so great
and violent that any but he had died of them, yet had he never
died of them unless he himself had pleased, and unless the fire
of his infinite charity had consumed his life.   He was then the
sacrificer himself, who offered himself unto his Father and immolated himself, dying in love, to love, by love, for love, and of
love.

   Yet beware of saying, Theotimus, that this amorous death of
the Saviour took place by manner of rapture, for the object
which his charity moved him to die for was not love-worthy
enough to ravish to itself this divine soul, which departed then
from his body by way of ecstasy, driven and forced on by the
abundance and might of love ; even as we see the myrrh tree
send forth its first juice by its mere abundance, without squeezing
or drawing in any way ; according to that which he himself said,
as we have declared : *No man taketh my life away from me but
I lay it down of myself.*   O God! Theotimus, what burning
coals are cast upon all our hearts to inflame us to the exercise
of holy love towards our all-good Saviour, seeing he has so
lovingly practised them towards us who are so evil !   *This charity
then of Jesus Christ presseth us !*

---

* Is. liii. 7.

BOOK XI.

SOVEREIGN AUTHORITY WHICH SACRED LOVE HOLDS OVER ALL THE VIRTUES, ACTIONS AND PERFECTIONS OF THE SOUL.

CHAPTER I.

HOW AGREEABLE ALL VIRTUES ARE TO GOD.

Virtue is of its own nature so amiable, that God favours it wheresoever he finds it. The pagans, though they were enemies of his divine Majesty, now and then practised certain human and moral virtues, which were not by their nature placed above the forces of the reasonable spirit. Now you may guess, Theotimus, how small a matter that was : for though these virtues made a great show, yet in effect they were of little worth, by reason of the lowness of the intention of those who practised them. They laboured for scarcely anything but honour, as S. Augustine says, or for some other object of light consideration, such as the upholding the social good, or from some weak inclination they had to good ; which inclination, meeting with no contradiction, carried them on to trifling acts of virtue—as for example, to mutual courtesy, to aid their friends, to live with moderation, not to steal, to serve masters faithfully, to pay hirelings' wages. And nevertheless though this was so slender, and accompanied with many imperfections, God took it in good part from those poor people, and recompensed it largely.

464

The midwives whom Pharaoh commanded to kill all the male children of the Israelites were without doubt Egyptians and pagans; for in the excuse they made for not having executed the king's pleasure, they said : *The Hebrew women are not like the Egyptian:* this would not have been to the purpose if they had been Hebrews : and it is not credible that Pharaoh would have granted so cruel a commission against the Hebrews to Hebrew women, being of the same nation and religion : besides Josephus testifies that they were in fact Egyptians. Now, Egyptians and pagans as they were, yet they feared to offend God by so barbarous and unnatural a cruelty as the massacre of so many little children would have been. The divine sweetness was so pleased with this that it *built their houses*, that is to say, made them fruitful in children and in temporal riches.

Nabuchodonosor, King of Babylon, had waged a just war against the city of Tyre, which the divine justice willed to chastise, and God signified to Ezechiel that in recompense thereof he would deliver up Egypt as a prey into the hands of Nabuchodonosor and his army, *Because*, said God, *he hath laboured for me.** Hence, adds S. Jerome in the commentary, we learn that in case the very pagans do some good thing they are not left unrewarded by God's judgment. So did Daniel exhort Nabuchodonosor, an infidel, to *redeem* his *sins by alms*,† that is, to ransom himself out of the temporal pains due to his sins, which hung over his head. Do you see then, Theotimus, how true it is that God makes account of virtues, though practised by persons otherwise wicked? If he had not approved the mercy of the midwives and the justice of the war of the Babylonians, would he have taken care, I pray you, to reward them? And if Daniel had not known that the infidelity of Nabuchodonosor would not prevent God from being pleased with his alms, why would he have counselled him to do them? Indeed the Apostle assures us that pagans *who have not the law do by nature those things that are of the law.*‡ And when they do so, who can doubt that they do well, and that God makes account of it? Pagans understood that marriage was good and

---

necessary, they saw that it was becoming to have their children brought up in liberal knowledge, in the love of their country, in the arts of civil life, and they did so. Now I leave it to your consideration whether this was not grateful unto God, since to this end he had given the light of reason and natural instinct.

Natural reason is a good tree which God has planted in us; the fruits which spring from it cannot but be good. They are fruits which in comparison with those which spring from grace are indeed of very small value, yet still, not of no value, since God has valued them, and for them has given temporal rewards. Thus, according to the great S. Augustine, he rewarded the moral virtues of the Romans with the grand extent and magnificent renown of their empire.

Sin unquestionably makes the soul sick, and then she cannot do great and laborious deeds; yet little ones she can do, for all the actions of the sick are not sickly: they still speak, they still see, they still hear, they still drink. The soul in sin can do good works, which, being natural, are rewarded with natural rewards; being civil, are paid in civil and human money, that is, with temporal advantages. The sinner is not in the state of the devils, whose wills are so steeped in and incorporated with evil that they can will no good at all. No, Theotimus; the sinner in this world is not in that state. Here, he is in the way between Jerusalem and Jericho, wounded to death but not yet dead; for, says the Gospel, he is left *half-dead*; and as he is half-alive so he can do half-living actions. 'Tis true he can neither walk, nor rise, nor cry for aid, no, not so much as speak, save only languishingly, by reason of the faintness of his heart; yet can he open his eyes, stir his fingers, sigh, make some word of complaint:—weak actions, and actions in spite of which he would miserably die of his wounds, had not the merciful Samaritan poured in the oil and wine, and carried him to the inn, where he gave charge that at his cost the man should be dressed and looked to.*

Natural reason is deeply wounded, and, as it were, half slain by sin; whence, being in such sad condition, it cannot observe

* Luke x.

all the commandments, which, however, it clearly sees to be good : it knows its duty but cannot acquit itself thereof; its eyes have more light to discover the way than its legs have strength to undertake it.

The sinner may indeed occasionally observe some of the commandments, yea all of them for some short time, so long as no great occasion for practising virtues commanded, or violent temptation to commit sin forbidden, present itself. But that a sinner should live long in his sin without adding to it new ones, is not a thing that can be done but by God's special protection, for man's enemies are ardent, active, and perpetually striving to cast him down, and when they see that no occasion of practising virtues commanded occurs, they excite a thousand temptations to make him fall into things forbidden ; at which time nature without grace cannot save itself from the precipice : for if we overcome, *God gives us the victory through Jesus Christ,** as S. Paul says. *Watch and pray, that you enter not into temptation.*† If Our Lord had said only *watch*, we might expect that our own power would be sufficient, but when he adds *pray*, he shows that *if he keep not* our souls in time of temptation, *in vain* shall *they watch who keep them.*

CHAPTER II.

THAT DIVINE LOVE MAKES THE VIRTUES IMMEASURABLY MORE
AGREEABLE TO GOD THAN THEY ARE OF THEIR OWN NATURE.

THE masters of husbandry admire the gracious innocence and purity of little strawberries, because, though they lie upon the ground and are continually crept over by serpents, lizards, and other venomous beasts, they yet receive no impression of poison, nor are infected with any malign quality ; a sign that they have no affinity with poison. Such then are human virtues, Theotimus ; which, though they may be in a heart that is low, earthly, and largely occupied by sin, yet are not infected with its

* 1 Cor. xv. 57.   † Matt. xxvi. 41.

malice, being of a nature so noble and innocent that it cannot
be corrupted by the society of iniquity, according to what even
Aristotle has said:—that virtue is a habit which no one can
make ill use of.   And though the virtues which are so good in
themselves are not rewarded with an eternal recompense when
they are practised by infidels or by such as are not in the state
of grace, this is not surprising, because the sinful heart from
whence they proceed is not capable of an eternal good
(being, as it is, turned away from God), and because no
one can receive the celestial inheritance belonging to the Son of
God, but such as are in him, and are adoptive brothers of his ;
to say nothing of this reason, that the covenant by which God
promises heaven refers to such only as are in his grace, while the
virtues of sinners have no worth nor value save that of their
nature, which, consequently, cannot raise them to the merit of
supernatural rewards.   Indeed these are for this very cause
called supernatural, that nature and all that belongs thereto can
neither give nor merit them.

But the virtues which are found in the friends of God, though
they be only moral and natural in themselves, are yet ennobled,
and raised to the dignity of being holy works, by reason of the
excellence of the heart which produces them.   It is one of the
properties of friendship to make the friend and all that is good
and honest in him dear to us : friendship pours out its grace
upon all the actions of him who is loved, however little ground
of favour there may be ; the bitternesses of friends are sweets,
and the sweets of enemies are bitter.   All the virtuous actions of
a heart at friends with God are dedicated to God, for the heart
that has given itself, how has it not given all that depends on
itself?   He that gives the tree without reserve, gives he not
also the leaves, flowers and fruit ?   *The just shall flourish like
the palm-tree : he shall grow up like the cedar of Libanus.   They
that are planted in the house of the Lord shall flourish in the
courts of the house of our God.** Since the just man is planted
in the house of God, his leaves, his flowers and his fruit grow
therein, and are dedicated to the service of His Majesty.   *He*

* Ps. xci. 13, 14.

shall be like a tree which is planted near the running waters, which shall bring forth its fruit in due season. And his leaf shall not fall off: and all whatsoever he shall do shall prosper.* Not only the fruits of charity, and the flowers of the works which it ordains, but even its very leaves, that is, the moral and natural virtues, draw a special power and efficacy from the love of the heart which produces them. If you are grafting a rose tree, and put a grain of musk in the cleft of the stock, all the roses that spring from it will smell of musk: cleave then your heart by holy penitence, and put the love of God in the cleft; then engraft on it what virtue you please, and the works which spring from it will be all perfumed with sanctity, without need of any further attention.

When the Spartans had heard an excellent sentence from the mouth of some wicked man, they never thought it right to receive it till it was first pronounced by the mouth of some good man: so that to make it worthy of acceptance they did no more than get it uttered again by a virtuous man. If you desire to make the human and moral virtue of Epictetus, Socrates or Demades become holy, cause them to be practised by a truly Christian soul, that is, by one which has the love of God. So God first had respect to the good Abel, and then to his offerings, these taking their favour and worth in the sight of God from the goodness and piety of him who offered them. Oh the sovereign goodness of this great God, which so favours its lovers that it cherishes their least little actions, so long as they have the slightest degree of goodness, and excellently ennobles them, giving them the title and quality of holy! Ah! this is in consideration of his beloved Son, whose adopted children he would honour, sanctifying all there is of good in them, their bones, the hairs of their head, their garments, their graves, yea, down to the very *shadow*† of their bodies; their faith, hope, love, religion, yea even their social life, their courtesy, the affability of their hearts.

Therefore my beloved brethren, saith the Apostle, *be ye steadfast and immovable, always abounding in the work of the Lord, knowing that your labour is not in vain in the Lord.*‡ And

---

* Ps. i. 3.   † Acts v. 15.   ‡ 1 Cor xv 58.

mark, Theotimus, that every virtuous work is to be esteemed the " work of the Lord," yea though it were even practised by an infidel ; for his divine Majesty said unto Ezechiel *that Nabucho- donosor and his army had laboured for him,** because he had waged a lawful and just war against the Tyrians : sufficiently showing thereby that the justice of the unjust is God's, and tends and belongs to him, though the unjust who work that justice are neither his, nor tend nor belong to him : for as the great prince and prophet Job, though of pagan extraction and an inhabitant of the land of Hus, did for all that belong to God, so moral virtues, though they proceed from a sinful heart, do none the less belong to God.   But when these same virtues are found in a truly Christian heart, that is in a heart endowed with holy love, then they not only belong to God, but they are not " in vain in the Lord," being rendered fruitful and precious in the eyes of his goodness.   " Add charity to a man," says S. Augus- tine, " and everything profits ; take charity from him, and what remains profits him no longer."   And : *To them that love God all things work together unto good,*† says the Apostle.

CHAPTER III.

THAT THERE ARE SOME VIRTUES WHICH DIVINE LOVE RAISES TO A HIGHER DEGREE OF EXCELLENCE THAN OTHERS.

BUT there are some virtues which by reason of their natural alliance and correspondence with charity are also much more capable of receiving the precious influence of sacred love, and consequently the communication of the dignity and worth of it. Such are faith and hope, which, together with charity, have an immediate reference to God ; and religion, and penitence, and devotion, which are employed to the honour of his Divine Majesty.   For these virtues, of their own nature, have so close a relation to God, and are so susceptible of the impressions of

* Ezech. xxix. 20.   † Rom. viii. 28.

heavenly love, that to make them participate in its sanctity they need only to be with it, that is, in a heart which loves God. So, to make grapes taste of olives it is but necessary to plant the vine amongst the olives; for by their neighbourhood alone, without touching one another at all, these plants will mutually interchange their savours and properties, so great an inclination and so strict an affinity is there of one to the other.

Truly all flowers, except those of the tree called Sad (*triste*), and a few others that are monsters in Nature, all, I say, rejoice, expand and put on beauty at the sight of the sun, and the vital heat which they receive from his rays; but all yellow flowers, and especially that which the Greeks term *Heliotropium*, and we sunflower, not only receive gladness and pleasure from his presence, but by an affectionate turning movement follow the attractions of his rays, keeping him in sight, and turning themselves towards him, from his rising to his setting. So all virtues receive a new lustre and an excellent dignity from the presence of holy love, but faith, hope, the fear of God, piety, penance, and all the other virtues which of their own nature particularly tend to God and to his honour, not only receive the impression of divine love whereby they are raised to a great value, but they wholly incline towards it, associating themselves with it, following and serving it on all occasions. For in fine, my dear Theotimus, the holy Word attributes a certain saving, sanctifying and glorifying property and force to faith, to hope, to piety, to the fear of God, to penance: which clearly shows that those virtues are of great price, and that being practised by a heart which is in charity they become more excellent, fruitful and holy than the others, which of their own nature have not so great an affinity with sacred love. And he who cries out: *If I should have all faith, so that I could remove mountains, and have not charity, it profiteth me nothing,** clearly shows that with charity this faith would greatly profit him. Charity then is a virtue beyond comparison, which not only adorns the heart in which it is, but by its mere presence also blesses and sanctifies all the virtues which it meets there, per-

---

* 1 Cor. xiii. 2.

fuming and scenting them with its celestial odour, by means of which they are made of great value in the sight of God; which, however, it does far more excellently in faith, in hope and in other virtues, which of themselves naturally tend to piety.

Wherefore, Theotimus, of all virtuous actions we ought most carefully to practise those of religion and reverence towards divine things, those of faith, of hope and of the most holy fear of God, taking occasion often to speak of heavenly things, thinking of and sighing after eternity, frequenting churches and sacred services, reading spiritual books, observing the ceremonies of the Christian religion : for sacred love is fed according to its heart's desire in these exercises, and in greater abundance spreads its graces and properties over them than it does over the actions of those virtues which are purely human ; as the lovely rainbow makes all the plants upon which it lights odoriferous, but the *aspalathus* incomparably more so than all the rest.

CHAPTER IV.

THAT DIVINE LOVE MORE EXCELLENTLY SANCTIFIES THE VIRTUES WHEN THEY ARE PRACTISED BY ITS ORDER AND COMMANDMENT.

THE fair Rachel had children by Jacob in two ways. She counted as hers the children of her handmaid Bala, and afterwards she had children of her own—namely, Joseph and the beloved Benjamin.

Now I say to you, my dear Theotimus, that charity and sacred love, a hundred times more fair than Rachel, ceaselessly desires to produce holy operations. She calls the operations of the other virtues her offspring because they are produced by her order, love being the master of the heart, and consequently of all the works of the other virtues done by its consent. But, further, this divine love has two acts which are her own proper issue and of her extraction. Of these the one is effective love, which, as another Joseph, using the plenitude of royal authority, subjects and reduces all the people—her faculties, powers, passions and affections—to God's will, that it may be loved, obeyed and served above all things, by this means putting the great celestial commandment in execution : *Thou shalt love the Lord thy God with all thy heart, with all thy soul, with all thy mind, and with all thy strength.* The other is affective or affectionate love, which, as a little Benjamin, is exceedingly delicate, tender, pleasing and amiable, but in this more happy than Benjamin, that charity its mother dies not in its bringing forth, but, so to say, gains a new life, by the sweetness she feels in it.

Thus then, Theotimus, the virtuous actions of the children of God all belong to charity ; some of them because she produces them of her own nature; others because she sanctifies them by her quickening presence ; and finally others, by the authority and command which she exercises over the other virtues, whence she makes them spring. And these last, as indeed they are not so eminent in dignity as the actions which properly and immediately issue from charity, yet incomparably surpass those which take their whole sanctity from the mere presence and society of charity.

A great general of an army having won some important battle, will without doubt have all the honour of the victory, and not unreasonably ; for he himself will have fought in the very front of the army, doing many great feats of arms, and for the rest he will have arrayed his troops, and ordained and commanded all that was done: so that he is considered to have done all, either by himself, fighting with his own hand, or by his direction, commanding others. And even if some friendly troops come unexpectedly and fall in with the army, yet the general is not deprived of the honour of their work, for though they have not received his commands, yet they have served him and followed his intentions. Nevertheless, although we attribute the glory as a whole to him, we do not fail to give each part of his army due credit for its own share ; we say that the vanguard did this, the main body that, the rearguard the other; the French behaved thus, the Italians thus, the Germans and the Spaniards thus : yea we praise the private individuals who have

distinguished themselves in the battle.   So, my dear Theotimus,
amongst all the virtues, the glory of our salvation and victory
over hell is ascribed to divine love, which, as prince and general
of the whole army of virtues, does all the exploits by which we
gain the triumph.   For sacred love has his proper actions which
issue and proceed from himself, by which he does wonders of
arms against our enemy, and withal he ranges, commands and
orders the actions of other virtues, which are therefore, termed
acts commanded or ordained by love.   And if, at last, some
virtues perform their operations without his order, yet if they
assist his intention, which is God's honour, he will still acknowledge them to be his own.   Nevertheless, though we say in general,
after the divine Apostle, that *Charity beareth all things, believeth
all things, hopeth all things, endureth all things,** in a word, that
it does all, yet we distribute in particular the praise of the
salvation of the Blessed to other virtues, according as they
excelled in each one ; for we say some were saved by faith,
others by alms-deeds, others by temperance, prayer, humility,
hope, chastity,—because the acts of these virtues have appeared
with lustre in these saints.   Yet again after we have extolled
these particular virtues we must reciprocally refer all their
honour to divine love, which to every one gives all the sanctity
which they have.   For what else does the glorious Apostle
mean when he teaches that charity *is kind, is patient, that it
believes all, hopes all, bears all,* save that charity ordains and
commands patience to be patient, hope to hope, faith to believe.
And truly, Theotimus, at the same time the Apostle intimates that
love is the soul and life of all the virtues, as though he would
say : patience is not patient enough, nor faith faithful enough,
nor hope confident enough, nor mildness sweet enough, unless
love animate and quicken them.   The same thing this same
vessel of election gives us to understand when he says, that
nothing profits him and he is nothing without charity ; for it
is as though he had said, that without love a man is not patient,
nor mild, nor constant, nor faithful, nor hopeful, in the way a
servant of God should be, which is the true and desirable being
of man.

* I Cor. xiii. 7.

CHAPTER V.

HOW LOVE SPREADS ITS EXCELLENCE OVER THE OTHER VIRTUES,
PERFECTING THEIR PARTICULAR EXCELLENCE.

I HAVE seen, says Pliny, a tree at Tivoli grafted in all the fashions that one can graft, and bearing all sorts of fruit; for upon one branch there were cherries, on another nuts, on others grapes, figs, pomegranates, apples, and, in a word, all kinds of fruit. This was wonderful, Theotimus, yet more so is it to see, in Christian man, heavenly love, with all virtues grafted thereon; in such sort that, as one might have said of this tree that it was a cherry tree, an apple, a nut, a pomegranate, so may one say of charity that it is patient, mild, valiant, just, or rather that it is patience, mildness and justice itself.

But the poor tree of Tivoli did not live long, as the same Pliny records, for this variety of productions dried up its essential sap, so that it withered away and died; whereas, on the contrary, charity is fortified and invigorated, so as to produce abundance of fruit in the exercise of all the virtues ; yea, as our holy Fathers have observed, it is insatiable in its desires of bringing forth fruit, and never ceases to urge the heart wherein it dwells, as Rachel did her husband, saying : *Give me children, otherwise I shall die.**

Now the fruits of grafted trees always follow the graft, for if the graft be apple it will bear apples, if cherry it will bear cherries ; yet so that these fruits always taste of the stock. In like manner, Theotimus, our acts take their name and species from the particular virtues whence they spring, but they draw the taste of their sanctity from holy charity, which is the root and source of all sanctity in man. And as the stock communicates its taste to all the fruits which the grafts produce, yet so that each fruit preserves the natural property of the graft whence it sprung, even so charity pours out in such sort her excellence and dignity upon the acts of other virtues, that she does not deprive them of the particular worth and goodness which they have by their own natural condition.

* Gen. xxx. I.

All flowers lose their lustre and grace amidst the darkness of night, but, in the morning, the sun, which makes them again visible and agreeable, does not however make their beauties and their graces equal, and its brightness, though equally spread over them all, yet makes them unequally bright and glorious, according as they are more or less susceptible of the effects of its splendour. And the light of the sun, equal as it is on the violet and the rose, yet will never make that so fair as this, or make a daisy as lovely as a lily. However, if the sun should shine very clearly upon the violet, and very mistily and faintly upon the rose, then without doubt it would make the violet more fair to see than the rose. So, my Theotimus, if one with an equal charity should suffer death by martyrdom, and another hunger by fasting, who does not see that the value of this fasting will not therefore be equal to that of martyrdom? No, Theotimus, for who would dare to affirm that martyrdom is not more excellent in itself than fasting? And as it is more excellent, and as superadded charity does not take away but perfects its excellence, charity will consequently leave to it the advantage which it naturally had over fasting. Surely no man of good sense will equal nuptial chastity to virginity, nor the good use of riches to the entire abnegation of the same. Who again would dare to say, that charity accompanying these virtues deprives them of their properties and privileges, since it is not a virtue which destroys and impoverishes, but betters, quickens and enriches all the good it finds in the souls which it rules. Yea, so far is charity from bereaving the other virtues of their natural pre-eminences and dignities, that, on the contrary, having this quality of perfecting the perfections which it meets with, it more greatly perfects where it finds greater perfection. It acts like sugar, which so preserves and so seasons fruits with its sweetness that, sweetening them all, it leaves them dissimilar in taste and sweetness, according as their natural taste and sweetness are dissimilar, nor does it ever make peaches and nut-fruits as sweet or agreeable as apricots and mirabels.

Still it is true that if love be ardent, powerful and excellent in a heart, it will also more enrich and perfect all the virtuous works which may proceed from it. One may suffer death and fire for God without charity, as S. Paul supposes,* and as I explain elsewhere: by better reason may one suffer them with little charity. Now I say, Theotimus, that it may come to pass that a very small virtue may be of greater value in a soul where sacred love fervently reigns, than martyrdom itself in a soul where love is languishing, feeble and dull. Thus the little virtues of our Blessed Lady, of S. John, of other great saints, were of better worth before God than the most exalted of many inferior saints; as many of the slight movements of love in the seraphim are more inflamed than the greatest in angels of the last order; or as the first essays of the nightingale are incomparably more melodious than the song of the best-trained finch.

Pireicus towards the end of his days painted only miniatures and trivial subjects, such as barbers' or cobblers' shops, asses laden with herbs, and similar petty matters; which he did, as Pliny conjectures, to lessen his great renown, whence in the end he came to be called a painter of rubbish; and yet the greatness of his art did so appear in his small works that they were sold at a higher rate than the great pieces of others. Even so, Theotimus, the little simplicities, abjections and humiliations in which the great saints so delighted, in order to hide themselves and put their hearts under shelter against vainglory, having been practised with a great excellence of the art and of the ardour of heavenly love, were found more grateful in the sight of God than the large and illustrious works of many others which were performed with little charity and devotion.

The sacred spouse wounds her beloved with a single one of her hairs,† of which he makes such great account that he compares them to the flocks of the goats of Galaad; and he has no sooner commended the eyes of his devout loving one, which are the most noble parts of the face, than presently he praises her hair, which is the most frail, worthless and mean; to teach us that in a soul captivated by divine love, exercises that seem very trifling are yet highly agreeable to his Divine Majesty.

* I Cor. xiii. 3.　　　　　　　† Cant. iv. 9.

CHAPTER VI.

OF THE EXCELLENT VALUE WHICH SACRED LOVE GIVES TO THE
ACTIONS WHICH ISSUE FROM ITSELF, AND TO THOSE WHICH
PROCEED FROM THE OTHER VIRTUES.

BUT you will say to me, what is this value, I pray you, which
holy love gives to our actions? Oh! Theotimus, verily I should
not have the assurance to say it, if the Holy Ghost himself had
not declared it in most express terms by the great Apostle S.
Paul, who speaks thus: *What is at present momentary and light
of our tribulation, worketh for us above measure exceedingly an
eternal weight of glory.** For God's sake, let us ponder these
words. *Our tribulations,* which are so *light* that they *pass in a
moment, work for us* the solid and stable *weight of glory.* I
beseech you, behold these wonders! *Tribulation* produces *glory,
lightness* gives *weight,* and *moments* work *eternity.* But what is
it that can give such power to these fleeting moments and light
tribulations? Red purple, or fine crimson violet is a most
precious and royal cloth, yet not by reason of the wool but of
the colour. The works of good Christians are of such worth
that heaven is given us for them; but, Theotimus, it is not
because they proceed from us and are the wool of our hearts,
but because they are dyed with the blood of the Son of God,—
I mean because our Saviour sanctifies our works by the merits
of his blood. The vine-sprig, united and joined to the stock,
brings forth fruit not by its own power but in virtue of the
stock. Now we are united by charity unto our Redeemer as
members to their head, and hence it is that our fruits and good
works, drawing their worth from him, merit life everlasting.
Aaron's rod was dry, and incapable by itself of bringing forth
fruit; but as soon as the name of that great high priest was written
upon it, in one night it brought out its leaves, its flowers and its
fruits.† We of ourselves are withered branches, unprofitable,
fruitless, *not sufficient to think anything of ourselves, as of ourselves, but our sufficiency is from God, who also hath made us fit*

* 2 Cor. iv. 17.   † Numb. xvii. 8.

ministers,* and able to do his will, and therefore as soon as by holy love the name of our Saviour, the great bishop of our souls, is engraven in our hearts, we begin to bear delicious fruits unto life everlasting. And as seeds which of themselves would only bring forth insipid melons, would bring forth sugared and musked ones, if they were steeped in sugared or musked water; so our souls, which of themselves are not able to produce one single good thought towards God's service, being steeped in sacred love by the Holy Ghost who dwells within us, produce sacred actions, which tend towards and carry us to immortal glory. Our works as proceeding from ourselves are but frail reeds; but these reeds become golden by charity, and with the same we measure the heavenly Jerusalem, which is given us by that measure :† for as well to men as to angels, glory is distributed according to charity and its actions. So that the measure used by men and that used by angels is the same,‡ and God *has rendered* and will *render to every man according to his works,*§ as all the divine Scripture teaches us, assuring us of the felicity and eternal joys of heaven in reward of the labours and good works which we have performed on earth.

A magnificent reward, and one that savours of the Master's greatness whom we serve. He indeed, Theotimus, if so he had pleased, might most justly have exacted our obedience and service without proposing unto us any salary or hire at all, because we are his by a thousand most legitimate titles, and because we can do nothing of worth save what is in him, by him, for him, and from him. Yet his goodness has not disposed thus, but, in consideration of his Son, our Saviour, has willed to treat with us at a set price, receiving us for hire, and engaging himself by promise to pay us, according to our works, eternal wages. Nor is it that our service can either be necessary or profitable unto him, for when we shall have accomplished all his commands, we are yet to avow with most humble truth or most true humility that indeed we are most *unprofitable servants,* and utterly useless to our Master, who by reason of his essential

---

* 2 Cor. iii. 5.   † Apoc. xxi. 15.   ‡ Apoc. xxi. 17.
§ Apoc. xxii. 12.

superabundance of riches can have no profit by us; but, converting all our works to our own advantage and good, he ordains
that we shall serve him with as little profit to him as there is
much to us, who by such small labours gain such great rewards.

He was not bound to pay us for our service if he had not
given his promise to do so. But do not think, Theotimus, that
he would so manifest his goodness in this promise as to forget to
glorify his wisdom; yea, on the contrary, he most exactly observed the rules of equity, mingling seemliness (*bienseance*), with
liberality in an admirable manner; for though our works are
indeed very small and in no wise comparable with glory by their
matter, yet in regard to their quality they are very proportionate thereunto, by reason of the Holy Ghost, who, by charity
dwelling in our hearts, works in us with so exquisite an art,
that the same works which are wholly ours are still more
wholly his, since he produces them in us as we again produce
them in him, he does them for us as we do them for him, he
operates them with us as we co-operate with him.

Now the Holy Ghost dwells in us if we be living members of
Jesus Christ, who therefore said unto his disciples : *He that
abideth in me, and I in him, the same beareth much fruit ;** and
this, Theotimus, is because he that abides in him is made par-
taker of his divine Spirit, which is in the midst of man's heart as
a fountain of living *water springing up unto life everlasting.*†
So the holy oil which was poured upon our Saviour as upon
the head of the Church militant and triumphant, spreads itself
over the society of the Blessed, who as the sacred beard of this
heavenly Master are continually attached to his glorious face,
and runs down upon the company of the faithful, who as garments are joined and united by love to his Divine Majesty ; and
both companies, as being composed of brethren of the same
family, have reason to cry out : *Behold how good and how
pleasant it is for brethren to dwell together in unity : like the precious ointment on the head, that ran down upon the beard, the
beard of Aaron, which ran down to the skirt of his garments.*‡

Our works, therefore, as a little grain of mustard-seed, are in

---

* John xv. 5.   † John iv. 14.   ‡ Ps. cxxxii. 1, 2.

no sort comparable in greatness to the tree of glory which they produce, yet they have the vigour and virtue to produce it, because they proceed from the Holy Spirit, who by an admirable infusion of his grace into our hearts makes our works his, and yet withal leaves them our own, since we are members of a head of which he is the Spirit, and ingrafted in a tree whereof he is the divine sap. And as he thus acts in our works, and we after a certain manner operate or co-operate in his action, he leaves us for our part all the merit and profit of our services and good works, and we again leave him all the honour and praise thereof, acknowledging that the commencement, the progress, and the end of all the good we do depends on his mercy, by which he has come unto us and prevented us, has come into us and assisted us, has come with us and conducted us, finishing what he had begun. But, O God! Theotimus, how merciful is his goodness to us in thus distributing his bounty! We give him the glory of our praise, forsooth! and he gives us the glory of possessing him. In fine, by these light and passing labours we obtain goods which endure for all eternity. Amen.

CHAPTER VII.

THAT PERFECT VIRTUES ARE NEVER ONE WITHOUT THE OTHER.

It is said that the heart is the first part of a man which receives life by the infusion of the soul, and the eye the last, as, contrariwise, in a natural death the eye begins first to die, and the heart is the last. Now when the heart begins to live, before the other parts are animated, life is certainly very feeble, frail and imperfect, but ever as it establishes itself more thoroughly in the rest of the body, it is also more vigorous in each part and particularly in the heart, and we see that when life is injured in any one of the members it is weakened in all the rest. If a man's foot or arm be hurt all the body is troubled, excited, disturbed and affected; if the stomach is disordered, the eyes, the voice and the whole countenance show the effects of it, so great is the sympathy amongst the organs of man's natural life.

All the virtues are not acquired together, in an instant, but one after another, in proportion as reason, which is like the soul of our heart, takes possession, first of one passion then of another, to moderate and govern them : and ordinarily this life of our soul begins in the heart of our passions, which is love, and spreading itself over all the rest it quickens at last the very understanding by contemplation; as, on the contrary, moral or spiritual death makes its entry into the soul by the want of reflection *—*death enters by the windows,*† says the sacred text— and its last effect is to destroy good love, which once perishing, all our moral life is dead in us. So then, although we may perhaps possess some virtues without others, yet are they but languishing, imperfect and weak virtues, since reason, which is the life of our soul, is never satisfied nor at ease in a soul unless it occupy and possess all the faculties and passions ; and when it is aggrieved and wounded in some one of our passions or affections, all the rest lose their force and vigour, and grow exceedingly weak.

You see, Theotimus, all the virtues are virtues by the proportion or conformity they have with reason, and an action cannot be called virtuous if it proceed not from the affection which the heart bears to the excellence and beauty of reason. Now if the love of reason possess and animate a soul, it will be obedient to reason in all occurrences, and consequently will practise all the virtues.   If Jacob loved Rachel in consideration of her being Laban's daughter, why did he despise Lia who was not only the daughter, but the eldest daughter, of the same Laban?   But because he loved Rachel by reason of her beauty, he could never equally love poor Lia, though a fruitful and wise maid, because to his mind she was not so fair.   He who loves one virtue for the love of the reason and comeliness which shine in it, will love all the virtues, since he will find the same motive in them all, and he will love each of them more or less, as reason shall appear in them more or less resplendent.   He who loves liberality and not chastity, shows sufficiently that he loves not liberality for reason's sake, because reason is

* *L'inconsideration*—i.e., failure of the spiritual eye (Tr.).
† Jer. ix. 21.

still more radiant in chastity, and where the cause is more strong the effects ought also to be more strong. It is, therefore, an evident sign that such a heart is not moved to liberality by the motive and consideration of reason; whence it follows that this liberality which seemed to be virtue is but an appearance of it, since it proceeds not from reason, which is the true motive of virtues, but from some other and foreign motive. It is sufficient for a child to be born in marriage to bear in the world the name, the arms, and the titles of his mother's husband, but to have his blood and nature he must not only be born in the marriage but of the marriage. Actions have the name, arms and badges of the virtues, because being born of a heart endowed with reason we presume them to be reasonable, yet they have neither the substance nor vigour of virtue when they proceed from a foreign and illegitimate motive, and not from reason. It may happen then, that a man may have some virtues and lack others; but they will either be virtues newly springing and as yet tender, like flowers in blossom; or else perishing and dying virtues, like fading flowers: for, in conclusion, virtues cannot have their true integrity and sufficiency unless they be all together, as all philosophy and divinity assure us. What prudence, I pray you, Theotimus, can an intemperate, unjust and cowardly man have, since he makes choice of vice and forsakes virtue? And how can one be just without being prudent, strong, and temperate, since justice is no other thing than a perpetual, strong and constant will to render to every one his own, and since the science by which right is done is called jurisprudence, and since, to give each one his own, we must live wisely and moderately, and hinder the disorders of intemperance in ourselves so as to give ourselves what belongs to us? And the word virtue, does it not signify a force and vigour belonging to the soul as a quality, even as we say that herbs and precious stones have such and such a virtue or property?

But is not prudence itself imprudent in an intemperate man? Fortitude, without prudence, justice and temperance, is not fortitude, but folly; and justice is unjust in the weak man who dares not do it, in the intemperate man who permits

himself to be carried away with passion, and in the imprudent man who is not able to discern between the right and
the wrong.   Justice is not justice unless it be strong, prudent
and temperate ; nor is prudence prudence unless it be temperate,
just and strong; nor fortitude fortitude unless it be just,
prudent and temperate; nor temperance temperance unless it
be prudent, strong and just.   In fine, a virtue is not perfect
virtue, unless it be accompanied by all the rest.

It is true, Theotimus, that one cannot exercise all the virtues
at once, because the occasions are not all presented at once ; yea,
there are virtues which some of God's greatest saints had never
occasion to practise: for S. Paul, the first hermit, for example,
what occasion could he have to exercise the pardoning of injuries,
affability, magnificence, and mildness?   Nevertheless, such souls
stand so affected to the rectitude of reason, that though they
have not all the virtues in effect, yet they have them all in
affection, being ready and prepared to follow and obey reason
in all occurences, without exception or reservation.

There are certain inclinations which are esteemed virtues and
are not so, but favours and advantages of nature.   How many
are there who are naturally sober, mild, silent, chaste and
modest ?   Now all these seem to be virtues, and yet have no
more the merit thereof than bad inclinations are blameworthy
before we have given free and voluntary consent to such natural
dispositions.   It is no virtue to be by nature a man of little meat,
yet to abstain by choice is a virtue.   It is no virtue to be silent
by nature, though it is a virtue to bridle one's tongue by reason.
Many consider they have the virtues as long as they do not
practise the contrary vices.   One that has never been assaulted
may truly boast that he was never a runaway, yet he has no ground
to boast of his valour.   He that has never been afflicted may
boast of not being impatient, but not of being patient.   In like
manner, some think they have virtues who have only good
inclinations, and as those inclinations are some without others,
they suppose that virtues may be so too.

In truth the great S. Augustine shows, in an epistle which he
wrote to S. Jerome, that we may have some sort of virtue
without having the rest, but that we cannot have perfect ones

without having them all; whilst, as for vices, we may have some without having others, yea, it is even impossible to have them all together : so that it does not follow that he who has lost all the virtues has by consequence all the vices, since almost every virtue has two opposite vices, which are not only contrary to the virtue but also to one another. He who has forfeited valour by rashness cannot at the same time be taxed with cowardice; nor can he who has lost liberality by prodigality, be at the same time reproached with niggardliness. Catiline, says S. Augustine, was sober, vigilant, patient in suffering cold, heat and hunger; so that both himself and his accomplices deemed him marvellously constant; but this constancy wanted prudence, since it made choice of bad instead of good; it was not temperate, for it gave the bridle to repulsive uncleanness; it was not just, since he conspired against his country: it was not then constancy but obstinacy, which to deceive fools bore the name of constancy.

CHAPTER VIII.

HOW CHARITY COMPREHENDS ALL THE VIRTUES.

There flowed a river out of the place of delights to water Paradise, and thence it was divided into four heads.* Now, in man there is a place of delights, whence God makes the river of reason and natural light stream out to water all the paradise of our heart, and this river branches out into four heads; that is, it makes four streams according to the four regions of the soul. For 1°. Over what is called the practical understanding, that is to say the part of the intelligence which discerns the actions we should do or avoid, natural light spreads prudence, which inclines our mind wisely to judge of the evil that we are to avoid and drive away, and of the good we are to do and pursue. 2°. Over our will it makes justice stream out, which is a continual and firm will to render to every one his own. 3°. Over the concupiscible appetite it makes temperance flow, moderating the passions which are therein. 4°. Over the irascible appetite or anger it

* Gen. ii. 10.

sends out fortitude, which stays and controls all the motions of
anger.   Now these four rivers, thus separated, afterwards divide
themselves into several others, in order that all human actions
may be duly fashioned to natural honesty and felicity.   But
besides all this, God, to enrich Christians with a special favour,
makes spring up on the very top of the superior part of their
spirit a supernatural fountain which is called grace, and which
comprehends indeed faith and hope, yet consists in charity.   It
purifies the soul from all sins, and then adorns and embellishes
it with a most delightful beauty ; and finally spreads its waters
over all the faculties and operations thereof, to give the understanding a celestial prudence, the will a holy justice, the concupiscible appetite a sacred temperance, and the irascible appetite
a devout fortitude, to the end that man's whole heart may tend
to the supernatural honesty and felicity which consist in union
with God.   And if these four streams and rivers of charity meet
with any one of the four natural virtues in the soul, they bring
it to their obedience, mingling themselves therewith to perfect
it, as perfumed water perfects natural water when they are
mixed together.   But if holy charity, spread out in this
manner, find not the natural virtues in the soul, then it alone
does all their operations as occasion requires.

Thus heavenly love finding certain virtues in S. Paul, S.
Ambrose, S. Denis, S. Pachomius, shed upon them an agreeable
brightness, reducing them all to its service.   But in Magdalen,
in S. Mary of Egypt, the Good Thief, and a hundred other such
penitents who had been great offenders, divine love, finding no
virtue, did the office and work of all the virtues, making itself
patient, gentle, humble, and liberal in them.   We sow great
variety of seeds in gardens, and cover them, as if burying them,
till the sun's greater heat makes them rise, and, as one would
say, resuscitates them, when they produce their leaves and their
flowers, with new seeds each one in its kind ; so that one sole
heat from heaven causes all the diversity of these productions,
by means of the seed which it finds hidden in the bosom of the
earth.   Verily, my Theotimus, God has sown in our hearts the
seeds of all virtues, which, however, are so covered with our
imperfections and weakness that they do not appear, or appear

very slightly, till the vital heat of holy love comes to quicken and resuscitate them, producing by them the actions of all virtues. So that as the manna contained in itself the variety of the tastes of all meats, and left a relish thereof in the mouths of the Israelites, even so, heavenly love comprehends in itself the diversity of the perfections of all the virtues in so excellent and sublime a manner, that it produces all their actions in time and place according to the occasions. Josue indeed valiantly defeated God's enemies by his good handling of the armies which were under his charge ; but Samson defeated them yet more gloriously, references, who by his own hand slew them by thousands with the jawbone of an ass. Josue by his command and good order making use of the valour of his troops did wonders, but Samson by his own force alone wrought miracles. Josue had the strength of many soldiers under him, but Samson had it in him, and could alone perform as much as Josue with many soldiers. Holy love is excellent in both these ways, for finding some virtue in a soul (and ordinarily it finds at least faith, hope and penitence) it animates, commands, and happily employs them in God's service, and for the rest of the virtues which it finds not, it does their work itself, having more strength by itself than they have all together.

The great Apostle not only says that Charity gives us patience, kindness, constancy, simplicity, but he says that *charity is patient, is kind,** is constant: and it is the property of the supreme virtues amongst angels and men, not only to order the inferior virtues to work, but also to be able themselves to do what they command others. The bishop distributes the charges of all the ecclesiastical functions :—to open the Church, to read therein, to exorcise, preach, baptize, sacrifice, give communion and absolve ; and he himself can do, and does, all this, having in himself an eminent virtue, which comprehends all the inferior virtues. So S. Thomas, on the strength of S. Paul's assurance that *charity is patient, kind, strong,* says : " Charity does and accomplishes the work of all the virtues." And S. Ambrose, writing to Demetrias, calls patience and the rest of the virtues

* I Cor. xiii. 4.

members of charity.   And the great S. Augustine says that the
love of God comprehends all the virtues and does all their
operations in us.   These are his words: " What is said about
virtue being divided into four (he means the four cardinal
virtues) is said in my opinion by reason of the different affections which proceed from love.   So that I do not hesitate to
define those four virtues thus : Temperance is a love which gives
itself entirely unto God ; Fortitude is a love which willingly
supports all things for God's sake : Justice is a love* which
serves God only, and therefore disposes justly of all that is
subject to man : Prudence is a love that makes choice of things
proper to unite itself unto God, and rejects such things as are
contrary to it."   He therefore that has charity has his soul
invested with a fair wedding garment, which, as that of Joseph,
is wrought with the variety of all the virtues : or rather he has
a perfection which contains the virtue of all perfections and the
perfection of all virtues.   And therefore *charity is patient, is
kind ;*† she *is not envious* but bounteous ; she is guilty of no
levities but is prudent ; she *is not puffed up* with pride, but is
humble ; she *is not ambitious* or disdainful, but amiable and
affable ; she is not eager to exact that which belongs unto her,
but free and condescending ; she is not irritable but peaceable ;
she *thinketh no evil* but is meek ; she *doth not rejoice in evil* but
in the truth, and with the truth she *beareth all things ;* she easily
believeth all the good that is said to her without any obstinacy,
contention or distrust ; she *hopeth all* good things for her neighbour without ever losing the hope of procuring his salvation ;
she *endureth all things,* expecting without disquiet that which is
promised her ; and in conclusion, charity is that pure fire-tried
gold, which our Saviour counselled the Bishop of Laodicea to
buy,‡ which contains the virtue of all things, which can do all,
and which does all.

* The French has *force,* but it is clearly an error; S. Augustine's word
is *amor,* as his argument requires.   See *De Morib. Eccl.* c. xv. [Tr.]

† 1 Cor. xiii.   ‡ Apoc. iii. 18.

CHAPTER IX.

THAT THE VIRTUES HAVE THEIR PERFECTION FROM DIVINE LOVE.

Charity is then *the bond of perfection,** since in it all the perfections of the soul are contained and assembled, and since without it, not only can one not have the whole array of virtues, but one cannot even have the perfection of any virtue. Without the cement and mortar which fasten the stones and walls, the whole edifice goes to rack; were it not for the nerves, muscles and sinews, the whole body would be undone; and without charity the virtues can never sustain one another. Our Saviour ever joins the fulfilling of the commandments to charity. *He that hath my commandments,* says he, *and keepeth them, he it is that loveth me; he that loveth me not keepeth not my words; If any one love me, he will keep my word:†* which the disciple whom our Saviour loved repeating, says : *He that keepeth his word, in him, in very deed, the charity of God is perfected;‡ and this is the charity of God, that we keep his commandments.§* Now he who should have all virtues, would keep all the commandments : for he that had the virtue of religion would keep the first three commandments; he that had piety would observe the fourth; he that had the virtue of mildness and gentleness would observe the fifth ; by the virtue of chastity one would observe the sixth; by liberality one would avoid the breach of the seventh ; by truth one would effect the eighth ; by frugality and purity one would observe the ninth and tenth. And if without charity we cannot keep the commandments, much less can we without it have all the virtues.

True it is, one may have some virtue, and live some small time without offending God, though wanting in divine love : but even as we sometimes see uprooted trees produce something, but imperfectly, and only for a short time, so a heart separated from charity, may indeed bring forth some acts of virtue but not for long.

All virtues separated from charity are very imperfect, since

* Col. iii. 14.   † John xiv. 21, 23, 24.   ‡ 1 John ii. 5.
§ 1 John v. 3.

they are not able without it to arrive at their end, which is to make us happy. Bees in their birth are little grubs and worms, without feet, without wings, and without shape ; but in course of time they change, and become little flies ; afterwards waxing strong, and being come to their growth, they are said to be formed, finished and perfect bees, because they have all that is wanted for flying and for making honey. The virtues have their beginning, their progress, and their perfection ; and I do not deny that without charity they may be born and even grow ; but that they should come to their perfection, and bear the name of formed, fashioned, and accomplished virtues, that depends on charity, which gives them the strength to fly in God, and to collect from his mercy the honey of true merit, and of the sanctification of the heart in which they are found.

Charity is amongst the virtues, as the sun amongst the stars ; she distributes to all their lustre and beauty. Faith, hope, fear and penitence ordinarily go before her into the soul to prepare her lodging ; and, upon her arrival, they with all the train of virtues obey and wait upon her, and she with her presence animates, adorns and quickens them all.

The other virtues can in turn aid and stimulate one another in their works and exercises : for who knows not that chastity requires and excites sobriety, and that obedience moves us to liberality, prayer, and humility ? Now by this communication which they have amongst themselves they participate in one another's perfections : for chastity kept by obedience has a double dignity, its own and that of obedience ; yea, it has even more of the dignity of obedience than of its own : for, as Aristotle says that he who stole for the sake of sensuality sinned rather against purity than against honesty, because all his affections tended to impurity, and he only used theft as a passage to it ; even so he who keeps chastity through obedience is more obedient than chaste, since he makes chastity serve obedience. Nevertheless, from the mixture of chastity and obedience a perfect and accomplished virtue cannot issue, since they both want the last perfection, which is love ; so that if it were possible that all the virtues were put in one man, and that he wanted only charity, this union of virtues would indeed be a most perfect and complete body in all its parts, such as Adam's was when God with his omnipotent hand formed it of the slime of the earth: yet would it be a body wanting motion, life and grace, till God should breathe into it *the breath of life,** that is, holy charity, without which nothing profits us.

For the rest, the perfection of divine love is so sovereign that it perfects all the virtues, and can receive no perfection from them, no not from obedience itself, which is the one most able to give perfection to the rest: for although love be commanded, and although in loving we exercise obedience, yet still love draws not its perfection from obedience, but from the goodness of him whom it loves; love not being excellent because it is obedient, but because it loves an excellent good. Truly in loving we obey, as also in obeying we love; but if this obedience be so excellently loveable, it is because it tends to the excellence of love; nor does its excellence consist in this, that loving we obey, but in this, that obeying we love. So that even as God is as much the last end as the first beginning of all that is good, so love, which is the source of every good affection, is likewise its last end and perfection.

CHAPTER X.

A DIGRESSION UPON THE IMPERFECTION OF THE VIRTUES OF THE PAGANS.

THOSE ancient sages of the world long ago made glorious discourses in honour of the moral virtues, yea, even in behalf of religion: but what Plutarch observes of the Stoics suits still better the rest of the pagans. We see ships, says he, which bear the grandest titles: some are called the Victory, others the Valour, others the Sun; yet, for all that, they remain dependent on the winds and waves: so the Stoics boast of being exempt from passions, without fear, without grief, without anger, unchanging and unchangeable, yet are they in fact subject to trouble, disquiet, impetuosity, and other follies.

* Gen. ii. 7.

I earnestly ask you, Theotimus, what virtues could those people have, who voluntarily, and of set purpose, overthrew all the laws of religion. Seneca wrote a book against superstitions, wherein he very freely reprehends pagan impiety. " Now this freedom," says S. Augustine, " was found in his writings, but not in his life; since he even advised that a man should reject superstition in his heart but should practise it in his actions; for these are his words: Which superstitions the sage shall observe, as being commanded by the law, not as being grateful to the gods." How could they be virtuous, who, as S. Augustine relates, were of opinion that the wise man ought to kill himself, when he could not or would not longer endure the calamities of this life, and yet were not willing to acknowledge that calamities were miseries or miseries calamities, but maintained that the wise man was ever fortunate and his life happy ? " O what a happy life," says S. Augustine, " to avoid which one has even recourse to death ? If it be happy, why do you not remain in it ?" Wherefore, that Stoic and commander who, for having killed himself in Utica to avoid a calamity which he considered it unworthy to survive, has been so praised by the worldly-minded, did this action with so little true virtue that, as S. Augustine says, he did not exhibit a high courage that wished to avoid dishonour, but a weak soul which had not the strength of mind to await adversity. For if he reputed it a dishonourable thing to live under victorious Cæsar, why did he tell others to trust to the clemency of Cæsar ? Why did he not advise his son to die with him, if death were better and more honourable than life ? He killed himself, then, either because he envied Cæsar the glory he would have gained by sparing his life, or because he feared the shame of living under a victor whom he hated : wherein he may have the praise of having a stout, perhaps a great heart, but not of being a wise, virtuous and constant soul. The cruelty which is exercised without emotion and in cold blood, is the most cruel of all. It is the same with despair; for the most slow, deliberate, and determined is the least excusable and the most desperate. And as for Lucretia (that we may not forget the valour of the less courageous sex), either she was chaste under the violence of the son of Tarquin, or she was not. If Lucretia were not chaste, why is her chastity so praised ? If she were chaste and innocent on that occasion, was not Lucretia wicked to murder the innocent Lucretia ? If unchaste why so much praised, if honest why was she slain ? But she dreaded reproach and shame on the part of such as might have thought that the treatment she had suffered through violence while she was in life had been undergone voluntarily, if after it she had remained in life. She feared to have been considered an accomplice in the sin, if what was done to her wickedly were borne by her patiently. But are we then to oppress the innocent, and kill the just in order to avoid the shame and reproach which depends upon the opinion of men ? Must we maintain honour at the cost of virtue, and reputation at the hazard of justice ? Such were the virtues of the most virtuous pagans towards God and towards themselves.

As to the virtues that refer to our neighbour, they trod under foot, and most shamefully, by their very laws, the chief of them, which is piety.* For Aristotle, the greatest intellect amongst them, pronounced this horrible and most pitiless sentence. " As to the question of exposing, that is, abandoning children, or of bringing them up, let this be the law : that nothing is to be kept that is deprived of any member. And as to other children, if the laws and customs of the city do not allow the abandoning of them, and the number of any one's children so increase on him that he has more by half than he can keep, he is to be beforehand, and procure abortion." Seneca, so praised as a wise man, says : " We kill monsters :—and if our children are defective, weakly, imperfect, or monstrous, we cast them off, and abandon them." So that it is not without cause that Tertullian reproaches the Romans with exposing their children to the mercy of the waters, to cold, to famine, to dogs ; and this not by the force of poverty; for as he says, the very chief men and magistrates practised this cruelty. Good God ! Theotimus, what kind of virtuous men were these ? And what was their wisdom, who taught a wisdom so cruel and brutal? Alas! said the great Apostle, *professing themselves to be wise they became fools, and their foolish heart was darkened,*† and delivered up to a reprobate

---

* That is, the mutual love of parents and children—*pietas* (Tr.)

† Rom. i. 22, 21.

sense.   Ah! what horrible counsels that great philosopher
Aristotle gives! and how greatly is he reproached for them by
Tertullian and the great S. Ambrose.

Indeed if the pagans practised some virtues, it was generally
for the sake of worldly glory, and consequently they had nothing
of virtue but the action, and not the motive and intention : now
virtue is not true unless it has a right intention.   " Human
cupidity has produced the fortitude of pagans," says the Council of
Orange, " and divine charity that of Christians."   " The virtues
of pagans," says S. Augustine, " were not true, but only resembled true ones, because they were not done for a proper end, but
for transitory ends.   Fabricius shall be less punished than Cata-
line, not because the former was good, but because the latter was
worse ; not because Fabricius had any true virtues, but because
he was not so far off true virtues.   So that the virtue of the
pagans will, at the day of judgment, be a kind of defence to
them ; not such as that they can be saved thereby, but such as
that they may be less condemned."   One vice was neutralized
by another amongst the pagans, vices making room for one
another, without leaving space for any virtue : and for this one
vice of vain glory they repressed avarice and many other vices.
Yea sometimes through vanity, they despised vanity ; whereupon
one of the furthest removed from vanity, treading under his feet
the rich bed of Plato,—What are you doing, Diogenes, said Plato
to him ?   I trample under foot Plato's pride, said he ; it is true,
replied Plato, but you trample it with another pride.   Whether
or no Seneca was vain may be gathered from his last words; for
the end crowns the work, and the last hour judges all : what
vanity, I pray you!—being at the point of death, he said to his
friends that he had not been able until then sufficiently to thank
them, and that therefore he would leave them a legacy of what
he had most desirable and most beautiful ; which, if they faithfully kept it, would bring them great praises ; adding that this
magnificent legacy was nothing else but the picture of his life.
Do you see, Theotimus, how offensive was the vanity of the last
breath of this man?   It was not love of honest virtue, but love
of honour which pricked forward those wise men of this world to
the exercise of virtue ; and similarly their virtues were as

different from true virtues, as the love of right and of merit is different from the love of reward. Those who serve their prince for their own interest, ordinarily perform their duty with more eagerness, ardour, and outward show; but those who serve for love, do it more nobly, generously, and therefore more worthily.

Carbuncles and rubies are called by the Greeks two contrary names, for they name them *pyropos* and *apyropos:* that is, fiery and fireless, or inflamed and flameless. They call them fiery, burning, red coals, or carbuncles, because in light and splendour they resemble fire: but they call them fireless, or, so to say, uninflammable, because not only is their shining without any heat, but they are not even capable of heat, there being no fire that can heat them. So did our ancient Fathers term the pagan virtues, virtues and non-virtues both together; virtues, because they had the lustre and appearance of them, non-virtues, because they not only lacked the vital heat of the love of God, which alone could perfect them, but they were not even capable of it, because they were in persons without faith. "There being in those times," says S. Augustine, " two Romans great in virtue, Cæsar and Cato, Cato's virtue came much nearer to true virtue than Cæsar's did." And having said somewhere that the philosophers who were destitute of true piety had shone with the light of virtue, he unsays it in his book of *Retractations*, considering this to be too great praise for virtues so imperfect as those of the pagans were: which in truth are like to shining fireworms, which only shine during the night, and day being come lose their light. For, even so, those pagan virtues are only virtues in comparison with vices, but in comparison with the virtues of true Christians, are quite unworthy of the name of virtues.

Yet whereas they contain some good, they may be compared to worm-eaten apples; for the colour of these, and such little substance as is left them, are as good as those of entire virtues, but the worm of vanity is in the core, and spoils them; and therefore he who would use them must separate the good from the bad. I grant, Theotimus, there was some firmness of heart in Cato, and that this firmness was praiseworthy, but he who would rightfully appeal to his example, must do so in a just and right matter, not inflicting death on himself, but suffering it when true virtue requires; not for the vanity of glory, but for the glory of truth: as was the case with our martyrs, who, with invincible hearts, performed so many miracles of constancy and resolution, that those of a Cato, an Horatius, a Seneca, a Lucretia, an Arria, deserve no consideration in comparison with them. Witness a Laurence, a Vincent, a Vitalis, an Erasmus, a Eugenius, a Sebastian, an Agatha, an Agnes, a Catharine, a Perpetua, a Felicitas, a Symphorosa, a Natalia, and a thousand others, who make me ever wonder at the admirers of pagan virtues; not so much because they unreasonably admire the imperfect virtues of the pagans, as because they do not admire the most perfect virtues of Christians, virtues a hundred times more worthy of admiration, and alone worthy of imitation.

CHAPTER XI.

HOW HUMAN ACTIONS ARE WITHOUT WORTH WHEN THEY ARE DONE WITHOUT DIVINE LOVE.

THE great friend of God, Abraham, had by Sara his chief wife a most dear only son, Isaac, who also was his sole heir: and though he had Ismael by Agar, and several other children by Cetura, who were wives of a servile and inferior condition, yet he bestowed upon these only certain presents and legacies whereby to put them off and disinherit them, because not being acknowledged by his chief wife, they could not succeed him : now they were not acknowledged, because, with regard to the children of Cetura, they were all born after Sara's decease; and as for Ismael, though his mother Agar had at first acted by the authority of Sara her mistress, yet afterwards she despised her mistress, and would not allow Sara's rights over the child. Now, Theotimus, it is only the children, that is the acts, of most holy charity, and the children or acts which the other virtues conceive and bring forth under her commandment and direction, or at least under the wings and favour of her presence, which

are *heirs of God, and joint heirs with Christ.** But when the
moral virtues, or even the supernatural virtues, produce their
actions in the absence of charity, as they do amongst schismatics,
according to S. Augustine, and sometimes amongst bad Catholics,
they are of no value towards Paradise, not even alms-giving,
though it should lead us to *distribute all our goods to the poor*,
nor yet martyrdom, though we *should deliver* our *body* to the
flames *to be burnt.* No, Theotimus, *without charity*, says the
Apostle, all this *profiteth nothing ;* as we show more amply elsewhere. Further, when in the production of moral virtue the
will proves disobedient to her mistress, which is charity (as
when by pride, vanity, temporal interest, or some other bad
motive, virtues are turned from their own nature), then those
actions are driven out and banished from Abraham's house and
Sara's society, that is, they are deprived of the fruit and of the
privileges of charity, and consequently are left without worth or
merit. For those actions, thus infected by a bad intention, are
in fact more vicious than virtuous ; they have virtue only on
their outside ; their interior belongs to vice, which serves them
for a motive ; witness the fastings, offerings, and other actions
of the Pharisee.

But finally, besides all this, as the Israelites lived peaceably
in Egypt during the life of Joseph and of Levi, and directly
after the death of Levi were tyrannically reduced to slavery—
whence arose that proverb of the Jews : One of the brothers
being deceased, the others are oppressed : [as is related in the
great Chronology of the Hebrews, published by the learned
Archbishop of Aix, Gilbert Genebrard, whom I name for honour
and with consolation, having been his disciple, though an unworthy one, when he was Royal Reader at Paris, and was
explaining the Canticle of Canticles]—so the merits and fruits,
as well of moral as of Christian virtues, most sweetly and
tranquilly subsist in the soul while sacred love lives and reigns
therein; but as soon as divine love dies, all the merits and
fruits of other virtues die at once. These are the works which
divines call killed (*mortifiées*), because, having been born alive under
the protection of charity, and, like Ismael, in the family of Abraham,

* Rom. viii. 17.

K K

they afterwards lose life and the right of inheritance by the disobedience and rebellion of the human will, which is their mother.

Alas! Theotimus, what an evil! *If the just man turn himself
away from his justice, and do iniquity according to all the
abominations which the wicked man useth to work, shall he
live? All his justices which he hath done shall not be
remembered : in the prevarication by which he hath prevaricated,
and in the sin which he hath committed, in them he shall die,*
says Our Lord in Ezechiel.* So that mortal sin ruins all the
merit of virtues: because, as for those which are performed
while sin reigns in the soul, they are born so dead that they are
for ever useless towards eternal bliss; and as for those which
were performed before the sin was committed, that is, while
sacred love lived in the soul, their value and merit perish and
die as soon as sin comes, not being able to preserve their life
after the death of charity which had given it to them. The
lake which profane authors commonly call Asphaltites, and
sacred authors the Dead Sea, has so heavy a curse upon it, that
nothing that is put into it can live : when the fish of the Jordan
come near it they die, unless they speedily return against the
stream; the trees upon its shore produce nothing that lives,
and although their fruits are in appearance and outward show
like the fruits of other places, yet when gathered they are found
to be only skins and rinds full of ashes, which are blown away
by the wind :—a sign of the infamous sins, in punishment of
which, this country, which contained four populous cities, was
of old converted into an abyss of corruption and infection : and
nothing, methinks, could better represent the evilness of sin
than this abominable lake, which had its origin from the most
execrable crime human flesh can commit. Sin, therefore, as a
dead and mortal sea, kills all that comes near it; nothing has
life of all that is born in the soul which sin possesses, or of all
which grows round about. Alas! Theotimus, nothing. For
sin is not only a lead work, but is moreover so infectious and
pestilential, that the most excellent virtues of the sinful soul
produce no action of life : and although the acts of the sinner have
oftentimes a great resemblance to those of the just man, yet are

* xviii. 24.

they in reality but rinds filled with wind and dust, regarded, indeed, by the divine goodness, and even rewarded with temporal presents, which are bestowed upon them as upon the children of servants; but rinds which neither are nor can be of so agreeable a relish to the divine justice as to be rewarded with eternal reward. They perish on the trees, and cannot be preserved in the hand of God, because they are void of true worth, as is said in the Apocalypse to the Bishop of Sardis, who was *considered* to be a *living* tree by reason of divers virtues which he practised, and yet was *dead*,[*] because he was in sin; his virtues were not true living fruits, but dead rinds and pleasing only to the eye, not savoury apples good for food. So that we may all utter this true saying, in imitation of the holy apostle : *Without charity I am nothing, nothing profiteth me ;* and that of St. Augustine : " Put charity in a heart and everything profits, take charity away and nothing profits." I mean that nothing profits for eternal life, for as we say elsewhere, the virtuous works of sinners are not useless for temporal life. But, my dear Theotimus, *what doth it profit a man, if he gain the whole world* temporally *and suffer the loss of his soul* [†] eternally.

CHAPTER XII.

HOW HOLY LOVE RETURNING INTO THE SOUL, BRINGS BACK TO LIFE ALL THE WORKS WHICH SIN HAD DESTROYED.

THE works then of a sinner, while he is deprived of holy love, are not profitable to eternal life, and therefore they are called dead works : on the contrary the good works of the just man are said to be living, inasmuch as divine love animates and quickens them with its life. But if afterwards they lose their life and worth by sin, they are said to be works in death (*amorties*), extinguished, or killed, but not dead works, especially with regard to the elect. For as our Saviour speaking of the little Talitha, the daughter of Jairus, said *she was not dead,*

---

[*] Apoc. iii. 1.   [†] Matth. xvi. 26.

but slept only,* because, being about to be raised to life, her death would be of such short duration that it would resemble sleep rather than a true death; so the works of the just man (and especially of the elect) which the commission of sin makes to die, are not called dead works but only deadlike, killed, stupefied or put into a trance, because upon the approaching return of holy love, they will, or at least can, soon revive and return to life again. The return of sin deprives the heart and all its works of life: the return of grace restores life to the heart and all its works. A sharp winter makes all the plants of the earth die down, so that if it always lasted, they also would always continue in this state of death: sin, that most sad and dreadful winter of the soul, kills all the holy works which it finds therein, and if it always continued, never would anything recover either life or vigour. But as at the return of the fair spring, not only do the new seeds which are sown under the favour of this beautiful and fertile season germinate and agreeably bring forth their plants, each one in its kind, but also the old plants, which the rigour of the past winter had bitten, withered, and made die down, grow green and vigorous, and take up again their strength and their life :—so sin being blotted out, and the grace of divine love returning into the soul,—not only do the new affections which the return of this sacred spring brings into the soul blossom and bring forth ample merits and blessings; but the works also that were dried up and withered by the rigour of the winter of past sins, delivered from their mortal enemy, resume their strength, grow vigorous, and, as if risen from the dead, flourish anew, and bring forth fruit of merits for eternal life. Such is the omnipotence of heavenly love, or the love of heavenly omnipotence. *When the wicked turneth himself away from his wickedness, which he hath wrought, and doth judgment and justice, he shall save his soul alive. Be converted and do penance for all your iniquities; and iniquity shall not be your ruin,*† says the Lord Almighty. And what means—*iniquity shall not be your ruin,* but that the ruin which it made shall be repaired? So, besides a thousand endearments which the

---

* Marc. v. 41.   † Ezech. viii. 27, 30.

prodigal son received from his father, he was re-established, even with advantage, in all his privileges, and in all the graces, favours and dignities which he had lost. And Job, that innocent image of a penitent sinner, in the end received *twice as much as he had before.** In truth the most holy Council of Trent desires that we should encourage penitents who have returned to the sacred love of the eternal God, in these words of the Apostle : Abound *in every good work, knowing that your labour is not in vain in the Lord.*† For God is not unjust, that *he should forget your work and the love which you have shewn in his name.*‡ God then does not forget the works of those who having lost love by sin recover it by penance. Now God forgets works when they lose their merit and sanctity by sin committed, and he remembers them when they return to life and vigour by the presence of holy love. So much so, that for the faithful to be rewarded for their good works, as well by the increase of grace and future glory, as by the actual enjoyment of eternal life, it is not necessary that they should never relapse into sin, but it is enough, according to the Sacred Council, that they depart this life in the grace of God and charity.

God has promised an eternal reward to the works of a just man. *But if the just man turn himself away from his justice* by sin, *God will no more remember his justices* and good works *which he hath done.*§ But yet if this poor fallen man afterwards rises and returns into God's grace by penance, God will no longer remember his sin : and if he do not remember his sin, he will then remember the former good works, and the reward which he had promised them ; because sin, which alone had blotted them out of the divine memory, is totally effaced, destroyed and annihilated. So that then the justice of God obliges his mercy, or rather the mercy of God obliges his justice, to regard anew the former good works, even as though he had never forgotten them ; otherwise the holy penitent would never have dared to say to his master : *Restore unto me the joy of thy salvation, and strengthen me with a perfect spirit.*‖ For, as

---

* Job xlii. 10.   † 1 Cor. xv. 58.   ‡ Hebr. vi. 10.
          § Ezech. xviii. 24.   ‖ Ps. l. 14.

you see, he not only demands a newness of *heart* and *spirit*, but he expects to have the *joy* given back to him which sin had bereft him of. Now this joy is nothing but the *wine* of heavenly love, which *cheers the heart of man.**

It is not with sin in this matter as with the works of charity. For the works of the just man are not effaced, destroyed or annihilated by the commission of sin, they are only forgotten; but the sin of the wicked is not only forgotten, but also blotted out, cleansed away, abolished and annihilated by holy penance. Wherefore the sin that is committed by the just man, does not cause the sin that was once pardoned to live again, because it was entirely annihilated: but when love returns into the penitent soul, it makes her former good works return to life again, because they were not abolished but only forgotten. And this oblivion of the good works of the just who have forsaken their justice and charity consists in this, that they are made unprofitable to us so long as sin makes us incapable of eternal life, which is their fruit; and therefore as soon as by the return of charity we are put back in the ranks of God's children, and consequently made capable of immortal glory, God recalls to mind our good works of old, and they again become fruitful. It were not reasonable that sin should have as much power against charity as charity has against sin; for sin proceeds from our infirmity, charity proceeds from God's power. If *sin abound* in malice to ruin us, *grace superabounds* to restore us; and God's *mercy*, by which he blots out sin, *is* continually *exalted* and becomes gloriously triumphant *over* the rigour of the *judgment*,† by which God had forgotten the good works which went before sin. So in the corporal cures which our Saviour wrought by miracles he not only restored health, but moreover added new blessings, making the cure far excel the disease, so bountiful is he to man.

I never saw, read, or heard, that wasps, gadflies, flies, and such little noxious insects when once dead could come to life and rise again, but that the dear bees, those virtuous insects, can live again, every one says, and I have often read it. It

---

* Ps. ciii. 15. † Rom. v. 20 ; James ii. 13.

is said (these are Pliny's words) that if one keep the dead bodies of drowned honey-bees all winter indoors, and expose them to the sunbeams the following spring, covered over with ashes of the fig tree, they will live again and be as good as ever. That iniquities and sinful works can return to life, after they have once been drowned and abolished by penance, truly, my Theotimus, never did the Scripture, nor, as far as I know, any theologian, aver it: yea the contrary is authorized by holy Writ, and by the common consent of all Doctors. But that good works, which, like sweet bees, compound the honey of merit, being drowned in sin, can afterwards regain life, when, covered with the ashes of penance, they are exposed to the sun of grace and charity, is held and clearly taught by all theologians: nor are we to doubt but that they become profitable and fruitful as before. When Nabuzardan destroyed Jerusalem, and Israel was led into captivity, the holy fire of the altar was hidden in a well, where it was turned into mud, but this mud being drawn out of the well and exposed to the sun after the return from captivity,—the dead fire kindled again, and the mud was turned into flames.* When the just man becomes a slave to sin, all the good works which he had done are miserably forgotten and turned into mud, but being delivered out of captivity, when by penance he returns into the grace of heavenly charity, his former good works are drawn out of the well of oblivion, and touched with the rays of heavenly mercy they return to life, and are converted into as clear flames as ever, to be replaced on the sacred altar of the divine approbation, and to have their original dignity, their first price, and their first value.

CHAPTER XIII.

HOW WE ARE TO REDUCE ALL THE EXERCISE OF THE VIRTUES, AND ALL OUR ACTIONS TO HOLY LOVE.

BRUTE beasts, being unable to know the end of their actions, tend indeed towards their end, but do not aim at it: for to aim at a thing, is to tend towards it by intention, before tending to-

* 2 Mac. i. 19.

wards it in action. They cast, as it were, their actions towards their end, but they have no forecast, simply following their instinct, without election or intention. But man is in such sort master over his human and reasonable actions, that he does them all for some end, and can direct them to one particular end, or several ends as he pleases: for he can change the natural end of an action;—as when he swears in order to deceive another, whereas the end of an oath is, on the contrary, to hinder deceit. He can also add another end to the natural end of an action;—as when, besides the intention of succouring the poor to which almsgiving tends, he adds the intention of inducing the poor man to do the like.

Now sometimes we add a less perfect end than is that of our action, sometimes we add an end of equal or like perfection, sometimes again an end that is more high and eminent. For besides helping a needy man, to which almsgiving specially tends, one may propose: 1°. to gain his friendship; 2°. to edify one's neighbour; and 3°. to please God. There are three differing ends, whereof the first is lower, the second not much better, and the third much more excellent than the ordinary end of almsgiving. So that, as you see, we have power to give different perfections to our actions, according to the variety of motives, ends and intentions which we have in doing them.

Be good exchangers,* says our Saviour. Let us be very careful then, Theotimus, not to change the motives and ends of our actions except to profit and advantage; and to do nothing in this matter save with good order and reason. Now, look at that man who enters on some office for the public service or to acquire honour: if his design be rather to honour himself than to serve the commonwealth, or if he be equally desirous of both, he is wrong, and does not escape being an ambitious man; for he overthrows the order of reason, in either preferring or equalizing his own interests to the public good. But if, proposing as his principal end the public service, he is very glad also at the same time to advance the honour of his family, truly one cannot blame him, because his designs are not only honest,

* These words are often quoted by the early Fathers as words of our Saviour; they are not found in the Bible (Tr.).

but also well ordered. Another communicates at Easter, in order to escape the ill-word of his neighbours, and to obey God: no one doubts that he does well. But if he communicate to avoid blame as much as, or more than, to obey God, who again can doubt that he acts unreasonably; equalizing or preferring human respect to the obedience which he owes to God. I may fast in Lent, either from charity in order to please God; or from obedience, because it is a precept of the Church; or from sobriety; or from diligence, in order to study better; or from prudence, to make some saving which is required; or from chastity, in order to tame the flesh; or from religion, the better to pray. Now, if I please, I may make a collection of all these intentions, and fast for them all together: but in that case there must be good management to place these motives in proper order. For if I fasted chiefly out of a sparing humour, rather than from obedience to the Church; if to study well rather than to please God;—who does not see that I pervert right and order, preferring my own interest before obedience to the Church and the pleasure of my God? To fast in order to save is good, to fast in order to obey the Church is better, to fast in order to please God is best: but though it may seem that with three goods one cannot make a bad; yet he who should place them out of order, preferring the less to the better, would without doubt commit an irregularity deserving of blame.

He who invites but one of his friends, gives no offence to the rest; but if he invite them all, and give the chief seats to those of lower rank, giving the more honourable the bottom places,—does he not offend both those and these?—these, because he lowers them against reason : those, because he makes fools of them. So, when we do an action for a single reasonable motive, however slight it may be, reason is not offended thereby; but he who will have many motives, must rank them according to their quality, otherwise he sins: for disorder is a sin, as sin is a disorder. He who desires to please God and our Blessed Lady does excellently well, but he who would please our Blessed Lady as much as God, or more than God, would commit an intolerable irregularity, and one might say to him, as was said to Cain: *If thou hast offered well but wrongly divided,—stop, thou hast* *sinned.** To each end we must give its proper rank, and consequently the sovereign rank to that of pleasing God.

Now the sovereign motive of our actions, which is that of heavenly love, has this sovereign property, that being more pure, it makes the actions which proceed from it more pure; so that the angels and saints of heaven love absolutely nothing for any other end whatever than that of the love of the divine goodness, and from the motive of desiring to please him. They all indeed love one another most ardently, they also love us, they love the virtues, but all this only to please God. They follow and practise virtues, not inasmuch as they are fair and delightful, but inasmuch as they are agreeable to God: they love their own felicity, not because it is theirs, but because it pleases God: yea, they love the very love with which they love God, not because it is in them, but because it tends to God; not because it is sweet to themselves, but because it pleases God; not because they have and possess it, but because God gives it them, and takes his good-pleasure in it.

CHAPTER XIV.

THE PRACTICE OF WHAT HAS BEEN SAID IN THE PRECEDING CHAPTER.

Let us purify, then, Theotimus, as far as we can, all our intentions, and since we are able to spread over all the acts of the virtues the sacred motive of divine love, why shall we not do it, rejecting, as occasion requires, all kinds of vicious motives, such as vain-glory, and self-interest, and considering all the good motives which we may have for undertaking the action which presents itself, in order to choose that of holy love, which is the most excellent of all, to pour it over all the rest, or steep them in it. For example, if I desire valorously to expose myself to the hazards of war, I can do it, considering various motives: For the natural motive of this action is that of strength and

* Gen. iv. 7. From the Septuagint (Tr.).

valour, which moves us reasonably to undertake perilous exploits : yet besides this I may have divers other motives ; as that of obeying the prince whom I serve, that of love for the common weal, that of magnanimity, which makes me rejoice in the greatness of this action. Now, coming to the action, I enter on the foreseen peril for all these motives together. But to raise them all to the rank of divine love, and perfectly to purify them, I will say in my soul with all my heart : O eternal God, who art the most dear love of my affections, if valour, obedience to my prince, love of my country, and magnanimity, were not agreeable unto thee, I would never follow the movements I now feel, but because these virtues please thee, I embrace this occasion of putting them in practice, and I will only follow their instinct and leading, because thou lovest and willest them.

You see plainly, Theotimus, that by this reflection of the spirit, we perfume all those other motives with the holy sweetness of love, since we do not follow them as motives simply virtuous, but as motives, willed, accepted, loved and cherished by God. He who steals in order to get drunk, is more a drunkard than a thief, according to Aristotle ; and he who practises valour, obedience, love of country, and magnanimity to please God, is rather a divine lover, than valiant, obedient, patriotic, and magnanimous, because his whole will in this action comes to terminate and be absorbed in the love of God, only using all the other motives to arrive at this end. We are not wont to say we are going to Lyons but to Paris, when we only go to Lyons in order to get to Paris : nor that we are going to sing but that we are going to serve God, when we only go to sing in order to serve God.

And if it chance that sometimes we are touched by some particular motive, as, for example, if we should love chastity on account of its lovely and delightful purity, at once we must pour out, over this motive, that of holy love—in this manner : O most honourable and most pleasing spotlessness of chastity, how worthy of love art thou, since thou art so beloved of the divine goodness ! Then, turning towards the Creator : Ah ! Lord, I demand only one thing of thee, this is what I aim at in chastity, to see and effect in it thy good pleasure, and to take the delight thou takest therein. And when we begin the practice

of any virtue, we should often say with all our heart : Yes,
eternal Father, I will do it, *for so hath it seemed good in thy
sight.** Thus are we to animate all our actions with this heavenly
good-pleasure, loving the honourableness and beauty of virtue
principally because they are agreeable to God : for, my dear
Theotimus, there are some men who excessively love the beauty
of certain virtues, not only without loving charity, but even with
contempt of charity.   Origen and Tertullian so loved the purity
of chastity, that for it they violated the great laws of charity ;
the one choosing to commit idolatry to preserve it,† the other
separating himself from the most chaste Catholic Church, his
mother, to establish the chastity of his wife more according to
his own fancy.   Who knows not that there were certain " Poor
men of Lyons,"who from praising mendicity excessively, became
heretics, and of beggars became lying vagabonds ?   Who is
ignorant of the folly of the Enthusiasts, Messalians, Euchites,
who forsook charity, to exalt prayer ?   And were there not
heretics, who to exalt charity towards the poor, put down
charity towards God, ascribing man's whole salvation to alms-
deeds, as S. Augustine witnesses, although the holy Apostle cries
out, *if I should distribute all my goods to feed the poor, and
have not charity, it profiteth me nothing ?*‡

God has set over me the standard of love,§ says the sacred
Sulamitess.   Love, Theotimus, is the standard in the army of
virtues : they ought all to range themselves by it ; it is the only
flag under which our Saviour, who is the true General of the
army, makes them fight.   Let us therefore reduce all the virtues
to the obedience of charity : let us love particular virtues, but
principally because they are agreeable to God ; let us excellently
love the more excellent virtues, not because they are excellent,
but because God loves them more excellently.   Thus will holy
love give life to all the virtues, making all of them full of love,
lovable, and lovable above all things.

* Matt. xi. 26.

† The only authority for this accusation against Origen is a statement of
S. Epiphanius (de Hær. lxiv. c. 2), which Baronius (ann. 253) rejects as an
nterpolation, and Tillemont (III. note xxii. on Origen) proves to be erroneous
Tr.).

‡ 1 Cor. xiii. 3.   § Cant. ii. 4.   From the Septuagint (Tr.).

CHAPTER XV.

HOW CHARITY CONTAINS IN IT THE GIFTS OF THE HOLY GHOST.

THAT man's heart may easily follow the motions and instincts of reason, in order to attain the natural felicity which it can aim at, by living according to the laws of rectitude, it requires to have :—1°. Temperance, to repress the rebellious movements of sensuality; 2°. Justice, to render to God, our neighbour and ourselves what is due; 3°. Fortitude, to vanquish the difficulties which occur in doing good and avoiding evil; 4°. Counsel, to discern what means are most proper to attain unto good and virtue ; 5°. Knowledge, to know the true good, to which we are to aspire, and the true evil which we are to fly ; 6°. Understanding, thoroughly to penetrate the first and main grounds or principles of the beauty and excellence of rectitude ; 7°. And finally, wisdom, to contemplate the divinity, the prime source o all good. These are the qualities whereby the spirit is rendered gentle, obedient, and pliable, with regard to the laws of the natural reason which is in us.

In like manner, the Holy Ghost, who dwelleth in us, wishing to make our soul supple, pliable, and obedient, with regard to his heavenly movements and divine inspirations, which are the laws of his love, in the observance of which consists the supernatural felicity of this present life, bestows upon us seven properties and perfections, nearly corresponding to those seven which we have just spoken of, and called, in the Holy Scripture and in the books of theologians, gifts of the Holy Ghost.

Now they are not only inseparable from charity, but, all things well considered, and speaking precisely, they are the principal virtues, properties and qualities of charity. For 1°. Wisdom is in fact no other thing than the love which relishes, tastes and experiences, how sweet and delicious God is ; 2°. Understanding is nothing else than love attentive to consider and penetrate the beauty of the truths of faith, to know thereby God in himself, and then descending from this to consider him in creatures; 3°. Science, on the other hand, is but the same love, keeping us attentive to the knowledge of ourselves and creatures, to make us reascend to a more perfect knowledge of the service which we owe to God; 4°. Counsel is also love, insomuch as it makes us careful, attentive, and wise in choosing the means proper to serve God holily; 5°. Fortitude is love encouraging and animating the heart, to put in execution that which counsel has determined should be done; 6°. Piety is the love which sweetens labour, and makes us, with good heart, with pleasure, and with a filial affection, employ ourselves in works which please God, our Father; and 7°. to conclude, Fear is nothing but love insomuch as it makes us fly and avoid what is displeasing to the divine Majesty.

So, Theotimus, charity will be another Jacob's ladder to us, consisting of the seven gifts of the Holy Ghost, as of so many sacred steps, by which angelic men will ascend from earth to heaven, to be united to the heart of God Almighty, and by which they will descend from heaven to earth, to take their neighbour by the hand and lead him to heaven. For, as we mount the first step, Fear makes us forsake evil; on the second, Piety excites us to will to do good; upon the third, Knowledge makes us discern the good we are to do, and the evil we are to fly; upon the fourth, by Fortitude we take courage against all the difficulties which occur in our enterprise; upon the fifth, by Counsel we make choice of suitable means; upon the sixth, we unite our understanding to God to behold and penetrate the features of his infinite beauty; and upon the seventh, we join our wills to God, to taste and experience the sweetness of his in- comprehensible goodness; for upon the top of this ladder, God bending towards us, gives us the kiss of love, and makes us taste the sacred breasts of his sweetness, better than wine.

But, if after we have deliciously enjoyed these favours of love, we desire to return to the earth, to gain our neighbour to the same happiness;—from the first and highest step, where we have filled our will with a most ardent zeal, and have perfumed our souls with the perfumes of God's sovereign charity, we must descend to the second step, where our understanding receives an incomparable light, and makes provision of the most excellent considerations and maxims, to glorify the divine beauty and goodness; thence we pass to the third, where, by the gift of Counsel, we consider by what means we may instil the relish and esteem of the divine sweetness into our neighbour's heart; upon the fourth, we take heart, receiving a holy Fortitude, to surmount the difficulties which might cross this design; upon the fifth, by the gift of Knowledge, we begin to preach, exhorting souls to follow virtue and fly vice; upon the sixth, we strive to emplant Piety in them, that acknowledging God for their loving Father, they may obey him with a filial fear; upon the last step, we urge them to fear the judgments of God, so that mingling this fear of being damned with filial reverence, they may more earnestly forsake the earth to ascend to heaven with us.

Charity, therefore, comprehends the seven Gifts, and is like to a fair lily, which has six flowers whiter than snow, and in the midst the beautiful little golden hammers of wisdom, which beat into our hearts the taste and loving relish of the goodness of the Father our Creator, of the mercy of the Son our Redeemer, and of the sweetness of the Holy Ghost our Sanctifier. And I place thus this double fear upon the two lowest steps, to reconcile all the translations with the holy and sacred Vulgate edition : for if in the Hebrew, the word fear is twice said, this is not without mystery, but to show that there is a gift of filial fear, which is nothing else but the gift of piety, and a gift of servile fear, which is the beginning of all the progress we make towards the sovereign wisdom.

CHAPTER XVI.

OF THE LOVING FEAR OF SPOUSES; A CONTINUATION OF THE SAME SUBJECT.

AH! *my brother Jonathan,* said David, *thou wast amiable to me above the love of women :** as though he had said, thou wast worthy of a greater love than that of wives for their husbands.

* 2 Kings i. 26.

All excellent things are rare. Imagine to yourself, Theotimus, a spouse of dove-like heart and having the perfection of nuptial love. Her love is incomparable, not only in excellence, but also in the great variety of beautiful affections and qualities which accompany it; it is not only chaste, but modest; it is strong, but gracious withal; it is violent and yet tender; it is ardent yet respectful, noble yet fearful, bold yet obedient, and all its fear is mingled with a delicious confidence. Such truly is the fear of a soul endowed with the excellence of love; for she has such assurance of the goodness of her spouse that she fears not the losing of him, but she greatly fears that she will not enjoy enough of his divine presence, and that some occasion may make him absent himself, though only for a moment. She is quite confident that she will never displease him, but she fears she may not love him as much as love requires: her love is too noble to entertain even the least suspicion of ever falling into disgrace with him, but still it is so sensitive that it fears it may not be closely enough united to him; yea, the soul sometimes arrives at such perfection that she no longer fears she may not be closely enough united to him, her love assuring her that she will be so for ever, but she fears that this union may not be so pure, simple and attentive as her love would desire. Such is that admirable lover, who would not love spiritual sweetnesses, pleasures, virtues, consolations, lest she might be diverted, be it ever so little, from her only love, which is the love she bears to her beloved; protesting that it is himself, not his gifts, which she seeks, and crying out to this effect:—Ah! *show me, O thou whom my soul loveth, where thou feedest, where thou liest in the midday, lest I begin to wander after** the pleasures which are outside thee.

With this sacred fear of divine spouses were touched the great souls of S. Paul, S. Francis, S. Catharine of Genoa, and others, who would not admit any mixture in their loves, but endeavoured to make them so pure, so simple, and so perfect, that neither consolations, nor the virtues themselves, should find any place between their heart and God, so that they might say:

---

* Cant. i. 6.

I live, not I, but Jesus Christ lives in me: my God is all things to me: what is not my God is nothing to me; Jesus Christ is my life: my love is crucified; and other such words of an ecstatic heart.

Now the love of beginners or learners proceeds from true love, but from a love which is as yet young, feeble and only beginning; filial fear proceeds from a constant and solid love, already tending to perfection; but the fear of spouses springs from the excellence and perfection of love already quite possessed: and as to servile and mercenary fears, they do not truly proceed from love, but ordinarily precede love, and are its harbingers, as we have already said, and they are oftentimes very profitable servants. You will see, Theotimus, an honourable lady who, not willing to *eat her bread idle,* any more than she did whom Solomon so much extolled,* will lay silk in goodly variety of colours on fine white satin, which afterwards she will richly embellish with gold and silver in suitable patterns: the work is wrought with the needle, which she inserts wherever she would lay her silk, silver, or gold; yet the needle is not put into the satin to be left there, but only to draw in after it and make way for, the silk, silver, and gold: so that when these are once laid upon their grounds, the needle is drawn out and taken away. Even so the divine goodness, wishing to place a great variety of virtues in man's soul, and afterwards to embellish them with his sacred love, makes use of the needle of servile and mercenary fear, with which our hearts are ordinarily first pricked. But still this is not left there, but ever as the virtues are drawn into and laid in the soul, mercenary and servile fear departs, according to the word of the beloved disciple: *Perfect charity casteth out fear.*† Yea, verily, Theotimus, for the fear of being damned and of losing heaven is dreadful and full of anguish: and how can it then stand with sacred love, which is all agreeable, all sweet?

* Prov. xxxi. 27.   † 1 John iv. 18.

CHAPTER XVII.

HOW SERVILE FEAR REMAINS TOGETHER WITH HOLY LOVE.

ALTHOUGH, however, the lady we spoke of will not leave her needle in her work after it is finished, yet as long as there remains anything to be done in it, if any other occurrence make her stop, she will leave the needle sticking in the pink, the rose, or the pansy which she is embroidering, so as to have it more ready when she returns to her work. In like manner, Theotimus, while the Divine Providence is about the embroidery of virtues and the work of divine love in our souls, there is always a mercenary or servile fear left in them, till charity, being come to perfection, takes out this pricking needle and puts it back, as it were, in its cushion. In this life, therefore, wherein our charity will never come to such perfection that it shall be exempt from peril, fear is always necessary, and even while we thrill with joy by love, we must tremble with apprehension by fear. *Serve ye the Lord with fear, and rejoice unto him with trembling.* *

Our great father Abraham sent his servant Eliezer to choose a wife for his only son Isaac: Eliezer went, and by Divine inspiration made choice of the fair and chaste Rebecca, whom he took back with him. But this wise maiden quitted Eliezer as soon as she met Isaac; and being introduced into the tent of Sara, she remained his spouse for ever. God often sends servile fear as another Eliezer (and Eliezer is interpreted, help of God) to arrange the marriage between the soul and sacred love. But though the soul comes under the conduct of fear, she does not mean to espouse it; for, in fact, as soon as the soul meets with love, she unites herself unto it, and quits fear.

Yet as Eliezer after his return remained in the house, in the service of Isaac and Rebecca, so fear, having led us to holy love, remains still with us, to serve both love and the loving soul as occasion requires. For though the soul be just, yet is she oft set upon by extreme temptations, and love, all courageous

* Ps. i. 11.

as it is, has enough to do to sustain the assault, by reason
of the disadvantage of the place wherein it is, which is the
heart of man, changeable and subject to the mutiny of the
passions. In that case, therefore, Theotimus, love employs fear
in the fight, making use of it to repulse the enemy. The brave
prince Jonathan, when going to attack the Philistines amidst
the obscurity of the night, would have his armour-bearer with
him, and those that he killed not, his armour-bearer killed.*
So love wishing to carry out some bold enterprise, uses not
only its own motives, but also the motives of servile and mercenary fear ; and the temptations which love does not strike
down are overthrown by the fear of being damned. If a temptation to pride, avarice, or some voluptuous pleasure attack
me :—Ah ! I will say, shall it be possible, that for things so vain,
my soul would quit the grace of her well-beloved ? But if this
will not serve, love will call fear to its aid :—Ah ! dost thou not
see, miserable heart, that if thou give way to this temptation
the horrible flames of hell await thee, and that thou losest the
eternal inheritance of heaven ? A man makes use of anything
in extreme necessities, as the same Jonathan did, when passing
the sharp rocks, which were between him and the Philistines,
he not only used his feet, but went scrambling *and creeping on
hands and feet* as best he could.

Even therefore as mariners who sail out with a fair wind
and in fair weather, do yet never forget the cables, anchors, and
the other things required in time of hazard and tempest, in like
manner the servant of God, though he enjoy the sweet repose
of holy love, must never be unprovided with the fear of
God's judgments, to help himself therewith amidst the storms
and assaults of temptation. Or, again, as the skin of an apple,
which in itself is of small esteem, is yet very useful for preserving the apple which it covers; so servile fear, which of its
own nature is of little worth in comparison with love, is yet
very serviceable for preserving it during the dangers of this
mortal life. And as he who gives a pomegranate gives it
indeed for the seeds and juice which are contained in it, but

* 1 Kings xiv. 1.

yet gives also the skin as a necessary accompaniment of it; so, although the Holy Ghost amongst his sacred gifts bestows a loving fear upon the souls which are his, that they may fear God in piety as their father and their spouse, yet does he not fail to add mercenary and servile fear, as an accessary to the other which is more excellent.   So Joseph sending to his father many loads of all the riches of Egypt, gave him not only the treasures, but withal the asses that bore them.

Now although mercenary and servile fear is very necessary for this mortal life, yet is it unworthy to have any part in the immortal, where there will be an assurance void of fear, a peace without apprehension, a repose free from anxiety.   Yet the services which this servile and mercenary fear shall have done to love will be there rewarded; so that though these fears, as another Moses and another Aaron, enter not into the land of promise, yet shall their posterity and works enter : and as to the fear of children and the fear of spouses, they will hold their rank and place, not to cause any distrust or trouble in the soul, but to make her admire and reverence with submission the incomprehensible Majesty of this omnipotent Father, and this Spouse of Glory.   *The law of the Lord is unspotted, converting souls. . . . The fear of the Lord is holy, enduring for ever and ever.**

CHAPTER XVIII.

HOW LOVE MAKES USE OF NATURAL, SERVILE AND MERCENARY FEAR.

LIGHTNING, thunder, thunderbolts, tempests, inundations, earthquakes, and other such unforeseen accidents, excite even the most indevout persons to fear God, and nature, which goes before reasoning in those occurrences, drives the heart, the eyes, yea the very hands heavenwards to invoke the assistance of the most holy Divinity, according to the common sentiment of man-

* Ps. xviii. 8, 10.

kind, which is, says Titus Livius, that such as serve the Almighty prosper, and such as contemn him are afflicted. In the storm which imperilled Jonas, the mariners feared with a great fear, and immediately each of them turned to his god. They were ignorant, says S. Jerome, of the truth, yet they knew there was a Providence, and believed it was by the judgment of heaven that they were in this danger ; as those of Malta, when they saw S. Paul, after the shipwreck, attacked by the viper, believed that it was from the divine vengeance.* And indeed thunder and lightning, tempests, thunderbolts, are called by the Psalmist, *Voices of the Lord ;* and he says further, that *they fulfil his word,*† because they proclaim his fear, and are as ministers of his justice. And again, desiring that the divine Majesty should make his enemies tremble, he says : *Send forth lightning and thou shalt scatter them : shoot out thy arrows, and thou shalt trouble them :*‡ where he terms thunderbolts the arrows and darts of God. And before the Psalmist, Samuel's good mother had already sung, that even God's enemies would fear him, if he would thunder over them from heaven.§ Indeed Plato, in his *Gorgias* and elsewhere, testifies that there was some sense of fear among the pagans, not only concerning the chastisements which the sovereign justice of God inflicts in this world, but also concerning the punishments which he inflicts in the other life upon the souls of those who have incurable sins. So deeply is the instinct of fearing the Divinity graven in man's nature.

This fear, however, when felt after the manner of a first movement, or natural feeling, is neither to be praised nor blamed in us, since it proceeds not from our free-will. Yet it is an effect from a very good cause, and a cause of a very good effect; for it comes from the natural knowledge which God has given us of his Providence, and gives us to understand how closely we depend on the sovereign omnipotence, moving us to implore his aid ; and when this feeling is found in a faithful soul, it much advances her in goodness. Christians (amidst the dread which thunder, tempests, and other natural dangers cause in

---

* Acts xxviii. 4. † Ps. cxlviii. 8. ‡ Ps. cxliii.
§ 1 Kings ii. 10.

them) invoke the sacred names of Jesus and of Mary, make the sign of the Cross, prostrate themselves before God, and make many good acts of faith, hope and religion. The glorious saint Thomas Aquinas, being naturally subject to terror when it thundered, was accustomed to say, as an ejaculatory prayer, the divine words which the church so much esteems : *The Word was made flesh.* Upon this fear, then, divine love frequently makes acts of complacency and benevolence : *I will praise thee, for thou art fearfully magnified.** Let every one fear thee, O Lord ! *O ye kings understand : receive instruction, you that judge the earth. Serve ye the Lord with fear : and rejoice unto him with trembling.*†

But there is another fear, taking its origin from faith, which teaches us that after this mortal life there are punishments fearfully eternal, or eternally to be feared, prepared for such as in this world have offended the Divine Majesty and die without being reconciled to him; that at the hour of death the soul shall be judged by a particular judgment; and that at the end of the world all shall rise and appear together to be judged again in the universal judgment. For these Christian truths, Theotimus, strike with an extreme dread the heart that deeply ponders them. And indeed how could one represent unto himself those eternal horrors without shuddering and trembling with apprehension ? Now when these sentiments of fear take such root in our souls that they drive and banish thence the affection and will to sin, as the sacred Council of Trent speaks, they are certainly very wholesome. *We have conceived* of thy fear, O Lord, *and have brought forth the spirit of salvation,* is said in Isaias.‡ That is, thy wrathful face terrified us, and made us conceive and bring forth the spirit of penance, which is the spirit of salvation ; so did the Psalmist say : *There is no peace for my bones, because of my sins,* yea, they tremble, *because of thy wrath.*§

Our Saviour, who came to establish the law of love amongst us, ceases not to inculcate this fear: *Fear him,* he says, *that can*

* Ps. cxxxviii. 14. † Ps. ii. 10, 11.
xxvi. 18, according to the Hebrew [Tr.] § Ps. xxxvii. 4.

*destroy both soul and body into hell.** The Ninivites did penance upon the threat of their destruction and damnation, and their repentance was agreeable to God; and, in a word, this fear is comprised amongst the gifts of the Holy Ghost, as many ancient Fathers have noted.

But if fear does not exclude the will of sinning and affection for sin, it is certainly evil, and like to that of the devils, who often cease to do harm for fear of being tormented by exorcisms, without ceasing to desire and will evil, which is their meditation for ever; or it is like to that of the miserable galley-slave, who would like to tear out his overseer's heart, though he dares not stir from the oar for fear of being lashed; or like to the fear of that great heresiarch of the last century,† who confessed that he hated a God who punished the wicked. Truly he who loves sin, and would willingly commit it, in spite of the will of God, though he will not commit it simply because he fears to be damned, has a horrible and detestable fear: for though he has not the will to execute the sin, yet he has the execution of it in his will, since he would do it if fear held him not back, and since it is as it were by force that he does not put his will into effect.

To this fear we may add another, less malicious indeed yet equally useless: such as that of the judge Felix, who, hearing God's judgments spoken of, was terrified;‡ yet he did not for all that give up his avarice; and that of Baltassar, who, seeing that miraculous hand which wrote his condemnation upon the wall, was so struck with dread that *his countenance changed, and his thoughts troubled him: and the joints of his loins were loosed, and his knees struck one against the other:*§ and yet he did not do penance. Now to what purpose do we fear evil, if our fear does not make us resolve to avoid it?

The fear, then, of those who as slaves observe the law of God to avoid hell, is very good; but much more noble and desirable is the fear of mercenary Christians, who, as hirelings, faithfully labour, yet not principally for any love they bear their masters

---

* Matt. x. 28.   † Luther [Tr.]   ‡ Acts xxiv. 25.
§ Dan. v. 6.

but to be paid the wages promised them. O! if the eye could see, if the ear could hear, or if it could enter into the heart of man what God hath prepared for those that serve him—Ah! what a dread would one have of violating God's commandments, for fear of losing those immortal rewards! what tears would be shed, what groans would be uttered, when they were lost by sin! Yet this fear would be blameworthy if it contained in it the exclusion of holy love; for he who should say: I will not serve God for any love I intend to have for him, but only to obtain the rewards he promises,—would commit blasphemy, preferring the reward to the master, the benefit to the benefactor, the inheritance to the father, and his own profit to God Almighty, as we have more amply shown in the second Book.

But, finally, when we are afraid of offending God not to avoid the pains of hell or the loss of heaven, but only because God being our good Father we owe him honour, respect, obedience, then our fear is filial, because a good child does not obey his father on account of the power he has to punish his disobedience, or because he might disinherit him, but purely because he is his father; in such sort that though his father might be old, powerless, and poor, he would not serve him with less diligence, but rather, like the bird of filial piety, would assist him with the more care and affection. So Joseph seeing that good man Jacob his father, old, in want, and brought under his son's government, ceased not to honour, serve and reverence him with a tenderness more than filial, and which was so great that his brothers having observed it, considered that it would even operate after the father's death, and therefore worked on it to obtain pardon from him, saying: Your *father commanded us before he died, that we should say thus much to thee from him: I beseech thee to forget the wickedness of thy brethren, and the sin and malice they practised against thee: we also pray thee, to forgive the servants of the God of thy father this wickedness. And when Joseph heard this, he wept,* so readily did his filial heart melt when his deceased father's wishes and will were represented to him. Those, therefore,

* Gen. l. 17.

fear God with a filial affection who fear to displease him purely
and simply because he is their most sweet, most benign and
most amiable Father.

At the same time, when it happens that this filial fear is
joined, mingled and tempered with the servile fear of eternal
damnation, or with the mercenary fear of losing heaven, it
ceases not to be agreeable to God, and is called a beginning
fear, that is a fear of such as are beginners and learners in
the exercises of divine love. For as young boys when they first
begin to ride, feeling their horse curvet a little, not only cleave
close to him with their knees, but also catch hard hold of the
saddle with their hands, but after they have had a little more
practice simply press their saddles close;—even so, novices and
apprentices in God's service, finding themselves in desperate
straits amid the assaults which the enemy delivers at the
beginning, not only make use of filial but also of mercenary and
servile fear, and hold themselves on as they can, that they may
not fall from their design.

CHAPTER XIX.

HOW SACRED LOVE CONTAINS THE TWELVE FRUITS OF THE HOLY
GHOST, TOGETHER WITH THE EIGHT BEATITUDES OF THE
GOSPEL.

THE glorious S. Paul speaks thus: *Now the fruit of the Spirit is
charity, joy, peace, patience, benignity, goodness, longanimity,
mildness, faith, modesty, continency, chastity.** But mark,
Theotimus, how this holy Apostle, counting these twelve fruits
of the Holy Ghost, reckons them as only one fruit; for he does
not say the *fruits of the spirit are charity, joy,* but *the fruit of the
spirit is charity, joy.* Now the mystery of this manner of speech
is this. *The charity of God is poured forth in our hearts, by the
Holy Ghost who is given to us:*† charity is truly the only fruit

* Gal. v. 22.   † Rom. v. 5.

of the Holy Ghost, but because this one fruit has an infinity of excellent properties, the Apostle, who wishes to mention some of them by way of example, speaks of this one fruit as of many, because of the multitude of properties which it contains in its unity, and conversely speaks of all these fruits as of one only, by reason of the unity in which is comprised this variety. So he who should say that the fruit of the vine is grapes, must, wine, brandy, the drink that rejoices the heart of man, the beverage that comforts the stomach :—would not mean that they were fruits of different species, but only that, although it was only one fruit, yet it had many different properties, according as it was differently used.

The Apostle, then, simply means to say that the fruit of the Holy Ghost is charity; which is joyous, peaceable, patient, benign, good, long-suffering, mild, faithful, modest, continent, chaste; that is to say, that divine love gives us an inward joy and consolation together with great peace of heart, which in adversity is preserved by patience, and which makes us benign and gracious in succouring our neighbour by a cordial goodness towards him; a goodness which is not variable, but constant and persevering, and which gives us a noble, long-suffering heart, by means of which we become mild, affable and condescending to all, we support their humours and imperfections, we keep perfectly faithful towards them, testifying a simplicity accompanied with confidence as well in our words as in our actions, we live modestly and humbly, cutting off all superfluities and irregularities in meat, drink, apparel, bed, games, pastimes and other such desires and pleasures, by a holy continency, repressing, especially, the inclinations and rebellions of the flesh by a vigilant chastity; so that our whole man may come to be engaged in holy loving, as well interiorly by joy, peace, patience, longanimity, goodness and fidelity, as exteriorly by benignity, mildness, modesty, continency and chastity.

Now charity is called a fruit inasmuch as it delights us, and inasmuch as we enjoy its delicious sweetness, the sweetness of a true apple of paradise, gathered from the tree of life, which is the Holy Spirit, grafted on our human spirits and dwelling in us by his infinite mercy. But when we not only rejoice in this heavenly love and enjoy its delicious sweetness, but also place all our glory therein as in the crown of our honour, then it is not only a fruit, delightful to our palate, but it is also a most desirable beatitude and felicity, not only because it assures to us the felicity of the next life, but also because even in this life it enriches us with a contentment of inestimable value, a contentment which is so strong that all the waters of tribulation and the floods of persecution cannot extinguish it. Yea, it is not only not extinguished, but it waxes rich amidst poverty, it is glorified by abjections and humiliations, it rejoices in tears, it gains strength by being forsaken of justice and deprived of the help thereof when it implores and no one will grant; compassion and commiseration recreate it, when it is surrounded by the miserable and suffering; it delights in renouncing all sorts of sensual and earthly delights to obtain purity and cleanness of heart; it places its valour in stilling wars, jarrings and dissensions, and in spurning temporal grandeurs and reputations; it grows strong by enduring all sorts of sufferings, and holds that its true life consists in dying for the well-beloved.

So that in a word, Theotimus, most holy charity is a virtue, a gift, a fruit and a beatitude. As being a virtue, it makes us obedient to the exterior inspirations which God gives us by his commandments and counsels, in the execution of which we practise all virtues; whence love is the virtue of all virtues. As being a gift, charity makes us docile and tractable to interior inspirations, which are, as it were, God's secret commandments and counsels, in the execution of which the seven gifts of the Holy Ghost are employed, so that charity is the gift of gifts. As being a fruit, it gives us an extreme relish and pleasure in the practice of the devout life, which is felt in the twelve fruits of the Holy Ghost, and therefore it is the fruit of fruits. As being a beatitude, it makes us repute the affronts, calumnies, revilings and insults which the world heaps upon us as the greatest of favours and a singular honour; and withal makes us forsake, renounce and reject all other glory save that which comes from the well-beloved Crucified, for which glory we glory in the abjection, abnegation and annihilation of ourselves, desiring no other marks of majesty than the thorn-crown of the Crucified, the sceptre of His reed, the robe of scorn which was put upon Him, and the throne of His cross, upon which sacred lovers have more content, joy, glory and felicity than ever Solomon had on his throne of ivory.

Thus love is oftentimes represented by the pomegranate, which, as it takes its properties from the pomegranate-tree, may be said to be the virtue of this tree; so again it seems to be its gift, which it offers to man by love; and it is its fruit, since it is eaten to please man's taste; and finally it is, so to speak, its glory and beatitude, since it bears the crown and diadem.

CHAPTER XX.

HOW DIVINE LOVE MAKES USE OF ALL THE PASSIONS AND AFFECTIONS OF THE SOUL, AND REDUCES THEM TO ITS OBEDIENCE.

LOVE is the life of our heart, and as the weights give movement to all the movable parts of a clock, so love gives to the soul all the movements it has. All our affections follow our love, and according to it we desire, we rejoice, we hope, we despair, we fear, we take heart, we hate, we avoid things, we grieve, we get angry, we triumph. Do not we see that men who have given up their heart as a prey to the base and abject love of women have no desires but according to this love, take no pleasure but in it, neither hope nor despair but on this account, neither dread nor undertake anything but for it, are neither disgusted nor fly from anything save what diverts them from it, are only troubled at what deprives them of it, are never angry but from jealousy, never glory but in this infamy. The like may be said of those who love riches or are ambitious of honours; for they become slaves to that which they love, and have neither heart in their breasts, nor soul in their hearts, nor affections in their souls, save only for that.

When therefore divine love reigns in our hearts, it royally brings to its empire all the other loves of the will, and consequently all its affections, because they naturally follow love ; this done, it tames sensual love, and bringing it to obedience, brings also after it all the sensual passions. For, in a word, this sacred love is the sovereign water, of which our Saviour said : *He that shall drink of the water that I will give him, shall not thirst for ever.** No truly, Theotimus, he that has love in any abundance, he shall neither have desire, fear, hope, courage, nor joy but for God, and all his movements shall be at rest in this one celestial love.

Divine love and self-love are in our hearts as Jacob and Esau in the womb of Rebecca : they have a very great antipathy and opposition to one another, and continually struggle in the heart ; whence the poor soul cries out: Alas! wretched that *I am, who will deliver me from the body of this death,* that the sole love of my God may peaceably reign in me ? However, we must take courage, putting our trust in our Saviour's word, who, commanding us to fight, by his command promises victory to his love ; and he seems to say to the soul that which he caused to be said to Rebecca : *Two nations are in thy womb, and two people shall be divided out of thy womb, and one people shall overcome the other, and the elder shall serve the younger.*† For as Rebecca had only two children in her womb, but because two peoples were to descend from these was said to have two nations in her womb, so the soul having two loves in her heart, has consequently two great troops of motions, affections and passions ; and as the two children of Rebecca by the contrariety of their movements made her suffer great convulsions and pains, so the two loves of our soul cause great travails to our heart. And as it was said of her two children that the elder should serve the younger, so has it been ordained that of these two loves of our heart the sensual shall serve the spiritual, that is, self-love shall serve the love of God.

But when was it that the elder of those peoples which were in Rebecca's womb served the younger ? Surely it was only

* John iv. 13. † Gen. xxv. 23.

when David overcame the Idumeans in war, and Solomon ruled over them in peace. Oh! when therefore shall it be that sensual love shall serve Divine love? It shall then be, Theotimus, when armed love, having become zeal, shall by mortification subject our passions; and far better then, when in heaven above, beatified love shall possess our whole soul in peace.

Now the method by which Divine love is to subject the sensual appetite is like to that which Jacob used when, for a good presage and beginning of what was afterwards to come to pass, he at the birth of Esau held him by the foot, as it were to seize Esau's right, supplant him and keep him down, or, as it were, to keep him tied up after the manner of a bird of prey, such as Esau was, being a hunter and a terrible man. For so holy love perceiving some passion or natural affection rising in us, must presently take it by the foot and bring it to its service. But what is meant by *taking by the foot?* To bind and reduce it to the service of God. Do you not see how Moses transformed the serpent into a rod, simply taking it by the tail? Even so, when we give a good end to our passions they turn into virtues.

But what method are we then to observe in order to bring our affections and passions into the service of Divine love. The Methodic physicians have always this aphorism in their mouths, —that contraries are cured by their contraries; the Spagyrists have another famous sentence opposed to this—that likes are cured by their likes. Howsoever it be, we know that two things make the light of the stars disappear,—the obscurity of the mists of night, and the light of the sun which is stronger than theirs; and in like manner we fight against passions, either by opposing to them contrary passions, or by opposing stronger affections of their own kind. If some vain hope present itself unto me, my way of resistance may be to oppose to it this just discouragement: O foolish man! upon what foundation do you build this hope? Do you not see that this great man in whom you trust is as near to his grave as thyself? Do you not know the instability, weakness and imbecillity of the spirit of man? To-day this heart from which you expect something is thine, to-morrow another will carry it away for himself: on what then is this hope grounded? I can also resist this hope by opposing to it a more solid one. Hope in God, O my soul! for it is he who delivers thy feet out of the snare; no man ever hoped in him, and was confounded: fix thy designs upon eternal and imperishable things. In like manner one may combat the desire of riches and temporal delights, either by the contempt they merit or by the desire of immortal ones; and by this means sensual and earthly love will be destroyed by heavenly love, either as fire is extinguished by water on account of the contrary qualities of water, or as it is extinguished by fire from heaven, on account of the stronger and overpowering qualities of this.

Our Saviour makes use of both these methods in his spiritual cures. He cures his disciples of worldly fear by imprinting in their hearts a higher fear: *Fear ye not them that kill the body, and are not able to kill the soul: but rather fear him that can destroy both soul and body into hell.** When he would another time cure them of a lower joy, he assigned them a nobler one: *Rejoice not,* said he, *in this, that spirits are subject unto you: but rejoice in this, that your names are written in heaven:*† and he himself casts out joy by grief: *Woe to you that now laugh: for you shall mourn and weep.*‡ Thus does Divine love supplant and bring into subjection the affections and passions, turning them from the end to which self-love would sway them, and applying them to its spiritual intentions. And as the rainbow touching the herb *aspalathus* deprives it of its own smell and gives it another far more excellent, so sacred love touching our passions takes from them their earthly end, and bestows a heavenly one in its place. The appetite for food is made very spiritual if before gratifying it we give it the motive of love:— Ah! no, Lord! it is not to content this wretched stomach, nor to allay this appetite that I go to table, but according to thy Providence to sustain this body which thou hast given me subject to this misery: yes, Lord! *because it hath so pleased thee.* If I hope for a friend's assistance can I not say: O Lord, thou hast so appointed our life, that we should have to take help,

---

* Matt. x. 28.   † Luke x. 20.   ‡ Luke vi. 25.

comfort and consolation from one another ; and because so it pleases thee, I will use this or that man whose friendship thou hast given me to this end. Is there some just occasion for fear? It is thy will, O Lord, that I should fear, in order that I may use fit means to avoid this trouble; I will do so, O Lord, since such is thy good pleasure. If the fear be excessive : Ah ! O God, my eternal Father ! what is it that thy children, or the chickens which live under thy wings can fear ? so then, I will take the means necessary to avoid the evil which I fear, but that done,—Lord, *I am thine, save thou me,* if it be thy pleasure, and what may befall me I will accept, because such will be thy good pleasure. O holy and sacred alchemy! O heavenly projection-powder ! by which all the metals of our passions, affections and actions are converted into the most pure gold of heavenly love.

CHAPTER XXI.

THAT SADNESS IS ALMOST ALWAYS USELESS, YEA CONTRARY TO THE SERVICE OF HOLY LOVE.

ONE cannot graft an oak upon a pear tree, of so contrary a humour are those two trees : nor can anger or despair be grafted on charity, at least it would be very difficult. As for anger, we have seen this in the discourse upon zeal; as for despair, unless it be reduced to the legitimate distrust of ourselves, or to a sense of the vanity, weakness and inconstancy of worldly favours, helps and promises, I see not what service Divine love can draw from it.

And as for sadness, how can it be profitable to holy charity, seeing that joy is ranked amongst the fruits of the Holy Ghost, coming next to charity? Still, the great apostle says: *The sorrow that is according to God worketh penance unto salvation which is lasting : but the sorrow of the world worketh death.* [*] There is then a sorrow or sadness according to God, which is employed either by sinners in penance, or by the good in com-

* 2 Cor. vii. 10.

passion for the temporal miseries of their neighbours, or by the perfect in deploring, bemoaning and condoling the spiritual calamities of souls. For David, S. Peter, Magdalen, wept for their sins; Agar wept when she saw her son almost dead of thirst; Jeremias over the ruin of Jerusalem; Our Saviour over the Jews; and his great Apostle sighing says these words: *Many walk of whom I have told you often (and now tell you weeping) that they are enemies of the cross of Christ.**

There is then also a sadness of this world, which likewise proceeds from three causes. For—1°. It comes sometimes from the infernal enemy, who by a thousand sad, melancholy and disturbing suggestions obscures the understanding, weakens the will, and troubles the whole soul: and as a thick mist fills the head and breast with rheum, and by this means makes respiration difficult, and greatly incommodes the traveller; so the evil spirit, filling man's mind with sad thoughts, deprives it of facility in aspiring to God, and possesses it with an extreme tedium and discouragement, in order to bring it to despair and perdition. They say there is a fish called the sea-toad, surnamed the sea-devil, which stirring and spreading the mud troubles the water round about it so as to hide itself therein as in an ambush, from whence, as soon as it perceives poor little fishes, it darts upon them, kills and devours them: whence perhaps has come the common expression—fishing in troubled waters. Now it is the same with the devil of hell as with the devil of the sea; for he makes his ambush in sadness, and then, having troubled the soul with a multitude of sad thoughts cast hither and thither in the understanding, he makes a charge upon the affections, bearing them down with distrust, jealousies, aversions, envies, superfluous apprehensions of past sins, adding withal a number of vain, sour and melancholy subtleties of the imagination, that all reasons and consolations may be rejected.

2°. Sadness sometimes also proceeds from one's natural disposition, when the melancholy humour predominates in us: and this is not vicious in itself, yet our enemy makes great use of it to weave and prepare a thousand temptations in our souls

* Phil. iii. 18.

For as spiders scarcely ever spin their webs save when the
weather is dull and the sky cloudy ; so this malign spirit never
finds as much facility in spreading the nets of his suggestions in
sweet, kindly and bright souls, as he has with the gloomy, sad
and melancholy ; for these he easily disturbs with vexations,
suspicions, hatreds, murmurings, censures, envies, sloth and
spiritual numbness.

3°. Lastly, there is a sadness which the various accidents
of life bring upon us. *What manner of joy shall be to me,*
said Tobias, *who sit in darkness, and see not the light of heaven ?*[*]
Thus was Jacob sad on the news of the death of his Joseph,
and David for that of his Absalom. Now this sadness is
common to the good and the bad ; but to the good it is moderated by acquiescence in and resignation to the will of God : as
we see in Tobias, who gave thanks to the Divine Majesty for
all the adversities which came upon him, and in Job, who blessed
the name of the Lord for them, and in Daniel, who turned his
griefs into songs of joy. As to worldlings, on the contrary,
this sadness is an ordinary thing with them, and spreads out into
regrets, despair, and deadness of soul : for they are like apes and
monkeys, which are always sullen, sad and peevish at the waning
of the moon, as, on the contrary, at the new moon, they
leap, dance and play their apish tricks. The worldling is out
of temper, uncivil, bitter and gloomy when temporal prosperity
fails him ; and in abundance he is almost always boastful,
foolishly elated and insolent.

Indeed the sadness of true penitence is not so much to be
named sadness as displeasure, or the sense and detestation of
evil ; a sadness which is never troubled nor vexed ; a sadness
which does not dull the spirit, but makes it active, ready and
diligent ; a sadness which does not weigh the heart down, but
raises it by prayer and hope, and causes in it the movements of
the fervour of devotion ; a sadness which in the heaviest of its
bitternesses ever produces the sweetness of an incomparable
consolation, according to the precept of the great S. Augustine :
"Let the penitent sorrow always, yet always rejoice for his

* Tob. v. 12.

sorrow." "The sadness," says Cassian, " which works solid penitence, and that desirable repentance of which one never repents, is obedient, affable, humble, mild, sweet, patient,—as being a child and scion of charity : so that spreading over every pain of body and contrition of spirit, and being in a certain way joyous, courageous, and strengthened by the hope of doing better, it retains all the sweetness of gentleness and longanimity, having in itself the Fruits of the Holy Spirit, which the holy Apostle recounts : *Now the Fruits of the Spirit are charity, joy, peace, longanimity, goodness, benignity, faith, mildness, continency.*" Such is true penitence, and such is right sadness, which in good sooth is not really sad or melancholy, but only attentive and earnest to detest, reject and hinder the evil of sin for past and for future. And indeed we often see repentances which are very eager, troubled, impatient, wet-eyed, bitter, given to groans, very crabbed and melancholy, which at last turn out fruitless, and lack all true amendment, because they do not proceed from the true motives of the virtue of penitence, but from selfish and natural love.

*The sorrow of the world worketh death,** says the Apostle ; we must, therefore, Theotimus, carefully avoid and banish it as much as we can. If it be from nature, we must repulse it by contradicting its movements, turning it aside by the practices suitable to that purpose, and using the remedies and way of life which physicians themselves may judge best. If it come from temptation, we must clearly open our mind to our spiritual father, who will prescribe for us the method of overcoming it, according as we have said in Part IV. of the *Introduction to the Devout Life.* If it arise from circumstances, we will have recourse to the teaching of Book VIII., in order to see how grateful tribulations are to the children of God, and how the greatness of our hopes for eternal life ought to make all the passing events of the temporal almost unworthy of thinking about.

At last, in all the sadness which may come upon us, we must employ the authority of the superior will to do all that should be done in favour of divine love. There are indeed actions

† 2 Cor. vii. 10.

which so depend upon the corporal disposition and constitution that we have not the power to do them just as we please : for the melancholy-disposed cannot keep their eyes, or their words, or their faces, in the same good grace and sweetness as they would do if they were relieved from this bad humour; but they are quite able, though without this good grace, to say gracious, kind, and civil words, and, in spite of inclination, to do what reason requires as to words and works of charity, gentleness and condescension. We may be excused for not being always bright, for one is not master of cheerfulness to have it when one will; but we are not excusable for not being always gracious, yielding and considerate ; for this is always in the power of our will, and we have only to determine to keep down the contrary humour and inclination.

BOOK XII.

CONTAINING CERTAIN COUNSELS FOR THE PROGRESS OF THE SOUL IN HOLY LOVE.

———◆◆———

CHAPTER I.

THAT OUR PROGRESS IN HOLY LOVE DOES NOT DEPEND ON OUR NATURAL TEMPERAMENT.

A GREAT religious of our age has written that our natural temperament much conduces to contemplative love, and that such as are of an affectionate and loving nature are best adapted for it. Now I suppose he means not that sacred love is distributed to men or angels according to, or much less in virtue of, natural conditions ; nor would he say that the distribution of divine love is made to men according to their natural qualities and abilities : for this were to belie the Scripture, and to violate the ecclesiastical canon, by which the Pelagians were declared heretics.

For my part, I speak in this treatise of the supernatural love which God out of his goodness pours into our hearts, and whose residence is in the supreme point of the spirit; a point which is above all the rest of the soul, and independent of all natural disposition. And withal, though souls inclined to love have on the one hand a certain propensity which makes them more ready to desire to love God, they are, on the other hand, so subject to set their affections upon lovable creatures, that their propensity puts them in as great danger of being diverted from the purity of sacred love by a mixture of other loves, as they have facility in wishing to love God; for the danger of loving amiss is attached to the facility of loving.

It is true that souls of this kind, being once well purified from the love of creatures, work wonders in holy loving, as love finds a great facility in diffusing itself throughout all the faculties of the heart: and thence proceeds a most delightful sweetness, which appears not in those whose souls are peevish, harsh, melancholy and churlish.

Nevertheless, if two persons, the one of whom is loving and sweet by nature, the other harsh and sour, have an equal charity, they will love God equally, but not alike. The heart naturally sweet will love more easily, more amiably, more sweetly, though not more solidly nor more perfectly; yea, the love which shall spring amongst the thorns and repugnances of a harsh and dry nature shall be the more noble and glorious, as the other shall be more delightsome and lovely.

It imports not much then, whether one have a natural inclination to love, when it is a question of a love which is supernatural and exercised supernaturally. Only this, Theotimus, I would gladly cry out to all men: O mortals, if you have hearts disposed for love, why do you not devote yourselves to celestial and divine love? But if you be hard and sour-tempered—since you are wanting in natural love, why do you not aspire to supernatural love, which shall be lovingly bestowed upon you by him who calls you to his so holy love?

CHAPTER II.

THAT WE ARE TO HAVE A CONTINUAL DESIRE TO LOVE.

*Lay up treasures in heaven.** One treasure is not enough for the pleasure of this divine lover, but he desires that we should have so much treasure that our treasure may be composed of many treasures; that is to say, Theotimus, that we are to

* Matt. vi. 20.

have an insatiable desire of loving God, adding continually love upon love. What is it that so strongly urges the bees to increase their honey but the love they bear to it? O heart of my soul, created to love the infinite good, what love canst thou desire but this love, which is the most to be desired of all loves! Ah! O soul of my heart, what desire canst thou love but the most lovely of all desires! O love of sacred desires! O desires of sacred love! Oh! how *have I coveted to long for* thy perfections.*

The disgusted sick man has no appetite for eating, yet has he an appetite to have an appetite; he desires no meat, but he desires to desire it. Theotimus, to know whether we love God above all things is not in our power, unless God himself reveal it unto us: yet we may easily know whether we desire to love him; and perceiving the desire of holy love in us, we know that we begin to love. It is our sensual and animal part which covets to eat, but it is our reasonable part which desires this appetite; and because the sensual part does not always obey the reasonable part, it frequently happens that we desire appetite and cannot have it. But the desire of loving and love depend upon the same will: wherefore as soon as we have framed the true desire of loving, we begin to have some love; and ever as this desire grows, love also increases. He who desires love ardently shall shortly love with ardour. Ah! who will give us the grace, Theotimus, that we may burn with this desire, which is the *desire of the poor*, and the *preparation of* their *heart*, which God willingly hears.†
He who has no assurance of loving God is a poor man, and if he desire to love him he is a beggar, but a beggar with the blessed beggary of which Our Saviour has said: *Blessed are the beggars of spirit; for theirs is the kingdom of heaven.*‡

Such a one was S. Augustine, when he cried out: "O to love! O to run! O to die to self! O to get to God!" Such S. Francis, saying: "Let me die of thy love, O thou friend of my heart, who hast deigned to die for my love." Such S. Catharine of Genoa, and the Blessed Mother (S.) Teresa when,

---

* Ps. cxviii. 20. † Ps. ix. 38.
‡ Matt. v. 3. From the Greek [Tr.].

panting as the hart pants, and dying with the thirst of divine love, they sighed out this word : *Ah Lord ! give me this water.**

Temporal covetousness, by which we greedily desire earthly treasures, is the root of all evil ; but spiritual avarice, whereby one sighs incessantly after the pure gold of Divine love, is the root of all good. He who truly desires love seeks it truly ; and he who truly seeks it, truly finds it ; and he who has truly found it has found the fountain of life, whence *he shall draw salvation from the Lord.*† Let us cry, night and day, Theotimus : Come, O Holy Spirit ! fill the hearts of thy faithful, and kindle in them the fire of thy love. O heavenly love, when wilt thou fill my soul ?

CHAPTER III.

THAT TO HAVE THE DESIRE OF SACRED LOVE WE ARE TO CUT OFF ALL OTHER DESIRES.

WHY do hounds, think you, Theotimus, more ordinarily lose the scent or strain of their quarry in the spring-time than at other times ? It is, as hunters and philosophers say, because the grass and flowers are then in their vigour, so that the variety of smells which they send out so fills the hounds' sense of smelling that they can neither take nor follow the scent of their game, among so many scents which the earth exhales. In sooth those souls that ever abound in desires, designs and projects, never desire holy celestial love as they ought, nor can perceive the delightful strain and scent of the divine beloved, who is compared to the roe, and to the little fawn of the doe.‡

Lilies have no season, but flower soon or late, as they are deeper or less deep set in the ground : for if they be thrust three fingers only into the earth they will presently blossom, but if they be put six or nine, they come up proportionately later. If the

* John iv. 15.   † Prov. viii. 35.   ‡ Cant. ii. 9.

heart that aims after Divine love be deeply engaged in terrene and temporal affairs, it will bud late and with difficulty ; but if it have only so much to do with the world as its condition requires, you shall see it bloom timely in love, and send out a delicious odour.

For this cause the Saints betook themselves to deserts, that being freed from worldly cares they might more ardently apply to heavenly love. For this the spouse shut one of her eyes,* to the end that she might keep the sight of the other alone more fixedly, and thereby take better aim at the very midst of her beloved's heart, which she desires to wound with love. And for this same reason she keeps her hair so plaited and gathered up in a tress that she seems to have one only hair which she makes use of as a chain, to bind and bear away her spouse's heart, whom she makes a slave to her love.

They who desire for good and all to love God, shut up their understanding from discoursing of worldly things, to employ it more earnestly in the meditation of divine things, and gather up all their pretensions under the sole intention which they have of loving only God. Whosoever desires something which he desires not for God that much less desires God.

A religious man demanded of the Blessed Giles what he could do most grateful to God; and he answered him by singing : "One to one, one to one ;" that is, one only soul to one only God. So many desires and loves in a heart are like many children at one breast, who, as they cannot all suck at once, struggle each one for his turn, so that at last the fount dries up. He who aspires to heavenly love, must sedulously reserve for it his leisure, his spirit and his affections.

* Cant. iv. 9.

CHAPTER IV.

THAT OUR LAWFUL OCCUPATIONS DO NOT HINDER US FROM PRACTISING DIVINE LOVE.

CURIOSITY, ambition, disquiet, the not adverting to, or not considering, the end for which we are in this world, are the causes why we have a thousand times more hindrance than business, more worries than work, more occupation than profit: and these are the embarrassments, Theotimus, that is, the silly, vain and superfluous undertakings with which we charge ourselves, that turn us from the love of God, and not the true and lawful exercises of our vocations. David, and, after him, S. Louis, in the press of the perils, toils and travails which they endured, as well in peace as in war, did not cease to sing in truth: *What have I in heaven, and besides thee what do I desire upon earth ?** S. Bernard lost none of the progress which he desired to make in this holy love, though he were in the courts and armies of great princes, where he laboured to bring matters of state to the service of God's glory ; he changed his habitation, but he changed not his heart, nor did his heart change its love, nor his love its object; and, to speak his own language, these changes were made in him but not of him, since although his employments were very different, yet he was indifferent to all employment, and different from them all, not receiving the colour of his affairs and conversations, as the chameleon does that of the places where it is, but remaining ever wholly united to God, ever white in purity, ever red with charity, and ever full of humility.   I am not ignorant, Theotimus, what the wise man's counsel is :

> He ever flies the court and legal strife
> Who seeks to sow the seeds of holy life :
> Rarely do camps effect the soul's increase,
> Virtue and faith are daughters unto peace.

And the Israelites had good reason to excuse themselves to

* Ps. lxxii. 25.

the Babylonians, who urged them to sing the sacred canticles of Sion : *How shall we sing the song of the Lord in a strange land ?** But do you not also mark that those poor people were not only among the Babylonians but were also their captives. Whoever is a slave to courtly favours, the prizes of the law, the honours of war,—Alas ! all is over with him, he cannot sing the hymn of heavenly love. But he who is only at court, in war, at the tribunals, by duty—God helps him, and heavenly sweetness is as an *epithem* on his heart, to preserve him from the plague which reigns in those places.

While the plague afflicted the Milanese, S. Charles never made any difficulty in frequenting the houses and touching the persons that were infected. Yet, Theotimus, he only frequented and touched them, so far forth as the necessity of God's work required, nor would he for the world have thrust himself into danger without true necessity, lest he should commit the sin of tempting God. So that he was never touched with any infection, God's Providence preserving him who had so pure a confidence in it, that it had no mixture either of fear or rashness. In like manner God takes care of those who go not to the court, to the bar, to war, except by the necessity of their duty ; and in that case a man is neither to be so scrupulous as to abandon good and lawful affairs by not going, nor so overweening and presumptuous as to go thither or stay there without the express necessity of duty and affairs.

CHAPTER V.

A VERY SWEET EXAMPLE ON THIS SUBJECT.

GOD is innocent to the innocent,† good to the good, cordial to the cordial, tender towards the tender, and his love often makes him do acts of a sacred and holy fondness (*mignardise*) towards

* Ps. cxxxvi. 4.   † Ps. xvii. 26.

souls who, out of an amorous purity and simplicity, make themselves as little children with him.

Upon a day S. Frances was reciting Our Lady's Office, and, as it commonly happens that if there is but one affair in the whole day, it presses most at time of prayer, this holy lady was called away by her husband for some household matter, and four sundry times thinking to take up again the thread of her Office, she was called from it again, and constrained to interrupt the same verse, till this blessed affair, for which they had so importunately interrupted her prayer, being finished at last, when she returned to her Office she found the verse, so often left by obedience and so often recommenced by devotion, all written in fair golden letters, which her devout companion, Madam Vannocia swore she saw the dear Angel-Guardian of the Saint writing, as S. Paul afterwards revealed to the Saint herself.

What sweetness, Theotimus, of this heavenly spouse towards this sweet and faithful lover! But meantime you see that necessary employments, according to each one's vocation, do not diminish Divine love, but increase it, and gild, as it were, the work of devotion. The nightingale loves her melody no less when she makes her pauses than when she sings; the devout heart loves love no less when she turns to exterior necessities than when she prays: her silence and her speech, her action and her contemplation, her employment and her rest, equally sing in her the hymn of her love.

CHAPTER VI.

THAT WE ARE TO EMPLOY IN THE PRACTICE OF DIVINE LOVE ALL THE OCCASIONS THAT PRESENT THEMSELVES.

THERE are souls that make great projects to do excellent services for Our Saviour, by eminent actions and extraordinary sufferings, but actions and sufferings of which there is no opportunity, and perhaps never will be, and who upon this apprehend they have done a great matter in love, in which they are very often deceived :—as appears in this, that embracing in desire, as seems to them, great future crosses, they anxiously avoid the burden of such as are present, which are less. Is it not an extreme temptation to be so valiant in imagination, and so cowardly in execution?

Ah! God preserve us from those imaginary fervours, which very often breed a vain and secret self-esteem in the bottom of our hearts. Great works lie not always in our way, but every moment we may do little ones with excellence, that is, with a great love. Behold that Saint, I beg you, who bestows a cup of cold water on the thirsty traveller; he does but a small matter in outward show, but the intention, the sweetness, the love, with which he animates his work is so excellent, that it turns this simple water into water of life, and of eternal life.

The bees gather honey from the lily, the flag, the rose; yet they get as ample a booty from the little minute rosemary flowers and thyme; yea they draw not only more honey, but even better honey from these, for in these little vessels the honey, being more closely locked up, is kept better. Truly, in the low and little works of devotion, charity is not only practised more frequently, but ordinarily more humbly too, and consequently more usefully and more holily.

Those condescensions to the humours of others, that bearing with the clownish and troublesome actions and ways of our neighbour, those victories over our own humours and passions, those renouncings of our lesser inclinations, that effort against our aversions and repugnances, that heartfelt and sweet acknowledgment of our own imperfections, the continual pains we take to keep our souls in equality, that love of our abjection, that gentle and gracious welcome we give to the contempt and censure of our condition, of our life, of our conversation, of our actions :—Theotimus, all these things are more profitable to our souls than we can conceive, if heavenly love have the management of them. But we have already said this to Philothea.*

* Devout Life, iii. 35.

CHAPTER VII.

THAT WE MUST TAKE PAINS TO DO OUR ACTIONS VERY
PERFECTLY.

OUR Saviour, as the ancients report, was wont to say to his disciples : Be good exchangers. If the crown be not good gold, if it want weight, if it be not struck with the lawful stamp, it is rejected as not current: if a work be not of a good species, if it be not adorned with charity, if the intention be not pious, it will not be admitted amongst the good works. If I fast, but out of sparingness, my fast is not of a good metal; if it be out of temperance, but I have some mortal sin in my soul, the work wants weight, for it is charity that gives weight to all that we do; if it be only through complaisance, and to accommodate myself to my company, the work is not marked with the stamp of a right intention : but if I fast out of temperance, and be in the grace of God, and have an intention to please his Divine majesty by this temperance, the work shall be current money, fit to augment in me the treasure of charity.

To do little actions with a great purity of intention and with a strong will to please God, is to do them excellently, and then they greatly sanctify us. Some eat much, and yet are ever lean, attenuated and languid, because their digestive power is not good ; there are others who eat little, and yet are always in good plight, and vigorous, because their stomach is good. Even so there are some souls that do many good works, and yet increase but little in charity, because they do them either coldly and negligently, or by natural instinct and inclination rather than by Divine inspiration or heavenly fervour ; and, on the contrary, others there are who get through little work, but do it with so holy a will and inclination, that they make a wonderful advancement in charity ; they have little talent, but they husband it so faithfully that the Lord largely rewards them for it.

CHAPTER VIII.

A GENERAL MEANS FOR APPLYING OUR WORKS TO GOD'S SERVICE.

All whatsoever you do in word and in work, do all in the name of Jesus Christ.* *Whether you eat or drink or whatever you do, do all to the glory of God.*† These are the words of the Divine Apostle; which, as the great S. Thomas says in explaining them, are sufficiently put in practice when we have the habit of holy charity, whereby, though we have not an express and set purpose of doing every work for God, that intention is implicitly contained in the union and communion we have with God, which dedicates all the good we can do, with ourselves, to his Divine goodness. It is not necessary that a child, while living in the house and under the authority of his father, should declare that all he gets is got for his father; for since his person belongs to his father, all that depends on it also belongs to him. So it suffices that we be God's children by love, to make all that we do entirely directed to his glory.

It is true then, Theotimus, that, as we have said elsewhere, even as the olive-tree set near unto the vine imparts unto it its savour, so charity being near the other virtues communicates unto them its perfection. Yet true it is also that if one engraft a vine upon an olive, it not only more perfectly communicates its taste but also makes it share in its sap; so do you not content yourself with having charity, and together with it the practice of virtues, but endeavour that it may be by and for it that you practise them, that they may be rightly ascribed unto it.

When a painter holds and guides a pupil's hand, the stroke that is made is principally attributed to the painter, because, though the pupil indeed contributed the motion of his hand and application of the brush, yet the master also for his part did so mingle his movement with the pupil's, giving the touch through him, that to the master is specially attributed the honour of whatever is good in the stroke, though yet the apprentice is also

---

* 1 Cor. x. 31.   † Col. iii. 17.

praised, because of the pliableness with which he accommodated his movement to the direction of his master. Oh! how excellent are the actions of the virtues when Divine love impresses its sacred movement on them, that is, when they are done out of the motive of love! But this happens in different ways.

The motive of Divine love pours forth a particular influence of perfection upon the virtuous actions of those who have in a special manner dedicated themselves to God to serve him for ever. Such are bishops and priests, who by a sacramental consecration, and by a spiritual character that cannot be effaced, vow themselves, as branded and marked serfs, to the perpetual service of God; such are religious, who by their vows, either solemn or simple, are immolated to God in quality of living and reasonable sacrifices; such are those who betake themselves to pious congregations, dedicating themselves for ever to God's glory; further, such are all those who of set purpose produce deep and strong resolutions of following the will of God, making for this end retreats of some days, that they may stir up their souls by divers spiritual exercises to the entire reformation of their life—a holy method, and ordinary among the ancient Christians, but since almost entirely left off till that great servant of God, Ignatius of Loyola, brought it into use again in the time of our fathers.

I know that some are of opinion, that such a general oblation of ourselves does not extend its virtue and carry its influence into the actions which we practise afterwards except so far forth as in the exercise of them we apply the motive of love in particular, by dedicating them in a special manner to the glory of God; yet all confess with S. Bonaventure, quoted by every one in this matter, that if I have resolved in my heart to give a hundred crowns for God's sake, though afterwards I make the distribution of this sum at leisure, having my mind distracted and without attention, yet is all the distribution made through love, because it proceeds from the first intention which Divine love made me make of giving it all.

But, prithee, Theotimus, what difference is there between him who offers a hundred crowns to God, and him who offers all his actions? Truly none, save that the one offers a sum of money, and the other a sum of actions. And why, I pray, shall they not equally be considered to make the distribution of the parts of their sum in virtue of their first purposes and fundamental resolutions? And if the one, distributing his crowns without attention, fails not to have the advantage of that first purpose, why shall not the other, in the distribution of his actions, enjoy the fruit of the first intention? He who has deliberately made himself a loving servant of his divine goodness has, by that act, dedicated to him all his actions.

Grounding himself upon this truth, every one should once in his life make a good retreat, therein to cleanse his soul from all sin, and should then make a determined and solid resolution to live wholly to God, as we have taught in the first part of the *Introduction to a Devout Life;* and afterwards, at least once every year, he must make the review of his conscience and the renewal of the first resolution, which we have put down in the fifth part of that work, to which on this point I refer you.

Indeed S. Bonaventure acknowledges that a man who has got so great an inclination and custom of well-doing as frequently to do it without any special intention, fails not to merit much by such actions; which are ennobled by love, because they spring from love as from the root and original source of this blessed habit, facility and promptitude.

CHAPTER IX.

OF CERTAIN OTHER MEANS BY WHICH WE MAY APPLY OUR WORKS MORE PARTICULARLY TO THE LOVE OF GOD.

WHEN pea-hens hatch in very white places their young ones are also white: and when our intentions are in the love of God whilst we project some good work, or undertake some vocation, all the actions that issue thence take their worth and derive their nobility from the love whence they have their origin; for who does not see that the actions which are proper to my vocation and requisite to my design depend on this first election and resolution which I have made?

Yet, Theotimus, one must not stay there; but to make excellent progress in devotion, we must not only in the beginning of our conversion, and afterwards every year, address all our life and all our actions to God, but we must also offer them to him every day following the Morning Exercise which we have taught Philothea; for in this daily renewing of our oblation, we spread the vigour and virtue of love upon our actions by a fresh uniting of our heart with the Divine glory, by means whereof it is ever more and more sanctified.

Besides this, let us a hundred and a hundred times a day unite our life to Divine love by the practice of ejaculatory prayers, elevations of heart and spiritual retirements; for these holy exercises, casting and lifting our spirits continually into God, bear also up to him all our actions. And how could it be, I pray you, that a soul who at every moment darts up unto the Divine goodness, and who incessantly breathes words of love, in order to keep her heart always lodged in the bosom of her heavenly Father, should not be considered to do all her works in God and for God?

She who says: "Ah! Lord, I am thine—My beloved is wholly mine, and I, I am all his—My God, thou art my all—O Jesus thou art my life—Ah! who will do me the favour that I may die to myself, that I may live only to thee—O to love! to advance! to die to self! O to live to God! O to be in God! O God, whatsoever is not thy very self is nothing to me!"—she, I say, does she not continually dedicate her actions to her heavenly spouse? O how blessed is the soul who has once for all made the offstripping and the perfect resignation of herself in and into the hands of God, whereof we have spoken above!—for afterwards she will only need to make one little sigh and one look at God, to renew and confirm her offstripping, resignation, and oblation, together with the protestation that she wishes nothing but God and for God, and neither loves herself nor anything in the world save in God and for the love of God.

The exercise then of continual aspirations is very useful for vivifying all our works with love; but especially does it most abundantly suffice for the small and ordinary actions of our life; for as to heroic works and matters of consequence, it is expedient, if we intend to make any great profit, to use the ensuing method, as I have already in brief declared elsewhere.*

Let us in these occurrences elevate our heart and spirit to God; let us with deep consideration and extended thought ponder on eternity, so holy and so glorious; let us behold how throughout eternity the Divine goodness tenderly cherished us, preparing all suitable means for our salvation and progress in his love, and in particular the chance of doing the good which now presents itself to us, or suffering the evil which has come upon us: this done, spreading out, if I may so speak, and lifting up, the arms of our consent, let us embrace dearly, fervently and most amorously, the good that presents itself to be done, or the evil that must be suffered, in consideration of this that it has been eternally willed by God, to please him and to obey his Providence.

Behold the great S. Charles, when the plague attacked his diocese. He lifted up his heart to God, and reflected attentively that in the eternity of Divine Providence, this scourge was prepared and determined for his flock, and that the same Providence had ordained that in this their scourge he should take a most tender care to serve, solace and cordially assist the afflicted, since in this occurrence he found himself the ghostly father, pastor and bishop of that province. Whereupon, representing to himself the greatness of the pains, toils and hazards which it would be incumbent on him to undergo in that behalf, he immolated himself in spirit to God's good-pleasure, and tenderly kissing this his cross, he cried from the bottom of his heart, in imitation of S. Andrew: "I salute thee, O precious cross, I salute thee, O blessed tribulation! O holy affliction, how delightful thou art, since thou didst issue from the loving breast of this Father of eternal mercy, who willed thee from all eternity, and ordained thee for my dear people and me! O cross, my heart wills thee, since the heart of my God has willed thee; O cross, my soul cherishes and embraces thee, with its whole affection!"

* Book viii. 14.

In this sort we are to undertake the gravest affairs, and to meet the sharpest tribulations that can befal us. But if they prove to be of long continuance, we must from time to time, and very frequently, repeat this exercise, that we may more profitably continue our union with God's good will and pleasure, pronouncing this short yet wholly divine protestation of his Son : *Yea, eternal Father, for so it hath seemed good in thy sight.** O God, Theotimus, what treasures are in this practice !

CHAPTER X.

AN EXHORTATION TO THE SACRIFICE WHICH WE ARE TO MAKE TO GOD OF OUR FREE-WILL.

I ADD to the sacrifice of S. Charles that of the great patriarch Abraham, as a lively image of the most strong and loyal love that could be imagined in any creature.

Certainly he sacrificed all the strongest natural inclinations he could have had, when, hearing the voice of God saying to him : *Go forth out of thy country, and from thy kindred, and out of thy father's house, and come into the land which I shall show thee,†* he went forth at once, and with speed put himself upon the way, *not knowing whither he went.‡* The dear love of country, the sweetness of the society of his kindred, the pleasures of his father's house, did not shake his constancy; he departs boldly and with fervour, and goes whither it shall please God to conduct him. What abnegation, Theotimus, what renunciation ! One cannot perfectly love God unless one forsake affections for perishable things.

But this is nothing in comparison with what he did afterwards, when God, calling him twice, and seeing his promptitude in answering, said to him : *Take thy only-begotten son Isaac, whom thou lovest, and go into the land of vision : and there thou shalt offer him for a holocaust upon one of the mountains which I will show thee.§*

* Matt. xi. 26.   † Gen. xii. 1.   ‡ Heb. xi. 8.
§ Gen. xxii. 1.

For behold this great man, setting out immediately with his so loved and amiable son, goes three days' journey, comes to the foot of the mountain, leaves there his servant and ass, loads his son Isaac with the wood necessary for the holocaust, himself carrying the sword and the fire; and as he ascends, this dear child says to him: *My father;* and he answers: *What wilt thou, son. Behold, saith he, fire and wood, but where is the victim for the holocaust? And Abraham said: God will provide himself a victim for the holocaust, my son.* And meanwhile they arrive at the top of the appointed mountain, where Abraham now constructs an altar, lays the wood in order upon it, binds his Isaac, and places him upon the pile; he extends his right hand, lays hold of and prepares his sword, lifts his arm, and as he is ready to despatch the blow in order to immolate the child, the angel calls to him from above: *Abraham, Abraham. And he answered: Here I am. And the angel said to him: Lay not thy hand upon the boy.* It is enough: *Now I know that thou fearest God, and hast not spared thy only-begotten son for my sake.* Upon this Isaac is untied, Abraham takes a ram which he finds hanging by the horns in the brambles, and sacrifices it.

Theotimus, *he who looketh on* his neighbour's wife, *to lust after her, hath already committed adultery with her in his heart,** and he who bindeth his son in order to immolate him has already sacrificed him in his heart. Behold then, for God's love, what a holocaust this holy man offered in his heart! Incomparable sacrifice, which one cannot fully estimate, nor yet praise to the full! My God! who is able to discern, which of the two loves was greater—Abraham's, who to please God sacrifices so amiable a child, or this child's, who to please God is quite willing to be sacrificed, and to that end permits himself to be bound, and extended upon the wood, and as a tender little lamb, peaceably awaits death's blow from the dear hand of his good father?

For my part, I prefer the father in longanimity, yet dare I withal boldly give the prize of magnanimity to the son: for on the one side it is indeed a marvel, but not so great a one, that Abraham, already old and accomplished in the science of loving

* Matt. v. 28.

God, and fortified with the late vision and word of God, should make this last effort of loyalty and love towards a master whose sweetness and providence he had so often tasted and relished; but to see Isaac, in the spring-time of his age, as yet a mere novice and apprentice in the art of loving his God, offer himself, upon the simple word of his father, to the sword and the flame to become a holocaust of obedience to the Divine will, is a thing that passes all admiration.

Yet, on the other side, do you not see, Theotimus, that Abraham tosses and turns in his soul, more than three days, the bitter thought and resolution of this sharp sacrifice? Do you not feel compassion for his fatherly heart, when, ascending alone with his son, this child, simpler than a dove, said unto him : *Father, where is the victim?* and he answered him : *God will provide* for that, *my son.* Do you not think that the sweetness of this child, carrying the wood upon his shoulders, and piling it afterwards upon the altar, made his father's bowels melt with tenderness? O heart which the angels admire and God magnifies! O Saviour Jesus, when shall it then be, that having sacrificed to thee all that we have, we shall also offer up to thee all that we are? When shall we offer unto thee our free-will, the only child of our spirit? When shall we extend and tie it upon the funeral pile of thy cross, of thy thorns, of thy lance, that as a little lamb, it may be a grateful victim of thy good pleasure, to die and to burn with the flame, and by the sword, of thy holy love?

O free-will of my heart, how good a thing were it for thee to be bound and extended upon the cross of thy divine Saviour! How desirable a thing it is to die to thyself, to burn for ever a holocaust to the Lord! Theotimus, our free-will is never so free as when it is a slave to the will of God, nor ever so much a slave as when it serves our own will. It never has so much life as when it dies to itself, nor ever so much death, as when it lives to itself.

We have freedom to do good or evil; yet to make choice of evil, is not to use, but to abuse our freedom. Let us renounce this miserable liberty, and let us for ever subject our free-will to the rule of heavenly love : let us become slaves of love, whose serfs are more happy than kings. And if ever our soul should offer to employ her liberty against our resolutions of serving God eternally and without reserve,—Oh! in that case, for God's sake, let us sacrifice our free-will, and make it die to itself that it may live to God! He that would for self-love keep it in this world shall lose it in the other, and he that shall lose it in this world for the love of God, shall keep it, for the same love, in the other. He that gives it liberty in this world shall find it a serf and slave in the other, and he that shall make it serve the cross in this world shall have it free in the other, where being in the fruition of the Divine goodness, liberty will be converted into love, and love into liberty—a liberty of infinite sweetness:—without effort, pain, or any repugnance we shall unchangeably, for ever, love the Creator and Saviour of our souls.

CHAPTER XI.

THE MOTIVES WE HAVE OF HOLY LOVE.

S. BONAVENTURE, Father Louis of Granada, Father Louis de Ponte, Father Diego di Stella, have sufficiently discoursed upon this subject. I will only sum up those points on which I have touched in this treatise.

The divine goodness considered in itself is not only the first motive of all, but also the greatest, the most noble and most mighty. For it is that which ravishes the Blessed, and crowns their felicity. How can one have a heart, and yet not love so infinite a goodness? This subject is treated to some extent in chapters i. and ii. of Book II., and from chapter viii. to the end of Book III., and in chapter ix. of Book X.

The second motive is that of God's natural Providence towards us, of creation and preservation, as we say in chapter iii. of Book II.

The third motive is that of God's supernatural Providence

over us, and of the Redemption he has prepared for us, as is explained in chapters iv., v., vi., vii., of Book II.

The fourth motive is to consider how God brings to effect this Providence and Redemption, giving every one all the graces and assistances required for salvation ; which we handle in Book II., from chapter viii., and in Book III., from the beginning to chapter vi.

The fifth motive is the eternal glory which the Divine goodness has provided for us, which is the crown of God's benefits towards us : of which we have said something from chapter ix. to the end of Book III.

CHAPTER XII.

A MOST USEFUL METHOD OF EMPLOYING THESE MOTIVES.

Now to receive from these motives a profound and strong heat of love, it is necessary, 1°, that after having considered one of them in a general way, we apply it in particular to ourselves. For example : O how amiable this great God is, who out of his infinite goodness gave his son for the whole world's redemption ! Yes, indeed for all in general, but in particular for me, *who am the first of sinners.** Ah ! he *hath loved me*, yea, I say, he hath loved even me, even me myself, such as I am, *and delivered himself* to his Passion *for me.*†

2°. We must consider the Divine benefits in their first and eternal source. O God ! Theotimus, what love can we have sufficiently worthy of the infinite goodness of our Creator, who from all eternity determined to create, preserve, govern, redeem, save and glorify all in general and each in particular ? Ah ! what was I then when I was not ? What was I ? who now being something am yet but a simple and poor worm of the earth ? And still God from the abyss of his eternity thought thoughts of benediction in my behalf ? He considered and

* 1 Tim. i. 15.   † Gal. ii. 20.

designed, yea determined, the hour of my birth, of my baptism, of all the inspirations that he would bestow upon me; in a word, all the benefits he would do and offer me. Ah ! is there a sweetness like unto this sweetness?

3°. We must consider the Divine benefits in their second and meritorious source; for do you not know, Theotimus, that the High Priest of the Law wore upon his back, and upon his bosom, the names of the children of Israel, that is, the precious stones upon which the names of the chiefs of Israel were engraven? Ah! behold Jesus our chief bishop, and see how, from the instant of his conception, he bore us upon his shoulders, undertaking the charge of redeeming us by his death, *even the death of the cross.* O Theotimus, Theotimus, this soul of Our Saviour knew us all by name and by sur-name; but above all in the day of his Passion, when he offered his tears, his prayers, his blood and his life for all, he breathed in particular for thee these thoughts of love: Ah! my eternal Father, I take to myself and charge myself with all poor Theotimus's sins, to undergo torments and death that he may be freed from them, and that he may not perish but live. Let me die, so he may live; let me be crucified so he may be glorified. O sovereign love of the Heart of Jesus, what heart can ever bless thee as devotedly as it ought!

Thus within his maternal breast his divine heart foresaw, disposed, merited and obtained all the benefits we have, not only in general for all, but also in particular for each one, and his breasts of sweetness provided for us the milk of his influences, his attractions, his inspirations, and the sweetnesses by which he draws, conducts and nourishes our hearts to eternal life. Benefits do not inflame us unless we behold the eternal will which destines them for us, and the Heart of Our Saviour who has merited them for us by so many pains, especially in his death and passion.

CHAPTER XIII.

THAT MOUNT CALVARY IS THE ACADEMY OF LOVE.

AND at last, as our conclusion,—the death and passion of Our
Lord is the sweetest and most constraining motive that can
animate our hearts in this mortal life: and it is the very truth,
that mystical bees make their most excellent honey within the
wounds of this Lion of the tribe of Judah, slain, rent and
torn upon the Mount of Calvary. And the children of the
cross glory in their admirable problem, which the world understands not : *Out of* death, *the eater* of all, *has come forth the
meat* of our consolation; *and out of* death, *strong* above all, *has
come forth the sweetness* of the honey of our love.* O Jesus, my
Saviour, how love-worthy is thy death, since it is the sovereign
effect of thy love !

So, in the glory of heaven above, next to the Divine goodness known and considered in itself, Our Saviour's death shall
most powerfully ravish the blessed spirits in the loving of God.
As a sign whereof, in the Transfiguration, where we have a
glimpse of heaven, Moses and Elias *talked with Our Saviour
of the Excess* † *which he was to accomplish in Jerusalem.* But of
what excess, if not of that excess of love by which life was
forced from the lover, to be bestowed on the well-beloved ? So
that in the eternal canticle I imagine to myself that this joyous
exclamation will be repeated every moment :

> Live, Jesus live, whose death doth prove,
> The might supreme of heavenly love.

Theotimus, Mount Calvary is the mount of lovers. All love
that takes not its beginning from Our Saviour's Passion is
frivolous and dangerous. Unhappy is death without the love
of the Saviour, unhappy is love without the death of the
Saviour ! Love and death are so mingled in the Passion
of Our Saviour that we cannot have the one in our heart

* Judges xiv. 14.　　　　† *Excessum*, Luke ix. 31.

without the other. Upon Calvary one cannot have life without love, nor love without the death of Our Redeemer. But, except there, all is either eternal death or eternal love : and all Christian wisdom consists in choosing rightly; and to assist you in that, I have made this treatise, my Theotimus.

During this mortal life we must choose eternal love or eternal death, there is no middle choice.

O eternal love, my soul desires and makes choice of thee eternally! Ah! come, Holy Spirit and inflame our hearts with thy love! To love or to die! To die and to love! To die to all other love in order to live to Jesus's love, that we may not die eternally, but that, living in thy eternal love, O Saviour of our souls we may eternally sing: *Vive Jésus!* I love Jesus. Live Jesus whom I love! I love Jesus, who lives and reigns for ever and ever. Amen.

May these things, Theotimus, which by the grace and help of charity have been written to your charity, so take root in your heart that this charity may find in you the fruit of good works, not the leaves of praises. Amen. Blessed be God! And thus I close this whole treatise in the words with which S. Augustine ended an admirable sermon on charity, which he made before an illustrious assembly.

THE END.

*If you have enjoyed this book, consider making your next
selection from among the following . . .*

Prices subject to change.

Little Book of the Work of Infinite Love. *de la Touche* 2.00
Textual Concordance of The Holy Scriptures. *Williams* 35.00
Douay-Rheims Bible. *Leatherbound*. 35.00
The Way of Divine Love. (pocket, unabr.). *Menendez* 8.50
Mystical City of God—Abridged. *Ven. Mary of Agreda* 18.50
Moments Divine—Before the Blessed Sacrament. *Reuter* 8.50
Miraculous Images of Our Lady. *Cruz* 20.00
Miraculous Images of Our Lord. *Cruz* 13.50
Raised from the Dead. *Fr. Hebert* 16.50
Life and Work of Mother Louise Margaret. *Fr. O'Connell* 12.50
Autobiography of St. Margaret Mary. 5.00
Thoughts and Sayings of St. Margaret Mary 5.00
The Voice of the Saints. *Comp. by Francis Johnston*. 6.00
The 12 Steps to Holiness and Salvation. *St. Alphonsus* 7.50
The Rosary and the Crisis of Faith. *Cirrincione & Nelson* 2.00
Sin and Its Consequences. *Cardinal Manning* 6.00
Fourfold Sovereignty of God. *Cardinal Manning* 5.00
Dialogue of St. Catherine of Siena. *Transl. Algar Thorold* 10.00
Catholic Answer to Jehovah's Witnesses. *D'Angelo* 10.00
Twelve Promises of the Sacred Heart. (100 cards). 5.00
Life of St. Aloysius Gonzaga. *Fr. Meschler*. 12.00
The Love of Mary. *D. Roberto*. 8.00
Begone Satan. *Fr. Vogl*. 3.00
The Prophets and Our Times. *Fr. R. G. Culleton* 12.50
St. Therese, The Little Flower. *John Beevers*. 6.00
St. Joseph of Copertino. *Fr. Angelo Pastrovicchi* 6.00
Mary, The Second Eve. *Cardinal Newman* 2.50
Devotion to Infant Jesus of Prague. *Booklet* 75
Reign of Christ the King in Public & Private Life. *Davies* 1.25
The Wonder of Guadalupe. *Francis Johnston*. 7.50
Apologetics. *Msgr. Paul Glenn* 10.00
Baltimore Catechism No. 1 . . . . 3.50
Baltimore Catechism No. 2 . . . . 4.50
Baltimore Catechism No. 3 . . . . 8.00
An Explanation of the Baltimore Catechism. *Fr. Kinkead* 16.50
Bethlehem. *Fr. Faber*. 18.00
Bible History. *Schuster*. 10.00
Blessed Eucharist. *Fr. Mueller* 9.00
Catholic Catechism. *Fr. Faerber* 7.00
The Devil. *Fr. Delaporte*. 6.00
Dogmatic Theology for the Laity. *Fr. Premm*. 20.00
Evidence of Satan in the Modern World. *Cristiani* 10.00
Fifteen Promises of Mary. (100 cards) 5.00
Life of Anne Catherine Emmerich. 2 vols. *Schmoeger* 37.50
Life of the Blessed Virgin Mary. *Emmerich*. 16.50
Manual of Practical Devotion to St. Joseph. *Patrignani* 15.00
Prayer to St. Michael. (100 leaflets). 5.00
Prayerbook of Favorite Litanies. *Fr. Hebert*. 10.00
Preparation for Death. (Abridged). *St. Alphonsus* 8.00
Purgatory Explained. (pocket, unabr.). *Schouppe*. 9.00
Fundamentals of Catholic Dogma. *Ludwig Ott* 21.00
Spiritual Conferences. *Tauler* 13.00

Prices subject to change.

Prices subject to change.